Economic evolution and structure

Frederic L. Pryor uses the concept of structural complexity to show how changes in the population, the labor force, the structure of industry, the financial system, foreign and domestic trade, and the government sector are related to the same general trend in the U.S. economic system over the past forty years and in the coming twenty years. He also investigates the impact of these changes on the functioning of the system, exploring such matters as the long-term rising unemployment rate, the alleged increasing volatility of the economy, the changing degree of competition, and the evolving economic role of the government.

The discussion is aimed at those who wish to view the economy as a whole and who are concerned with problems of understanding an economy that is becoming increasingly complex along many different dimensions. For specialists a number of appendices discuss a variety of technical issues.

Economic evolution and structure

The impact of complexity on the U.S. economic system

FREDERIC L. PRYOR
Swarthmore College

CAMBRIDGE
UNIVERSITY PRESS

Published by the Press Syndicate of the University of Cambridge
The Pitt Building, Trumpington Street, Cambridge CB2 1RP
40 West 20th Street, New York, NY 10011-4211, USA
10 Stamford Road, Oakleigh, Melbourne 3166, Australia

© Cambridge University Press 1996

First Published 1996

Printed in the United States of America

Library of Congress Cataloging-in-Publication Data
Pryor, Frederic L.
   Economic evolution and structure : the impact of complexity on the U.S.
economic system / Frederic L. Pryor.
      p. cm.
   Includes bibliographical references and index.
   ISBN 0-521-55097-1 (hc). – ISBN 0-521-55924-3 (pb)
   1. United States – Economic conditions – 1945- 2. Economic
forecasting – United States 3. Economic indicators – United States.
4. Organizational change. I. Title
HC106.5.P78   1996
330.973—dc20   95-13037
                                                        CIP

A catalog record for this book is available from the British Library

ISBN   0-521-55097-1   Hardback
ISBN   0-521-55924-3   Paperback

"I Wished a Simpler Life for Me" (poem) copyright © 1996 by Alberta J.
Bontemps.

To Shannon and Dan

Contents

viii   **Contents**

List of tables and diagrams

Tables

Diagrams

Acknowledgments

This book could not have been written without the intellectual and financial help of many people and institutions. I must emphasize the importance of the usual disclaimer that none are responsible for my interpretations or errors.

The Alfred E. Sloan Foundation and the Swarthmore College Research Fund financed the research for this book, and I carried out much of the research at the Brookings Institution in Washington, DC. I am grateful to all of these organizations for their support and encouragement.

Various people supplied me with data, computer programs, and research materials. I especially would like to thank Karl E. Cass, Richard E. Caves, Robert W. Crandall, Richard DuBoff, Kenneth Goldstein, Thomas D. Hopkins, Lynn Jenkins, Lawrence Katz, Mary F. Kokoski, John Mazzeo, Göran Östblom, Chad Shirley, Charles F. Stone, Susan D. Tuck, Clifford Winston, and Martin Wolfson. I would also like to express my appreciation to Wilbur G. Lewellen, Nell Minow, Robert C. Ochsner, and Robert Williams for interviews or letters on particular issues. I have had three hard working and competent research assistants and would like to thank Chang-Tai Hsieh, Elliott Sulcove, and Joshua Teitelbaum. The poem by Alberta J. Bontemps that begins the text is reprinted with permission of the author.

A number of friends and relatives have generously given me their time to read and comment on all or part of the manuscript. John Caskey, Richard DuBoff, Dan Pryor, Mil Pryor, Zora Pryor, Bernard Saffran, and F. M. Scherer read the entire book. Henry Aaron, Philip Bagnoli, Margaret Blair, Ralph Bryant, Jed DeVaro, Claudia Goldin, Harold Hochman, Lynn Karoly, Mark Kuperberg, Ellen Magenheim, Stephen O'Connell, Lee Perlman, Marshall Reinsdorf, and Daniel Sichel read individual chapters. I am most grateful to all for their patience and assistance. I also appreciate the aid given to me at various brown bag lunches at both Swarthmore College and the Brookings Institution, where parts of this book were presented.

This book originated as a course I gave at Swarthmore College in 1991 on the future of the U.S. economic system and I would like to thank my students for their comments and reactions. In the following years I continued to rework these materials and, with all the help I received, I hope by this time that I finally got things right.

Frederic L. Pryor
Swarthmore, Pennsylvania

CHAPTER 1

Complexity in the economy

I wished a simple life for me.
The web I see is too complex to be.
I wish that I might un-
    wind this web I've made.
The knot is twisted and hard.
To cut it would destroy
    the whole and make discord.
This cannot be.
Spinning tighter and tighter until it breaks.
This life I have begun to
Make.

Alberta Bontemps

Our society is becoming more complex, not just our personal lives. These two developments stem from many of the same causes, and reversing such trends does not seem feasible in either sphere. Indeed, with solemn mien politicians, preachers, futurists, and fanatics have told us so often that the world, in general, is becoming more complex that the idea seems commonplace. Nevertheless, in particular situations the meaning of this idea is often obscure: What do such pronouncements concretely mean, for instance, regarding the economy? Under what specific circumstances is the assertion true? Most importantly, how does it affect our daily lives?

I have written this book because I believe that the concept of complexity is crucial for understanding the evolution of the U.S. economic system. Defined precisely and used as a tool of quantitative research, it leads us to ask new questions about the economy, as well as to give us new answers to many old questions. It allows us to see how the population is becoming more heterogeneous, an important factor underlying the decline of social cohesiveness in the United States. It provides perspective about the long-term rising unemployment rate in the economy. It leads us to explore more carefully than before whether volatility in the economy is increasing. It suggests to us some important clues for understanding the changing business strategies by large corporations. It forces us to look, in a quite different manner, at the changing international competitiveness of particular American industries. It shows us more clearly how the government sector has both responded to, and created, the

increasing complexity of the economic system. It guides us to greater understanding about a number of processes underlying economic growth. It permits
us to see more clearly the direction in which the institutions of the economy
have been changing and to make predictions about the future evolution of the
economy in a more disciplined manner. Complexity, let me emphasize, is not
a theory but a perspective; it is not an ideology, but an approach to help us see
how a number of seemingly different changes in the economy are related.[1]

In analyzing the structural complexity of the economic system, three quite
different phenomena must be considered: the structure itself, the processes
generating the complexity of this structure, and the impact of this complexity
on the operation of the system. The first question is primarily descriptive and
requires the development of a set of quantitative indicators. The second question is both descriptive and analytic. The descriptive task involves following
the indicators of structural complexity over time; the analytic task involves
exploration of those mechanisms that have created the changing complexity.
The third question involves linking particular aspects of the behavior of the
economic system to its structural components. In some cases, this can be carried out in a rigorously deductive fashion; in other cases, more intuitive methods of inference must be employed. In both cases, however, I do not rest with
the theory but attempt to test the propositions empirically. It is this link
between theory and behavior that, in turn, allows us to say something about
the future of the economic system in an organized fashion. It is this link upon
which I focus in this book; the policy prescriptions must be left for others.

The first task of this chapter is to explore the meaning of the term *complexity,* especially since it is used in a number of different ways in the social science literature. This is followed by a discussion of some of the major results
in the rest of the book that show how an increase in complexity of the economic system influences the behavior of the economy. The final two sections
of the chapter explore how complexity can be measured and the motives that
guide my approach. In order to maintain continuity in both this chapter and the
rest of the book, I present detailed evidence on a variety of particular points in
a series of appendices. Although annoying for those wishing to pursue all
aspects of the argument in depth, this procedure lessens the burden on those
who are willing give the author the benefit of doubt at particular points of the

---

1. Complexity of the economy is the central focus of a book by Warsh (1984) and, under other
   rubrics, of a number of articles by others. While sharing a common vision about the importance
   of complexity in understanding the operations of economic systems, these authors have applied
   the concept in much different ways than I. Of course, predictions about increasing complexity
   are common to all these studies. Nevertheless, it is what the analyst does with the concept for
   developing understanding of the operation of the economy that is crucial. Much closer to the
   approach taken in this book is an analysis of the structural complexity of exchange systems in
   tribal and peasant societies by Stodder (1995).

argument. Above all, this book is not aimed at the specialist in particular
fields, but rather to those who wish to see how the specialized knowledge in
one branch of economics is related to that in another branch.

The meaning of structural complexity

As I will discuss in greater detail in Appendix Note 1.1, the concept of complexity has several different but related meanings. In this study I use the term
only in the sense of structural complexity, which relates to the organization
of a system at a single point in time. Structural complexity is, of course, a
concept that can be employed to describe many different phenomena and we
have only to look around us to find examples. In the field of technology, for
instance, the original turbojet engine of the 1930s had a few parts, of which
only one moved; by 1990 jet engines had a much superior performance but,
at the same time, had almost 20,000 parts.[2] In the field of business organization, the division of labor has increased so that the number of interactions
within a firm have greatly increased. Or, as I show in Chapter 2, the population has become increasingly heterogeneous and this, in turn, increases difficulties of governance.

Problems arise in trying to understand the concept of structural complexity
because particular investigators have employed different definitions tailored to
their own analytical tasks. In some cases the definition is highly abstract, for
instance, Herbert Simon characterizes a complex system in terms of a large
number of parts interacting in a nonsimple way.[3] For our investigation of the
evolution of the economic system, it is difficult to employ this definition
empirically. Others have defined complexity in a very narrow fashion, for
instance, in terms of the number of distinct units within a system. This does
not easily serve our purposes either.

Our analytic problems are compounded because the various phenomena
we are studying can be examined from different perspectives so that the concept of complexity can be applied in different ways and can yield seemingly contradictory results. That is, according to one perspective, complexity
might be increasing; but according to another perspective, it may be decreasing. Such difficulties are not confined to economics. For instance, the biologist George C. Williams points out that in some respects, such as with brain

---

2. Arthur (1993).
3. Simon (1969), p. 86. In other sciences these conceptual problems also appear. For instance,
   Murray Gell-Mann (1994), a Nobel laureate in physics, derives a highly abstract definition of
   structural complexity that is useful for his purposes but is difficult to apply to many problems
   in the physical sciences. Gell-Mann's approach toward complexity is sufficiently different
   from that of Ilya Prigogine, a Nobel laureate in chemistry, that he does not even mention the
   latter in his survey of complexity.

structure, a mammal is structurally more complex than any fish.[4] But in other respects, such as the integumentary histology of the species, the average fish is much more complex than any mammal. Both perspectives are useful, even if the conclusions appear at odds. The definition of complexity, as Nobel laureate Murray Gell-Mann is wise to remind us, is necessarily context dependent.

The definition of structural complexity used throughout this book starts with the notion that complexity relates either directly or indirectly to the information necessary for those in the system to function effectively. Three different but related sets of indicators capture this notion: the direct information requirements, the elaborateness of the internal configuration of the system and the accompanying interactions, and the heterogeneity of the elements of the system. Each of these three indicators captures at least one facet of the concept of complexity used in ordinary discourse.

Direct information requirements

Any system requiring more immediate information for a person to function effectively is more complex. In the economic system as a whole, this greater demand for information is due, in part, to the rising level of technology; and it is reflected in the greater specialization of labor and a higher per capita income. The latter, in turn, is accompanied by greater information requirements on the consumer side that reflect the greater number of products and product attributes: We not only have a number of different types of VCRs on the market from which to choose, but each has a wide number of different features. Advanced technology has also lowered costs of communication and transportation, a major factor in the expansion of the size of individual markets. All of these aspects of the increasing informational requirements of the system have influenced not only how institutions are structured, but the strategies they pursue to survive.

Unfortunately, measurement problems to capture aspects of this type of complexity are severe. Although information requirements or knowledge per se are difficult to measure from the output side, they have often been investigated by measuring the inputs – especially the labor force – used in gathering, analyzing, and disseminating information. The latter approach is obviously imperfect. Measurements of the size of markets and the degree to which additional information must be taken into account are also difficult. If market prices are the only information producers consider in their decisions, the size of markets would make no difference. But if producers base their decisions on richer information than price, then an increase in exports and imports places a greater information burden on them.

4. Williams (1966), p. 43. The next reference is to Gell-Mann (1994), p. 33.

Industry or department	Situation 1				Situation 2				Situation 3			
	A	B	C	D	A	B	C	D	A	B	C	D
A	X				X	X	X	X	X	X	X	X
B		X				X	X	X	X	X	X	X
C			X				X	X	X	X	X	X
D				X				X	X	X	X	X

X = for organizations, an order sent from a department listed in a row to a department listed in a column; for an economy, a flow of products sent from an industry listed in the column rows to an industry listed in the heads for further processing.

The meaning of these diagrams is discussed in the text. The structural complexity of situation 1 is less than structural complexity of situation 2 that, in turn, is less than the structural complexity of situation 3. Situation 2 represents an arrangement of the rows and columns such that the Xs are "triangulated" completely.

Figure 1.1 Intrafirm or intraeconomy interactions.

More elaborate interactions or internal configuration

As the internal organizations of economic units within the economy increase in specialization and interdependence, more elaborate internal interactions occur. In certain cases an increase in scale also gives rise to more internal interactions. A simple but unrealistic case arises when an organization requires every individual to be in contact with every other individual. In this situation, when the number of employees increases one unit from $n - 1$ to n, the number of interrelations between employees rises by $n - 1$ units. More realistically, a larger organization often has more hierarchical levels and, to the extent that this signifies a greater volume of interrelations between all levels, structural complexity increases. If, however, department B within the organization deals only with department A above it and with department C below it, then in a meaningful sense the complexity faced by the members is only slightly greater than if the department were self-contained and dealt exclusively with a market. If, however, a department B must also deal with departments C and D below it and also with department A above it, and if A, C, and D must also deal with each other, then complexity has increased considerably in this particular structural sense.

This idea can be easily graphed by creating a matrix with every industry or department on both the vertical and horizontal axes. In the first example, the letters stand for departments within an organization, the rows indicate the department giving orders, and the columns indicate the department receiving them. An X is placed in the matrix if department A sends orders to department B. Within a department orders are both sent to and received by department members, so there is always an X in the diagonal element. This matrix, shown in Figure 1.1, can have different configurations. In Situation 1, the matrix is completely decomposable and each department is self-contained. In Situation 2, the matrix can be triangulated; that is, department A sends orders to all other departments, department B to all departments but A, and so forth. In Situation 3 the matrix is totally undecomposable. If complexity is defined in terms of internal interactions, then the increasing structural complexity in moving from Situation 1 to Situation 3 should be readily apparent.

Such an approach can also be used to examine one aspect of the complexity of the economy as a whole. In such a case, instead of considering the axes to be different departments, we define them as different industries, with the Xs indicating one industry sending products to another for use as inputs in further processing. The final use of these products (consumption, investment, government purchases, and exports) and the factor inputs (labor, land, and capital) and imports are not included. If they were, we would have an input–output table; such tables are available for many countries and over a considerable period of time. As I'll show in the following section, some simple measurements can be developed from such a matrix that allow us to generalize about the changing complexity of the interindustry flows of the U.S. economy.

Greater differentiation or heterogeneity of units

As the particular units of the economy become more differentiated, diverse, or heterogeneous, more information is required to understand the system. Inequality of income for example, is one type of diversity. For policy makers, a system with quite similar units is much easier to deal with than a system with quite different units. In the former case, one policy might be suitable for all units; in the latter case, different policies may be required to deal with dissimilar units. For instance, it requires less information for a government to make policy where the incomes of the population are roughly equal than if there is great inequality.

A summary of these three meanings of structural complexity and various examples to illustrate them are presented in Table 1.1. I discuss each example in detail in later chapters. Let me repeat that all three aspects of structural complexity – increasing direct information requirements of the system, increasing interactions within the system, and increasing heterogeneity of the units within the system – reflect the increasing information requirements necessary for us to function effectively in the system and, on a personal level, deal with the increasing complications of life.

Impacts of structural complexity

In the final chapter of this book I will examine various scenarios for the development of capitalism in the United States in the light of the four most impor-

Table 1.1. *Meaning and examples of increasing structural complexity*

Increasing direct information requirements of the system:

- Skill levels (and information processing) of the labor force rises (Chapter 3)
- Share of labor force engaged in creation, processing, and interpreting information increases (Chapter 3)
- Sizes of markets and variety of products increases (Chapters 6, 8)
- Businesses take into account more governmental regulations (Chapter 9)

Increasing interactions within the system:

- Interrelations between various sectors of the economy become more extensive (Chapter 1)
- Larger share of individual wealth is created directly by the government or through government institutions (Chapter 5)
- Financial interrelations become more intricate as ratio of financial to tangible assets rises (Chapter 5)

Increasing heterogeneity of the economic system:

- Ethnic differences within the population become more important (Chapter 2)
- Differences in income and wealth become greater (Chapter 2)
- Differences in the size distribution of firms become greater (Chapter 6)

tant – and interrelated – trends that I believe are driving change in the society. Two of these trends are economic – increasing structural complexity of the economic system and increasing internationalization of the economy; and two are social-cultural – a decreasing social cohesiveness and an enervation in the capitalist spirit. The exact impact of structural complexity on the operation of the economy is controversial and is a major concern of this study.

In recent years some have used the complexity approach as a telescope to examine entire economic systems at a single glance. In such analyses it is often an article of faith that greater complexity leads either to a greater chance of a malfunctioning of the system or a greater volatility of behavior. An analogy is often drawn with the frequency of breakdown of complex machinery. More careful scholars generally confine their generalizations to a relatively narrow range of phenomena and phrase their proposition more cautiously.[5] In some cases this argument is also tied to decelerating growth because coordination costs to avoid such breakdowns are rising faster than other costs. For instance, G. J. Mulgan tells us that "... as institutions, economies, and soci-

5. For instance, Gell-Mann (1994), p. 28, notes that complex ecosystems are apparently less resilient to changes in the external environment than comparatively simple ones, but that this is still a matter of controversy among specialists. If the general linkage between increasing structural complexity and volatility or lack of resiliency is true, then under certain conditions limits are placed on the general increase of complexity. The next reference is to Mulgan (1991), p. 2.

eties grow and become more complex, the costs of coordination and control tend to rise faster than their material capacities."

This type of systemic approach toward complexity can be easily abused and from such global propositions about the relation between structural complexity and greater fragility of the system as a whole, we can "prove" the proposition by selecting a few vivid examples. For instance, in July 1993 an obscure plant of the Sumitomo Chemical Company in Nihama, Japan, blew up and destroyed 65 percent of the world's capacity for producing an epoxy resin, cresol novalac, used to seal most computer chips into their plastic packages. Shortly thereafter spot prices for computer memory soared. Other "chokepoints" can be specified in the manufacture of computer chips or of equipment making the chips as well.[6] Orio Giarini approaches the global proposition about increased fragility in a different manner by arguing that since both insurance costs and accident prevention costs have grown much faster than production, this must reflect increases in the vulnerability of the system to breakdowns. Unfortunately such evidence is insufficient to prove this proposition.

Those interested in general systems theory have also used the concept of complexity to speculate about the general deceleration of growth in industrialized nations in the last few decades. According to this argument, increased complexity of an economy requires more resources devoted to information gathering, processing, and analysis; which means that fewer resources can be devoted to investment. For example, a measure of the information required for a market system to function might be the production of those sectors such as wholesale and retail trade plus finance and real estate, where the primary function is to serve as an intermediary between buyers and sellers. In the period between 1950 and 1990, the share of the GDP originating from these sectors rose from 25 to 39 percent (1982 prices).[7]

Although this kind of telescopic approach toward complexity is interesting, it is usually much too grandiose. For instance, the linkage between resources devoted and investment and to the information sector is far from clear. As shown in Chapter 4, measurement of the information sector is considerably more complicated than the use of such simple data might suggest; and more careful measures yield much less dramatic results. Nevertheless, the telescopic approach does yield useful results if we are more careful with both the theory and the evidence than is usually the case. For example, a fruitful study by Abhijet V. Banerjee and Michael Spagal uses an interesting mathematical model to argue that the increasing structural complexity, measured by a trian-

6. *The Wall Street Journal*, August 27, 1993, p. 1. The citation in the next sentence comes from Giarini (1985).
7. The data come from U.S. Department of Commerce, Bureau of Economic Analysis (1986), pp. 254–5; and *Survey of Current Business*, 73, No. 5 (May 1993), p. 54. The series are spliced using 1977 as the pivot.

gularized input–output table (see Figure 1.1) accompanying an increase of per capita income, makes central planning increasingly difficult and the economy more prone to supply breakdowns. This leads to the proposition that the centrally planned economies manifested a greater deceleration of growth than market economies, a prediction supported by empirical evidence.[8]

In studying changes in structural complexity, the microscope is often a more useful instrument than the telescope and this is an approach adhered to in much of the following discussion. I start with relatively concrete problems, draw upon empirical studies of my own and of others, and attack the complexity problem from the ground up. In some cases where an acceptable theory is lacking, I adopt an inductive approach. For instance, in my study of economic volatility, I compute indicators of the actual volatility of a large number of financial and production indicators over a forty-year period to see what has actually happened. Only then do my speculations about the future begin. Although definite answers are not always possible, the attempt to match the various conjectures and propositions against data advances our understanding because we can remove a clutter of irrelevant theoretical models from the table.

Chapters 2 through 4 deal with the population and the labor force. As shown in Chapter 2, the complexity of the population structure, as measured by various indicators of heterogeneity, has increased over the last forty years. Under certain conditions, such heterogeneity leads to greater problems of governance, long-run planning, and higher government expenditures (Chapter 9).[9] It appears to be an important factor in the decline of social cohesiveness. Some aspects of this population heterogeneity also have a direct impact on the determinants of economic growth.

As discussed in Chapter 3, the complexity of the structure of the labor force also has increased in two senses: the overall level of skill required for the various jobs is higher and the heterogeneity of the jobs has increased. An important consequence is that structural unemployment has become more important over the years, in major part because of imbalances in the supply and demand for unskilled workers. A crucial indicator is the ratio of earnings of skilled and unskilled workers, which has widened in the last decade and a half. In one respect, however, structural complexity in the labor force has declined. This is in the area of labor-management relations, where labor unions have declined in importance. Such a change has a number of implications and I present evidence that these include a decline in fringe benefits and greater wage inequality.

Chapters 5 and 6 deal with the financial structure and the structure of production. The former chapter documents a rising structural complexity defined in terms of the structure of physical and financial assets. Discussion focuses

8. Banerjee and Spagal (1991). Pryor (1994b) provides the empirical evidence for the proposition.
9. Kirby (1985) argues the proposition about governance; Michael (1968) discusses governmental expenditures.

on the empirical evidence that such increasing complexity has led to greater financial distress, for instance, bank failures and bankruptcies, but not greater volatility, a result with some important implications for monetary policy. Chapter 6 documents an increasing structural complexity defined in terms of the informational burden on productive units, the heterogeneity of productive establishments and enterprises, and also the separation of ownership and control. The chapter begins with an analysis of a survey on the various strategies used by enterprises to deal with the increasing complexity of the economic environment in which they must operate. I then investigate evidence from a large number of empirical studies that ownership and control of U.S. corporations are becoming increasingly separated and that this separation has an important impact on executive compensation and also on firm profits.

Chapters 7 and 8 deal respectively with the behavior of markets for U.S. and foreign products. Chapter 7 explores the increase in domestic competition that has come about by the extension of the market – one indicator of structural complexity – arising from a greater amount of foreign trade. The chapter shows how the increase in complexity of domestic markets has acted against the law of one price so that the expected price convergence in different domestic markets has not occurred. It also documents how volatility of prices of raw materials has increased, largely because of the increase in the volatility of exchange rates. Chapter 8 shows how the increase in openness of the U.S. economy has increased in the past at a rapid rate, and how it probably will not continue in the future. It also examines the sources of U.S. competitiveness on the world market and the particular role played by products that are technologically advanced or that require highly skilled workers.

Chapter 9 deals with the government sector. It analyzes the differential growth of particular governmental expenditures to demonstrate how, in this respect, the government responds to changes in structural complexity. It also shows how the government has generated structural complexity in markets through an extension of its regulatory activities. Finally it documents how rising structural complexity has increased the difficulty of setting both micro- and macroeconomic policies. As the economy becomes more differentiated and heterogeneous, the goals of policy may increase in number because of the varied demands of the different groups. The greater heterogeneity and competing demands increase information requirements of the system and, in addition, lengthen decision-making lags of policy. At the same time, the policy tools available to the government for influencing the course of the economy may diminish as markets increase in scope and the nation becomes more integrated into the international economy.

Chapter 10 presents in detail the argument that increasing structural complexity is one of four major interrelated trends that are shaping the evolution of the society along with increasing internationalization of the economy, decreasing social cohesiveness, and enervation of the capitalist spirit. The manner in which these trends interact with each other and are countered by particular policy actions are analyzed with the aid of a scenario analysis that sketches five possible futures of the economic system. The two extremes of course, are, no change and exhaustion of the system; the other three scenarios provide more interesting possibilities.

Measurements of structural complexity

Before ending this introduction, two methodological issues deserve brief discussion. The first is the actual measurement of complexity which, given my emphasis on confronting theories with data, is a crucial problem. Edward O. Wilson, a leading biologist, once remarked:[10] "It is not difficult to recognize complexity ... The difficulty comes in how you measure it." Depending upon the phenomena under investigation, it is possible to use several different measures of complexity since each of the three different approaches for defining complexity has several dimensions.

An example of this multidimensionality of structural complexity can be given for the economy as a whole in terms of the definition focusing on the elaborateness of the internal configuration of the system. One approach to the problem uses input–output tables for the United States in 1947 and 1977, employing two simple measurements of structural complexity that come to mind:

- The first is the ratio of the interindustry flows of production to final use of the products: For any given level of GDP, the greater the flows of production from one industry to the other, rather than the end-user, the greater the structural complexity. This measure of complexity shows no essential change in the U.S. economy during the postwar era.
- Another measure focuses on the degree to which the interindustry matrix can be triangulated. By systematically moving the rows and corresponding columns around, we can try to increase the sum of the interindustry flows above the diagonal and decrease the sum below (as shown in Figure 1.1, Situation 2). In this case, the measure of complexity is the ratio of below-diagonal to above-diagonal flows. For the United States between 1947 and 1977, the ratio slowly increased from .317 to .325 when highly aggregated input–output tables are used; this indicates that structural complexity has slowly increased.[11] Since the input–output table of developing nations contain many more zeros than industrialized nations, this type of com-

---

10. Cited by Lewin (1992), p. 136.
11. I triangulated comparable 23 by 23 transaction matrices of the 1947 and 1977 input–output matrices of the United States (from Miller and Blair, 1985, Appendix B). A fuller description of the calculation is presented in Pryor (1994).

plexity must have increased much faster at lower stages of the industrialization process, a phenomenon receiving some exploration in the economic literature.[12]

The two different measurements of complexity of the U.S. production structure lead to different conclusions, but this should not cause alarm if we bear in mind that complexity is multidimensional; indeed, still other measures of structural complexity based on the input–output tables can be devised as well. In the specific case under consideration, it can be easily shown that the two particular measurements of structural complexity lead to different behavioral properties of the system, so that the multidimensional procedure is justified. Indeed, any satisfactory theory about complexity must explain the behavior implications of each measure.

In many cases, structural complexity is most usefully measured by indicators adopted for the occasion with a particular theory in mind. For instance, in the examination of complexity of the organization of labor in a factory, it is generally believed that higher levels of skill are tied to more complicated interactions between the parts of the system. In this case we can use the general level of skill of the work force as a measure of this type of complexity. For studying the complexity of the financial system, it is generally believed that the relative size of financial to real assets is an important indicator of financial interactions with the system; therefore, appropriate indicators can be easily devised (see Chapter 5).

Although these ad hoc measures of complexity are useful, we cannot stop at this point. Given the importance of information flows in the general definition of structural complexity, we can draw upon some simple ideas from information theory to obtain a more general measure of complexity. The *Theil statistic* turns out to have the properties needed to measure structural complexity from an information standpoint. For those unfamiliar with this statistic, it is discussed in greater detail in Appendix Note 1.2.

For our purposes the *Theil coefficient* (designated *H*) can be used in many different ways. It can be employed to measure both heterogeneity and inequality, although these two aspects of structural complexity are quite different. If we wish to compare complexity calculations from different types of data sets, it is often convenient to normalize the coefficients by the highest value that *H* can take so that the homogeneous–heterogeneous scale or the inequality-equality scale run from 0 to 1. I call this the *relative Theil statistic*. The Theil statistic also can be decomposed easily so that the impact of the individual parts can be examined. This means, for example, that in studying the distribu-

---

12. Lamet, Richter, and Teufelsbauer (1972) have the most extensive discussion. They, as well as Yan and Ames (1965), discuss alternative indicators of structural complexity using input–output tables.

tion of income, we can determine what part of the total inequality is due to inequality within particular classes defined by race or gender and what part of the inequality is due to differences in average income between these groups.

Final remarks on methodology

The last methodological issue concerns the approach, in general, and my motives for selecting and attacking the various problems in the manner that I have chosen. For the most part the method of analysis of structural complexity represents a more general application of the paradigm followed by specialists in industrial organization relating behavior to market structure, or by biologists relating anatomical structures to the adaptiveness of the plants or animals. As such, it requires little justification.

I do not try to make an exhaustive study of the evolution of the economic system. Instead, I select a series of issues to discuss that provide insight into important problems of economic institutions and, at the same time, illustrate different aspects of changing structural complexity in the post–World War II era. While it would be possible to study changing structural complexity for a longer period, I prefer to sacrifice temporal depth for a greater breadth of coverage. It also is possible to explore the evolution of behavior at a lower level (for instance, at the level of the individual firm) but this also must be left for others.[13] The analysis of both structural complexity and evolution can deal with many different aspects of the economy, but this study focuses primarily on the institutional structure of the system as a whole. This means, for instance, that although many problems of developing technology have an impact on structural complexity and the evolution of the economy in different ways, I deal primarily with those impinging on the system.

It also might be satisfying to develop an abstract theory about complexity and the functioning of an economic system, but this is not my aim. Herbert Simon posed a deep question when he asked,[14] "Is there anything nontrivial, yet quite general, that can be said about complexity?" With regard to complexity in the structural or morphological sense, I suspect that the answer is "not a great deal" and that Simon himself has well covered the field. Unfortunately, most purely theoretical discussions about complexity in the social sphere suffer from tediousness, pomposity, or both. Moreover, the level of abstraction is sufficiently high that the relation of the resulting theory to

---

13. One first-rate piece of work along these lines is by Nelson and Winter (1982), but their book explores the economic evolution at a different level of abstraction and asks quite different questions than this study, which is more concerned with institutional structure. The same may be said about studies such as Arthur (1994) or other analyses briefly mentioned in Appendix Note 1.1 or in an extremely useful study by Nelson (1995).

14. Simon (1977), p. 170.

real-world phenomena is tenuous at best and nonexistent at worse. Such theorizing, which can be carried out easily in the comfort of one's armchair, has the advantage of avoiding the hard work necessary for concrete economic research; but it hardly serves to advance our state of knowledge.

My purpose is much different: to use the various concepts of complexity to examine in an empirical fashion different aspects of the evolving U.S. economic system. Unlike some observers, I do not see the U.S. economic system evolving in the next few decades into some type of postcapitalist economy that is qualitatively so different from that to which we are accustomed that all we need to do is to sketch its major outlines.[15] Moreover, unlike many, I do not believe that societal and historical change is accelerating in the world today. Rather, I believe that we are evolving slowly and that it is necessary to be as specific as possible in our discussion of the future, particularly to avoid general propositions with dubious empirical relevance. Given the constraints of space, the disadvantage of my approach is that only a few problems in the various areas of the economy can be discussed. I hope, however, that the particular economic problems receiving attention will serve to stimulate others to employ the approach to analyze problems that they believe are important.

Since I am concerned not just with the past but also with the future of the economic system, let me add yet another caveat. We must follow Talleyrand's maxim that above all we must avoid overenthusiasm (*"surtout pas trop de zèle"*). Therefore, I try to abstain from the uncritical and irresponsible gusto of many practitioners of futurology, especially the wishful thinking, the confusion of the "will be" and the "ought to be," and the sermonizing. I also try to adopt work habits quite different from futurologists who, like theorists of complexity, are also addicted to sitting in their armchairs and, on the basis of miscellaneous anecdotes and statistics picked up during the day, letting their imaginations freely roam. Without feeling it necessary to examine systematically all the available data, these futurologists can generate all sorts of "interesting" predictions but, as Bertrand Russell once remarked in a different context, this type of scholarly endeavor has all of the advantages of theft over honest toil. Also it is unfortunate that the writings of many who believe they are blessed with the gift of prophesy are so breathless, pretentious, smug, and moralistic that the literature is an ordeal to read; I also try to avoid these traps.

An old Chinese proverb tells us that prediction is difficult, especially about the future. Most forecasts are actually observations about what has happened in the past and present, and which trends in this period are likely to have an impact on tomorrow. Thus, our knowledge of the present and the future is inextricably mixed. Since our comprehension of the present is in continual

---

15. Carnevale (1993), Drucker (1993), and Toffler (1981) are typical of those believing that we are evolving into a qualitatively different economic system. Attali (1991), p. 3 is typical of those asserting that social change is accelerating.

flux, we can understand one important meaning of Paul Valéry's oft-cited aphorism, "The Future is not what it used to be." And we also understand why a thorough understanding of the present is necessary for prediction.

Despite the pitfalls, the complexity approach has several advantages in studying the future. It forces the analysis to be sufficiently specific about what is happening in the present so that meaningful predictions can be made. It also provides an alternative to most of the current economic studies of the future that focus on such problems as the future level of the GDP, population, pollution, raw material stocks, or the forthcoming discoveries and innovations that allegedly will alter our lives. Instead, it directs our attention to a much different set of problems concerning the changes in economic institutions and in policies that influence their behavior.

To avoid confusion about my aims and methods, let me also explain briefly what I do not argue in this book:

- I do not believe that complexity of the economy always increases and, in this case, we can find an analogy in the field of biology. Although it has been part of the conventional biological wisdom from Charles Darwin and Herbert Spencer to the present that life is becoming more complex, some biologists and geologists have argued recently that in important dimensions, this is not the case. In a survey of these issues Daniel V. McShea shows that it is not only difficult to measure complexity but that decreases in biological complexity are common.[16] This should serve as a warning to social scientists, where it is part of the conventional wisdom that societies relentlessly and continuously evolve into more complex forms.

- I also do not argue that complexity is some type of exogenous phenomenon that "just happens." Often the degree of complexity of an

16. Some of the types of evidence in this debate are useful to note. McShea (1991) examines three different measures of the complexity of the vertebrae of four classes of aquatic animals and compares the results with similar measures for surrogates of their terrestrial ancestors. He finds a drift away from complexity, not toward it, in most cases. Boyajian and Lutz (1992) show an increase in the complexity of ammonoids (an extinct class of swimming, shelled mollusks), as measured by the lobs and saddles of their internal chambers, for about 200 million years; thereafter, this measure of complexity levels off. Bonner (1988) points out that complexity is often related to size and he makes a case for a generalized version of Cope's rule (over geological time organisms generally increase in size). But he also points out numerous exceptions to this rule. Moreover, he shows that although a positive relationship between size of animals and certain measures of complexity such as number of cell types exists, the relationship is weak. Attempts to link complexity, as measured by the size of the genome or the coding DNA per genome, to some types of gross measures reflecting the hierarchy of the species give rise to even more problems (Bonner, 1988, p. 123; Smith, 1988, p. 220). Some recent studies suggest that the increasing ability for information processing of the brains of certain mammals, which is yet another sign of increasing structural complexity, appears an exception, rather than a rule of nature (Lewin, 1992, Chapter 7)

economy is a function of policies taken by governments or private individuals that can be reversed. For instance, complexity in the financial system, as manifested by a high ratio of financial to physical assets, is in large measure a function of governmental regulation of financial intermediaries. In some cases, as I argue in detail in Chapter 9, the government creates structural complexity through its regulatory activities. In still other situations institutions develop that allow complexity to be reduced in certain dimensions, for instance, the market.[17]

- Moreover, I do not believe that economic or social problems necessarily increase with complexity. For instance, although no ethnic problems occur when the population is ethnically homogeneous, the most severe ethnic problems may not be most acute with the maximum heterogeneity, but somewhere between the two extremes. More specifically, such problems may be most acute, not in a situation where the population is evenly divided among two ethnic groups, but in a situation where one is 15 percent and the other is 85 percent. In the latter case, the predominance of one group may give rise to inappropriate behavior on its part toward the other group (for instance, the activities of the Hutu in Rwanda) that would never occur either where the ethnic groups are 50–50 or where the minority group has only 1 or 2 percent of the population. Similarly, ethnic tensions may be much higher when there are few ethnic groups than when there are many.[18]

- I do not use the complexity perspective for normative purposes – to argue for or against particular governmental policies or to provide advice on how best an individual can face the future. Rather, this is

From the discussion of Gell-Mann (1994), pp. 227–31 and 244–46, three additional considerations become important to take into account: First, we must not confuse the average complexity of the entire population with the complexity of a particular species. Second, certain types of complexity can increase simply as a result of a random genetic walk that have no correlation with biological fitness. Third, decreases in social complexity are not only possible but have also occurred often in history, for instance, in Central America after the collapse of the Classic Maya civilization or in Europe after the collapse of the Roman empire. This kind of statement, however, depends upon a special definition of complexity and in some respects, for instance, heterogeneity of ruling groups, structural complexity increased.

17. This argument does not necessarily mean that fewer resources for information processing and dissemination are utilized in market than in centrally planned economies. My own calculations (Pryor, 1977) have shown that these costs were roughly similar in the two types of economies, although I believe that more useful information was transmitted through the market mechanism.

18. For instance, in Malaŵi where the major ethnic groups number less than ten, there seems to be a much greater sense of ethnic identification than in Madagascar, where there are almost fifty. In an investigation (Pryor, 1990) of both countries I attempted to identify the ethnicity of some seventy-five cabinet ministers; in Malaŵi the task was easy and could be accomplished with the aid of several informed observers. In Madagascar the task proved extremely difficult and required many more interviews.

an exercise in positive economics – to identify past and future trends and to investigate the performance of particular sectors of the economy. In Chapter 6, for instance, I am more interested in how managers actually deal with increased structural complexity, rather than how they should deal with the problem, a question that I leave to well-paid business advisors to discuss. Although the policy implications of the findings in this study are important, it would take a separate book to work them out.

- Finally, I do not argue that increased structural complexity necessarily reflects progress in some general sense.[19] In economics the notion of progress in a general sense is not very useful. Instead, discussion focuses on the behavior of economic systems according to such concrete criteria as economic growth or the distribution of income. If economies have increased in complexity to adapt to certain circumstances, it is not clear that economic performance along many other dimensions has improved; this is a matter for empirical investigation, since theory often tells us little about the nature of the tradeoffs.

Having briefly noted what this study is not about, let me conclude by emphasizing that this study is about empirical questions of positive economics: In what ways is structural complexity increasing or decreasing in the U.S. economic system? If such changes are occurring, how do people deal with them and what impact do they have on the functioning of the economy? The concept of structural complexity provides a useful framework to examine these questions for different sectors and institutions of the economy. Each chapter constitutes a relatively self-contained essay, tied with the other chapters primarily with regard to approach and the use of the same conceptual framework.

I am not trying to provide a general theory of how the economy works, but rather to use the concept of structural complexity to ask questions about the economy that have not been previously posed and to show how diverse economic phenomena in different sectors are related. My aim is to use the concept to examine changes in institutions throughout the economy in a more systematic and fruitful fashion than up to now.

---

19. A biological analogy offers insight. In this discipline the notion of progress is suspect and has given rise to considerable debate (for instance, among the various authors in Nitecki, 1988). Furthermore, the linkage between progress and complexity is even more problematic. For instance, Boyajian and Lutz (1992) show that among the ammonoids, no relationship can be found between extinction rates and complexity. Moreover, if complexity of the brain and its information processing capacity is measured by mass, it is not clear that porpoises, elephants, and blue whales, all of which have larger brains than humans, are somehow smarter. In any case the notion that human intelligence is related to brain size has been long discredited (Gould, 1981).

CHAPTER 2

Population

Heterogeneity is one of the three aspects of structural complexity discussed in the previous chapter. Focusing on this theme directs attention to the way in which the population is divided into groups that make the operations of the economy and government more information intensive and complicated. This chapter analyzes changes in both demographic and economic heterogeneity. For the latter I give particular attention to inequalities of income and wealth that act to stratify the population into clusters with quite different needs and interests. Through a variety of mechanisms discussed in the following sections, these changes in this heterogeneity have an important impact on the performance and operation of the economy.

For the four decades following World War II, I document the increasing demographic heterogeneity, as defined by ethnicity, family structure, and age. These appear to be relatively recent trends; in the four decades before World War II, it seems likely that the situation was different. Only heterogeneity of the population defined by education has remained the same or declined. This trend, however, has not had the expected result either of raising the average level of literacy or of decreasing the variation of literacy skills in the population. I also document the increasing economic heterogeneity, especially the rising inequalities of income and wealth since the mid- or late 1970s and examine some possible causes. These trends in inequality also appear to be a post–World War II phenomena. I also argue that the causal forces underlying such changes in demographic and economic heterogeneity are likely to persist in the near future. Moreover, the impact of public policy to influence these various trends is usually weak and/or uncertain, at least in the short run, so that it is difficult for the government to offset such changes in structural complexity.

Increases in structural complexity of the population have both social and economic consequences. The increase in economic heterogeneity, as manifested by greater inequalities of income and wealth, not only feeds back upon the demographic heterogeneity, but also has an adverse impact on economic growth. The increase in demographic heterogeneity acts to decrease social cohesiveness. These themes receive attention at the end of the chapter and, from other perspectives, in later chapters of the book.

Table 2.1. *Trends in race and ethnicity*

Year	Racial composition		American Indian[a]	Asian and Pacific islanders	Theil statistics		Foreign born as percent of population
	White	Black	American Indian[a]	Asian and Pacific islanders	White– nonwhite	Black– nonblack minority	Foreign born as percent of population
1950	89.5%	----------10.5------------------			.336	n.a.	6.9%
1960	88.6	10.6	-------- .9----------		.357	.274	5.4
1970	87.6	11.1	--------1.3---------		.375	.336	4.7
1980	85.9	11.8	--------2.3---------		.407	.445	6.2
1990	83.9	12.3	.8	3.0	.441	.546	8.7
Projections							
2010	79.6	13.6	.9	5.9	.506	.637	9.9
2030	75.8	14.8	1.0	8.4	.553	.668	10.2
2050	71.8	16.2	1.2	10.7	.594	.681	10.2

[a]The American Indians are defined to include Aleuts and Eskimos. Larger Theil statistics reflect greater structural complexity, as defined by heterogeneity.
Data: see Appendix Note 2.5. The absolute Theil statistic increases as heterogeneity increases; it is discussed in Appendix Note 1.2.

Demographic structures: Ethnicity, family structure, education, and age

For our purposes the most important dimensions of demographic heterogeneity are race and ethnicity, family structure, education, and age. The indicators for each type of heterogeneity are quite straightforward and, in most cases, show an increase in recent decades.

Race and ethnicity

Trends in the racial and ethnic composition of the population depend not only upon relative birth and death rates, but also upon immigration policies and their enforcement. The projections in Table 2.1 are based on conservative assumptions about immigration; the projections show several clear trends. The share of the white population has declined and, according to the projections, will continue to decline further. Both the shares of the black and American Indian populations show rising trends, but the shares of Asian and Pacific Islanders are rising even faster. This means not only that minority racial groups are increasing in relative importance, but that the minority racial groups are also becoming more heterogeneous, trends that are clearly revealed by increases of the Theil statistic measuring heterogeneity. (The statistic is explained in detail in Appendix Note 1.2.)

The Hispanic population, which constituted 9 percent of the population in 1990, is not defined as a separate group in these statistics. According to recent Census Bureau projections, their share in the population will reach 21.5 percent by the year 2050.[1] In the same period, the remaining white population shrinks from 75.7 in 1990 to 52.7 percent in 2050. For such a calculation to have meaning, however, we must assume that the Hispanic population retains its ethnic identity, a trend encouraged by a variety of governmental measures encouraging diversity.

Table 2.1 also presents data on the share of foreign born in the population. This percentage has varied over the country's history. In 1870, for instance, it was 17.3 percent; and in the twentieth century the high point was reached around 1910 when 15.1 percent of the population was foreign born.[2] The projections of foreign born used in Table 2.1 assume that net immigration into the United States will be 880,000 a year from 1990 to 2050; if it is 1,370,000 instead, the percentage of foreign born will be roughly 13.3 percent by 2050. From 1992 to 1994, legal immigration was roughly one million a year.

The demographic forces underlying this trend toward greater structural complexity, as defined by racial and ethnic heterogeneity, are not difficult to understand since they are based on differential birth, death, and immigration rates of particular groups. Some of the economic impacts of these trends, which raise more subtle issues, are discussed at the end of this chapter.

Household structure

Households in the United States range in composition from two-parent families with children (formerly the dominant mode) to a single person living alone, which occurs in all age brackets but particularly among the elderly who have lost a spouse. Such data, shown in Part A of Table 2.2, reveal an increasing heterogeneity of living arrangements. The increasing importance of one-parent families is due both to rising divorce rates and illegitimacy; and I present some relevant data on this matter in Part B of the table. For perspective, the divorce rate in the 1921–23 period was 10 per 1,000 married women in the relevant age group. Such data also reveal that increasingly more children in the United States are living in single-parent households.

These trends are not likely to be reversed in the near future. Indeed, many argue that as women enter the labor force in greater number and as the gap between wages of men and women narrows, women are less economically

1. Day (1993), middle series.
2. Calculated from U.S. Department of Commerce, Bureau of the Census, 1975, pp. 8, 19.

Table 2.2. *Trends in living arrangements*

Part A: Percentage of population in different types of households[a]

	1960	1970	1980	1988
Married couples with children under 18	44.2%	40.3%	30.9%	27.0%
Married couples without children under 18	30.3	30.3	29.9	29.9
Subtotal: married couples and children	74.5	70.6	60.8	56.9
Other family types with children	4.4	5.0	7.5	8.0
Other family types without children	6.4	5.6	5.4	6.6
Subtotal: other family types and children	10.8	10.6	12.9	14.6
Living alone	13.0	17.1	22.6	24.1
Other nonfamily households	1.7	1.7	3.6	4.4
Absolute Theil statisticb	1.37	1.41	1.53	1.57
Relative Theil statistic[b]	76.4%	78.7%	85.5%	88.0%

Part B: Some factors underlying the growth of single-parent families

Year	Illegitimate births	Families with two parents in household	Divorce rates Three-year period	Divorces per 1,000 married woman, 15 to 44
1950	3.9%	86.2%	1948–50	17
1960	5.3	87.8	1950–62	16
1970	10.7	87.1	1969–71	26
1980	18.4	78.5	1978–80	40
1990	26.6	71.9	1987–89	37

[a]The data on percentage of population living in different types of households exclude the population living in nonhousehold arrangements (institutions or other types of group quarters). Such persons were an increasingly small share of the U.S. population between 1950 (3.8 percent) and 1980 (2.5 percent).
[b]A larger Theil statistic reflects greater heterogeneity. The absolute Theil coefficient is open-ended and the upper bound is determined by the size of the population. The relative Theil statistic is the absolute Theil coefficient divided by its highest possible value so that it ranges from 0 to 1.
Data: see Appendix Note 2.5.

dependent upon men and have fewer economic incentives, either for marrying or for preserving their marriages. The decline in job opportunity among men with low education (see Chapter 3) has also contributed to a decline in marriage rates in the relevant social groups. This changing household structure has many implications discussed in various parts of this book. Of immediate relevance, the rising share of children raised in one-parent households is correlated with the rising inequality of income discussed below, because such households are much more likely also to have low incomes. Since girls from such families are more likely to have illegitimate children of their own and to raise them in single-parent families and since boys in such families are less likely to complete their education, poverty may persist through generations of a family, a matter discussed in greater detail in the following section.

Education

Heterogeneity in education can refer either to inputs or outputs. One input is, of course, the years of schooling received by the population. According to the data presented in Appendix Note 2.1, differences are narrowing so that educational heterogeneity is decreasing. Similarly, differences in other easily measurable inputs such as teacher–student ratios or teachers salaries have narrowed over time across the nation.[3]

Educational outputs can be measured either in terms of test scores or of wages and jobs achieved after the student joins the labor force. In looking at outputs, as measured by test scores, a peculiar problem of interpretation immediately arises. We read daily in the newspaper about the low quality of schools. For instance, in Virginia, one-fourth of the students in the state college system must attend remedial courses in reading, writing, and arithmetic; and in the community colleges of this state over one-half of the courses are remedial. But do these reflect just a lower general level in high school education for all? Or do they indicate that the distribution of educational skills has become more unequal? Or do such data simply indicate a decrease in funding for remedial education for high schools? We also read that in the 1980s, about 20 percent of the total number of college graduates were holding jobs that did not require a college degree. Does this mean that jobs were not available to them or that the differences in the quality of higher education have become so great that these "graduates" did not have an actual level of education to hold jobs requiring college level skills? Again we face the interpretative problem of determining whether such data mean that educational inequalities are increasing or decreasing.[4] Finally, the relationship between what students learn in school and what they actually retain thereafter is problematic.

To get around many of these problems, Table 2.3 presents statistics on both averages and inequality (dispersion), as indicated by the coefficient of variation of educational test scores. The data in Panels A and B present results of a study of literacy defined in terms of what skills people can apply to various tasks. The sample covers the entire population in 1992 including immigrants and school dropouts. The skill levels (the table notes reveal the tasks corresponding to the skill levels) are depressingly low, and the youngest three decade cohorts appear quite similar. This indicates that basic literacy is not greatly different for those

3. Betts (1993).
4. The discussions based primarily on data from public schools are not invalidated by the existence of a private school sector since the share of pupils in these schools is small – about 15 percent – and has not greatly changed over the postwar period (Bureau of the Census, annual-b, 1992, p. 138).

Table 2.3. *Indicators of variation of educational quality*

A. National Adult Literacy Test (NALT) scores: Averages and variation

Age group	Median years of schooling	Reading (Prose scale)		Information processing (Document scale)		Quantitative (Quantitative scale)	
		Average score	Coefficient of variation	Average score	Coefficient of variation	Average score	Coefficient of variation
25–34	12.9	282	22%	281	22%	281	23%
35–44	13.1	289	23	283	23	288	24
45–54	12.8	282	23	273	23	282	24
55–64	12.6	260	24	249	25	261	26
> 65	12.2	230	29	217	29	227	36

B. National Adult Literacy Test (NALT): 1992 levels of ability

	Reading			Information processing			Quantitative		
	At or below		At or above	At or below		At or above	At or below		At or above
Scores	225	275	376	225	275	376	225	275	376
Age group									
25–34	16%	41%	4%	14%	41%	4%	17%	41%	5%
35–44	14	35	6	16	39	5	15	36	6
45–54	16	41	5	17	37	3	17	41	5
55–65	26	57	1	30	64	1	25	55	2
> 65	44	76	1	53	85	0	45	71	2

C. National Assessment of Educational Progress (NAEP) reading test: trend of 17-year-old pupils in school

	Age in 1992	Average score, reading	Coefficient of variation	Average scores, other tests					
				Science		Mathematics		Writing	
1971	38	285.2	16%	1970	305		n.a.		n.a.
1975	34	285.6	15	1973	296	1973	304		n.a.
1980	29	285.5	15	1977	290	1978	300		n.a.
1984	25	288.8	14	1982	283	1982	299	1984	212
1988	21	290.1	13	1986	289	1986	302	1988	214
1990	19	290.2	14	1990	290	1990	305	1990	212

Notes: All scales run from 0 to 500. The scores for those sixty-five and over are biased downward because of difficulties with the test caused by visual and other physical impairments. The coefficient of variation is the standard deviation divided by the mean.

Prose skills on NALT scale. Prose scale 225: Underline meaning of a term given in a government brochure on supplemental social security income. Prose scale 275: Interpret instructions from an appliance warranty. Prose scale 374: Compare two metaphors in a poem.

Information processing skills on NALT scale. Document scale 230: Locate intersection on a street map. Document scale 277: Identify information from a bar graph depicting source of energy and year. Document scale 378: Use information in a table to complete a graph including labeling axes.

Quantitative skills on NALT scale. Quantitative scale 238: Calculate postage and fees for certified mail. Quantitative scale 278: Use a calculator to determine difference between regular and sale price from an advertisement. Quantitative scale 383: Determine shipping and total costs on an order form for items in a catalog.

Sources: see Appendix Note 2.5.

in the ages between twenty-five and fifty-five. The test scores for the older populations may reflect, in part, visual and other physical impairments in taking the test.[5] For our purposes it is most noteworthy that the dispersion of these test scores is roughly the same for all age cohorts except the oldest; and that the tails of these distributions, at least for the first three decade cohorts, look roughly the same as well. What all this suggests is that within the last three decades or so, inequalities of educational outputs, as measured by a standardized test, have not greatly changed. Thus the output data lead to quite different conclusions about changing structural complexity than the input data.

We might interpret such cross-section data to mean that the schools have produced roughly the same actual literacy skills over the last three decades. Or the results could mean that schools have imparted more education over time, but that the older generations have been able to improve their literacy skills out of school and to close the gap. Using the National Assessment of Educational Progress (NAEP) test scores presented in Panel C of Table 2.3. I could find no evidence of any dramatic trends in test scores from 1970 to 1990: reading scores increased slightly, science scores decreased slightly, and mathematics remained roughly the same.

So it appears most likely that schools have produced roughly the same actual literacy skills for several decades, even though the actual years in school has changed.[6] More specifically, it seems likely that if there has been an increase in the average quality of education over the last three decades, it has been very small and that the inequalities of literacy among the population have also not greatly changed. Any increase in the overall level of literacy has come about through the retirement of older generations who have had considerably less formal education than the current generation. Although this cohort effect was undoubtedly very important during the 1950s to the mid-1970s, thereafter this source of change of average literacy skills has become less important. These conclusions have some important implications on income inequalities (discussed in the following section) and unemployment (see Chapter 3).

5. It could be argued that such impairments would bias the average test scores downward in the fifty-five to sixty-five cohort. But such a bias would probably be partially offset by the fact that those with lower levels of literacy tend to have a lower life expectancy so that a greater share died during the last decade of their normal working life and did not take the test.

   These data also show that the additional years of formal education of the generation that was thirty-five to forty-four at the time of the test yielded only a very slight improvement in test scores; and that the slightly greater education of the twenty-five to thirty-four-year-old cohort in comparison to the forty-five to fifty-four-year-old cohort made absolutely no difference at all.

6. According to Kirsch and Jungeblut (1986), who directly compare the Adult Literacy Test for reading of a sample of young adults with the NAEP tests for seventeen-year-old students, the average scores of the latter are lower, presumably because "reading skills increase with use in practical situations after termination of formal education or during the pursuit of higher education." This is offset by the impact of the omission of drop-outs from the study of seventeen-year-old students.

The major puzzle raised by this discussion is why heterogeneity in educational inputs is decreasing, while heterogeneity in educational outputs is not. Two explanations come readily to mind:

Impact of measurable and nonmeasurable inputs: A well-known early and highly disputed study by James Coleman and his colleagues presents evidence that school quality, as measured by easily available statistics, makes little difference on student achievement as measured by test scores.[7] Subsequently, many have reexamined the problem using other data sets. One survey of more than 140 of these studies shows that most attempts to relate teacher–pupil ratios, teacher experience, teacher education, teacher salaries, or expenditures–pupil with educational outcomes reveal few significant relations.[8] Nevertheless, these issues are far from settled in a number of ways and the current literature is showing few signs of agreement.

Such mixed statistical results suggest that equalizing measurable inputs such as expenditures per student will probably not be sufficient to reduce inequalities of educational outcomes. Moreover, many state and local governments are not even equalizing such expenditures. For instance, many governments give lower per capita subsidies to innercity community colleges than community colleges in more favored areas. In addition, state governments give more aid per student to the prestige flagship universities in the state than to community colleges, which have a higher share of students from low-income families. All these practices, of course, have been – and will continue to be – subject to a plethora of law suits. At the primary and secondary level, schools in poor areas are often in a worse position to obtain grants from governmental bodies or private foundations than schools in more affluent areas with staff members trained to obtain such funds. Finally, federal funds do little to even out educational expenditures per students in different states.

Although school quality may not be easily measured in terms of inputs, there is general agreement that schools vary greatly in the efficiency with

---

7. James Coleman et al. (1966).
8. Hanushek (1986). Recently Card and Krueger (1992a) have challenged James Coleman's results using cross-state evidence to show that white men educated in states with higher quality education, as measured by such indicators as pupil–teacher ratios and relative teacher pay, have on the average earned more than in states with low-quality schools, holding years of education and other factors constant. In another article they (1992b) also show that improvements of the quality of schools with predominantly black student bodies explains about 20 percent of the narrowing of the black–white earnings gap of those attending school in the south. By way of contrast, Betts (1993) uses a longitudinal study of high-school students and finds that the Card–Krueger results are not replicable when input data about the high school of the person is used instead of statewide averages; and using several longitudinal studies, Grogger (1993) finds similar results to those of Betts. A conference in 1994 at the Brookings Institution showed no convergence of views about the actual economic effects of increased expenditures in education.

which they use these inputs to impart skills and knowledge. Unfortunately, public policy acts in a very uncertain manner when it tries to take such intangible factors into account.

Neighborhood effects: The neighborhood of the school has some important influences. For instance, Susan E. Mayer presents evidence that, holding race and the socioeconomic status of the child constant, the lower the average social–economic level of children in a school, the greater the probability of that child dropping out and, if a girl, bearing a child in her teens.[9] For those remaining in these schools, another study presents data suggesting that the quality of education (measured by wages received after school) is negatively affected by percentage of minority students in the school and positively influenced by the interest of the parents of children, other factors including race and parental background held constant. Children of families taken out of high poverty neighborhoods and placed in other neighborhoods, a feature of the Gautreaux Assisted Housing Program in Chicago, are more likely to stay in school. Such results indicate that educational outcomes are related to cultural and other factors characterizing the location of the school.

These neighborhood effects have many other consequences as well, particularly on employment; the causal mechanisms of these linkages are also different. Neighborhood effects are exacerbated by a growing spatial differentiation of poverty and nonpoverty families. More concretely, poverty is becoming increasingly concentrated in certain innercity areas; indeed, some evidence is available that such growing spatial differentiation has occurred at all income levels.[10] Such spatial isolation has consequences such as a lack of role models for the children, a lack of information about the wider world, and a lack of

9. The two studies are respectively by Mayer (1991) and Grogger (1993). The latter study uses raw data that have a variable reflecting the interest of the respondent's parents in the education received; this is directly related to the measure of educational success of he students. If, however, individual students from the same school are compared, this parental variable no longer has statistical significance. This suggests that aggregate interest of the parents in the education of their children is the key variable for a given school. Davis (1993) summarizes some of the results of the Gautreaux Assisted Housing Program on the educational performance of the children.

10. For instance, in recent years the percentage of families in poverty has risen in the central cities and has fallen in the suburbs and nonmetropolitan areas (Peterson, 1991). It appears that the urban poor have become increasingly concentrated into particular census tracts, and that areas classified as ghettos (according to various criteria of social pathologies) are not only increasing but include a higher percentage of the poor. The most difficult analytic problem is separating out the factor of race, emphasized particularly by Massey and Denton (1993) and income, But as Massey and Denton show (p. 129), in "hypersegregated cities" the percentage of poor in "low-income neighborhoods" increased for both whites and blacks between 1970 and 1980. This was especially evident among African-Americans, who had already a higher concentration of poverty. More recent statistics are found in Harrison and Bennett (1995).

exposure to a wider range of ideas and attitudes. Among other things, these lead to the reinforcement of a "culture of poverty" discouraging the development of a work ethic, a matter discussed in greater detail in the final chapter.

In sum, the discrepancy between a growing homogeneity of the population, when classified by educational inputs, and the roughly similar degree of heterogeneity, when individuals are classified by educational outcomes, seems due in major part to neighborhood effects. These can be traced, in turn, to the growing stratification of neighborhoods by income.

Age

Heterogeneity of the age structure means simply that the population is less concentrated in a given number of age groups and is more evenly spread over the entire age range. Although this can occur for a number of different reasons, for the United States and other industrialized nations this means, as we all know, that the relative share of older people is becoming greater. This trend arises from two circumstances: a fall in the birth rates so that the share of children in the population is smaller and a fall in the mortality among the aged so

Paul Jargowsky (cited by Kaus, 1992) has investigated the problem of spatial separation by income groups in a more general by devising a sorting index to measure the extent to which households are grouped into neighborhoods by income. Between 1970 and 1980 in 237 metropolitan areas, the degree of sorting by income groups increased slightly; but for the northern states, this increase in economic sorting appears marked. Massey and Eggers (1990) analyze the same data set in a different manner and find that such an increase in sorting was much more characteristic of African-Americans than other racial groups where the trend did not occur or was less marked.

Some argue that this growing spatial isolation is also accompanied on the top end of the income scale by a growing estrangement of the elite from the mass of people. Christopher Lasch argues convincingly that there has always been a privileged class in America, but it "has never been so dangerously isolated from it surroundings" (Lasch, 1995, p. 4). His major concern is that this elite lacks comprehension of the fragility of civilization, that it lives primarily for its own well being and in the assurance that tomorrow's world will be better, and that it lacks any sense of its obligations to help preserve its historical heritage and its community. Herrnstein and Murray (1990) approach this matter from a different angle in their suggestion that accompanying an increasing stratification of cognitive ability in society is an increasing geographical segregation along the same lines. This observation parallels those by authors such as William Julius Wilson, who argue that the exodus of individuals with high education or high cognitive ability from traditional African-American communities into more middle class areas has left these communities impoverished for role models and on a downward spiral. Of course, the same can be said for communities of poor whites as well. All of these approaches are related to my argument in Chapter 10 that social cohesiveness is declining.

It should be added that these trends about increasing spatial distances of different groups are not completely unambiguous and others have obtained somewhat different empirical results, for instance White (1987, p. 189) and Farley (1991). Nevertheless, the increasing spatial concentration of poverty generally seems accepted.

Table 2.4. *Key data on the age distribution*

| | 1950 | 1960 | 1970 | 1980 | 1990 | Projections | | |
						2010	2030	2050
Share of population under six (%)	12.6	13.5	10.3	8.6	8.8	7.9	7.6	7.7
Share of population, six through seventeen (%)	18.6	22.3	24.0	19.5	16.7	16.2	15.8	15.5
Share of population sixty-five through eighty-four (%)	7.8	8.6	9.1	10.3	11.3	11.4	17.8	16.0
Share of population eighty-five and over (%)	.4	.5	.7	1.0	1.3	1.9	2.4	4.6
Median age (years)	30.1	29.5	28.1	30.0	33.0	37.4	39.0	39.3
Dependency ratio (%)	65.1	81.5	79.0	65.1	61.7	60.0	77.5	77.9
Absolute Theil statistic[a]	4.33	4.34	4.36	4.38	4.41	4.45	4.49	4.53
Relative Theil statistic[a]	93.9%	94.0%	94.5%	95.0%	95.5%	96.3%	97.3%	98.1%

Note: To obtain data for all 101 age groups, I made some small estimates for several census series where data on the oldest segment of the population are presented only in five-year intervals. Data sources are given in Appendix Note 2.5.
[a]A larger Theil statistic reflects greater heterogeneity. The absolute and relative Theil statistics are discussed in the notes to Table 2.2; a fuller explanation is found in Appendix Note 1.2.

that this age cohort maintains its numbers for a longer time. Some relevant data are presented in Table 2.4.

The data show that age heterogeneity, as measured by the Theil statistic, has increased very slowly. With the fall in the birth rate, the relative share of those under eighteen has fallen, while both the young–old (sixty-five through eighty-four) and the old–old (eighty-five and over) has risen dramatically. The dependency rate (the ratio of those under eighteen and over sixty-four to those between eighteen and sixty-five) has fluctuated considerably since it is strongly affected by the birth rate.. In 1960 it reached historic highs as a result of the high birth rate since the end of World War II; in the twenty-first century it rises as the relative number of aged rise faster than the relative number of children falls. These trends are well-known and need no additional elaboration.

Brief summary

This discussion documents the increasing structural complexity of the population in the four decades following World War II, as indicated by measures of heterogeneity of ethnicity and race, family structure, and age. The heterogeneity of educational attainment has either decreased or remained the same, depending upon whether we are examining educational inputs or outputs. Some important implications of these trends are discussed later in this chapter.

Economic structures: The distribution of income and wealth

Heterogeneity of the population is also manifested by the degree to which it is stratified according to different levels of incomes and wealth. Such inequality is the subject of a considerable amount of wishful thinking. For instance two well-known futurists joyfully inform us:[11] "By 2000 there will be no mistaking the trend toward a more comfortable, more equal America. The richest and poorest segments of the American population will be much smaller than they are today, the middle class correspondingly larger." It is useful to take a flint-eyed view of the actual trends. The following argument suggests that inequalities of wealth have steadily increased since the early 1960s and that the inequalities of income have steadily increased since the late 1970s. Both will probably continue in this direction for some years to come, thereby leading to greater population heterogeneity.

The size distribution of income

Over its history the United States has experienced considerable movements in the degree of income inequality.[12] In the early nineteenth century, income inequality appeared to increase considerably in the four decades preceding the Civil War. After the Civil War income inequality seemed to remain relatively constant until the turn of the twentieth century, when it began to rise again. World War I brought a sudden shift toward equality, but this effect wore off by 1929. Between 1929 and the middle of the century, however, income inequality, as well as wage and salary inequalities, declined significantly. In various decades these long-term trends have reflected the influence of quite different underlying causes. These diverse trends in different periods suggest that it is useful to be modest in our projection of income and wealth inequalities into the future.

Current trends

As shown in Figure 2.1 the measures of income inequality reveal an irregular decrease from 1950 to 1967–1968. Thereafter, inequality increases, accel-

---

11. Cetron and Davies (1989), p. 22. Other futurists might be cited as well.
12. Willliamson and Lindert (1980) give some data for the nineteenth century. Levy and Murnane (1990) and Goldin and Margo (1992) present evidence for the period from 1929 to the present.

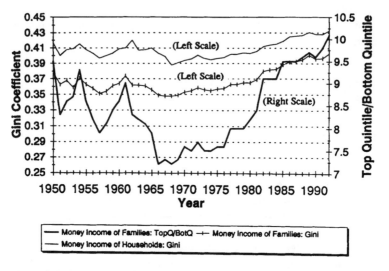

Notes: Quintile ratios and Gini coefficients rise with increasing inequality. The data are pretax income including money transfers. Data sources are found in Appendix Note 2.1.

Figure 2.1. Inequality indicators

erating upward in the early 1980s. This generalization holds for all three annual measures of income inequality presented in the figure. Two of these measures are based on Gini coefficients, which run from .00 (total equality) to 1.00 (total inequality) and focus respectively on families (related people living together) and households (families plus unrelated individuals residing with the family). The third measure is the ratio of average incomes in the top and bottom quintiles of the income distribution of families.

Other definitions of inequality reveal similar trends.[13] If the inequality data are recalculated to take account of the size, composition, and age of family members, the same trends in inequality emerge. If we continue along this line of inquiry and examine the inequality of consumption, taking account of the fact that consumer durables are consumed over a period of years, the same trends also appear. The pattern of inequality of wages and salaries follows a roughly similar pattern as well (see Appendix Note 2.2).

Such data on income inequalities reflect income only in a single year, rather than a lifetime. Some argue that current spells of poverty lead to lower rela-

13. Karoly (forthcoming) presents calculations of the income distribution where she takes family size and composition into account. Cutler and Katz (1991) carry out a similar calculation and, moreover, calculate the inequality of consumption "per equivalent person." Although these distribution calculations reveal inequalities considerably less than those shown in Figure 2.1, the trends are the same.

tive incomes only at a single point in time. If these spells of poverty are only temporary and do not reflect equality of incomes over longer periods, then a declining equality of annual income is not as serious as it might first appear. Although we must rely on some difficult estimates, this argument appears to fall to the ground when confronted with the evidence.[14] Using income tax returns Joel Slemrod presents evidence that the average income of taxpayers for the seven.year period from 1967 through 1973 was somewhat more equal than in the seven.year period from 1979 through 1985. This tax sample omits, however, a significant proportion of low-income families. Using income data over time from the University of Michigan's Panel Study of Income Dynamics (PSID), Charles F. Stone and Larry Radbill show in some preliminary calculations that average incomes over the ten.year period from 1969 to 1979 were more equal than over the nine.year period from 1979 to 1987. For this they use two samples: labor income of prime-age males and total family income. Thus, from 1980 onward lifetime incomes are becoming more unequal as well. Jonathan R. Veum shows that year-to-year mobility in the income distribution has significantly declined between 1972 and 1986 for family income, for equivalent incomes (taking family composition into account) and for earnings of the family head. These long-term inequalities are somewhat less than the inequalities for a given year since people have low or high incomes in a particular year that do not occur in other years. Steven V. Rose presents some interesting results based on two ten-year samples. He shows that the same families in the lower income quintiles were much more likely to experience low or negative income growth over the decade than families in the higher income quintiles; moreover, this gap in income growth widened over time.[15] He also presents evidence that differential income growth was lower among black families than white families, that they were more likely to experience income declines over the decade, and that these black–white differences increased over time.

All these studies of long-term income point toward greater lifetime inequalities of income in the 1980s than in the previous decade. Most also show a decline in long-term income mobility and reveal a greater income stratification. As for their results concerning the poorest segment of the population, they add support to more traditional studies that show an increase in long-term poverty.[16]

14. Slemrod (1992) makes the calculations from the tax returns. The other studies that I mention are Stone and Radbill (1993a and 1993b), Veum (1992), and Rose (1993).
15. Reporting some preliminary results, Isabel V. Sawhill and Mark Condon (1992) use two nine-year samples and present data suggesting a contrary conclusion, namely that although lifetime incomes are becoming more unequal, income mobility from quintile to quintile has not greatly changed. But this study is criticized on a number of technical grounds by Stephen V. Rose, who points out, among other things, that it is necessary to adjust to take into account random fluctuations of income in a single year by comparing several year averages of incomes ten years apart in order to avoid bias.
16. For instance, Jencks (1991).

Although the trend in annual and decade data toward greater income inequality reflects an increasing lifetime income stratification of the population, does it extend over generations as well? One measure employed in the literature about this problem is the income elasticity of income of fathers and sons: if the father's income is 1 percent above the median income, what percent above the median income is the son's income? An elasticity of 0 indicates no relation at all between the income of fathers and an elasticity equal to one means that income inequalities are completely inherited. An elasticity between zero and one, which we would expect, shows a certain regression toward the mean.

The results of two recent studies deserve attention.[17] Drawing data from the PSID, Gary Solon shows that this elasticity is probably between .4 and .5. An elasticity of .4 means that if the father's income is in the lowest quintile, the son has a .49 chance of also having an income in the lowest quintile and a mere .17 chance of rising to the median. Using quite different statistical methods and a sample of incomes of fathers and sons from the National Longitudinal Survey, David Zimmerman obtains roughly the same elasticity results for wages and salaries. In sum, intergenerational income elasticities are higher, and intergenerational income mobility is lower than commonly believed. Thus the increasing lifetime inequality of income also may be transmitted to future generations.

In examining the increase in structural complexity of the demographic variables, the causes are relatively clear. By way of contrast, the underlying causes of this increase in the inequality of income since the early 1970s are obscure. As previously noted, some part may be due to changes in the family structure and the relative rise in importance of single-parent families. Some part may be due to the apparent increase in marriage between those with roughly equal earning potentials ("assortive mating"). Aside from these, some economic factors also seem important and it is worthwhile to investigate clues provided by changes in major income components, as well as in individual earnings.[18]

17. The two studies to which I refer are Solon (1992) and Zimmerman (1992). From theoretical evidence Solon also demonstrates that previous studies of intergenerational income mobility that show an elasticity of about .2 are biased downwardly.
18. Herrnstein and Murray (1994), Part I, provide convincing evidence of an increasing stratification of the U.S. population by cognitive ability, which represents the rise of meritocracy. If an individual's income is determined by two factors, education and I.Q., then such a stratification leads to a more unequal distribution of income for reasons argued by Tinbergen (1975). Although such stratification by cognitive ability does not explain the U-shaped pattern shown in Figure 2.1, it could have an extremely important impact on secular changes. As Herrnstein and Murray note (p. 541), "Deciphering complexity is one of the things that cognitive ability is good for." This argument would fall under the demand-side factors for skills that is discussed in Chapter 3.

Underlying causes – Changes in major income components: Income inequality can increase if the share of property income, which is much more unequally distributed than labor income, becomes a larger share of national income. Property income (profits, rent, net interest) has accounted for about 20 percent of that part of national income attributable to distinct factors of production.[19] Between the 1950s and 1990, its share in the national income decreased slightly, and more detailed analyses have found no important shifts in property income that would explain the increasingly unequal division of income in the population.

As I document in the following section, the distribution of wealth has become more unequal over most of the postwar period, which suggests, in turn, that even a constant share of property income could contribute to the increase in income inequality. Recent microevidence suggests, however, that so far this impact of such changes on inequalities of income have been relatively small.

Underlying causes – Changes in relative labor earnings of individuals: Labor income (wages and salaries) accounts for about 80 percent of that part of national income that can be attributed to distinct factors of production. Here a problem of interpretation arises, since most data refer to inequalities of individual wages and salaries, while family labor income depends in part on how many members of the family are working. Although this demographic factor has played a certain role, changes in the relationships between family and individual incomes do not appear to number among the most important causes of the increasing inequality of labor incomes.[20] As a result, we can focus our attention on the underlying causes of changes in inequalities of individual earnings.

19. Proprietors' income (both farm and nonfarm) is difficult to attribute to either capital or labor. Such income fell from 14.1 percent in the 1950s to 7.7 percent in the 1980s (U.S. Department of Commerce, Bureau of Economic Analysis, 1992/3). Cutler and Katz (1992) analyze in further detail the impact of shifts in labor and property income on the size distribution of income. Karoly (forthcoming) presents the empirical evidence showing the contribution of changing inequality of property income to changes in overall income inequalities.

20. Karoly and Burtless (1994) have a detailed empirical analysis of the relation between individual and family income; for trends of income inequality over time, this relationship does not play an important role. Some economists have argued that changes in the types of families has played a certain role. For instance, Mishel and Bernstein (1993, pp. 40–2) point out that between the late 1960s and 1990, the only type of family experiencing a significant increase in median family income were married couples with the wife in the paid labor force; married couples without a wife in the labor force or family groups with no spouse present experienced a relatively low real income increase. This covered a period in which wives of middle- and upper-income families entered the labor force in a far faster rate than wives of low-income families who had a labor force participation rate that was initially much higher. Given the fact that men and women tend to marry people similar to themselves in ability, the entry into the labor force of high-skilled, high-ability women would not only increase the income of married couples with wives working but would also increase the inequalities of incomes of fam-

Two dates are important in understanding trends in the level and the inequality of labor income. Nineteen seventy-three marked the end of a rapid rise in aggregate productivity and in real wages, and the beginning of a rise in the ratio of foreign trade to GDP (discussed in detail in Chapter 8). Nineteen seventy-nine marked the beginning of an acceleration of earnings inequality, particularly among male workers. Although different studies assess the magnitudes of these trends somewhat differently, this trend in inequalities of wages seems unmistakable.[21]

Explanation of the changes in the inequality of labor income of wages and salaries can be approached from several analytic perspectives: examination of between-group and within-group wage differences, study of changes in the institutions of wage determination., and isolation of supply and demand elements for different types of labor. All of these are discussed in Appendix Note 2.2. The most revealing analysis, however, focuses on changes in the supply and demand factors.

On the supply side, a rapid increase in college-educated workers from the end of World War II up to the end of the 1970s led to a decline in the wage differentials between high- and low-educated workers. After 1980, however, the entry of college graduates into the labor force slowed markedly and the educational differential began to rise. Further, in the 1970s and 1980s, a shift in immigration patterns toward a larger share of lower skilled workers played a certain role in pulling down wages at the low end of the scale of native workers.[22]

On the demand side, technological change in recent years has had a bias toward highly skilled workers so that the demand for these workers has risen much faster than for unskilled workers. This issue is explored at greater depth in Chapter 3, where I show that the rise in unemployment is particularly evi-

ilies with two working members. This hypothesis however is controversial (Veum, 1992, confirms it but does cites conflicting evidence). As discussed in the next chapter, the increase in the female participation rate in the labor force is tapering off and so this factor, if it every played a role, should not be important in the future.

21. Norton W. Grubb and Robert H. Wilson (1992) find an irregular but upward trend in wage and salary inequalities from 1967 to the early 1980s, a sharp increase up to 1986, and then a slight reversal. Lynn Karoly (1988) finds an upward trend throughout the period, although not so marked during the 1980s. Both studies use the March Current Population Samples and the same measure of inequality. Although their numerical results are quite similar for the early part, such results diverge considerably by the end of the period. The underlying reasons for such different results are not clear. Karoly also calculates inequality using other aggregate measures such as the Gini coefficient and the variance of the logarithms of income; all measures show the same trends.

22. Borjas, Freeman, and Katz (1992) provide empirical evidence on this matter. The change in the composition of immigrants arose from a variety of causes including changes in U.S. immigration laws in 1965 that favored relatives of those living in the United States over skilled workers, a shift in the countries of origin of the immigrants, and a rise in illegal immigration. Borjas (1994) has further analysis of the quality of the immigrants.

dent among the unskilled. Another factor is the decline in demand for U.S. produced goods that embody large amounts of unskilled labor. This, in turn, is due partly to shifts in domestic demand patterns and partly to the increasing imports that are crowding out U.S. production in these low-wage industries. As I show in Chapter 8, the U.S. industries with high ratios of unskilled to skilled workers have been hard hit. Several mechanisms can be offered to explain this turn of events. The most popular explanation is that U.S. unskilled workers are facing increased competition from "low-wage workers" abroad. From a glance at trade statistics, however, this explanation seems problematic and is probably of secondary importance.[23]

Aside from these demand and supply factors, some institutional causes can be adduced, although they seem to be of secondary importance. For instance, the penetration of imports of industries with high industrial concentration has lowered the economic rents of the high-wage, low-skilled workers in these industries. Moreover, the decline in the relative power of labor unions (Chapter 4), which have acted in the past to compress the wage distribution, has also led to wider wage differentials.[24]

It should be added that none of these various supply, demand, or institutional explanations explain very well the differential behavior of wage inequality among male and female workers.

The size distribution of wealth

From the early 1950s to the early 1980s, the distribution of wealth revealed no marked trends; thereafter, it became increasingly unequal. Before turning to the data I must emphasize that the estimation of changes in the distribution of wealth over time is fraught with difficulties due to both conceptual and data problems. Moreover, in most cases, such data refer only to physical and financial wealth, rather than broader definitions covering human capital or wealth held in the form of pension and Social Security rights. The two major sources of raw data – estate tax returns for individuals and household surveys – yield somewhat different results; and the sources of these differences are not clear.

23. First, the share of imports from the low-wage developing nations has not greatly changed in the post–World War II period (as discussed in Appendix Note 8.2). Second, the share of imports in the GDP did not greatly change during the 1980s when real wages of low-wage workers in the United States continued to fall. Third, wages in a number of industrialized nations such as Japan and Germany, when converted into dollars by the exchange rate, became higher than wages in the United States as the dollar fell in the late 1980s and early 1990s. Most studies (for instance, Lawrence and Slaughter, 1993) place secondary importance on this trade factor as a explanation for the rising inequality of wages.

24. These institutional factors receives greater attention in Appendix Note 2.2. My stress on supply and demand factors is consistent with the results of the analysis in Chapter 3 about the changing composition of skills of the labor force.

Table 2.5. *Measures of the inequality of wealth*

A. *Net worth held by wealthiest individuals: Estate multiplier method*

	Lampman–Smith estimates		Wolff–Marley estimates			
			Narrow definition		Broad definition	
	Top 0.5%	Top 1.0%	Top 0.5%	Top 1.0%	Top 0.5%	Top 1.0%
1922	29.8%	—	26.8%	—	28.0%	—
1929	32.4	—	—	—	—	—
1933	25.2	—	—	—	—	—
1939	28.0	—	—	—	—	—
1945	20.9	—	—	—	—	—
1949	19.3	—	—	—	—	—
1953	22.7	—	—	26.6	—	21.3
1956	22.5	—	—	—	—	—
1958	21.4	26.6%	20.8	25.9	16.4	20.7
1962	22.2	28.2	23.0	29.1	17.5	22.4
1965	25.4	31.3	25.4	31.3	18.9	23.6
1969	21.8	27.4	22.5	28.2	16.4	20.9
1972	21.9	27.2	21.8	27.6	15.8	20.3
1976	14.4	19.2	12.6	17.3	9.8	13.4
1981	—	—	19.7	28.4	14.0	20.4

B. *Net worth held by wealthiest families: household survey method (Wolff estimates)*

	Top 0.5%	Top 1.0%	Top 10%	Top 20%	Gini coefficients[a]
1962	25.9%	33.4%	67.0%	80.9%	.80
1983	26.2	33.7	68.1	81.3	.80
1989	31.4	38.9	72.3	84.6	.84

[a]Gini coefficients increase with rising inequality.
For other notes and data sources, see Appendix Note 2.5.

Furthermore, data on estate tax returns exist for the entire country only since the early part of the twentieth century and reliable nationwide household surveys only began to be made in the post–World War II years. The imperfect data on the distribution of wealth reveal considerable swings in inequality over the last 200 years in the U.S.[25]

25. Piecing together a variety of data sources for particular localities, Jeffrey G. Williamson and Peter H. Lindert present evidence that wealth inequalities remained roughly the same from the middle of the seventeenth century up to the beginning of the nineteenth century. In the half-century preceding the Civil War, by way of contrast, the inequality of wealth increased considerably (Williamson and Lindert, 1980). After a fall of inequality in the 1860s, due in good measure to the redistribution of wealth in the South after the Civil War, wealth inequalities changed little until World War I, when they declined again.

From the data in Table 2.5 several conclusions can be drawn about the distribution of wealth in more recent times. First, the definition of wealth is a crucial factor determining the degree of inequality. The Lampman–Smith and Wolff–Marley estimates (narrow definition) define *net worth* and *wealth* in a relatively conventional sense; and the degree of inequality is much higher than if claims on the Social Security system are included (Wolff–Marley, broad definition). Second, whatever the measure of wealth used, the inequality of wealth is very high; and this seems true not only in an absolute sense, but also in comparison to certain other industrialized nations such as France.[26] Finally, wealth inequalities decreased in the 1950s and then, in recent years, increased although the exact turning point depends on the definition of wealth.

The data on net worth held by the wealthiest individuals suggest a relative constancy until World War II; the various ups and downs of the series are more an artifact of the basic data and a certain randomness in the death of some very wealthy individuals than of variations in the distribution *per se*. The most significant change occurred during World War II, with the share of net worth of the wealthiest individuals revealing a dramatic reduction. To a considerable degree this appears due to changes in the share of wealth held by individuals within a given family. With some heroic assumptions, several economists have estimated the share of the wealthiest families (not individuals), manifested a much smaller decline.[27] After that, the estate tax data show a slight rise in inequality up to the late 1960s and a slight decline thereafter, so that the level of inequality in the early 1980s was roughly the same as in the 1950s. The sharp dip in inequality in 1976 appears more an artifact of the raw data, rather than any real phenomenon.

The household survey data show a rough constancy of the share of wealth held by the wealthiest .5 or 1 percent of households from 1962 to 1983, and then a sharp rise in inequality in the next six years. The calculations of Gini coefficients of inequality for the entire distribution yield the same results.

In isolating the causes of these changes in the distribution of wealth over the last half-century, several possible factors can be ruled out quickly.[28] Although under some circumstances, a shift in the age distribution can affect the distribution of wealth, Daphne T. Greenwood shows that these effects were quite

26. Wolff–Marley (1991).
27. Lampman (1962) and Wolff–Marley (1989).
28. Greenwood (1987) analyzes the impact of the changing age distribution. Pryor (1973a) presents a simulation model analyzing the impact of changing inheritance, marriage, and savings practices on the distribution of wealth. Although inheritance laws were liberalized in the mid-1970s, it does not seem likely that such changes explain the marked changes in the 1980s. It should be added that the 1993 budget bill raised inheritance taxes so that the long-term effects of the changes in the 1970s would probably be offset. The analysis of causes of changes in the distribution of wealth in the 1980s is based on the empirical analysis of Wolff (1994).

small. Although changes in inheritance practices also could have an important influence, it does not seem likely that these played a significant role. Although much needs to be learned about the causes of the distribution of wealth in the past, three factors appear to have caused the changes in the 1980s.

First, since high-income earners save a larger percent of their disposable incomes than low-income earners, it seems likely that a change in the inequality of income would be paralleled by a similar change in the distribution of wealth. During the 1980s this effect was undoubtedly reinforced by an increase in disposable income to total income by the rich and the reverse by the poor. More specifically, in the 1980s tax rates on the incomes of high-income families fell and more regressive taxes such as Social Security and sales taxes increased. In the period from 1950 up to the mid-1970s, wealth inequalities remained roughly constant during a period in which the distribution of income became somewhat more equal.

Second, in the 1980s relative asset prices changed in favor of those assets most likely to be held by the wealthy such as corporate stocks. More specifically, between 1983 and 1989, prices of stocks increased much more rapidly than the prices of homes, the chief asset held by the bottom 80 percent of the wealth distribution. In the period from 1962 to 1983, the reverse was true. It does not seem probable that the differential price change of assets in the 1980s will continue indefinitely into the future.

Third, during the 1980s the rate of inflation slowed. Since the ratio of debts to monetary income is generally higher for the poor than the rich, inflation during the 1960s and 1970s aided the poor relatively more than the rich. In the 1980s, this effect was not as strong.

Brief summary

Since the early 1970s income inequalities have increased. Of particular importance, the demand for skilled and educated workers has increased faster than the supply and the reverse applied to the unskilled. Inequalities of wealth have increased since the early 1960s, a trend traceable in part to greater disposible income and saving by the wealthy and to relative changes in the prices of assets held by the wealthy. Both trends have contributed to a greater statification of the population and, as I argue in the following section, both are likely to continue.

The future

I have documented increases in structural complexity, as manifested by rising demographic and economic heterogeneity. Although heterogeneity has increased with regard to race and ethnicity, family structure, and age, this has not necessarily occurred for all possible dimensions by which the population can be divided, for instance, religion.[29] Although it also is possible to have increasing demographic heterogeneity without increasing inequality of income and wealth, this possibility is not very likely in large measure because such variables as race, education, and age, play a crucial role in explaining work force status and wages. As I have noted, most of these trends in increasing structural complexity are relatively recent and date from 1950 or beyond. To what extent are they expected to continue in the future?

Ethnic and racial heterogeneity will undoubtedly continue to increase, in part because of higher birth rates of the nonwhite population, in part because it seems unlikely that the immigration stream will decelerate, at least in the near future. Several factors underlie this assertion. The economic forces attracting immigrants to the United States, especially from the Third World, will continue as long as income gaps between these nations and the United States remain. The process is reinforced by the communications revolution allowing peoples of these nations to see the lifestyles of others in the world. Prevention of illegal immigration will remain difficult, given the porousness of U.S. national borders and the unwillingness of the United States to adopt draconian measures to prevent illegal immigration that have been carried out by nations such as Japan. Some commentators, such as Paul Kennedy and Jacques Attali, see illegal immigration as a crucial problem for most industrialized nations in the twenty-first century.[30] Finally, it does not seem likely that immigration quotas will be greatly changed in the coming years. Of course, U.S. public opinion about the desirability of immigration into the United States has waxed and waned over the decades. Given trends to greater income inequality, the resistance of lower income voters toward a greater influx of perceived competitors for jobs will

29. It is usually assumed that religious heterogeneity is increasing because of the rising share of population with no religious preference. More specifically, from 1957 through 1990, the share of the population giving Protestant as their religious preference fell from 66 to 56 percent of the population; Jews and Catholics roughly maintained their share while those claiming "other" religious preference rose from 1 to 6 percent and those giving no religious preference rose from 3 percent to 11 percent (U.S. Department of Commerce, Bureau of the Census, annual-b, 1992, Table 75). Church and synagogue members as a share of the adult population also declined. Moreover, public opinion polls show that persons attending church and synagogue within the last week also fell in the same period, but to a much slower degree.

This rising heterogeneity also is supposed to be manifested by a growth of fringe religions. More specifically, in the postwar period mainline religions have lost their dominance and certain religions new to the United States increased in importance, for instance, by 1990 the United States had more Muslims than Jews (National Council of the Churches of Christ in the U.S.A., annual-1992). Assuming that religious heterogeneity can be measured by membership in various churches, religious diversity has decreased in the postwar period, primarily as a result of church mergers. This may be one dimension where cultural heterogeneity did not increase. Further discussion and the relevant data are given in Appendix Note 2.1.

30. Kennedy (1993) and Attali (1991). The Census Bureau estimates come from Spencer (1989).

undoubtedly increase, as it sometimes has in the past under similar circumstances; but the translation of such discontent among groups with a relatively low voter turnout into actual legislation seems problematic. Such arguments give plausibility to the belief that it quite possible for net immigration into the United States to exceed the Census Bureau's high estimate of 1,370,000; after all, their high estimate in 1988 was roughly their middle estimate for the 1993 projections. All this means that the share of foreign born in the U.S. population may again reach the levels of the 1870s by 2050.

It is more difficult to predict changes in family structure. Although divorce rates appear to have tapered off somewhat in the 1980s, the rise in the rate of illegitimate births shows no sign of decelerating and the single-parent households with children reveals an irregular but upward trend since the 1960s. As I'll point out, children from single-parent households are more likely to live in such arrangements when they have children, so that the process is self-reinforcing.

The inequality of education of the labor force, as measured by output, appears roughly the same over the last few decades and this is likely to continue in the future. In the early 1990s the federal and state governments began to undertake some initiatives such as setting national educational goals and establishing a nationwide testing system to equalize educational outcomes. Successful lawsuits in a handful of states also have led to state governmental programs to equalize educational expenditures in the various districts. Nevertheless, by the mid-1990s these measures have not led to a reversal of the general trend starting in 1980 of the states placing more of the economic burden of school financing on the districts themselves; this leads to greater inequalties of educational expenditures per student. Moreover, neighborhood effects arising from increasing segregation of the poor would also have to be offset. This would require higher educational expenditures per student than in the wealthier districts, a consideration that has not yet entered into discussion. Finally, the rising proportion of children with educational impairments arising from the impact of single-parent households also would somehow have to be reversed.

With regard to age heterogeneity, the simple demographic factors underlying past changes point toward a continuation of these trends for the next few decades. If the birth, death, and immigration parameters continue to hold, the age distribution should reach a new equilibrium sometime toward the end of the first third of the twentieth century. Since these critical demographic parameters seldom remain constant for very long, such an equilibrium will probably never be achieved.

The increasing inequality of the distribution of income will probably continue in the coming years. A reversal seems unlikely as long as educational outputs do not become not equalized. An upsurge of unskilled illegal immigrants or a rise in the share of children suffering from the effects of divorce or living in single family households could accelerate such a trend toward greater income inequalities. It is impossible to predict the bias of future technological change toward high- or low-skilled work; but no signs of any reversal of current trends are available. Moreover, little evidence is at hand to suggest that imports will not continue to adversely effect those U.S. industries with a high share of unskilled workers which, in turn, will place additional downward pressure on low wages. Finally, if the nightmares predicted by the ecologists actually happen and raw material shortages occur, the relative rise in their prices will further widen the distribution of real income. This is because a much higher percentage of the consumption budgets of the poor than the rich can be attributed to raw materials embodied in commodities that they consume. These impacts are considerable and Appendix Note 2.3 presents some quantitative estimates.

It is difficult for the government to adopt policies that will reverse current trends, especially in the short run, for two reasons. First, most policy tools to influence massively the distribution of income are either ineffective or politically infeasible. In the short run the direct fiscal influences are small. From the detailed emperical evidence, we know that changes in the structure of taxes and governmental transfers during the 1980s exacerbated the increasing income inequality, although not to a major degree.[31] Such governmental measures might be reversed in the late 1990s and future years, although political forces manifested in the mid-1990s make such measures unlikely. The government also can take other obvious steps on the expenditure side to reduce real income inequality. Nevertheless, it does not seem that these would make a great deal of difference, at least in the next decade or so. Probably the most effective tool to influence the distribution of real income would be a national health program, but whether this is politically feasable remains to be seen. Second, although policy tools that focus on labor skills or other aspects of human capital can effectivedly change the distribution of income, these take a long time to have an impact.

Some causes underlying the spurt in the inequality of wealth in the 1980s, particularly the relative increase in the value of assets most likely to be held by the wealthy, are likely to abate. But the increasing inequality of income suggests that the rising inequality of wealth will persist in the near future, if only because it is the wealthy who save and invest the largest share of their income.

The impact of trends of structural complexity

The trends in demographic and economic heterogeneity have many implications. In some cases, the impact can be tied directly to the increase in one type of heterogeneity. For instance, the increasing age heterogeneity, as reflected by

---

31. Gramlich, Kasten, and Sammartino (1993) present a useful analysis of this problem.

the aging of the population, means that relatively more resources are likely to be devoted to support the aged – a topic taken up in greater detail in Chapter 9. The increasing ethnic heterogeneity, resulting from increased immigration, has some direct implications on the quantity and quality of the labor force. In the following discussion, I wish to focus on two broader issues, namely the impact of increasing demographic and economic heterogeneity on the rate of economic growth and on social cohesiveness.

Impact on the rate of economic growth

In recent years economists have begun to focus attention on the ways in which the distribution of income can influence investment and economic growth. Traditionally it has been believed that more unequal income distributions lead to more aggregate saving, given the fact that high-income people save a larger share of their income than those with low income.

This type of saving effect is probably more than offset by several other important causal forces.[32] For instance, due to imperfections in the capital market, children from poor families find it difficult to borrow in order to finance their education and this, in turn, leads to an underinvestment in education for the community as a whole. Moreover, due to the spatial clustering of housing by income levels and reliance on property taxes to finance education, low-income communities may underinvest in education for all of their citizens. Finally, spatial clustering by income may lead to reinforcement of the "culture of poverty" and an unevaluation of the benefits of education. It should be noted that such housing segregation by income level appears more marked in the United States than in other industrialized nations.

Demographic heterogeneity also has some important impacts on the rate of growth. For instance, in so far as the increasing heterogeneity of family structure, as manifested by the rise of the single-parent family adversely influences the work ethic, this culture of poverty is reinforced. That is, economic growth is reduced both because the quality of the labor force will increase less rapidly and because the intensity of work will decrease. In the following remarks, however, I focus on age hetergeneity because, according to the conventional wisdom, the aging of the population is supposed to reduce economic growth because of falling saving rates. I'll argue that the general conclusion about economic growth is right, but the hypothesized mechanism is wrong and that the more important causal links are different.

The argument about age and saving rates can be approached in several different ways. Using the lifecycle model of saving, we can derive the results that with a low population growth and a low increase in productivity, saving in the

---

32. I draw from the ideas of Galor (1993) and Benabou (1993).

United States will fall in the next few decades for two reasons: the stable population structure will result in gross dissaving by the aged that would be equal to the gross saving of those in the working ages. And the lifetime incomes of the working population and the retired population are roughly equal so that the saving of those in the labor force would not differ greatly from those who have retired. According to Jean Crockett, such a simple model has certain implications about the fall of aggregate saving in the 1970s that did not actually occur.[33] But with some sophisticated modifications to this model she also concludes: "In the absence of substantial recovery in real wage growth [and a low population growth rate: *FP*], saving rates fall below those of the 1980s under a wide range of parameter assumptions." David M. Cutler and his colleagues also find a fall in saving and growth rates for somewhat different but related reasons.

But no theoretical model does a very good job in predicting actual saving by decade cohorts. My own model employs a more empirical approach toward saving by assuming that saving rates in the different ten-year age cohorts remain the same as those in 1990. This approach means that we can take account of a crucial economic reality: people in the fifty-five to sixty-five-year cohort have a saving rate several times higher than any other age group, an empirical fact not taken into account by other models. Such saving behavior apparently occurs because this age cohort has finished putting their children through college and sees considerably more clearly than before the implications of saving for retirement. This says something about the usual assumption of infinite planning horizons for individual savers!

My simulation model, described in detail in Appendix Note 2.4, moves a population through time, taking account of differences between age cohorts of saving rates, labor force participation rates, and rates of productivity due to age and education. Total production is a function of effective labor and capital, and the latter, in turn, is a function of saving and depreciation rates. Given the complicated interactions between the age distribution, labor force participation, GDP, saving, and growth, it is necessary to employ a simple simulation model to work out the implication of any particular set of assumptions.[34]

The base line simulation assumes full employment, constant saving rates by decade cohorts, the same number of immigrants per year as in the late 1980s,

33. This conclusion and the quotation come from Crockett (1990). The next study mentioned is Cutler et al. (1990).
34. It is well known that gross business saving accounts for the largest share of total gross saving. As a percent of either total GDP or GDP originating from the business sector, these shares were roughly constant from 1950 up to the early 1970s and from the mid-1970s up to 1993 the shares trended slightly downward. From the early 1970s to the mid-1970s, these shares experienced a one.time increase. These data come from Tables 5.1, 1.1, and 1.7 of the national income and product accounts. I have modeled business and government saving as a constant share of the GDP in order to focus attention on the impact of personal saving and the population structure.

and decade changes of total factor productivity (reflecting disembodied nonbiased technological change) equal to 10 percent. I focus on economic growth rather than average saving rates per se since changes in the population affect not just saving but overall productivity and labor force participation rates as well.

With such a model it can be shown that future economic growth is much lower than in previous decades. More specifically, the annual rate of per capita growth falls from 1.50 percent in the 1990s to a low of 1.22 percent in the 2010s. The primary reason is that saving rates fall considerably in all age groups in the 1980s so that the base saving rates are much lower than historic averages. Of course, changes in the age structure influence the rate of personal saving, but only within a small band; for the first forty years the saving impact of the elderly is more than offset by the rising share of people in the fifty-five to sixty-five-age bracket, which have the highest saving rate since they are putting aside funds for their retirement.

The decline in growth rates over time also occurs for two additional and important reasons: The ratio of labor force to total adults falls with the aging of the population and the share of the population over sixty-four rises. Further, as the ratio of capital to labor rises, depreciation also rises in comparison to gross saving so that net capital formation declines. If we vary some key assumptions of the baseline projection, some other useful results are obtained (all quantitative results of the simulation model are presented in Appendix Note 2.4).

- *Birth and death rates:* Changes in age specific birth and death rates do not greatly influence future growth rates of per capita GDP.
- *Change in the saving rate:* The 1980s witnessed a general decline in saving in all age groups, as well as by corporations (see Chapter 5). If this continues, it is a much greater threat to economic growth than the aging of the population per se. The growth rates of per capita GDP are quite sensitive to changes in these age cohort saving rate.
- *Technological change:* Technological change has varied considerably over the decades, falling particularly in the 1970s. The results from the simulation also are quite sensitive to this factor. I argue in Chapter 10 that the declining rate of technological change is also related to an enervation in the "spirit of capitalism."

The model is not a complete picture of reality, particularly because it places so much attention on measurable influences. But more subtle influences of the age distribution also can be specified. For instance, Ben Wattenberg argues that a greater share of the elderly population leads to a decline in investment caused by "old people living in old houses [and] ruminating about old ideas."[35] As noted in Chapter 1, insurance costs have also grown much faster

---

35. Wattenberg (1987). Habib (1985) discusses geographical mobility of the aged. Hacker (1992), p. 109, has statistical measures of entrepreneurship immigrants by country of origin.

than income; it is possible that this reflects a rising rate of risk aversion. Moreover, the elderly are considerably less geographically mobile than the young; and under certain conditions this might discourage particular invest-ment activities. Though we can speculate upon these matters, the empirical basis for any type of definite conclusions is small. Andrew Hacker suggests these tendencies might well be offset by the dynamic entrepreneurial drive of certain subgroups of immigrants.

Impact of Demographic and Economic Heterogeneity on Social Cohesiveness

A crucially important impact of these trends of increasing structural com-plexity of the population are social and cultural, not economic. The United States is becoming an increasingly stratified society, which negates the American dream of economic mobility. The endpoint of this process is, as Benjamin Disraeli decried in his novel *Sybil*[36]: "Two nations; between whom there is no intercourse and no sympathy; who are as ignorant of each other's habits, thoughts, and feelings, as if they were dwellers in different zones, or inhabitants of different planets' who are formed by a different breeding, are fed by a different food, are ordered by different manner, and are not governed by the same laws ... the Rich and the Poor." I present cer-tain empirical evidence in Chapter 10 that the United States is experiencing a breakdown in social cohesiveness; and the growing heterogeneity of the population and the economic inequalities within this population have undoubtedly played an important role in this process. Unfortunately, in the confines of this discussion, a tight causal relation between increasing struc-tural complexity of the population and decreasing social cohesiveness can-not be established. But the proposition has plausibility, and it is reinforced by the following discussion of some the impacts of particular types of het-erogeneity and inequality.

The impact of increasing ethnic heterogeneity through immigration can lead to greater social and cultural heterogeneity. The impact on social cohesiveness depends on the assimilation process, a process that can take place at very differ-ent rates, depending upon political conditions.[37] Peter Drucker, an immigrant, has worried about the lack of assimilation of recent immigrants and has noted that: "Now 'diversity' is the message preached and practiced. Any attempt to make new groups into 'Americans' is considered discrimination, yet only sixty years ago the attempt to prevent such groups from becoming 'Americans' would have been considered discrimination." Incentives are also declining for immi-

---

36. Disraeli [1845 (1981)], p. 65.
37. The first citation in the paragraph comes from Drucker (1993), pp. 152–3; the second, from Ravitch (1993).

grants to establish an American identity, since the courts have established the rights for welfare and other benefits to resident groups without citizenship.

Of course, the problem of assimilation arises even with citizenship, as illustrated by one immigration judge administering the oath of citizenship in Spanish. Along the same lines Diane Ravitch adds: "Today social science frowns on assimilation, seeing it as a form of cultural coercion, so state systems of education are likely to eschew cultural imposition. In effect, the state schools may encourage trends that raise doubts about the purpose of necessity of a state system of education ... [moreover] ... as populations grow increasingly diverse in ethnic backgrounds, immigrants become less willing to adopt the culture of the new country. And it becomes increasingly difficult to define the culture of the host country when it is not broadly shared." I return to the problem of the public education system in the following discussion.

The language problem is particularly acute.[38] The U.S. government has adopted a program to encourage bilingual programs to teach children with limited English proficiency. But many critics, such as Linda Chavez, claim that the program has shifted from its original goal to become a "native-language maintenance program." Moreover, recent immigrants have tended to cluster in areas with large concentrations of previous immigrants, a pattern that appeared more marked than in the past. As one might suspect, living in such concentrations reduces the probability of mastery of English. Although the impact of poor English proficiency on income is deadly and the economic incentives to learn English are strong, many immigrants do not manage to break out the circle of poverty through mastery of the language.

The language issue is not confined to recent immigrants however.[39] In a massive study of the historical processes generating segregation of African Americans in the twentieth century, Douglas S. Massey and Gary Denton provide evidence that "Black English has become progressively more distant from Standard American English, and its speakers are at a clear disadvantage in U.S. schools and labor markets." The high degree of racial segregation in housing, means that "People growing up [in a hypersegregated environment] have little direct experience with the culture, norms, and behaviors of the rest of American society and few social contacts with members of other racial groups." The authors provide evidence that many South Side residents of Chicago, a predominantly black housing area, had never been downtown to the Loop. It should be no surprise that their links to white society and jobs are

---

38. The quotation about bilingual education is from Chavez (1992). Altonji and Card (1989), p. 26 discuss spatial clustering if recent immigrants; and Goldin (1993) analyzes the problem in historical perspective. Chiswick and Miller (1992) discuss the language problem.

39. The information and quotations about language and housing segregation come from Massey and Denton (1993), pp. 13, 64, 77, and 163. Orfield (1993) presents data on racial compositions of schools.

weak and that: "Growing up in a ghetto increases the likelihood of dropping out of school, reduces the probability of attending college, lowers the likelihood of employment, reduces income earned as an adult, and increases the risk of teenage childbearing and unwed pregnancy." Arising from such housing segregation we have, in other words, a growing cultural heterogeneity accompanied by some tenacious self-perpetuating features. It should be added that such housing segregation increased steadily throughout the twentieth century until 1970; between 1970 and 1980, segregation by racial groups appeared to decline slightly. Nevertheless, Gary Orfield presents more recent data showing that segregation of black students in primary and secondary schools increased from the mid-1980s to the early 1990s – for the first time in two decades – and was at the same level as in the early 1970s. Moreover, the percentage of Latino students in schools that predominantly were minority has been increasing since the late 1960s.

The impact of the increasing heterogeneity of the family structure also is likely to have more serious consequences on both social cohesiveness and the income distribution. Although many women gain greater happiness after divorce, there is a cost to society and the economy.[40] Diane Ravitch comments: "As families dissolve under the pressures of modern life, many children lose their emotional anchor and are thrown into a world where peer pressure shapes values and behavior ... Where will children learn the virtues of restraint, moderation, and responsibility that are necessary ... The schools can teach them, but only as a complement to what children learn at home ... If no one is home, or if no one there takes responsibility for the children, neither schools nor technology can take the place of the [intact: *FP*] family." One major consequence occurs in the area of crime, a useful indicator of social cohesiveness. For instance, 70 percent of juveniles in state reform institutions come from fatherless homes.

Various studies have shown that other things being equal, the children of divorced parents or in single-parent families have a higher incidence of poverty. Indeed, the incidence of poverty in this type of family has soared and the percentage of poor families headed by single females has risen from 28 percent in 1959 to 64 percent in 1988. Moreover, these children are less likely to finish high school or attend college; they have lower occupational achievement; and the girls also are more likely both to marry in their teens or to bear children outside of wedlock.[41] According to some recent studies, the psycho-

---

40. The quotation comes from Ravtich (1993); Whitehead (1993) presents the data on juvenile crime and fatherless families.
41. The poverty data come from Jencks (1991). Data for the other propositions come from: Blanckenhorn (1995), McLanahan and Bumpers (1986), McLanahan (1989), and Garfinkel and McLanahan (1986). Studies about psychological injury include: Wallerstein and Blakesely (1989) and McLanahan (1989).

logical injury to children of divorce often lasts many years, even if the care-giving parent remarries. In some cases, the impact of single-parent families is considerably less if the parent is widowed. Nevertheless, these impacts on the children can lead to a type of increasing cultural heterogeneity and an inter-generational transmission of poverty.

The breakup of the traditional family has other influences that deserve men-tion. Since the children of these families have impairments that make them more difficult to educate, equalizing educational inputs will not equalize edu-cational outputs. This is undoubtedly one explanation for the divergence between educational inputs and outputs. This increasing heterogeneity of fam-ily structure also places greater pressures for more government expenditures, a topic discussed in Chapter 9.[42]

Final word

This survey of structural complexity of the population, defined in terms of demographic and economic heterogeneity, has touched on a variety of issues. Two main messages emerge from the discussion. First, the structural com-plexity of the population has increased and, in most respects, will continue to rise in the near future. Furthermore, these trends have important impacts, not just on such economic variables as economic growth but on the social and cul-tural bonds that tie the nation together.

On the demographic side I document the increasing heterogeneity of race and ethnicity, family structure, and age since 1950. On the economic side I establish the rising inequalities of income and wealth in the 1980s; trends which stratify individuals and families will continue in the near future as well. Of course, many of these issues have received attention in quite different con-texts and I draw deeply upon this research. The complexity approach has the advantage of forcing us to ask broader questions covering a variety of differ-ent types of heterogeneity and to allow us to see more clearly how these vari-ous issues are related.

In most instances, government policy has little short-run effect on the prob-lems that arise from this increasing structural complexity. Many of these prob-lems are also interrelated so that policy changes to ameliorate these impacts must proceed on a broad front. Moreover, in certain cases, such as the equal-

---

42. It might be argued that the greater poverty rate among single mothers places pressure on the government to redistribute income to provide certain services to the children of these poor families that the single parent taking care of the child cannot provide. I argue in Chapter 9 that this is not necessarily the case. However, scattered evidence suggests that children of bro-ken families are less likely to support their parents in their old age, and this may place pres-sure on the government to redistribute income to provide certain services to the older popu-lation that their children do not provide, an argument that appears to have more merit.

ization of educational outputs, the links between policy means and ends are controversial. These observations mean that no sitting President who undertakes such measures, either to reduce structural complexity of the population or alleviate its impact, can hope to gain political profit from the results. For this reason I am pessimistic that such problems will be frontally attacked by the federal government. Financial constraints on state and local government also limit the impact that they may have.

CHAPTER 3

The labor force: Complexity and unemployment

Consideration of structural complexity raises a variety of questions about the labor force and the market for labor. In this chapter I focus on the complexity of the job structure and its implications for unemployment. In the following chapter I deal with the shift of labor into the "information sector" and the reduction of structural complexity in the institutions of labor–management relations.

In the following discussion I document that structural complexity of the job structure is rising according to two of the three definitions of the concept offered in Chapter 1. First, and more importantly, the direct information requirements of the system, measured in terms of the skill requirements of jobs, are increasing. Second, the heterogeneity of the labor force, which is one measure of the division of labor, appears to have an upward trend. In the next chapter I discuss the labor market in terms of the third aspect of complexity, the interactions within the system.

After considering the secular rise in the rate of the unemployment rate since 1950, I take up the argument advanced in the previous chapter that the demand for skilled labor has risen faster than the supply and that the reverse has occurred for unskilled labor. These factors are crucial in explaining not just shifts in the wage structure but also the rising unemployment rate. For empirical support I explore evidence on literacy levels of employed and unemployed workers, and data on changes of the rates of unemployment among workers with different skill levels.

To round out the argument, I also examine five competing explanations of the secular rise in the unemployment rate to show their inadequacies. In the course of such an investigation I show that the severity of business-cycle fluctuations has not greatly changed over the postwar period. This means that increasing macroinstability of the economy cannot serve as an explanation of the long-term rise of the unemployment rate. I also examine and reject a proposition beloved by most futurists that the accelerating pace of change has caused this secular trend.

Structural complexity and the skill levels
of the job structure

Many discussions of the changing skill level of jobs in the U.S. economy are muddled because they do not carefully distinguish different types of skills. I focus particular attention on substantive skills that require the processing of information, since information requirements are a crucial part of the definition of structural complexity. Another source of confusion is the schizophrenic nature of the discussion. On the one hand, the rising "skill level," not to mention the expressed "need for ever more highly skilled workers," has been repeated enough times to become banal. Many serious empirical studies also support this claim.[1] On the other hand a vociferous group has claimed – at least before the competitive threat of Japan and the benefits of flexible production methods received so much publicity – the exact opposite, namely that the U.S. labor force is becoming "deskilled," although the meaning of this term is not carefully specified so that it is unclear what skill is at issue. Indeed, some members of the left have argued that this deskilling has been an integral part of capitalism: The attempt by American employers to break down each job into its simplest components ("Taylorism") and to structure the work force in an assembly line under a centralized control ("Fordism") reduces all skill levels, increases the interchangeability of workers, and thereby reduces the bargaining power of labor. Although such views now seem quaint, more recently some have worried about technological displacement of skilled workers, drawing evidence from selected case studies.[2] Still another group has taken the position that labor force shifts from manufacturing into services imply "a future of lousy jobs" and that such changes are turning America into a nation of hamburger flippers at fast food restaurants.

These various arguments fail to take account of a powerful counterargument.[3] According to well-known management specialist, Peter Drucker: "The function of organization is to make knowledge productive. Unskilled labor is not an asset; manual work in making and moving things weakens a developed economy." Anthony Carnevale adds that in the evolving world economy "... our national competitiveness is based not only on productivity but also on quality, variety, customization, convenience, and timeliness. People are demanding high-quality goods and services that are competitively priced, available in a variety of forms, customized to specific needs, and conveniently accessible. In addition, people do not want to wait patiently for state-of-the-

---

1. For instance, Johnston and Packer (1987).
2. A typical example is Rochell (1989). Murnane (1988) has a useful summary of this literature. The "lousy jobs" refers to a book edited by Burtless (1989).
3. The quotations come respectively from Drucker (1993), p. 40; and Carnevale (1991), p. 2. "Toyotaism" is the subject of an interesting report by the OECD (1992b).

art goods and services ... Central to the new economy are flexible and infor-mation based technologies." This means that workers must be creative, flexi-ble, and knowledgeable, able to accept responsibilities and change. In short, Toyotaism is challenging Fordism.

But lingering fears remain about the degree to which automation will even-tually eliminate the need for skilled workers, once the transition period is over and "most work is automated." Underlying such apprehensions is the assump-tion that particular technologies require a particular kind of worker, which does not seem to be the case.[4] For instance, Shoshana Zuboff discusses how a given technology can be organized either to enhance or degrade workers' skills. In these cases the degree to which the key decisions concerning pro-duction are centralized is crucial. Along these lines Fred Block also provides examples of how Japanese and American factories use flexible manufacturing systems in quite different ways and with quite different skill levels, with the Japanese decentralizing major decisionmaking concerning production to a much greater extent than most American enterprises using the same technolo-gy. Block emphasizes that although automation may reduce skill depth (that is, the skills associated with a single task), it increases the variety of tasks per-formed and the necessity for skill breadth.

In the end these matters can only be resolved in an empirical fashion that requires us to study the skill content of the changing occupation structure. The key to my analysis is a determination of particular characteristics of the skill content of the various occupations listed in the U.S. census from 1950 to 1990. These estimates are based on ratings of the skill characteristics of thousands of highly specific jobs, as established by committees of specialists for the U.S. Department of Labor and published in various editions of the *Dictionary of Occupational Titles*. Although we can carp at many individual ratings, they are the most comprehensive and detailed such attempt available. An important study presents the results of weighted averages of these characteristics for each of the 500-plus occupations listed in the U.S. census, so that it is possible to cal-culate changes in the skill requirements over the years arising from changes in the structure of occupations.[5] In the empirical analysis I follow closely the method pioneered by David R. Howell and Edward N. Wolff, but pursue the calculations in somewhat greater detail and for a longer time period.

4. The references are to Zuboff (1988) and Block (1990).
5. I discuss other aspects of this study, by Roos and Treiman (1980), in Appendix Note 3.1. The method I use follows that of Howell and Wolff (1991). Howell (1994) qualitatively describes the results of his further calculations of the skill level of the labor force, namely that there is a "deceleration in skill growth between the 1960s and 1980s." My calculations in Table 3.1 show exactly the opposite results, at least for substantive and interaction skills. The sources of our differences are not clear; my statistical source (census data) and methods are described in Appendix Note 3.1.

Table 3.1. *Characteristics of all U.S. jobs*

	1950	1960	1970	1980	1990	Male/female gap over time
Substantive skills	3.65	3.76	3.96	4.16	4.40	Gap small, closing (men higher)
Interaction skills	1.90	2.04	2.22	2.39	2.64	Gap small, no trend (men higher)
Motor skills	5.06	5.08	5.12	5.03	4.89	Gap small, no trend (women higher)

Notes: The scales run from 0 (low) to 10 (high). A short description of the estimation technique and sources is given in the text. In Appendix Note 3.1 I present a more detailed discussion of the estimation procedures and sources, as well as data on other types of skills.

Before turning to the data, it is necessary to emphasize that the calculations are based on one key assumption: the skill content within any particular occupation has remained roughly the same in the 40-year period under consideration. Research on the validity of this assumption is hardly conclusive. The available evidence of several studies, however, provides evidence that although certain occupations have shown an upgrading or downgrading of the skill requirements, the *net changes* have been slight and can be neglected.[6] If, as some suggest, the skill levels within individual occupations have risen, then my calculations in Table 3.1 underestimate the long-term rise in the overall levels of particular skill of the job structure; if, on the other hand, increasingly less qualified people are occupying these occupations, my calculations overestimate the rise of skill levels.

Table 3.1 presents the results of such a statistical exercise for three types of skills for the job structure in the census years. In interpreting these data, we must avoid two traps. We must be careful not to confuse the skill levels of the job structure with years of formal education discussed in the previous chapter; many college graduates have jobs that do not require their formal ("paper") educational credentials.[7] To look at the problem from a different angle, any change in the skill characteristics reflects the characteristics demanded by employers, and not the skills of the labor force per se. For certain short periods, Howell and Wolff have an interesting empirical demonstration that the demand for high skills, as reflected in the job structure, may be quite different

6. I refer particularly to a study by Spenner (1983) and Horowitz and Herrnstadt (1966). I do not find Bishop's qualitative argument (1993) convincing that skill levels within individual occupations has risen. Other qualitative assessments, for instance, Mishel and Teixeira (1991), conclude that skill levels in given occupations have not changed.
7. Nasar (1992) discusses this phenomenon. Later in the paragraph I refer to Howell and Wolff (1991).

than the formal supply of educational credentials. By itself, this suggests either that many workers are working at jobs for which they are overqualified or else the content of the formal education received has declined. Given the discussion in the previous chapter showing that in the early 1990s the different age cohorts show few differences in basic literacy skills, even though the average years of formal education have gradually increased over time, the latter interpretation seems closer to the truth.

Table 3.1 presents time-series data for three measures of occupational skills:[8]

1. *Substantive skills* are a composite measure created by a factor analysis examining a number of different characteristics of DOT variables associated with particular occupations. It is correlated with general educational development, specific vocational preparation, data skills, general intelligence, verbal skills, and numerical skills. The level of these skills has increased steadily over time. Howell and Wolff show that, in 1970, this skill rating was significantly correlated with average wages and formal education for those with these various occupations.
2. *Interaction skills* or "people skills" define the degree of ability required for the personal interactions on the job. Arranged on a spectrum from high to low skills required these include: mentoring, negotiating, instructing, supervising, diverting, persuading, speaking and signaling, serving, and taking instructions. Again, the level of such skills required in the job structure is increasing, but at a decreasing rate. These skills are modestly correlated with substantive skill; they are, however, considerably less correlated with income than substantive skills.
3. *Motor skills* are another composite measure created by means of a factor analysis and is correlated with a variety of characteristics such as manual dexterity, motor coordination, and skill in dealing with things. This variable is of particular relevance to the debate on deskilling at

8. What I call "substantive skills" is usually designated as "substantive complexity" in the literature, but I do not wish to burden the term "complexity" with an additional meaning.

   Table A.7 in Appendix Note 3.1 presents additional data on the characteristics of the set of occupations. These include data skills, skills in using things, general educational development, specific vocational preparation, strength required (heavy work to sedentary), other physical demands (a composite variable taking into account the climbing, stooping, kneeling, crouching, crawling, reaching, handling, fingering, feeling, and seeing required for the job), environmental conditions (a composite variable taking into account extreme cold or heat, temperature change, humidity, noise, atmospheric conditions, other hazards), physical demands (a composite variable created by a factor analysis that embraces the variables included in both the strength and other physical demands indicators), and undesirable working conditions (a composite variable created by a factor analysis that includes variables reflecting temperature, humidity, and other similar indicators).

the workbench level. Unlike the two other variables, motor skills within the U.S. job structure show no particular long-term trend since the level rises in the first half of the period and falls in the second half. Such skills are also not correlated with substantive or interaction skills or, for that matter, with the formal education or wages.

For lack of data some important skills are not covered in the table, especially the ability of people to work effectively in teams, to take initiative, and to exercise creativity or foresight. Certainly these types of skills are both more difficult to measure and also more important for the development of the economy in the future.

The results of this statistical exercise for the job structure can be quickly summarized. The skill levels of jobs in the United States, as measured by the required substantive or the interaction skills, have been rising. Since higher substantive and interaction skills require more information processing, structural complexity in the sense of direct information requirements of the system has increased. A rising trend of substantive skills is also found by earlier investigators who have followed such an approach for shorter time periods, particularly Howell and Wolff. Although deskilling in terms of substantive skills has occurred in certain industries, the notion of a general deskilling process for the economy as a whole represents a triumph of ideology over common sense.[9] The fears about a fall in levels of substantive skills arising from the shift into services also are groundless. On the contrary, the evidence shows clearly that the entire job structure is shifting toward work requiring more data analysis, more general education, and also more specific vocational preparation. The occupations increasing in relative importance also involve a higher level of interaction with people. From detailed evidence presented in Appendix Note 3.1 it is also clear that the evolving job structure requires less skill in dealing with things, less strength, and less physical demands, although the aggregate measure of motor skills has not greatly changed.

The increasing skill requirements reflected in the data in Table 3.1 raise some questions about the arguments of those who, basing their analyses on U.S. Labor Department projection of the demand for jobs, claim that the U.S. labor force is becoming overeducated. Given the rising substantive skills of the job structure, coupled with the apparently slow growth in basic literacy and mathematical skills discussed in Chapter 2, the reverse seems to be the case.

9. It is possible for skill X to decline in every industry, and yet the average level of skill X to rise if the industrial mix shifts toward those industries using higher levels of skill X. The average skill level also can rise if low-skilled workers do not obtain further employment when they are replaced by machines, so that their skill levels are no longer included in the average. Although both of these processes occurred to a certain extent, neither of these extreme cases determined what actually happened.

John H. Bishop reviews this literature and shows not only that Labor Department projections have grossly underestimated the demand for educated workers in the past, but also that projections of a surplus of educated workers are in conflict with the rising wage premium that skilled workers have received, especially since 1980.[10]

We have much to learn about the causes underlying the results presented in Table 3.1. Howell and Wolff decompose a similar set of data and show that between 1960 and 1985, roughly half the change in the overall level of substantive skills can be explained by the change of mix of industries (a function of demand for goods and services), and the remaining half can be explained by a change in the job mix within particular industries. What is less clear is the extent to which these trends in various skill characteristics are either the result of changes in technology and other factors influencing the demand for labor, or the outcome of adaption of existing technology to the labor skills produced by the educational system. Moreover, it is also unclear to what degree the skill mix is influenced by the centralized manner in which the American productive enterprises are managed, in contrast to the system used in some countries such as Japan that allegedly give more decision-making authority to workers at lower levels of the administrative hierarchy.

To determine the impact of the rising participation of women in the labor force, I also carried out this exercise with the job structure of men and women separately and the results provide few surprises: for most, but not all, indicators, overall levels of skills of men and women are closing over time.[11]

Despite our lack of a clear understanding of the underlying causes, at a descriptive level the overall trends over the last four decades seem unambiguous: Structural complexity has increased in the sense that those jobs requiring greater substantive and interactive skills are also those with greater requirements for information.

Structural complexity and the heterogeneity of occupations

According to Adam Smith, occupational heterogeneity reflects, in essence, the division of labor that should be increasing with rising levels of economic development. It can be measured by a Theil statistic in the same manner as the statistical exercises in the previous chapter. The statistic, however, is normalized by

---

10. Bishop (1990). A number of studies, for instance, Mishel and Teixeira (1991) rely on these BLS projections. The reference in the next paragraph to Howell and Wolff still refers to their 1991 study.
11. From the perspective that the gap between the skill requirements of jobs held by men and women is decreasing, the structural complexity of the labor force is decreasing. Although this change in structural complexity has little importance for the operation of the economy as a whole, the social implications, of course, are of interest.

Table 3.2. *Measurement of labor force heterogeneity*

| Year | Chained Theil statistics[a] | | Number of occupational categories |
	Absolute	Relative	
1950	5.264	87.8%	401
1960	5.326	86.3	480
1970	5.339	86.5	480
1980	5.331	88.1	426
1990	5.328	89.5	384

[a]A rising Theil statistic shows increasing heterogeneity and the calculations parallel those presented in Chapter 2. The absolute Theil statistics run from 0 to some upper limit defined by the number of categories and, in this case, can not be compared from year to year because the number of occupational categories differs. Each census publication presents the occupational distribution for the year of the census and for the year of the last census. Since the categories for the census of occupation varied with each census, pairs of Theil statistics were calculated and then chained, using the categories of the 1970 census (the 1960–70 data) as the base to achieve comparability over time. The relative Theil statistic allows comparisons to be made between the years. It is defined as the ratio of the absolute Theil coefficient to the upper limit, so that it runs from 0 (where the entire labor force is in one occupation) to 1, where the entire labor force is equally divided among all occupations.

Sources of data and other comments about the calculations are presented in Appendix Note 3.1. The Theil statistic is discussed in Appendix Note 1.2.

the number of occupational categories so that the results are more easily comparable for the entire period. As expected, the data in Table 3.2 reveal that occupational heterogeneity has been quite high for the entire period under examination, in contrast to earlier times where most of the labor force was primarily in one occupation, agriculture. Although occupational heterogeneity increased between 1950 and 1990, the pattern is irregular because the Theil statistic dipped in 1960 and 1970. Nevertheless, for the forty-year period, the long-term trend appears to be slowly upward, although we can not be completely sure.

The rising long-term level of unemployment

The rising level of structural complexity in the labor force has many implications. For instance, an increasingly high share of jobs requiring a long training period raises the costs of firing workers. Moreover, the higher the skill levels required, the greater the difficulties for management to monitor and control these workers; this, in turn, raises increasingly serious problems about work incentives. To relate this discussion to some general themes of the book, I focus on the macroeconomic issue of unemployment, especially since the evidence presented in Chapter 2 suggests that this increasing structural complexity has played an important role in the changing distribution of income.

The argument below is straightforward: the unemployment rate has been increasing over the long term, such unemployment is concentrated among the unskilled, and the basic cause of unemployment can be understood with a simple model of the supply and demand for labor with different skill levels. More specifically, an important clue to this secular rise of the unemployment rate comes from information about the composition of labor skills. The demand for labor with greater substantive and people skills, as measured by the indicators presented in Table 3.1, has been rising much faster than the supply, as measured by the indicators discussed in the previous chapter showing a relatively flat level of average literacy skills in different age cohorts.

I also examine a number of other theories purporting to explain the long-term growth of unemployment based on other factors. These alternatives do not appear to play very important causal roles in the unemployment picture. But in the course of exploring these hypotheses, I must deal with certain issues about the changing severity of macroeconomic fluctuations and the acceleration of change that have relevance to some general themes about the evolution of the economy.

Unemployment trends

As shown in Table 3.3, the conventionally measured rate of unemployment increased at an average annual rate of about 1.5 percent over the four decades from 1950 through 1990. It has, of course, fallen below or risen above the trend, depending on business cycle conditions. If this trend continues, the average 5.7 unemployment rate in the 1950–90 period should rise to 10.3 percent in the next forty years. Such a secular increase in the unemployment rate does not appear due to changes in the relative importance of various subgroups of the labor force that have differential rates of unemployment. Table 3.3 shows that a recalculated unemployment rate (holding the age, gender, and racial composition of the labor force constant) rises at roughly the same rate. Moreover, this long-term rising unemployment rate also does not appear to be due to a narrow definition of the labor force. If we recalculate the unemployment rate to include "discouraged workers" (those not in the labor force because they don't think they can obtain a job) and part-time workers who wish to work longer hours, roughly similar results are obtained. I might add that part-time workers constitute an increasingly important segment of the labor force.[12] Finally, the long-term upward trend in the unemployment rate shows no sign of tapering off: a quadratic trend factor added to the normal trend calculations provides very little explanatory power. In short, the secular

---

12. Recent studies of part-time and discouraged workers include those by Abraham (1990), Blank (1990), and Tilly (1991).

Table 3.3. *Trends in U.S. unemployment from 1950 through 1990*

Unemployment Definition	Average annual value	Trend increase of average annual value (not absolute percentage crease)[a]
Civilian unemployment rate (conventional statistic)	5.7%	+1.5%
Rate using expanded definitions of unemployment and labor force[b]	8.4%	+1.1%
Rate holding age, sex, race constant (eight categories)[c]	5.8%	+1.3%
Average duration of unemployment (weeks)	12.4	+ .8%

[a]All trends are statistically significant at the .05 level and are calculated by fitting an exponential curve to the data using an ordinary least-squares technique.

[b]Data using expanded definition of the labor force data run only from 1955 through 1990. They include all military (not just resident) plus those people not looking for work because they did not believe they could find any jobs (discouraged workers). The expanded definition of unemployment includes discouraged workers plus one half of those who are working part time but who wish to be working considerably more hours.

[c]For the estimate holding labor force structure constant, the rates taken into account are for all combinations of two races (white and nonwhite), men and women, and young (sixteen through nineteen) and older (twenty and over). The weights for the index are the average share of these eight groups from 1965 through 1975.

Further notes on sources and methods are presented in Appendix Note 3.3.

increase in the unemployment rate since the middle of the twentieth century is due neither to measurement nor to end-point problems.

Data on the unemployed classified by length of unemployment at the time the labor force survey show that each category defined as a ratio to the entire labor force has risen. Even more disturbing, the secular rate of long-term unemployment (over fifteen or twenty-six weeks) has increased the fastest. This is reflected in the data in Table 3.3 showing a rise in the average length of unemployment. Such a statistic has a downward bias since it takes into account only the unemployment at the time of the survey. Estimating completed spells of unemployment is a difficult task, but average duration of completed spells of unemployment appear to have risen about 1 percent a year between 1948 and 1978.[13] These depressing phenomena are well known to labor specialists.

13. These results are based on the data of Akerlof and Main (1980). It must be noted that such estimates raise some very difficult conceptual and estimation problems and that the Akerlof–Main estimates are quite different from a shorter series by Bowers (1980) or some point estimates by Clark and Summers (1979).

Table 3.4. *Literacy levels of different segments of the labor force (ages sixteen and above)*

	Labor force share 1992	Reading (prose scale) Average score	Information processing (document scale) Average scorer	Quantitative (quantitative scale) Average score
Full-time employed	76.0%	288	284	290
Part-time employed	16.6	284	277	280
Unemployed	7.4	260	257	256
Not in labor force	—	246	237	241
Total	100.0	272	267	271

Notes: All scales run from 0 to 500; totals may not add because of rounding. Other data from the same survey are presented in Table 2.3, which also indicates to what level of skills these scores correspond.
For data sources, see Appendix Note 3.3.

Unemployment rates among the unskilled are higher than other groups of the population.[14] Moreover, the unemployment rate among the unskilled has increased faster than among more skilled workers, at least among men in the prime-age working ages. In particular sectors such as manufacturing, the proportion of unskilled jobs has also fallen, while total employment in the sector has fallen as well. If the U.S. labor market is the same as that in Canada or Sweden, average spells of unemployment are also longer for the least educated workers. Finally, in a massive study of some half a million prime-age males, Chinhui Juhn, Kevin M. Murphy, and Robert H. Topel show not only that the long-term unemployment rate of the unskilled has risen rapidly, but that their rates of nonparticipation in the labor force have risen as well. In short, the unskilled adults are more likely than the skilled to be found both among the unemployed and also among those not formally in the labor force.

The relation of skills and unemployment can also be seen in a different way by examining the data in Table 3.4 on literacy skills of those with different labor force status. The data show a clear ranking with full-time workers having the highest average literacy skills and those not in the labor force, the lowest. People not in the labor force are a heterogeneous group and include those with visual and other physical impairments, those still in school, homemakers, and also many who became discouraged and have stopped looking for formal

14. Blackburn, Bloom, and Freeman (1990) present data on relative increases of unemployment among unskilled and skilled in the United States. Berndt, Morrison, and Rosenblum (1990) analyze the proportion of unskilled jobs. The studies for Canada and Sweden are respectively by Beach and Kaliski (1997) and Löfgren and Engström (1989). The last reference is to Juhn, Murphy, and Topel (1991).

work in the labor force. Moreover, detailed data show a rising share of the labor force without basic skills as we move from full-time workers to those not in the labor force.

Of crucial importance, if those not currently employed had been able to find work, their real wages would have fallen. More specifically, using information on measurable skills and other characteristics of individuals both in and out of the labor force, Juhn, Murphy, and Topel show that the men who are unemployed or who have dropped out of the labor force would have received wages which, if they were employed, would have fallen in real terms in the postwar decades. In brief, for this group the opportunity cost of idleness has fallen. All of this suggests that the increase in the demand for skilled and educated labor affects the entire labor force, rather than just the top end.

Microeconomic mechanisms for explaining long-term unemployment

The general causal forces underlying the rising demand for more literate and skilled workers, as manifested by the rising level of substantive skills in the structure of employed workers and the roughly constant level of basic literacy skills, as argued in the previous chapter, has led to a fall in real wages and a rise in the unemployment rate among workers with low skills or literacy levels. But the exact mechanisms by which the unemployment has come about deserves closer attention and several hypotheses, none mutually exclusive, have been advanced.

Demand changes and the impact of the minimum wage: Due to shifting of the demand for unskilled labor, fewer jobs suitable for unskilled labor are available at or above the minimum wage. This means, in contrast to the next explanation, that the rise in unemployment and withdrawal from the labor force has not been voluntary. Unfortunately, most studies of the relationship between the minimum wage and aggregate unemployment show only a weak relationship, and, moreover, this linkage is usually specified in terms of short-run changes. My argument focuses on long-term changes and the notion that the productivity of an unskilled worker remains roughly the same. Over the long run, as the minimum wage rises, the probabilities of employment of such a worker decrease. This phenomenon is not picked up in studies focusing on short-run changes of the minimum wage and unemployment.

Supply changes: Some argue that the decline in relative wages of low-skilled workers has reduced the quantity of such labor supplied.[15] Since the opportu-

---

15. For instance, Juhn, Murphy, and Tobel (1991).

nity cost of leisure has fallen (that is, the cost of not working is lower because wages are lower), more low-skilled group of prime-age males have decided either to withdraw completely from the labor force or to prolong their spells of unemployment. Only the latter, of course, leads to an increase in measured unemployment. Such an explanation assumes that unemployment is voluntary and also that these workers choose not to upgrade their skills to obtain jobs requiring higher qualifications. This type of supply choice is often based on the availability of alternative sources of income: either from a family member; from certain types of governmental benefits, such as the disability insurance program of the Social Security system; or from remunerative activities not covered in governmental employment surveys, such as crime.

Impact of job search: Janet Yellen has raised the possibility that nonmarket-clearing mechanisms may also be at work.[16] If, for instance, wage dispersions exist so that some high-wage jobs for unskilled workers exist, many of those losing their work may prefer to remain unemployed in the hopes of eventually landing such a "good job," rather than accepting a low-paying "bad job." Such an interpretation receives support from the fact that little relationship exists between changes in regional unemployment rates and overall regional employment growth; by way of contrast, there is a strong negative relation between regional unemployment and employment growth in high-wage industries. In other words, it is not rising employment in general that reduces the unemployment rates, but only the growth of high-wage employment. Not enough evidence is available to determine whether the importance of this factor has increased over time.

Without additional detailed empirical work, we cannot determine the relative weight of the three explanations. I suspect that the demand-side explanation is most important, although the other factors undoubtedly played a role.

The role of coordination mechanisms for explaining long-term unemployed

Before leaving explanations of the rising unemployment rates based on increasing structural complexity, it is useful to consider the role of the increasing heterogeneity of the job structure and the coordination problems that this might generate.

Microeconomic coordination problems refer to the difficulty of filling a job requiring a specific set of different skills with a person who happens to possess this bundle of skills. Such problems can arise because the skills that are taught are not those sought by employers. But the mechanisms for matching

16. Yellen (1991). These mechanisms are studied by those interested in "efficiency wages."

the demand and supply of skill bundles might also be imperfect, due in large part to the high costs experienced by potential employees in learning about such job openings and of potential employers in evaluating the skills of these job applicants.[17]

Both parts of this matching problem become more difficult as the occupational structure increases in heterogeneity, as skills become more diverse, and as the training requirements to achieve these skill levels become greater. In bygone years, it might have been easier to find engineers with a general training than now when a producer is searching for engineers with experience, let us say, in both electronics and solid-state chemistry.

Unfortunately, empirical evidence for this hypothesis is ambiguous. At least at a single point in time, as noted previously, unemployment spells are longer for the less-skilled workers than the more skilled. This, however, cannot be easily distinguished from effects associated with higher average levels of unemployment of low-skilled workers. As a result, we must be content merely with raising the possibility of matching problems increasing in severity with the increasing heterogeneity of the labor force. When the data necessary to carry out a more complete investigation are available, a more definitive evaluation can be given.[18] If such problems do become more serious, they can be

17. Bishop (1993a) has a pioneering study of this matter.
18. Readily available data on vacancy rates for jobs embodying different levels of skill provide some empirical evidence. Using data for the United States in 1980 and 1982, Holzer (1990) shows that vacancy rates are much higher, for instance, for jobs requiring craftworkers than laborers, concluding that "skill requirements of jobs generally have significant positive effects on vacancy rates, in particular, higher average occupational compositions of industries are associated with higher vacancy rates" (p. 4). Abraham (1987, p. 216) provides some evidence for Canada showing, for instance, that the vacancy rate among professional/technical workers is higher than among clerical or sales.

   But there is less to this empirical evidence than meets the eye. Many exceptions occur in this positive relation between vacancy rates and skill levels, and, moreover, these differences in vacancy rates are not great. For other countries such as Japan (Brunello, 1991, p. 143) the relation receives no empirical support at all. These mixed results arise because the statistic under examination – job vacancy rates – is influenced by job turnover rates, unemployment rates, and rehiring rates that, in turn, vary according to occupation so that various causal influences are confounded. For instance, Abraham points out that high-skilled jobs feature a lower turnover rate and, moreover, unemployment rates among the highly skilled are less so that vacancy rates are pulled in opposite directions. That is, they are pulled lower because of lower turnover, but higher because they are harder to fill once jobs become empty. Furthermore, the time patterns of job turnover, unemployment, and rehiring are sufficiently complicated that the rank order of job vacancy rates for various occupations varies considerably over time (Konstant and Wingeard, 1968).

   Moreover, as noted in the text, both unemployment and length of unemployment is less for the skilled than the nonskilled. Without estimating a multiequation model that takes into account both vacancies of high- and low-skilled jobs and unemployment of high- and low-skilled individuals, it is impossible to sort out the various causal factors at work. Unfortunately, the requisite data for such an investigation do not appear available.

surmounted with innovations in the labor market that would make it substantially easier for a matching of skills wanted with skills possessed, for instance, computerized employment registers on a national level. But in the last four decades under examination, U.S. labor markets have functioned in roughly the same basic manner and no significant innovations along these lines have occurred.

Other possible causes of the long-term rise of the unemployment rate

To judge the plausibility of the structural complexity explanation of the long-term rise of the unemployment, it is important to explore some alternative propositions. In this brief discussion I would like to show that five common hypotheses have little explanatory power. These other arguments focus on increasing economic turbulence, increasing incentives encouraging unemployment, tradeoffs between job vacancies and unemployment, increasing wage rigidity, and changes in the work ethic.

Increasing economic turbulence: Economic turbulence arises from the impact of various types of shocks to the economy that displace workers and create unemployment. On the supply side these shocks include changes in technology used in particular industries, changes in the degree of import competition for particular goods, and changes in raw material prices. On the demand side these shocks include changes in domestic or foreign preferences for such goods, either by private individuals or the government. The impact of such shocks to the economy can be seen by shifts in employment between various areas, various industries, or various occupational groups. This argument has considerable intuitive appeal since such turbulence is most clearly manifested in the United States by the rapid creation and elimination of jobs: roughly 11 percent of all jobs are lost each year because of layoffs or plant closures.[19]

This kind of argument has appeared in one form or another in the economic literature for more than a century. For instance, in his theory about the growing industrial reserve army of the unemployed, Marx argued that in capitalist economies the workers displaced by technological advances would form an increasingly large proportion of the population.

Blaming the secular rise in unemployment on technological shocks is not convincing. In the United States the rate of technological change, at least as measured by productivity calculations, has been decelerating, not accelerating. More specifically, the rise in labor productivity was 2.2 percent in the 1950s, 1.6 percent in the 1960s, .9 percent in the 1970s, and .3 percent in the

---

19. Davis and Haltiwanger (1992).

1980s.[20] Moreover, as long as aggregate demand is maintained, displaced workers can be absorbed into other sectors of the labor force over time unless their skills are completely industry-specific and cannot be upgraded; both assumptions appear dubious.

In recent years David Lilien has revived the turbulence argument in a much more sophisticated garb that includes all types of shocks and that focuses on unemployment over the business cycle.[21] As I'll discuss in more detail, my own macroeconomic calculations do not show any increase in the severity of the business cycle for the period after 1950. And as I show in Chapter 5, short-term volatility of production is also not increasing in intensity. We can also measure turbulence directly and examine the degree to which such shocks have lead to changes in the share of the labor force in different regions, industries, or occupations either in the short run (from year to year) or long run (from decade to decade). These calculations for seven different measures along three different dimensions are shown in Table 3.5.

20. These results are obtained by fitting a quadratic exponential trend to the data on GDP per employee or resident member of the armed forces, calculating the predicted labor productivity every ten years and then determining the growth rates between these years. The data came from U.S. Council of Economic Advisors (annual-1993). If labor and capital are combined to estimate total factor productivity (a more complete measure of technological change) by means of a Cobb–Douglas production function, the deceleration of technical change is even more striking.

21. Lilien's (1982) thesis is controversial and several recent studies have approached the problem from quite different perspectives, for instance, Davis and Haltiwanger (1992) or Parker (1992). The turbulence thesis (sometimes called the "mismatch hypothesis," although this term is a misnomer) also has received considerable criticism. Some such as Johnson and Layard (1986) have focused on the statistical problems arising from the reduced form of equation used to test the idea; others such as many of the authors in Padoa–Schioppa, ed. (1991) have not found the relationship between turbulence and unemployment for other countries that Lilien and Parker have found for the United States.

As an explanation for long-run changes in unemployment, we can skip over many of the statistical problems of the short-run models and set up a simple empirical test. The shifts in the composition of the labor force that arise from various shocks can be easily measured by calculating changes in the relevant shares of the labor force from one period to the next by employing the following simple formula:

$$T_t = .5 \sum{}^i \mid s_{i,t} - s_{i,t-1} \mid,$$

where T is turbulence, s is the share under examination, i is the particular group (geographical, industrial, or occupational), and t is the year. The turbulence statistic holds the degree of unemployment for the economy as a whole constant and measures the share of the labor force that must be changed from one place, industry, or occupation to another in order to maintain this assumption. Turbulence in the short run is measured every year; and in the long run, every ten years.

In the economic literature some objections have been raised against such a statistic, especially because it focuses on actual employment shares, rather than desired employment shares (e.g., Abraham, 1991); and other, less intuitive measures, are used. Experiments with these other measures reveal roughly the same trends over the long run as my own statistic.

Table 3.5. *Possible causes of long-term unemployment, 1950 through 1990*

Variable	Average annual index value	Average annual rate of change of index value[a]
Turbulence:[b]		
Geographical: Short run (48 states)	.007	No significant trend
Geographical: Long run (48 states)	.050	No significant trend
Industrial: Short run (66 industries)	.014	−1.1%
Industrial: Long run (66 industries)	.086	No significant trend
Occupational: Short run (12 groups)	.010	No significant trend
Occupational: Long run (12 groups)	.058	−1.8%
Occupational: Long run (census data, 380–480 groups)	.136	No significant trend

	Average annual ratio value	Average annual rate of change of ratio value
Labor force incentives on demand or supply side:		
Minimum hourly wage to average hourly wage	.388	−1.3%
Minimum hourly wage to average hourly compensation	.346	−1.7%
Weekly unemployment benefits to average weekly wage	.335	−.2%
Weekly unemployment benefits to average weekly compensation[c]	.297	−.6%
Average length of unemployment when benefits are exhausted	21.7	+.4%
Ratio of help-wanted index to total nonagricultural employment:[d]		
Unadjusted index	—	+.6%
Index adjusted for comparability	—	No significant trend

[a]Only those trends that appear statistically significant at the .05 level are included in the table; the trend values are calculated by fitting an exponential curve to the data by an ordinary least-squares technique.

[b]The turbulence index indicates the percentage of the labor force that must be transferred to achieve the employment pattern in a later year. It is discussed in the text. The annual series run from 1954 through 1990 and are adjusted to achieve comparability after the definitional changes in the early 1980s. For the series indicating ten-year changes, such changes were calculated for the years only starting 1958 or 1959 so as to avoid problems of comparing changes with employment structure during or immediately after World War II. For the calculations using census data, the data cover 1950 through 1980; because of a limited number of data points, no trend regression is calculated.

[c]Compensation includes not only direct wages and salaries, but also various types of fringe benefits and Social Security payments.

[d]The help-wanted index runs from 1951 through 1990. The adjustments to the help-wanted index follow those of Katherine G. Abraham.

Further explanations for other indicators, as well as sources and methods of estimation, can be found in Appendix Note 3.3.

The results of such calculations are quite clear: turbulence along all dimensions and measures has not increased; indeed, in certain cases the reverse occurred. Although turbulence in the U.S. economy appears considerable, increasing turbulence does not appear to underlie the rising long-term rate of unemployment according to these indicators.[22]

These calculations of turbulence have a broader significance, namely with regard to the fatuous and self-serving pronouncements by many futurists and political gurus that "change is accelerating." The turbulence calculations in Table 3.5 suggest that such accelerating change has not trickled down into our daily lives, at least as reflected by increased turbulence of job places. Of course, it is possible that change is accelerating along certain other dimensions, for instance, our stock of scientific knowledge. But this does not mean that Americans are reeling increasingly unsteady along the sidewalks, trying to recover equilibrium after the latest "future shock."

Increased incentives for unemployment: Various incentives on both the demand and the supply side of the labor market act to encourage unemployment by influencing the tradeoff between labor and leisure. Other than lower wages for unskilled workers, which I discussed previously, are these incentives increasing in sufficient importance to cause a secular increase in unemployment rates?

On the demand side, a rising ratio of the minimum wage to the average wage can create an increase in the unemployment rate by preventing the employment of a rising number of people who are willing to work at low wages but who lack the skills to bring their productivity to a level at least equal to this minimum wage. These workers either become unemployed or drop out of the labor force. The data in Table 3.5 show, however, that over four decades, the reverse was the case. As a percentage of the average, the minimum wage actually fell.

On the supply side, it is generally believed that the higher the unemployment compensation or the longer that such benefits are available, the greater the incentive for the worker to remain unemployed; and the longer they might extend their periods of unemployment. Moreover, the empirical microeconomic evidence is generally consistent with these propositions, at least at a single point in time.[23] For the unemployment rate to rise over time,

---

22. Some evidence is available that job turnover of individuals has increased. For example, Marcotte (1994) uses survey data and finds that probabilities of job separation (combined voluntary and involuntary) of individual workers increased somewhat between 1976 and 1987. This is, however, different from the turnover of job places, which is the focus of my analysis. Moreover, my rough estimates using Marcotte's results suggest that this increase in employment turnover accounted for only a very small fraction of the increase in the rate of unemployment.

23. The results of almost two dozen studies are summarized by Hammermesh (1982); and subsequent studies (e.g., Corson and Grossman, 1986; Feldstein and Poterba, 1984; Katz and Meyer, 1990; Nicolson, 1981; Solon, 1985) add additional evidence. International evidence is provided by various authors in Grubel and Walker (1978). One skeptical voice to all of these studies, however, is Atkinson, Gomulka, and Mickelwright (1984).

however, such disincentives for employment must increase and, for the period from 1950 through 1990, this does not appear a very promising explanation. Table 3.5 shows a downward trend in the ratio of such benefits to both average wages and salaries and to total compensation. Although the share of the population covered under such unemployment programs has risen, this occurred mostly in the early part of the period and probably played a small role thereafter. For less inclusive measures of wages and salaries with which I experimented (not shown in the table), the share of benefits showed a slow rise; such mixed results suggest that the incentive effect depends considerably upon the type of wages that unemployed workers are likely to obtain. The length of benefits, as measured by the average length of unemployment of those exhausting their benefits, rose; most of this occurred also in the earlier part of the period, an impression given statistical support when a quadratic factor is added to the trend calculations. Thus, it is possible that changes in the unemployment compensation payments acted to increase unemployment. The mixed results I obtain suggest, however, that the effect has probably not been very strong.

The incentive approach comes in another garb: the rising share of taxes and costs of governmental regulations in the employment process means a rising gap between the take-home wages of a worker and the cost to the employer of hiring that worker. The burden of such taxes and governmental measures on the employer reduces the demand for labor; similarly, the lower take-home wages of the worker reduce the number offering their services at a given market wage. The overall result is a smaller employed labor force. While this effect undoubtedly reduces participation in the labor force, it does not increase the measured unemployment rate, which is based on those who are actively looking for work.

Tradeoffs between job vacancies and unemployment: According to current discussion about the Beveridge curve, an economy faces a tradeoff between unemployment and job vacancies. If job vacancies are high, unemployment is low, and vice versa. Although the causation appears to run from unemployment to job vacancies, the reverse causation also can be argued, namely that the increasing unemployment is somehow due to a secular reduction in job vacancies. This situation, in turn, can only be alleviated by additional investment and job growth.

For the sake of argument let us accept this approach for the United States and ask about the behavior of job vacancies over the period. Unfortunately the U.S. government does not do a good job in collecting such data and we must be satisfied with a proxy variable instead. More specifically, although data on jobs reported to employment offices in various states are available for 1950 to the present, this series has two major difficulties. The methods of collecting the statistics have differed significantly over the years; and the job openings supplied to these agencies are usually for the unskilled and do not reflect the overall job vacancy situation.[24]

A much better measure of job vacancies is the Conference Board series on the number of help-wanted advertisements published in newspapers in fifty-one cities in the United States. Katherine G. Abraham has subjected this series to several tests against pilot studies of job vacancies in particular cities and other statistics.[25] She shows that the help-wanted series tracks the data quite well from the more detailed surveys. In using the help-wanted series over the long run, Abraham also makes three additional adjustments for the 1960–85 period to take into account: the shifting composition of jobs (the intensity of advertising varies according to the job); the decline in newspaper competition; and changes in advertising practices to adapt to pressures of the Equal Employment Opportunity and affirmative action regulations. In Table 3.5 I extend her adjustments and data series to cover the entire four decades. It also is necessary to "normalize" the help-wanted series; following Abraham, I have calculated the ratio of this series for nonagricultural employment.

According to Table 3.5, the unadjusted help-wanted data reveal a secular increase, but no significant trend can be found in the adjusted series, which is more useful for our purposes. This latter result lies at the basis of Abraham's more sophisticated argument that in the United States, the Beveridge curve has not remained constant but has been shifting over time; so that job vacancy and unemployment rates have both increased. The message is that the secular increase in unemployment does not seem attributable to a secular decline in job vacancies, that is, by shifts along the Beveridge curve.

Institutional factors increasing unemployment: Two quite different types of arguments about the influence of institutional factors have been advanced to explain the long-term growth in the rate of unemployment. The first concerns the hiring process; the other, labor markets, and the rigidity of wages.

Sometimes it is claimed that unemployment is increasing because, at a given wage level, the demand for labor has decreased because of rising hidden wage costs. These include the costs associated with the increasing administrative difficulties in firing workers, either if the economy takes a downturn or if particular workers do not perform at the expected level. This increasing job protection has arisen both from governmental legislation providing employ-

---

24. An initial attempt to compare such different sources of information about job vacancies and want ads is U.S. Department of Labor, Employment and Training Administration (1978).
25. Abraham (1987).

ment protection and, in a few cases, from contracts negotiated with labor unions. The greater employment protection in various West European nations over that in the United States also accounts for their lower employment response to short-term changes in production.

Although this line of argumentation has considerable intuitive appeal, several problems arise. First, a firm's labor force adjustment can take place not only through changes in employment, but changes in hours. Katherine Abraham and Susan Housman show that in Belgium, France, and Germany, changes in work hours are much more sensitive to business-cycle conditions than employment, a situation quite different than in the United States.[26] More relevant to the problem of secular changes is their finding that labor force adjustments to short-term changes in production do not seem to have been markedly influenced by the differences in employment protection measures in the three countries. This result, which runs counter to the conventional wisdom on the subject, suggests that the changes in U.S. employment protection legislation had little effect on the U.S. unemployment rate in the long run.

Of course, labor unions have played a role in protecting workers from what they perceive as discharges without cause. Moreover, the higher wages received by union members in certain industries allegedly have forced a larger number of workers to look for jobs in lower paid industries that have a limited capacity to absorb them. But this line of argument does not seem promising as an explanation for the secularly increasing unemployment rate when we realize that the relative importance of unions has declined, not increased, over time. Moreover, the wage differential between union and nonunion members has not changed greatly (data are presented in Table 4.2). I discuss both topics in much greater detail in the next chapter.

A much different type of institutional argument arises from labor market considerations, where it can be shown easily that rigid wages raise unemployment in economic downturns so that the average unemployment over the cycle is larger than when wages are more flexible.[27] Although theoretical objections can be made against this argument, it seems worthwhile to examine empirically the flexibility of wages over the post–World War II period to determine whether this factor might play a role in the secular rise in unemployment.

---

26. Abraham and Housman (1993). The most important impact of such job protection laws may be in long-term hiring. Anecdotal evidence suggests that in the face of such laws, employers are more willing to substitute machines for workers.

27. Some economists (for instance, Hahn and Solow, 1986; or De Long and Summers, 1986) have argued that flexible wages actually increase the severity of business cycles and average unemployment rate over the cycle, in good measure because such flexible wages make aggregate demand more flexible as well. A useful simulation model of the various issues involved is by Caskey and Fazzari (1992).

My own calculations of wage flexibility in Appendix Note 3.2 over the four-decade period from 1950 through 1991 show no significant changes in wage flexibility. I attack the question using a model proposed by Robert J. Gordon.[28] He specifies an equation that explains changes in average nonagricultural gross hourly wages in the private sector by the ratio of actual to potential GDP ("the gap") and a number of control variables. I modify his approach slightly so as to test for changes in wage rigidity. The regression calculations reveal little evidence that either real or nominal wages have become less flexible over time. Economists such as Steven G. Allen, who have examined wages for a century long period, also find no significant change in the sensitivity of nominal wages in the earlier and the later decades of this period. The wage rigidities approach to explain a secular rising unemployment rate also does not seem very promising.[29]

This data set also allows us to calculate whether the business cycle has increased in severity, a question related to one of the major themes of this book. Measuring severity by the percentage gap between actual and potential GDP, I find no evidence of any change over the four-decade period. Such a result (details are presented in Appendix Note 3.2) provides bad news to theorists of

28. Gordon (1983); the later reference is to Allen (1991). Gordon's model, described in detail in Appendix Note 3.2, includes the following explanatory variables: the ratio of actual to potential GDP ("the gap"); the change in the ratio of the gap from last year to this year; changes in annual prices; and three factors influencing aggregate supply, namely dummy variables reflecting the extraordinary situation during the Korean War, another dummy reflecting the period of the wage and price controls under President Richard Nixon, and finally a variable reflecting change in producer prices for crude materials for further processing. To this model I have added a variable to reduce serial correlation and two variables to allow investigation of changes over time of some of the key parameters.

29. The wage-rigidity argument comes in one last variation, namely that high unemployment in a past period partly causes high unemployment in this period. This hysteresis effect or path dependent process is supposed to occur for one or more of three reasons: unemployed workers lose their skills as their period of unemployment increases; in past periods of high unemployment, investment was not made that would have resulted in productive capacity to employ current unemployment; or currently employed workers collectively bargain to achieve a wage level that insures their own employment but discourages new hiring because the wage is higher than the marginal productivity achieved by hiring new workers. The argument about the depreciation of human capital may have some merit for periods of unemployment lasting several years, but for shorter periods I have been unable to find any supporting evidence. For the second argument, I have not been able to find any systematic evidence. And the third argument hardly seems relevant for a long-term period in a country where labor unionism is decreasing in importance and where the rise in productivity and the stagnation of the level of real wages could counteract any extra high wages in a given year. A quantitative analysis of this wage effect is carried out by Blanchard and Summers (1988), who examine unemployment and wages in the United States and certain West European nations. They conclude that such effects are relatively small in the United States, especially in comparison to Western Europe. In brief, short-term hysteresis effects hardly explain the long-term increase in the unemployment rate.

various stripes. The business cycle has not diminished in severity as our knowledge of macroeconomics increases, as optimistic Keynesians have preached. Capitalism also does not seem threatened by increasing macroinstability, as Marx and his epigones have argued. And we do not face an increasing tendency toward systemic breakdown, at least along this dimension, as some grand theorists of complexity have predicted. I return to this theme of instability in other chapters of the book, but primarily from a microeconomic standpoint.

Changes in the work ethic: In the American business press, numerous commentators have asserted that American workers are becoming lazier in comparison to the golden past. Of course, other than isolated anecdotes no evidence is ever supplied, thereby providing yet another indication that pop-sociology is the last refuge of scoundrels. More serious commentators argue a parallel thesis, namely that work frictions have increased and, correspondingly, the effort of workers on the job has decreased. They offer data for various short time periods on strikes, absenteeism, and quit rates.[30] Other aspects of the work ethic find discussion in Chapter 10.

The question of work frictions as manifested by strikes can be put to rest quickly. As a percent of total work time in the economy, the days lost in strikes have decreased dramatically over the forty-year period.[31] Data for short-term periods used in these discussions simply do not reflect the long-term trends. Some additional aspects of this issue are discussed in the Chapter 4.

Turning to more direct indicators of the work ethic, the U.S. Bureau of Labor Statistics (BLS) has tabulated data on the rate of voluntary absenteeism due to sickness and to "other" reasons. The series started in 1957 when the Current Population Survey began to include questions asked of the population about their work attendance.[32] The available data lead to a clear conclusion: From 1957 to the present, no upward trend in absenteeism is visible; indeed,

---

30. This argument is raised by Weisskopf, Bowles, and Gordon (1983)
31. Table 4.2 presents data on this matter.
32. Unpublished data on absenteeism from 1957 to 1967 come from Naples (1982), p. 282. The 1957–66 data are not strictly comparable with later data due to changes in the Current Population Survey concepts and designed. Data for 1967–74 come from Hedges (1973, 1975); a slightly different series for 1973–89 come from Hedges (1977), Taylor (1979), Klein (1986), and Meissenheimer (1990). For the series from 1967 to 1973, the reported data use one universe for reporting the rate of absenteeism for part of the week and a slightly different universe for reporting absenteeism for one week or more. From the data for the overlap years 1973–4, we can see that the error introduced by adding the results from the two universes is small so that we can speak definitely of trends for the period from 1967 onward; and with considerable assurance about trends from 1957 through 1967. In general, absenteeism for reasons other than sickness has fluctuated from 2.3 percent to 2.6 percent from 1967 to 1980; in 1986 and 1989 the rates were, respectively, 2.1 and 2.0 percent. Total absenteeism fluctuated from 6.0 to 6.6 percent from 1967 to 1980; in 1986 and 1989, the rates were respec-

from the mid-1980s on, the rate of absenteeism declined markedly. Attempts to collect similar data from enterprises and establishments have proven fruitless since many do not collect such statistics in a usable form.[33] My own sample survey work on this matter shows that the impressions of manufacturing production managers about changes in absenteeism over time differ considerably from the published data of the government. These managers most likely suffer from "nostalgia bias," namely that all things (including absenteeism) were always better in the good old days.

Another possible indicator of the work ethic is the degree of job turnover due either to voluntary quits or to what is euphemistically named "other" reasons. Although data are available only for the manufacturing sector and only for the years 1950 through 1981, no statistically significant trend can be observed.[34]

I make the argument in Chapter 10 that an enervation in the spirit of capitalism is occurring in the United States. This trend is not manifested, however, by the quantitative indicators of the work ethic, but rather in more subtle ways that seem to influence labor force participation rates considerably more than actively looking but not finding employment. For the purpose at hand, we must look elsewhere for an explanation of the secular increase in the unemployment rate.

Conclusions and implications for the future

This chapter examines structural complexity of the labor force in two different ways: the heterogeneity of the job structure, which reflects the division of labor, and the average skill levels, which reflect the informational requirements of the production process. Both types of structural complexity increased over the postwar period.

Trends in the skill levels of the job structure depend upon the skill in question. For substantive skills, a composite variable embracing general education, specific vocational preparation, as well as data and verbal skills, the level of skill embodied in the occupational structure has increased steadily. The same can be said for "people skills." The motor skills embodied in the job structure, on the other hand, have declined. These increases in intellectual skills show conclusively that technology is not "deskilling," at least with regard to generating, gathering, and analyzing information.

tively 4.7 and 4.4 percent. Although it might be argued that with the rising share of women in the labor force, the rate of absenteeism should show a secular increase, according to the calculations of Leigh (1983), the higher rate of absenteeism among once other factors influencing absenteeism are taken into account.

33. This is discussed by Folger and Belew (1985). My survey work is found in Pryor (1983).
34. The data come from U.S. Department of Commerce, Bureau of the Census (1975), p. 181; and U.S. Department of Labor, Bureau of Labor Statistics (1983), p. 180.

If the supply of skills is growing more slowly over the long run than the demand that is generated by higher levels of technology, then we can expect a relative decline in wages of low-skilled workers and a secular increase in the unemployment rate. And these trends are exactly what we find since the mid-1970s. Furthermore, the long-term upward trend in the unemployment rate shows no sign of tapering off. The causal nexus between skills imparted by education and unemployment also is revealed by data showing that literacy levels among the unemployed are much lower than those who have full-time work.

Although the relative importance of the various mechanisms by which such unemployment comes about can be disputed, the basic causal forces are relatively simple. I also spend considerable efforts in this chapter to determine if other approaches have much explanatory power, but to no avail. Those hypotheses linking the long-term rise in unemployment to increasing economic turbulence, increased incentives for unemployment, trade-offs between job vacancies and unemployment, institutional factors, and changes in the work ethic do not prove promising.

The most general policy implication of these finding is clear: if we continue on the same educational trajectory, long-term unemployment is likely to continue to rise in the future. And, as argued in the previous chapter, allocating more resources to an unchanging educational system is not likely to have much effect. Specifying exactly what measures we must take to tailor the educational system to increase the skill level of the labor force, particularly those in the lower half of the skill distribution, would take us far from the theme of this study.

CHAPTER 4

The labor force: Changes in sectors and organization

The structural complexity of the labor force and labor market can be studied from many viewpoints and in this chapter I focus on two changes with considerable importance to the evolution of the entire economic system. The first is the shift of the labor force toward information-intensive sectors and occupations. This indicates an increase in the direct informational requirements of the system, one of the three aspects of structural complexity offered in the first chapter. The second is a change in the structure of labor–management relations occasioned by the decline of unionization of the labor force. From at least one important perspective, this change represents a decline in structural complexity because it indicates fewer interactions between key economic institutions comprising the system. This change in interactions within the system is another of the three aspects of structural complexity.

The information sector contains those workers engaged in creating, processing, and interpreting the information necessary for the economy to operate. Its relative size provides a sensitive indicator of both information flows and interrelations between different parts of the economic system. The information sector can be measured in terms either of specific industries or of specific occupations dealing with information flows. Although this compositional change of the labor force is, in part, also manifested by the well-known increase in the share of the labor force in the service sector, the underlying causes of this changes are controversial. I argue in the following discussion that future shifts toward the information sector should be slower in the future than in the past.

In one important sense the organization of labor–management relations has become structurally less complex since the labor unions, a major actor in the system, represent a declining share of the labor force. After exploring the underlying causes of this change, which I expect to continue, I focus on some of some important economic implication of this critical institutional change.

The shift of the labor force to the "information sector"

An increase in the resources devoted to the gathering, processing, and producing of information represents both a rise in the general information requirements of the system and also a rise in specific transaction costs; that is, the costs

75

of negotiating economic transactions, of learning about prices, quantities, qualities, and technology of goods and services, and of monitoring and enforcing these agreements. Various estimates of the development either of the "information sector" or of the transaction costs in the United States strikingly reveal this relatively faster increase of the information sector.[1] Indeed, some have elevated this development into a general law. G.J. Mulgan, for instance, declares that: "As institutions, economies, and societies grow and become more complex, the costs of coordination and control tend to rise faster than their material capacities." If true, this generalization has some grave consequences. For instance, pursuing this idea, Jean Voge investigates various physical and social systems and comes to the conclusion that these rising information and organization costs eventually result in a deceleration of growth. All this may seem too scary to be true; and my own estimates about these shifts, which are presented in the following discussions, reveal a less dramatic picture.

These alleged relationships, nevertheless, deserve empirical attention. Certainly the relative rise in transaction and organization costs can reduce the resources available for investment, and in this way economic growth can decline. But such an argument implicitly assumes that information technologies have a slower growth of productivity than production of other goods and services. If the reverse is true, then in real terms, the information sector can grow faster than the rest of the economy and yet not crowd out resources used for investment. Moreover, decreasing information costs allow an economic organization to become more productive.

This shift of resources to the information sector is but one manifestation of the march to the so-called postindustrial society. In the following discussion, I provide evidence that such a development has indeed happened, but at a much slower pace than commonly believed. Further, I argue that such a development should occur even more slowly in the future. Before focusing directly on the shift of the labor force toward the information sector, it is important to deal with several key issues in the general shift of labor toward the service sector.

Barebones of the theory of postindustrial society:
the shift of labor into the services

Daniel Bell's discussion of the postindustrial society is a brilliant book that has served as the classical text on the subject.[2] He based his analysis in part

1. These estimates include those by Machlup (1962), Porat (1977), and Wallis and North (1986). The citation comes from Mulgan (1991). Voge (1983) ties organization costs to economic growth with an analysis of alternative allocation of resources to investment or economic organization. Unfortunately, in his enthusiasm he stretches the empirical evidence available to him far beyond its limits and darkly hints that the post–1973 productivity slowdown in the United States was an important sign that this organizational limit to growth had been reached.
2. Bell (1973).

Table 4.1. *Industrial and occupational shares of labor force*

Part A: Military and homemakers excluded	1950	1960	1970	1980	1990
Share of labor force classified by industry					
Goods	55.9%	50.2%	45.3%	41.0%	36.1%
Services	44.1	49.8	54.7	59.0	63.9
Information services	34.4	39.1	46.1	51.0	53.1
Other services	9.7	10.7	8.6	8.0	10.8
Share of labor force classified by occupations					
Workers producing goods	50.5%	43.3%	34.7%	30.1%	26.6%
Workers producing services	49.5	56.7	65.3	69.9	73.4
Workers producing information	37.5	41.5	50.3	54.6	56.6
Personal services	11.9	15.2	15.0	15.3	16.8
Part B: Military and homemakers included					
Share of labor force classified by industry					
Goods	35.2%	32.7%	31.2%	31.2%	29.6%
Services	64.8	67.3	68.8	68.8	70.4
Information services	21.6	25.5	31.7	38.8	43.5
Remaining services	43.2	41.8	37.1	30.0	26.8
Homemaking	36.0	33.1	29.7	22.3	16.8
Armed forces	1.1	1.7	1.5	1.6	1.2
Other services	6.1	7.0	5.9	6.1	8.9
Share of labor force classified by occupations					
Workers producing goods	32.0%	28.5%	23.8%	22.9%	22.0%
Workers producing services	68.0	71.5	76.2	77.1	78.0
Workers producing information	23.8	27.5	34.6	41.6	46.9
Remaining services	44.1	44.0	41.5	35.6	31.1
Homemakers	35.6	32.4	28.7	22.3	16.0
Armed services	1.1	1.6	1.5	1.6	1.2
Personal services	7.5	10.1	10.3	11.7	13.9

Note: The sources and methods are described in Appendix Note 4.1.

upon the discussion surrounding the "law" named either after the seventeenth century political economist Sir William Petty or after the twentieth-century economist Colin Clark. This law says that with economic development, the share of the GDP (and the share of labor) in agriculture, mining, and other "primary industries" declines over time, while the share of the tertiary sector such as services and government rises. The share of the secondary sector comprising manufacturing, utilities, construction, and transportation first rises and then, at some later stage of economic development, declines. Bell combines the primary and secondary sectors to focus attention on the increasing shares of labor in the service sector.

If we look at the structure of the labor force, as commonly defined, the data discussed in detail later (Table 4.1) show the service industries rising from 44.1 percent to 63.9 percent of the labor force from 1950 through 1990. Within the service sector, however, the change in the share of the labor force was very uneven: the rise was greatest for business services; finance, insurance, and real estate; legal services; and social services (health, education, and welfare services). The labor force share of workers in personal services actually declined. For distributional services (wholesale and retail trade) the share of workers increased only slowly.

This is not, however, the end of the story since the conventional measure of the labor force omits those engaged in the military and in homemaking. If these are included, the share of workers in the services increased much more slowly, from 64.8 percent in 1950 to about 70.4 percent of the labor force in 1990, because the share of the population providing housekeeping services on a full-time basis declined considerably in the period. This phenomenon, in turn, occurred in part because of changes reducing the necessary time for performing such work. That is, housework has become increasingly mechanized; for instance, vacuum cleaners, automatic washing machines, and air filter devices, all reduce cleaning and dusting time. Moreover, many services have been transformed into goods, for instance, factory-prepared foods reduce family food preparation time. As wages rise, the opportunity costs of homemaking also increase and create incentives for moving into the paid labor force.

By the early 1990s, however, the rising participation rate of women in the labor force appeared be decelerating. Ben Wattenberg presents public opinion data showing that the percentage of women wanting to stay home has recently stopped falling. This may presage a leveling of the female participation rate in the labor force in the future.[3] In turn, this change will probably act to slow the growth of the service sector as measured excluding homemakers.

Thus far I focus attention only upon industries; but the same kind of argument can be made for occupations as well. More specifically, in the production of goods, many people are really engaged in service occupations, for instance, clerks, and bookkeepers. As I show in the following discussion, the share of these service occupations has increased also; the rate is also much slower if homemaking services are included.

These white-collar occupations are not, as often assumed, immune to the currents of foreign trade. G.J. Mulgan argues the extreme view that as much as 85 percent of white-collar work could be done remotely, rather than at the site of the office; and a good share of these jobs might be less expensively car-

3. Wattenberg (1991), p. 85.

ried out abroad.[4] For instance, some data-entry work, processing of insurance claims forms, and other routine clerical work of enterprises in the United States are now being performed outside the United States with the results transmitted electronically to the home office. Hewlett-Packard took a more extreme step and transferred the head office of its personal computer branch from California to France; less dramatically, Swiss Air announced in 1993 that its entire accounting office would be transferred from Zurich to Bombay, where it would be carried out by skilled and less-expensive Indian accountants. Now that communications technology permits the export of service jobs, these incidents appear as harbingers of the future. Service jobs in the United States that do not depend on face-to-face interactions and are information intensive might increase considerably more slowly in the United States than in the past, since they would be produced by less expensive labor abroad.

Are these shifts in the structure of the labor force toward services due to changes in supply or demand factors? At this point, the theory of the postindustrial society becomes uncharacteristically mute. A crude approach for isolating demand factors can be made from national accounts data, where the various types of consumption are classified according to whether they are goods or services. In the period between 1950 and 1990, the average annual increases in the consumption of goods and services were respectively 2.9 and 3.8 percent.[5] These estimates are based on a narrow definition of consumption, but if we broaden the definition by including as consumption the production of the government (unevenly split between goods and services), investment (goods), and exports (unevenly split between goods and services), we obtain roughly the same results.

A major problem with this type of analysis is that the results are sensitive both to the manner in which the sectors and occupations are classified and to the measurement of growth in the individual sectors. Using a more sophisticated input–output approach to measure both growth of production and measurement of sectoral shifts, William J. Baumol, Sue Anne Blackman, and Edward N. Wolff show that between 1960 and 1980, less than 10 percent of the change of employment in the service industries can be attributed to changes in the overall structure of final demand (consumer or investment).[6] Although a change in the direct demand for services explains a share of the increasing relative importance of services, it is necessary to look at other factors as well. Three conflicting theories engage our attention.

---

4. Mulgan (1991), p. 81.
5. In the period of six decades between 1929 and 1990, the average annual increases in the personal consumption of goods and services were roughly the same. These estimates are based on data from Table 1.2 from the national accounts (U.S. Department of Commerce, 1986, and *Survey of Current Business,* various issues).
6. Baumol, Blackman, and Wolff (1989), p. 155.

Increasing transaction costs: In the mid-1980s John Joseph Wallis and Douglass C. North proposed a demand-side explanation.[7] They argued that the increase in services reflects the fact that increasing levels of economic development are accompanied by increasing transaction costs accompanying the rising structural complexity of the organization of the economy. These transaction costs, in turn, require more resources to information creation, processing, and interpreting; an argument that is very much in accord with the major theme of this book. They specified that such complexity arises from several sources:

1. The division of labor is increasing (a variant of my job heterogeneity argument in the last chapter) and coordination problems within an enterprise are becoming increasingly severe.
2. With the falling transportation and communication costs, markets are becoming broader in geographical scope. Such internationalization of the economy requires greater information costs since domestic producers must take into account a much larger market area with many more competitors (and governments) involved. Moreover, with the rise in discretionary income, consumers are demanding more heterogeneous goods, which increase the information requirements of production and sales. In short, the business environment is becoming structurally more complex. I present further evidence on this matter in Chapter 6, showing that enterprises are following organizational strategies to adjust to such a changing environment. I also discuss further aspects of the problem with regard to foreign and domestic trade in Chapters 7 and 8.
3. The level of technology is becoming increasingly complicated and has greater information requirements. Further, the number of products and their variants and the possible technologies to produce these goods and services are greatly increasing. This is manifested not just by the rising level of automation but, as discussed in Chapter 3, by increasing demands for skilled labor.
4. Government intervention into the economy is becoming more extensive, both in scope of coverage and depth of application. Firms are facing a greater number of health, safety, environmental, wage and pension rules, and other regulations. I discuss this theme in much greater detail in Chapter 9.

From such considerations Wallis and North argue that transaction costs – the information resource costs of maintaining and operating the institutional framework associated with the gains from trade – are increasing in comparison to the costs of making and transporting production. They focus particular-

---

7. Wallis and North (1986).

ly on the implications of these costs for the changing nature of property rights.They also carry out the useful task of measuring these transactions costs from the beginning of the twentieth century to the present.[8] Such empirical results also suggest that these transactions costs are increasing faster than they can be offset by the rise in produtivity in information processing.

Differential productivity growth: William J. Baumol, Sue Anne Blackman, and Edward N. Wolff propose a supply-side explanation.[9] Their key assumption is that labor productivity has grown much faster in the production of goods than of services. Because the final structure of demand between goods and services has not greatly changed, this differential productivity growth produces a shift of the labor force into services. As a simple numerical example, suppose that the economy is initially producing fifty units of goods and fifty units of services, that fifty workers are initially engaged in the production of each, and, finally, that productivity triples in the production of goods and remains the same in the production of services. If the volume of goods and services is to remain *in the same proportion*, workers must be shifted to the service sector. The result is twenty-five workers are producing seventy-five units of goods and seventy-five workers are producing seventy-five units of services. Further, if wages of workers in the two sectors remain in the same proportion, the share of the GDP in the service sector, measured in current prices, will also rise.

The differential productivity increases can be calculated from national account data, and the faster rise in the labor productivity of goods than of services receives statistical support.[10] But several serious problems arise. The first is the determination of what is the volume of a service, especially if that service has dimensions difficult to quantify.[11] For instance, what exactly are

8. Their statistical exercise is controversial. For instance, Davis (1986) points out difficulties in the manner that Wallis and North have operationalized their concepts. For example, why do they distinguish between farm managers (transactions sector) and farmers operating their own farm alone who also keep records (transformation sector)? Why don't they distinguish between clerks writing reports and keeping records (transactions sector) and clerks maintaining inventories and others whose activities enhance production (transformation sector)? Or for the government sector, how meaningful is their distinction between those providing transactional services and those providing transfers?

9. Baumol, Blackman, and Wolff (1989).

10. From specially constructed productivity indices of different industries that take inputs into account, Baumol, Blackman, and Wolff (1989) document a productivity lag in the production of services in comparison to the production of goods. Since relative wages in the two sectors have remained roughly the same, this means that the relative cost per unit of service is rising in comparison to a unit of goods, which acts to offset a shift toward the consumption of services due to higher incomes alone.

11. Problems in the measurement of services can be seen in the discussion about the decline in time devoted to housework. Some argue that the decline is merely statistical and is due to lower standards of house cleanliness. Although some evidence suggests such a decline occurred dur-

hospitals producing? Government statisticians are often able to measure the service output only by the inputs, which is obviously an unsatisfactory procedure. Problems sometimes arise in distinguishing goods and services. For instance, is a fax a good or a service? Additional problems occur in distinguishing the growth in labor productivity due solely to the workers in that industry and that due to workers in other industries producing inputs for that product because costs fall and productivity rises if, for instance, raw materials become less expensive. Finally, within any specific industry, the key assumption about the productivity lag becomes more controversial since many types of office automation and computerization raise productivity of the service workers.

To explain shifts in the job structure, the Baumol team uses a decomposition analysis to separate the relative importance of the productivity lag, the substitution of white-collar for blue-collar work within narrowly defined industries, and the change in the composition of final demand.[12] Between 1960 and 1980 in the production of goods, the first two factors had a roughly equal effect and accounted for almost all of the decline of employment growth. The increase in traditional services was relatively small and, according to their estimates, was due almost completely to the productivity lag effect. For information services, slightly more than half of the growth in their share of the labor force was accounted for by the substitution of white-collar for blue-collar work, and most of the remainder was due to the productivity lag effect.

This kind of empirical demonstration is impressive, but the accuracy depends very much on whether they have measured productivity correctly.[13] An extreme view is expressed by Michael Darby, the former Chief Economist of the U.S. Department of Commerce: "At our present state of knowledge, we don't really know what's happening to service-sector productivity. It could be growing faster than manufacturing productivity, instead of much slower." His ideas are seconded by Michael Harper, Chief of Productivity Research of the Bureau of Labor Statistics, who notes that productivity in many sectors is "simply impossible to measure." The conventional academic wisdom among most economists is that productivity in the service sector has been underestimated but that it still has not risen at the rate in the goods-producing sector. Baumol and his colleagues were using the best data available to them; but if

ing the 1980s (e.g., O'Neill, 1993), the reduction in housework began to occur a number of decades before then. Traditional measurements of the production of the banking sector do not adequately take into account the additional banking services and the greater speed with which many services are carried out (for instance, through automatic teller machines).

12. Baumol, Blackman, and Wolff (1989), p. 155.
13. Both citations come from Malabre and Clark (1992), p. A1. The conventional wisdom of economists on this matter can be found in Griliches (1992).

they have underestimated the real rise in service productivity, which is quite possible, then their argument is greatly weakened and the Wallis-North approach receives greater support.

Technological complementarities: For several decades economists have argued the proposition that capital is complementary to white-collar labor and a substitute for blue-collar labor.[14] For instance, some types of flexible manufacturing systems either replace blue-collar workers with engineers or increase the number of engineers. In a sophisticated econometric study Ernest R. Berndt, Catherine J. Christensen, and Larry S. Rosenbaum extend this argument by using cross-section data for two-digit manufacturing industries to show that an increasing share of high-tech capital is associated with a rising employment of white-collar labor and with a declining or level employment of blue-collar labor. In other words, such investment is complementary to white-collar labor and is a possible substitute for blue-collar labor. Berndt and his colleagues also obtain roughly similar results when they examine complementarities of such communication technologies and labor with different degrees of formal education. Although such econometric work is impressive, the causal mechanisms are unclear. As discussed in Chapter 3, automation and computer technology can be used with different skill levels, depending upon how the work is organized. Although information technology might be correlated with employment of those with higher education, this does not seem to me to be a necessary requirement. After all, almost anyone can be trained to use a computer for most common shop or office tasks in a relatively short time.

At present, it is impossible to decide to what degree the transaction costs, the differential productivity growth, and the technological complementarities approaches explain the shift into services in general or into information occupations in particular. Everything hinges on measuring productivity in the service sector, which is very difficult. If Wallis-North are most correct, the higher share of workers producing services is due to the increasing requirements of the knowledge society; if Baumol-Blackman-Wolff are most correct, this shift is due primarily to a shift in the relative productivity of blue and white collar workers; and if Berndt-Morrison-Rosenbaum are most correct, these changes are really due to the nature of technological change. It may seem wishy-washy to declare that the theses of all three teams have some grain of truth; but since no detailed data exist to resolve the dispute, I can provide no definite answer. So with this uncertainty in mind, it is time to turn to the information sector.

14. An early study is by Berndt and Christensen (1974). The recent study is Berndt, Morrison, and Rosenbaum (1992).

The increasing importance of the information sector

The top part of Table 4.1 presents data on production sectors. The information sector includes all of such industries as telecommunication, trade, finance and real estate, and education plus part of such industries as medical, business services, and public administration. Although this classification includes some arbitrary decisions, the overall trends should not be greatly affected. The data show that the information services appear to have experienced a dramatic growth in the last four decades. This has occurred along a broad front, and not to the growth of any single industry composing the information sector.

One problem of focusing exclusively on industries is that the data are muddled by the shuffling of particular functions between and within particular industries. For instance, using a classification by industry, if the advertising department within a manufacturing firm becomes an independent company selling its services exclusively to that manufacturing firm, the share of workers in the service industry rises; and the share in the goods industries falls.

Therefore, the lower section of each part of the table presents data on occupations, classified as to whether these workers deal directly with the material production of goods or services. The data also reveal roughly the same picture as the data on industrial sectors. Again, a number of arbitrary classification decisions must be made; and in many occupations the activities embrace several categories (for instance, a building superintendent processes data but also provides a service). In such cases, the personnel were simply evenly split between the two categories. These calculations also show a movement into the service sector, and, moreover, at a faster rate than the industrial data.

From such empirical regularities, an interesting ideological superstructure can be built about entry into the "knowledge society;" indeed, this has been standard grist for the mills of futurists for the last several decades. David R. Howell and Edward N. Wolff take the argument a step further by distinguishing between information-creators (for instance, teachers, lawyers, engineers), information-managers (administrators, supervisors), information-analysts (accounts, computer-programmers, electricians), and information-transformers (for instance secretaries, clerks, sales representatives, registered nurses) and compare these groups with people-centered occupations (for instance, sales clerks, barbers), and material-centered occupations (machinists, truck drivers, food service workers).[15] They show that information-centered occupations have increased as a share of all occupations at the expense of material-centered occupations, with the share of people-centered occupations remaining roughly constant. From 1950 through 1985, all four types of infor-

15. Howell and Wolff (1993).

mation-centered occupations increased in relative importance, although at quite varied rates in the different decades.

This increase in information-centered occupations has occurred at the same time as investment in computers and other information-handling machinery has soared. By the late 1980s, such equipment accounted for about 40 percent of all investment in producer durables. Given their much more rapid depreciation, computers are, of course, a much smaller percentage of the total stock of producer durables. Nevertheless, this raises the question of why this machinery has not provided a sufficient productivity increase so that fewer workers could handle the same quantity of information.

The computer productivity puzzle

Nobel Prize laureate Robert Solow has defined the computer productivity puzzle in the following manner:[16] "We see the computer everywhere but in productivity statistics." It has been often pointed out that although computers and communication equipment comprised roughly one-sixth of the net stock of all producer durable equipment in the service sector by the late 1980s, productivity increases in this sector have been very low in the late 1970s and 1980s when such investment was taking place. Most empirical studies show relatively low productivity gains from computers and one highly technical production function study of manufacturing comes to the conclusion that on the margin, the benefits of investment in information and computer technology have been less than the costs. Erik Brynjolfsson argues that many of these studies are so severely impaired by measurement problems that the results mean less than meet the eye. To explain the computer productivity paradox, economists have offered some ingenious explanations. Since the topic bears on our understanding of the future development of the economy, it is worthwhile to consider them briefly.

To a certain extent computer usage can produce services that are not captured in the production or productivity statistics. An analogy is found in the introduction of electricity, where data to measure the productivity increases resulting from the use of electricity do not capture the qualitatively better services produced, for instance, brighter lights or more reliable sources of energy. Similarly, the data to measure the productivity increases resulting from the use of computers do not capture the saving of time of consumers (for instance, ATMs or electronic data bases) or the qualitative improvement of

16. Solow is cited by Paul David (1990). Baily and Gordon (1988) explore computers and productivity in the services; and the list of reasons explaining the computer productivity puzzle comes mainly from their essay.. The generalization drawn from thirty empirical studies of the computer productivity puzzle comes from Brynjolfsson (1993). Morrison and Berndt (1991) carry out the highly technical production function study to which I refer.

working conditions by eliminating certain highly repetitive work (for instance, retyping letters).

It takes time to absorb new technologies and to rearrange the work process around it. Paul David (1990) draws an historical parallel with the dynamo and electricity generation, which also did not yield their potential for increased productivity for a number of decades.[17] In part, this lag occurred because initially the innovations had to be laid on top of old production systems. To be used to maximum advantage, entire manufacturing systems had to be redesigned. For instance, the vertical factories had to give way to one-story factories, which allowed more efficient material handling systems. In the same way many enterprises introducing computers have also maintained the old systems as well; and one reads in the business press stories about the insurance industry, which embraced computers many years ago but only began in the early 1990s to eliminate workers whose jobs were still tied to traditional systems. This story is told in other industries, although systematic evidence on the matter was not available at the time of this writing. In my enterprise survey reported in Chapter 6, one respondent wrote a margin note that it is necessary for his enterprise to elevate computers and communication to a vital strategic resource and away from the traditional data processing tasks, a sign that his company had not yet fully utilized the potential of the new technology.

Of course, some of the use of information technology is not to enhance the process of production. In some cases computer technology is used to take customers or profits away from competitors by serving a marketing purpose in the same manner as advertising expenditures. In other cases computer outputs might be wasted either because the computers are producing unnecessary information by those whose pay is tied to the quantity of computer output or because companies do not know how to use the additional information obtained with computers. Service industries that were shielded from competition by regulations and that did not, at least until recently, face global competition in particular were likely to use the new information processing technology in an inefficient manner.

Finally, and perhaps most importantly, because computing equipment constitutes only a small part of total capital, it is often econometrically difficult to pick up the effect of computers in production function studies unless they are carried out with highly detailed statistics.[18] Another promising approach is a standard type of growth accounting exercise, where the capital stock in computers is sep-

---

17. Paul David (1990).
18. For instance, using firm-level data both Frank R. Lichtenberg (1993) and Brynjolfsson and Hitt (1993) are able to detect an important productivity effect resulting from the use of computers. Up to the mid-1990s, however, this type of microeconomic study was rare and the generality of these results remains to be seen. The growth accounting study is by Oliner and Sichel (1994).

arated from other types of capital. Following such an approach Stephen Oliner and Dan Sichel show that computer capital has been too small to have a great influence on overall growth, even if investment in such equipment obtains an extra-high return. For instance, if overall investment accounts for one percentage point of annual growth, if the computer stock comprises one-fifth of producer durables, which in turn constitute one-half of total business capital, and if the investment return to computers is twice as high as other types of capital, then investment in computers will account for only .09 percentage points of growth.

This contribution to growth by computers is barely detectable and may be too high, especially if we include as part of computer investment the cost of computer software. It is also worth emphasizing that the use of computers has not even enhanced the productivity of information workers to a degree necessary to offset requirements for additional workers needed to fulfil the needs for the additional creation, processing, and interpreting of information accompanying the rise of structural complexity. In short, although the use of computer technology may offset part of the decline in U.S. economic growth rate, little systematic macroeconomic evidence is available to suggest that this offset will be complete in the near future or that growth will accelerate.

Changes in the labor–management environment

The perspective offered by the concept of structural complexity leads us to ask questions about other aspects of the labor market. Of considerable interest and importance to the evolution of the economic system is the changing environment of labor–management relations.

The share of the U.S. labor force enrolled in labor unions has declined, as I document in the following discussion. In turn, this development represents an important decline in the structural complexity of the organization of labor–management relations, at least in the sense that one layer of organization is eliminated and, without a union, enterprise managers do not need to go through the long and complicated process of collective bargaining.[19] Thus interaction between two major institutions has declined. On some issues, management can now deal with the workers on a take-it-or-leave-it basis. This situation is expressed by the sentiment often found in the business press that without a union, life for management is much "simpler." This does not necessarily mean raw exploitation, but rather that many issues do not need to be subject of bargaining.

A problem of viewpoint arises in defining the decline of unionization as a reduction of structural complexity. In so far as unions discipline workers and

---

19. It also represents a decrease in the heterogeneity of the labor force with regard to labor union membership, as measured by the Theil statistic.

Table 4.2. *Labor union membership, union/nonunion wage differentials, and strike activities*

	Share of union members in nonagricultural labor force	Wage differentials: union/nonunion workers		Percentage of work time lost in strikes		Average annual unemployment rate
		P-H estimates[a]	Pryor estimates	More than 6 workers involved	More than 1000 workers involved	
1950–4	30.3%	23.5%	n.a.	.278%	.206%	4.0%
1955–9	30.2	26.9	n.a.	.252	.198	5.0
1960–4	27.2	27.5	n.a.	.128	.084	5.7
1965–9	26.3	25.8	n.a.	.214	.148	3.8
1970–4	25.2	16.0	n.a.	.232	.162	5.4
1975–9	22.5	n.a.	24.6%	.168.	.102	7.0
1980–4	19.1	n.a.	30.1	n.a	.064	8.3
1985–9	15.6	n.a.	23.6	n.a.	.038	6.2

[a]The P-H estimates are by Pencavel and Hartsog. Their estimate for 1975–9 is omitted both because it is so different from other estimates and because they also believe that it is not reasonable. The wage differential estimates attempt to hold the industry constant.
Sources of the data and methods of estimation are presented in Appendix Note 4.1.

prevent such actions as wildcat strikes, they might make life simpler for management. In the present era in the United States, however, this disciplinary function of unions does not seem very important; and, as I document later, strikes are decreasing in importance. Some might claim that a nonunion situation represents greater complexity because now management must deal with every individual worker, rather than a single bargaining unit. This gives a misleading picture. Of course, there is bargaining with individual members of the work force, but such bargaining also occurs with unionization as well. What is important is that management resources devoted to dealing with workers have declined.

The declining role of unions

In comparison to other industrialized nations in the late 1980s, the United States had the lowest share of union membership among its nonagricultural wage and salary employees.[20] Table 4.2 shows, moreover, that in the United States the relative importance of union membership in the nonagricultural labor force has been decreasing since the mid-1950s. If public sector unions were excluded from the calculations, then the decline of the share of union membership would be even more dramatic. Among other industrialized

20. Blanchflower and Freeman (1992) and Chang and Sorrentino (1991) discuss these international comparisons.

nations, a declining share of union membership appeared in only a few nations during the 1970s; in the decade of the 1980s, however, this movement became more pronounced and appeared in eight of the eleven industrial nations for which comparable evidence is available.

The decline in union power is manifested not just by declining membership, but by other factors as well.[21] The percentage of union victories in National Labor Relations Board (NLRB) elections has fallen dramatically over time, public approval of labor unions as manifested by survey data has declined, and union political influence appears to have diminished. Five quite different types of explanations have been advanced to explain this trend, each of which provides an important piece to the puzzle:

Changes in the structure of the work force: The structure of the work force is changing in ways that signal a decline in unionism. For instance, women now constitute a higher percentage of the labor force and, in the United States, they have traditionally been less unionized. Manufacturing, the base of the labor movement, is declining in relative importance in the economy and, moreover, is moving toward the South and West, where historically unions have found it more difficult to organize. The labor force has shifted toward services, which have always been less unionized than manufacturing, in part because of the smaller size of the work units. As previously noted, the occupational structure is shifting toward white-collar work and also part-time work; these two occuaptional groups are more difficult to organize than blue-collar or full-time occupations.

Although these arguments seem self-evident, the empirical evidence on unionization and the changing structure of the labor force is mixed.[22] Most empirical studies of the problem suggest that changes of the sectoral mix of production, of the gender mix, or of the mix of occupations in the labor force have not been the dominant causal force of the decline of union membership. This problem of causation, however, is complicated because the relative importance of these structural factors seems to vary from period to period. In addition, unions in other nations have succeeded in organizing both men and women, both white-collar and service workers, and workers in both small and large plants, which suggests that most of these factors appear to be of secondary importance in the United States and that deeper causes are at work.

Increasing job heterogeneity might, however, play a role in declining unionization in the long run since it works against labor solidarity. More specifical-

---

21. This paragraph draws upon the work of Goldfield (1987), especially pp. 23, 35.
22. The first reference is to Troy (1992); the reference to "most studies" include those by Blanchflower and Freeman (1992), Farber and Krueger (1992), Goldfield (1987) and Neuman and Rissman (1984).

ly, as work becomes more heterogeneous, unions find it more difficult to represent all of the interests of the work force within a factory. For instance, if a union tries to reduce wage differences between occupations, highly skilled workers are disaffected; but if it tries to increase wage differences, low-skilled workers are angry. The correct balance is difficult for any union, no matter how skillful, to achieve.

Increasingly competitive economy: In a highly competitive market, the economic role played by unions is quite restricted. Any wage increases unions can gain in a particular plant that are not offset by productivity increases will result in a decrease in employment in that plant.[23] In the United States, in the 1970s and 1980s, competition in the economy increased as imports rose, a phenomenon I document in detail in Chapter 8. Another contributing factor was the decline in government regulation of various sectors, especially airline or trucking industries. This increased competition in these sectors because with governmentally regulated rates, unions could obtain higher wages for their members, which the companies would then pass on to consumers. Such deregulation became important, however, only since the late 1970s. More importantly, perhaps, the decline in transportation and communication costs has made it easier for enterprises either to transfer production abroad or to contract out to nonunion plants located in low-wage areas in the United States.

In the coming decades these competitive pressures will continue, at least in manufacturing and in those services that can be imported. Although many studies show that unionized factories are more productive than nonunionized plants, this productivity different usually does not offset the union-wage differential so that enterprise profits are lower.[24] This means that unionized factors are less competitive against imports and, since union wages are generally believed to be more rigid, they are also economically are more vulnerable during business downturns. These factors could have an adverse impact on enterprise growth, a conjecture receiving positive support from a recent study of factories in California showing that unionized plants grew more slowly than nonunion plants. If this latter study is valid for the entire United States, it suggests that the role of labor unions in obtaining wage increases will be increasingly restricted and, as the most likely result, fewer workers

23. If unions cannot raise wages, they can still provide some valuable services to the workers. For instance, they can increase the participation of workers in plant decision making, as well as disseminate information not just about plant policies but also about conditions in the labor market and training opportunities outside the plant. But, of course, many such informational services can be supplied by the administration of the enterprise, one of the aims for adopting certain Japanese management methods.

24. Freeman and Medoff (1984), Chapters 11 and 12, present evidence that unionized enterprises have higher productivity than nonunionized factories, other things such as capital stock remaining the same, and that profit rates are lower. The California study is by Leonard (1992).

may find it worthwhile to belong to unions because of the threat of unemployment in business downturns.

Decline in demand for unionization: Henry S. Farber and Alan B. Kreuger analyze survey data on attitudes toward unions and conclude that changes in the worker demand for union representation accounts for virtually all of the decline between 1977 and 1991, rather than the relative supply of union jobs.[25] Another study finds a drop in unionization of new establishment so that loss in union jobs due to structural shifts is not offset; in part this appears related to the demand for unions. Further, a recent cross-section study also shows that U.S. states with a higher proportion of younger workers have a lower rate of unionization, other things remaining equal; this appears another manifestation of the decreasing demand for unions. Finally, the increasing importance of employment of temporary help, outside contractors, and part-time workers who could not easily benefit from services provided by unions also acts to reduce the demand for union representation.

For the public at large, Gallup public opinion polls have shown a falling public approval of labor unions from the late 1950s through the mid-1980s.[26] This has held true even when the respondents have recognized the need for some organization to discuss and resolve legitimate concerns with employees. Even analysts highly sympathetic to the labor movement ruefully note that many workers no longer view unions as effective agents for them.

This fall in demand for union representation by workers seems paradoxical in light of the considerable differential in wages between union and nonunion workers within industries, as shown in Table 4.2. Indeed, David G. Blanchflower and Richard B. Freeman provide evidence that, other things being equal, this differential is greater in America than in five other industrial nations for which comparable microdata are available.[27]

But this greater wage differential has an important negative implication for the workers as well, namely that they are in greater danger of being laid off after the higher wages take effect, especially if they do not have seniority. It is known, for instance, that layoff rates and cyclical swings in employment are greater in union than in nonunion plants, in part because the union wage differential makes the plants more vulnerable to competition.[28] For many

25. Farber and Kreuger (1992). The other two studies to which I refer are by Freeman and Rebick (1988) and Moore and Newman (1988). This rising importance of temporary workers and outside contractors is documented by Abraham (1990). Blank (1990) and Tilly (1991) also have useful discussions of the issue.
26. Goldfield (1987), p. 35, analyzes the Gallup data. The other two studies to which I refer are by McDonald (1992) and Edwards (1993), p. 90.
27. Blanchflower and Freeman (1992).
28. Farber (1986).

risk-averse workers, the wage differentials are simply not worth the greater chance of unemployment.

Substitution of roles traditionally played by unions: Many of the gains for which unions have fought on the plant level have now been enshrined in national legislation. In other cases, such as welfare payments, the government has taken over union functions, a result shown in a sophisticated statistical study by William J. Moore and his colleagues (1989).[29] Federal pension legislation (ERISA), job safety regulations (OSHA), judicial restrictions on termination at will, and plant closing laws, as well as federally mandated family leave policies have also preempted union activity in these areas. In many cases management has also decided to preempt the union role by offering workers most of the benefits of unionism without the associated costs. Such changes might also underlie the fall in demand for union representation discussed previously.

Although Richard B. Freeman and James L. Medoff, among many labor economists, have made convincing arguments that unions provide the employee with a "voice" in the affairs of the company, this function also can be structured by the company itself.[30] For instance, one study notes that over half of the companies surveyed by the New York Stock Exchange claimed to have introduced various types of employee involvement programs. Undoubtedly with the emergence of increasingly complex and flexible production, such communication between workers and management will increase, thereby reducing the importance of the "voice" provided by labor unions.

An intrinsic difficulty arises, however, in replacing some traditional functions of labor unions with governmental legislation. As Richard Edwards argues, worker rights enshrined in law and enforced by the government have a limited reach.[31] The regulations are complicated and ambiguous and, as a result, reporting costs are high for the enterprise. Further, their enforcement is often sporadic, slow, and expensive. Penalties for violations are often light so that these regulations do not serve as a strong disincentive. Finally, workers are often ill-served by the cumbersome mechanisms, particularly when high-cost and unpredictable litigation must be undertaken.

But many unorganized employees find it difficult to protect their rights. Of course, worker rights in nonunion shops differ greatly from company to company, but even in those where joint labor–management decide over many personnel issues, worker rights are uncertain and can be unilaterally withdrawn at any time. It was not until the 1980s, for instance, that employee handbooks specifying the rights and responsibilities of workers were given legal recogni-

29. Moore et al. (1989). Some previous studies with less statistical sophistication also showed the same results, at least for recent years (Neumann and Rissman, 1984).
30. Freeman and Medoff (1984). The next study is by Jacoby and Verma (1992).
31. Edwards (1993).

tion.[32] But even as these handbooks gain force of law, simple conflict-resolution mechanisms are often insufficient or unfair, so that legal costs must escalate as problems move to the courts.

Rising costs of organizing unions: Certification elections for union representation have fallen considerably over time and, moreover, the success rate has fallen as well. In part, this phenomenon can be ascribed to a failure of aggressive organizing by unions;[33] in part to greater resistance by employers; and in part to changes in the legal and political structure that make union organizing more difficult.

The lack of aggressive union organizing has been attributed to the monopoly position of many unions and to their increasing bureaucratization. A higher percentage of certification elections have been won where several unions are competing against each other than if only one union is attempting to get recognition.[34] Regarding bureaucratization, James T. Bennett has gone so far as to argue that it is of little advantage for unions to be aggressive in their organizing, especially since with the rise in union dues, they are in better financial shape than ever before and have no need to add new members. Indeed, investment in organizing other factories even might weaken the financial status of the union!

Some analysts have emphasized the importance of rising employer resistance, as manifested by an increase in the number of labor complaints to the NLRB about unfair labor practices.[35] As noted previously, the wage differential between union and nonunion workers is higher in the United States than in other nations. Since employer costs rise and profits fall considerably faster than this differential, managers have a greater incentive to resist unionization than in other countries. Moreover, given the present confrontational nature of labor relations in the United States, factories with unions have much more structured workrules, which reduces flexibility of production.[36] The impact of some of this management resistance, however, is open to question. For instance, one study tries to relate violations of Taft-Hartley Act as reported to the NLRB (normalized by the number of employees eligible to vote) to certification outcomes for unionization, but finds no relationship.

Legal and political factors influencing the degree of unionization are varied. Some cross-section evidence shows that unionization is much higher in those states with laws that provide exceptions to employment-at-will doctrine, that

32. Ibid, Chapter VIII.
33. Chaison and Dhavale (1990).
34. Goldfield (1987), p. 210. The next two references are to Bennett (1991) and Neumann and Rissman (1984).
35. Freeman (1992) and Goldfield (1987), pp. 51–2, 196.
36. Farber (1986). The contrary evidence is provided by Moore and Newman (1988).

is, laws that make it more difficult to fire workers. Such laws appear both a cause and effect of union strength. Furthermore, some states have passed right-to-work laws banning union shops, which makes union organizing more difficult. Labor unions have tried a variety of solutions to the problem including much greater training of union organizers. Whether these measures will have any noticeable effect in the future remains to be seen.

On the political side, the top personnel of the NLRB are appointed by the U.S. President. For twenty-eight of the forty years between 1952 and 1992, they have been Republicans and, of course, this party has traditionally been more friendly toward business. Occasioned by new appointments by the Reagan administration in the 1980s, costs of organizing or maintaining unions rose because of changes in the direction of NLRB rulings that made union busting and resistence to union organizing easier. For instance, it became easier for employers to replace strikers, to engage in massive resistance against unionization, and to delay certification elections. Such latitude on the part of management in the United States is in dramatic contrast to that allowed in many other industrial nations.The degree to which this situation will continue under the Clinton and later administrations remains to be seen. Certainly in the first two years of the Clinton administration, such changes did not have a high political priority.

The impact of a declining union representation

The declining importance of union representation has had an impact on many different facets of economic life in the postwar era. Before taking these up, I must immediately dispel one myth. It can be argued that the decline in the share of the labor force represented by labor unions means that wages would fall in comparison to profits. As pointed out in Chapter 2, this does not seem to be the case. Over the four decades from 1950 through 1990 the relative share of wages to profits has slightly risen. Although it might be claimed that the ratio of aggregate wages to aggregate profits would have risen even faster if unions had maintained their previous strength, little empirical evidence supports this argument.

Among the effects of declining unionization of the labor force, it is useful to consider the evidence with regard to fringe benefits, strikes, job turnover, and more general aspects of production.

Fringe benefits: In their classic study on the role of unions, Richard B. Freeman and James L. Medoff suggest that labor unions raise the relative ratio of pensions, health care, and other fringe benefits to salaries.[37] A quantitative

---

37. Freeman and Medoff (1984). The quantitative study is: Bloom and Freeman (1991).

analysis of the problem provides evidence that 10 to 25 percent of the fall in private pension coverage in recent years is explained by declining unionization. The extent of company pensions, however, can be considerably influenced by federal tax laws and other regulations, so that this type of impact of declining unions can be offset by governmental action.

Strikes: Although many studies have focused on changes in the frequency of strikes over the business cycle, less attention has been paid to long-run changes in strikes. As a result, the causal relations are much less clear.

Examining the matter from an international perspective, several studies present evidence that the United States has a high degree of labor conflict, as manifested through strikes.[38] Labor conflicts have always been high and data on the number of strikes, as a ratio of the nonfarm civilian labor force, remain roughly the same between 1900 and 1950. Data on days lost in strikes as a ratio of the nonfarm civilian labor force do not extend back so far. Between 1927 and 1950, however, these data show a rise. Table 4.2 shows considerable fluctuations in the average number of labor-days lost in strikes over the period from 1950 to 1990. Nevertheless, the data suggest that the incidence of strikes generally has decreased in this four decade period, especially in the 1980s. It appears that in the long term, the degree of open labor–management conflict has begun to trend downward.

Different causal factors seem to influence the relationship between labor unions and strike frequency in the United States[39] Over the long run, the relative degree of unionization appears positively related to the number of days lost in strikes, which rise in the thirties, peak in the immediate postwar years, and then trend irregularly downward thereafter.[40] Such a relationship by no means tells the entire story, witness the high degree of strike activity in the period from 1890 to 1910, when unions were scarce. Strike frequency also appears to depend in part upon governmental aid such as the availability of unemployment insurance to strikers or other measures such as job guarantees for strikers after a settlement is reached. In the last few decades, this type of governmental support appears to be ebbing, especially with the decline in the

38. These studies include those by Paldam and Pederson (1984) and Hibbs (1987). The strike data from 1900 to 1950 come from U.S. Department of Commerce, Bureau of the Census (1975), pp. 126–7 and 179.

39. Cross-country comparisons by Paldam and Pederson (1984) and Hibbs (1987) provide evidence for the proposition that high unionization reduces strikes, particularly with social-democratic governments. This is because the battle for changes in the distribution of income shifts from the industrial to the political arena. This type of relationship is irrelevant to the United States, where social-democratic parties have little influence.

40. Kaufman (1982) examines in detail this positive relation between strike frequency and union density. Schor and Bowles (1987) show that the incidence of strikes depends in part on government transfer payments such as unemployment insurance.

political influence of labor unions. Finally, in recent years with increasing competition from imports, workers and management may be learning to accommodate each other without strikes.

Job turnover: Various empirical studies provide evidence that by giving workers a "voice" in their worklife, labor unions have reduced labor turnover.[41] This suggests that labor turnover should have increased with the decline in unionization, but the facts are quite different. Although U.S. quit rates and also total separation rates are very high by international standards, over the last four decades they have tended downward.[42] Of course, the union voice approach can be salvaged with the proposition that labor turnover would have decreased much faster if unionization had remained at the same level, but no supporting evidence has been advanced. Any statistical analysis would require sorting out a number of other causes underlying the changes in the quit rate as well. For instance, in recent years, job turnover has declined because workers have not wanted to risk losing their health benefits by taking a job elsewhere.

Broader aspects of production: Labor unions have influenced other aspects on the quality of work life that receive comment elsewhere.[43] Economists have also carried out many cross-section studies to measure the impact of

41. For example, Freeman and Medoff (1984) and Freeman (1992).
42. For this generalization I am relying on data from manufacturing to represent the entire economy, taking data from data come from *Employment and Earnings,* 29, No. 1 (January 1982) and Bureau of the Census (1975), p. 181. Although the downward trend in these rates have been interpreted in an alarming manner as demonstrating a "new industrial feudalism," with workers immobilized on their jobs because of seniority and negotiated fringe benefits. The evidence supporting this hypothesis is positive but weak (Pencaval, 1970); an earlier study by Ross (1958) is even more negative.

What appears more striking to me is that despite the downward trend, the quit rate is still at a relatively high level with roughly one worker in five quitting every year. This lowers the incentive of firms to invest resources in the training of their work force, since other firms not making such payments have the resources to pay higher wages to the newly trained workers, since they do not need to recover these costs.
43. For instance, Belman (1992) summarizes nine statistical studies about the relationship between the quality of worklife and unionization: most but not all show that unions increase quality of worklife, reduce wildcat strikes, and limit turnover. Other studies show that within plants unions act to reduce the inequality of wages and, as I discuss in Chapter 2, the decline in unions is one of the reasons adduced for an increasing inequality of wages for the economy as a whole. Freeman (1992) presents additional data on the matter and also argues that unionized companies are more likely to have health and safety committees. These various factors seem much less susceptible to influence by legislation than some of the other matters discussed previously. On the other hand, the increasingly competitive environment suggests that firms may have greater incentive to increase those aspect of the quality of worklife that have a positive impact on productivity. The cross-section studies to which I refer in the text are also summarized by Belman (1992).

unions on production. In his review of statistical studies Dale Belman points out that most find a positive relationship between unionization and labor productivity, other factors held constant. Most, but not all, studies also show that unions reduce profit margins.[44]

Conclusions and implications for the future

This chapter asks questions about the structural complexity of the labor force from two perspectives: the share of the labor force in information services, which reflects the information requirements of the economy as a whole; and the degree of unionization, which reflects the interaction between organized groups in labor relations.

The information sector

In the post–World War II era, the share of the labor force in the service sector increased. The rate depends, however, on how the labor force is defined. The major source of this increase lay in the information sector and in the information occupations, that is, those involved in the creation, processing, and analysis of information The underlying reasons for these trends are not entirely clear, and three competing, but not mutually exclusive, arguments appear to have some explanatory power. The Wallis-North explanation focuses on increasing structural complexity of the economic system so that information needs grow faster than the GDP. The Baumol-Blackman-Wolff explanation highlights the differential productivity changes in the production of goods and services which, combined with slow changes in the demand structure, lead to a shift of the labor force into services. The Berndt-Morrison-Rosenbaum explanation concentrates on technological complementarities of computer technology and service personnel. I also point out that if homemaking is considered a service, then the increase in the service sector is much smaller than previously believed because the increase of women into the labor force has led to many services in the market place merely replacing those services previously performed at home.

The rising share of the labor force in the service sector, in general, and the information sector, in particular, will undoubtedly continue in the future. I believe, however, that the pace of change in the United States will be considerably slower for three reasons. First, modern technology has made it increas-

---

44. Several studies show that unionized firms carry out less research and development. Any study linking R and D expenditures to unionization has to overcome the difficulties of holding other factors constant. For instance, considerable unionization occurs in mature industries, such as steel, that never had much R and D. Furthermore, little systematic evidence is at hand that unions reduce the rate of introduction of new machines or work practices.

ingly possible to import services that do not require physical contact with the customers, and examples of this trend are provided. Incentives to import services to take advantage of lower paid workers abroad will increase if real wages in the U.S. economy rise. Second, the increase in the number of women entering the labor force is tapering off, which means that the substitution of measured services produced in the market for unmeasured services produced at home will slow. Finally, as we enter the middle years of the computer era, computers may finally begin to realize their full productivity-enhancing potential. If this occurs in the information sector itself, then the rising share of the labor force in this sector may begin to taper off.

The most important macroeconomic implication of this shift into services is the impact on the rate of growth of the economy as a whole and two factors need to be considered. In so far as productivity in the service sector is rising more slowly than in the production of goods, then growth of the entire GDP is likely to decelerate. In so far as the measurable impact of computers has not been great, this technology will probably serve only as a partial offset to this decelerating productivity increase. In short, we must base our views of the future on a lower rate of economic growth than in the first two postwar decades.

Institutions of labor relations

The decline in the share of the labor force represented by labor unions can be traced to a number of factors. These include changes in the sectoral, gender, and geographical composition of the labor force; an increase in competition in domestic markets due to increased imports; a decline in demand for unionization; a substitution of roles traditionally played by unions by other actors; and a rise in the cost of organizing labor unions.

Clearly, some of these causal factors will not play the same role in the future. As I argue in Chapter 8, we should not expect the relative importance of foreign trade in the GDP to increase at the same rate as in the 1970s and 1980s, so competitiveness on domestic markets should not change as much. The demand for unionization by workers can change, particularly if they begin to believe more strongly than now that management is taking unfair advantage of them. This ideological element is difficult to predict. The substitution of roles played traditionally by union by other actors has limits, particularly with regard to actions by the federal government. Finally, the change in the political climate can reduce the costs of organizing labor unions. I might add that approached in the proper manner, unions can have success in organizing white-collar, service, and government workers. According to John B. Judis: "Today, union leaders have discovered it is quite possible to organize ... [service] workers, because the owners of hotels, hospitals or grocery stores can't respond to organizing drives by threatening to move their businesses abroad."[45] But competition in many services is high so that unionization would not necessarily lead to higher wages.

The change in the political climate as an encouragement for unionization also has limits. In several European nations, wage bargaining is carried out on a sectoral basis and, in some of these countries such as Austria, unions play an important role in the semicorporatistic economic systems.[46] As I argue in Chapter 10, this type of institutional development appears highly unlikely in the coming decades in the United States. Moreover, the downturn in the union representation in the 1980s in an increasing number of other industrialized nations suggests that such a labor–management system is no guarantee against a decline in the importance of unions.

In the near future, the trends in the share of the labor force represented by labor unions will probably decelerate, but not reverse. This downward trend can be encouraged if enterprises continue to adopt work methods to provide more participation of their workers in decision making and to devise alternative institutions for structuring labor–management relations to improve worker attitudes toward the company.[47]

The downward trend in unionism in the future may not have the same impact as in the past few decades. For instance, given increasing recognition of problems of financing social security, the elimination of private pension plans may not be as easy as in the past. If the new participatory management methods take root, workers may have sufficient "voice" so that the downward trend in strike activity will continue at a faster rate.

The impact on productivity is problematic because the positive relationship between unions and productivity that is found in cross-section studies does not necessarily hold over time. For instance, if unionism increases productivity by raising wages in a single enterprise, this option is not open for the economy as a whole. It seems prudent to remain skeptical that the declining level of unionization will have any significant impact on productivity, research and development expenditures, or introduction of new technology.

The perspectives afforded by the exploration of the concept of structural complexity have led us to ask a number of important questions about the evolution of the labor force and the labor market. This and the previous chapter document an increasing structural complexity of the labor force in terms of

---

45. Judis (1994).
46. These are discussed by Pryor (1988).
47. This assertion is based on Edwards' extended argument (1993) about the necessity to develop new institutions for exercising some of the functions unions used to fulfill, particularly in the area of conflict resolution mechanisms between labor and management. He also urges creation of other quasilegal mechanisms to protect worker rights so that workers will have a minimum degree of job security.

skill levels and heterogeneity of jobs and in terms of a shift of the labor force into the information sector. Decreasing structural complexity has occurred in the sphere of labor–management relations. In the following chapters I move from the population and labor force to other aspects of the economic system, both to explore the changing structural complexity and determine the impact of such changes on the operation of the economy.

CHAPTER 5

Wealth, ownership, and the financial structure

Applying the concept of structural complexity to the financial structure leads us to explore questions of vital interest to the future of the some key financial institutions and policies. This chapter focuses on three such topics: documentation of some important changes in the structure of wealth and ownership; determination of the relationship these changes to increases in the structural complexity of the financial system; and empirical investigation of the impact of the increasing structural complexity on financial distress and the volatility of the financial system.

The analysis starts with a discussion of the types of wealth in the economy, who owns it, and in what forms it is held. I show that an increasing share of personal wealth is intangible, and that much of this intangible wealth is either created directly by the government or generated by governmental activities. At the same time, the direct share of the government in the ownership of the nation's tangible wealth is decreasing. Focusing on just one type of wealth, I provide evidence that financial intermediaries are holding an increasing share of financial assets, a trend that I contend is closely tied to the increasing structural complexity of the financial system.

The financial superstructure, through which personal wealth is accumulated and maintained, is an integral part of U.S. capitalism. I argue that an appropriate indicator of structural complexity of this part of the economic system is the ratio of financial claims to the value of the actual physical assets that are ultimately involved. Such an indicator is sometimes called *leverage*. This approach also links structural complexity to the potential fragility of the financial system. I show that structural complexity (and, as a result, potential fragility) has increased over time. Given the general proposition that increasing structural complexity leads to increased instability of the system, we are directly led to focus on two types of instability – distress and volatility. Either phenomenon might lead to a cascade of financial problems that could greatly exacerbate the business cycle.

Indicators of financial distress include financial crises, bankruptcies, bank failures, and delinquent loans of both businesses and individuals. I show that over the four decades from 1950 though 1990, almost all indicators of financial stress have increased. The government is not helpless and has some policy instruments to combat this type of financial instability. By way of contrast, I also find that the increasing structural complexity of the financial system is not accompanied by its increasing volatility, a result contrary to common belief.

Trends in the ownership and composition of wealth

In this discussion, I outline briefly some major trends in the ownership of wealth and the changing form in which wealth is held. Appendix Note 5.1 provides quantitative evidence to support this qualitative discussion.

Formal ownership is a bundle of rights associated with some asset that is enforceable by law. Traditionally, ownership has implied powers to dispose and to use wealth, that is, to be able to sell or transfer it to others as well as to control its employment and to earn income from it. In more recent times, these various functions of ownership have been separated and are often held by different persons or groups. For instance, the holder of a share in a pension fund may be the ultimate owner of some physical asset and can earn income from it without controlling or disposing of it. Indeed, some financial instruments such as a bundle of securitized mortgages are explicitly designed to separate the management of the assets from the receipt of income from them. At this point I only discuss the ownership of wealth at different points in time, without concern about the impact of this separation except how it reflects increasing structural complexity. In the next chapter I focus on such problems in the corporate nonfinancial sector and, moreover, discuss in considerable detail the impact of the separation of ownership and control in the manufacturing sector on profits and other performance indicators.

The following trends in the ownership and composition of wealth deserve note:

Composition of tangible wealth: Over the post–World War II period the relative shares of different types of tangible wealth – residential structures, consumer durables, nonresidential buildings and equipment, and land – have not greatly changed.

Importance of intangible wealth: For households, intangible wealth includes human capital (the investment made in the education of individuals), claims on pensions and Social Security, and holdings of various types of income-producing privileges. The government generates a large share of this intangible capital, either by financing it (for instance, education) or by creating institutions through which it is administered (for instance, Social Security). The stock of human capital has been much larger than the stock of tangible household wealth and, in the period from 1950 to 1990, increased somewhat faster. Further, the net claims on pensions and Social Security (current claims plus the discounted value of future claims minus future payments) are roughly equal in value to total personal tangible wealth and, moreover, have also increased faster than total tangible wealth. This means that in the post–World War II era, the government role in the creation of household wealth has gradually increased.

Ownership of fixed reproducible wealth: Over the postwar period the share of fixed reproducible wealth (tangible wealth excluding land, inventories, and durables) directly owned by individuals has remained roughly the same. The share owned by corporations has increased, while the share held by various levels of government has declined, particularly after 1970. Fears of "creeping socialism" in the United States are groundless, at least along this dimension.

Ownership of total private financial assets: Private households have held the largest share of private financial assets, but this share has steadily decreased over the postwar period. By way of contrast, the share held by private financial institutions has steadily increased, in part because of the rising importance of pension funds. As I show in the following discussion, financial assets are an increasingly important share of total wealth and the shift in the holding of these financial assets is an important factor associated with the increased structural complexity of the financial system.

Internationalization of wealth: The share of wealth physically located in the United States but owned by foreign residents has increased dramatically, especially since the early 1970s, and, in 1990, such foreign investment amounted to 8 percent of total domestic assets. Assets physically located abroad but owned by U.S. residents have slowly increased as a ratio of total domestic wealth, and, in 1990, amounted to 5.8 percent. In 1950, the United States was a net creditor to the world; in 1990, it was a net debtor.

Trends in the structural complexity of the financial system

Defining the structural complexity of the financial system raises some conceptual problems and a brief historical exegesis is useful. Most tribal societies have few financial instruments. Wealth is owned directly and there are few recognized claims on the ownership of this wealth by anyone not directly holding such wealth. By way of contrast, in advanced capitalist-market economies, many claims on wealth physically held by one person circulate so that the actual wealth and the ultimate claimant are sometimes remote. A person has a claim on wealth from a bank in the form of a bank account; the bank has a claim on wealth in the form of a loan agreement to a financial group; and the particular financial group may, in turn, hold a claim on wealth in the form of a stock certificate on the company which actually holds and manages the asset. The volume of interactions, both between the various claimants on the wealth, and between this group and those managing it rises as the ratio of financial claims to physical assets rises.

The volume of interactions reflects two of the three definitions of structural complexity discussed in the first chapter: the direct information requirements of the system and the elaborateness of interactions within the system. Therefore, it seems appropriate to measure the structural complexity of the financial system either in terms of the ratio of financial to physical wealth or in terms of the relative importance of financial intermediaries, whose activities are reflected in the financial instruments.[1] For the financial system, therefore, the measure of complexity corresponds to what is commonly known as leverage and, as a result, we can draw upon a vast literature on the topic. Given this approach, two possible indicators are available to measure the complexity of the financial superstructure:

- The first is the ratio of total financial assets to total physical assets. This is sometimes called the *financial interrelations ratio*.
- The second is the ratio of assets of financial institutions to all U.S. financial assets. This measure of the relative importance of financial institutions (banks, insurance companies, and private pension funds) is sometimes designated as the *financial intermediation ratio*.

From comparisons of national balance sheets for twenty countries, some of which go back 300 years, Raymond Goldsmith argues that the financial interrelations ratio rises in the early stages of economic growth and then levels off.[2] For the United States, for instance, Goldsmith argues that this ratio reached a peak in the 1930s and has declined slightly thereafter. The same behavior also is true of the financial intermediation ratio, which, according to Goldsmith, achieved a peak sometime between 1939 and 1950. Using more recently published data that extend to 1990, a quite different picture emerges. I group the data in the same categories as the volatility data in the following discussion so that direct comparisons can be made later in the discussion.

1. The creation of financial intermediaries to specialize in tasks previously carried out by individual banks may simplify the tasks of individual banks or of banking clients. Looking at the structure as a whole, however, complexity increases in these cases since interactions within the system become more elaborate. Walsh (1984) has a similar argument.
2. Goldsmith (1985). The definitions used in my calculations are slightly different from those of Goldsmith (1985) so that the absolute value of the ratios for the overlapping years is somewhat different as well. For the period up to the late 1970s, however, the trends appear roughly the same.

Table 5.1. *Structural complexity of the financial system*

	Annual averages (percentages)			
	1950 through 1959	1960 through 1969	1974 through 1978	1983 through 1990
Aggregative data:				
Financial interrelations ratio[a]	136%	154%	129%	152%
Financial intermediation ratio[b]	26.1	28.4	34.9	38.1
Sectoral data:				
Financial ratios for households[c]				
Total liabilities to total assets	9.1	13.3	14.7	17.0
Interest payments to disposable personal income	1.4	2.1	2.2	2.7
Total liabilities to disposable personal income	46.6	68.2	71.0	85.5
Financial ratios for nonfinancial, nonfarm corporate businesses[d]				
Total assets to net worth	151.7	162.4	155.2	166.0
Gross interest payments to cash flow	11.4	20.0	33.4	62.2
Liabilities to GDP originating	78.1	85.3	80.7	92.6
Financial ratios for all commercial bank members of the FDIC				
Cash assets to total assets (percent)	22.5	17.9	17.1	12.4
Ratio of total assets to net worth (not a percent)	12.9	11.9	14.0	14.6

[a]Financial interrelation refers to the ratio of total financial assets of the private sector to total tangible assets of the private sector.
[b]Financial intermediation refers to the ratio of financial assets held by the private financial sector to the total financial assets held in the economy.
[c]Households include personal trusts and nonprofit organizations as well.
[d]For nonfinancial, nonfarm corporate businesses, cash flow is estimated as the sum of profits after taxes and depreciation. Interest payments are gross and exclude imputed interest. Disposable personal income includes transfer.
All ratios are calculated from current dollar data. The time periods are selected to include only "normal" years, that is, to omit those years in which special exchange rate or interest rate policies were being pursued by the Federal Reserve. In this way the data are comparable with those in Tables 5.2 and 5.3.
Data sources are given in the Statistical Notes in Appendix Note 5.3.

According to the aggregative calculations in Table 5.1, the financial interrelations ratio reveals an irregular upward direction in the forty-year period, but with a significant downward dip in the 1970s. The financial intermediation ratio shows a relentless upward movement for the entire period. By both measures, therefore, structural complexity of the financial system increased.

In part, the changes in both ratios seem driven by changes in banking institutions and financial instruments. For instance, recent developments in the securitization of assets have blurred the line between commercial and investment banking. Creation of money market accounts has blurred the line between checking and savings accounts. Development of many new types of financial instruments, such as derivatives, creates an increasing number of alternative assets for investors. These institutional changes paralleled the rising indicators of structural complexity.

These indicators of structural complexity number among the series most used to study the potential fragility of the financial system. To strengthen the argument, I include in Table 5.1 some other series for individual sectors that give a closer look at this potential fragility. For the households, the picture is one of increasing indebtedness, with all indicators rising steadily over time. A major portion of the liabilities are mortgages, but installment debt has also risen from 8.4 percent of *disposable personal income* (DPI) in 1951–5 to 18.1 percent of DPI in 1986–90.[3] The rise in total liabilities to DPI is paralleled, of course, by a rise in the ratio of interest payments to disposable personal income, which is still a relatively low percentage of income. The interest payments, of course, do not include debt amortization which amounts roughly to 10 percent of the debt per year. Thus, the combined interest and amortization payments rose from roughly 5 percent in the 1950s to roughly 10 percent of DPI in the 1980s.

For nonfarm, nonfinancial corporations financial leverage is the ratio of total assets to net worth. This ratio has increased over the forty-year period, although it took a dip from 1976 through 1985. The ratio of liabilities to the GDP originating in this sector followed the same pattern. It is alarming that gross interest payments as a percentage of cash flow have risen dramatically and, in the late 1980s, accounted for about three-quarters of total cash flow.[4] Although in the early 1990s this ratio fell to the average of the previous decade, any sudden downturn in profits and many corporations would find it difficult to pay the interest on their loans. Most of these results are also found when data from a large fixed sample of individual enterprises are examined instead.

Liquidity in the financial sector, as measured by cash assets to total assets, has steadily declined. This means that without outside assistance, the ability of these institutions to withstand bank runs and other sudden withdrawals of funds is reduced, other things remaining equal.[5]

3. Data on installment debt as a percentage of personal income comes from *Survey of Current Business,* 71, No. 10 (October 1991), p. C-40. The percentages were then recalculated as a percentage of disposable personal income.
4. Other relevant data are presented in Appendix Note 6.1, Table A.11. Warshawsky (1991) obtains roughly the same results when using a large fixed sample of individual enterprises.
5. It can be shown easily with a simple probability model that larger banks have less need for a given liquidity ratio than small banks. Further, larger banks might be more able to diversify their risks than smaller banks. In so far as economic development is accompanied by larger banking institutions, somewhat less liquidity may be needed in the economy. It is unclear whether the trends documented in Table 5.1 exceeded this amount, hence the ceteris paribus clause.

Thus, potential financial fragility has probably risen. As a gross generalization, almost all of the various series took an especially high jump in the 1980s, which many have labeled as the "decade of debt." It is this growth in debt that is a major cause underlying the rise in complexity of the financial system, as manifested by the rise of the financial interrelations and the financial intermediation ratios.

Such trends have received extensive commentary, as has the tripling of debt of the federal government between 1980 and 1990.[6] It is useful to step back from the political debate and examine some economic reasons for this increase in the various forms of private debt comprising these consumer and business liabilities. Discussion is facilitated by separating demand and supply factors and the contributing role of the government.

Supply factors: Some increase in debt arose from a greater availability of credit.[7] For instance, the globalization of financial markets has widened the sources of credits. Moreover, the deregulation of the U.S. banking industry has enabled banks to make more loans, many of which are riskier but which pay higher interest rates. In addition, the supply of bank credit has increased, in part because of a change in bank management ideology and the shift from an emphasis on *asset management* to *liabilities management.* Using the latter approach, banks have been more willing to leverage their assets since they can use funds borrowed from other banks or nonbank financial institutions (for instance, negotiable certificates of deposits) to meet reserve and/or liquidity requirements.

On the consumer side, an increase in the availability of credit has come about from the securitization of some forms of consumer debt. This has meant that many banks and other institutions are willing to extend credit since they can package and resell such debt to transfer the risks of default to others. One manifestation of this phenomenon has been the surge in credit card debt.[8]

Demand factors: Some increase in debt arose from changes in management techniques and in the economy allowing more debt to be taken on without increasing the overall risk to production. For instance, Richard B. McKenzie and Christina Klein argue that computerization has given firms an increasing ability to manage their financial affairs and their debt structure by providing them with more timely financial information. Furthermore, the decline in union power and militancy has made labor costs less fixed, which allowed greater debt to be taken on. Outsourcing of production may have also reduced risk to individual firms. In other cases, industries that are less sensitive to the

6. Council of Economic Advisors (1992), p. 394.
7. McKenzie and Klein (1992).
8. Ibid.

business cycle, such as the service industry, have become relatively more important; and such industries can safely take on more debt. There is, as I discuss in the Chapter 3, little evidence that the microeconomy as a whole has become less sensitive to business cycle conditions.[9]

Some increase in debt also arose from a surge in demand to finance corporate restructuring through such devices as *leveraged buy-outs* (LBOs). Many economists have argued that these changes increase the efficiency of the firm by reducing the problems of control of owners over managers by giving the latter a greater stake in the profitability of the firm. It is quite unclear that things have worked out in this way and, in the next chapter, I review the economic impact of the separation of ownership and control of industrial corporations.

On the consumer side Robert Pollin presents evidence that the increase in demand for debt cannot be traced to demographic shifts or to a consumption binge by the public or even, citing public opinion data, to a dramatic shift in attitudes toward debt.[10] Rather, he contends that such debt has arisen from increased borrowing to maintain living standards as real incomes have fallen for a significant portion of the population, an argument predicated on an increased ability of the low income population to obtain credit. He utilizes data revealing that the proportion of households in debt and also debt–income ratios have risen especially among those in the lowest quintiles of the income distribution where such real income declines have been the greatest, as I discuss in Chapter 2. While his analysis is hardly definitive, it is highly suggestive.

Contributing role of the government: Roughly half of the increase in financial fragility in the nonfinancial, corporate sector, can be traced to an increase in dividends relative to profits.[11] Correspondingly, retained earnings have declined and investment financed by debt has increased. The reasons for this trend are difficult to unravel, but surely tax laws favoring debt over equity financing have played a role. The corporate buy-outs financed by debt were also strongly influenced by the tax laws and the ability of firms to deduct interest on such debt when declaring taxable profit income. The alarming increase in the ratio of interest payments to cash flow of nonfinancial corporations (discussed in detail in Appendix Note 6.1) can be attributed in the 1980s in roughly equal degrees to this increase in debt and to the rising interest rates.

---

9. Some have even argued that internationalization of the economy has reduced risks to individual firms by spreading their sales over many nations so that they need not rely on just one market. My own evidence on increasing annual volatility of international raw material prices discussed in Chapter 7 casts doubt on such claims.
10. Pollin (1990).
11. In Appendix 6.1, I explore this phenomena using a simple simulation model.

Changes in tax laws during the 1980s increased incentives for investing in real estate, which has been mainly financed by borrowing. The overinvestment in commercial real estate in the late 1980s was accompanied by defaults and, as discussed in greater detail later, bank failures. The tax laws have also supported the rise in consumer credit, at least until such interest was no longer a deductible expense in declaring taxable income.

Since taxes and financial regulations touch almost all of the demand and supply factors for credit, the increase in debt is not necessarily an immutable trend, but could be reversed by changes in governmental policy. For instance, some simple changes in the tax code could considerably reduce the frequency of LBOs financed from borrowed funds. As discussed later, such changes would be in some cases quite desirable for the economy as a whole, although they would face a formidable opposition by those who have so greatly benefited from the current laws. The spate of recent books on reform and the possible futures of the financial system attests not just to the urgency of the task but also belief by specialists that meaningful changes are possible.[12]

Whatever the cause, the increase in the structural complexity of the financial system, especially in the 1980s, raises some obvious problems. The first is the simple problem of debt burden. Another is the increased fragility of the economy that such debt might occasion.

The burden of debt is particularly onerous when it is used to finance current consumption rather than investment to increase assets. In the United States in the 1980s, as domestically financed investment declined and the foreign debt soared, the country turned from a large creditor to a large debtor nation in a decade. The counterargument is unconvincing, namely that many of the assets gained from this borrowing were intangible, for instance, increased efficiency in companies purchased in LBOs. For the 1990s the increased external debt burden means, in turn, that domestic consumption to pay the interest costs to foreign creditors must be further cut back if domestically financed investment is to be increased. In other words, economic growth becomes more painful and is yet another reason to believe that the GDP will rise more slowly in the future than in the past.

But a second and more practical problem concerns the policies of the government to deal with this increased fragility, in particular if it has adverse effects on the economy. Certainly tax policy and banking regulations can have an important influence. For nonfinancial firms, for instance, such measures strongly affect the relative costs of equity and debt capital. For financial firms the amount of leverage can be easily limited. The problem is not one of policy tools, but of political will.

12. For instance, Pierce (1991) and Barth et al. (1992).

Implications: Financial distress

Two critical questions about the impact of such structural complexity need to be asked: Have the higher debt ratios led to greater financial distress, that is, to more market crises and crashes or to more bankruptcies, foreclosures, and loan delinquencies? And has it also led to greater volatility, not just of critical financial variables but production series as well? Or, to put these questions in a more general way, has the increase in potential fragility of the financial system arising from greater structural complexity led to economic instabilities? Or has such potential fragility been offset by innovations that allow the financial system to function effectively with less liquidity, greater leverage, and a greater debt burden?

It is not at all obvious that the potential fragility of the financial system, as manifested by increased structural complexity, leads to increased actual fragility of the system, and economists have quite different views. Some, particularly those close to the business community, argue that important institutional innovations in the financial system, particularly in the area of liabilities management, allow the financial system to function smoothly with much greater leverage. Others, such as Hyman Minsky, argue from theoretical considerations that potential financial fragility leads to financial crises, other types of financial distress, and financial volatility.[13] I also must note the inchoate notion mentioned briefly in Chapter 1 that any type of increasing complexity leads to greater instability in any system. My purpose in this discussion is to examine such indicators of financial instability empirically, rather than to explore either the theory or the exact mechanisms by which these instabilities have come about. Several definitions are necessary to clarify further discussion.

Fragility means that economic shocks can cascade and magnify through the economy so that the system is vulnerable to financial distress. Increasing fragility can also lead to increasing volatility of important financial and other economic variables. Although this fragility may be caused by high structural complexity of the financial system, it can also come about from other causes such as government policy or high interest rates.

Financial distress (sometimes called *financial instability*) is a collective term for a number of acute financial problems. The most dramatic such problem is a banking crisis. This is an episode of intense demand for money, due to an abrupt widening of the gap between the supply and demand of credit, that threatens to spread rapidly through the financial system.[14] Indicators for such

13. For instance, Minsky (1992).
14. This follows the argument of Wolfson (1986 and 1990). Wolfson has recently made a detailed study of all financial crises in the post–World War II period (1986). Among these he includes: the credit crunch of 1966; the Penn Central bankruptcy panic in 1970; the threatened failure of the Franklin National Bank and the Real Estate Investment Trusts (REITs) in 1974; the

a crisis include a rapid liquidation of short-term debt, a scramble for safety (which, for instance, would widen interest rate spreads between different kinds of bills and bonds), a sharp decline of the net worth of borrowers, and possibly even bank runs leading to a decline in the money supply. Other and less dramatic types of financial distress include financial insolvency such as illiquidity, bankruptcies, loan foreclosures, and loan payment delinquency.

Financial volatility describes the month-to-month or the year-to-year variation in key financial variables such as security prices, the stock of money and credit, and so forth. Financial volatility is the focus of the discussion in the next section.

Table 5.2 presents several indicators of financial distress. All show a considerable increase over the last forty years. They are grouped in time periods to permit comparisons with the volatility data discussed in the next section.

Financial crises increased markedly. Business failures also reveal an irregular but imporant rise. Such failures have increased much faster than the new business starts, so this latter factor does not underlie the dramatically rising failure rate. Bank failures measured in terms of the assets involved and loan failures, as measured by loan writeoffs, have shown an unambiguous increase as well. A critical underlying factor is the increasing ratio of interest payments to cash flow, a phenomenon that I have previously discussed and that seems partly driven by the tax structure.[15] In a recession, the higher the ratio of fixed-income payments to total income, the greater the risk of bankruptcy. This occurs becomes if income falls for any substantial period, the interest payments cannot be met; and one bankruptcy can trigger others. Evidence on this matter is presented for the nonfinancial corporate sector in Appendix Note 6.1. Moreover, if consumers or companies have fully leveraged their assets, aggregate demand can fall as they set aside funds for repayment, so that increased debt can cause a recession in the same manner as excess inventory accumulation; indeed, the two phenomena often accompany each other.

The data in Table 5.1 may not suggest immediately that the consumer sector would experience increasing financial distress. But the rising levels of personal bankruptcies and delinquent or foreclosed mortgages shown in Table 5.2 tell us otherwise. Readily available evidence does not suggest that such an increase in such mortgage problems is due to an increase in the share of these mortgages held by low-income families since housing ownership among such

Hunt Brothers silver speculation episode in 1980; the crisis occasioned by the failures of the Drysdale Government Securities, Inc. and Penn Square Bank; the threatened default of Mexico in 1982; the troubles of Continental Illinois Bank and also the Financial Corporation of America (the holding company for American Savings and Loan Association – at the time, the largest thrift bank in the country) in 1984; the run on state-insured thrifts in Ohio and Maryland in 1985; and the stock crash in 1987.

15. Many aspects of the problem are discussed by various authors in Friedman (1991).

Table 5.2. *Indicators of financial distress*

	Annual averages			
	1950 through 1959	1960 through 1969	1974 through 1978	1983 through 1990
Financial crises				
Number in designated time period	0	1	1	5
Other indicators of financial distress				
D&B, business failures: Failure rate per 1,000 listed firms, annual average	41.9	52.1	33.6	98.9
D&B, business failures: short-term liabilities to estimated total short-term liabilities of nonfarm, nonfinancial businesses (%)	.5%	.8%	.8%	3.0%
FDIC, commercial banks: Deposits of failed banks to total deposits (%)	.01	.01	.12	.76
FDIC, commercial banks: Gross writeoffs of loans to total loans and leases (%)	.16	.23	.50	1.07
Savings and loan banks: Assets of bankrupt banks to total assets (%)	.01	1.89	.04	2.44
MBA: Delinquent mortgages (% of total)	2.32	3.20	4.53	5.27
MBA: Foreclosed mortgages (% of total)	n.a.	.32	.39	.89
SAIF: Value of delinquent mortgages (% of total)	n.a.	n.a.	1.12	3.98
SAIF: Value of foreclosed mortgages (% of total)	n.a.	.68	.29	1.94
AOUSC: Personal bankruptcies per 10,000 people 20 and over	4.7	13.1	13.5	25.8

Notes: D&B is Dun and Bradstreet; FDIC, Federal Deposit Insurance Corporation; MBA, Mortgage Bankers of America; SAIF, Savings Association Insurance Fund; AOUSC, Administrative Office of the United States Court. The business failure data exclude farms.
The time periods are selected to include only "normal" years, that is, to omit those years in which special exchange rate or interest rate policies were being pursued by the Federal Reserve. Thus, they are comparable with the data in Table 5.3.
Sources and further explanation of some of the data are presented in Appendix Note 5.3.

families has declined. Part of this increase in consumer financial distress may be due to the rising proportion of household wealth held in risky assets, particularly since 1980. This gives consumers greater exposure to market swings and the possibility of bankruptcy. Indeed, some observers such as Henry Kaufman (known on Wall Street as Dr. Doom) argue that these small investors also act in ways to make the market more volatile because they do not understand the nature of risk and frantically tend to dump stocks onto the market when prices are falling, or headlessly buy when prices are rising.[16] Although this proposition may not always hold, it is nevertheless worrisome.

16. *Economist,* October 9, 1993, p. 90.

In short, in both the household and the nonfinancial corporate sector, a rising potential financial fragility (see Table 5.1) is associated with a rising incidence of financial distress (see Table 5.2). Although other explanations for the rising financial distress can be offered, the positive association of fragility and distress in all three sectors is too strong to be ignored.

Martin Wolfson has carried out a thorough statistical analysis of the relationship between potential financial fragility and financial distress (which he calls *instability*) for the period 1946 through 1987.[17] His indicator of financial distress is a composite variable (the principal component of several different series) of four variables: financial crises, commercial bank failures, failures of savings and loan banks, and insolvent savings and loan banks. He tries to explain this annual series with four causal variables:

1. A composite variable reflecting potential financial fragility (composed of two series: for nonfinancial corporations, the relation of interest payments to cash flow; and for commercial banks, the ratio of loan losses to total loans). This is positively related to financial distress.
2. A composite variable representing the availability of funds for borrowing outside regular borrowing channels. These include Eurobank loans, commercial paper, and the like. Such a variable is negatively related to financial distress.
3. A composite variable representing the adverse impact of various regulations on savings and loan banks. In situations when market interest rates rose, these regulations placed these banks in a competitive disadvantage and led to withdrawals by their depositors.
4. A dummy variable indicating the few years after the founding of the money market mutual funds when a large volume of funds flowed into these new institutions.

The four explanatory variables account for almost twice the variance of a composite variable representing financial distress and crises than a simple time trend. All are statistically significant and have the right sign. This statistical demonstration is impressive. It is gratifying to see that despite various types of financial innovations, the a priori expectation about a positive relation between potential financial fragility and financial distress and crises receives empirical support.

Nevertheless, this kind of statistical exercise is hardly the final word and it is also possible to think of other causes at work. For instance, laws on personal bankruptcy were loosened in 1978 to make such actions easier. Moreover, the higher interest rates in the 1980s undoubtedly led to more delinquent mortgages. Such a statistical demonstration also cannot tell us the degree to

17. Wolfson (1990).

which the system of bank regulation itself was responsible for the increased distress of the banking system. The increasingly lax regulation, combined with a highly generous system of deposit guarantees, certainly encouraged banks to take loan risks to achieve a higher profit.

An even more difficult question is the relation between these bank crises and episodes of financial distress with changes in production. Although financial crises preceded four of the six most important major economic downturns in American economic history, it is generally agreed that the Federal Reserve possesses sufficient policy tools to prevent such a cascading catastrophe.[18] For instance, the major stock market downturn in October 1987 had no major effect on production. The relationship of volatility in the productive sector to volatility in the financial sector is a much more delicate and interesting matter to investigate, as I illustrate later.

Implications: Volatility of production and financial variables

Some well-known and respected American central bankers such as Paul A. Volcker or E. Gerald Corrigan have expressed concern that short-run volatility of financial variables has increased over time.[19] Allegedly, such greater volatility has created more financial crises and has increased problems facing monetary authorities in managing the financial system. Unfortunately, these public officials do not specify the exact nature of their concerns nor do they offer any empirical evidence to support such a dramatic contention, other than the belief that their work as central bankers to stabilize the economy has become more difficult over the years. Sean Becketti and Gordon H. Sellon, Jr. also note a "widespread perception" that financial market volatility increased during the 1980s, although these concerns are generally not clearly specified either.

Such a belief about increasing financial volatility among central bankers or the general public is not confined to this side of the Atlantic. In an apparent reference to monetary and financial variables, Charles Goodhart notes that "...it was a regular occurrence for senior officials at the Bank of England (and for pundits elsewhere) to complain that ... volatility was higher at the present time (as each year went by) than in previous periods."

Volatility in the productive sphere is also an important worry for policy makers. Stability or low volatility is a useful property for markets because short- and long-run price signals are more congruent, price spreads are generally smaller, and the operation of the market requires fewer resources since information costs are lower. Volatility of economic variables also increases

18. Two discussions along these lines are by Friedman (1991) and Summers (1991).
19. Volker (1991) and Corrigan (1991). The citation comes from Becketti and Sellon (1989). In the next paragraph the citation is from Goodhart (1988).

risk and adversely affects domestic investment and consumption, as well as foreign trade. Moreover, the setting and administration of both monetary and fiscal policymaking by various levels of government and the Federal Reserve become more difficult if volatility increases.

The economic literature contains a number of studies of financial volatility. Some of these focus on the stock market and investigate whether this market is efficient; others focus on foreign exchange markets and investigate other phenomena.[20] But these questions about the secular trends of volatility have received relatively little attention. Moreover, the few relevant studies that I could locate deal with only a few series. By focusing on the economy as a whole and selecting a broad range of series, we can gain the perspective necessary to provide some answers to these questions.

In the following discussion I obtain several important results.[21] On the financial side, the various monetary and financial variables show a very mixed long-term pattern of volatility from month to month, contrary to the claims of some central bankers. On the production side volatility is generally decreasing over time. Further, no evidence is found of feedback from the financial to the production variables.

Trends in volatility: Possible causes

In this empirical analysis volatility refers to month-to-month or quarter-to-quarter variations. Although daily, weekly, and annual volatility are also of interest, they receive no attention in the following discussion, in major part because the causal forces appear much less interesting. Daily and weekly volatility are much more strongly influenced by highly short-term influences, which often have more speculative than economic causes.[22] Economic factors appear to play a sufficiently important role in determining monthly or

20. I refer to studies by Shiller (1992) and Frenkel and Mussa (1980). Garner (1990b) presents evidence that stock market volatility adversely affects consumption and Maskus (1990) provides evidence that exchange rate volatility reduces foreign trade. Garner (1990a) has also argued that volatility of prices of financial instruments has an impact on the demand for money, but the empirical evidence is much weaker.

21. This empirical analysis was carried out jointly with Elliott Sulcove and is presented in Pryor and Sulcove (1995). The Becketti and Sellon study (1990) is close in spirit and method to ours, although we had not read it until our manuscript was submitted for publication. Both their study and ours measure volatility in the same manner. Their results and ours differ, however, for several reasons. Most importantly, we have omitted two periods over the post–World War II period where volatility occurred because of policy shocks that we consider nonrepeatable and exogenous to the system. Our series also extend somewhat later in time than theirs and this, in turns, modifies the impact of the 1987 stock market crash on the statistical results.

22. Peters (1991), pp. 173–4 explores stock market returns over different time periods using the tools of chaos theory. He finds that the estimated Hurst exponents stabilize when periods of thirty days or longer are examined. He attributes the instability of this structural statistic for shorter periods to random fluctuations due to such phenomena as short-term speculative movements.

quarterly volatility to deserve investigation. Annual volatility is strongly influenced by macroeconomic factors that have received discussion elsewhere. For instance, considerable attention has been given to the macroeconomic policies of the Reagan administration that led to an increase in annual volatility in the 1980s, that is, to the rise and fall of the dollar in foreign exchange markets. But the monthly or quarterly volatility presents some quite different problems of analysis.

Secular trends in volatility, about which the central bankers have expressed anxiety, are rather mysterious. It is useful to list briefly some common explanations of the phenomenon:

External shocks: If trends in volatility were related solely to external shocks, then we would have to explain why these shocks are increasing in severity. A story could be told about the increasing openness of the U.S. economy and the greater impact on the domestic economy of shocks in foreign nations that influence our exports and imports. But since it is generally argued that the increasing scale of markets for goods reduces volatility, the mechanism underlying these shocks would have to be specified in an imaginative fashion. Furthermore, such a mechanism would have to explain why the shocks in the real sphere do not cause echo shocks in the monetary sphere. A more likely source of shocks comes from the international financial sector. I refer particularly to the massive increase in foreign exchange transactions that occurred after the loosening of capital flow restrictions in the late 1970s and the completion of the process in the late 1980s in a number of West European nations.[23] As a result, foreign exchange transactions soared: in March 1986 the daily net foreign exchange market turnover in the United States was $59 billion; by April 1989, such daily turnover rose to $128 billion dollars; and by April 1992, it was $192 billion. These amounts were much higher than total foreign reserves of the Federal Reserve Bank and, indeed, by 1992 this daily turnover in the foreign exchange market amounted to 58 percent of total assets of the Federal Reserve Bank. This is part of the internationalization of the economy that I describe in the final chapter as one of the four major social-economic forces acting upon the economic system.

Policy shocks: Certain types of policy measures have an immediate effect on volatility of particular variables and it is worthwhile to consider three different and important policy shocks over the period:

1. The introduction of floating exchange rates in the 1970s has increased volatility in other spheres, a phenomenon receiving attention from several economists. Rudiger Dornbusch, for instance, presents a sim-

23. Goldstein and Mussa (1993). The data come from Goldstein et al. (1993).

ple model showing that fluctuations of exchange rates induce fluctuation in prices of homogeneous commodities. The hypothesized increase in annual volatility of raw material prices is confirmed in Chapter 7.[24] Ronald I. McKinnon also argues that floating exchange rates led to a secular increase in the volatility of interest rates, a result that does not receive confirmation in our empirical analysis.

2. A different type of policy shock occurred in the late 1970s when the Federal Reserve Bank experimented with policies to stabilize the growth of the money supply, rather than interest rates.

3. And a final policy shock has been the gradual loosening of controls over capital movements in various countries and the dramatic rise in the volume of activity in foreign exchange markets. Under certain conditions, funds moving rapidly from country to country can introduce volatility both in financial and real variables.

Falling information costs: The costs of obtaining and processing information have exhibited a long-term decline. This means that both supply and demand curves shift faster in response to any shock that is particularly relevant and, moreover, that a greater range of shocks will be taken into account. The resulting increased volatility is, of course, reinforced by any greater flow of financial resources or any greater flexibility of factors of production. And, it should be added, computerization and the fall of information costs have served as a powerful stimulus for the development of these new financial instruments.[25] The ever greater flow of investment funds into some of these instruments, such as exotic derivatives, may lead to increasing financial volatility and distress, although the exact relationships have not yet been rigorously clarified.

Potential financial fragility: The increasing potential financial fragility might directly lead to greater volatility or indirectly through increasing financial distress. For instance, an increase in financial distress in the form of bank failures or bankruptcies would provide a series of shocks to other parts of the economy. Further more, reciprocal relationships might exist between financial fragility, financial distress, and volatility of financial series as well. Certainly it is possible that increased volatility in both the production and financial sectors could lead to financial distress as enterprises find themselves hit with a sudden drop in sales or a sudden increase in interest payments.

I have sketched four possible reasons why volatility might have increased over the post–World War II period. Separating out their individual impacts

24. The references in this paragraph are to Dornbusch (1985) and McKinnon (1990).
25. This relationship and the future of banking are analyzed by Sanford (1994).

raises some difficult econometric problems and, instead, I have set a more modest goal, namely determining empirically whether volatility in either the financial and the real sphere has actually increased.

The empirical analysis

I have been unable to locate in the relatively small literature investigating trends in volatility over long time periods any convincing study showing an increase in volatility. The most sophisticated study is by Rodney Dickens who uses an ARCH model and finds evidence of cyclical behavior of monthly volatility, but not long-term changes of volatility, of several bond yield, stock yield, and exchange rate series.[26] Unfortunately, this study and others analyzing volatility coefficients have focused on only a few indicators. It could be argued, however, that the most important patterns of volatility have appeared in other indicators.

Rather than an intensive analysis of a few series for a short period, I investigate many monthly and quarterly series for a forty-year period, but use relatively simple statistical techniques.[27] Selecting the proper descriptive statistic requires dealing with such problems as the occurrence of sudden spikes that often dominate the results for decades and the occurrence of long-run increases in the underlying variable that increase the apparent variation. To meet these difficulties, the following three-step process is employed to estimate the key descriptive statistic:

1. I first calculated the monthly (or quarterly) percentage changes in each series.
2. Then I determined the squared deviation of such percentage changes from the average monthly change for the year centering on the month under investigation.[28] Such a procedure is an attempt to hold constant annual swings in the variable under examination that do not relate to monthly volatility per se. For instance, if exchange rates are trending

---

26. Dickens (1987). The other studies to which I refer include Wilson et al. (1990), Frenkel and Mussa (1980), and Becketti and Sellon (1990). I discuss the latter in note 21.
27. By examining variations in month-to-month volatility, rather than average volatility per se, I minimize the problems arising because some series represent averages of the data for days within the month, while others represent end-of-month data, while still others represent some composite such as the average of the end-of-week data.
28. The measured variance (V_t) at each point is:

$$V_t = \sum_{j=-6}^{j=+6} (\overline{X}_{t+j} - X_t)^2/12$$

where

$$X_t = \sum_{j=-6}^{j=+6} X_{t+j}/13$$

and X_t is the percentage difference of X at times t and $t-1$.

upward, a simple measure of month-to-month changes would catch such an upward trend, which does not represent any type of increased monthly volatility around the trend.

3. Finally, I calculated the mean of these sample variances for the period under review and tested whether this measure of dispersion of percentage changes was significantly different from another period, using a simple test of differences between two means.[29]

One last adjustment turned out to be necessary. To avoid confounding the transition stages of two important policy changes in policy regimes (that most likely will not be repeated) with secular changes in the empirical analysis below, I omit two periods. These are the months from the beginning of 1970 to the end of 1973 when the fixed exchange rate system was collapsing and the flexible exchange rate system was being introduced, and the months from the beginning of 1979 to the end of 1982 when the Federal Reserve was following a policy of stabilizing the money supply, rather than interest rates. The division between the 1950s and the 1960s is arbitrary.

The results

Summary results of the investigation for sixty-four quarterly and monthly series are presented in Table 5.3. In the table I only compare the 1983–90 to the 1950–9 period to determine if volatility increased. More detailed comparisons by decades are presented in Appendix Note 5.2. For each set of comparisons, the percentage of series showing a statistically significant increase (at a .95 level of confidence) is designated in the column labeled with a plus; no statistically significant change, in the column labeled with a zero; and a statistically significant decrease, in the column labeled with a minus sign. If volatility is increasing steadily over time, the results should show that in all cases, the 1983–90 series reveal more volatility than the earlier series, so that the plus column has 100 percent of the cases. For instance, for the 17 stock and bond

---

29. Such a test appeals to the Central Limit Theorem by assuming that the sample mean variances are distributed normally. For this theorem to be valid, I assume that the monthly calculated variances are independent and distributed identically. Clearly this is not the case since one month's calculated variance shares eleven out of twelve observations with the previous month's. However, this should not be a problem for two reasons: The Central Limit Theorem is fairly robust with respect to violations of the conditions. Moreover, there is complete independence between the variance calculations of more than a year apart.

    This kind of simple procedure appears suited for the descriptive task at hand. It also sidesteps statistical nightmares arising from nonstationarity or nonconverging variances as the time period increases. More specifically, it is possible that some of these series have no variance in the sense that calculations of the variance would not converge as the series used in the calculations became longer. But I use the variance, not as a measure of some intrinsic property of the system, but merely as a description of what happened to the system in a particular time interval. Becketti and Sellon (1990) adopt a similar procedure.

Table 5.3. *Changes in volatility over time*

Monetary and Financial Indicators

	Number of series	Significance tests: 1983–90 to 1950–9		
		+	0	−
Stock and bond yields: total[a]	M 17+	50%	12%	38%
Bonds, 3 years and over	M 8	62	25	12
Bills, commercial paper, prime rate, federal funds rate, discount rate	M 6*	0	0	100
Stock indexes[b]	M 3	100	0	0
Money and credit: total	M 7*	20	20	60
Money[c]	M 5*	33	0	67
Credit[d]	M 2	0	50	50
Exchange rate index[e]	M 1	100	0	0
Exchange rates	M 10	90	10	0

[a]The bond yields include: Aaa corporate bonds, Aa corporate bonds, A corporate bonds, Baa corporate bonds, Aaa state/local bonds, Baa state/local bonds, long term government bonds, 5 year government bonds, 3 year government bonds, 1 year T bills, 6 month commercial paper, the discount rate, the prime rate, the effective rate on federal funds.
[b]The stock indices include: Standard and Poor 500, Dow Jones industrial average, NYSE common stock price index.
[c]The money series include: M1, M2, M3, liquidity, monetary base.
[d]The credit series include: commercial and industrial loans outstanding, consumer installment credit.
[e]The exchange rate series include: Belgium, Canada, France, Germany, Japan, Italy, Netherlands, Sweden, Switzerland, United Kingdom. The Federal Reserve Bank exchange rate index, which started in 1967, was extended back to the late 1940s using the same weights.
[f]The GDP components include: consumption, investment, government expenditures, exports, and imports.   *(Notes continued on next page.)*

yield series, half of them show significantly more volatility in the later period, but 38 percent show less volatility, and 12 percent show no significant difference. Taking the results of Table 5.3 and the more detailed results in Appendix Note 5.2 into account, we can draw the following conclusions:[30]

30. Purists might argue that these exercises with descriptive statistics are inadequate and that the only real way of proving an increase in volatility is to look at prediction errors in macroeconomic models. Such an approach would allow us to separate shocks originating from the demand and supply sides. Unfortunately, because of structural changes in the economy, the results of such an exercise using any of the many fixed coefficient models available have lit-

Table 5.3. *(cont.)*

Production, Price, and Labor Indicators

	Number of series	Significance tests: 1983–90 to 1950–9		
		+	0	–
GDP, current, NSA	Q 1	0%	0%	100%
Major components*f*	Q 5	0	0	100
GDP, constant, NSA	Q 1	0	0	100
Major components*f*	Q 5	0	0	100
Major physical production series*g*	M 5	50	25	25
Major price indices	M 3	100	0	0
GDP deflator, NSA	Q 1	0	0	100
Employment/unemployment*i*	M 3	0	0	100
Manufacturing hours, hourly wages	M 2	0	0	100
Help wanted ad index	M 1	100	0	0

*g*The major physical production series include: industrial production, housing starts, production of electrical power, new plant and equipment.
*h*The major price deflators include: consumer price index, producer price index, index of sensitive material prices.
*i*The employment and unemployment series include: nonagricultural employees, total civilian unemployed, unemployment rate.
M = monthly; Q = quarterly; NSA = not seasonally adjusted. The asterisk indicates that some series do not fully extend from 1950 through 1990. The + column indicates the percentage of cases where the volatility was significantly greater in the later period than the earlier; the column indicates the percentage of cases where the volatility was significantly smaller in the later period than the earlier; and the 0 column indicates where no significant trend could be found.
Sources, other comments, and tables showing comparisons between individual decades are presented in Statistical Note 5.2 and 5.3.

- *Stock and bond yields.* The volatility picture is quite mixed. Bonds with longer maturities, which normally show more volatile, are somewhat more likely to show an upward trend in volatility than bonds and bills of shorter maturities. Looking at the individual series,

tle meaning for a forty-year period. Although it is possible also that volatility of financial and production variables had other causes that have dampened the increase in volatility expected from greater financial fragility, I could find no plausible candidates that would have had such a strong impact. The descriptive approach used in the discussion appears as a necessary first step for any more sophisticated analysis.

bonds with different risk ratings show roughly the same volatility so that no apparent relation between risk and volatility is apparent. Stock volatility show little relation with the bond markets and also reveal an irregular increase over the period.

- *Money and credit.* Although the pattern of volatility of the money and credit series also is mixed, they show a somewhat greater tendency toward greater volatility over time. The credit series are somewhat more likely to show this upward trend in volatility than the money series.

- *Exchange rates.* The gradual collapse of the fixed exchange rate system in the 1960s and the introduction of floating exchange rates in the early 1970s should have led to a greater volatility in the latter period.

Moreover, with the gradual relaxation of capital flow restrictions in the 1980s mentioned previously, it seems likely that exchange rate volatility would be greater in the 1980s than in previous periods. Such expectations are confirmed, not just for the Federal Reserve index of ten currencies but also for most of the individual exchange rates composing this index. The results are overdetermined since the increase of volatility of these dollar exchange rates in the 1980s might also be tied to the macroeconomic policies of the Reagan administration that allowed the dollar to rise and fall out of proportion to historical changes. An important implication of the increasing volatility of exchange rates is the increasing volatility of raw material prices on the world market, a phenomenon investigated in detail in Chapter 7.

- *GDP and major aggregates.* By and large, volatility in GDP aggregates, measured either in current or constant prices, has decreased. Similar results are also obtained for the national income. Explaining this declining volatility raises some problems. The conventional wisdom tells us that the gradual shift into services would lead to a decrease, rather than an increase, in volatility. But series for the production of goods and for services reveal few important differences and both show a roughly equal and declining volatility.[31] Such results

31. These results are for seasonally adjusted constant price series, using my own seasonal adjustment estimates since an official adjustment in constant prices for this seasonality factor was not available. I believed that such an adjustment was necessary since the changes in the seasonality might lead to a measure of volatility that did not properly reflect long-run changes. As it turned out, the seasonal and nonseasonal adjusted series for components of the GDP give very similar results, this should not be a problem. Comparisons of the relative volatility of two series are made by the coefficients of variation of their running-average deviations of quarterly change. It should be noted that the volatility statistic is independent of the size of the macroeconomic indicator under investigation, so this factor does not play a role in the results.

also do not appear traceable to changes in governmental policy in dealing with short-term fluctuations.

- *Unemployment and production.* The volatility of employment and unemployment shows a general decrease over time. This is quite consistent with the results of the GDP and national income series.

- *Behavior of disaggregated series.* The four major physical production series (total industrial production, electricity production, housing starts, and new plant and equipment) show a mixed pattern so that no unambiguous trend can be discerned. In general, however, these results do not appear consistent with the results for the GDP and major aggregates. This micro–macro difference can also be seen in the differences in volatility between the GDP deflator and the three major price indices. Although no ready explanation comes to mind, this warns us that volatility patterns on the micro and macro levels can be quite different.

- *Other.* I also examined volatility for shorter series for other types of assets, but patterns were similarly difficult to discern. A dramatic case occurs in a comparison of housing prices in the 1980s to the 1970s for five cities using Case-Shiller weighted repeat sale indices. I expected to find the same general patterns of volatility in the five different markets since the asset is the same. But instead, I found some cities experienced significant changes in volatility of the index, while in other cities, no such changes occurred.[32] Local conditions are crucial determinants of volatility in this market.

In summary, no upward trend in overall volatility is apparent. Although some indicators such as the stock market and exchange rates are becoming more volatile, many of the other series are decreasing in volatility. The decline in volatility of the GDP and employment aggregates suggests that no important feedback occurs between any increased volatility in particular financial variables and the production sphere.

Conclusions and implications for the future

Looking at structural complexity in the financial sector allows us to raise a number of issues of vital concern to the evolution of the economic system. Turning first to wealth in its broadest sense, several important trends appear likely to persist in the coming decades. Intangible wealth will undoubted remain the most important type of capital and, as the level of technology rises,

---

32. I am grateful to Karl E. Case for supplying these data. The results also are highly sensitive to whether current price data or price data deflated by the GDP deflator are used. In both cases, however, no general patterns could be discerned.

may increase in importance in comparison to tangible wealth. A large share of type of wealth either arises from, or is highly influenced by, public policy. Thus, the government's role in wealth creation may increase, even while its actual share of tangible wealth decreases. Foreign ownership of wealth located in the United States will undoubtedly increase as will ownership by U.S. nationals of wealth located abroad. For a more narrow definition of wealth – private financial assets – it seems likely that the share held by financial institutions will increase, unless the govern ment takes certain policy measures discussed later.

Structural complexity of the financial system can be measured by either the ratio of total financial assets to total tangible assets (the financial interrelations ratio) or the ratio of financial assets held by the private financial sector to total financial assets. Both measures show an increase in structural complexity of the financial system in the postwar period. This change in the financial structure in turn, has, been a critical causal factor underlying the increasing financial distress, as measured by financial crises, business failures, failed banks, delinquent mortgages, and personal bankruptcies.

Increasing structural complexity of the financial system is not necessarily bad, if such changes only reflect better techniques for managing financial assets so that fewer reserves are needed. And if financial institutions learn from their mistakes in the 1980s, some of their errors associated with a rising structural complexity of the financial system that led to greater financial distress will not be repeated. But, as noted previously, since governmental policy decisions exacerbated the increase in financial distress, it is appropriate to review briefly some policy steps the government might take to reduce the potential fragility of the system.

Certainly the government can make changes in the tax system to discourage high rates of borrowing. For instance, interest on bonds to finance leveraged buy-outs does not need to be deductible on corporate taxes. Other tax changes can shift corporate incentives away from dividends and borrowing for investment and toward self-finance and equity financing. Monetary and security policies can limit the introduction of increasingly exotic derivatives and can also raise the margin requirements of those who buy such instruments. In so far as large government deficits lead to higher interest rates, at least during periods of prosperity, a more responsible fiscal policy might reduce the possibilities of financial distress in the private sector occurring from this cause. Bankruptcy laws can be tightened so that it is not used as an alternative for paying one's debts. Other policies come readily to mind. The important point is that the government can influence the structural complexity of the financial system and reduce the potential fragility of the system with a variety of policies. These are undoubtedly more effective if combined and coordinated, but this policy advice is more easily said than done. If, on the other hand, no measures are taken to reduce the potential fragility of the financial system, financial distress will probably increase in the future.

The first chapter refers to a conjecture that increased structural complexity leads to greater instability of the system. Although this speculation appears to have merit, at least with regard to financial distress, the increased structural complexity does not seem to have led to a general increase in volatility of important financial and production indicators. As shown in Chapter 2, business cycles have not changed in severity since the early 1950s, at least as measured by the deviation of GDP from the full employment production of goods and services. Combined with the results of this chapter, the empirical analysis shows that although the business cycle has not greatly changed in magnitude, its path is less bumpy, as shown by the decreased volatility from quarter to quarter. This should continue in the near future as well.

For most financial series the empirical tests reveal a mixed picture, but only for the stock indexes and the exchange rates could a definite increase in volatility be seen. Such a general result is good news in the sense that the effectiveness of instruments of public policy is much less certain in dampening volatility than in reducing potential fragility of the financial system.

Several implications of these empirical results also deserve emphasis. Of greatest importance, the feedback between the volatility of the monetary and financial variables appears negligible, since the two groups of series reveal quite different temporal patterns of volatility. Feedback between the volatility of exchange rates and production also appears low. For instance, as I note in Chapter 7, a major impact of the increased volatility of exchanges rates is in the increasing volatility of raw material prices; but this increased volatility is not paralleled by greater volatility of production of these goods. Moreover, even though the volatility of the exchange rates was reaching historic highs in the 1980s, neither exports nor imports (measured either in current or constant prices) showed an increase in validity.[33]

If the vague and ex cathedra remarks of central bankers about increasing volatility refer to month-to-month or quarter-to-quarter periods, they must be taken with a grain of salt. Indeed, some cynics might argue that we can save our salt because these pronunciamentos have such a strong element of self-interest that they deserve no attention at all. Such a testy reaction, perhaps, is too hasty. Particular asset markets such as commercial real estate, silver futures, and certain derivatives for which I could not obtain long-term series did manifest some disturbing boom-and-bust symptoms during the post–World War II period that involved volatility lasting longer than the one-month interval that I investigate. Moreover, high volatility occurred for a num-

---

33. In part, this may have been due to exporters and importers pricing according to the domestic markets in which the goods were sold. This phenomenon is discussed in greater detail in Chapter 7.

ber of financial and real variables in the two periods where major changes in policy regimes occurred. As noted, I omit these two periods from the calculations in an attempt to focus attention on volatility arising from "basic" economic factors. If, contrary to my assumption, major shifts in policy regimes are becoming more frequent because of endogenous factors, then these conclusions must be modified.

CHAPTER 6

Production institutions and management

Application of the concept of complexity to production institutions and management raises many interesting issues of which this chapter deals with three: The first is the extent to which managers are changing their organizations to deal with the structurally more complex business environment. The next focuses on the heterogeneity of the structure of enterprises and establishments, especially the changing relative importance of the largest units, that is, "big business." The final issue deals with that type of structural complexity manifested by the separation of ownership and control, and the implications of this phenomenon on enterprise profits and remuneration of managers.

If skills of the labor force and the level of technology are increasing, if the legal framework, the scope of markets, and other phenomena affecting decision making within enterprises are becoming more complicated, how does management adjust to such an evolution of the economic environment? I outline several basic strategies for dealing with this increasing structural complexity and then present the results of my own survey of Chief Financial Officers and Directors of large corporations to explore these matters. The results show that managers are deeply concerned and are pursuing three distinct strategies to face these problems.

If the sizes of establishments and enterprises are becoming more heterogeneous, government policy makers would have a greater informational burden and would face increasingly difficult problems in dealing with this more variegated universe of productive units. We can measure such heterogeneity, one of the three aspects of structural complexity defined in the first chapter, in the same manner as population heterogeneity is handled in the second chapter. I also examine a number of other aspects of the size distribution of establishments and enterprises, focusing particular on trends among the largest enterprises that dominate the economy.

As discussed in the previous chapter, the holding and managing of assets is becoming increasingly separated from their ownership, so that interactions between different groups in the economy are becoming more extensive. I explore the degree to which this aspect of increasing structural complexity is occurring in the manufacturing sector and show that the trend is difficult to discern since two offsetting causal forces are at work. Turning to the impact of managerial control, the evidence is quite mixed. The discussion suggests – but hardly proves – that the impact of "managerialism" is much less than generally feared.

Managing complexity: changes in internal corporate structures

The economic environment in which enterprises operate is becoming more structurally complex in many ways. As argued in Chapter 3, technology has required increasing skills of the labor force. As discussed in Chapters 8 and 10, internationalization of the economy has widened markets and increased competition. As analyzed in Chapter 9, the scope of governmental regulation rose during much of the period. As described in the business press, the rise in discretionary income of the population has increasingly forced producers to be more flexible and to customize their goods and services. To what extent do managers recognize these changes and how are they reorganizing their enterprises to deal with this increasing structural complexity?

To obtain quantitative evidence on these questions, I carried out a survey of American managers on the ways in which they have, and will be, reorganizing their enterprises to face these problems. I also obtained some useful qualitative evidence in the remarks about particular aspects of their problems and solutions written in the margin of the questionnaire by the respondents.

For corporate executives to meet the challenges of increasing structural complexity, three general and nonexclusive strategies can be envisioned:

- Mastering structural complexity through increased use of information and increased reliance on more powerful information-managing technologies.
- Reducing structural complexity handled by top management by decentralizing in various ways, altering and simplifying relations with suppliers, or changing the degree of vertical integration.
- Evading structural complexity by streamlining and simplifying procedures, processes, products, and the process of change.

The purpose of this survey of U.S. enterprises is to determine the extent to which each of the three strategies has been pursued in the past decade and will be followed in the coming decade. The survey shows that enterprises in the United States have been following all three of these strategies and, to a considerably lesser extent, plan to pursue such strategies in the future. The answers reported in the following section to certain questions also raise doubts about the accuracy of the conventional wisdom about changes in organizational structures.

Mechanics of the survey

The survey covers only enterprises with 500 or more employees that are outside of the agricultural and governmental sectors. Because many smaller firms deal primarily within local markets, where the problems of structural complexity may not be as severe, they are excluded. Such larger firms employed 43 percent of all workers and employees in the sectors covered.

At the beginning of September 1993 I sent questionnaires addressed by name to 750 Chief Financial Officers (CFO: if the enterprise did not have a person with such a job title, then to Treasurers or Controllers) and also to 750 outside members of the Boards of Directors of corporations. The names of the enterprises were drawn randomly from the files of a direct mailing company that had somewhat over 85 percent of the total number of corporations with over 500 workers in its data bank.[1] Since it is possible for the CFOs and outside directors to supply different answers, given their different perspectives, I first examined the samples separately. As it turned out, there were no statistically significant differences in the answers, so I could combine the two samples. To check for bias arising from a differential response rate from different industries, I calculated a weighted average of the responses, where the weights corresponded to the total labor force in enterprises with 500 and more employees in the various industrial branches. These weighted-average results were practically the same as the unweighted results and, for simplicity, the unweighted replies are used in all tables to follow.

I hoped to maximize responses by means of a questionnaire that fit onto one side of a legal size sheet of paper. This meant that I was limited to a small number of questions and could not ask about ways to meet the challenge of complexity falling outside the simple framework presented here. Because those in the sample have little time to answer such an over-the-transom letter from an unknown person, I aimed at a 10 percent response rate; the actual response rate was 14.4 percent (17.9 percent for the CFOs, 11.0 percent for the Directors). The firms responding to the questionnaire employed roughly 2.5 percent of all those working in enterprises with a labor force of 500 or more in the sampled industrial sectors.

Results and some interpretations

For the CFOs, the questions required them to make estimates of trends in their company for the last decade and to predict probable trends in their com-

1. Information on the universe of such firms comes from U.S. Department of Commerce, Bureau of the Census (1991b). In selecting the particular firms for the sample, I did not take into account whether the enterprises were domestic or foreign owned. In checking information about such ownership in those companies that responded, it turned out that the number of foreign-owned enterprises was too small to be separated for statistical purposes.

panies for the next decade. For the members of the Boards of Directors the questions required them to make similar estimates of trends in all companies in which they were a director.

The responses for the aggregated sample are presented in Table 6.1 and, in more detail, in Appendix Note 6.4. I have scored the replies so that plus scores represent the kinds of adaption to increasing complexity that follow one of the three strategies mentioned previously. Minus answers are those opposite to such a response.

Two important conclusions can be drawn quickly. First, in the late 1980s and early 1990s, U.S. enterprises adopted all three of the basic strategies for meeting the challenges of complexity. Second, a considerably smaller percentage of firms will make such changes in the future than those who made them in the past. The first conclusion receives a more extensive examination below, where attention focuses on each question. The second conclusion deserves some consideration before turning to the detailed results.

The smaller percentage of firms planning to make the organizational changes in the future suggests that the respondents believed most of the organizational changes necessary to meet foreseeable competitive challenges were already carried out. In turn, this conclusion might reflect either the massive changes that were already made in the 1980s and early 1990s or a certain short-sightedness by management. However, such results could also mean that enterprise leaders are unwilling to commit themselves to further change until they learn how the changes introduced in the past decade are working out. In either case, this difference between past and future suggests that the respondents are talking about actual changes in the past or actual plans for changes in the future, rather than answering to reflect the latest management fad or the conventionally "right" answers.

Although I have no simple way of determining whether the changes specified by the respondents actually occurred, the respondents also had no obvious motive to waste ten minutes of their busy lives by giving misleading answers and returning the questionnaire. The major problem is selection bias, that is, that the representatives of those enterprises returning the questionnaire are changing their organizations differently than most others and that they wish the world to know about it. Unfortunately, few outside indicators exist that would allow an evaluation of such a bias.

Mastering structural complexity through increased use of information

U.S. enterprises clearly have been attempting to keep up with the everincreasing amount of business information. Table 6.1 shows that both the status of information managers and the share of resources (to sales) used for information processing increased in the decade 1983–93. Further, both are expected to increase in the coming decade, albeit at a slower pace. The status of the information officers follows a similar pattern.

With the increasing computerization of American enterprises, it may seem strange that the relative costs of data processing are increasing, rather than decreasing. In Chapter 4 I examine this problem with regard to the rising number of workers in the information sector for the entire economy. From this extensive discussion, two quite different interpretations of the rising relative costs of data processing expenses are relevant: First, computers have not yet yielded their expected productivity increase, the so-called *computer productivity paradox*. Second, the amount of information to be processed has increased faster than computer technology. Without much more detailed data, it is impossible to determine the relative importance of these or other explanations of the rising expenditures on information processing.

Reducing structural complexity through increased decentralization and related steps

U.S. enterprises are battling complexity along this front as well. As shown in Table 6.1, a significant share of firms attempted to decentralize by creating more profit centers in the past decade and this trend is continuing into the future, but at a slower pace. In addition, a significant share of firms attempted to decentralize by grouping divisions and creating overall group leaders, a trend that will continue more slowly in the future. The replies to these questions, particularly about the future, might vary between the CFOs and the Directors, since the latter have more information about where the firm is going. But in reality the answers are not significantly different.

The creation of more profit centers and group executives means, other things being equal, that an extra layer is added to the bureaucratic hierarchy. Taken alone, this suggests that the hoary notion about decentralization always bringing a broader span of control and a flatter administrative pyramid might be wrong. But other things may not be equal and such an additional administrative level could be offset either by eliminating a hierarchical level somewhere else in the administrative pyramid or by thinning out higher levels of the administrative hierarchy. Whether such an offset is occurring cannot be determined with the data from this survey. Nevertheless, the conventional wisdom among futurists that firm hierarchies are becoming flatter and broader may be too simplistic.

Another facet of this trend toward pushing operational responsibilities lower in the hierarchy is the tying of compensation more closely to indicators related to the enterprise's success. Such use of an incentive system is supposed to encourage the worker or employee to take more responsibility to improve the performance of the entire enterprise. Contrary to myth, U.S. firms – at least in manufacturing – do not have a close tie between compensation and results

Table 6.1. *Overall results of the enterprise survey*

	Average scores		
Questions	Past decade	Future decade	Difference
Mastering structural complexity through increased use of information:			
1. How has (will) the ratio of expenditures for data processing as a percent of sales change(d)?			
Scale: decreased = –1; same = 0; increased = +1.	+.44*	+.18*	–.25*
2. How has (will) the status of information officers change(d)? Same scale as above.	+.46*	+.29*	–.17*
3. How has (will) the budget of the controller's office as a percent of sales change(d)?			
Same scale as above.	–.28*	–.45*	–.17*
4. How have expenditures for legal matters as a percent of sales change(d)?			
Same scale as above	+.77*	+.41*	–.35*
Reducing structural complexity at the top by decentralization:			
5. Has (will) responsibility for operations been (be) decentralized by creating more profit centers? Scale: fewer profit centers = –1; same = 0; more profit centers = +1.	+.50*	+.18*	–.32*
6. Has (will) responsibility for operations been (be) decentralized by grouping operating divisions and creating overall group leaders?			
Scale: fewer groupings = –1; same = 0; more groupings = +1.	+.41*	+.22*	–.19*
7. Has (will) the relation between compensation of workers and employees in different operations and the results of their work been changed?			
Scale: less closely tied = –1; same = 0; more closely tied = +1.	+.61*	+.61*	.00

8. Have (will) relations between suppliers change(d) so that there are more competitive relations with more suppliers or closer relations with fewer?

    Scale: More competitive with more = −1; same = 0; closer relations with fewer = +1.

+.46*	+.26*	−.20*

9. How has (will) vertical integration change(d)? Scale: more vertical integration = −1; same = 0; less vertical integration = +1.

+.07	+.05	−.02

Evading structural complexity by simplification:

10. Has (will) attention to the core or closely related businesses change(d)?

    Scale: less focus on core = −1; same = 0; more attention on core= +1.

+.60*	+.46*	−.14*

11. How has (will) product standardization change(d)? Scale: less standardization = −1; same = 0; more standardization = +1.

+.48*	+.43*	−.05

12. How has (will) process standardization change(d)? Same scale as above.

+.66*	+.65*	−.01

13. How has (will) standardization of procedures change(d)? Same scale as above.

+.58*	+.54*	−.04

14. How has (will) the process of change change(d)? Scale: more large changes = −1; same = 0; more incremental changes = +1.

−.08	+.54*	+.63*

Note: In the first two columns an * means that the average scores are significantly different from zero (.05 level of confidence); in the third column, it means that the scores of the first two columns are significantly different. Sample size = 206 enterprises outside of agriculture and government with 500 or more workers and employees. Other details are supplied in the text. Totals may not add because of rounding. See also Appendix Note 6.4.

(measured by any indicator) at low levels of the hierarchy and, as indicated later, at high levels of the hierarchy the linkage is becoming increasingly weaker.[2] The attempted changes, appearing in a significant share of the sampled enterprises, may be a belated attempt to rectify their compensation situation and the survey respondents expect such efforts to continue apace in the future. Unfortunately, such a step is difficult to carry out, especially since more complex technologies often raise the costs of measuring and monitoring individual performance. Given the similarity of the answers for both the past and the future decade, the responses might also signify that the respondents believe that such incentive pay is the "right" policy to follow, even though they are not doing so at present. I did not ask about whether enterprises are decentralizing by increasing employee involvement; but evidence from a study by Edward E. Lawler and his colleagues suggests no discernible trend, at least in the latter part of the 1980s.

Two other aspects of the organization structure deserve brief attention. A significant number of enterprises reported that during the past decade, they began to have fewer suppliers and they dealt with them at less of an arms-length distance. Although it may be desirable to deal with fewer suppliers on a more competitive basis, the question to the respondents was phrased as if this were a dichotomy; and only one respondent explicitly objected. Such a move toward closer relations with fewer supplies does not necessarily indicate that American enterprises are moving toward a keiretsu model, as found in Japan. Rather, it appears consistent with the drive in many firms to adopt just-in-time inventory systems. When done carefully, such a change in supply relations could lead to a reduction in structural complexity, but this is by no means assured.

At the same time as enterprises were dealing with fewer suppliers, they claim not to have changed significantly their degree of vertical integration. That is, they are producing roughly the same share of their needed raw materials and intermediate inputs as they did in the past, rather than contracting out this function. This reply is consistent with more macroeconomic evidence on the question discussed in Appendix Note 6.2. Moreover, companies do not plan to change the degree of vertical integration in the future.

Evading structural complexity through simplification and related measures

Evading structural complexity through simplification also seems important to U.S. enterprises. As shown in Table 6.1, most enterprises claim that they have begun to pay greater attention to the core and related businesses and that this trend will continue in the future. This appears to accord with information

---

2. For workers at lower levels, data are presented in Pryor (1984a). The next reference is to Lawler et al. (1992).

discussed later in the chapter about the declining relative importance of the largest enterprises, because they have divested themselves of parts of their companies unrelated to their major mission.

The degree to which U.S. enterprises have diversified or consolidated their production lines has shifted dramatically over time. David J. Ravenscraft and Frederic M. Scherer find that the average number of lines of business for the top 200 manufacturing enterprises (ranked by sales) rose from 4.76 in 1950 to 10.89 in 1975.[3] But Frank R. Lichtenberg presents evidence that the peak of industrial diversification was probably in the early 1970s and that since then, the degree of enterprise diversification has significantly decreased. A considerable fraction of this change came through divestitures of units previously acquired in mergers. His own calculations also show that productivity within a given branch of industry was inversely related to the number of industries in which the firm was engaged, other variables held constant. This is a telling instance of diseconomies of scope.

Although my survey results parallel recent national trends in reduction of diversification, the replies are stated in terms of "core business" and this raises the linguistic problem that the definition of core business by these top executives may have changed and become broader. This could occur either because economies of scope are becoming more important or because the necessity of entering new lines of business are critical when existing lines reach maturity. One respondent to the survey noted, for instance, that his "core business" is expanding into allied areas, so that for him the "core business" might include those lines with the same critical inputs. Another problem of interpretation is that this allegedly greater focus on the core business also suggests a reduction in the degree of vertical integration since supply of an input to the main production does not constitute part of the "core." As noted previously, a reduction of vertical integration has not occurred.

According to the survey replies, a significant share of firms tried to reduce structural complexity by simplifying products, processes, and procedures. The simplification of product lines appears curious in light of the alleged necessity to customize products because of the splintering of taste, the transformation of the mass market into micro markets, and the introduction of new methods of flexible production. To a certain extent the question about product simplification is ambiguous since it is possible for firms to simplify design and functionality of their products, while increasing the number of their features to appeal to niche markets. To some, simplification might mean focusing most production on a few products, even though a great many variants for niche markets are produced.

Finally, although the respondents claimed that the process of change in their enterprises remained roughly the same in the past decade, a significant share of them intended to focus on incremental, rather than large-scale change. Such

---

3. Ravenscraft and Scherer (1987), p. 30. The further reference is to Lichtenberg (1990).

a borrowing of Japanese techniques (which originated in the United States), under the proper circumstances, will lead to a reduction of complexity of the process of change. This reply reflects the most dramatic increase of any activity attempting to reduce structural complexity. It also suggests, by the way, that the respondents are not impressed with the recent management fad of "reengineering the firm," which implies a total reorganization of the firm's activities from top to bottom.

Concluding comments

The survey results suggest two general conclusions. First, the respondents certainly claim their companies are acting as if executives were responding to increasing complexity of the business environment. The results of the survey that these enterprises are simultaneously following the three basic strategies reinforces this conclusion: mastering structural complexity through increased expenditures on information; reducing structural complexity by cutting down on information handled by top management by decentralization; and evading structural complexity by simplifying procedures, processes, products, and the process of change to reduce information requirements. Second, most respondents saw more change occurring in the past decade than in the next decade and this either implies a certain unwarranted complacency or indicates a caution in continuing the process of change until the results of past organizational changes become clearer.

The process of organizational change to meet the increasing structural complexity of the business environment is not easy. It also cannot be implemented by following recipes from traditional management textbooks since the necessary concrete steps differ considerably by industry.

The size distribution of productive units

Two aspects of the size distribution of productive units deserve attention: the relative importance of the largest firms and the heterogeneity of the mix of large and small enterprises and establishments. As noted in Chapter 1, heterogeneity is one of three indicators of structural complexity and any increased structural complexity, in turn, places a greater information burden on any governmental agency attempting to regulate such units.

Aggregate concentration

I discuss the relative importance of enterprises and establishments in terms of the share of production or of inputs of the largest units, a phenomenon often called "aggregate concentration." Such an approach, while useful in examining certain phenomena such as the concentration of power or the alienation of workers, is incomplete since it does not take the entire distribution into account. Nevertheless, it is useful first place to start the analysis.

As a result of the merger boom in the 1960s and also in the late 1970s and 1980s, the usefulness of studying aggregate concentration should be apparent.[4] Many worry about the impact of enterprise size per se on the behavior the rate of innovation, work satisfaction, and similar performance factors. They also raise concerns about the political implications of such a concentration of economic power.

It is important to note that the impact of aggregate concentration has received considerably less attention by economists than its measurement. Unfortunately, the attempt to isolate the impact of bigness per se gives rise to sufficient statistical difficulties that the conclusions from empirical studies are often relatively obvious and are seldom earthshaking or dramatic.[5] The daily press, of course, gives more spicy treatment to the problem of aggregate concentration. For instance, we often find the assertion that because such concentration is rising, industrial competition on a microlevel must be decreasing. Such a claim is wrong for three main reasons. As I show later, aggregate concentration is not increasing; as I demonstrate in the next chapter, competition is increasing, not decreasing; and as I have shown elsewhere, no logical connection exists between concentration on the level of individual markets and on the level of the industrial sector as a whole.[6]

Marxist economists label the increase in the absolute size of establishments and enterprises as the concentration of capital and the relative importance of the largest enterprises as the centralization of capital. According to Marx, both the concentration and centralization of capital increase over time in capitalist economies because of the consequences of long-run competitive forces operating in an environment with limitless economies of scale. This theory, in turn, plays an important role in his prediction about the downfall of capitalism. In recent years this theory about the concentration and centralization of capital has been supplemented by the notion that the information revolution allows firms to become even larger than before. As I show in a following discussion, both hypotheses of revolution – Marxian and informational – prove to be poor descriptions of events in the United States, at least for the post–World War II

---

4. Some useful data are presented in Blair and Uppal (1993), p. 43.
5. Weiss (1983) has a useful summary of the literature. Although the writings on the impact of aggregate concentration by John Kenneth Galbraith (1967) have probably enjoyed the most public attention, Weiss shows that few of Galbraith's novel claims have received empirical verification. Frederic M. Scherer (1977) advances an interesting proposition that although compensation in large firms is more than in small firms, worker satisfaction (as indicated by job turnover, absenteeism, and strikes) is lower. Thus, workers face a tradeoff between monetary and nonmonetary income.
6. Pryor (1973b).

period. Given its frequent misuse, the word "revolution" should be retired from the social science vocabulary.

Before turning to the data, I must raise one caveat. With the increasing number of corporate alliances, cooperative arrangements, joint investment projects and joint ventures, the boundaries of a single enterprise have become fuzzier in recent years.[7] For the following discussion, however, I still use the traditional definition.

Aggregate concentration for the universe of U.S. firms excluding those in the agricultural and governmental sectors reached a peak in the late 1970s and then declined dramatically in the next decade (the data are presented in Appendix Note 6.2). It is useful, however, to focus attention on the manufacturing sector alone since comparisons with the rest of the world can also be made. For this sector aggregate concentration can be most easily measured in terms of value added or employment of the top 100 or 200 enterprises. I avoid measuring aggregate concentration with production statistics because of problems arising from the double accounting of production at different stages of the production process.[8] And for other reasons, using asset data also seems inappropriate.[9]

---

7. Badaracco (1988).
8. The production approach leads to some bizarre statistics. For instance, According to Piel (1992, p. 246) the combined sales of 3,560 largest transnational corporations in 1985 amounted to almost one-third of the combined GNP of all the industrial countries and exceeded the aggregate GNPs of all developing countries including China. The use of value-added or labor-force statistics yield much lower relative shares of the large corporations because of the double-accounting problem. Piel also estimates of the GDP the developing nations based on exchange rate conver sions, which considerably understate the purchasing power equivalent in dollars of these GNPs.
9. The asset data include not just domestic manufacturing activities, but domestic nonmanufacturing as well as foreign production activities. If these large firms exported all goods produced by their foreign subsidiaries back into the United States, then the asset statistic might be an appropriate measure of aggregate concentration. But this is not the case, although it must be added that the exports of U.S. owned factories abroad back to the United States are considerable in some industries. The asset approach has other problems as well: for instance, it is difficult to evaluate foreign assets in a meaningful sense when exchange rates are fluctuating. Moreover, a significant change in the basis of calculating the share of assets of the largest manufacturing corporations occurred in the middle 1970s. Although the trend in asset concentration still seemed upward (Scherer and Ross, 1990, p.62), my labor force measure avoids these problems. Another source of confusion about trends in aggregate concentration arises from the common use of the assets of the top 100 manufacturing firms as a ratio of total manufacturing assets. The numerator is overstated in comparison to the denominator because it embraces nonmanufacturing activities to a greater extent.

  A number of economists present data on aggregate concentration extending back before the period in my table, e.g., Collins and Preston (1961); Herman (1981), p. 191; and Weiss (1983). For assets of nonfinancial corporations, aggregate concentration of the largest 100 or 200 corporations rose from 1909 to 1933, but declined since then so that there is little difference between 1909 and 1975. For industrial (manufacturing plus trade, construction, and some services) corporations or for manufacturing corporations alone, the share of assets of the largest 100 or 200 corporations rose from 1909 to 1958 and has remained roughly constant ever since.

Table 6.2. *Trends in aggregate concentration*

	1947	1958	1963	1972	1982
Data for the U.S. manufacturing sector alone					
Shares of value added:					
Largest 100 firms	23%	30%	33%	33.1%	32.8%
Largest 200 firms	30	38	41	43.1	43.2
Share of employees:					
Largest 100 firms	—	—	—	25.8	23.8
Largest 200 firms	—	—	—	34.6	32.7
Data for employees in all activities of the largest 100 manufacturing and mining firms					
As share of economically active in manufacturing and mining:					
United States	—	33.0	36.2	44.8	44.1
22 industrial nations	—	11.3	13.3	16.7	18.5
World capitalist system	—	7.2	8.2	9.6	8.5

Notes on sources and methods of calculations are found in Appendix Note 6.5.

The data in the top part of Table 6.2 show that the relative importance in the largest firms in the manufactur ing sector of domestic economy has not changed much since the mid-1950s; the largest change was between 1947 and 1954 (not shown in the table), rather than during the various merger boom in post–World War II era. In recent years a wave of divestiture accompanied the merger boom.[10] Among large firms included in Table 6.1, such divestitures appear roughly equal in value to the mergers. In other words, the share of value added and the labor force of the largest manufacturing enterprises to the total universe of manufacturing firms remained roughly the same between 1963 and 1982.

Because of the offsetting impact of mergers and diversitures, certainty about trends in aggregate contration in the the next few decades is unwarranted. Some empirical evidence is available that heavy investment in information processing is often followed by enterprise downsizing since the firm is able to contract out many functions previously carried out inhouse because of high transaction costs.[11] But this may be offset by public policy measures encouraging mergers, for instance, favorable tax treatment toward junk bonds used by one firm to acquire another.

Another determinant of the merger wave is the profitability of such actions, and in this regard the available evidence presents a complicated picture.[12]

For sales or net income, a slight decline in aggregate concentration of nonfinancial corporations occurred between the late 1920s or early 1930s and 1975.

10. Lichtenberg (1990) presents some useful data on the matter. Blair and Uppal (1993), pp. 43, 52 have data on the total value of mergers.
11. A pioneering empirical study on this problem is by Brynjolfsson et al. (1993).
12. The references in this paragraph are: Lichtenberg (1992), Ravenscraft and Scherer (1987), Long and Ravenscraft (1993), and Blair (1993b).

From comparisons of productive establishments before and after a change in ownership (merger, acquisition, or leveraged buy-out) with plants experiencing no change in ownership, Frank Lichtenberg argues that the former show a statistically significant gain in relative productivity. But from merger data from 1950 through 1975, Ravenscraft and Scherer present evidence that profitability of the acquiring firm has usually suffered following the merger. William F. Long and David J. Ravenscraft, who focus just on leveraged buyouts (LBOs), present evidence that for the early 1980s, various financial indicators improved after the change in ownership, Nevertheless, they also find that by the late 1980s, this was no longer the case. Moreover, some improvement in the behavior of the financial indicators occurred as a result of a decline in research and development expenditures, which would probably have a long-term negative impact on financial performance. From this and other empirical evidence of the profitability of mergers, Margaret M. Blair concludes, "What started as a rational exercise in restructuring firms ... seems to have become a fad driven by the machinery invented to facilitate the deals and possibly encouraged by tax changes."

The statistics in the bottom part of Table 6.2 look at the situation from a more global perspective. They compare total labor force of large firms classified as manufacturing and mining, regardless of the sector or the country in which they are employed, to total sectoral employment in domestic manufacturing and mining. It is noteworthy that the trends of aggregate concentration for the United States alone using the different approaches in the two parts of the table are different. More specifically, the aggregate concentration for all activities (manufacturing and nonmanufacturing, domestic and foreign) of the 100 largest firms appeared to be increasing in the United States, at least until 1972, because their nonmanufacturing and foreign operations increased faster than their domestic manufacturing activities.

Table 6.2 also shows that for the industrialized capitalist world as a whole, aggregate concentration increased for the entire period. But when the developing nations are included so the data embrace the entire capitalist world, aggregate concentration increased only until 1972. At this point, manufacturing in certain developing nations began to increase dramatically, thereby reducing the market share of the large firms in the industrialized nations.[13]

13. More specifically, in the 1972–82 decade, employment of the 100 largest firms in the capitalist world increased about .6 percent per year, while the total economically active in mining and manufacturing increased at an average rate of 1.9 percent.

One caveat must be added. These international data refer to specific companies only. In some countries, however, a number of companies have sufficiently strong links with each other to form a "group" that exercises considerable power. For instance, according to Kearns (1992), the six major keiretsu in Japan (Sumitomo, Mitsui, Sanwar, Mitsubishi, Dai-Ichi Kangyo, and Fuyo) directly account for about 27 percent of industrial assets.

Size distribution of productive units

In Appendix Note 6.2 I analyze in detail the size distribution of productive units throughout the economy, not just manufacturing. In this discussion, I briefly summarize the results.

Average size: Although the average size of productive units increased from the early part of the century up to the 1960s in some sectors such as manufacturing, the average employment size of both enterprises (firms) and establishments (plants) began to decline in the 1980s. One factor underlying this change was the decline in the share of the labor force working in manufacturing, where the sizes of production units are larger than in most other sectors. Since the optimal size of the enterprise or establishment depends upon technology, it is difficult to determine whether trends in the 1980s will continue. As noted previously, there is some empirical evidence to support the facile claims of many futurists that computerization will reduce the average sizes of productive units, but we cannot be sure.

These data allow us to explode certain ideological shibboleths. Fears about an increasing concentration of capital giving a greater political power base to an ever smaller group of managerial elite seem premature. The argument that worker alienation, which appears higher in larger enterprises, is increasing for the economy as a whole with the growing size of enterprises also does not have a sound basis, either from these data or from studies focusing particularly on the problem.[14]

Such data, however, do not allay our fears that the current average size of enterprises is too large and that this breeds an unhealthy symbiosis with government. More particularly, the pressures on the federal government are extremely strong to bail out those very large companies finding themselves in financial difficulties because of the large employment effects.

This should not lead us to romanticize small businesses. The belief that small businesses in the United States generate the vast majority of new jobs and are the keys to economic growth is overstated. As Charles Brown and colleagues demonstrate, this enduring political myth has little basis in fact, primarily because it focuses only on the creation and not the rapid disappearance of small firms.[15] In sum, gross job creation is not net job creation. Furthermore, their data show that small business is no more important a generator of new jobs than large business; indeed, in recent years the relative importance of small business in new job creation has somewhat declined.

We can conjecture from these data that many U.S. enterprises and establishments have reached the point where the diseconomies of scale in large

14. For instance, Quinn et al. (1974).
15. Brown, Hamilton, and Medoff (1990).

organizations arising from increasing structural complexity outweigh the economies of scale of large scale production. A shard of supporting evidence is cited previously on the impact of computers and information processing investment on firm size. The data for a more rounded and complete argument supporting the conjecture, however, are not yet at hand. Among other things, economies of scale are closely tied to other aspects of technology as well and it is unclear where we are headed along this dimension.

Structural complexity: Using the Theil statistic as a measure of heterogeneity, I find that structural complexity of the size distribution of both productive establishments and enterprises has slowly and irregularly increased. Another measure of structural complexity takes into account vertical communications within an enterprise and looks at the extent of multiplant firms. This also shows a slow increase in structural complexity. Both sets of data supporting these conclusions are presented in Appendix Note 6.2.

In short, the data reveal a simultaneous increase of structural complexity of the size distribution of productive enterprises and establishments and a decrease in the degree of aggregate concentration. This represents a unique type of change of the size distribution of productive units.

The separation of ownership and control

The discussion in Chapter 5 points to two aspects of increasing structural complexity of the structure of wealth. First, the financial leverage is rising; second, the control and management of assets are increasingly removed from ownership. The more elaborate financial superstructure and the separation of ownership and control both increase direct informational requirements of the system and the interactions within the system. In particular, the owners have increasing difficulties – called agency problems – in controlling the actions of managers.

The financial trends in the nonfinancial, corporate sector parallel those in the economy as a whole and are discussed in detail in Appendix Note 6.1. After considering briefly some basic propositions, the following analysis deals with three important questions about the separation of ownership and control: the extent and trends of manager-dominated firms; the impact of such manager domination on executive compensation, which seems the easiest type of nonprofit maximizing behavior to investigate; and the more difficult issue of the impact of the separation of ownership and control on profits. Readers must be warned that because of the mixed evidence for all three questions, we can draw few solid conclusions. The discussion has bearing, however, on many issues about structural complexity.

Some basic propositions

According to a well-known thesis expounded by Adolf A. Berle and Gardiner C. Means (1933), the development of capitalism features an increasing separation of ownership and control.[16] Furthermore, such a separation leads not only to the firms operating according to goals other than profit making, but also to the rise to power of a new class of nonowning managers – a phenomenon designated by the term "managerialism." Three quite different causal forces underlie this separation of ownership and control.

First, in modern capitalist societies, the corporate form comes to dominate production, a topic that has received extensive treatment.[17] Second, as corporations grow in absolute size, they far outstrip the ability of most wealthy people to own a significant share of the voting stock. This is because it requires an increasingly large amount of wealth to own a given fraction of equity of a firm. Third, as the sale of shares becomes more widespread, it also becomes rational for investors to diversify their portfolios to reduce the risk inherent in placing a major share of wealth in a single asset or enterprise.

According to this approach, with increasing dispersion of ownership, managers are more able to control the composition of the Board of Directors.[18] Although in recent years outside Directors constitute a majority in most large U.S. corporations, it is argued that these Directors cannot obtain the information effectively to monitor the CEO. For instance, Jeremy Bacon and James K. Brown argue: "Unless the Chief Executive Officer wants his [outside] Directors to become actively involved, it is all but impossible for them to become very effective." Or a decade later Andrei Shleifer and Robert W. Vishny claim that such Directors "are rarely effective in stopping the nonvalue maximizing [activities that do not maximize the value of the stockholders wealth: *FP*] of the managers."

16. Berle and Means (1933).
17. Some data are presented in Table A.13, Appendix Note 6.2. Scherer (1988) has an extensive discussion of the phenomenon.
18. Of course, the actual degree of managerial domination is inversely related to the degree of ownership concentration, and on this issue certain evidence is available. Common sense, as well as econometric studies (e.g., Demsetz and Lehn, 1985), show that concentration of ownership is inversely related to the size of the firm. Other variables also influence ownership concentration and Demsetz and Lehn (1985) argue that in a relatively stable economic environments or in regulated industries, less resources are required to monitor the activities of managers. As a result, ownership is more dispersed than in economic environments where profits are variable and the environment is "noisy." They also find some empirical evidence to support this approach. The relation between ownership concentration and instability of profits or variability of stock prices are, as Demsetz and Lehn predict, also positively correlated with increasing ownership concentration. However, the square of these variables is negatively correlated, a result which they never adequately explain.

Brown (1990) presents data on the numerical importance of outside directors. The citations come from Bacon and Brown (1975) and Shleifer and Vishny (1988).

Control by managers, rather than owners, allegedly has some important consequences. For instance, managerial control may not necessarily lead to profit maximization because these managers might administer the firm to further their personal goals, rather than the goals of the stockholders (for instance, profits) or of other stakeholders such as the employees. In a classic work Robert A. Gordon argues one implication in a blunt form:[19] "The Chief Executive is in a sense his own employer. Within broad limits he frequently sets his own compensation. Even if the Board of Directors or a minority stockholding group is active and powerful, the Chief Executive's salary may continue to be considerably larger than that commanded by men of seemingly comparability ability in companies of similar size and profitability." Although this proposition appears easy to test, it is not, as I indicate later.

The theory of managerial control (hereafter called *managerialism*) has other important implications. For instance, Robert A. Gordon has argued that managers are risk averse since they seldom receive commensurate rewards for accepting large risks that lead to high profits and they place their job at stake if such risks lead to high losses.[20] In elaborating the behavior of managerial dominated firms, economists such as Robin Marris and William J. Baumol also stress that executive compensation in such firms is generally more closely tied to sales than to profits or other measures of the increase in shareholders' wealth, the basis of elaborate theory about the sales-maximizing or the growth-maximizing firm.

Some economists strongly reject these arguments. Among other things, they claim that the functioning of the market imposes sufficiently tight constraints that a significant deviation of a manager-dominated firm from the activities of an owner-dominated firm is unlikely. This market approach comes in several variants. Some argue that the market for capital operates with sufficient efficiency that any firm not maximizing profits would not receive the necessary outside capital to survive. Others claim that the market for corporate control would lead to any elimination of a salary differential between executives of manager- and owner-controlled firms. Still others focus on the market for top corporate managers or even on the product market, which, it is argued, gradually eliminates firms with high overhead costs. Other aspects of the theory of managerialism have been subject to intense attack as well.

Although considerable theoretical evidence can be adduced to argue either side of these issues, it seems more fruitful to turn to the available empirical evidence, first to whether manager control is increasing and then to whether managerial compensation is higher and profits are lower in manager-dominated firms.

19. Gordon (1945), p. 277.
20. Ibid. The other references are to Marris (1964) and Baumol (1967).

Table 6.3. *Some data on trends in corporate ownership and control*

Part A: Holdings of Corporate Equities

	1952	1960	1970	1980	1990
Institutional					
Private pension funds	1.1%	3.9%	7.8%	14.2%	18.6%
State and local government retirement funds	.0	.1	1.2	2.8	8.4
Other insurance companies	3.3	3.0	3.2	5.0	5.1
Mutual fund holdings	2.0	3.5	4.6	2.7	6.6
Bank personal trusts	.0	.0	9.4	8.1	5.2
Closed-end funds; brokers and dealers	.4	.1	9.6	8.3	5.5
Commercial banks and savings institutions	.2	.3	.3	.3	.3
Total institutional	8.2	12.1	27.3	33.7	44.7
Foreign investors	2.2	2.2	3.2	4.1	6.3
Private individuals	89.7	85.8	69.6	62.2	49.1
Market value of equities (billion dollars)	169.9	425.0	859.8	1,568.9	3543.7

Part B: Ultimate control of 200 largest nonfinancial corporations: Larner estimates

	Percentage of Firms	
Type of control	1929	1963
Private ownership	6.0%	.0%
Majority ownership	5.0	3.0
Minority control	23.2	9.0
Legal device	20.5	4.5
Management control	44.2	83.5
Receivership	1.0	.0
Total	100.0	100.0

*a*For Part B, the data are taken from a study by Robert J. Larner, who has drawn from an earlier study by Berle and Means for his 1929 data. He considers a firm privately owned if a single family or group owns 80 percent of more of the voting stock; for majority ownership, between 50 and 80 percent; minority control, 20 to 50 percent in 1929 and 10 to 50 percent in 1963. In the text, I criticize these estimates. It should also be noted that he may have omitted certain privately held firms because of lack of data.
The sources are presented in Appendix Note 6.5.

The extent of manager-dominated enterprises

Part A of Table 6.3 shows that the share of market equities held by institutional investors has increased dramatically between 1952 and 1990. In this way, the holding of stock is becoming more, not less, concentrated. Part B of the same table reports estimated by Robert J. Larner, following the Berle-Means approach, of the separation of ownership and control over a thirty-four-year period.[21] Similar estimates including some from later years are also available. These data lead to a conclusion opposite from that drawn from the data in Part A, namely that the holding of stock is becoming less concentrated, not more. The Berle-Means approach can be criticized from several standpoints.

Omissions: The lists of the largest firms used to determine the degree of manager control often omit closely held firms of considerable size because they do not release data on their sales or assets, for instance, Cargill Inc. (grain processing), Hearst Corp. (newspapers), the Bechtel Corporation (construction), Hallmark (greeting cards), or Mars (candy). The omission of these closely held family firms skews the data toward manager-dominated firms. The extent of this sample bias is difficult to determine.[22]

Determination of control: Owner control may be exercised by a group and it is often difficult to determine without inside information how much stock belongs to a cohesive voting bloc. Some careful studies reveal a much greater degree of ownership concentration than the simple Berle-Means approach would lead us to believe.[23] Moreover, when the investigator is unable to determine if the firm is dominated by one or several groups of stockholders, it is generally placed in the residual category of manager-controlled, which also skews the results.

The Berle-Means approach requires the selection of arbitrary cutoff points, for instance, a firm is owner dominated if more than 10 or 20 percent of the stock is held by a single owner or group, and this leads to biased estimates. More specifically, using data from the United States and the United Kingdom, several studies show forcefully that the results obtained by such a methodology depend very much on the cutoff points selected.[24] Equally important, since the degree of potential managerial control depends not just on the dispersion of ownership among many holders of small blocs of stock, but also upon the degree of concentration of large blocs of stock, both must be taken into account by some sort of continuous variable. For instance, in a study of some 500 enterprises in the late 1970s, Harold Demsetz and Kenneth Lehn find that, on the average, the top five stockholders (including institutions) own 25 percent of the firm and the top twenty stockholders own 38 percent. Such concentration provides the potential for a coalition among these owners that would offset the power of the manager. Thus the concentration of ownership

21. Larner (1970). Scott (1986), p. 137, has data for later years.
22. Burch (1972) Chapter 2; has a useful discussion of this problem.
23. Such studies include those by Burch (1972), Dye (1983), Pedersen and Taub (1976), and Reinemer (1979).
24. These include essays by Cosh and Hughes (1987), Leach (1987), and Leach and Leahy (1991). Later references in the paragraph are to Demsetz and Lehn (1985) and Herman (1981), p. 87. The argument in the next paragraph is also due to Herman (1981).

appears significant, even though at times the share of the voting stock directly held by the directors appears small. Of course, it is also an open question
whether potential control is translated into actual control, that is, whether
holdings of large blocs of stock act as a cohesive group against the managers.

In any case, "control" is a tricky concept and difficult to operationalize.
Moreover, it is useful to distinguish between active versus latent control which
is manifested only in crises, or control in terms of policy initiation versus control in terms of veto power, or control according to different functions such as
financial or operative. But these reasonable procedures are seldom followed
because of lack of accessible evidence.

Congruence of interests: The issue of whether owners or managers control the
enterprise may be nugatory if the interests of the groups are the same. Top managers usually own a considerable amount of the shares of their corporation, so
that their long-term interests are tied to those of the stockholders.[25] In a careful
empirical study Michael C. Jensen and Kevin J. Murphy show that even in the
largest firms where managers own a relatively small percentage of the stock,
the dividend and capital gain income from the shares they own in their own
firm are much larger than their salary, bonuses, and other incentives. Previous
studies have also revealed that this has been the case for many decades.[26]

The role of financial intermediaries: The degree of owner control of enterprises is further complicated by the growth of stock ownership by financial
institutions, which, in turn, are indirectly owned by others. These holdings by
financial intermediaries, shown in Table 6.3, have centralized ownership considerably. A great deal of controversy has arisen, however, about what this
means and how this power is exercised.

Numerous studies point out that representatives from financial groups can
be found on almost all boards of directors and that they hold "strategic positions" of ownership in many firms.[27] Some, such as David M. Kotz, defend
the view that the degree of bank control is massive in good measure because
of such board memberships. Others such as Edward S. Herman firmly reject
this position, claiming that bank and financial control is important usually only

25. Lewellen (1971). The next reference is to Jensen and Murphy (1990). Other evidence on these
problems is supplied by Benston (1985), Cosh and Hughes (1987) and Kostiuk (1990).
26. The evidence on the relationship between the ownership stake of managers and profits is
mixed. Some investigators such as Stano (1975) have found a significant and positive relation between enterprise profits and this ownership stake; others such as Mueller (1986) or
Charreaux (1991) find such a relation either small or nonexistent.
27. Bacon (1990) has recent data on the relative number of bankers on these boards. Dye (1983)
and Kotz (1978) argue that actual influence exercised is great. Herman (1981) Chapter 4
backs away from such a position. The business press reference is Business Week, March 15,
1993, pp. 68–75.

when these large corporations get into serious financial difficulties. In the early 1990s, however, some large institutional holders of stock began to exercise the power of their holdings to remove Executive Officers when the firm began to flounder. Although the role of the California Public Employees Retirement System (CalPERS) in the removal of the President of General Motors attracted considerable attention, other cases can be cited as well. The business press hailed this as a new trend toward "relationship investment," and, according to a cover story in *Business Week*, such institutions are becoming "patient and involved" investors. A 1993 SEC ruling that such institutional investors can informally confer without prior notification or proxy statements reinforces this trend. Although these changes appear as important steps toward "finance capitalism," they are hesitant steps. For instance, after a change in the top executive, CalPERS appeared much less willing to take such an aggressive role. I discuss the possibilities of the trend continuing, as well as the impact of such changes, in Chapter 10, where I consider various scenarios of the future of capitalism.

Currently it is difficult to judge the impact of the increase in power of institutional investors on the performance of firms. Several small-scale studies provide evidence, however, that the voting of large blocks of stock by bank trust departments has a statistically significant and positive impact on the profit performance of large firms.[28] I must emphasize, however, that the exercise by institutional investors of their ownership rights to influence enterprise policies is still severely circumscribed.[29] Banks are limited in the assets they can hold in their portfolios and bank holding companies are allowed to hold only up to five percent of the voting shares in nonbanking companies. Mutual funds owning more than 10 percent of any firm are subject to regulatory and tax restrictions, some of which would apply to their entire portfolio. Forty states limit the percentage of investment of insurance companies in the common stock of a single firm to a range between 2 and 25 percent. Pension funds lose their tax-free status if they actively engage in providing direction to a company in which they own stock; and they are further constrained by the "prudent man" rule that requires a highly diversified portfolio. Many other constraints for institutional investors could be added to this list. Still other types of institutional investors are limited in other ways.[30]

28. Finnerty, Choo, and Sufrin (1979) and also Levin and Levin (1982).
29. Roe (1990, 1993). Of course, such institutions are required to vote their shares, but this occasional act by no means allows them to control the firm.
30. One ownership trend often touted in the popular press is the increasing role of employee stock ownership plans (ESOPs). Allegedly these new owners will play an increasing role in corporate control in the coming decades. This judgment, however, appears premature although ESOPs have grown phenomenally in recent years. According to data in Table 10.1, members of ESOPs comprised about 10 percent of the nonagricultural work force in 1990. In the late 1980s, such ESOPs held 4 percent or more of the stock in one third of the Fortune 100 and

These legal restrictions are important, I believe, and considerable skepticism is warranted regarding the claims about the control of top policy making in most U.S. corporations by various financial intermediaries, especially since the direct evidence is limited and anecdotal. Perhaps the most important control that many financial intermediaries exercise is indirect: By buying or selling large blocks of stock, such financial institutions affect the price of the stock. As long as managerial behavior is influenced by stock prices and the fear of a takeover, this indirect influence can be considerable. Unfortunately, it also makes for a certain short-term perspective by managers. More specifically, they have an incentive to neglect long-term investments that would hurt profits in the short run in order to pump up current earnings.

This list of difficulties determining the degree to which ownership is separated from control or who exactly controls the enterprise is long; from the previous summary it should be clear that the empirical evidence is contradictory. Attempts to derive other indicators of this phenomenon also lead to ambiguous results.[31] Although many large enterprises are controlled effectively by their managers, we must be careful in making predictions. Philip H. Burch has cautiously opined, "...it would certainly appear that while there has been a definite trend toward managerial control of big business over the years, the magnitude of this shift in economic authority has generally been overstated." But even this discreet assessment might not take full account of the increasing concentration of ownership by financial and other institutions. Furthermore, the role played by these financial intermediaries is very dependent upon governmental regulations, which can change considerably in the future. In short, recent trends in the separation of ownership and control are unclear, and the future is even more clouded. About this aspect of increasing structural complexity, we can say little.

Compensation of top executives

If managers control the firm, rather than the owners, many argue that these hired executives would receive a much higher compensation than they would if the owners actually controlled the enterprise. Such a compensation differential allegedly occurs because total executive compensation is only a minus-

27 percent in the Fortune 500 (Blasi and Kruse, 1990, p. 14 ff.). But in most cases the shares in such ESOP plans are not voted by the members, but by trustees who are usually appointed by management. The impact of these plans on corporate performance does not seem great, although this is a matter of some controversy in the literature. I discuss these matters in greater detail in Chapter 10 when considering various scenarios of the future of capitalism.
31. For instance, Lazonick (1988) argues that the greater dividends and the decline in retention of profits for financing new investment shows an increase in the power of owners over managers. As I indicate in Chapter 5, profit retention is a function of many factors of which the tax treatment of debt and equity capital is crucial. The citation is from Burch (1975), p. 102.

cule fraction of total sales and makes little difference on the profit performance, so managerial decisions about their own salaries have little aggregate
impact. Furthermore, according to this argument, with the increasing separation of ownership and control, executive compensation should be increasing
relatively to the compensation of others in the firm. These hypothesized
trends, which are related to the increasing inequality of income documented in
Chapter 2, are possible to verify empirically.[32]

In turning to the empirical evidence on these matters, we must view the data
on executive compensation with caution, because a full evaluation must take
into account not only salary, cash and stock bonuses, but also corporate contributions to savings, stock purchase plans, stock options, and job perquisites
such as homes, cars and planes, club memberships, and the like. Data for some
components, such as salary and current bonuses tied to the current performance of the firm (perquisites are an exception), are readily available. But it
is often quite difficult to determine the present value of those parts of the compensation package tying the manager's interests to the long-term financial performance of the firm, for instance, stock options.[33]

Trends in relative managerial compensation: The data presented in Table A.14
in Appendix Note 6.3 measure the compensation of the CEOs of the top fifty
largest industrial corporations in the United States as a ratio of the average
compensation of full-time employees.

For salaries and direct bonuses, which are easiest to measure, the ratios
reveal a U-shaped pattern over time, falling from 1940 until 1970 and then rising sharply, although not reaching the 1940 level by 1990.[34] Michael C. Jensen

32. Of course, executive compensation is determined by many other factors that I do not have
    space to discuss. For instance, both Williamson (1963) and Auerbach and Siegfried (1974)
    show that managerial compensation is related to degree of market concentration and entry
    barriers, even though these two studies disagree on whether managerial control is an impor-
    tant additional variable in understanding the total picture. Almost all find the size of enter-
    prise an important determinant of the salaries of top managers.

    There is also a large literature on whether sales or profits are the major determinant of man-
    agerial compensation, for instance, studies by Bartlett, Grant and Miller (1992); Deckop
    (1988); Jensen and Murphy (1990); Larner (1970); Lewellen and Huntsman (1970); Masson
    (1971); and Meeks and Whittington (1975). The results of these studies are very mixed.

33. In readily available data on executive compensation such as those appearing in Forbes, which I
    use in my calculations for later years, the value of the stock options are determined only from
    those options that are actually exercised, rather than the current and future accrued value of
    unrealized options. More serious academic studies such as those by Lewellen, which I use for
    earlier years, attempt the latter course. Valuation of contributions to pension plans requires deter-
    mination of life expectancy and future interest rates and *Forbes* does not specify its methods.

34. I must also note that the compensation data for the CEOs in the top fifty firms do not neces-
    sarily parallel those for all firms; some have suggested that the compensation of executives in
    these largest companies is increasingly out-of-line with corporate executives of smaller com-
    panies. The reference later in the paragraph is to Jensen and Murphy (1990).

and Kevin J. Murphy obtain a similar result and provide evidence that salary and bonus of CEOs in the top quartiles of the NYSE corporations has declined, in real terms, from 1934–8 to 1974–86 period.

For total compensation, which includes both salaries, deferred payments, and stock options, the picture is more murky because the pretax and posttax trends diverge. On a pretax basis, the ratio of total compensation of the top executives to average compensation was irregular in the fifty-year period and, in 1990, was roughly the same as in 1940. On a posttax basis, ratio of total compensation of the top executives to average compensation followed a U-shaped pattern, falling from 1940 to 1970 and then increasing sharply so that it was well above the 1940 level by 1990.

It should be noted that the median compensation is considerably lower than the average, due to extremely high compensation received by a few executives. Some well-publicized examples of high executive compensation, primarily in the form of these deferred payments, come readily to mind. For instance, Steven J. Ross, the Chief Executive of Time-Warner, had an annual compensation that averaged over $16 million a year in the period from 1973 through 1989.[35] But even the median compensation of these top executives, measured as a ratio of the average compensation of all workers, more than doubled in the twenty years from 1970 to 1990.

The patterns over time, either of total compensation or various key components certainly do not reflect the allegedly steady increase in the separation of ownership and control over the same period. Although the separation of ownership and control may play a role in the high compensation of corporate executives, many other causal factors are also at work and high CEO salaries reflect more than just this structural change.[36]

In my view the key problem is not the level of these salaries, outrageous as they may be, but the relation of executive compensation to enterprise performance. Often such compensation is often not closely tied to performance of the firm. Even in firms showing considerable losses, executive salaries and bonuses seldom fall, as gleefully reported by Graef S. Crystal and the annual *Business Week* roundups of executive salaries.[37] Even more worrisome is the evidence provided in two recent studies that the relationship between pay and performance has become looser, not tighter, over the last few decades. This is undoubtedly related to the rising ratio of compensation of these executives to the average compensation of all workers over the same time period.

---

35. Crystal (1991), p. 84.
36. The standard theories about corporate compensation need extension in a number of ways, for instance, to explain why and how outside directors in certain corporations pay themselves six-figure fees (*Business Week*, June 20, 1994, p.6).
37. Ibid. Studies relating CEO salaries and enterprise performance include those by Santerre and Neun (1989) and Jensen and Murphy (1990).

Relative compensation in manager- and owner-dominated firms: The argument is simple: Corporations with dispersed stock ownership (and manager domination) are much more likely to give larger bonuses (not salaries) to executives than firms with concentrated ownership. This is because stockholders are less able to monitor executive behavior and the bonus ties the long-term interests of the managers more closely with their own. These conclusions tie in with some results obtained by Dennis Mueller that bonuses, not salaries, are more likely to be tied to profits, rather than sales.[38]

But is the level of executive compensation higher in manager-dominated firms than owner-dominated firms? Although early studies suggested that there was no statistically significant differences, later studies provide evidence that top executives in manager-dominated firms do receive higher compensation than in owner-dominated firms.[39] The problem is holding constant the other determinants of executive compensation and, given the mixed evidence on these matters, however, we cannot be completely sure about these recent results.

Some final words: This brief review shows a complicated relation between managerialism and CEO compensation. Although CEOs in manager-dominated firms might receive higher compensation than hired executives in similar positions in owner-dominated firms, this result is not yet certain. Furthermore, any alleged increase in managerialism cannot explain either the long-term time pattern of CEO compensation or the rapid rise in such compensation since the 1960s. The increasingly loose linkage of corporate performance to compensation from the 1960s to the present is probably related to the rise in managerial compensation and also may be due, in part, to increasing difficulties in monitoring managerial performance and determining who and what is really responsible for certain changes in profits.

38. Mueller (1986), Chapter 7.
39. Based on his sample of firms in the 1960s, Robert Larner (1970) claims that little difference appeared in CEO pay in the two types of firms; unfortunately, he did not present his evidence in sufficient detail to evaluate his results. For several samples of enterprises spanning the late 1920s and early 1930s, George J. Stigler and Claire Friedland (1983) provide additional support to this conclusion by showing no correlation of executive salaries and the type of control (owner or manager), holding asset size of company constant. More recently, Rexford E. Santerre and Steven Neun (1989) show that if the profit rate is added to the Stigler-Friedland regression as another explanatory variable, manager-dominated firms had higher executive compensations, other factors being equal Dyl (1988) provides more support for this conclusion. Leach and Leahy (1991) use a sample of U.K. firms to show that managerial remuneration is higher in manager-dominated firms, and Holderness and Sheehan (1988), who find that in companies with the dominant stockholders occupying the position of CEO, compensation to these managers is higher.

Profits and risk

The proposition that manager-dominated enterprises earn lower profits than owner-dominated enterprises is based on several assumptions, of which three deserve mention: First, the managers are maximizing their own utility and enterprise profits are not their dominant interest. Second, the market does not strongly constrain managerial behavior. Third, the major difficulties in monitoring performance are those experienced by owners in relation to the top managers, rather than those of the top managers in relation to their subordinates.

The first two assumptions have been challenged seriously and the third is controversial. With regard to the first, Harold Demsetz provides some theoretical arguments that this is simply not the case.[40] And with regard to the second assumption, John P. Palmer was the first of many investigators to find differences in profit performance between manager- and owner-dominated firms only when the degree of imperfect competition, measured by concentration ratios or barriers to entry, are relatively high. Or, to put it in a different way, managerialism is possible only when the markets are sufficiently imperfect that enterprise managers can pursue their own goals without endangering the long-run financial health of the firm.

Besides problems in measuring manager- and owner-dominated enterprises, other statistical problems arise in determining the differences in profit performance. It is necessary to take risk explicitly into account, either by means of some type of risk-adjusted profit rate or by including some measure of risk as an explanatory variable. Most of the studies in the literature do not take this precaution. Results are also strongly affected by the manner in which profit rates are defined; that is, the manner in which the numerator (profits) is adjusted and whether the denominator is net worth, total assets, or sales. For instance, James L. Bothwell finds that owner-controlled firms have higher profit rates when defined as a percent of total assets, but not as a percent of net worth.[41] Results are affected by the manner in which control is defined; and some studies also show that it is useful to distinguish quite carefully the different combinations involved.[42] We also must hold constant other causal factors such as the degree of imperfect competition, the size of the firm, the industry, the role of imports, and so forth that influence profits. Since various

40. The references in this paragraph are to Demsetz (1983) and Palmer (1973a).
41. Bothwell (1980).
42. For instance, this would include separating: (a) firms managed by their owners; (b) firms with a hired manager but with a dominant bloc of stockholders; (c) firms with a hired manager but with a dominant bloc of stock held by financial intermediaries; (d) firms with a hired manager who owns a large block of stock; and finally (e) firms with little ownership concentration with a hired manager who has little stock ownership.

contributors to the literature have held quite different factors constant, the results from the different studies are difficult to compare.

For profit performance, the results from more than a dozen econometric studies of the problem are quite mixed. About half show little or no statistical difference in profit rates between manager- and owner-controlled firms in the United States.[43] And the other half show that owner-controlled firms do have higher profit rates than manager-controlled firms. Various studies of managerialism and risk also show mixed results so that no conclusions can be drawn at this time.[44]

A final note

The theory of managerialism has detractors on both the right and the left. Many Marxists claim that because the basic class and power mechanisms are the same, the behavior of all firms is roughly the same, regardless of whether the firm is dominated by owners or managers. Many adherents of the Chicago school claim that the efficiency of the capital market and the market for corporate control allows little leeway for managers to follow interests different from those of stockholders. Frederic M. Scherer speaks for many including myself when he notes:[45] "Theoretical thought on the ownership and control of

43. Studies showing little or no difference in profit performance of manager- and owner-dominated firms include those by Demsetz and Lehn (1985), Elliott (1972), Kammerchen (1968), Kania and McKean (1976), Larner (1970), Sorensen (1974), and Stigler and Friedland (1983). Scherer (1988) cites a study by Morck, Shleifer, and Vishney (1985), who replicate the study of Demsetz and Lehn but specify the equation somewhat differently and show that maximum profitability is achieved when directors hold 5 to 20 percent of the companies shares, with higher or lower inside shareholding resulting in a lower profitability; such a result defies a simple interpretation. Lawriwsky (1984) shows that profit performance does depend on the share of stock held by the firm directors; he concludes, however, that "there is no simple formula tying control type and performance" since internal structure of the firm and incentives are crucial (p. 220).

   Studies showing a difference in profit rates of manager- and owner-dominated firms include those by Boudreaux (1973), Holl (1975), Leach and Leahy (1991), McEachern (1976), Monson, Chiu and Cooley (1968), Neun and Santerre (1986); Palmer (1973a), and Radice (1971). Mueller (1986) explores differences between predicted long-run returns on assets in firms with different proportions of shares held by top managers and also identifiable outside owner groups. He finds little impact of the outside owners but lower profits in firms with significant inside ownership.

44. Some find that profit variability or other measures of risk are not statistically different in the two types of enterprises. These include studies by Kania and McKean (1976), Larner (1970), and Palmer (1973b, 1975). Others find that profit variability or other measures of risk are lower in manager dominated firms. These include studies by Boudreaux (1973) and McEachern. Kamin and Ronen (1978) introduce another complication, namely that in manager-dominated firms, the accounting process is carried out in a manner deliberately to smooth variations in profits, so that all such studies using this type of accounting data are flawed.

45. Scherer (1988).

the modern corporation is in a state of turmoil. There is lack of agreement on how seriously the goals of owners and managers diverge ... 'Chicagoans' hold, that the surviving ownership structures will be those efficiently adapted to the mandates of the market place ... Greater intellectual unease is the lot of those like myself who, following Berle and Means, believe that ownership structure can make a difference but are uncertain what difference it makes."

Managerialism raises many useful questions about the impact of a special type of structural complexity. But this also is a case where we cannot easily predict the future because we do not understand the present.

Summary and implications for the future

This chapter focuses on three facets of structural complexity as it influences the enterprise sector and is revealed by it. One part of the discussion concerned the increasing structural complexity of the economic environment and the impact this has had on the organization of business. My survey of officials in large U.S. corporations shows that, as a group, they clearly recognize the problems arising from this change in their decision-making environment. Furthermore, a majority seem to have followed three strategies to meet the challenges of these changes: mastering structural complexity through increased use of information; reducing structural complexity handled by top management; and evading structural complexity by simplifying procedures, processes, products, and the process of change.

I argue in Chapter 10 that the type of economic system toward which we are evolving depends very much on whether, and how, enterprises will change to meet the problems raised by still greater structural complexity in the future. In this respect it is worrisome that the executives in my survey claim to have placed more emphasis on following these strategies in the past decade (1983–93) than they plan to do so in the future decade (1993–2003). Of course, what they say they will do and what they will actually do are two quite different things. Whatever happens, public policy will not play an important role. The government has few policy tools available to influence organizational reorganization. Moreover, the government is unclear on how to solve its own organizational problems. Only the business sector can save itself.

The structural complexity of the productive sector itself is also increasing. Employing a measure of heterogeneity, I find that the size distributions of both enterprises and establishments reveal a slowly rising structural complexity over time. This has not been accompanied by a parallel increase in the importance of the largest enterprises, because aggregate concentration ratios rose to the mid-1960s or mid-1970s (depending on the indicator) and then began to fall. This fall in importance of the largest enterprises came about partly because a change in the structure of production toward the services (Chapter 4). But another part of the story comes from the actions of the enterprises themselves, as they began to divest themselves of operations not directly related to their core business. We might conjecture that increasing structural complexity has caused some diseconomies of scale underlying such actions, but sufficient evidence is not available to provide any certainty about this matter. In the near future, a marked deviation from current trends does not seem likely.

One implication of the slowly rising heterogeneity of the size distributions of enterprises and establishments is that public policy toward the productive structure becomes more difficult because of higher information requirements. That is, it becomes increasingly difficult to develop uniform policies to deal with all companies because they are increasingly different. I discuss this issue in considerable detail in Chapter 9. Another important implication relates to a critical assumption of some studies of economic evolution that technological complexity is associated with increasing economies of scale and scope.[46] In some respects such an assumption has a grain of truth, particuarly in some industries. Nevertheless, such an argument implies that enterprises should be becoming larger and the degree of industrial concentration should be increasing. As shown in this chapter, the first prediction does not describe the current situation and, as documented in the next chapter, the second prediction is incorrect as well.

The structural complexity of the ownership pattern, as manifested by the separation of ownership and control, may have slowly increased, although it is difficult to know if that was offset by the increasing concentration of ownership among financial intermediaries. Moreover, it is difficult to predict what will happen since the role of these institutional investments is strongly constrained by legislation that may change. In the final chapter I discuss a number of possible scenarios of the changing role of these financial intermediaries that could have a major impact on the economic system.

Whatever the trend, I must emphasize that the impact of a changing degree of managerialism is quite unclear. It does not seem to have had a direct impact on the time pattern of CEO compensation, even though it might have influenced compensation of manager-dominated firms at a single point in time. Since 1960, CEO compensation as a ratio of average compensation for all

46. Some exciting and promising work has been carried out that focuses on increasing returns in the economy, particularly with regard to path dependent processes featuring positive feedbacks (for instance, Arthur, 1994). If this assumption were generally true for all parts of the economy, then it would undermine much of orthodox economics, which is based on the assumption of diminishing returns. As noted previously, the indicators covering the entire economy are not favorable for the increasing returns hypothesis. My major objection to neoclassical economics is that it is too narrow and does not give proper attention to my interesting economic issues, rather than it relies too heavily on any assumption about diminishing returns or economies of scale and scope associated with changing technology. Arthur's approach certainly has validity for certain sectors of the economy, however.

workers in the economy has increased, a contributing factor to the increasing inequality of income discussed in Chapter 2. Evidence on the impact of the separation of ownership and control on the profit performance and risk taking of enterprises is so mixed that no firm conclusions can be drawn.

A key result of this exploration is the finding that since 1970, CEO compensation relative to average compensa tion of full-time workers in the economy as a whole has increased, while the relationship between this compensation and enterprise performance is becoming weaker. These trends are not easily amenable to public policy. If they continue, it bodes ill, not just for U.S. productivity, but also for social tranquility.

CHAPTER 7

The behavior of markets

The concept of structural complexity provides a useful tool to examine certain types of market behavior, especially since market activity and the structural complexity of the economy mutually influence each other. Although many aspects of these relationships deserve attention, in this chapter I address three particular questions that focus on the impact of this market structure on economic processes: To what extent has the increased structural complexity offset the action of the law of one price? To what degree has the increased structural complexity caused by the internationalization of the economy influenced the degree of competition on domestic markets? And to what extent has increased structural complexity of the economy influenced the volatility of market prices, particularly for internationally traded basic materials?

In an important sense, markets represent a structurally less complex organization of the economy than central planning. This is because markets do not feature most of the intricate interactions between various levels of government and producers. In a market economy the primary interaction is between buyers and sellers and, as a result, information is generated and used decentrally. These information flows are crucial for the functioning of markets and can be used to measure the structural complexity.

Of course, various markets are organized in quite different ways and measurements of the structural complexity can be made along many dimensions. As discussed in Chapter 6, for instance, such complexity can increase as products become more intricate or customized, as the level of technology embodied in the product rises, as markets increase in their geographical reach (internationalization), or as governmental regulation of these markets expands. All these changes impose additional information burdens on the participants in the system. The measurement of the complexity of markets raises many interesting problems that require investigation. In this chapter, however, I do not deal with these quantitative issues; instead, I handle the direction of change of structural complexity in a qualitative fashion so as to investigate other problems. The problems of the origins, impact, and measurement of market complexity can not be handled in a single chapter.

The increasing structural complexity arising from greater customization of products works against the *law of one price*. This law, which stems from Adam Smith, says that as transportation costs fall, prices between various regions tend to converge.[1] Increasing structural complexity, however, makes arbitrage between markets more difficult so that such price convergence may not occur. With a sample of retail prices in five quite separated cities in the United States I show that the expected price convergence for particular product groups does not take place and that price differentials between these cities have remained roughly the same over the forty-year period.

The internationalization of the economy represents a widening of markets; it also indicates an increase in their structural complexity, since producers must consider in their decisions a larger range of consumers and rival producers. Using a data set of the market share of the top four domestic producers plus imports for more than 400 markets. I measure the increase in competition resulting from such an expansion of foreign trade.

Although it is commonly argued that this widening of markets should lead to greater price stability, I show that market price volatility, at least for internationally traded basic commodities, has increased. The major underlying cause, I argue, is the increase in volatility of exchange rates, a phenomenon first explored in Chapter 5. This trend in price volatility has not been reflected, however, in increased volatility of production. In this case, increased structural complexity has an asymmetric influence on price and quantity variables of the particular markets.

Some retail price behavior in domestic markets

The law of one price says that in relatively competitive markets (for instance, without regional monopolies), prices will tend toward equality, plus or minus costs reflecting such factors as differential transportation costs of goods to various parts of the market. Although other factors such as costs of information or store location can be specified that would lead to retail price differences within particular cities, they have little impact when comparing average prices of particular commodities between various cities. In this section I show how predictions based on the law of one price conflict with predictions based on the ideas discussed in Chapter 6 that the economy and markets are increasing in structural complexity. Using retail price data on seventeen product groups in five U.S. cities, I demonstrate empirically that these forces are of relatively equal strength.

Among international economists a fierce battle has raged about whether the law of one price holds for raw materials and other relatively homogeneous commodities in international trade. Various investigators have invoked a variety of complications arising from trade lags, rational expectations, and exchange rate considerations to explain why the action of the law of one price

---

1. Kindleberger (1989) has a fascinating analysis of the history of this doctrine.

is not immediately apparent in this type of foreign trade. For nonhomogeneous goods in international trade, most observers agree that the law of one price simply does not hold. This is because exporters often price to the markets in which they are selling, that is, they set prices competitive with those prevalent in the foreign market and they take little account of changes in the exchange rate, at least in the short and middle run. Paul Krugman explores some important empirical support for this contention with an examination of changes in exchange rate and import price indices, showing that the foreign exchange rates are much more volatile than the import prices.[2] Supporting microeconomic evidence is also available. This strategy of *pricing to market* may be quite rational to a profit maximizing firm, especially where its market share is important for future sales.

I should add that the long-run fate of the pricing-to-market strategy is currently unclear because in the early 1990s it was challenged in a U.S. court. Eastman Kodak accused Fuji Films of violating the antidumping laws by maintaining its dollar price of its film when the Japanese yen rose. Since the film was made in Japan and Holland, the cost of production denominated in dollars rose as well. Although the U.S. courts handed down a preliminary ruling in favor of Eastman Kodak, Fuji later settled out of court so that the basic issue could not be resolved at that time. Nevertheless, these considerations suggest that the law of one price does not seem to hold in a significant share of products in international trade.

By way of contrast, economists studying the domestic economy implicitly assume that the law of one price applies, at least in some form, in almost all cases. Unfortunately, they have not tested this article of faith empirically because of difficulties of obtaining the relevant data, namely data on the prices of particular goods or product groups in many different localities.

Price dispersion across space: the issue at stake

Although prices for the same quality good vary across space for a variety of reasons, it is difficult to quantify these factors for an economic analysis of a static version of the law of one price.[3] Fortunately, it is much easier to test a dynamic version of the law, namely that as the share of transportation costs

---

2. Krugman (1989). Supporting microeconomic evidence comes from Engel (1992) and Marston (1990). Froot and Klemperer (1988) analyze the rationality of pricing-to-market strategies in international trade. The Kodak–Fuji case mentioned in the next paragraph is discussed in *The Wall Street Journal* and the *Washington Post,* both on March 31, 1994.

3. In the economic literature a number of articles dealing with search costs explore differences in prices of particular goods and services within a relatively confined geographical area, for instance, Pratt, Wise, and Zeckhauser (1979). I have been unable to locate, however, any that deal with variations in average prices between large market areas for a long time period.

falls in comparison to the sale price of a good or service, price differences across space should diminish.

Since 1950 this fall in relative transportation costs appears to have occurred. More specifically, producer prices of transportation services rose from 1950 through 1990 at an annual rate considerably lower than the increase of the consumer price index.[4] Except for clothing, it was also lower than for any commodity group under consideration in the statistical analysis to follow. Such data on relative price trends say nothing, of course, about changes in cost shares. But if we assume that the transportation component of various goods increased only slowly in real terms in response to these changes in relative prices, these price trends reflect a decline in the share of transportation costs, measured in current prices, as well. Although I was unable to locate data on the changing share of transportation costs in total retail sales to justify this assumption, indirect evidence from foreign trade accounts and also national income accounts provide solid support for it.[5]

Five reasons can be offered why the dynamic version of the law of one price does not apply in the domestic economy at the retail level when comparing average prices of a particular commodity group across large cities. The first two relate to particular aspects of the increasing structural complexity of markets:

Rising search costs: The narrowing of price differences across space assumes that consumers shop for the lowest price. For relatively expensive and homogeneous commodities or services, this seems likely to occur since consumers easily can make price comparisons and they might be able to save considerable money. For instance, some consumers wishing to buy a new car are will-

4. Transportation prices alone rose at an average annual rate of 3.2 percent, which is calculated from current and constant price data from the NIPA that are published in *Survey of Current Business,* 73, No. 6 (July 1993) and, for previous years, various volumes of U.S. Department of Commerce, Bureau of Economic Analysis, *National Income and Product Accounts of the United States.* This is compared to the rise in the *consumer price index* (CPI) for the various commodities sold at retail. Although the implicit GDP deflators are not strictly comparable to the CPI data (the former more closely approximate a *Paasche index;* the latter, a *Laspeyres index*), the differences in the rates of change are sufficiently great that the generalization about declining relative transportation costs seems safe. For clothing I am informed by Marshall Reinsdorf of the Bureau of Labor Statistics that the series had an unintentional downward bias in past years.

5. More technically, I am making the reasonable assumption that the price elasticity of demand for transporta tion services on the producer and retail level is less than unity. Some indirect evidence can be offered in support. According to IMF data (annual, various editions), the ratio of foreign trade measured CIF and FOB fell over the period under investigation, which suggests that transportation costs as a share of foreign trade declined. National account data from the U.S. Department of Commerce (1992/93, Tables 6.1B and 1.3) also show that the share of value added in transportation to total value added in private industry fell or to the total production of goods fell over the period.

ing to search a considerable distance from their home if they can buy one for a significantly lower price. If, however, the goods or services are heterogeneous, the costs of search are much higher since it takes longer to learn the various features of the commodity. Similarly, if the good is relatively inexpensive, it is not worthwhile spending much time shopping for the lowest price unless the good is bought repeatedly. In the course of economic growth, the value of shoppers' time rises since the alternative uses of time increases with an expanding per capita income.[6] Over time, other things being equal, we would expect search time to decrease, especially for heterogeneous goods; we would also expect price dispersions between cities to increase.

Declining arbitrage possibilities: Price dispersion should be less for those goods or services for which arbitrage is easy, so that people can buy where the price is low and sell where the price is high. But arbitrage is difficult at the retail level for several classes of goods and services: those where the relative selling costs are high, for instance highly heterogeneous goods; and those that cannot be easily transported, for instance, housing and many personal services. With rising per capita and discretionary incomes, consumer purchases move away from relatively standardized to more heterogeneous goods, or from relatively simple models of a commodity to more complicated and higher quality versions. On the consumer level, therefore, arbitrage becomes increasingly difficult and, as a result, price dispersion should become greater for particular commodities.

The remaining three reasons for believing that the law of one price may not hold are unrelated to complexity per se: They also provide, I believe, much weaker forces for offsetting the law of one price.

Changes in local and state government actions: At a single point in time, price dispersion across different governmental units should be greater for those goods and services for which the share of sales taxes is relatively significant. It is unclear, however, whether sales tax rates in different states have converged or diverged over time, and the same might be said for other types of governmental actions, for instance, the setting of public utility prices. With the data set available to me, it was not possible to take this type of offsetting fac-

---

6. The increasing importance of catalogue sales, which lower search costs, does not appear to have had a great impact on regional price convergence, at least for the goods that I examine here. The sales volume of computer shopping, which also reduces search costs, is rising rapidly. Other marketing innovations to lower search costs could be mentioned as well.

Allegedly, more educated people spend less time shopping because they can process information more efficiently, and this reduces search costs. The magnitude of this effect is not clear. The rising per capita income effect that raises the opportunity cost of search time was not very important in the 1980s when average real incomes barely rose. Linder (1970) has a useful analysis of the rising value of time.

tor systematically into account; nevertheless, it seems unlikely that such actions would have markedly influenced price dispersion across the five cities.

Changes in rents of retail outlets: In the long run, land rents of retail outlets are part of the costs factored into the retail price. If the dispersion of these rents across space changes over time, then the divergence of retail prices should change in the same direction, other things remaining equal. It is difficult to generalize about these matters from first principles because several factors must be considered. Unfortunately, the empirical evidence is also ambiguous. Although I have no direct evidence on retail rents, I do have data on the relative prices of all rental units, as well as shelter costs including rents, household insurance, and similar expenses. On the one hand, the dispersion of the shelter costs reveals no secular trend; on the other, the dispersion of house rents alone has increased. With such mixed evidence, it is difficult to draw a firm conclusion. Nevertheless, the broader concept of shelter expenses seems to me more relevant for considering retail expenses than rents alone since the former include utilities and taxes. Creating additional problems is the shift of retail sales from high-rent, central-city areas to low- and medium-rent shopping malls in the suburbs. I make the reasonable assumption that this change occurred at roughly the same rate in the five cities so that it does not have a marked impact on price dispersion between cities.

Changes in the degree of imperfect competition: If the sale of certain goods on the retail markets is dominated by oligopolies or monopolies in certain localities, and if the degree of imperfect local competition changes over time, then price dispersions over space can be affected. Little information is available on these matters, but to sidestep the problem, I have confined myself to large metropolitan areas where retail market imperfections are presumably not great enough to influence the comparisons.

No theory tells us whether the five factors acting in the opposite direction to the law of one price are stronger or weaker than the impact of the law, so it is necessary to turn to the data to decide the issue. Unfortunately, this medicine also turns out to be easier to prescribe than to take.

The data and some problems in testing

The basic data come from a special study by the U.S. Bureau of Labor Statistics, which investigates differences in absolute price levels of a limited number of product groups during the late 1980s in many urban areas. For this study I selected five cities: New York, Philadelphia, Detroit, Chicago, and Los Angeles. Using price indices for these cities for each of the product groups, I projected the price levels both forward and backward. Because of special problems mentioned later, I made two sets of calculations: one from the earliest year of the series (or 1950, whichever came first) up to 1993; the other from 1976 to 1993.

Although data on only a limited number of product groups are available, they allow us to gain some idea of price differences across various cities around the country, and also, in some cases, within metropolitan areas. Within these metropolitan areas prices for some categories of goods such as food are quite similar, as we would expect. For other categories – particularly hetero-geneous goods – prices can be quite different. For instance, retail prices for household furnishings and operations in the Connecticut suburbs are about 60 percent of those in New York. Or stores in the county where Los Angeles is located charge 10 percent more than those in the surrounding counties for boys clothing, while medical services are 45 percent more in the surrounding coun-ties than in Los Angeles county. Many of these differences are difficult to explain and the data set comes with a disclaimer: The calculations were made for an experimental program and since no standard errors were calculated, we cannot definitely say if any such differences are statistically significant.

Since prices of all commodity groups are rising, it is necessary to standard-ize for these trends. The basic statistic used here is the unweighted coefficient of variation of prices (CV, the standard deviation divided by the mean) in five large urban areas. I test whether this statistic has increased or decreased over time.[7] To avoid making seasonal corrections, for each year I average the monthly statistics. The statistical test is whether the *CV* series increased or decreased over time.

An interesting problem in interpreting the results arises from the nature of shocks to the system. In looking at graphs of the various series of *CV*s over time, most appear to have an evident trend. It is also clear that the calculated

---

7. In the statistical analysis I have assumed that the distribution of the coefficients of variation is such that standard tests of statistical significance can be employed (for instance, the *t* test in the regression equations). Since the general interpretations of the results are not greatly differ-ent if other significance levels are used, the errors introduced on this account should be small.

It is also necessary to consider what bias my statistical methods might impart to the results. The data used in this study are average prices from many different outlets for product aggre-gates, each composed of relatively substitutable products. It is difficult to see any major impact such aggregation should have on the trend of the spatial variation. Other data problems also arise, but they do not seem fatal.

More intractable is the problem arising from the weighting of the aggregates. The average prices for each aggregate are calculated for a one-year period in the late 1980s according to the Consumer Price Index weights in use at that time. The time series used in the extrapolations were periodically reweighted and it is impossible to determine the bias imparted by this procedure. This is the reason why, as noted previously, I made all calculations for two time periods.

The results do not appear to be influenced by changes in the measurement of goods and ser-vices included: Except for rental equivalents of owner-occupied housing, major changes have not been made; moreover, any such changes would occur in all cities where the data were col-lected and should have less impact on the *CV* between cities than in the price increases per se.

I discuss several other problems in Appendix Note 7.1 and Pryor (1995).

trends are highly sensitive to the time interval selected for calculating the trend statistics. Moreover, most of the series reveal irregular up-and-down movements lasting for a number of periods that differ from commodity to commodity. This suggests that random shocks are persistent and that some series can be best described as a type of random walk. In other words, in some cases the value of the CV in period t is equal to the value in period $t - 1$ plus a random factor, so that there is no underlying trend, even though the series drifts up or down. Fortunately, some statistical procedures are available to deal with the problem. I have calculated regressions with the CVs as the dependent variable and lagged values of the CVs plus time as the independent variables to permit use of a Dickey-Fuller test determine whether a random walk occurred. This calculation also allows us to separate the impact of random shocks causing random drift to the series from deterministic trends; I designate these as the "corrected trend values."

The results

The following discussion summarizes the statistical results in a qualitative fashion. Table A.18 in Statistical Note 7.1 reports in detail the actual results.

Average spatial variation: For the most part, relative levels of price dispersions among various goods and services accord with expectations. For instance, clothing and household furniture, which are much more heterogeneous than foods, have a greater price variations between them. Given the quite different supply and demand conditions for housing in different cities, the price variations over space are also high. All services show considerable spatial price variation: in some cases because they cannot be easily arbitraged (for instance, medical and entertain ment services), in other cases because of the influence of government taxes or price setting regulations (for instance, piped gas and electricity).

Presence of a random walk:[8] For the longer series from 1950 up to 1993, we can be relatively sure of the presence of a random walk in only two out of the eleven series. For most of the others series, however, the results suggested that

8. Before turning to the calculations testing for the presence of a random walk and/or persistent shocks that might underlie such results, it is worthwhile to consider what economic factors might underlie such behavior of the coefficient of variation of prices across space. I ran a series of regressions for each series to test if price divergences were related to business cycle conditions, changes in real per capita income, changes in the Consumer Price Index, and changes in the price of the commodity or service under consideration. In a number of cases such correlations were found, but they were not consistent with regard to sign from commodity to commodity. Although a number of economists have argued that in inflationary situations, price changes have less informational value than in periods of price stability, I found no systematic evidence that spatial dispersion of prices was related to inflation.

Table 7.1. *Measurements of retail price behavior*

Good or service	First year of series	"Corrected" average annual change of coefficients of variation	
		First year to 1993	1976 to 1993
Alcoholic beverages	1976	—	None
Cereal and bakery products	1950	None	Significant +
Dairy products	1950	None	Significant −
Fruits and vegetables	1950	None	None
Meat, poultry, fish, eggs	1976	—	None
Canned and prepared foods, baby foods, snacks, and other foods	1976	—	None
Men and boys clothing	1950	Significant +	None
Women and girls clothing	1950	None	None
Footwear	1950	None	None
Motor fuels	1978	—	None
Private transportation	1950	None	Significant −
Piped natural gas and electricity	1950	None	None
House furnishings & operations	1976	—	Significant +
Housing rents	1957	Significant +	None
Shelter (rents & rental equivalent)	1953	None	None
Entertainment (e.g., books, movies) and so forth)	1976	—	Significant +
Medical services	1967	None	Significant +

Notes: A dash indicates no data are available. "Significant" refers to statistical significance with a .95 level of confidence; otherwise, no trend is reported. + indicates a divergence of the prices over space (an increasing coefficient of variation); − indicates a convergence of price over space (a decreasing coefficient of variation).

The series most appropriate for making tests of price convergence are: cereal and bakery products; meat, poultry, fish, and eggs; canned and prepared foods; men and boys clothing; women and girls clothing; footwear; and house furnishings and operations.

Motor fuels are one part of the private transportation series; housing rents is one part of the shelter series.

Data sources and a full presentation of the calculated coefficients on which this table is based are presented r in Appendix Note 7.1.

shocks to the system persist for many years. These signify that competitive forces and arbitrage mechanisms on the retail level take a number of years to have an impact. For the shorter series from 1976 or beyond to 1993, the statistical tests also reveal the presence of random walks in two cases.

Trends in spatial variation of prices: In calculating simple trends of the longer series of *CV,* four of the eleven series show a statistically significant divergence of prices over space, while five show a statistically significant convergence (and the remaining two show no significant trend). Focusing on the five series where such a test is most significant, two show a significant divergence and three show significant convergence. For the shorter time series, the results are not much different. An obvious problem arises because, in comparing the calculated trend values for the two time periods, many are quite different. This shows that the trend value often depends upon the choice of the end points, so that we must take into consideration the irregular cyclical movements mentioned previously.

Data on the "corrected trend values " are presented in Table 7.1 and represent the key results. For the longer series, only two of the eleven series show a statistically significant trend, and in both cases price divergence over the sample of five cities is occurring. For the 1976 to 1993 period, four series show a statistically significant divergence, two show a statistically significant convergence, and the remaining eleven reveal no statistically significant trend toward convergence or divergence. Confining the comparisons to just the most appropriate goods (the "true test"), similarly mixed results are obtained.

I should add that the trends in price convergence or divergence revealed are often not intuitively clear. Although it seems possible that prices of services might diverge, as they appear to do, plausible reasons do not come readily to mind for explaining why average prices of cereals and bakery products diverge between the five cities.[9]

A conclusion

The strongest message of these statistical experiments is that for most products, variations of prices across space reveal no distinct trend in the post–World War II period. This seems to have occurred because two offsetting forces are at war. On the one hand the declining transportation costs are acting to decrease spatial variations of prices. On the other hand, the increasing complexity of markets, especially arising from the increasing heterogeneity of goods, act to widen price differences across space. This is because such product heterogeneity reduces the possibilities of profitable arbitrage, and because shopper incentives to search are reduced by the rising opportunity costs of shopping time. In general, the two sets of forces have canceled each other out, although for individual commodities one set of forces may be stronger than the other.

Changes in the degree of market competition

The widening of the markets occurring in the process of the internationalization of the economy represents an important increase in structural complexity

9. Although milk prices, which are governmentally controlled in a number of states, might differ, their downstream impact on total dairy products should be small. For the large cities constituting the sample, such aspects as private labels or local monopolies should not play a role for either dairy products or bakery products.

Table 7.2. *Weighted concentration ratios, 1958 and 1982*

| | Domestic concentration ratios | | | |
| | Largest four firms | | Largest eight firms | |
	1958	1982	1958	1982
Manufacturing sector (weighted)	36.2	35.8	48.2	47.6
	Trade adjusted concentration ratios			
	Largest four firms		Largest eight firms	
Manufacturing sector (weighted)	35.7	32.6	47.4	43.5

Note: The calculations by two-digit industries are found in Table A.19 in Appendix Note 7.2, along with a brief description of sources and methods of the calculation.

because the information requirements for carrying out business increase. In the final chapter I argue that such internationalization should be considered as one of the four most important trends influencing future changes in the economic system. The purpose of this discussion is to explore an important impact of this increasing foreign trade in the economy, namely a rise in the degree of competition in domestic markets in the United States. I focus only on the manufacturing sector, where relevant data are available.

The standard measure used in discussing the degree of competitiveness is the concentration ratio, the share of domestic production (or shipments) accounted for by the four or eight largest producers. Although such an approach truncates the size distribution of market shares, it allows us to take advantage of data extending back several decades. Usually, industries are defined at a four-digit level in the standard industrial classification, which means that we are dealing with about 400 separate industries. The weighted averages for the manufacturing sector as a whole are presented in Table 7.2.

The trends on domestic production-concentration ratios can be quickly summarized. Weighted averages of conventional concentration ratios (hereafter designated as domestic production concentration ratios or DP-CRs) increased slightly between 1954 and 1958 (these calculations are not presented in the table). However, between 1958 and 1982, as shown in the table, these weighted concentration ratios declined about .4 (1.1 percent) on a four-firm level and .6 (1.2 percent) on an eight-firm level.[10] To jump ahead of the argument for a

10. To calculate the weighted average of 1958 using the 1982 SIC, I rearranged the industrial classes and, whenever a four-digit concentration ratio for 1958 was missing, assumed that it changed at the same rate as other concentration ratios in the three-digit category containing it. If the value-added weights of the respective years are used, the weighted ratios also decline between 1958 and 1982, but the change is slightly smaller.

moment, if these DP-CRs are recalculated to take imports into account (these are henceforth designated as trade-adjusted-concentration ratios, or TA-CRs), the weighted averages fell about 3.1 (8.7 percent) on a four-firm basis and 3.9 (8.2 percent) on an eight-firm basis between 1958 and 1982. These differences in percentage changes between the DP-CRs and the TA-CRs are considerable.

To develop a measure of competition that takes imports into account, it is useful to consider briefly some problems with the DP-CRs. Measures of competition, not just DP-CRs but other statistics using data of domestic production such as Herfindahl-Hirschman indices, have several important upward biases: First, the largest firms are generally the largest exporters so that, for instance, although the top four firms may account for 60 percent of total shipments, they may only account for 40 percent of domestic goods reaching buyers at home. Second, these domestic concentration ratios exclude the competitive effect of imports so that although only one firm in the United States may make a particular product, it may face considerable competition from imports and cannot act as a monopoly. These biases have often been discussed and some governments have published concentration ratios taking foreign trade competition into account;[11] unfortunately, the U.S. government does not number among them.

I estimate the TA-CRs for each individual commodity by multiplying the DP-CR by the ratio of the share of domestic shipments to the total goods potentially available to the consumer (domestic shipments plus imports). For this purpose I employ trade data classified at the same four-digit group as the production data. Several well-known problems arise when such a seemingly simple procedure is employed, none of which seem fatal to the estimates.[12]

11. For instance, Sweden (1968). A more extensive discussion of trade-adjusted-concentration ratios is found in Pryor (1994a).
12. First, this type of calculation understates the degree of monopoly facing the consumer because some of the top four firms in a particular industry may import similar goods produced either by their own subsidiaries abroad or by foreign manufacturers under their license, selling the goods under their own label in the United States. As a result, these imports would not be counted as a domestic "shipment" in the available statistics, a phenomenon occurring, for example, in the automobile and electronic equipment industries. This type of foreign sourcing by domestic firms can be included in the calculation; but only the U.S. Census Bureau, which has access to the relevant trade data, could carry out such a calculation. As a result, this bias can not be taken into account. I do not believe, however, that such a bias would greatly distort the results reported here except for a handful of industries.

Second, it is possible that a particular importer is one of the top four suppliers of a commodity. In these rare cases, neither the DP-CRs nor the TA-CRs record such a phenomenon.

Third, the imports are measured at their customs value, that is, excluding transportation, insurance, and tariffs (Abowd, 1991, p. 415); and this introduces some statistical noise into the calculations. This also probably makes relatively little difference.

Finally, this procedure does not take exports into account and the upward bias to both sets of concentration ratios that result.

The relationship between an increase in imports and the trade-adjusted-concentration ratios is not as simple as it might appear at first glance. For instance, in 1958 the TA-CRs for four-digit industries were 1.4 percent lower than the DP-CRs, while in 1982 they were 8.9 percent lower, a change of 7.6 percentage points. In the same period the ratio of merchandise imports to production of goods increased from 5.6 percent to 18.9 percent, a change of 13.3 percentage points. Of course, if domestic concentration changes in response to imports, there is no need for changes in the ratio of imports to domestic production to parallel exactly the changes in TA-CRs. But, as I demonstrate at considerable length elsewhere, a more subtle factor, namely variations in the importance of changes in both exports and imports of the same goods, also play a role.[13]

Although it is not relevant for the immediate purposes of this exposition, the causes of these changes in TA-CRs between 1958 and 1982 are relatively easy to explain.[14] In brief, about 50 percent of the change of the individual concentration rates can be explained by nine factors: the initial concentration ratio, changes in the size of the market, changes in productivity, three variables reflecting changes in the barriers to entry, and three artificial variables reflecting short-term trade adjustment conditions.

One last but crucial factor must be introduced, since this argument from microeconomic factors alone does not take into account the types of mergers being carried out both inside and outside the United States. As I show in the previous chapter, the merger boom up to 1980 in the United States had little effect on aggregate concentration, because of the divestitures that simultaneously took place. The data in Table 7.2 show that such mergers have not led to a decline in competition in individual markets, in large measure because most domestic mergers were conglomerate or vertical, rather than horizontal, which would raise antitrust issues. In sum, the increasing structural complexity arising from internationalization of the economy has lead to markedly greater competition on domestic markets, at least up to the early 1990s. The impact of enterprise mergers abroad on competition in U.S. domestic markets is discussed in the conclusions to the chapter.

Market volatility

In previous chapters I examine various situations to test the proposition that increasing structural complexity leads to greater volatility or instability; in most cases, the proposition does not seem to describe current trends. Nevertheless, a total rejection of the proposition is premature because, under certain conditions, such structural complexity can lead to a rise in market

13. Pryor (1994a)
14. Ibid.

volatility, either of prices, quantities, or both. As I argue later, these conditions seem to occur, in part, in the world market for basic materials.

In the following discussion I show that volatility in basic material prices has markedly increased from 1950 through 1990, but that volatility of production has not greatly changed. The increasing volatility of foreign exchange rates underlies such price behavior; a number of factors discussed here seem to underlie such quantity behavior. Since production of basic commodities does not quickly respond to short-term changes in demand, the brunt of adjustment to equate supply and demand lies more heavily on price changes.

The behavior of raw material markets and the special role of exchange rates

A basic commodity is generally a homogeneous product featuring a world-wide market with roughly similar dollar prices throughout the world. These markets are particularly suited for examining price volatility because, unlike industrial commodities, the available price data reflect actual transaction prices and, moreover, the data are not contaminated by changes in quality. Other things being equal, changes in the volatility of prices and quantities should reflect either basic changes in the organization of their markets, for instance, the introduction of international commodity cartels or changes in structural complexity.

The data used to explore price volatility are summary indices derived from annual international price series of more than fifty basic commodities covering raw materials, fuels, and foodstuffs, as well as animal, forest, and fishery products. The data used in exploring quantity volatility are summary indices derived from worldwide production data for a somewhat smaller set of products.

What factors would lead us to believe that volatility of international prices or of production of basic materials has changed? It is generally argued that price volatility for such commodities should be decreasing because of the increase in market size, the development of forward markets, and the decline in macroeconomic volatility.[15] I believe that the changing behavior of exchange rates has the most important influence on the changing volatility of prices and production of basic materials. Several theoretical studies, most notably an essay by Rudiger Dornbusch, argue that fluctuations of exchange rates induce fluctuations in prices of homogeneous commodities, at least on a short-term basis. This seems intuitively reasonable and the proof is relatively simple.[16] And, as shown in Chapter 5, exchange rate volatility has increased over time. This phenomenon is due, most likely, to the introduction of a float-

15. The arguments about these matters are spelled out in greater detail in Appendix Note 7.1.
16. Dornbusch's argument (1985) is elegant and is summarized in Appendix Note 7.3.

Table 7.3. *Annual volatility of dollar exchange rates*

	Average percentage deviations from a five-year moving average					
	1950–69 Nominal E.R.	1970–9 Nominal E.R.	1980–9 Nominal E.R.	1950–69 Real E.R.	1970–9 Real E.R.	1980–9 Real E.R.
USA (weighted)	.7	2.2	18.3	2.7	2.1	6.6
USA (weighted excluding Mexico)	.6	2.2	4.1	2.9	2.1	4.6

Notes: For each year the exchange rates are annual averages. The nominal exchange rates are deflated by GDP price deflators to estimate the real exchange rate. The measurement of volatility is somewhat different from that employed in Table 5.3 but is, I believe, more suited for the current price data.

Data for the fifteen nations included in the index are presented in Appendix Note 7.3, Table A.20. Because Mexico has a relatively high weight in the index, and shows extremely high currency fluctuations, the index is calculated both with and without that nation.

ing exchange rate system in the early 1970s and the liberalization of capital flows in the late 1980s and 1990s.

The increasing volatility of exchange rate deserves some consideration. Sometimes the argument is raised that although floating exchange rates may exhibit considerable volatility on a daily, weekly, or even monthly basis, such an exchange rate system should stabilize exchange rates in the longer term.[17] According to this approach, the month-to-month data presented in Chapter 5 are irrelevant.

Table 7.3 presents calculations of an annual volatility index summarizing the bilateral exchange rate volatility of the currencies of fifteen large trading partners with the U.S. dollar. The results show clearly that differences in trends between short-term and longer-term exchange relations are small. More specifically, annual volatility of exchange rates increased over the forty-year period both in current and constant dollar terms, just as the volatility in the monthly and quarterly data increased over the same period as well (see Table 5.3). For most individual bilateral exchange rates with the dollar, the same is also true.

The causes of the increase in volatility of the annual average exchange rates with the dollar include two critical institutional changes, namely the introduction of floating exchange rates in the early 1970s and the increased liberalization of international capital flows in the late 1980s. In addition, the economic policies pursued by the Reagan administration, which allowed the dollar to

17. This argument is made, for instance, by Bakrone-Adesi and Yeung (1990), who provide certain supporting empirical materials.

soar during the 1980s and then to decline almost as sharply may have also played a causal role. Some more technical reasons explaining greater annual volatility can also be offered. For instance, an increasingly complicated lag structure of markets that causes greater overshooting or undershooting of the equilibrium might have also had some influence in these results, although it is difficult to be very certain about these matters.

Volatility of annual prices of basic materials

According to a well-known proposition of microeconomic theory, prices become more stable as markets expand in scope and size, other things being equal, for three reasons: First, particular external shocks on the supply side (such as floods or strikes) or on the demand side (such as changes in tastes or income) become less important since they are diffused over a broader market area; furthermore, they may be offset by shocks in the opposite direction in other parts of the market. Second, information networks about prices becomes more developed in larger markets so that producers can make their decisions more carefully on the basis of more accurate information. Third, forward markets develop, which allow the risk to be shifted from producers to professional risk takers and which permit, under normal conditions, stabilizing speculation to take place.[18]

The proposition about market stability can also be examined from another perspective. If markets are narrowed, price volatility should increase. Theoretical evidence indicates that certain types of trade barriers such as quotas or the European Community's variable levy on agricultural goods narrow markets and increase price volatility in the rest of the world.[19]

These considerations lead to the conclusion that because the role of international trade has become increasingly important over the last four decades and because markets in various nations have become increasingly integrated, price volatility should be decreasing, other things held equal. This proposition is, of course, just the opposite of the argument I raised before, namely that increasing volatility of exchange rates should lead to greater volatility of prices of basic materials as well. Only a look at the relevant statistics can resolve the conflict.

The data in Table 7.4 show that basic material prices were more volatile on a year-to-year basis at the end of the period than at the beginning, measured either in current or deflated prices.[20] Thus, the exchange rate linkage is the

18. Sarris (1984).
19. A model with simulation results is presented by Pryor (1981).
20. The deflation procedure implicitly assumes that the main direction of causation is from volatility of ex change rates to price volatility to quantity volatility. If this were not the case, then the deflator would be inappropriate because it would confound several different effects.

Table 7.4. *Annual price volatility of basic commodities*

	Number of products	Average percentage deviation of prices from a five-year moving average							
		1950 through 1954	1955 through 1959	1960 through 1964	1965 through 1969	1970 through 1974	1975 through 1979	1980 through 1984	1985 through 1989
Current prices									
All basic commodities	55	9.8	7.5	7.0	7.9	19.3	14.4	13.1	13.9
All basic commodities except fishery products	48	9.7	7.4	7.0	7.8	19.4	14.5	13.2	14.0
Deflated prices									
All basic commodities	55	9.6	7.4	7.1	7.7	18.8	14.1	13.1	13.8
All basic commodities except fishery products	48	9.5	7.4	7.0	7.7	18.9	14.1	13.2	13.9

Notes: For each year the prices are annual averages. The constant prices are current prices deflated by GDP deflators. Appendix Note 7.3 includes a discussion of sources and methods, as well as price volatility data by product group.

most appropriate way to look at the problem. Any hope for increasing commodity price stability on a year-to-year basis has not been realized, at least in the period from 1950 through 1989. After the introduction of a general system of floating exchange rates in the early 1970s and the oil shock of 1973, price volatility of basic commodities increased considerably in the following years. In the 1980s the degree of volatility decreased little from their level in the 1970s and, indeed, was slightly greater in the second half of the decade than the first.

The differential price volatility of the various product groups does not correspond to intuitive expectations: price volatility was, on the average, highest for crops and, in decreasing order, tree and forest products, animal products, fuels, raw materials, and fishery products. This ordering seems unrelated to any type of production lags that might lead to a cobweb phenomenon. Within each product group, it should be added, the differences in average annual price variations are considerable.

Volatility of annual production of basic materials

If prices are becoming more volatile and if production responds to these changes in prices, then production should also become more volatile as well.

Table 7.5. *Annual production volatility of basic commodities and of several aggregate series*

	Average percentage deviation of prices from a five-year moving average							
	Number of products	1950 through 1954	1955 through 1959	1960 through 1964	1965 through 1969	1970 through 1974	1975 through 1979	1980 through 1984	1985 through 1989
All commodities except fishery products	46	n.a.	n.a.	3.6	3.0	2.6	3.2	3.3	3.7
U.S. GDP volume	—	2.1	1.4	.8	1.0	1.9	1.9	1.8	.8
Combined GDP volume, 31 nations	—	.9	1.1	1.2	.8	1.2	1.1	1.2	.6

Notes: The individual product series are weighted by the same weights as the price series. Appendix Note 7.3 includes a discussion of sources and methods, as well as production volatility data by product group.

Exploring such a possibility requires series of annual production for the world as a whole for various basic commodities. Unfortunately, such data are less readily available for the entire forty-year period than the price data and, as a result, the sample is somewhat smaller.

The volatility statistics presented in Table 7.5 are calculated in the same manner as in Tables 7.3 and 7.4. Whenever possible, the same commodities are used in the quantity sample as in the price sample. In some cases, however, a related commodity (for instance, copper ore, rather than copper bars) had to be used because completely comparable data were lacking. For comparison I also include a similar calculation of annual fluctuations for the U.S. GDP as well as the combined GDP for thirty-one nations.

In general, annual volatility of total production is considerably lower than price volatility. And, as one might suspect, annual fluctuations of the aggregate GDP of either the United States or of thirty-one nations are even lower. Of greatest importance, production volatility does not reveal any important trend over the four-decade period and the pattern of changes is quite different from that of prices. For instance, production volatility was lower in the 1970s when price volatility increased.

Because of different price elasticities of demand and supply, we should not expect relative changes in production and price volatility to be correlated. Crop products, which show the greatest price volatility over the forty-year period, have only an average production volatility over the thirty-year period. By way of contrast, tree and forest production, which show the greatest production volatility, reveal only an average price volatility.

Two factors appear important in understanding why trends in production volatility have not paralleled those of price volatility:

First, in most types of raw materials the production lags are long, the marginal costs of significantly changing the level of production are often high, so that the risks of responding to short-term price increases are great, especially if aggregate production overshoots the rise in demand so that prices would then fall and losses would be incurred.

Second, given the long-run nature of production of raw materials, it is likely that when price volatility increased, producers place less weight on recent price changes since these prices contain less useful information than price trends over the past. Rather, it would make better sense to base their production decisions on a weighted average that considers a longer history of prices. So the increased volatility of prices could have led to a situation where raw material producers were considerably less sensitive to any short-term price changes in making their production decisions. It is also possible that changes in the relative importance of long-term supply contracts, where payment is based on current market prices, also played a role. I could not find, however, any relevant statistics on this matter.

What all this means is that quantity volatility is much smaller than price volatility and, moreover, does not respond to increases in foreign exchange volatility. As a result, the adjustment process in the international markets for basic materials falls primarily on prices, rather than on quantities.

Implications for volatility in retail markets

The increased volatility of basic material prices has several serious implications, not just to producers of these materials, but also to users of these basic materials for further processing.[21] Although most of these implications must be left for others to analyze, it is useful to explore briefly how such volatility could influence retail prices.

Under certain conditions, for instance, the increased volatility of basic material prices could pass through and cause increased price volatility of finished goods. Of course, many factors can intervene to dampen such price influences. In agriculture, for instance, government price setting programs can nullify such an effect. In industries with a high value added, the influence of basic material prices is small. For other products, there are considerable costs to constantly changing the price (so-called *menu cost*). In many indus-

---

21. Given the ready availability of annual data on raw material production, prices, and trade (e.g., Manthy, 1978), it is surprising that such information has not received more analysis. Much of the research that has been carried out has focused on such questions as "excess" volatility; relation of spot and futures market price behavior; the impact of speculation; or, more recently, the greater weekly volatility of commodity prices than exchange rates (Bui and Pippenger, 1990).

tries, firms meet changes in demand, not by changing the price, but by changing the delivery time.

But most important, as Nhoung Bui and John Pippenger have argued in their study of basic material prices, retail prices tend to be sticky because these markets are not as "well organized" as basic materials markets.[22] In the latter markets, information costs are lower, arbitrage is frequent, price changes are less costly, the opportunities for sellers or buyers to negotiate on nonprice considerations are less, and the markets are more competitive. In terms of the information requirements and intricacy of interactions, the basic materials markets are less structurally complex.

Volatility on the retail level can be easily analyzed. Taking consumer price series for goods at a four-digit level from 1950 through 1989, I constructed price volatility series in the same manner as that used for the raw material prices.[23] As we would expect, the annual volatility of the series that included fifty-six different categories of consumer goods showed slightly more than twice the annual price volatility as the series with fifteen different categories of consumer services. Most importantly, neither series showed any increase in volatility over the period.

One last issue deserves mention, although no resolution can be attempted. On the international level, these volatility calculations suggest that prices play a crucial role in allocation. On the domestic level, however, some specialists in industrial organization, such as Dennis W. Carlton, argue that on an interfirm level, price rigidity for long periods is very common, even for very homogeneous products.[24] Among other things, this means that nonprice rationing methods such as waiting lines play a more important role in the functioning of domestic markets than commonly believed.

Conclusions and implications for the future

The structural complexity of markets is a function of a number of factors including the level of technology, domestic laws and international agreements, the type of product and the degree of competition. This chapter focuses on three types of impacts of the increasing structural complexity of markets.

The increase in structural complexity, viewed in terms of the heterogeneity of goods, has acted to offset the price convergence within the domestic market that one would expect through the operation of the law of one price. The degree of retail price dispersion between U.S. cities did not greatly change in the last forty years, even though the declining costs of transportation should have led, according to the law of one price, to price convergence. The increas-

22. Bui and Pippenger (1990).
23. The data were supplied on computer disks by the Bureau of Labor Statistics.
24. Carlton (1986, 1989).

ing heterogeneity of goods makes arbitrage of goods from one city to another more costly so that such a price convergence did not occur.

Market innovations can lower search costs, and the possibility of shopping by computer or interactive TV screen is becoming increasingly easy. If these innovations, now in their infancy, diffuse rapidly, then it is possible for the law of one price to gain strength over the complexity factors operating in the opposite direction. In short, the law of one price may have relevance, not just for economic historians but for futurists as well.

The fall in trade barriers and costs of transportation has widened the market by increasing foreign trade, and in this way structural complexity has increased because information requirements are higher. This greater foreign trade, in turn, has increased competitiveness on domestic markets. The data on concentration ratios show a slight increase in competitiveness when the domestic economy is examined in isolation and a considerably greater increase when imports are taken into account.

The increased competition may serve to revitalize American capitalism. I argue in the final chapter that the "spirit" of U.S. capitalism is becoming enervated, but this development in international trade could well serve as a counteracting force, at least if American managers win the fight for their competitive existence. It is also possible, however, that the effect will level off. I argue at length in the next chapter that it does not seem likely the ratio of trade to GDP will increase very much in the next few decades in the United States. Moreover, from a detailed regression analysis of the causes underlying the change in concentration ratios, it also appears that the factors most influential in the change in concentration ratios between 1958 and 1982 will not be so important in the future.[25] If these arguments are correct, then the divergence between the behavior of trade-adjusted and domestic production-concentration ratios should narrow, the increase in competition occurring from trade should decelerate, and the impetus toward a revitalization of American capitalism will slacken.

Another factor that may act to decrease competition also deserves consideration. As I point out, the merger boom up to 1980 had little visible effect either on aggregate concentration or on competition in individual markets. This occurred largely because most of these mergers were conglomerate or vertical, rather than horizontal. But two opposite scenarios for the future of competition can be imagined.

The pessimistic scenario rests on the fact that the merger boom between large foreign producers and the growing economic strength of the multinational enterprises may not prove so benign in the future. This is because these mergers are primarily horizontal, rather than conglomerate, vertical, or outside

25. Pryor (1994a).

the manufacturing sector. If such international horizontal mergers continue, then actual industrial concentration may increase while the domestic production or trade-adjusted-concentration ratios, as I have calculated them, will become increasingly irrelevant since neither takes into account the linkages between domestic production and the production of foreign subsidiaries. For example, let us assume away foreign transplants in the United States and posit a situation where the big three U.S. auto makers are producing 50 percent of domestic consumption, so that the DP-CR is 100 and the TA-CR is 50. If, however, one fifth of the imports are from foreign factories of the big three, then the TA-CR is really 60, and if imports of foreign automobile into the United States are increasingly dominated by three foreign manufacturers, then six manufacturers effectively control the entire U.S. market. We can easily conjure other situations where increasing foreign trade can lead to less competition on domestic markets, rather than more. In such cases, however, this scenario implies that the world concentration ratios are much higher than concentration ratios on the domestic market and that imports from abroad displace domestic producers.

The optimistic scenario assumes that competition from the newly industrialized nations will more than offset any decrease of competition among the mature industrialized nations. Some evidence for this scenario is shown in Table 6.1. Aggregate concentration for the entire capitalist world market decreased between 1972 and 1982, driven by the rapid rise in industrial employment in the developing nations. If this trend continues and these nations move into lines of production competing with those from the industrial nations (for instance, cars and electronic equipment from Korea), then increasing world trade will be accompanied by greater competition on a domestic level as well. This trend may well be reinforced with the reintegration of some of the former Marxist nations of East Europe and elsewhere into the world capitalist system. The increased competition on a domestic level is likely to elicit increasingly loud calls for trade protection by domestic industries that are unable or unwilling to meet this threat.

Since it is unclear which of these scenarios is more likely, it hardly seems appropriate for the U.S. government to relax its antitrust measures and rely on the forces of international trade to increase industrial competition. Indeed, which of these two scenarios is occurring can only be determined by calculating concentration ratios that take not just the level of our imports into account (as I have done), but the origins of these imports as well.

An increase in structural complexity arising from a growing internationalization of the economy has several other important impacts. As noted in Chapter 5, exchange rates are one of the few series exhibiting a rising level of monthly volatility. The annual data presented in this chapter provide evidence that such increased volatility occurred in the longer-term as well. Some simple theoretical considerations lead to the proposition that price volatility of internationally traded basic commodities should increase, a proposition also receiving empirical support in this chapter.

If this explanation is correct, then what can we say about the future? If the liberalization of international trade and capital markets have caused this increase in exchange rate volatility, then the end of the increasing volatility is in sight since complete liberalization does not have far to go. But the assumption underlying this prediction is controversial. For instance, if the international trading system breaks into several large trading blocs, then we have to ask about what happens to the stability of exchange rates between these blocs. This, in turn, requires some determination about whether the political element in these exchange rates will increase or decrease.

An exchange rate system without political interference is utopian, of course. So the question really comes down to the different forms and extent of political interference with the exchange rate in single countries and trading blocs with a single currency. A judgment about this matter is impossible to make, at least until we have information about the governance of these future trading blocs. At the time of writing, the future of the Maastrich treaty is cloudy, and the probability of the emergence of a European trading bloc with a single currency within the next decade is low, but not zero.

In this chapter I define three impacts of greater structural complexity on the operation of markets in a narrow fashion, primarily because the impact on larger issues is difficult to analyze. If the increase in structural complexity caused by a rising internationalization of the economy continues, American producers have a strong incentive to revitalize their organizations. As indicated, the persistence of this trend toward increasing competition remains in doubt. I do not believe that economic growth will be affected by the other two impacts of increased structural complexity, namely the rising volatility of basic material prices or the importance of the offset to the law of one price. The increasing volatility of basic material prices is not being transmitted upward to U.S. final consumers and is not destabilizing the economy. As a result, this effect is inconvenient, but not worrisome. The internationalization of the economy that underlies several of these microeffects does have some much more important effects, particularly about international competitiveness of particular industrial branches. But this is the topic of the next chapter.

CHAPTER 8

The foreign trade sector

Internationalization of the economy is a general concept referring not just to the foreign trade sector and the openness of the economy, but also to a broader set of issues such as world market integration (goods, services, labor, capital), the economic vulnerability to foreign nations (sometimes called *mutual dependence*), and the sensitivity to economic events and policies abroad (sometimes called *economic interdependence*). Such internationalization leads to increasing structural complexity in many dimensions. Markets become more extensive and heterogeneous; interactions between different parts of the economic system become more elaborate; and the direct and indirect information requirements of the economic system increase. The increased structural complexity has a strong influence on enterprises, whether they are formally multinational or domestic. It also has an important impact on governments since national economic policies must now be more closely coordinated with those of foreign nations if they are to be effective.

At several points in this study I draw attention to particular aspects of internationalization, for instance, increased immigration (Chapter 2), foreign ownership (Chapter 5), and the impact of foreign trade on domestic competition (Chapter 7). I spotlight the impact of internationalization on the weakening of the effectiveness of domestic monetary and fiscal policy in the next chapter and discuss still other aspects in the final chapter. In Appendix Note 8.1 I relate the various concepts of internationalization with each other and briefly discuss some empirical work concerning the impact of internationalization on the U.S. economy. More extended treatments of the topic can be found in both the technical and popular literature.[1] Internationalization is so important and so pervasive that in the final chapter I choose to treat it separately as one of the four major trends influencing the future of the economic system, although in many respects it overlaps with the trend of increasing structural complexity.

This chapter focuses on foreign trade, one particular aspect of internationalization; and it deals with three different topics related to the structural com-

---

1. For instance, in 1994 and 1995, the Brookings Institution published a twenty-one-volume set of monographs examining various problems of internationalization and integrating the world economy. McRae (1994) discusses many interesting aspects of the process of internationalization and its impact on the functioning of the economy in the coming decades on a more popular level.

plexity of the economy: the growing importance of trade, the changing skill content of trade, and sources of U.S. trade competitiveness.

Of course, it is, well known that the relative share of foreign trade in the GDP has increased, especially during the 1970s. But determining whether this trend is expected to continue in the future proves a difficult question to answer. My analysis suggests that the rapid growth in the share of foreign trade in the domestic economy will probably be slower in the coming decades.

The rising skill content of U.S. trade relates to the informational requirements of production. Analysis of this topic provides a link to the discussion in Chapter 3 of the changing skill level of the U.S. labor force in general. It also introduces the exploration of the changing competitiveness of particular U.S. exports and imports.

The analysis of the sources of competitiveness of different U.S. industries on the international economy focuses particularly on the technologically advanced industries or those that require highly skilled workers. Such an exercise provides some useful insights into the reciprocal causal relations between trade and the technological level of domestic production. Moreover, it shows the degree to which the nation's production institutions have responded to, and mastered, more advanced technologies.

Changes in the relative share of foreign trade in the GDP

Openness refers to the relative share of foreign trade in the economy, and it is usually measured as a ratio of trade to some indicator of aggregate production. The greater the openness, the broader the markets and the greater the resulting structural complexity of these markets because of the increased direct requirements for information. In the United States, from the mid-nineteenth century to the early 1920s, the export/GNP ratio fluctuated from 5 to 8 percent, with the highest ratio in the 1877–81 period and the lowest in the 1920s.[2] Part A of Table 8.1 presents some indicators of trade openness from 1929 to the present.

The most striking feature, of course, is the increase in openness of the economy from the early 1970s to the mid 1980s; thereafter, the trend tapers off. Some perspective on this trend can be gained from data for the world as a whole, where the trade–GDP ratio rose from 1950 to 1980 and then declined slightly in the next decade.[3] The last four columns in Part A of the table show that in their respective branches of production, trade openness for the production of both goods and services has generally increased over time. This sug-

2. U.S. Department of Commerce, Bureau of the Census, 1975, pp. 231, 883–4. Calculations by Simon Kuznets (1959, p. 102) yield somewhat different results, showing the highest export–GDP ratio to have occurred in the years 1909–18, while the highest import–GDP ratio occurred in the years 1869–78.
3. This generalization is based on data for exports in current prices, GDP in constant prices, and a GDP price deflator from various issues of International Monetary Fund (annual).

Table 8.1. *U.S. trade openness and some underlying factors*

Part A: Aggregate trade ratios

Year	Share of total GDP		Share of total goods production		Share of total service production[a]	
	Total exports	Total imports	Merchandise exports	Merchandise imports	Service exports	Service imports
1929	5.7%	5.4%	9.4%	8.0%	1.7%	3.1%
1939	4.3	3.4	6.7	4.9	1.7	2.0
1950	4.3	4.0	6.3	5.6	2.4	2.8
1958	4.5	4.4	7.1	5.6	2.3	4.2
1963	4.8	4.2	8.0	5.8	2.4	3.4
1967	4.8	4.7	7.8	6.8	2.6	3.5
1972	5.5	6.0	9.2	10.4	3.3	3.2
1977	7.8	9.1	13.7	17.3	3.7	3.1
1982	8.5	9.3	16.1	18.8	3.8	3.1
1987	7.0	11.1	13.9	22.8	4.7	4.1
1990	9.8	10.9	18.0	23.0	5.4	3.6
1993	10.4	11.4	18.2	23.6	4.6	3.0

Part B: An index of intraindustry trade and other key ratios influencing aggregate trade

Ratios

	4 digit IITS					
	For total duties to trade	Only for manufacturing duties trade	Transportation and insurance to total imports	Duty free imports to total imports	Assessed duties to dutiable imports	Assessed duties to to total imports
Year	1	2	3	4	5	6
1929	n.a.	30.7%	n.a.	66.4%	40.1%	13.5%
1939	n.a.	28.4	12.5%	61.4	37.3	14.4
1950	n.a.	28.4	7.2	54.5	13.1	6.0
1958	n.a.	36.1	9.2	41.9	11.1	6.4
1963	n.a.	39.6	8.2	36.8	11.5	7.3
1967	n.a.	44.8	6.9	38.2	12.2	7.5
1972	43.1	45.0	6.7	34.2	8.5	5.7
1977	n.a.	49.2	5.9	29.7	5.3	3.7
1982	40.4	47.7	4.5	31.3	5.2	3.6
1987	n.a.	n.a.	4.4	32.9	5.2	3.5
1990	n.a.	n.a.	n.a.	n.a.	n.a.	3.3

[a]Service exports and imports exclude factor payments. IITS = intraindustry trade statistic (a modified Grubel-Lloyd index defined in footnote 7). The IITS = 1.00 when there is complete intraindustry trade (balanced exports and imports); the IITS = 0 when there no intraindustry trade so that there are only imports or exports). Data for 1929, 1939, and 1950 are estimated by assuming the same ratio of two-digit to four-digit IITS in these years as in 1960.
n.a. = not available.
All data in both parts of the table are in current prices and are the sources are described in Appendix Note 8.5. For the second half of table, imports are general imports measured FOB, port of shipment.

gests that the shifting composition of the GDP toward sectors with less trade openness is partly responsible for the behavior of the aggregate measure of trade oppenness. Moreover, as a share of total exports and imports, the share of services has increased.[4] Another aspect of this increasing openness is that U.S. trade is generally becoming more sensitive to price and income considerations. As I show in Table A.23 in Appendix 8.1, price elasticities of both exports and imports appear to have increased and, moreover, the price elasticity of imports (but not exports) has increased as well.

Although the basic facts about increasing openness (or income elasticities of demand for imports and exports greater than unity) are relatively clear, explaining their causes is not so simple. Before trying to isolate some of these factors, it is useful to heed a warning by Andrew Rose in his empirical study of openness of twelve countries over a thirty-four-year period:[5] "There are few economically sensible and statistically significant results for the larger countries. Thus, existing trade theory does not appear to provide a good explanation for the growth of the trade ratio [trade openness; *FP*]." A generation before, Simon Kuznets argued that changes in the trade–GDP ratio depend not only on changes in comparative advantage but on technological changes, social inventions, policies taken for political purposes, and other factors that may swamp the impact of any economic factors under consideration. With these warnings in mind, let us cautiously examine the most important economic factors to which this increase in openness might be attributed, realizing that the analysis may be incomplete.

Explanatory variables

It is useful to separate the possible economic causal factors into three groups: correlates of income, policy factors, and exhaustion of natural resources. Although other causal variables (such as population increases) have been proposed, they seem less useful for this analysis.[6]

Correlates of income: Three correlates of income are alleged to lead toward an increasing openness of the economy:

4. In Chapter 4 I discuss briefly the impact of the communications revolution on stimulating the trade of services. For instance, Bangalore, India is becoming a major center for computing programming. Both instructions from the home office and the completed programs can be transmitted almost instantaneously.
5. Rose (1991). The later reference is to Kuznets (1959, p. 106).
6. A well-known proposition, shown in many cross-section and time-series regressions of trade–GDP ratios (e.g., Bliss et al., 1962) is that this ratio is inversely proportional to the country's population. Although this may be important for relatively small nations where the domestic market is too small to allow economies of scale to be achieved, it hardly seems relevant to the U.S. economy.

- *Lower natural barriers of trade.* In part, the rising openness seems due to declining relative prices of imports because of the declining transportation and communication costs accompanying economic growth. As Column 3 of Part B of Table 8.1 reveals, transportation costs, which act as a "natural" barrier to trade, have fallen considerably in the post–World War II period. In the last decade, however, this decline seems to have leveled off. Moreover, such costs are now sufficiently low that further declines in transportation costs should have relatively little impact on an increase in openness.
- *Increasing discretionary income.* In part, the rising openness seems due to increasing discretionary income and the desire of consumers to buy more sophisticated and variegated goods. One measure of this phenomenon is the intraindustry trade statistic (IITS). This statistic focuses attention on those categories of trade where the heterogeneous nature of the goods is important and which, as a result, the United States both imports and exports (for instance, goods such as computers or automobiles). As shown in columns 1 and 2 of Part B of Table 8.1, for U.S. manufacturing trade the relative importance of intraindustry trade rose from the 1950s through to the late 1970s; but since then this rise has leveled off. A similar phenomenon occurred in most other countries as well during the same period.[7] The causes for this leveling off of the IITS are not yet fully understood, although certain offsetting factors in the rise of trade such as the increasing importance of just-in-time inventory systems in manufacturing, which make it useful for suppliers to be close-by, may have played some role.
- *Relative prices of tradables and nontradables.* In part the rising openness can be attributed to a shift in the prices of tradable and nontradable goods and services. Accompanying a higher level of per capita income is a relative rise in prices of those goods and services for which, for one reason or another, productivity has increased more slowly than average. These include many different types of personal services and other goods and services not entering foreign trade. This means that the purchases of tradable goods from those industries

7. Two recent studies attempting to explain changes in the intraindustry trade are Scherer (1992) and Globerman and Dean (1990). In a recent note (Pryor, 1992a), I present evidence to challenge the Globerman-Dean interpretation.

  The formula I have used to calculate the IITS (intraindustry trade statistic) is a modification of the standard formula (presented below in formula 2) in order to take into account that aggregate exports and imports may not be balanced, namely: $IITS = 1 - \Sigma \mid (x_i/X) - (m_i/M) \mid$, where x_i and m_i are respectively the exports and imports of commodity i, and X and M are respectively total exports and imports. This modification is not used for the cross-section analysis carried out later in the chapter.

where productivity has increased faster than average are particularly favored over the course of economic growth.[8] This shift in relative prices may account for the relatively slow rise of services as a share of consumption, as noted in Chapter 4.

Policy factors: Although many policy factors influencing the degree of openness can be mentioned, the fall in trade barriers appears the most important.[9] Three imperfect measures are provided in Columns 4, 5, and 6 of Part B of Table 8.1, more specifically, the share of nontaxed goods in imports and the relative importance of tariffs to the total value of imports; they show a decline in the relative importance of this type of barrier. These data do not, of course, reflect the change in nontariff barriers (NTBs) such as quotas, voluntary export restrictions, "buy national" laws, and other restrictions. Unfortunately, for this exercise these NTBs proved too difficult to quantify so as to determine their direction of change.

Given the relatively high unemployment in most Western nations, the political climate does not seem propitious for a dramatic fall in current trade barriers, except perhaps through the mechanism of free trade agreements between small groups of nations. Although the GATT agreement initialed in late 1993 contained some important measures, its impact on overall trade should be small, particularly in the 1990s when the agreement will be implemented. A good deal of attention has been paid to the Canada–U.S. Free Trade Agreement (ratified January 1989) and the North American Free Trade Agreement (NAFTA) which came into effect in January 1994. Since much of the rhetoric urging the adoption of NAFTA foresaw a rapid increase in trade between these nations, several unfortunate facts are worth bearing in mind.

According to the data presented in Appendix Note 8.2, U.S. trade with Mexico and Canada has generally hovered between 20 and 30 percent of total trade for half a century, with no noticeable trends in the post–World War II period. Although some trade frictions arose between the United States and these nations, U.S. trade barriers for goods from these nations were relatively low and this has an important implication. In the late 1980s, the United States produced roughly 80 percent of the agricultural, mining, and manufacturing

---

8. Although Rose's (1991) regressions show a perverse effect of a proxy variable for the relative price of tradable and nontradable goods and services (the ratio of the producer price index to the Consumer Price Index), such an empirical result might be attributable to his specification, where he also included a variable representing total GDP. Since total GDP is a function of per capita GDP and population, the hazards of time-series analysis with collinear variables might have been responsible for these results.

9. The exchange rate regime allegedly has some influence on the openness of the economy, at least in so far as fluctuating rates create risks that can not be hedged, so that trade is discouraged. The actual impact of the floating exchange rate system on the volume of trade is a matter of considerable controversy.

goods in the three country area. If absolutely no trade barriers existed and if domestic consumers bought randomly with no attention paid to the origin of goods, at this time the United States would have imported and exported about 20 percent of its agricultural, mining, and manufactured goods, which in turn amounted to roughly 4.6 percent of the U.S. GDP.[10] This is the "theoretical limit" of U.S. trade with its NAFTA partners. Since the actual U.S. trade with Mexico and Canada amounted to roughly 2.5 percent of the GDP around 1990 and since it seems highly unlikely that its trade with these NAFTA partners would realize anywhere near its theoretical limit, the increase in U.S. trade openness occasioned by NAFTA – or GATT – appears relatively small. The most important result of NAFTA will probably be a change in investment, rather than trade, even though investment flows across national borders induce some increase in trade.

Exhaustion of natural resources: The decline in net exports of natural resources seems to me to be crucially important explanation of the rising degree of openness in the 1970s. Without taking into account particular conditions within the U.S. economy, however, such a factor in itself cannot explain which direction trade openness will change.

The argument is simple. Suppose that a country has a comparative advantage in natural resources that are gradually exhausted so that the nation increasingly becomes a net importer, rather than a net exporter of these basic products. This means that the trade surplus in another category, either agricultural products or manufacturing products, must increase for overall balance in the current accounts to be maintained. Of course, in the short run the imbalance could be financed by foreign loans and direct investment, but such a capital inflow can not last forever. In the United States the trade surplus in agricultural products has been relatively small for some decades and, moreover, the share of such trade in the total trade turnover has been declining. Thus our attention must focus on the balance of manufacturing trade and the magnitude of changes in exports and imports that must occur for the current accounts to come into balance again.

The country would have to move down the ladder of goods and services for which it has a comparative advantage to increase its manufactured exports; and it would have to move up the same latter so that fewer manufactured goods are imported. Several possible responses might occur:

10. This calculation started with an estimate of the 1988 GDP of the three countries in comparable prices (Summers and Heston, 1991). From national accounts data from United Nations (1992), I determined the percentage production of agriculture, mining, and manufacturing in the GDP and, assuming the percentage in comparable prices would be roughly the same, made the calculation reported in the text. The assumption, however, is not strictly correct; but since the purpose of the calculation is to determine orders of magnitude, it seems acceptable.

1. Total manufactured imports might fall so much that less pressure would be placed on the exporter of manufactured goods to find new foreign markets. In this case, openness would decline.
2. The additional manufactured exports might roughly equal the fall in the export of natural resources while, at the same time, the fall in imports of manufactured goods might roughly equal the increased imports in natural resources. In this case, trade openness would remain the same.
3. Manufactured exports might rise more rapidly than manufactured imports would fall, so that when balance is once again achieved, trade openness has increased.

Falling trade barriers abroad, combined with the willingness of foreign exporters of manufactured goods to the United States to lower their prices so as to remain competitive in the hard won foothold they had gained in U.S. markets, suggests that the third possibility occurred in the 1970s.[11] In the 1980s, however, this process of adjustment was interrupted by the rise in the dollar that, in turn, was brought about by the Reagan government's experiments in supply-side economics and the massive governmental deficit that was incurred.

Detailed data on these trends for a half century are presented in Table 8.2. The table shows that raw material imports have been increasing as a share of total merchandise imports in the half century from 1929 to 1980, while raw material exports have remained relatively low, so that the trade balance in raw materials is becoming increasingly negative. Moreover, both raw material imports and the balance of U.S. raw material trade are becoming increasingly larger shares of domestic production. Of the different types of raw materials, the import of crude petroleum is the driving force, especially after the 1960s when the country became a large net importer of this source of energy. This was the crucial structural break in the postwar U.S. trade pattern. As a share of GDP originating in manufacturing, both exports and imports have increased dramatically over the last half century, with the balance of trade remaining roughly the same. This means that trade openness has increased since the expected fall in manufacturing imports has not offset the increase in raw material imports. The data on the composition of exports shows that manufactured exports have increased faster than natural resource exports have decreased. At the same time, the share of manufactured imports has decreased more slowly than the rise in the share of natural resource imports.

These changes in the composition of exports and imports due to exhaustion of natural resources, especially the acceleration after 1970, represent important structural changes in the U.S. economy. Among other things this argument

11. Although commentary on this matter is quite extensive in the business press, analysis in the technical literature is not extensive. One important exception is Krugman (1989).

Table 8.2. *Trends in the commodity structure of trade*

	1929	1939	1950	1960	1972	1982	1991
As percent of GDP originating from corresponding sector							
Raw materials including petroleum, coal products, and primary metals							
Exports	17.9	20.6	6.9	8.4	7.1	9.8	16.4
Imports	−11.4	−9.5	−12.7	−15.0	−23.3	−43.2	−46.4
Trade balance	6.5	11.1	−5.7	−6.7	−16.2	−33.3	−30.0
Agriculture, forestry, fishing							
Exports	16.1	9.2	13.7	22.3	17.6	35.3	23.1
Imports	−8.8	−6.8	−7.9	−10.2	−10.4	−14.2	14.3
Trade balance	7.3	2.3	5.8	12.1	7.2	21.0	8.8
Manufacturing production except petroleum, coal products, and primary metals							
Exports	11.5	8.8	7.9	10.4	14.1	26.4	34.9
Imports	−11.9	−7.0	−7.0	−6.7	−14.4	−24.6	41.1
Trade balance	−.4	1.8	.9	3.7	−.3	1.8	−6.2
Exports as percent of total merchandise exports							
Raw materials	20.0	27.8	13.2	11.8	7.4	10.1	7.3
Agriculture, forestry, fishing	30.6	20.4	28.5	23.5	13.9	13.4	6.3
Manufacturing excluding raw materials	49.4	51.8	58.3	64.7	78.7	76.4	82.0
Imports as percent of total merchandise imports							
Raw materials	15.7	18.6	26.0	28.9	21.5	36.7	16.3
Agriculture, forestry, fishing	20.7	22.0	17.7	14.6	7.3	4.5	3.1
Manufacturing excluding raw materials	63.6	59.4	56.2	56.5	71.2	58.9	76.8

Notes: Imports are "general imports" valued at FOB and are assigned a negative sign. GDPs originating for all sectors before 1950 were estimated from data on national income originating from these sectors. Additional estimates were made for GDP originating from primary metals sector before 1950.
Sources are discussed in Appendix Note 8.5.

implies that mechanical extrapolations based on calculated elasticities provide a questionable basis for quantitative forecasting.

It is worthwhile to note that this exhaustion of natural resources increases the vulnerability of the U.S. economy to private and governmental actions of foreign nations. Moreover, management problems of the domestic producers become more complex because they must now take into account a whole new set of considerations such as the exchange rate and the conditions in foreign markets before making their decisions about raw material purchases.

Although the factors listed previously provide insight into why the degree of openness of the economy increased during the 1970s, it is worthwhile to consider why openness did not increase very much during the 1980s. Certainly the impact of lower barriers to trade, either natural or policy-induced, appears to be diminishing. Changes in the pattern of production, particularly the increasing focus of U.S. manufacturers on micromarkets and faster responses to changing domestic demand, appeared to be limiting increased imports in the late 1980s and early 1990s, aided, of course, by a falling dollar. Rising protectionism abroad, due in part to the high long-term unemployment rate in many of these nations, slowed the growth of U.S. exports, despite the impact of the falling dollar.

In short, although the economy is gradually adjusting to its exhaustion of natural resources, no plausible factors can be adduced to suggest that the share of trade in the GDP will begin to rise again in the rapid fashion as in the 1970s. If I am correct about these trends, increases in structural complexity arising from increased openness of the economy will also taper off.

The skill content of exports and imports

As argued in Chapter 3, the level of substantive and interaction skills embodied in a good or service is an indicator of the structural complexity of that production because these skills require a higher degree of information generation, gathering, and processing. Substantive skills are a composite measure created by a factor analysis of many different characteristics associated with the occupations used in production that require general educational development, specific vocational preparation, data skills, general intelligence, verbal skills, and numerical skills. Interaction skills designate "people skills," that require instructing, negotiating, supervising, and other activities for personal interactions on the job. Contrast is provided by the calculation of embodied motor skills, a composite variable also created by a factor analysis that indicates a variety of manual skills.

The same type of empirical analysis presented in Chapter 3 can be employed to examine changes in skills embodied in foreign trade. For imports, we can calculate the domestic skills that would have been used if the United States had produced the imported goods.[12] Although these may not represent the skills of the foreign labor used in producing these goods, it is a good first approximation since roughly more than three quarters of U.S. imports come from traditionally or newly industrialized nations where the education and training systems are advanced. This descriptive exploration provides some building blocks for the more analytical approach in the next section. For reasons of data availability, this study focuses on the period between 1958 and 1982.

12. If the purpose of this exercise were to calculate some type of trade balance of skills, then the embodied skills of the labor employed abroad in producing these products would have to be used. My purpose is to focus on the competitiveness of U.S. manufacturing industries so that the skill content of competing products made in the United States is important.

The detailed data (presented in Appendix Note 8.3) show that over the twenty-four-year period total manufacturing production embodied rising levels of substantive and interaction skills, but slightly declining levels of motor skills. Skills in handling data increased the most and total physical demands of production decreased the most. The detailed data show that these changes in embodied skills, for the most part, were due to changes in production methods (that is, the occupational mix for a particular industry, rather than the product mix). People skills were a notable exception to this generalization. These results are not surprising and are analyzed by others.[13]

For foreign trade, the most important result is that in both 1958 and 1982 U.S. manufacturing exports generally embodied more of all three skills than manufacturing production as a whole and the reverse was generally true of imports. These results suggest that during this period the United States had a comparative advantage in the products requiring more of these three general labor skills and a comparative disadvantage in products requiring less of them. This confirms the conventional wisdom on the subject.

Turning to the particular skills, the embodied substantive skills have increased in both trade and production. The more detailed data in Appendix Note 8.3 and also Table 8.3 show that in trade, data skills increased fastest, then substantive skills, and then general educational development. Such an ordering suggests not just that the nation is entering the information age, but that breadth of skills, rather than depth, is becoming increasingly important for both trade and production.

The greatest changes for production, exports, and imports that occurred in embodied people skills came about primarily as a shift in the composition of production, rather than changes in production methods. This means that the consumption of manufactured goods is shifting toward less standardized products requiring more negotiation, supervision, and instruction than traditional mass-produced objects. I should add that these interaction skills are measured by reference to work within an administrative hierarchy; and the measurement tells us nothing about the ability of the American work force for teamwork. Since teamwork and the ability to take initiative at the shop level appear important factors in the rapid rise of manufacturing productivity in Japan, the calculations may not measure what is truly important for the future of U.S. foreign trade. Unfortunately, data on changes in these skills over time are not available.

The embodied motor skill – a composite variable – also behaves interestingly, decreasing for production as a whole and even more so for exports, while increasing for the import competing industries. For both exports and imports as a whole, the detailed data show that such characteristics physical strength required, other physical demands, and jobs requiring undesirable

---

13. Howell and Wolff (1991) discuss these matters in detail.

Table 8.3. *Relative skill content of trade and production*

	Percentage differences: Imports to exports		Percentage differences: Exports to production		Percentage differences: Imports to production	
	1958	1982	1958	1982	1958	1982
Substantive skills	−13.9%	−13.4%	+7.5%	+9.7%	−7.5%	−4.9%
Interaction skills	−5.6	−8.5	−.7	+9.3	−6.2	.0
Motor skills	−4.7	−.4	+3.2	+1.1	−1.7	+.7

Notes: For imports the embodied skills are for workers in import-competing industries.
For 1958, these calculations are based on the data in data set W in Table A.27 (Appendix Note 8.3); for 1982, data set X. In all cases, the labor force weights of the year for which the comparisons are made are used. In the text the comparisons made with a situation with constant trade and production structures use comparisons similar to these, but taken from data sets Y and Z in Table A.27.

working conditions are declining. Several forces seem to underlie these results. The composition of trade and production is moving away from goods requiring such skills, more so for exports than for imports. For imports, however, the increase in the average level of embodied motor skills reflects changes in the methods of production for particular products, which apparently the United States is unable to match. In other words, these differential changes in embodied motor skills in exports and imports suggest (but do not prove) that the state of vocational education in the United States is declining in relation to its leading trade partners. Such an inference provides support for the qualitative findings of many who have argued that the major foreign competitors of the United States have a superior type of vocational training.[14]

Preliminary steps to determine factors underlying changes in U.S. competitiveness

If markets function so that the changing patterns of U.S. exports and imports reflect changes in U.S. comparative advantage, rather than changes in particular barriers to trade such as tariffs and quotas, then these calculations raise some concerns about the changing trade pattern of the United States. Some relevant data are presented in Table 8.3.

The first two columns in the table show the difference in relative skills embodied in exports and import-competing goods in 1958 and 1982. The relative gap in substantive skills in import-competing goods in comparison to exports remained roughly the same. Interaction skills and motor skills embodied in imports were lower than exports in 1958; for the former the gap

14. For instance, Dertouzos, Lester and Solow (1989).

increased, for the latter the gap closed. From similar comparisons when the production mix is held constant, we see that these results occurred because of changes in the occupational mix of particular industries. Except for motor skills, there is no indication of a convergence between skills embodied in exports and imports.

The last four columns in Table 8.3 show the skills embodied in exports and import-competing goods in comparison to the total production. These results suggest that, with the exception of motor skills, exports are becoming more dissimilar to overall production, while imports are becoming more similar in skill content to domestic production. Holding the productive mix constant and making similar calculations, it appears that most of this increasing similarity is due to changes in the occupational mix within individual industries. This conclusion can also be drawn from an examination of most of the other skills (listed in Appendix Note 8.3).

What these results suggest is that the U.S. comparative advantage in manufacturing is increasingly based on goods that are different from the average type of manufactured product in that they require more advanced skills.[15] At the same time, imports are increasingly challenging domestic production in the commodities embodying the average level of skills. In other words, the rest of the world is catching up to the United States in embodied skills and job characteristics of overall manufacturing production.

At a given exchange rate, the United States can maintain its foreign trade competitiveness only in those products requiring an extra amount of embodied skills. Such results are reflected in part in the studies by others analyzing changes in U.S. net exports. These show a rising importance of education, measured primarily in terms of workers in the sciences and engineering (embodying substantive skills and general educational development) in those products for which the United States has maintained its competitiveness.

Competitiveness and structural complexity

Structural complexity can increase, not just because more foreign trade occurs, but also because such foreign trade can lead to a change in the structure of production. More specifically, if the United States has a comparative advantage in more technologically advanced goods, the structure of domestic production changes as these exports become an increasingly important part of total trade and production. Investigating whether this has actually occurred requires us to isolate the determinants of the nation's international competitiveness in a more

15. Of course, in so far as the export pattern is different from the pattern of domestic production, for instance, a greater share of aircraft and defense products, the measured comparative advantage will always the pattern of domestic production. But the analysis of the skill content points to something deeper.

exact fashion than the previous analysis. The nation's competitiveness in technologically advanced products also tells us how well the production institutions can adapt to greater complexity.

In this discussion, "competitiveness" is used somewhat differently than in
most discussions and refers to the ratio of net exports (exports minus imports)
to domestic production in particular industries. One purpose of this descriptive
exercise is to use the available data in a systematic fashion to point the direction in which rigorous theorizing about the dynamics of changing trade patterns must take. To this end I explore two questions: What are the major factors underlying the shifts in competitiveness that have occurred in the last
quarter century? What difference does it make to the future of the U.S. economy that such changes have occurred? The major statistical tool for answering
these questions is a regression analysis of four-digit manufacturing industries.

Approach

One common measure of a nation's shift in competitiveness is its changing
share of world trade in particular product groups. Given the state of the available statistics on the commodity structure of trade for the world as a whole,
such an exercise is usually carried out on a relatively aggregative basis, which
is not helpful to us. Additional problems arise because of the difficulties of
linking the trade statistics with the attributes of the individual manufacturing
industries, since the latter are based on a different product nomenclature.

I have chosen instead to approach the problem by relying on U.S. data
alone, and by examining the share of net exports to total domestic production
and the shifts of this ratio over time. Competitiveness is not quite the same as
comparative advantage, but if the comparative advantage of the U.S. shifts
away from an industry, imports of the product generally increase, and the ratio
of net exports to production generally falls. If used carefully various theories
of the determinants of *static* comparative advantage can allow us to explain
changes in competitiveness.

A glance at the data

The most useful data set for this investigation includes 400 four-digit manufacturing industries between 1958 and 1982, a twenty-four-year period.
Before turning to the various theories and thence to the empirical analysis, it
is useful to gain some intuitive notion of the phenomena under investigation
by considering briefly the score of industries experiencing the greatest change
in competitiveness. Data for this exercise are presented in Appendix Note 8.4.
Aside from the fact that all of the industries turn out to be either durable goods
(consumer or producer) or raw materials, rather than nondurables, the various
industries are a very heterogeneous lot.

Of those industries showing the greatest positive change in net exports, some are high-tech industries (aircraft and aircraft equipment, devices to carry electricity or to measure it, measuring and controlling devices, electronic computing equipment, and oil field machinery); some are raw-material intensive industries (log production and pulp manufacture); and some lie in between (turbine and turbine generator sets). Of those industries showing the greatest fall in relative net exports, several are associated with low-tech leather processing and shoe industries (women's handbags, women's footwear, luggage, and rubber and plastic footwear); several are high-tech industries (textile machinery, radio and TV receiving sets, engineering and scientific equipment); and still others fall in between (calculating and accounting machines, miscellaneous ordinance and accessories, watches and clocks, and power hand tools).

Although the growth of production of industries experiencing the greatest increase in net exports is greater than those showing the greatest decrease, the difference is not large when electronic computing equipment is omitted from the list. The industries showing the greatest decrease in net exports appear to have a greater increase in total factor productivity. No causal relation is apparent and such a counterintuitive result suggests we should be careful in generalizing from just a few industries.

The endpoints for these comparisons are hardly ideal, since both years were years of recession. In 1958 the average annual unemployment rate was 6.6 percent and in 1982 it was 9.5 percent. In both cases the unemployment rate was between one and two percentage points higher than the previous year. This means that the measure for competitiveness is higher than it would normally be since imports generally decreased more than domestic production for the same commodities. However, 1982 was the last year before the rising U.S. dollar led to a massive influx of imports and an artificial fall in U.S. competitiveness. And 1958 was the earliest year for which comparable data are readily available on imports, exports, and domestic production, all classified according to the Standard Industrial Classification (SIC). Both 1958 and 1982 are years during which a Census of Manufactures is available, so that the data on the characteristics of the manufacturing sector are very detailed. Other aspects of the data are discussed briefly in Appendix Note 8.5.

Possible causes of the changes in competitiveness

Although we are trying to understand changes in competitiveness, rather than the pattern of competitiveness that existed in any particular year, it is useful to start by considering a set of theories to explain comparative advantage at a single point in time. Then we can decide how useful these theories might be for explaining the phenomenon at hand. A static approach dealing with factor endowments, a more dynamic approach focusing on declining costs, and a heterodox approach dealing with the end uses of the traded commodities prove most useful in explaining changes in competitiveness. I explore each in turn.

Factor endowment: According to the classical *factor-endowment theory* of comparative advantage, now sometimes called the *Heckscher-Ohlin-Vanek theory,* nations tend to export those goods embodying a relatively greater amount of those factors of production in which the particular nation is relatively abundant. Thus, in a world with only two factors of production, a country with a relatively greater endowment of capital would tend to export capital-intensive goods and import labor-intensive goods. The problems in using this approach to determine the structure of trade are manifold and have been discussed often.[16]

When the static factor endowment theory of comparative advantage is used to try to explain shifts in the pattern of trade, rather than the pattern at a particular point in time, further difficulties arise. We must not only consider factor intensities at one point in time, but changes in the relative factor intensities as well. The former approach showed some promise, as indicated later; but the latter approach did not and was eventually dropped.

Susan Hickok provides a useful discussion to illustrate some problems involved.[17] In a two-nation world, the nation with relatively more capital (and relatively less labor) might experience as faster growth of imports of capital intensive goods if the other country has a capital–labor ratio increasing more rapidly than the home country. In turn, this means that the relative comparative advantages of the two nations is shifting. Such an argument is a straightforward implication of the *Rybczynski theorem.*

This meaning of a statistically significant relationship between some measure of factor intensity at any particular point in time and a changing pattern of trade can have either a causal or a noncausal interpretation:

1. If the relationship is positive and causal, the changing trade pattern is being driven by an established comparative advantage that, during the time period under investigation, has been unchallenged. If the

---

16. See especially Leamer (1984, 1992). Several difficulties deserve particular emphasis. Theoretical problems arise because the assumptions underlying this approach are very restrictive; moreover, when more than two factors of production are taken into account, the theory becomes considerably more complex. Measurement problems are also formidable. For instance, relative factor endowment of a particular nation must be measured against the world supply of the various factors under consideration. In addition, the factor intensity of particular goods becomes ambiguous in many cases where the good is most profitable to produce with quite different factor ratios, depending on the relative prices of these factors (factor reversals). It should not be surprising that attempts to use the Heckscher-Ohlin-Vanek approach to explain the pattern of trade at any particular time have often not been very encouraging (e.g., Feenstra, 1988).
17. Hickok (1990).

relationship is negative and causal, the changing trade pattern is being driven by the loss of a comparative advantage.

2. If the relationship is noncausal, it may still be important to know on a descriptive level what is happening to gain some idea about the specific impact of the changing trade pattern on the domestic pattern of production and employment. Although we have no test to determine whether the relationship is causal or not, we can decide whether the results are consistent with a story told about shifts in the structure of trade from other types of evidence.

In the regression experiments I examined the role of seven different skill levels of labor embodied in the traded commodities at a single point in time. Only the variable representing low-skilled workers (operatives, laborers, and service workers) had a statistically significant (and negative) relation to changes in competitiveness. This shows what we already know, that the United States has been losing competitiveness in those industries where unskilled workers are a significant share of the labor force. Nevertheless, the mixed nature of the results obtained in these experiments suggests it is more useful to examine the types of skills, rather than occupational categories.[18]

I also explored the roles of ten different kinds of raw materials and land embodied in the traded goods at a single point in time. I measured such raw material inputs both in terms of direct usage as well as direct and indirect usage, that is, taking account of the use of the raw materials in the inputs of the traded product. The most meaningful results were obtained by using the direct and indirect usage of these raw materials; and the experiments revealed a statistically significant relationship of changes in competitiveness with products of the land (positive) and iron ore (negative). These results are to be expected. On a static level, the competitiveness of U.S. crop products reflects the nation's low population density, rich earth, and government policies toward agriculture.[19] Over time, the increasing competitiveness in products embodying land probably occurs because diminishing returns in such products are increasingly serious abroad as population densities increase in all nations. At the same time, the United States has been exhausting its iron ore resources,

18. Using an input–output table, these calculations were made for the embodied skills both in direct production of the commodity, as well as direct and indirect production; that is, taking account of the intermediate products. Since the results are not greatly different for the two sets of calculations and since the estimates for direct production allow much more disaggregative results, only the directly embodied job characteristics are used in the regression calculations presented in Table 8.4. The simpler approach dealing only with specific types of labor (unskilled, skilled, clerical, technical, etc.) is exemplified in an elegant study of static determinants of comparative advantage by Sveikauskas (1983).

19. The McKinsey Global Institute (1993) presents evidence that the U.S. competitiveness in food processing industries, at least in relation to Germany and Japan, is very high. With my statistical techniques it is impossible to take this factor into account.

especially in comparison to the rest of the world, and has not (as in the case of Japan) massively invested in facilities on the seacoasts to take advantage of lower priced iron ore imports. Because of intense labor union activity, wages in the iron and steel industries are also quite high. So we would expect the land intensiveness of U.S. products to increase, and the iron ore intensiveness to decrease, a result confirmed by the data.

Technological factors: This more dynamic approach toward foreign trade competitiveness places greater analytical weight on technological factors such as the growth of productivity of an industry, economies of scale, and the impact of sunk costs and other first-mover advantages.

The most direct approach is to explore changing total factor productivity in the United States to changes in competitiveness. Given the results discussed above when first glancing at the data, it should not be surprising that this type of frontal assault did not work.[20]

A more indirect approach is required and it is useful to start with the notion that many manufacturing industries manifest declining average costs with increasing volume. These declining costs are caused not just by static economies of scale. At a single point in time they can also occur with high fixed costs in comparison to marginal costs. And over time, they can occur by moving rapidly down the learning curve as volume of production increases.

Since the United States has a large internal market, at first glance it seems reasonable that exports would increase most rapidly where these economies of scale can be attained. But we should note that foreign industries taking advantage of falling costs occurring with greater volume could penetrate U.S. domestic markets so that the United States might lose competitiveness in such industries as well. This means that the U.S. net exports would either increase the most or decrease the most in those industries where the falling costs were most important.

In such cases we cannot simply add a variable reflecting falling costs to the regression since it is the value of the variable, rather than its sign, which is important. The effect can, however, be studied by examining the statistical

---

20. This approach raises a serious problem of interpretation, namely that it is not the growth of productivity per se that is important, but rather the growth of productivity vis-à-vis potential trade competitors in each industry. Since data are not readily available on the growth of productivity elsewhere in manufacturing industries in the world, however, alternative approaches are necessary. Because it seems most likely that the United States's relative technological advantage is preserved in those industries where the investment is increasing the fastest, it can be conjectured that competitiveness in these industries should increase. This phenomenon is measured both by changes in the ratio of the gross capital stock to the total labor hours in each industry, as well as by changes in the ratio of gross capital stock to the value of output. Neither these nor the total factor productivity change variable appeared significantly related to changes in competitiveness.

relation between various measures for falling costs and the absolute value of the regression residuals from the equations linking competitiveness to other explanatory variables such as relative factor endowments. As shown later, two measures of economies of scale – one on the plant level, the other on the enterprise level – are significantly related to these regression residuals.

Falling costs accompanying an increase in volume can be measured on both a plant and an enterprise level at a single point in time. For the former I experimented with a number of indicators on both the plant and the enterprise level.[21] Although these proxies are not exactly what we need, two of them have explanatory value in the two-stage procedure, namely the median number of workers in a production establishment and the economies of scale as measured differences in eight-firm and four-firm concentration ratios. An indicator of changing economies of scale looks at the difference in these measures at two points in time, but such dynamic measures did not prove to have explanatory value.

Another approach to the problem of measuring first-mover advantages starts with the simple notion that economies of large scale production are achieved in those industries where either fixed or sunk costs are high in comparison to marginal costs. This means that those entering the market first have a considerable advantage over newcomers since their average costs will be lower when the new competitors enter the market. This idea has received considerable attention in recent years and appears promising.[22] But for the purpose at hand, some problems arise.

For some of these variables indicating high fixed costs, for instance, selling costs, the advantages might be important in the short run, but not in the long run. An example is provided in the automobile industry: it took over a decade for Japanese cars to penetrate U.S. markets; but once a certain critical level was reached, the increase in market share was rapid. Although in the first decade and a half after World War II, the United States might have had a com-

---

21. On the plant level, I measured economies of scale in 1958 with three indicators: the labor force in a median size plant; the share of the total domestic production accounted for by a median sized plant; and the ratio of labor productivity in plants above the median to plants below the median. These indicators are often found in the industrial organization literature (e.g., Caves 1988).

    On the enterprise level for 1958, I employed a measure proposed by Wright (1978), who compares the market share of the largest four producers of the product to the market share of the fifth through eighth largest producers. Some account, however, must be taken of the fact that if the level of seller concentration of the top four producers is high, then the next four leading producers can not have a high market share. The actual formula employed at a static level is:

$$\text{Scale economies} = \left[\frac{CR8_t - CR4_t}{100 - CR4_t} \right] \qquad (1)$$

22. For instance, Kessides (1990) and Sutton (1991).

petitive advantage in products with high sunk costs to marginal costs, the United States lost this first-mover advantage with the rebuilding of the European and Japanese economies, especially where selling costs are important. This conjecture receives support by the following regression results.

The search for other variables reflecting first-mover advantages that would lead to changes in competitiveness did not prove successful. Although it seems reasonable to conjecture, for instance, that U.S. competitiveness would hold its own or increase in those industries where such research and development expenditures were a significant share of sales, this did not prove to be the case. Other proxies representing still different types of high fixed costs and first-mover advantages also did not prove to have any statistical relationship with changes in competitiveness.[23]

In summary, the technological approach leads to several interesting predictions that receive support in the regression experiments: changes in competitiveness are related to sunk costs, as measured by the relative importance of selling costs, and to economies of scale of production. Since the sign of economies of scale is uncertain, their impact can only be measured in a regression using the absolute value of the residuals.

Heterodox approaches: These include a grab bag of conjectures and hypotheses. In preliminary experiments I focused particular efforts on trying to relate changes in competitiveness to changes in trade barriers and also to "sclerosis"

23. For research, development, and technical personnel, I found that for most of the period under examination, there was no statistical relationship with the change in this first-mover proxy to changes in competitiveness. For the other proxies for first-mover advantage, I only had information for one year and, as a result, could not examine the changes in these variables with changes in competitiveness. I tried a number of other ways to introduce research and development into the regression explaining changes in competitiveness, but without success. This was surprising, given the important role of R and D that other such as Dosi, Pavitt, and Soete (1990) have found in their regression experiments.

This first-mover approach has an interesting variant, namely that for product lines where tastes are heterogeneous, the initial postwar market share has eroded as foreign competitors are able to gain sales by focusing on just a subset of the many product lines. A measure of product heterogeneity is the intraindustry trade statistic (IITS). This can be used on an aggregative level, as in Part B of Table 8.1, or for each industry and can be most easily measured with the Grubel-Lloyd formula:

$$IITS = 1 - \frac{|\text{Exports} - \text{Imports}|}{.5 * (\text{Exports} + \text{Imports})} \qquad (2)$$

According to this approach, changes in U.S. competitiveness should be related inversely to the IITS. No such relationship could be found, although another measure for heterogeneity associated with product usage, which is discussed below, does appear significantly related to changes in competitiveness. Taking a more dynamic approach, increases in heterogeneity, as measured by changes in the IITS ratio, appear related to increases in U.S. competitiveness; in the final regressions, however, the degree of statistical significance did not meet the predetermined level and the variable was dropped.

of certain American industries. Neither proved promising.[24] But one other approach based on commodity usage did yield some interesting results.

It seems more promising to look at commodity usage. For instance, using data on shares of exports and imports for various purposes, Susan Hickok shows that the United States is losing market shares in production of finished goods (capital goods plus automobiles and consumer goods).[25.] We might infer from these

24. *Trade barriers approach.* Several different types of trade barriers deserve mention. A direct measure, of course, is the level of tariffs. I experimented with this variable, but without success. Testing some of the measures for quantitative restrictions raised difficulties since these restrictions are sometimes a result of a loss of competitiveness, not a cause; and the data available to me allowed no easy way to set up a simultaneous equations model to separate out these effects. What is needed is an exogenous factor that affects American competitiveness and, of course, costs induced by governmental, environmental, and other regulations appear as promising candidates. Measures of these costs as a percent of sales have been made by Joseph Kalt (1988) for fifty-two manufacturing industries. Although this is a relatively high degree of aggregation (the two- and three-digit level of classification), I have assumed that these relative costs are roughly the same for the individual four digit industries within each broader class. Although Kalt found a significant relationship of these variables with changes in U.S. trade at an aggregative level (two- to three-digit level), I was unable to find such a relationship at the more detailed level on which I was working, although this negative result may have occurred because of the drastic assumptions I had to make with regard to the data.

   "Sclerosis" approach. In an influential and seminal book Mancur Olson (1982) has argued that for various reasons U.S. industry has become sclerotic; and Murrell (1982, 1983) has shown how these ideas can be applied to explain certain aspects of the trade structure. Since sclerosis can not be measured directly, we must employ indirect tests and proxies. For instance, Mueller and Hamm (1974), as well as others, have argued that barriers to entry are much lower in fast-growing domestic industries, other things being equal. In this case, the sclerotic domestic firms are simply unable to keep up with the changing market. A broader variant of this idea focuses on income elasticities of demand, namely that in those products with high growing world demand, the older and sclerotic U.S. firms lose market share to younger and more flexible foreign firms and U.S. competitiveness falls. In the experiments I carried out, the results did not appear promising, at least with the proxy variables that I employed.

25. Hickok (1990). Some confirming evidence is provided by Hampden-Turner and Trompenaars (1993) in a study of managerial values, who note (p. 20): "The American idea is of the Universal Product, reducible to parts ... and infinitely replicable ... What is aspired to is the widest possible product appeal (universalism) combined with a manufacturing process that is reduced to simple steps so that the parent company can manufacture wherever costs are lowest and sell to as many people as possible. It is the vision of the world's Cookie Cutter, or breakfast-food-for-everyone ... The headlong pursuit of the Universal Product ... tends to eclipse ... special circumstances and exceptional requests."

   Another commodity-usage approach is exemplified in a study by Andrew Warner (1992), who provides evidence from a time-series approach that on an aggregative level, the level of investment of major U.S. trade partners is a crucial determinant of U.S. exports. Given the overall growth of investment over the last quarter century, one might infer that U.S. capital goods are particularly competitive in the world economy, at least in the short term. Of course, an increase in world investment is generally associated with prosperity and it might have been U.S. consumer goods that were increasing when world investment rose. My regression results do not confirm Warner's hypothesis since the sign of the variable representing fixed investment is negative. It is not, however, statistically significant.

results that the United States is losing its competitiveness in those industries where the products must be tailored to individual tastes of the user. Let me emphasize that this inference, however, cannot be proven by the data that Hickok employed. An alternate interpretation could focus on the necessary processing or assembly of these goods at the final stage of production. Nevertheless, Hickok's conjecture is interesting and deserves further examination.

To test the basic factual statement, I calculated the relative share of total domestic usage of the products of all industries accounted for by intermediate usage and by various end-usages. For consumption goods, Hickok's insight receives confirmation.

Results of the statistical analysis

Given the type of approach, an ordinary least squares regression seems appropriate, where each four-digit industry is treated as a single case. Significance tests are applied to protect us from data errors that introduce spurious correlations and from actual causal factors that have a relatively small impact. Given the fact that I had to experiment with a number of proxy variables, I only consider results with very robust t statistics. Table 8-4 presents the results of the experiments explaining changes in net exports (changes in competitiveness). Following the procedure discussed previously, I also display the calculations linking the absolute value of the residuals of this regression to the variables reflecting economies of scale.[26] Although the causal nature of the variables in these regressions that proved statistically significant cannot be firmly established, such an exercise does allow us to isolate certain trends for further research and to focus discussion about whether such trends will continue into the future.

Of the six variables that have a statistically significant relationship with the change of competitiveness, four are related to factor proportions: the general educational development level embodied in production, the level of manual skills embodied in production, the relative extent that the goods of the industry contain crop products, forestry and fishing products, and products made from iron ore. The positive and significant value of the general educational development variable provides additional support for the conclusions obtained in the previous section, namely that in those products incorporating a high level of training, the United States is well able to compete on a worldwide basis and, indeed, has a comparative advantage. The negative value of the manual skills variable supports the conclusion of the previous section that we are losing our competitiveness in those industries that require a high degree of training in manual skills. It appears that we are seeing the impact of the long

26. For the first regression I only report results with a .99 level of significance. For the second regression, where I carried out many fewer experiments, I accept results with a .95 level of significance.

Table 8.4. *Results of the statistical analysis*

		Variable to be explained			
		Regression 1		Regression 2	
Variable to be explained		Change in the ratio of of net exports to production: 1958–1982		Absolute values of regression residuals of Regression 1	
		Regression results			
Explanatory variables	Unweighted average	Calculated coefficient	*t* statistic	Calculated coefficient	*t* statistic
Constant	—	.163	1.02	.0636	6.15
General educational development of labor force engaged in production in each industry, 1960 (scale 1 to 6)	3.13	.139	4.16	—	—
Motor skills of labor force engaged in production in each industry, 1960 (scale 0 to 10)	5.36	−.113	3.39	—	—
Dollar value of all direct and indirect usage of all crop products in a dollar of the product of the industry, 1958	.0378	.259	3.17	—	—
Dollar value of all direct and indirect usage of iron ore in a dollar of the product of the industry, 1958	.00516	−1.94	3.37	—	—
Ratio of total selling costs to total sales, 1976	.118	−.102	3.17	—	—
Ratio of total domestic usage going for end-use consumption (including usage an input for further production), 1958	.266	−.141	5.97	—	—
Median number of workers (1,000s) in a production establishment, 1958	222	—	—	.0471	2.23
Scale economies of enterprise, 1958	.244	—	—	.0736	2.03
Coefficient of determination		.2118		.0466	
Adjusted coefficient of determination		.1991		.0402	
Sample size		380		301	

Note: The sources of data are described in Appendix Note 8.5.

emphasis on the formal teaching of vocational skills by trade competitors of the United States in comparison to the various learning-on-the-job programs in the United States These regression results for the educational and manual skill variables also suggest that the United States is likely to be less competitive in industries with a high share of low-skilled workers, a conjecture that is confirmed in experiments where the education and manual skills variables are replaced with a variable representing the share of low-skilled workers.

The theoretical arguments previously discussed predicting an increasing competitiveness in products embodying land resources and a decreasing competitiveness in those products embodying iron ore receive confirmation. As a result, the country has increasing net exports in land and forest products and increasing net imports not just in iron ore, but finished iron and steel as well. These results, however, must be cautiously interpreted because other causal factors may be at work.[27] Some also have argued that the extra high wages that existed in the U.S. steel industries until recently and the subsidies given by some of our competitors to basic metallurgical industries have also contributed to the problem.

The negative sign for the relative importance of end-use consumption as a share of total domestic usage has several interpretations. Most likely, these results suggest that during the 1958–82 period, the United States was losing competitiveness in those products that must be tailored to individual tastes and special usage. Such goods are becoming increasingly important as family incomes rise and discretionary expenditures become more important. In many cases these goods are produced in shorter production runs than the more homogeneous products that are consumed by lower income families, that are used as intermediate inputs for further production, and that are more amenable to mass production.

Finally, the first-mover argument receives several kinds of confirmation. As noted previously, the ratio of the total selling costs to sales is one proxy among many reflecting different types of first-mover advantages. This advantage, which played an important role in the 1950s, has gradually eroded over time as other nations have a chance to invest in developing a sales network and brand loyalty. Consequently, the calculated regression coefficient has a negative sign. As argued previously, economies of scale variables, which reflect another type of first-mover advantage, should be positively related to the absolute value of the prediction errors of the variable reflecting changes in competitiveness. This receives a confirmation in the second regression. Proxy variables of other first-mover advantages such as research and development expenditures did not prove to be statistically significant.

27. I refer particularly to the impact of relative changes in the productivity of the food-processing industry. Some have suggested to me that this land and forest product coefficient might also reflect changing U.S. public policy toward these industries, but any such policy changes do not seem likely to have caused such a difference in net exports.

Economy of scale variables, both on the establishment and enterprise level, also are significantly related to changes in competitiveness. More specifically, the greater the economies of scale measured in this fashion, the more net exports rose (if the United States took advantage of these economies) or fell (if foreign competitors took advantage of these economies). The key question of why the United States was able, or not able, to take advantages of such economies of scale remains a subject for future research.

Some interpretations

For the study of structural complexity, the lack of statistical significance of the various research and development variables is of particular interest.[28] This suggests that it is not the volume of R and D per se embodied in a commodity that has increased America's competitiveness, since other nations have increased their capabilities in high-tech industries and could catch up during the twenty-four years under examination. Rather, as the skills variables suggest, it is the cognitive skills embodied in the production process that is crucial.

The coefficient of determination of .198 means that only about one-fifth of the variation of the net export to total production ratios can be explained by the regression. Although this coefficient of determination is statistically significant, its relatively low value means that it is quite difficult to determine what specific industries will experience a rise or fall in competitiveness. As indicated later, such a result has implications for the implementation of any type of industrial policy. To explore this problem in greater depth, I examine the largest prediction errors in Appendix Note 8.4.

Some of these cases of large prediction error can be attributed to changes in the relative quality of products produced in the United States and abroad. For cases of overoptimistic predictions, where foreign producers had caught up or surpassed the United States's lead, these might include radio and TV receiving sets, calculating and accounting machines, textile machinery, and engineering and scientific equipment. For cases of overpessimism, where the United States was able to maintain or widen its technological lead, these might include civilian aircraft and aircraft parts, current carrying wiring devices, pharmaceutical preparations, and instruments to measure electricity.

In other cases of large prediction errors, the technology of production appears to have changed. For the greatest negative prediction errors this might

---

28. It should be added that when the R and D variable did have statistical significance in some of the preliminary regressions, the calculated coefficient was quite low. That is, a considerable difference in the relative importance of R and D expenditures to sales had a relatively small impact on the change in competitiveness. This result may have occurred because the R and D variable was too aggregative. For instance, Audretsch and Yamawaki (1988) argue that some types of these expenditures have a much stronger impact on changes in foreign trade than others.

include watches, clocks, and watch cases. In still other cases, we must turn to very standard types of explanations. For instance, some cases of overoptimism in prediction occur for products that are very labor intensive. These might include women's handbags and purses, luggage, women's footwear, and cut stone and stone products. It should be noted, however, that some labor intensive industries did not experience marked declines in competitiveness so that this must be considered a contributory, rather than a sufficient condition for trade problems. Still other cases of overpessimism occur for products that are intensive in raw materials that are relatively abundant in the United States. These might include pulp mill products and logging mill products. Again, this type of cause appears a contributory, rather than sufficient cause, for an increase in competitiveness.

Some of the largest prediction errors defy easy explanation. These include the improvements in competitiveness that were much greater than expected in the production of miscellaneous hosiery, lawn and garden equipment, and women's and children's underwear. These are hardly high-tech industries and, it might be added, use imported machinery. Of course, these prediction errors undoubtedly could have been reduced if systematic consideration could have been taken of changes occurring among the United States's trade competitors in the various industries included in the statistical analysis. But this regret highlights the nub of the prediction problem: meaningful forecasts of the future competitiveness of all of the individual United States. Instead, it requires information that is simply not available. Although the regression analysis allows us to specify certain trends, the factors over which we have little information are considerably more important.

Conclusions and implications for the future

Internationalization of the economic system influences many different aspects of the economy. In the next chapter, for instance, I argue that such a trend reduces the effectiveness of monetary and fiscal policy. In this chapter I focus primarily on the implications of increasing internationalization for foreign trade.

The relative importance of trade, as measured by the ratios of exports or imports to total production, increased considerably during the 1970s. But since then these increases have slowed and, in the near future, no dramatic increase in openness is expected, even while the NAFTA and new GATT treaties are implemented. In past years, several causal factors seem to underlie this long-term increase such as correlates to rising income (falling transportation costs, rising discretionary income and the desire for more differentiated goods, and changes in relative prices between tradable and nontradable goods), the gradual depletion of U.S. raw material resources, and falling trade barriers. But in the near future, the impact of most of these should be considerably less. Even the depletion of U.S. raw material resources, which I believe to have played a crucial role, should decline in importance as the raw material content of goods decreases and as consumption patterns turn increasingly to services.

If no natural or policy-induced barriers to trade existed in the world, then the probability of a person purchasing a good from a given country would depend solely on that country's share of total world production. In 1980 the United States produced and consumed roughly one-fifth of the gross planetary product and, for simplicity, let us assume that this held for manufacturing as well. With random buying of goods, this means that imports (and exports) should amount to roughly 80 percent of manufacturing production, or about 16 percent of the GDP. Under similar assumptions, if mining and agriculture are added to this calculation, the theoretical limit of trade would very roughly be about 20 percent.

The United States is far from the theoretical limit of openness and it seems likely that the ratio of foreign trade to its production should increase, not just for manufactured goods but also for services. The absolute level of trade should increase at a lower rate than from 1950 through 1990, primarily because the rate of economic growth, both in the United States and abroad, is also tapering off, an issue discussed in the final chapter.

The conclusion that trade openness should not greatly increase in the next few decades has several immediate implications. It means that the spurt in competitiveness, as reflected in the trade-adjusted-concentration ratios in Chapter 7, will not soon be repeated. The increasing imports of foreign raw materials, that appears to have driven part of the increase in trade openness, also means that the nation's economic vulnerability to disruptions of international markets for these raw materials will continue to increase. Nevertheless, as shown in previous chapters, this greater openness has not led to greater macroeconomic instabilities. The evidence from previous chapters also suggests that the microeconomic instabilities introduced by increasing volatility of exchange rates and raw basic material prices have not destabilized the domestic economy.

Structural complexity of the foreign trade structure, as reflected in cognitive and people skills embodied in each unit of trade is increasing. This is true not just of U.S. exports, but of imports as well. Indeed, the skill content of a unit of imports is increasingly becoming similar to the U.S. manufacturing production system as a whole, while at the same time the skill content of a dollar of U.S. exports is increasingly different from a dollar of domestic manufacturing products general. This kind of analysis provided the introduction to a more systematic examination of the sources of U.S. trade competitiveness.

Some causes of the changes in the composition of net exports can be isolated, and several of these concerned factor intensities. The United States lost competitiveness in those industries incorporating raw materials where U.S.

reserves are being exhausted, such as iron ore; and it gained competitiveness in crop and forestry products embodying land resources which remain relatively abundant. These trends should continue. The United States gained competitiveness in those industries using a high share of workers with high substantive skills and it lost competitiveness in those industries using a high share of unskilled workers or workers with high manual, but not cognitive, skills. These trends should also continue. As noted in Chapter 3, this trade factor, combined with a slower shift in supply away from the unskilled jobs, appears to have had an important influence in the fall of relative wages of the low paying jobs.[29]

The degree to which U.S. competitiveness will continue to decline for consumer products with is quite unclear. Much depends upon the speed at which the United States's manufacturing sector can accommodate to heterogeneous consumer tastes and can adapt its production methods for shorter production runs of more varied products, a matter discussed in greater detail in the last chapter.

For those industries where the United States has had a comparative advantage primarily because it was the first major producer, the situation is more complicated. Although it seems most probable that for many industries with first-mover advantages, the U.S. trade position will ebb as other nations catch up, for instance, in industries requiring high selling costs and extensive trade networks. The situation is not so clear, however, for products that are intensive in research and development. Nevertheless, some indicators suggest that U.S. predominance in R and D, especially that relevant to foreign trade, is ebbing. For instance, R and D expenditures in certain nations such as Germany and Japan have increased considerably faster in the last two decades than in the United States and the relative world share of scientific papers and patents of the United States is decreasing. In the two-decade period between 1965 and 1985, the United States maintained roughly its share of the world's technology-intensive exports, but it is unclear how long this will last.[30]

The relatively low degree of predictive power of the regressions explaining changes in competitiveness means that attempts of the government to pursue a broad-scale industrial policy should not be very effective. Indeed, recent evidence from Japan, one of the few nations believed to have had a successful industrial policy, shows little relation between the strength of the measures taken

---

29. At the time of writing, the economics profession is split on these matters. Some such as Lawrence and Slaughter (1993) argue that the impact of foreign trade on industries with a high proportion of low-skilled jobs is not very important. Others such as Sachs and Shatz (1994) argue that it has had an impact on these industries, but they argue further that this impact has not had a very important effect on wages or the income distribution. My own empirical results with regard to industries parallel Sachs and Shatz, but the argument in Chapter 3 suggests that the major impact has been on unemployment which, in turn, has had an influence on the distribution of income.

30. Baumol et al. (1989) p. 104.

to aid particular industries and their resulting export performance.[31] These results, however, may be biased in the sense that although the Japanese government supported "winners," they gave relatively more support to "losers."

It should be added that even if the government encourages "winners" by means of general policies, rather than those tailored for particular industries, it must still treat "losers" in a differentiated fashion, depending upon the source of failure. This requires a highly heterogeneous set of policies to implement since the causes of failure are quite different in, let us say, the leather using industries than in the consumer electronic industries. (This observation is, of course, merely the economic implication of Tolstoy's famous dictum that all unhappy families are unhappy for different reasons.) Few governments have this kind of finesse. The theme of greater structural complexity increasing the difficulty of government policy making is explored at greater length in the next chapter.

The foreign trade sector acts to increase the structural complexity of the economic system, not just by widening markets and increasing the interactions between various parts of the economic system, but also by stimulating the production of technologically advanced goods that embody highly skilled occupations. Maintenance of this technological dominance is a crucial challenge for the future.

31. Beason and Weinstein (1993).

CHAPTER 9

The government sector

Many believe that shifts in the line between the public and private realms are the key determinants of the changes in the economic system. For instance, Robert Heilbroner states the matter bluntly:[1] "In my opinion no single issue will be more profoundly determinative of the future of the system than the relation of its two realms. I do not mean by this that there exists some 'optimal' mix of public and private spheres ..." Although I believe that shifts in the boundary between the public and private sectors are important, I argue in this chapter that I do not believe these shifts will be very significant in the United States in the next few decades. The next chapter focuses on other changes in the economic system having greater importance in the years to come.

The perspective afforded by the analysis of structural complexity leads us to ask three important questions about the behavior of the government sector. In what way is the shifting line between the public and private sector influenced by changes in structural complexity of the economic system? To what extent does the U.S. government act as a generator of structural complexity? And what is the impact of structural complexity on the effectiveness of governmental actions?

As enterprise managers must face and respond to an increasingly complex economic environment, discussed in detail in Chapter 6, so must the government. In so far as the government is expected to take measures to help its citizens respond to the more complex world, the governmental response to increased structural complexity is broader than that of the business world. In this chapter I focus particular attention on the ways in which governmental expenditures have served this purpose. This, in turn, provides a useful vantage point to examine some arguments about the possible expansion of these expenditures in the future.

The government is not just a passive reactor to increasing structural complexity but contributes to the increase in structural complexity as well. This occurs through its tax legislation, its day-to-day regulation of certain economic activities, and its actions defining the legal status of particular economic actions. To make this more concrete, I examine certain quantitative measures of changes in this regulatory activity and, more briefly, the costs of such regulations to the economy as a whole.

1. Heilbroner (1993), p. 90.

Increasing structural complexity can also influence the effectiveness of governmental activities, especially as such complexity is associated with greater information costs necessary for policy making. This requires us to examine the influence of such complexity on the completeness, timeliness, and accuracy of the data available to government policy makers. Such a discussion is complementary to the examination in Chapter 6 of the impact of structural complexity on productive enterprises in the private sector.

Evolution of the size of the government sector

Before turning to the three topics under review, it is useful to document briefly some traditional measures of the size of the government sector after World War II. These data are presented in Table 9.1. Although many detailed aspects of these and related series are discussed later, it is necessary at this time to draw four quick but crucially important conclusions.

First, generalizations about the direction of the trends in the size of the public sector in the four decades depend critically upon the indicator. As measured by public expenditures as a ratio of GDP, the public sector has increased in relative size. As measured by the relative number of full-time equivalent workers in the government sector, the relative size of the public sector has remained roughly the same. As measured by its relative share of the nation's net fixed reproducible tangible wealth owned by the government, the public sector has decreased in relative size. Thus, it is crucial to specify the indicator when analyzing changes in the public–private boundary.

Second, the relative size of different levels of government also depends upon the indicator. With regard to expenditures, the state and local government sector has been smaller than the federal; but with regard to the labor force and capital stock, for most years the state and local government sector has been larger. For all indicators, however, the state and local government sector grew relative to the federal sector over the period. This means that although we focus attention on the federal government in most discussions of the public sector, generalizations derived from this sector alone do not necessarily reflect the public sector as a whole.

Third, the composition of public activities has changed considerably. Among public expenditures, the share of expenditures on goods and services has declined, while that of transfers, interest, and net subsidies has risen. The relative share of workers in education on the state level increased considerably between 1950 and 1990, while those in defense on the federal level decreased.

Finally, the rate of change in the various indicators is quite different in the different decade. Thus we must be wary about making sweeping generalizations about quantitative magnitudes that cover all periods.

Table 9.1. *Traditional indicators of the size of the government sector*

A. *Government expenditures: Percent of GDP, current prices*

	1952	1960	1970	1980	1990
Federal	20.6%	18.0%	19.0%	20.9%	23.3%
State and local	7.1	9.4	12.6	12.4	12.7
Total	27.8	27.4	31.6	33.3	36.0
Goods and services	21.4	19.4	21.0	18.7	18.9
Transfers	4.0	5.6	7.6	11.1	11.2
Interest	1.3	1.5	1.9	1.7	3.1
Net subsidies	1.0	.9	1.0	1.7	2.8

B. *Full-time equivalent workers: Government employment as a percent of total employment*

	1950	1960	1970	1980	1990
Federal	7.8	8.9	8.6	6.1	5.1
Defense	3.7	4.8	4.6	2.9	2.2
Other	2.9	3.0	2.8	2.2	2.1
State and local	7.7	9.8	12.0	14.2	12.6
Education	3.2	4.4	5.9	7.4	6.3
Other	4.0	4.7	5.3	6.1	5.5
Total	15.4	18.7	20.6	20.3	17.7
Government enterprises	1.1	1.2	1.2	.9	.8

C. *Net fixed reproducible tangible wealth: Government owned as a percent of total tangible wealth*

	1950	1960	1970	1980	1989
Federal	13.8	12.1	9.1	6.3	6.5
Military	9.0	7.8	5.5	3.3	3.8
Infrastructure	2.0	1.8	1.6	1.5	1.2
Housing	.3	.3	.2	.4	.4
Other	2.5	2.2	1.7	1.1	1.1
State and Local	14.6	15.9	18.0	16.5	15.1
Infrastructure	9.1	9.4	10.1	8.9	8.0
Housing	.3	.6	.6	.6	.5
Other	5.1	6.0	7.3	7.0	6.6
Total	28.4	28.0	27.1	22.8	21.7

Notes: Total may not add because of rounding. For expenditures, grants in aid to state and local governments are excluded from the federal sector. For net fixed reproducible tangible wealth, infrastructure for the federal government includes highway and streets as well as conservation and development structures; for state and local governments, highways and streets, conservation and development structures, local sewer systems, and local water supply facilities. Data sources are discussed in Appendix Note 9.3.

Government expenditures as a response to structural complexity

Governments respond to increasing structural complexity of the economy in several different ways. The same as enterprises (Chapter 6), they must master complexity by devoting more resources to information processing, reduce complexity by decentralization, and evade complexity by simplification. Of course, such government efforts always receive lip service. For instance, in the 1980s the Grace Commission approached the problem by proposing the elimination of many programs, as well as streamlining administrative procedures; and in 1993, the Gore Commission made many proposals for simplification and decentralization.

Public expenditures reflect the manner in which the government responds to increasing structural complexity by creating programs helping both itself and the citizenry to meet the challenges of the changing economic environment. In this regard it is useful to begin with the observation that the most dramatic institutional change in the industrialized capitalist nations in the post–World War II period has been the rise in government expenditures as a share of the GDP. Among the OECD nations in the early 1950s this ratio (both current and capital expenditures of the government to the factor price GDP) was roughly 29 percent; by 1990, it had risen to roughly 52 percent.[2] In the United States, the upward trend was also important but not so dramatic: as shown in Table 9.1, government expenditures as a share of GDP rose from 28 percent in 1950 to 36 percent in 1990.

Before turning to the causes underlying this increase in public expenditures, I must emphasize that the growth of governmental expenditures (and taxes to pay for them) represents not merely a reallocation of resources from the private to the public sector. It also adds some additional costs to the private sector. For instance, under most conditions, increasing levels of taxation introduce ever greater distortions into the functioning of the market economy. The impact on work incentives, for example, depends upon the outcome of two economic forces operating in opposite directions: higher taxes lead to a substitution of leisure for work, while the lower posttax income leads to more work to make up for the income loss. Nevertheless, as the tax rate becomes higher, the first effect probably dominates since the number of hours to make up the income lost by paying taxes accelerates as the tax rate rises. Under these circumstances, many citizens make greater efforts to avoid taxes, either by exploiting tax loopholes or by engaging in nontaxed activities such as do-it-yourself projects (higher taxes, like tariffs, can lead to self-sufficiency), barter deals, or illegal activities such as participating in the underground economy. Distortions can be introduced from higher governmental expenditure side as well. For example, as in some countries such as Sweden, it is argued that the extraordinary high rate of absenteeism can be traced to overgenerous health benefits. The combination

2. The data are drawn from OECD (1970 and 1992a) and include the United States For the early 1950s, unweighted averages were calculated for 1950 and 1952. For 1990, unweighted averages were calculated from the data for the latest available year which, in most cases, was 1990. The U.S. data cited in the next sentence differ slightly from the OECD definitions, but the differences are not important for my argument.

of high taxes and generous transfers provides incentives to the immigration of workers and the emigration of capital. Furthermore, some individuals are said to develop a type of "learned helplessness" or dependent mentality. Moreover, all these effects become greater as the tax and expenditure levels rise.[3] The size of these effects is, however, controversial.

A brief review of theories about public expenditures

For the United States the explanations for the rise in government expenditures are varied, and four quite different types of explanations have been offered. Although it is not my intention to rehearse these various theories in detail, a brief discussion is useful to provide perspective for my own approach.[4]

Demand side: Some analysts argue that public expenditures are like most services, that is, their income elasticity of demand is greater than unity, so that the quantity demanded grows faster than income. This feature could come about either from some aspect of the preference structure of individuals in isolation or from the functional requirements of the system, for instance, the increasing structural complexity associated with economic growth. I explore this latter approach in the following discussion. Others trace the increase in expenditures to shifts in preferences, as occasioned by changes in ideology, understanding of the economy and society, or changes in the economic environment. Still others focus on the demand for particular expenditures, for instance, Lorenzo Kristov and his colleague argue that social affinity is crucial in forming preferences of the voters for income transfers.[5] Since the middle-income voters hold the balance of power, the wider the income disparities between them and the poor, the less likely they are to support governmental transfer programs to the poor. Similarly, the wider the income disparities between them and the rich, the more likely they are to back such transfer programs, especially if the costs can be financed by higher taxes on the rich. Thus, changes in the income distribution are causally linked to changes in voter demand for such redistributive transfers.

Supply side: Many analysts point to such supply factors as uncontrollable entitlement programs, bracket creep on the taxation side, or the irreversible tendencies of public bureaucrats and politicians to enlarge their sphere of influence. For instance, cross-section regressions show that for many decades the

3. Lindbeck (1987) has an interesting analysis of "learned helplessness" in Sweden.
4. I have reviewed the various theories about the increase in public expenditures at length elsewhere (Pryor, 1968); and more recent surveys are readily available, for example, Larkey et al. (1984); Lybeck and Henrekson (1988), Mueller (1989); or Lindert (forthcoming).
5. Kristov, Lindert, and McClelland (1992).

relative extent of both governmental health and welfare expenditures in different nations were strongly related to the number of years elapsing since the founding of the Social Security system.[6] In the past many have argued that since productivity of the government sector grows more slowly than in the private sector, the relative costs of this production increase, so that the ratio of public goods and services rises as a share of the GDP. The productivity assumption is open to question and, as shown in Table 9.1, the share of governmentally produced goods and services in the GDP actually fell from 1952 through 1990.

Bureaucratic: In previous years analysts attempted to explain changes in the relative importance of public expenditures in terms of changes in ideology, voter values, or party politics. More recently, attention has turned to models of the behavior of voters, legislatures, bureaucrats, and interest groups. For instance, some argue that legislators making public expenditure decisions often do not consider them as a coherent whole with interrelated implications over the long run, but rather in terms of seriatim decisions about particular programs, often with short-sighted "solutions" to their financing so that the true costs are manifested only in later years when different politicians are in office.[7]

Political economy: Some, particularly Marxists, argue that public expenditures are necessary to keep the system together and that as more systemic difficulties arise, more expenditures become necessary. For instance, as the distribution of income becomes more unequal, more transfers are required to pacify those who might rebel against the system. Others have claimed that the political mobilization of particular groups is particularly important.[8] For instance, elsewhere I have shown that the formation of the social insurance system in industrialized nations was strongly related to the relative importance of labor unions. Gøsta Esping-Andersen has a much broader theory that links political mobilization of workers, class alliances, and the nature of the polity to both quantitative and qualitative aspects (for instance, access to benefits and range of entitlements) of the welfare state. Dennis C. Mueller and Peter Murrell show that the absolute number of interest groups is correlated with the relative size of the public sector, although the nature of the causal links, I must add, is not entirely clear.

The political-economy approach for democracies also leads to an analysis of voter resistance to increased public expenditures. More specifically, voters are aware of these expenditures and their benefits, as well as of the direct costs to

6. Pryor (1968).
7. Larkey et al. 1984).
8. The three references are: Pryor (1968), Esping-Andersen (1991), and Mueller and Murrell (1986).

finance them and of the indirect costs to the economy of such higher expenditures. Three quite different analyses of voter behavior in presidential elections in the post–World War II period include a variable indicating increases in the volume of public expenditures.[9] They show that increases in these expenditures in previous years have resulted in a reduction of votes for the incumbent party. Such results suggest that any president who wants to be reelected would, other things being equal, work to reduce expenditures. Sam Peltzman, who has the most extensive such study, shows that these results also obtain both in senatorial elections and in gubernatorial elections, where the key variable in the latter elections is the increase in the volume of state expenditures.

The demand, supply, bureaucratic, and political-economy approaches, as they are commonly employed, can be criticized because, for the most part, they look at public expenditures as a whole. Such hyperaggregation obscures the fact that governmental budgets are usually voted upon program by program. Moreover, the most important causal elements seem to influence individual types of public expenditures. Thus, considerably more insight on the public sector as a whole is gained by studying the various expenditures separately to see which are growing most rapidly.[10]

It also should be clear from this brief review that the growth of public expenditures is the result of opposing forces. It is quite possible that welfare states can "overshoot" and that, as the long-term costs become evident, measures will be taken to reduce the ratios of such transfers to the GDP. This is occurring in several West European welfare states during the early 1990s. Whether the large transfers in such welfare states are responsible for the serious Euroslump in the same period, or whether instead the causes are traceable to ill-considered macropolicies or overregulation, particularly of the labor market, must be left for others to decide.

Possible impacts of structural complexity on public expenditures

In what manner is the increase in public expenditures a response to an increase in structural complexity, especially as manifested by the increased het-

9. These studies are by Niskanen (1975), Peltzman (1992), and Winston and Crandall (1994). All three of these studies also show that voters place considerably more weight on the performance of the economy than on public expenditure increases.

10. It must be emphasized that causal forces influencing public expenditures operate differently across space than over time and, moreover, such forces may act differently in the short and long run. For instance, the income elasticity of an expenditure may be greater than unity over time, but not among similar types of governments at a single point in time (many examples of this are provided in Pryor, 1968). Moreover, such elasticities are quite different in the short and long run for many different types of expenditures. Similarly, party politics may play a role in the increase of a given public expenditure at a given time; but the programs underlying this increase may persist for quite different reasons.

erogeneity of the population? Two clusters of causal relations between structural complexity and public expenditures can be isolated which, for convenience, are designated economic and social linkages.

Economic linkages: Government expenditures are directly affected by changes in population heterogeneity either when these expenditures are directly linked to a heterogeneity indicator or when these expendi tures are allocated differentially to a group whose increase signifies an increase in heterogeneity. The most obvious example of the latter, of course, is pension payments from the Social Security system. Given the current age distribution, increasing heterogeneity is reflected by a greater share of the aged in the population. If the social insurance system pays recipients a pension equal to a specified percentage of the average wage, then obviously the higher the share of aged in the population, the higher the social insurance tax on those in the work force. But the underlying assumption is important. As a share of GDP such payments need not rise if the age of eligibility to receive such payments rises over time or if the share of social insurance payments to average wage declines as the share of the aged in the population rises. Of course, both are politically difficult to carry out if the electorate becomes increasingly aged and if the aged have a higher participation in elections than younger voters.[11]

This kind of principle applies to other types of governmental expenditures that are directed disproportionately toward the aged. An example is health care: in both the late 1970s and the late 1980s, various public sources financed roughly 38 percent of total expenditures, but for those over sixty-five, this percentage was roughly 64 percent.[12] The shift in the age distribution, magnified by the greater per capita health expenditures of the aged, means growth in governmental health expenditures. If public and private real health expenditures per age group had remained the same in the period from 1950 through 1990,

11. Richard B. McKenzie (1990) argues that the political clout of the elderly has begun to decline in the United States, as manifested by the recent decline in per capita benefits. He offers as a theoretical justification the "law of the many," namely, that as the number of elderly increases, it becomes increasingly difficult to organize them, the common goals become increasingly diffuse, and the free-rider problem becomes increasingly severe. Although I find his application of public choice theory dubious, he does point out from a number of different indicators that after 1980 net total benefits to the aged are growing less fast than the elderly population; and the data presented below show a fall in the ratio of retirement benefits to the factor price GDP.

12. Waldo et al. (1989). For the calculations in this paragraph health expenditures per age group come from this source and the population data come from the same sources used earlier in this chapter. If 1977 health expenditures per age group are used instead, the results are of the same order of magnitude.

total health expenditures due to the change in the age distribution and size of the population would have risen 0.36 percent a year; but health expenditures by the government would have risen 0.65 percent a year. Although both rates are far below the average annual increase of real health expenditures of 5.1 percent during the period, the increasing aging of the population, combined with the disproportionate per capita payments to the aged played a causal role that must not be neglected.

For educational expenditures the role of structural complexity is also straightforward. As I argue in Chapter 3, as technology becomes increasingly complex, the need for a labor force with greater and more heterogeneous skills increases as well. This increasing structural complexity of the labor force, in turn, requires greater expenditures on education.

As the distribution of income becomes more unequal, it might be argued that the need for redistributive transfer payments by the government becomes greater. But this raises the problem of how such a need is translated into actual expenditures. As noted previously, social affinity appears to play an important causal role and the presence of an underclass with incomes much lower than the rest of society may discourage such transfers. In a multiple regression analysis using series for the United States covering almost a hundred years, Peter H. Lindert finds that welfare expenditures redistributing income are positively related to such economic variables as unemployment, share of old and per capita GDP. They are also negatively related to the ratio of average incomes of those in the middle to the bottom quintile of income; the wider the gap, the less the expenditures, other things remaining equal.[13]

Other more indirect economic linkages can also be specified.[14] But these do not yet have much empirical support and would lead us too far afield.

---

13. Lindert (1993).
14. For instance, if heterogeneity per se of the population is greater, we can make the argument that the demands placed on government would increased since a more heterogeneous population can have many more different demands on the public sector than a homogeneous population. Again, the problem is how these demands get translated into actual expenditures.

   If voters are completely selfish, the majority would out-vote the minority so that it would be as if such minority voters never existed. If the various minority groups hold the balance of power on other issues so that coalitions are important or if voters take note of "community effects" then the heterogeneity of the voters might be reflected in greater expenditures. Unfortunately, the public finance literature is only beginning to explore in an empirical fashion the formation of community preferences and the relation between the public expenditure preferences of various groups and actual expenditures (Cutler, Elmendorf, and Zeckhauser, 1993). The situation is further complicated because traditional public finance theory tells us that in cases where citizen preferences are heterogeneous, we are more likely to find a multitude of special districts that provide or do not provide the single service in question, a proposition for which some interesting support is available (Nelson, 1990).

   The shards of direct empirical evidence on these matters also are mixed and confusing. In the late 1950s economists carried out a study of public expenditures of municipalities in

Social linkages: One type of social linkage of structural complexity and public expenditures occurs between inequalities of income or wealth and expenditures for police protection.[15] Isaac Ehrlich has carried out cross-sectional empirical studies of U.S. municipalities to show a direct linkage between crimes, particularly against property, and income inequalities. Others such as Edward N. Muller have used international evidence to show linkages between income inequalities and political stability. Whenever insecurity, arising either from criminal or political factors, occurs, an obvious response is a demand for greater police and protection by the state.

A different kind of social linkage resulting from greater structural complexity occurs with governmental health expenditures. Gregory Pappas and his colleagues present data showing that lower socioeconomic groups have higher mortality rates and, furthermore, this inverse relationship was more pronounced in 1986 than in 1960.[16] Given the increasing inequality of income that has occurred in recent years, this trend is likely to continue, at least for the next decade. Under certain political conditions, such a growing disparity may also act as an important force to increase government health expenditures, especially for the group whose health has been falling relatively behind.

A final type of social linkage looms on the horizon. As noted in the next chapter, family savings rates declined during the 1980s for adults of all ages. The children of this generation may be forced to tax themselves to make up for the profligacy of their elders, at least if the former do not want the latter to live in destitution. Given the nation's declining social cohesiveness, however, this assumption might be questioned.

Wisconsin (Schmandt and Stephens, 1960) as well as of counties in the same state (Shapiro, 1961), in which the variable to be explained was the number of public services (from a list of 550 such services), rather than the total amount of expenditures. In both studies, the number of different public services was highly correlated with the population of the unit. Since it seems reasonable to assume that a key aspect of heterogeneity of the population, namely particular groups reaching a critical mass for political action, is related to the population size of the unit, some relationship is established between heterogeneity and number of services. Moreover, alternative interpretations in terms of economies of scale do not seem promising.

Attempts to examine the matter directly by including measures of population heterogeneity, for instance, the percentage of nonwhites or the percentage of people over sixty-five into the determinants of public expenditures give quite mixed results. In particular, such heterogeneity seems to have an opposite impact on local than on state governmental expenditures. State and county demographic characteristics also play quite different roles in explaining county expenditures (Cutler, Elmendorf, and Zeckhauser, 1993). On a national level, public expenditures may be inversely related to ethnic heterogeneity because of ethnic heterogeneity raises the transactions costs of reaching collective decisions about such spending (Mueller and Murrell, 1986). Until more research is carried out, this linkage between population heterogeneity and public expenditures must be considered "interesting, but not proven."

15. The two sources cited in this paragraph are: Ehrlich (1973) and Muller (1988).
16. Pappas et al. (1993).

For completeness, it is necessary to emphasize that many governmental expenditures do not seem related at all to structural complexity in general or population heterogeneity in particular. These would, for example, include expenditures for defense and diplomacy or for interest on government debt. Given the ruling ideology that the U.S. government should not directly intervene into production except in very special occasions, it also does not seem likely that governmental expenditures for economic purposes are directly related to complexity. Similarly, governmental expenditures for general administration, fire, and city services should not reveal a strong relation with heterogeneity of the population or, for that matter, more general measures of complexity.

Some data on U.S. public expenditures

Classifying governmental expenditures according to the arguments presented previously, we would expect that those expenditures more strongly tied to some aspect of structural complexity would show a greater increase. Although many of these expenditures have other determinants as well, the purpose in this exercise is to establish a presumption that structural complexity is an important causal force underlying public expenditure growth.

The data presented in Table 9.2 show that the ratio of most types of governmental expenditures to the factor price GDP increased significantly, particularly between the mid 1950s and the early 1980s. For the entire thirty-eight-year period covered in the table, the ratio of all expenditures grew at an average annual rate of .7 percent. The ratio of those expenditures identified previously as strongly related to complexity increased at an average annual rate of 2.5 percent, in contrast to the −.7 average annual growth rate of those public expenditures less directly related to population heterogeneity.

The ratio of GDP governmental expenditures for health, hospitals, and medical care increased more rapidly than other major expenditure categories, namely at average annual rate of about 5.1 percent for the period. This is considerably higher than the annual increase of about 3.5 percent for the ratio of total health expenditures to the GDP during roughly the same period. The shift in age structure discussed above accounted for less than 10 percent of this increase.[17] Among the new programs introduced during the post–World War II period that have led to an increase in governmental expenditures for health, Medicare (health expenditures for the aged) and Medicaid (health expendi-

---

17. The current price governmental expenditures for health, hospitals, and medical care was deflated by a price index of which 90 percent was represented by the implicit price deflator of medical expenditures in general (national income and product account (NIPA), Tables 2.6 and 2.7) and 10 percent was represented by the implicit price deflator for nonresidential construction (NIPA, Table 7.1). Such a deflator is, of course, very rough and, as a result, so is the estimate of the growth of real government expenditures.

Table 9.2. Public expenditures as a percentage of factor price GDP

	1952–5	1956–60	1961–5	1966–70	1971–5	1976–80	1981–5	1986–90	Average annual percent increase of ratio
All public expenditures	28.6%	28.5%	30.0%	32.4%	34.4%	34.1%	36.2%	36.0%	.7%
Public expenditures more directly related to population heterogeneity									
Health, hospitals, medical care	1.0	1.0	1.2	2.2	3.1	3.5	4.0	4.4	5.1
Retirement and disability	2.3	3.5	4.4	4.7	6.2	6.7	7.0	6.3	2.8
Police and correction	.5	.6	.6	.7	.9	.9	1.0	1.2	2.5
Education and training	3.2	3.8	4.5	5.6	6.5	6.2	5.7	5.7	1.7
Welfare, unemployment insurance, other income support, housing community development	1.8	1.9	1.9	1.8	2.9	3.0	2.9	2.6	1.6
Subtotal	8.8	10.8	12.6	15.0	19.5	20.4	20.7	20.2	2.5
Public expenditures less directly related to population heterogeneity									
Interest payments (net)	1.4	1.5	1.5	1.5	1.6	1.8	2.8	3.3	2.3
General government, fire, city services, recreation, unallocated expenditures	1.7	1.9	2.0	2.2	2.8	2.9	2.7	2.8	1.6
Economic functions (energy, agriculture, transportation natural resources, postal, economic development, regulation, commercial activities)	3.2	3.5	3.7	3.6	3.3	3.0	2.9	2.6	– .8
Defense, foreign affairs, foreign aid, space	13.6	10.9	10.1	10.0	7.2	6.0	7.2	7.1	– 2.0
Subtotal	19.8	17.8	17.4	17.4	14.9	13.7	15.6	15.8	– .7

Note: Expenditures include all levels of government and current, capital, transfer, subsidy and all other types of expenditures. The sources of data are discussed in Appendix Note 9.3

tures for the poor) have been particularly important. Both the aged and the poor, I should add, have particularly high health expenditure needs.

With regard to general health expenditures, Joseph P. Newhouse points out that the major source of increase of medical expenditures lies in the area of hospital costs. It is noteworthy that patient admissions levels have not greatly increased since 1950; moreover, bed–days per patient peaked around 1970 and were roughly the same in the 1980s as in the 1950s and 1960s.[18] He argues that much of the increase in general health expenditures lies in the willingness to pay for the new medical technology, much of which was financed by government research grants. The faster growth of public than private expenditures for health care, of course, represents something more than this, namely the assuming by the public sector of an increasing burden of health expenditures of the aged and the poor. Thus, increasing population heterogeneity plays an important indirect role in the growth of governmental expenditures for health and hospitals.

For retirement and disability payments, the direct role of increased aging is more apparent. If such payments kept up with the general rise in labor productivity (1.8 percent a year from 1950 through 1990) and the rise in the ratio of those 65 and over to the labor force (.4 percent a year for the same period), this would add up to 2.2 percent, which is little different from the actual rise in such expenditures. It is noteworthy that the ratio of retirement and disability expenditures (as shown in Table 9.2) to GDP declined in the latter part of the 1980s at a time when the ratios of the aged to the labor force or population rose. This suggests that the political linkages between the relative importance of the aged as a voting bloc and the actual retirement payments are not as firm as commonly believed.

The 2.5 percent annual increase in the ratio of expenditures for police and correction represents most graphically the increasing social heterogeneity and an erosion of social cohesiveness.The 1.7 percent annual increase of the ratio of expenditures for education and training is roughly equal to the general rise in labor productivity.

Of the public expenditures more directly related to population heterogeneity, welfare and income support expenditures have increased the least. These expenditures increased fastest between 1970 and 1980, a period in which the distribution of income showed a rough stability, rather than between 1980 and 1990 when all indicators showed a deterioration in income inequality (see Figure 2.1). Furthermore, such expenditures as a share of the GDP decreased in the 1980s at a time when the inequality of income was increasing. Underlying this greater acceptance of income inequalities was the increasing social distance between the poor that was discussed previously. If the ratio of

18. Newhouse (1992).

average income of the middle to lower quintiles of the income distribution continues to rise, we should not expect a significant rise in welfare expenditures in the near future, at least if the social affinity explanation of welfare expenditures continues to hold.

To what extent do the governmental expenditures shown in Table 9.2 represent a movement toward a welfare state? According to Assar Lindbeck, a welfare state adds four additional functions to the traditional roles of a capitalist government: mitigation of destitution; equalization of lifetime income and wealth, investment in human capital, and reduction of economic uncertainty facing individuals.[19] Clearly education expenditures and Social Security fill the last three functions; but the elimination of destitution has hardly been met. Moreover, according to data presented in Appendix Note 9.1, social security expenditures per family are roughly the same absolute amount for each income group. Only about 40 percent of these payments go to families with incomes less than $20,000. For expenditures not directed toward the aged (which constitute about 40 percent of total transfers) this share is about half. In 1990, transfer expenditures of the federal government amounted to about 9.6 percent of total personal income; nevertheless, the share of all transfers going to families with incomes less than $20,000 amounted to about 4 percent of total personal income. In short, the U.S. transfer system has only three of the four functions of the welfare state; and, as noted previously, it seems unlikely that welfare expenditures as a share of GDP will take a significant leap upward.

Turning to expenditures not strongly related to structural complexity, within the general government expenditures, the fastest growing component was "unallocated expenditures" (4.3 percent a year), followed by fire protection (2.6 percent annually) and recreation/culture (2.3 percent annually).[20] These

---

19. Lindbeck (1987). Other additions to the "classical" functions of the state in a capitalist society include: expenditures to stabilize the economy, to encourage economic development and trade, and to provide transfers (rents) to particular groups that have no welfare need.

   It might be added that other parts of the federal budget do not serve this redistributional function in a very notable function either. For instance, *tax expenditures* (the cost of particular tax breaks) in 1990 amounted to about 6.6 percent of personal income. Although the impact on the income distribution is not known, they are generally believed to be much more regressively distributed than transfers. For instance, for tax expenditures due to deductions of mortgage interest, local property tax exclusions, and Social Security income exclusions, which amount to almost a quarter of these tax exclusions, amounted to $99 and $259, respectively, in 1993 for households with incomes of $10,001 to $20,000 and $20,001 to $30,000, while they amounted to $1,401 and $2,854 respectively for households with incomes of $75,001 to $100,000 and over $100,000. These estimates are rough and are designed to give some idea of the orders of magnitudes involved; they are based on data from U.S. Congress, Joint Committee on Taxation (1993).

20. Fire protection expenditures includes certain costs not related to fire fighting such as the paramedical services administered by fire departments.

three expenditures, however, represented only a small ratio of the GDP. Defense expenditures are clearly related to the state of international tensions and throughout the period in the table, they reflect the state of the Cold War. Interest expenditures, which have risen dramatically in recent years, reflect the cumulative budget imbalances, a matter treated below in a broader context.

For each of the public expenditures discussed previously, causal factors other than structural complexity are also at work. Nevertheless, the clear association of different types of increased structural complexity with an increasing share of public expenditures in the GDP should be evident. This, in turn, leads us to believe that the share of public expenditures as a share of GDP will slowly continue to rise.

The government as a generator of structural complexity

In many different ways the government can change the complexity of the economic environment. In certain cases particular types of government activity can reduce economic complexity, for instance, by setting standards to reduce the amount of information buyers need to process. But in other cases the promulgation of economic regulations can increase complexity of management by requiring producers to carry out production in a more costly way and in a manner requiring more information to be collected and processed.

Determinants of regulation

The positive theory of government regulation is far less developed and the tests are far more ambiguous than for the positive theory of public expenditures. Consequently, I only sketch the main kinds of arguments advanced.[21] As in the case of expenditures, we need to distinguish causal factors on the demand and supply side.

Demand factors for regulation are reflected in the old-fashioned view that government regulation arises from the need to correct some type of market failure, real or imagined. This approach sometimes has been called the *normative analysis as a positive theory* and the clearest cases are in the area of environment, health, and safety. I must add that problems in these areas can also be attacked by means other than direct regulation, for instance, by changes in tax or liability laws. Market failures also arise from natural monopolies where the market distortions can only be resolved by government production or regulation. The existence of a particular natural monopoly is partly a function of technology and, in some industries, such as transportation and

---

21. A more complete and nuanced analysis can be found in Peltzman (1989).

communications, traditional monopoly positions are eroding. In transportation, for instance, considerable competition now exists between railroads, trucks, and air transport; and in communications, recent technological developments in broad channel satellite and fiber-optic cable communication have increased competition as well.

Supply factors might be considered for those types of regulation that allow extra-high profits (rents) to be gained by participants in the regulated industry. This approach is sometimes called the *economic theory of regulation.* These rents could arise from the regulatory agency being directly captured by the industry (for example, barbers inducing a licensing agency to set extra-high educational standards to reduce entry into the industry). Or the capture could be indirect, for instance, by the industry supplying the resources for the winning margin of politicians friendly to the industry. Problems arise, however, in specifying the exact mechanisms by which these rents are gained and the degree to which politicians are willing to risk placing costs on one group to obtain the money and votes of another.

Other approaches that focus on ideological elements sometimes are offered to explain the growth of regulation that focus on ideological elements. For instance, as I show later, the relative resources devoted to regulation fell during the Reagan and Bush administrations.

Unfortunately, none of these approaches is adequate. For instance, they do not really explain why governmental regulatory activities took their greatest leap during the Nixon administration (for instance, the Environmental Protection Agency and the Occupational Safety and Health Administration were both founded early in this presidency), why significant deregulation began during the Carter presidency, or why deregulation took the particular form that it did in later years. Another problem in using these approaches is that the quantitative dimensions of benefits and costs of regulation are difficult to pin down. For instance, it is often pointed out that such regulations give rise to "deadweight losses." As the regulations move output away from the efficient level (either because of regulation changes or because the economy changes), these losses to the economy increase. Although economists can quantify some of these costs, most voters do not read the technical journals in which such estimates appear and we can not specify the point at which they become unbearable so that deregulation begins.[22]

Despite the lack of hard evidence, some evidence suggests that voters are aware, nevertheless, of these costs. More specifically, from a regression analysis of voting behavior in presidential elections and an assumption that government expenditures on regulation measures in an approximate fashion regulatory activities, Clifford Winston and Robert W. Crandall argue that increased

---

22. Winston (1993) summarizes these costs in a number of industries.

economic regulation resulted in a small loss in the share of votes for the incumbent parties in the post–World War II era, other things being equal.[23] They also note that in the same period, increased social regulation (which they define to include pollution abatement, enforcement of wage and hour standards, enforcement of pure food and drugs, transportation regulation, coast guard, and agricultural marketing regulations) resulted in a small increase in votes for the incumbent party.

Extent and impact of regulation

In this brief discussion I focus only upon federal government regulations of production of goods and services. I make the simplifying assumption that the extent of regulation is proportional to the direct costs of the regulatory agency, as measured either by labor force or costs. Although this seems a more defensible procedure than counting pages in the *Federal Register* or the *Code of Federal Regulations,* it must be considered only as a first approximation. The approach is based on a simple idea: the more regulations that must be enforced, the more regulators there will be.[24] Although considerable regulation also is carried out by state and local governments, information about the expenditures and personnel for such purposes and the impact of such expenditures, unfortunately, has not been collected on any systematic and extensive basis.

Problems in isolating governmental expenditures on regulation arise because of difficulties in separating regulation from other activities such as policy implementation or police functions. Thus, in drawing up lists of the relevant agencies and bureaus, it is necessary to include only those whose activities significantly influence individual decision making of businesses and consumers, which means that we must sometimes separate expenditures for particular bureaus within agencies. For instance, only part of the Federal Reserve is devoted to regulation of the monetary sector. Three different time series are available to examine these matters.[25] Given the different causal factors at work, I also distinguish seven different groups of regulatory agencies. Table 9.3 presents the relevant data.

23. Winston and Crandall (1994).
24. Clearly this assumption is only a rough first approximation. It is certainly possible, for instance, to enforce more regulations by reducing the number of regulators, but raising the amount of fines for those who are caught.
25. These are by DuBoff (1993), Warren and Lis (1992), and Winston and Crandall (1994). I am grateful to Richard DuBoff, Robert W. Crandall, and Clifford Winston for allowing me access to their unpublished worksheets. Warren and Lis publish the details of their calculations, but their series do not extend as far back in time as the other two. I have selected the most extensive, which is by Winston and Crandall, but have followed the procedure of DuBoff in separating them into two groups, depending on whether they are "pure regulatory" or "partial regulatory." Although this procedure is subjective, it allows us to gauge the margin of error in the calculations.

Table 9.3. *Some direct costs of federal regulation agencies as a share of GDP*

	1951–5	1956–60	1961–5	1966–70	1971–5	1976–80	1981–5	1986–90
Part A: Broad definition								
Global total	.063%	.074%	.098%	.113%	.205%	.229%	.209%	.197%
Consumer protection	.024	.029	.031	.035	.051	.052	.044	.037
Job safety/working conditions	.006	.007	.010	.011	.020	.027	.024	.019
Environmental protection	.001	.001	.001	.005	.041	.053	.056	.067
Financial regulation	.007	.008	.012	.016	.017	.019	.020	.025
Energy regulation	.001	.005	.010	.008	.014	.022	.019	.011
Industry and trade regulation	.010	.011	.013	.012	.013	.013	.011	.011
Transportation/communication regulation	.013	.014	.022	.026	.050	.044	.035	.028
Part B: Narrow definition								
Global total: narrow definition	.018	.023	.038	.044	.102	.132	.123	.117
Consumer protection regulation	.002	.002	.005	.007	.013	.016	.013	.011
Job safety/working conditions	.004	.004	.006	.007	.017	.023	.021	.016
Environmental protection	.000	.000	.000	.004	.038	.049	.053	.063
Financial regulation	.003	.003	.006	.008	.009	.010	.010	.010
Energy regulation	.001	.005	.010	.008	.014	.022	.018	.011
Industry and trade regulation	.005	.006	.007	.006	.006	.007	.005	.003
Transportation/communication regulation	.003	.003	.004	.004	.004	.005	.004	.002

Notes: The data represent the regulatory activities of particular bureaus and offices of the federal government. The distinction between broad and narrow definitions of regulation follows the procedure outlined by Richard DuBoff; the former group includes fifty-eight different agencies; of these only thirty are included in the latter group. The sources of the data are discussed in Note Appendix 9.3.

As shown in both sets of data, the total expenditures of the regulatory agencies are a very small share of GDP. The changes in these costs, as a share of the GDP, give some idea about changes in the degree of regulation. It is noteworthy that this ratio increased steadily throughout most of the period, taking a particularly large jump in the early 1970s and reaching a peak in the 1976–1980 period, before declining in the 1980s. Certain data, not completely comparable with those in Table 9.3, suggest that regulatory expenditures as a percent of GDP increased very slightly in the early 1990s.[26] A majority, but not all, of the various regulatory expenditures (again measured as a fraction of the GDP) followed the same pattern. By way of contrast, relative environmental expenditures increased steadily through the period, as did the broadly defined expenditures for financial regulation. Industry and trade regulations either remained constant or decreased (depending on the definition); and expenditures on transportation and communication regulation took a particularly dramatic fall in the 1980s.

The crucial issue is: to what extent have these increased expenditures on regulatory activities by the government resulted in increased structural complexity for the economy? One possible indicator is the cost that they entail for the particular regulated enterprises. Such an approach, however, brings us face to face with the problem that a particular enterprise may have higher costs, even though the regulation has a net benefit to the economy as a whole. Although expenditures on pollution abatement and control amounted to 1.4 percent of the GDP in 1990, the benefits to consumers and businesses of such expenditures in terms of the resulting cleaner air and water, as well as more effective solid waste disposal, may have been much more.[27] The various federal laws and regulations about seat belts, windshield wipers, head restraints, fuel evaporation systems, exterior protection, catalytic converters, emission control systems, and other safety and health measures, added $666 (1976 dollars) to the cost of an average automobile between 1968 and 1978. Consumers, however, may have been willing to pay at least some of these added charges on their own free will so that such additional costs can not be characterized as a total loss to them. Finally, government regulations, particularly for standardization, might actually reduce costs; as noted later, hospital administration costs in Canada's regulated system as a share of total hospital expenditures are much lower than in U.S. hospitals.

Measuring the costs imposed by regulation on producers involves distinguishing four different types of costs: direct compliance costs (the capital and current costs), process costs (the paperwork involved), the losses in overall efficiency and economic growth in the economy, and the transfer costs (the

26. Melinda Warren (1994), p. 4.
27. Rutledge and Leonard (1992). The regulation costs on automobiles come from Weidenbaum (1978).

costs shifted from the producer to someone else). Since neither of the last two types of costs would greatly affect the structural complexity, we need to focus our primary attention on the first two costs. For purposes of this discussion, the analysis can be informal; some detailed quantitative estimates of the magnitudes of these costs are presented in Appendix Note 9.1.

The several sets of estimates available for the late 1970s and 1980s show that the direct compliance and process costs of regulation are very roughly 4 to 5 percent of the GDP. These estimates also suggest that $1 of federal expenditures on regulation results very roughly in $25 to $50 of additional costs of the private producers, a ratio that depends on the type of regulation. Although such quantitative estimates leave much to be desired, it seems reasonable to conclude from the data in Table 9.3 that the structural complexity introduced into the economy by governmental regulation increased considerably between 1950 and 1980. The extent to which such structural complexity decreased in the 1980s is more controversial, since the decline in relative federal expenditures was small and might have been offset by a change in the ratio of costs imposed on private enterprises for every dollar of federal expenditures on regulation.

Complications of laws and governmental regulations

Greater complications in laws and governmental regulations increase the structural complexity of the economic environment by raising the information costs facing producers of goods and services. It is useful to enquire briefly why governmental regulations are becoming more complicated.

Anne O. Krueger and Roderick Duncan have an interesting approach, arguing that increasing complications of regulation over time is a regular empirical phenomenon. It arises whenever political authorities attempt to control economic activity.[28] In the initial stages the rules are often relatively straightforward and simple. These laws, however, become increasingly convoluted, not just from some primal urge for government regulations to expand, but for several practical and specific reasons:

Correction of inequities: When the laws are initially implemented, certain groups find themselves disadvantaged, often in ways not foreseen by the drafters of the legislation. Some unforeseen and serious problems of fairness invariably arise, and attempts to address these and to reduce inequities lead to more complicated rules. An import licensing scheme discriminates between producers who had large inventories at the start of the base period and those who had low inventories; a wage freeze law discriminates in favor of those whose new contracts were signed before the cutoff date and against those

28. Krueger and Duncan (1993).

Table 9.4: *Indicators of the activities of the Internal Revenue Service*

	Administration costs of IRS as percent of GDP		Different number of forms		Text pages explaining law
1951–5	.08%				
1956–60	.07				
1961–5	.08				
1966–70	.08				
1971–5	.09				
1976–80	.09	1977	368	1976	682
1981–5	.09				
1986–90	.10	1989	392	1986	1379

Note: Sources of data are presented in Appendix 9.3.

whose contracts become due after the cutoff date. Correcting these inequities leads to a host of amendments and additional complications.

Self-interest of bureaucrats and intermediaries: once corrections of inequities begin to be made, the number of bureaucrats to administer the laws increases. Moreover, the more complicated the set of laws, the more likely it is to find a set of specialized intermediaries (lawyers and accountants), who understand the law and sell their aid to others. For instance, given the complications of the income tax law (see the following discussion), a whole industry of tax preparers has arisen. It is to the advantage of both bureaucrats administering the law and the specialized intermediaries to preserve the complicated structure of the law – indeed, to make them even more difficult to understand.

Market responses to regulation: the market responds to laws in many ways that are unforeseen by the original drafters. Krueger and Duncan point out the case where the lower U.S. tariffs on vests than on jackets meant that foreign countries sent "vests" to the United States plus additional material used to sew sleeves on them. Similarly, sugar quota laws ("sugar" defined as any product with more than 94 percent cane or beet sugar content) led to Canada exporting to the United States a sugar "substitute" composed of 93 percent sugar and 7 percent high fructose corn syrup (which is not sugar).

The operation of these three underlying causes of increasing complication of legislation can be seen in income tax legislation. Initially it was a proportionate tax of 1 percent on income plus some simple surtaxes. Table 9.4 provides some indicators of the way in which this law has become more complicated, even after the tax "simplification" laws of 1976–7 and 1985–6. Some data are available, namely the number of hours to fill out the forms, suggesting that some reduction in their complication may have taken place.[29] It must be added, however, that these compliance numbers are very rough estimates and must be taken with a grain of salt.

The tax system is the most egregious and obvious example of the increasing complications of U.S. laws. Many other government programs such as the sugar quota laws – or for that matter, agricultural price support regulations – reveal the same pattern. This tendency is not, of course, inevitable and periodically steps are taken to simplify or to deregulate.[30]

The impact of structural complexity on governmental policy effectiveness

As shown by the survey results presented in Chapter 6, increasing structural complexity influences the operations of enterprises in the private sector and forces them to adopt particular strategies of survival. In the government sector it also has an important impact, particularly on the effectiveness of government policy. More specifically, this structural complexity is reflected by deficient information for policy making, slowness in decision making and difficulties in policy implementation; and each deserves brief attention.

Information deficiencies

As argued in Chapter 1, increased structural complexity is both caused by, and is reflected by, higher information costs. It becomes more difficult to understand what is currently happening to the system. As Hilary Stout has noted:[31] "In fact, as the economy grows more complex, it also gets harder to measure by current methods." Decision makers in both the private and public sector must rely on incomplete, inaccurate, and late information. These problems can be easily illustrated with several examples of common U.S. macroeconomic statistics.

Incomplete information: In recent years, many have pointed out the incompleteness of U.S. macroeconomic statistics. In certain cases, for instance, the national accounts do not include production of "bads" such as pollution. They also do not include production of the underground economy, which various economists have estimated to amount to 2 to more than 20 percent of the GDP.[32] Moreover, in recent years these omissions appear to becoming more important in relation to the total GDP.

29. Hopkins (1992).
30. There are also a few other recent articles on the origin and impact of legal complications; these include studies by Bezeau (1979), Milliron (1976), and Daly and Omer (1990).
31. Stout (1989).
32. Schoepfle et al. (1992) surveys various estimates. According to O'Neill (1983), omission of the underground economy from the national accounts has reduced measured growth of the published GDP from 1950 to 1981 by .2 percentage points a year.

Inaccurate information: as illustrated in the next chapter, savings and investment statistics from the Commerce Department and the Federal Reserve Bank differ considerably, and only partially can these differences be attributed to the different concepts on which the statistics are based. Moreover, the trends in these two sets of savings statistics are often different. A gap, albeit much smaller, exists between labor force statistics, as published by the Census Bureau in its Current Population Survey and as published by the Bureau of Labor Statistics in its survey employment of business and governmental establishments. In the short term these two series have shown quite different trends. Many various price or output series do not take properly into account quality changes; and the Consumer Price Index is said to overstate actual inflation by one percentage point. The most egregious case of inaccurate price data on the producer side was computers, where such a correction raised production of producer durable equipment as a whole by a significant amount, especially between 1977 and 1984.[33] As noted in Chapter 4, measurements of service productivity are highly uncertain. In recent decades the quality of the data in the U.S. decennial censuses appears to have declined. Many other cases can be cited.

Late information: For many key statistics used in policy making, the final estimates are quite different from the estimates originally announced. For the constant price GNP, for instance, the standard deviation of change between the estimate announced by the Commerce Department 15 days after the end of the quarter and the final revised estimate is 2.2 percentage points.[34] Since the average quarterly change (annualized) is 2.4 percent, this means that if the average quarterly change is announced in the original estimate, there is a 28 percent probability than the actual change of GNP will either be negative or more than twice the original estimate. Even more disturbing, this probability falls only to 18 percent when comparing the estimate made 45 days after the end of the quarter and the final estimate. The accuracy problem is even worse for many components of the GNP or GDP, and the explanations of the annual revisions of these macroeconomic statistics are disturbing.

In recent years comparisons have begun to be made of other important government statistics as well. For payroll employment growth estimates by the Department of Labor, the accuracy appears slightly better than the GDP estimates.[35] For both the Federal Reserve Board's initial estimate of the growth of

33. Data on the extent of the correction come from *Survey of Current Business,* 66, No. 3 (March 1986), p. 10, and amounted to .4 percent a year.
34. Mankiw and Shapiro (1986). Young (1987) surveys the accuracy of the estimates of the components of GDP. The annual revisions of the GDP usually appear in *Survey of Current Business* (July issue).
35. Neumark and Wascher (1991). The estimates of the money supply, industrial production, and housing sales are examined respectively by: Mankiw, Runkle, and Shapiro (1984); Kennedy (1993); and Stout (1989).

the money supply and of industrial production, the accuracy of the original estimate appears worse than for the GDP. The worst case that I could find is housing sales, where the standard deviation of difference between initial and final estimates is 9 percentage points.

Clearly both public and private policy makers relying on the most recent government statistical estimates have a difficult job in trying to figure out what is happening to the economy. As Martin Zimmerman, the chief economist of Ford Motor Company, once noted in talking about the role of business economists:[36] "In theory, you're trying to find out what the future is going to be like. That's difficult when the past keeps changing."

Slow decision speeds

The increasing structural complexity of the economy gives rise to two major factors acting as a brake to policy making. The problems of selecting a solution are more complicated. And with increasing heterogeneity of the population, it is difficult to arrive at a policy solution.

More difficult policy problems: The more structurally complex the economy, the more difficult it is to gain an understanding of what solutions might be effective for any given problem.

One part of the problem is in understanding what to do. In the case study presented in Chapter 8 of the changing degree of competitiveness, a regression analysis using readily available information on a large number of explanatory variables was able to predict only about 20 percent of the variance of the change in competitiveness. To understand the problem of changing competitiveness in greater detail, an enormous amount of analysis and information processing is required on a highly microlevel. A quantitative perspective is provided by a study of the Japanese government's aid to particular industries by Richard Beason and David E. Weinstein.[37] According to their calculation, noted in passing in the previous chapter, there is little relationship between the use of four industrial policy measures (cheap loans, transfers, trade protection, and tax relief) and the growth of the industry. These results can be interpreted as meaning that even the Japanese government has considerable difficulty in selecting "winning industries" and, in the process, supports a great many "losing industries" as well. In a massive reassessment of the role of the Japanese government in the financing of "strategic industries," Kent E. Calder notes the "well-appreciated" conclusion that because of the increasing structural complexity of governmental operations, "the Japanese state is slowly losing control capabilities over time."

36. Cited by Stout (1989).
37. Beason and Weinstein (1993). The quotation at the end of the paragraph comes from Calder (1993), p. 17.

Another part of the problem arises because the linkages between the policies and results appear weaker. Much, but not all of this, is because the U.S. economy has become increasingly integrated with the rest of the world. Under normal conditions, the effectiveness of national macroeconomic fiscal and monetary policy making declines as global economic integration increases. An extreme situation arises for the individual states within the United States in which an attempt by any individual state government to carry out an independent and aggregate fiscal or monetary policy to raise the domestic product of the state would be ineffective. For fiscal policy, this is because increasing economic integration is generally accompanied by a higher marginal propensity to import, as shown in Appendix Note 8.1. This, in turn, limits the effectiveness of fiscal policy because the government expenditure and tax multipliers are lowered through leakages of domestic purchasing power through imports. For monetary policy, increased economic integration leads to an equalization of interest rates so that the effectiveness of monetary policy is lowered. If exchange rates are floating, additional problems arise.[38]

Internationalization of the economy also has an impact of many microeconomic policies as well. Conflicts of law of one nation and another become endemic, especially as nations claim extraterritoriality of their regulations.

38. If exchange rates are fixed, interest rates will equalize throughout the integrated area despite the efforts of any policy maker in a particular subarea to raise or lower exchange rates. If exchange rates are fluctuating, the funds searching for the highest interest rates play a major role in the determination of the exchange rate, so that monetary policy to raise the interest rates also raises the exchange rate. Moreover, if additional government expenditures lead to an increase in interest rates, this also leads to an appreciation of the exchange rate and foreign capital rushes to the nation to take advantage of the higher interest. Some econometric studies (e.g., Bryant and others, 1989) show a close linkage between the government deficit, an appreciation of the currency (through both the interest rate and increased imports induced by the government deficit), and a deficit on the balance of current account, a result that comes as no surprise to those having lived through the Reagan era with its "double deficit." This is, however, a controversial matter and such results, although they seem reasonable to me, are disputed.

Two uncertainties that arise in predicting exactly what will happen must be noted. First, depending on the response of investment and consumption to changes in the money supply within a country induced by a government budgetary deficit, the inflow of foreign funds can have a stimulative effect that might offset to some degree the decline in exports accompanying the appreciation of the currency. Second, the relative price elasticities of demand and supply for exports and imports in our country and abroad can magnify or diminish the impact of the trade deficit brought about by any given initial fiscal impulse.

Clearly, in an interdependent world, effectiveness of the macroeconomic policy also requires coordination with the policies of other nations. But in many cases it is not in the national interest of a foreign government to cooperate; for instance, the refusal of the Bundesbank to lower interest rates in Germany eventually led to the collapse of the European monetary system in July and August, 1993, and to policy chaos in a number of neighboring nations. Other problems of policy coordination have received considerable attention (e.g., Cooper, 1968, 1985).

For instance, in 1993 the National Labor Relations Board ruled that the secondary boycott provisions of U.S. labor law extended to conduct by Japanese labor unions operating in Japan, when the conduct was undertaken on behalf of a U.S. union in order to pressure U.S. employers.[39] But enforcement is difficult. The U.S. Department of Justice began to investigate cartel practices of foreign firms in so far as they affected trade and competition in the United States. Again, enforcement problems arise. All sorts of domestic regulations, for instance, on pollution, have a major impact on the pattern of international trade. Further, a U.S.-based company that is operating abroad may find its employment policies constrained by U.S. law so as to place it at a competitive disadvantage with other companies in that nation or even, in some cases, at variance to the local laws. Although such problems are being resolved on a case-by-case basis, they raise the more general point that problems facing policy makers in the United States have been made more difficult by internationalization.

In a structurally complex world the relationships between policy tools and their economic consequences become increasingly obscured in the domestic economy as well. It becomes more difficult to anticipate the complicated interactions and responses to particular measures, and the relationship between particular indicators and the rest of the economy become loosened. For this reason, for instance, the Board of Governors of the Federal Reserve Bank announced in July 1993 that it would no longer pursue monetary expansion targets because the money supply no longer told very much about the current state of the economy.

Heterogeneous interests: Clearly, the more heterogeneous the population, the more group interests must be taken into account and the more complicated the bargaining process to arrive at a solution. The criticism of the gridlock in the U.S. Congress in the 1980s and 1990s is misplaced; this difficulty in achieving agreement on legislation reflects not only the increasing difficulty of the policy problems but also the growing diversity of the population and a seeming hardening of group lines arising from a decline in social cohesiveness. Thus, it becomes more difficult to reach agreement both within and between groups.

Michael J. L. Kirby, a Senator in the Canadian Parliament, noted another aspect of the problem:[40] "Many citizens do not believe that there is such a thing as a problem for which the government cannot find a solution ... [without personal pain to them].... The governance problem is caused therefore in part ... by the failure of the governed and the governing to reach a consensus on what constitutes reality and hence on what is truly possible." Political par-

39. Brill and Halem (1994).
40. Kirby (1985).

ties, of course, can take advantage of such complexity by promising solutions that are infeasible. For instance, in 1994 the Republican Party's *Contract with America* promising a balanced government budget, decreased taxes, higher defense expenditures, and no indication of what other measures were necessary to realize these three goals. This contract exploited voter confusion about political and economic reality.

Problems of implementation

Although policy implementation is impeded by inadequate information and slow decision speeds, other problems also arise. One is the rise of other powerful institutions. For instance, as Hamish McRae has noted:[41] "Governments are weaker because many other things have become stronger: financial markets, large corporations, the international media and entertainment industries." To this might be added the vulnerability of structurally complex systems to disruptions at key points. Although in previous chapters I find little evidence of this on a macrolevel, on a microlevel the possibility is open. As Donald N. Michael argues, complexity leads to greater opportunities that low probability events will occur,.and one consequence occurs in urban environments where small groups can disrupt an entire system.[42] In light of the decreasing social cohesiveness discussed in the next chapter, this is a chilling thought.

These problems do not necessarily lead to the conclusion that we should have less government. An optimist might argue that some of these difficulties can surely be overcome by more resources devoted to information gathering and a restructuring of governmental decision processes to increase policy effectiveness. But a pessimist might counter with the claim that the government will have to focus more attention on fewer problems and that we must accommodate ourselves to a larger government acting with less effectiveness.

Conclusions and implications for the future

Between the early 1950s and 1990 the government sector, as measured by the ratio of public expenditures to the GDP, increased on all levels of government. In terms of labor inputs, however, the aggregate increase was slight and primarily at the state and local level. The cause for this divergence in trends of expenditures and labor inputs was the marked increase in the relative importance of transfers, rather than direct purchases of goods and services. In separating different types of governmental expenditures, I show that those associated with increasing structural complexity of the economy as a whole, particularly in the sense of population heterogeneity, have increased faster than those without this linkage.

41. McRae (1994), p. 205. The next citation is by Michael (1968).
42. Michael (1968).

Prediction of the future level of public expenditures is hazardous. Part of the problem is statistical and arises because it is often arbitrary whether a particular government program is included in the public sector. For instance, if the United States had adopted a Canadian-style single-payer health insurance program, the resulting expenditures would be counted as "public." If the United States had adopted a program financed exclusively by employer mandates, then the entire new set of taxes and expenditures would be off the federal books and not included in the public sector.

Another part of the problem arises from the moral hazard issues arising from certain programs, particularly concerning health and welfare. That is, given the existence of a welfare program, many people will begin to take advantage of it, even though it is not aimed at them. For instance, evidence is available showing that liberalizing the financing of nursing homes for the aged to aid the poor encourages many who are not destitute to move from the care of their family into such homes.[43] And many instances are known where a slight change in regulations regarding sickness leave has led to a jump in the number of those claiming such benefits. Although governments can counter such responses by ever more complicated eligibility regulations, it is seldom clear in advance whether the costs associated with moral hazard outweigh costs of the changing eligibility requirements and enforcement.[44]

The disaggregated data presented in Table 9.2 show that the growth of those public expenditures tied to increasing structural complexity more than offsets the relative decline in expenditures not tied to complexity. As I have shown in previous chapters, structural complexity along most dimensions should continue to rise in the future and, therefore, we might expect the relative share in the GDP of these governmental expenditures to rise as well.

It is possible that the private sector could carry out many of these functions that arise from increasing structural complexity. Several cross-section studies

43. Cutler and Sheiner (1993). In some cases incentives are such that the managers of these nursing homes are motivated to turn away some destitute aged with serious health problems in favor of nondestitute, healthy aged because the costs to the nursing home will be lower. Howe and Longman (1992) have some useful remarks on how many aspects of these programs and the tax measures to finance them, turn out to be highly regressive and quite different than originally intended.

44. It is often argued that the savings in administrative costs of allowing a program to be completely open more than outweighs the costs of over use. For instance, Woolhandler et al., (1993) compare hospital administrative costs in the United States and Canada, which has a single-payer type of national health insurance. In the United States where eligibility rules are quite important, such costs amount to about 25 percent of total hospital spending; in Canada, between 9 and 11 percent. But what is usually not emphasized in such arguments is that such administrative systems have hidden ways of rationing the service and, moreover, the percentage of the population trying to take advantage of the system increases over the years as more information about the system becomes available. Putting the matter in a different way, the short-run and long-run costs of a particular entitlement may be quite different, as experience from more developed welfare states such as Sweden have shown us (Lindbeck, 1993).

using nations as the unit of analysis demonstrate that the volume of private pensions (both individual and group pension plans) is inversely related to the relative volume of public pensions. But Gøsta Esping-Anderson shows in this type of regression analysis that the private share of pensions also is related inversely to the percentage of the aged, which suggests that an increasingly aged society turns increasingly toward public pensions.[45] Even though the United States lags other nations such as The Netherlands or France in the share of the labor force participating in private pension plans, it does not seem likely that the public share will decrease, especially since private savings rates have declined (discussed in more detail in the next chapter).

For health insurance, it is certainly possible that some relatively small changes could result in an increase in private health insurance coverage. But although an increase in the private sector activities in these two fields could replace a major part of the rise in public expenditures, this seems unlikely. The resistance of the private sector to such changes and the competitive forces leading to skimming the cream of the low-risk population, while leaving the high-risk population without coverage, will undoubtedly generate pressures for further governmental involvement.

One last set of considerations deserves brief mention. Some economists, such as Robert Heilbroner, raise the old fear of secular stagnation in which the one means of maintaining full employment is through governmental investment and other expenditures to maintain aggregate demand.[46] In the next chapter I argue that this scenario does not seem likely – that the twenty-first century will bring much different problems. But if he is correct, then public expenditures will increase for yet another reason.

What is the impact of a long-term increase in public expenditures on the government debt and governmental interest payments? It is useful to focus on the federal government for two reasons: it finances most of these expenditures and, moreover, the state and local governments are limited on the amount that they can borrow – most of their expenditures must be financed by taxes; these state and local governments are also more open to tax payer revolts and other actions to slow the growth of government expenditures.

These issues can be easily handled with a simple simulation model that examines various scenarios (discussed in detail in Appendix Note 9.2). For purposes of this discussion, the qualitative results can be summarized quickly. Contrary to the alarmists, under any kind of reasonable assumptions, federal expenditures on interest payments are not going to gobble up total federal expenditures. In most simulations, the share of interest expenditures changed less than 10 percentage points of total expenditures.

45. Esping-Anderson (1990, p. 121). The lag of the U.S. workers in private pension plans is discussed by Turner and Beller (1992), p. 10.
46. Esping-Anderson (1990), p. 121.

The model does show that raising taxes to finance higher governmental expenditures can reduce the growth rate of the economy markedly if we postulate that such taxes have a disincentive effect on investment.[47] Under extreme assumptions, the model shows that the GDP growth rate can fall short of past trends by about one-third of a percentage point annually. Two other important effects of higher governmental expenditures that are not shown by the model also deserve note. Any increasing deficit of the government budget, combined with the falling savings of both private individuals and enterprises generally leads to increased balance of payment deficits and greater foreign ownership of U.S. assets. In addition, under certain circumstances, increasing governmental deficits can also lead to greater inflation.

The government not only responds to structural complexity, but it creates such complexity in the form of increased regulation or more complicated laws and rules. The relative importance of such regulation appears to have risen and then, in the 1980s slightly declined. Because the determinants of government regulation are considerably more difficult to specify than public expenditures, it is difficult to say whether this change will be one of the few lasting aspects of the Reagan administration. But whatever the future, it is clear that such increasing government regulation has increased the structural complexity facing producers: In the 1990s the production of a bottle of catsup requires much more information and paperwork than in the 1950s, not only because of changes in technology and a widening of markets, but also because the regulatory environment in which such production takes place is now more complicated and the manufacturer must take into account many more considerations.

Some polar predictions have been made about the future of governmental regulations, in part because such regulations cover such a broad area of government activity. Two examples from well-known and capable economists deserve brief consideration.

Murray Weidenbaum argues the case of decreased regulation in the future.[48] He notes public opinion data showing a relatively small share of the U.S. pop-

---

47. The analysis in this paragraph is in terms of hypothetical relations, because determining empirically the impact of the level of public expenditures and taxes on economic growth is very difficult. Higher levels of public expenditures may have an impact on economic growth, but empirical studies to isolate such an effect lead to quite contradictory conclusions or statistical difficulties. To take one example among many, Barro and Lee (1993) find that the ratio of total government expenditures (excluding defense and education) to GDP is negatively related in a significant fashion to economic growth in ninety-five nations for the period from 1965 to 1985 (their Table 5). However, this variable loses its statistical significance when only upper income nations are used in the sample. Furthermore, if Japan – which is an outlier – had been eliminated from the sample, the derived results would have provided even less support for the hypothesis that a large government sector reduces economic growth. The authors omit defense and education expenditures on the weak grounds that they do not constitute "consumption."

48. Weidenbaum (1979). The various examples of the costs of regulations to prevent one premature death are cited by Morrall (1992).

ulation favoring increased governmental regulations. Furthermore, he claims that the public is gradually becoming increasingly aware of the high costs of many regulations. Some bizarre examples have received public notice as a result of the many recent studies, especially regarding the costs of regulation designed to prevent premature deaths. For instance, the atrazine–alachlor drinking water standard adopted in 1991 is said to cost $92 billion dollars per life saved. For the limits of formaldehyde exposure adopted in 1987, one study reveals that the cost of a saved life is $86 billion. Weidenbaum claims that the realization of such costs will gradually lead to a reduction in the relative volume of regulation. Such a prediction implies optimism about overcoming the difficulties in repealing regulatory laws. In the decade following the publication of his book, however, Weidenbaum was correct about increasing deregulation.

Nevertheless, this demand-side approach implicitly assumes that the ratio of social benefits to social costs of all new regulatory activity is, and will continue to be, low. The first part of the assumption is far from proven; and the second part does not necessarily follow from the first unless the economic environment in which production and consumption take place does not change.

Robert Heilbroner argues the case for increased regulation in the future.[49] He is influenced greatly by the increasing attention to environmental problems occasioned by pollution and argues that market failures, particularly with regard to externalities tied to global warming, will become increasingly important. He claims that the "resolution of these problems will have to be political ... the prospect adds one last, perhaps most powerful reason to anticipate that the market mechanism in the twenty-first century will sorely be supplemented, and in some areas, supplanted by planning of one kind or another." In as far as environmental regulations are the most rapidly increasing regulatory expenditure (Table 9.3), there is an element of plausibility in his prediction.

Nevertheless, this argument also has several weaknesses. Among other things, it assumes that governmental policy making is effective. As indicated previously, increasing structural complexity acts to reduce this effectiveness and, as a result, the public's demand for such regulation also may be reduced. Furthermore, Heilbroner's argument implies that governmental regulation is the only tool at the disposal of policy makers to solve a particular problem, which is certainly not so. Often, for instance, pollution can be controlled by special taxes, rather than direct regulation.[50]

The cost of either regulation or tax solutions is tied to the technology of control, which often is the same. For instance, justifiable concern has been raised

---

49. Heilbroner (1993).
50. In the past, government ownership was argued as a solution. The high pollution in Eastern Europe during its phase of central planning casts doubt on this assertion; further, a markedly increased nationalization of the means of production in the United States does not seem likely, at least in the coming decades.

about depletion of the Oglalla aquifer under the Great Plains. Today, either regulations limiting the drawing of water from this aquifer or a special tax on this water would require a small army of inspectors to enforce. But with technologies allowing monitoring of fields from an airplane, then enforcement costs are of either a regulatory or a tax system on this water would be greater reduced, so that regulation might be feasible.

It is noteworthy that aside from environmental regulations, financial regulation (defined broadly) was the only other regulatory expenditure to grow faster than the GDP during the entire period. This is undoubtedly related to the problems of financial distress and bankruptcy related to increasing financial fragility, a phenomenon discussed in Chapter 5. Again, the government can attempt to control the situation by supplementing traditional types of regulation with other measures placing more weight on use of the tax system.

I believe that the aggregative approaches of both Weidenbaum and Heilbroner are not amenable to very meaningful predictions. The situation is similar to that of public expenditures: it is necessary to examine individual sets of regulations, the changing economic environment, and the changing technologies of enforcement before predictions can be hazarded. As Sam Peltzman forcefully has reminded us, few predicted in the early 1970s the deregulation that took place in the late 1970s.[51] It seems likely, however, that increases in environmental and financial regulations will more than offset deregulation in other fields so that the net mass of regulation will increase.

These considerations lead to the overall conclusion that the government's role in the economy in response to its growing structural complexity will probably increase and, moreover, that the government's role as a regulator will probably lead to greater structural complexity for the rest of the economy as well. More certain than these conjectures is the conclusion that the increasing structural complexity will lead to increasing difficulties of the government in effectively accomplishing any of its tasks. Problems in increasingly incomplete, inaccurate, and delayed information lead to greater difficulties in policy making. The problems faced by such policy actions are more intricate, and problems of implementation are more intractable. Furthermore, just as individual states cannot carry out effective monetary and fiscal policy, the growing internationalization of the economy will make fiscal and monetary policy on the federal level more problematic.

Traditional ideological guideposts are becoming outdated. For both policy makers and citizens, the key intellectual task is to determine which governmental tasks are appropriate and feasible in an environment of increasing structural complexity and internationalization.

51. Peltzman (1989).

CHAPTER 10

The future of U.S. capitalism

According to a well-known aphorism, "When mortals speak of the future, the gods smile." The difficulties of understanding the most important causal forces influencing changes in the economic system today are daunting, and the problem is compounded by the adventitious character of many aspects of historical change. Nevertheless, the task is necessary to attempt, subjective as it may be, so that we can gain some idea of problems that are looming on the horizon. I leave policy prescriptions to another book; this is primarily an exercise in positive analysis. In this chapter I approach the problem of sketching the future of capitalism in three steps.

The first step of the argument is to investigate how the current system is performing and to ask whether the projected performance will be sufficiently poor as to force a change in the economic system. From a review of the evidence, this does not appear a promising approach.

The second step is to explore directly the sources of systemic change, either internal or external. For this purpose, I isolate four key changes: increasing structural complexity, increasing internationalization, decreasing social cohesiveness, and an enervation of the "spirit of capitalism."

The final step is link these sources of systemic change to particular scenarios. With regard to changes in the structural complexity of the economy, this has already been carried out in previous chapters where I have tried to show the impact of increasing structural complexity on a variety of economic institutions. More specifically, I have explored a variety of different institutional changes arising from increased structural complexity influencing the division of the population into separate groups, the market for labor, labor–management relations, the financial system, the management of enterprises, foreign and domestic trade, and the line between the public and private sectors. Each of these changes contributes to the evolving economic system, but in isolation none changes the texture of economic life as we know it. Depending upon one's optimism regarding the impact of certain of these changes, they point either toward a set of quantitative changes that do not lead to a qualitative change in the system, or toward a special kind of systemic stagnation. I briefly discuss both of these alternatives in this chapter.

The changes in the organization and control of the basic units of production seem to me a more basic institutional transformation, for these structure the way in which the economy impinges upon our daily lives during most of our waking hours. In the previous chapters, embryonic evidence of some possible transformations can be seen, and these, for convenience, can be labeled finance capital, atomic capitalism, and remodeled capitalism. For any of these three to come to fruition, however, one or more of the basic four causal forces designated above that drive the economic system must be reversed. In this chapter I briefly sketch the three scenarios; and in Appendix Note 10.3, I discuss each in considerably more detail.

Economic performance as a stimulus to systemic change

The basic argument is simple: Crises generate critical changes in the economic system and if an economy becomes increasingly dysfunctional, changes in the economic system will inevitably occur. Among nineteenth-century economists, Karl Marx was the fiercest exponent of this approach. He argued the inevitable overthrow of the capitalist system because of the everincreasing severity of business cycles, the increasing inequality of income, the gradual immiseration of the mass of workers, and the centralization and concentration of capital. Others who have followed have differed on the mode of change (evolutionary or revolutionary) and the type of performance inducing systemic change. But all have accepted the basic notion that dysfunctional behavior of the system leads to institutional change. In the following brief discussion I present some skeptical remarks about the relevance of this argument for the United States in the coming decades. Appendix Note 10.2 discusses in greater detail the performance of the economy.

Dysfunctional behavior

Is the U.S. economic performance so bad that popular reaction will force systemic change? For recent decades it is useful to glance at the most important indicators.

Economic growth: Over the four post–World War II decades, the rate of economic growth has declined, not just in the United States but in most economically advanced nations. In comparison to twenty-eight other industrial nations for the period from 1950 through 1988, however, the United States experienced the most rapid deceleration of growth of labor productivity.[1] Although the productivity spurt in the early 1990s has been much touted, it appears due in good measure to cyclical factors as well as to some one-time changes that

1. Pryor (1994b).

should have little further impact. A small part of the four-decade productivity deceleration can be traced to the decline in investment, particularly in the 1980s. More important causal factors, however, are at work.

In various chapters I advance different reasons for expecting a slowdown in economic growth. The aging of the population should reduce net savings and growth, and the decline in the labor participation rate should also have an adverse impact on growth as well (Chapter 2). Increasing inequality of income and wealth may have an adverse impact on rising productivity and economic growth (see Chapter 2 and the following discussion). The skills bottleneck is likely to lower economic growth (Chapter 3), as well as the shift of labor into the service sector, which may have a lower productivity growth than the goods sector (Chapter 4). The increasing level of potential financial fragility and the rising financial distress (bankruptcies and business failures) can act to discourage investment (Chapter 5). Increasing levels of taxes to finance the rising relative level of governmental expenditures also, under certain conditions, can have an adverse impact on economic growth (Chapter 9).

Some trends adversely influencing economic growth in the future, however, can be influenced by government policy. The decline in savings and the fall in relative research and development expenditures (discussed later) can be reversed. The rising level of economic distress (such as corporate bankruptcies and bank failures) that discourages investment (Chapter 5) also can be influenced by governmental policies. Indeed, governmental policy measures taken in the 1980s may played some role in reducing such economic distress in the first few years of the 1990s, although stronger policy measures may still be necessary.

I must stress that a slowdown in economic growth does not necessarily lead to dramatic systemic changes. For instance, the United Kingdom has experienced a relatively low growth of productivity and for some decades has moved steadily down in the national rankings of per capita income. But the British did not turn into revolutionary mobs as a result. If a nation is not losing its relative position in the world's distribution of income, the chances of such declining growth leading to systemic change is even less. The U.S. citizenry may have a similar response as the British and simply lower their sights and write witty and learned books about the age of diminished expectations.[2]

Inflation: During the 1980s the inflation rate declined (see Table A.34). It seems premature to say that the government knows how to deal with inflation. But barring any major supply disturbances such as the oil shocks in 1973 and 1989, the necessity of controlling inflation also does not appear to be the key to predicting systemic change.

2. This is the title of a book by Paul Krugman (1990).

Unemployment: Cyclical activity causing large swings in unemployment are not sufficiently serious to serve as an impetus for systemic change. Most economists believe the severity of business cycles is attenuating. My own evidence (Appendix Note 3.2) suggests that in terms of deviation from the full employment, their severity has not significantly changed since the mid-1950s. In any case, taming the business cycle is not at the top of the political agenda. The secularly rising rate of unemployment (Chapter 3) does not seem due to the lack of aggregate demand or secular stagnation, but rather to a lack of appropriate skills for the new technologies of production (Chapter 3). This problem can be solved, I believe, without a change in the economic system.

Volatility and market breakdowns: The investigations in several chapters show that economic volatility probably will not be a problem of increasing importance in the future. Macroeconomic and financial variables reveal no long-term upward trend in volatility (Chapter 5), and the increase in financial distress that has arisen because of increased leverage can be handled by existing policy tools. Although exchange rates and raw material prices show rising volatility (Chapter 7), this seems due in part to a one-time liberalization of trade and finance and should not increase so much in the future. Further, this volatility has not led to an increase in fluctuations of domestic retail prices (Chapter 7). Market breakdowns due to pollution and other externalities, as I argue in Chapter 9, do not require systemic change for resolution. One arguable exception, however, is the area of health care. Monopolies are not taking over the economy and, according to the data in Chapter 7, the U.S. economy is becoming more competitive.

Increasing inequality: To me the aspect of economic performance most likely to have a significant impact on the economic system is the secular increase in the inequality of income. As shown in Chapter 2, this rising inequality has occurred not just for yearly income, but for long-term income as well. Indeed, I also present some empirical evidence that such income differences are transmitted through the generations. As shown in Chapter 3, an increasing share of Americans also appear to lack the necessary skills for long-term participation in the labor force. Unless education and training programs are greatly strengthened, there is no plausible reason why these trends in inequality will not continue in the future. Moreover, empirical evidence from budget studies shows that if the environmental crisis leads to a rise in the prices of raw materials and foodstuffs, real income differences will widen even more (Appendix Note 2.3).

The increasing income stratification has some serious political consequences. As Irving Kristol cogently contends:[3] "The results of the political

3. Kristol (1978), p. 267. The second quotation comes from Bok (1993), p. 213.

process and of the exercise of individual freedom – the distribution of power privilege and property – must also be seen as in some profound sense expressive of the values that govern the lives of individuals ... If the principles that organize public life seem to have little relation to those that shape private lives – you have 'alienation' and anomie, and a melting away of established principles of authority." Derek Bok adds the following gloss: "The ultimate reason why we cannot ignore unjustified wealth is that it weakens the public's faith in the fairness of the economic system. Such faith is essential if we are to maintain support for the social order and inspire individuals to observe the laws, undertake the duties of citizenship, and extend the minimum of trust toward institutions necessary for communities to prosper."

These arguments, although they have a pleasing ethical ring, can be challenged. Because the levers of political power are in the hands of the privileged group, nations can tolerate a high degree of economic inequalities before social difficulties force a change in the economic system. Although many in the disadvantaged group may be seething in discontent, high police expenditures, privately guarded suburbs, and other institutions to keep the destitute away from more advantaged groups can be set up within the existing economic system so that political stability is maintained.[4]

It might be thought that discontent can be bought off through welfare expenditures, but this does not appear politically feasible. The evidence presented in Chapter 9 suggests that, other things being equal, the greater the income gap between those in the middle and lower income groups, the less the redistributional transfers by the advantaged group, in part because of the decreasing empathy that occurs because of the widening social distances. On the other side, a would-be leader attempting to politically mobilize the disadvantaged group would have to combat not only their apathy, but also his own cooptation by the advantaged group.

Increasing inequalities of income and wealth can lower economic growth. For instance, because of imperfections in the capital market, such inequalities can lead to lower investment in human capital both by low-income individuals and low-income communities, which has a cumulative effect of the generations. In so far as such inequalities are associated with greater absolute poverty and crime, such income stratification can also lead to a reallocation of funds from investment to expenditures for social welfare and crime fighting. If such inequality is accompanied by greater geographical stratification by income, a

---

4. Increasing structural complexity does mean that a small group of determined individuals can create enormous amounts of damage, as the 1993 bombing of the New York Trade Center demonstrated. Moreover, rising productivity has lowered the relative cost of firearms so that disadvantaged groups are more heavily armed. So the fragile social equilibrium becomes more costly to maintain in other dimensions as well, and the increasing share of the GDP devoted to police and protection (Chapter 9) is but one manifestation of this higher cost.

culture of poverty might be created in low-income areas that has an adverse effect on the work ethic. Most dangerously, such inequalities can lead to a disintegration of social cohesiveness, which has important economic implications. I discuss this topic later.

An unchanged economic system

Implicit in most current discussions of the economic system is the argument that in the coming decades the U.S. economic system will not greatly change at all. In its most vulgar version, we often hear the claim that the world has reached the end of history. According to this reasoning, the downfall of communism proves that late twentieth-century capitalism, particularly in its U.S. variant, provides the best of all possible economic worlds. Moreover, in the period from 1910 through 1950 few fundamental changes to the United States occurred, other than an expansion of the role of government, so why should we expect dramatic changes in the future? If serious economic problems are invoked as reasons for systemic change, we need merely intone about capitalism what Henry Hope, a leading seventeenth-century Amsterdam businessman said about trade in general:[5] "It is often ill but it never dies."

The previous discussion presents an intellectually more respectable argument leading to a variant of this conclusion: The performance of the economy is not such as to provide incentives for undertaking major systemic changes. That is, no economic crisis of sufficient urgency will occur that would kindle a flame for systemic change and the trends documented in this book will continue in the future as they have in the past. But such a humdrum scenario of the future of U.S. capitalism presupposes that other sources of change leading to a restructuring of U.S. economic institutions, either within or without the economic system, are not not sufficiently strong to derail current trends. It is necessary to explore this matter in greater detail.

Forces in the socioeconomic environment stimulating systemic change

Change in the economic system can be stimulated not just by economic crises – or political crises such as wars – but also by socioeconomic forces operating within or outside the economy. In the following discussion, I focus on four such forces crucial to our understanding of the evolution of the U.S. economic system: changes in structural complexity; rising economic integration of the world economy; declining social cohesiveness; and changing cultural values affecting the "spirit of capitalism." These four forces are broad and, as a result,

5. Cited by Braudel, 1982, p. 623.

are interrelated. Although certain aspects of each have been discussed in the analysis of increasing structural complexity, it is useful to review briefly each of these forces alone, focusing particularly on those dimensions not yet receiving attention.

Increasing structural complexity

The theme of this book is that structural complexity – the information required for the economic system to function – is generally increasing. For this discussion, I need only to summarize my major results in previous chapters for the post–World War II era. Such a task can be most easily accomplished by grouping the results according to the three aspects of structural complexity outlined in Chapter 1.

Heterogeneity of the system: The population is becoming increasingly heterogeneous according such criteria as age, family structure, ethnicity (induced by immigration), income and wealth (Chapter 2), and occupation (Chapter 3). Productive units, both enterprises and establishments, are becoming more heterogeneous according to their size (Chapter 6).

Direct information requirements of the system: The skill level of the labor force is increasing, both for production as a whole (Chapter 3) and also for production of exports and import-competing goods (Chapter 8). The share of the labor force devoted to creation, processing, and interpretation of information for a functioning economy is rising, albeit slowly (Chapter 4). Enterprises are facing an environment that is increasingly difficult to understand, and are being forced to adopt appropriate business strategies (Chapter 6). Because of the increasing variety of products and the rising costs of sale, the price convergence over time accompanying a fall in transportation that is predicted by the law of one price is no longer dominant in some important markets (Chapter 7). Markets are becoming broader as foreign trade becomes ever more important and this requires more information (Chapter 8). Government policy making is becoming less effective because of information that is incomplete, inaccurate, and late, problems arising from the increasing structural complexity of the economy (Chapter 9). Moreover, by increased regulatory activities, the government has also added to the structural complexity of the system (Chapter 9).

Internal interactions within the system. The interrelations between various sectors of the economy are becoming more extensive (Chapter 1). Wealth creation is becoming more elaborate with an increasing share of individual wealth created either directly by the government or through government institutions in recent years (Chapter 5). Ownership of the means of production is slowly becoming more separated from control (Chapter 6). Financial interrelations are becoming more intricate, as manifested by the ratio of total financial assets to total tangible assets; and the same trends are occurring for financial intermediation, as manifested by the increasing ratio of financial liabilities to real assets (Chapter 5) or by the rising financial leverage in the nonfinancial sector (Appendix Note 6.1).

In certain respects structural complexity has decreased, for instance, the system of labor relations (Chapter 4) or the distribution of formal education (Chapter 3). But this should not blind us to the more important conclusion that in most ways, structural complexity of the system has increased over the decades. In some cases this increased complexity has had an impact on the functioning of the economy; in other cases, not. I give considerable efforts in the previous chapters to exploring this impact, so that the significance of the increasing complexity can be placed in perspective.

Increasing internationalization of the economy

To a certain degree, increasing internationalization is an aspect of increasing structural complexity since markets expand in scope and much greater information is required for the conduct of business and consumption. But internationalization is a sufficiently important topic to deserve special attention as a crucial factor underlying the evolution of U.S. capitalism.

This internationalization is the result, in part, of declining transportation and communication costs that serve as a natural barrier to trade. But this trend also has occurred, in part, as the result of determined political actions by national decision makers to reduce restrictions to world trade in goods, labor, and capital. As a result, world trade has increased faster than world production in most periods since the end of World War II, a process sometimes called *shallow integration.* In the United States the ratio of exports and imports to GDP rose dramatically, especially in the 1970s, although in the 1980s some deceleration in this increase became apparent. As argued in Chapter 8, in the coming decades this ratio should rise but only very slowly.

As shallow integration has proceeded, various types of domestic policies and practices have become increasingly important in influencing the direction and volume of international trade and, as a result, have become the focus of considerable international discussion.[6] Attempts to standardize or harmonize these policy measures, a process sometimes called *deep integration,* have occurred in such areas as governmental tax, expenditure, and subsidy policies;

<hr/>

6. The most important aspects of deep integration will be covered in a series of twenty-one monographs in the *Integrating National Economies* series published by the Brookings Institution. This brief discussion draws from the statement of general themes of the project by Henry J. Aaron, Ralph C. Bryant, Susan M. Collins, et al.

monetary and interest rate policies as well as capital market and banking standards; competition, technology, and antitrust policies; product and process standards; environmental standards; and regulations covering hours, health, and safety conditions of workers.

Such deep integration often proceeds in stages, starting with mutual consultation, then moving toward national coordination, and finally toward explicit harmonization. This process occurred over a 200-year period between the various states comprising the United States, and, internationally, it has been occurring for some decades. For instance, under the leadership of the International Labour Office, certain labor regulations began to be harmonized in the 1920s.

It is neither likely nor desirable for such a convergence of the economic environment in various nations to become complete. Although such measures are often taken within the context of an economic union, it is not necessary for the dissolution of the nation state to occur for the process to continue. Nevertheless, such a deep integration does undermine the autonomy of national governments, just as the federal government in the United States has undermined, in many ways, the autonomy of the state and local governments.

The increasing internationalization of the world economy also means that national governments have fewer policy tools at their disposal to influence economic activity. On the macroeconomic level, national monetary and fiscal policies will become increasingly less effective in the same manner that macroeconomic policies of a particular state government require much more intervention to obtain a particular outcome (as argued in Chapter 9). On a microeconomic level, special governmental protection of particular national industries will become more difficult to achieve, market competition will become sharper (Chapter 7), and the very nature of industrial policy will change.[7] The fall in barriers to international capital flows makes it more difficult to tax capital without adverse effects on new investment. This increasing world economic integration also means that the imperatives of global economic integration and the counter-imperatives of national political integrity may clash, causing both political and economic difficulties.

Although the continued pace of economic integration of the world economy is difficult to foresee, the direction of change should be evident. Such internationalization of the U.S. economy has been quite evident in the last forty years; and there is no reason to believe that the trend in the future will be any different (Appendix Note 8.1).

Decreasing social cohesiveness

To a certain extent the decreasing social cohesiveness in the United States is a reflection of the increasing heterogeneity of the population documented in Chapter 2. But it is also a reflection of social forces independent of the econ-

7. Reich (1991).

omy and, as such, deserves to be treated separately, especially as these social forces have important implications for the economy.

As Fernand Braudel cogently argues:[8] "The worst error of all is to suppose that capitalism is simply 'an economic system,' whereas in fact it lives off the social order, standing almost on a footing with the state, whether as adversary or accomplice; it is and always has been a massive force, filling the horizon. Capitalism also benefits from all the supports that culture provides for the solidity of the social edifice.... And lastly capitalism can count on the dominant classes who, when they defend it, are defending themselves." It is useful to separate certain social-structural aspects, which are discussed in this section, from cultural aspects, which receive attention in the following section.

The declining social cohesiveness examined here is much more than merely the widening of social distance caused by increasing economic inequalities. It also concerns a loss of trust, not just in other people but in basic economic, political, and social institutions; the structures within which we live. It is difficult to isolate the causes of this declining social cohesiveness for many factors can be cited: the growing population heterogeneity; the disjunction between economic expectations and reality occurring as a result of the dramatic slow down in economic growth starting in the early 1970s; the cumulative effects of the increasing income inequalities beginning in the late 1970s; the logical result of certain cultural changes (discussed later); and so forth.

This decline in trust is manifested in many ways. Gallup survey data show downward trends since the 1960s or 1970s in the trust people say they place in major economic and political institutions in both the public and private sector.[9] Derek Bok, for instance, points out that between the mid-1960s and the 1980s, the percentage of people declaring that they could not "trust government officials to do the right thing most of the time" rose from 22 to 73 percent. It should be clear that such attitudes make attempts by the government to solve certain problems more difficult, especially if these problems arise from market failures or other misfortune arising in the private sector.

This decline in trust applies not just to institutions, but to other people as well. For instance, since the mid-1970s public opinion polls show that ratings of the honesty and ethics of most professions have declined as well. Steven Knacks cites survey data showing that since the mid-1960s people agreeing with the statement "most people can be trusted" has fallen roughly 15 percentage points.[10] Since the early 1950s a declining percentage of respondents reported that religion is important in their lives. Daniel Yankelovitch summarizes public opinion data showing that less value is placed on observing the rules of the society. He adds, moreover, that "we have come to experience the

---

8. Braudel (1982), p. 623.

9. These are reported in various issues of the *Gallup Poll Monthly*. The next reference is to Bok (1993), p. 271.

10. Knacks (1990). The next references are to Yankelovitch (1994) and a study by Easterlin and Crimmins (199).

bonds of marriage, family, children, job, community, and country as constraints that were no longer necessary ... and ... so strong is the appeal of greater freedom to express one's individuality that, once experienced, people find it very difficult to return to a more constricted world." Such a loss in trust and social cohesiveness also has shaped life goals. In listing their life goals, an ever decreasing percentage of first-year university students mention "helping others," while those listing becoming welloff financially has soared.

But such verbal statements to polltakers may not reflect behavior, and here the problem of measuring social cohesiveness begins. The increasing breakdown of the traditional family, the soaring number of children born ot wedlock, and the rising share of children raised in one-parent families, all documented in Chapter 2, are the most obvious indicators. On a civic level, the decline in the share of eligible population voting in elections is supposed to reflect, in part, a decline in the sense of civic obligation and social cohesiveness. Dishonesty appears to have increased: since the mid 1960s an increasing percentage of first-year university students report having cheated in high school; and for adults, income tax compliance has fallen.[11] Certain signs of social anomie – the opposite of cohesiveness – such as suicide among teens have soared since the early 1960s. The explosion of litigation reflects not just a decline in social cohesiveness but also a rising degree of structural complexity of the economic environment (Chapters 6 and 9), so that it is difficult to separate the two factors. Nevertheless, such litigiousness has led to a situation where, in 1990 lawyers constituted 0.59 percent of the labor force, while in 1950, they numbered only 0.27 percent – an annual increase of 1.9 percent. In quite a different social sphere, most observers believe that an increase in ethnic tension has occurred since the mid-1960s, despite many corrections of past inequities.

Criminality statistics provide another readily available measure of social cohesiveness. The causes of crime, to a certain extent, are tied to changes in the economy, for instance the growing inequality of income and wealth, but this lies beyond the scope of this discussion.[12] For our purposes we can simply use the crime rate as a social indicator that records the violation of the rules of the society.

Pollsters report that a large majority of Americans believe crime has increased in their own community, although this evidence is problematic.[13]

11. Knacks (1990). Bennett (1993) discusses anomie. The data on lawyer comes U.S. Department of Commerce, Bureau of the Census (1953 and 1992a).
12. Ehrlich (1973) presents statistical evidence linking crime to income inequalities. For any discussion on crime rates over time, it is necessary to consider the possibility that the number of laws have increased and made more activities illegal. This, however, does not seem to be an important aspect of the trends discussed in the text.
13. According to a *New York Times*/CBS poll in early 1994, almost three quarters of all Americans believed that crime in the country as a whole has increased and 58 percent believed that crime

The most meaningful crime statistics are taken from surveys in which people are asked whether they or their home have been victimized by crime in the last year. These data show a falling overall crime rate since the early 1970s. More specifically, in 1973, 16.8 percent answered affirmatively to the question posed by the survey takers; by 1975 this was 18.2 percent; and thereafter the figure has slowly declined to 14.3 percent in the 1986–90 period.[14] This measure, of course, lumps together all types of crimes, unweighted according to serious ness. The rate of violent crimes, however, has remained roughly constant in the same period.

Although the crime rate alone does not suggest a decline in social cohesiveness since the early 1970s, this reflects only part of the problem. Most importantly, increasing costly measures have been taken to isolate or prevent crime. For instance, between 1950 and 1980, the number of adult prisoners as a percentage of adults between twenty and sixty-five rose at an average annual rate of roughly 2.5 percent.[15] Crime has also been contained over time by enormous expenditures in crime prevention. From a recent scholarly estimate of the costs of transfers in the United States we can derive the cost of fighting crime at 5.3 percent of the GDP.[16] In the private sector these include the purchase of locks, security systems, guards at factories, systems to prevent theft

had increased in their own community (Berke, 1994). But verbal opinions vary considerably from the beliefs on which people act. When asked whether there was any area within a mile of their homes where they would be afraid to walk alone at night, the percentage has declined over the two decades: In the middle 1960s, about 32 percent of the respondents answered affirmatively to this question; this response rose to about 46 percent in the mid-1970s; and since then it slowly declined to about 42 percent in early 1994. This decline may be due in part to movement of fearful people living in the cities to the safer suburbs.

14. All data on crime, victimization, and prisoners come from Department of Commerce, Bureau of the Census (1975; and annual-b, various issues). The FBI crime rate data were adjusted for rough comparability over the period, especially the change in the coverage of property crimes and, in the early 1950s, the shift from crime in the major urban centers to crime in the entire nation.

   Two reasons can be offered why perceptions and incidence of crime have diverged. First, the victim statistics of the rate of violent crimes show no trend between 1973 and 1990. The murder rate, which rose from 4.6 per 100,000 in 1950 to 9.6 in the 1970s has declined only very slowly, so that in the 1986–90 period it was 9.2. Second, the widely reported (and misleading) FBI crime rate, which is based on crimes actually recorded by the police, rose steadily from 1.6 percent in the 1951–5 period to 5.7 percent in the 1986–90 period (I have tried to adjust the FBI data in the early years to conform to the definitions used in later years). Clearly, a higher percentage of crimes are being recorded by the police, although in the latter part of the 1980s, they only amounted to about 40 percent of the crimes reported to survey takers.

15. Data come from U.S. Department of Commerce, Bureau of the Census (annual-b). According to Bennett (1993), p. 3, since the median prison sentence for all serious crimes dramatically decreased, in part because of prison overcrowding, those on parole or probation numbered about three times those incarcerated in all prisons in the late 1980s.

16. Laband and Sophocleus (1992).The data on private guards and watch personnel come from U.S. Department of Commerce, Bureau of the Census (1953 and 1992a).

in libraries and stores, safety deposit boxes, and other measures; in the public sector, the costs of crime detection and prevention. The private costs have risen steadily over time, for instance, between 1950 and 1980, the private guards and watch personnel as a percent of the civilian labor force increased from 0.39 percent of the labor force in 1950 to 0.74 percent of the labor force in 1990, an average annual increase of 1.9 percent. The trend is even more pronounced in the public sector, where the share of governmental police and correction expenditures in the GDP has risen at an average annual rate of 2.5 percent (Table 9.2). These cost calculation omit, of course, the direct costs of crime and corruption that are even higher.[17]

The decline in social cohesiveness influences the economy in many ways. In the short run the breakdown of the traditional family requires increased governmental resources either for welfare benefits, special educational programs for disadvantaged children from such families, or for orphanages – the social panacea *du jour* in 1995. The decline in civic spirit makes governing more difficult. The resources reallocated from productive investment to protection against crime, of course, reduces economic growth.

In the long run the decline in trust also has a high cost. Most important, social cohesiveness and trust allow decision makers to operate with much longer time horizons, since short-term results are not necessary to appease those who must make sacrifices to finance such measures. For the nation as a whole, trust and social cohesiveness also lead to lower social tensions and less civil strife, thereby reducing investment risks. For the economy trust is, in the words of the nineteenth century Italian social commentator Gaetano Filangieri:[18] "...the soul of commerce and the credit it alone can generate must be regarded as a 'second species of money.'" Rephrased in dryer but more modern terminology, trust and social cohesion reduce information and transaction costs (negotiating and enforcing a contract), and also reduce perceived economic risks – the enemy of investment. As Wall Street pundits never cease to remind us, credit is man's trust in man.

Enervation of the "spirit of capitalism"

A change in cultural values is the final major source of structural change to the economic system that I consider. Of the four most important trends influ-

---

17. Laband and Sophocleus (1992) estimate the actual extent of crime, as reflected by the illegally transferred assets in 1985 as equal to 8.4 percent of the GDP. Although their estimating procedure contains, I believe, an upward bias, it should be clear that orders of magnitudes that are involved are enormous. These costs of crime also do not reflect the adverse economic effects of governmental corruption. Such corruption reflects a different facet of the loss of social cohesiveness and some have claimed that it is increasing not just in the United States but in many other capitalist nations as well (Cotta, 1991, pp. 85–130).
18. Cited by Pagden (1988).

encing the evolution of capitalism, this has the least relation to structural complexity per se. It is also, I might add, the most difficult to quantify. This does not mean that these values are irrelevant for the economy, for the effective functioning of bourgeois society and a capitalist system depends upon such values as a respect for hard work, saving for the future of oneself and one's family, and honest economic achievement. These values seem to be eroding. I must add that merely wanting to become rich is irrelevant – greed has an important place in all economic systems. It is the way in which people want to achieve wealth that is important, and this is where the "spirit of capitalism" becomes important.

For a moment it is useful to step back, to consider culture in general, and to start with Friedrich Nietzsche's startling statement:[19] "I describe what is coming, what can no longer come differently: *the advent of nihilism*. This history can be related even now, for necessity itself is at work here ... for some time now, our whole European culture has been moving as toward a catastrophe ..." He traces this not to "social distress" or "physiological degeneration" but to skepticism regarding morality, which is the outgrowth of the rationalistic Western tradition of religion and philosophy. Daniel Bell (1976) recasts the insight to argue that such nihilism arises from the triumphal victory of the modernist impulse in culture that destroys the intense moral zeal for self-regulation of everyday conduct characterizing early capitalism and replaces it with the desire for self-expression, gratification, and fun. It can be called the triumph of the traditions of Western rationalism in which all assumptions are challenged.

Nietzsche's basic argument about the rise of nihilism is taken closer to home by a number of social commentators: For instance, Jacques Attali speaks about the rise of a nihilistic indifference resulting from the constant flux of change of twentieth-century Western civilization.[20] Kenneth Gergen focuses on the reflection of this nihilism within individuals, namely the loss of their core identity because their lives are oversaturated with disconnected relationships and experiences. Irving Kristol argues that this is a prominent feature of our modernist culture, and that it features a denigration of bourgeois values that, in turn, destroy the moral underpinnings of a successful market system.

These arguments about changes in cultural values are provocative and, with regard to the economic system, focus our attention on those aspects of culture most directly related to the functioning of capitalism. In particular, it is useful to consider the elements of what Max Weber called the "spirit of capitalism." This designates a frame of mind where value is placed on the accumulation of wealth from productive economic activities, rather than on political power,

19. Nietzsche [1901 (1968)] p. 3).
20. Attali (1991), p. 16. The other references in the paragraph are to Gergen (1992) and Kristol (1992).

military glory, personal majesty, consumption, social approval, or personal holiness that provide a basic motivating force in other economic systems. In the period following World War II, the issue of the spirit of capitalism has been discussed in two quite different contexts.

One offshoot of the discussion stems from the ideas of Joseph Schumpeter, a staunch but pessimistic defender of the capitalist system, who wrote:[21] "Capitalism creates a rational frame of mind which, having destroyed the moral authority of so many other institutions, in the end turns against its own: the bourgeois finds to his amazement that the rationalist attitude does not stop at the credentials of kings and popes, but goes to attack private property and the whole scheme of bourgeois values. The bourgeois fortress thus becomes politically defenseless. Defenseless fortresses invite aggression especially if there is rich booty in them." He argued that the mechanism for the decline in the defense of private property lies in the separation of ownership and control, the rise of the independent power of paid managers against the owners of the means of production, and the bureaucratization of the entrepreneurial function. The system becomes increasingly difficult to defend on ideological grounds (in Kristol's phrase, "virtue loses its loveliness"), especially when the entrepreneurs, who embody the crucial element of change in capitalism, settle down for a secure existence as highly paid corporate bureaucrats.

From the vantage point of the 1990s, this approach seems dated. During most of the post–World War II era, the ideology of capitalism faced competition from both Marxism and the ideology of social democracy. With the collapse of communism in the late 1980s and the economic stagnation of many nations embracing a social-democratic ideology, the strength of these competing ideologies has considerably weakened. To many, the triumph of the ideology of capitalism appears complete, but this judgment seems premature: The weakening of various socialist ideologies may be only temporary, especially in those nations unable to navigate successfully the transition from communism to capitalism. Six years after the "collapse of communism" in the U.S.S.R. and East Europe, neocommunist parties were in power in most successor states; and in one of the exceptions to the generalization, Russia, the situation was uncertain. Nevertheless, it also does not seem likely that alternate ideologies will threaten the capitalist ideology in the United States for the next few decades. Indeed, the greatest threat to the capitalist ideology is no ideology at all, an ideological confusion that might have some serious consequences.

The other offshoot of the discussion stems from the question of whether the spirit of capitalism is waning because the economic system is becoming sclerotic. Such sclerosis represents, as it were, a triumph of politics over culture since it arises from the political activities of special groups to protect their eco-

---

21. Schumpeter (1942), p. 143.

nomic interests by placing restraints on the economic activities of others.[22] While some signs of this sclerosis have appeared, this issue is of secondary importance.

The most fruitful approach to the spirit of capitalism focuses on the cultural suppositions of capitalism. Daniel Bell points out a "radical disjunction" between the technical-economic order and the cultural order. The former is ruled by principles defined in terms of efficiency and rationality.[23] The latter

22. In a stimulating book Mancur Olson (1982) argues that stable societies with unchanged boundaries tend over time to accumulate more collusive groups and organizations for collective action (for instance, unions, professional associations, farm organizations, trade associations, lobbies, cartels). These groups attempt to reduce the level of competition in some manner beneficial to themselves or to exploit any deviation from competitive market standards that raise their income. Such activities not only create a one time loss to the economy, but reduce the society's capacity to adopt new technologies or innovations and/or slow down reallocation of resources in response to changing conditions. In both cases, economic growth is reduced.

This sclerosis increases over time and is observable both directly (the number of interest groups, which are measured by Mueller and Murrell, 1986) and indirectly. From this approach a number of testable propositions can be derived which allow us to assess the validity of the theory. Most importantly, countries that have existed the longest time with unchanged boundaries and no foreign invasions tend, other things being equal, not only to have the slowest rates of economic growth, but also more unequal distributions of income. Elsewhere (Pryor, 1983, 1984) I present results from cross-country regressions to show that the proposition about growth is simply wrong. Nevertheless, Weede (1990) presents some interesting supporting evidence for the second part of Olson's proposition, although it seems likely that the phenomenon may be explained by other causal factors. Although impressive support for other propositions derived from the sclerosis approach has been presented (for instance, Murrell, 1983), my own attempts to use this approach to explain changes in industrial concentration (Pryor, 1994b) and competitiveness in foreign trade (Chapter 8) were unsuccessful.

Although the basic proposition undoubtedly has a kernel of truth, it assumes that societies are unable to renew themselves and to reduce the power of such special interest groups without some major crises such as foreign invasion. However, Prime Minister Margaret Thatcher was able to reduce significantly the power of British labor unions and President Clinton was able to induce Congress to reduce domestic tariffs with the adoption of NAFTA, which suggests that the growth of special interest groups is not irreversible (although, I must add, some powerful interests were able to obtain some loopholes in this law). Moreover, as I argue later in the chapter, the increasing integration of the world economy and the falling tariffs means that the advantages of special privileges are undercut by competition from imports.

23. Bell (1976). The citation is from p. 37.

Myron Magnet (1993) takes this argument one step further. The ideas of the "cultural revolution of the youth" in the United States in the 1960s, with its critique of traditional bourgeois values and of its stress on freedom from societal constraints, filtered quickly to the certain low-income groups and minorities. The youth in these latter groups, in turn, became members of the underclass whose values make them both incapable of productive participation in the labor force as well as irresistible role models to other disaffected youth, who join them in increasing numbers. Translated into economic terms, this means that a change in cultural values have led to an increase in the reservation wage (the lowest wage at which a person will take a job) of the young, for which Magnet cites only some causal supportive evi-

is "prodigal, promiscuous, dominated by antirational, antiintellectual temper in which the self is taken as the touchstone of cultural judgement.... The character structure inherited from the nineteenth century, with its emphasis on self-discipline, delayed gratification, and restraint ... clashes sharply with the culture where such bourgeois values have been completely rejected – in part, paradoxically, because of the workings of the capitalist economic system itself." As Saul Bellow has recently noted, rage is the reverse of bourgeois prudence and is now brilliantly prestigious.

If these diagnoses are correct, then we should look at such crucial features of the system as the desire to save and invest, to innovate, and to work at high intensity. Reviewing the scanty empirical indicators provides evidence more ambiguous and mixed than these broad generalizations about culture might indicate. Of the four forces influencing the evolution of the economic system discussed in this chapter, the cultural trend is the most problematic because of the mixed nature of the evidence.

Although it appears that average annual hours in paid employment in the United States have slowly declined since the 1950s and 1960s, one study presents evidence that for men, work hours per week have remained roughly the same; and another study provides data that such work may have actually increased.[24] Whatever the trend, by 1990 Americans worked significantly longer hours in paid employment than workers in most European nations. Similarly, although several surveys, in which I have confidence, suggests that a relatively high share of Americans would like to work even longer hours, at least one survey shows that a relatively high share wish to work fewer hours. If people are working fewer hours, but wish to work more, then generalizations about changes in the "capitalist ethic" that is based on such evidence is problematic.

dence. Cross-section evidence from two surveys presented by Holzer (1985) shows a more complicated picture for 1979–80. The reservation wages for white and black young men as well as the types of jobs that they sought were roughly the same. Nevertheless, this reservation wage as a ratio of wage received in the past (which presumably reflects both the quality of the respondent and any possible discrimination) was higher for young black males than for whites. Moreover, the reservation wage of young blacks was less responsive to factors reflecting the job market demand for workers than of young whites. Such evidence hardly supports Magnet's thesis, although time-series evidence is needed for a conclusive evaluation.

24. Studies showing a decline in average hours of paid employment in the United States in the post–World War II era include: OECD (1994), p. 280; and Maddison (1977, Table A.9). John Owen (1986) shows no trend in annual work hours, at least for men. Julia Schor (1991, p. 29) shows an increase, at least for labor force participants, but her estimates have been severely criticized by specialists on time–budget studies, which served as the basis of her estimates. Although the survey data on subjective attitudes toward work cited by Bell and Freeman (1994, Tables 4, 5, and 7) appear conclusive, another survey cited by Wuthnow (1994, p. 65) shows quite different results and a much higher percentage of respondents wished to work fewer hours.

Attitudes toward hard work is another crucial aspect of the work ethnic and the spirit of capitalism and in this respect, the evidence about changes over time is also ambiguous. Daniel Yankelovitch claims that public opinion data show:[25] "...a shift from the Protestant ethic valuation of work as having intrinsic moral value to work as a source of personal satisfaction, and therefore less tolerance for work that does not provide personal satisfaction."

Readily available behavioral indicators on this matter provide some confirmation. It might seem encouraging that college and university enrollment has increased, since this suggests that America is providing the necessary human capital for the coming decades. But the quality of this human capital investment raises questions. For instance, in a 1993 nationwide survey of entering first-year university students (allegedly the cream of the high-school crop), only 33.7 percent reported spending more than six hours a week studying or doing homework during their last year in high school. This was down from 43.7 percent from a similar survey in 1981 and represents far less time than that spent on watching TV. It might be added that although 53.6 percent of incoming students to universities rated themselves in the highest 10 percent of academic ability and 27 percent had a high school grade average of A– or higher (up from 12.5 percent in 1969), over a quarter required remedial work in mathematics (up at least 10 percentage points from the 1970s) over a sixth needed extra help in reading, literature, and grammar. In part, this complacency seems a consequence of the gradual downplaying of individual achievement and academic competition toward more emphasis on cooperative or group cooperative or group education, life adjustment courses, and other excesses of the progressive education movement.

Although such surveys reveal some disturbing trends in the nation's high school and university students, these young people are still in their formative years and can change, so that it is necessary to look at the changes in the work ethic of adults as well. In this regard the data are much more problematic. My own attempts to measure changes in work intensity over time by means of a survey of production managers ended in failure because of "nostalgia bias" – the belief that things were always better in the past.[26] More specifically, about the same proportion of managers believed not only that work was being carried out with less intensity and with less attention to quality, but that absenteeism had increased as well. According to the statistics cited in Chapter 3, absenteeism rates do not appear to have greatly changed from the late 1950s to the late 1980s, when such rates began to fall. So the opinions of managers about changes in the work habits of their employees were biased. Moreover, as discussed in Chapters 3 and 4, some aspects of the work ethic, as manifest-

25. Yankelovitch (1994). The data on schools and homework in the next paragraph come from Cage (1994).
26. Pryor (1983).

ed by such indicators as the declining strike rates or job turnover, do not bolster the case of the decline of the work ethic either. These various measures of the work ethic are suggestive; but, I must emphasize, they are also too indirect to be convincing.[27]

Another approach focuses on the morale of the work force. It can be argued that the corporate downsizing occurring since the late 1980s destroys not only the bond of trust between workers and their enterprises alleged to have been enjoyed ("everyone is now scared") but also the incentive of workers to invest in firm-specific human capital. Of course, this trust and long-run commitment are both important elements of the work ethic.[28] To put the matter in a different way, Michel Albert notes that "a diligent and devoted management of a stable work force is one of the decisive ingredients for achieving a competitive edge" and in this respect, the cultural element is a crucial binding force.

Survey instruments to determine employee attitudes toward their work yield equivocal results. For instance, everyone agrees that major differences exist between work attitudes of average American and Japanese workers, in large respect because of cultural differences. James R. Lincoln reviews the evidence from various surveys and presents his own data as well.[29] but concludes that such data "...hardly offers clear and consistent support" to the common beliefs about such matters. A complicating factor is the separation of factors influencing the work ethic in general and in particular situations where work habits are strongly influenced by management practices. He summarizes his own studies on the matter by concluding "...our research has uncovered some firm evidence that certain putative Japanese management practices ... produce significant dividends in employee motivation, regardless of whether the work setting is Japan or the United States." So I must end this brief review of the prob-

27. It might be argued that the increase in female participation in the labor force shows an increase in the capitalist spirit. This phenomenon, however, may have other explanations. It should also be noted that in comparison to twelve major industrialized nations, the United States has the second lowest level of absenteeism; the lowest is Japan (Bosch, 1993, p. 11). This may, however, be less of a function of work ethic than the ease of being fired for cause in the United States.

28. Survey results (for instance, cited by Reich, 1993) provide some support for the notion that corporate downsizing does not often achieve the expected results. It might be added that the rapid reshuffling of parts of companies from one owner to another might also destroy the social bonds that allow particular organizations to function productively. Unfortunately, little evidence is available that the ill effects of these changes have increased over time. The citation comes from Albert (1993), p. 80.

29. Lincoln (1989). It is difficult to evaluate the work ethic from generalizations about values, where one finds extreme generalizations in the literature with little attention paid to how widely or deeply such values are held. For instance, McRae (1994), p. 81 argues that Japan's brand of Buddhism celebrates work as divine and cites one person saying: "Unlike Christian societies, where work is a necessary evil, we believe labour is an act of God, that working allows us to become closer to God." Among those attempting and failing to determine the impact of a declining work ethic in the United States is Edward Denison (1979), pp. 134–5.

lematic nature of the declining work ethnic by throwing up my hands, as have others examining the problem before me.

Less ambiguous evidence comes from data on saving's behavior. National account data (Appendix Note 10.2) show a dramatic decrease both in personal and governmental saving rates, especially since the early 1970s. On the personal level the decline in voluntary saving has occurred in all age brackets and all important demographic groups. This occurred, it should be added, in spite of many supply-side economic policies of the Reagan presidency designed to skew the income distribution so as to encourage saving.

It is, however, difficult to find any convincing economic reason to explain this decline.[30] A more likely candidate for the shift is a change in social values, but here the empirical evidence becomes more slippery. James Q. Wilson discusses some experimental data that present-mindedness among members of the underclass has increased; but, as he notes, little weight can be placed on such results until such experiments are replicated for other groups. Gilles Lipovetsky speaks of the growth of narcissistic, hedonistic, and self-centered behavior and a nation populated with people whose "world view has been emptied of all but the quest to satisfy the ego, to serve the interests of the self, to experience the ecstasy of personal liberation, and to indulge sexuality and the cult of the body." Contributing to such a change in values has been an increasing lack of understanding of the economic system in which we live and its complexities, a cognitive phenomenon that encourages alienation and the flight toward hedonism. This cognitive confusion is not only enforced by a decline in the quality of education but by such institutions as commercial television, which lead peopple to scorn complexity and to focus attention on feelings, rather than ideas.

These data on saving, however, are not defined to allow us to make the proper inferences about the capitalist spirit.[31] If, for instance, we add to the personal saving data in the national account involuntary personal saving such as net contributions (contributions minus benefits) of both employees and employers to the social security fund, employer contributions to private pension funds, and net purchase of consumer durables (a type of saving), the picture does not seem to change (Table A.34, Part C). With these corrections the total saving rate rose until the early 1970s and then declined precipitously. If, however, we employ a different data set and handle the insurance and pension

---

30. Such an exercise is carried out by Bosworth, Burtless, and Sabelhaus (1991). The major puzzle is why savings has declined when the growth of income has slowed down, when the lifetime income hypothesis suggests that savings should increase under such circumstances. That is, if people anticipate high income growth in the future, they save less today; the reverse should hold when they foresee lower income growth. The evidence on the underclass comes from Wilson (1994), p. 61. The citation at the end of the paragraph is approvingly cited by Albert (1993), p. 202.

31. This is discussed by Block (1990). My reading and his of the evidence differ, however.

funds in the manner used in the flow-of-funds accounts of the Federal Reserve System, personal saving is greater and the fall in the savings rate since the early 1970s still occurs, but is much less dramatic.

It is not the purpose of this chapter to resolve some very serious issues about the proper measure of saving, but some remarks are necessary. Although it seems likely that the appropriate saving rate has declined, the readily available evidence is not sufficiently strong to provide conclusive support to the argument about the enervation of capitalism. However much personal saving has declined, the fall in the aggregate saving rate is due less to the enervation of the capitalist spirit on the personal level and much more to the drop in business and especially government saving.

This decline in future orientation on the part of business is particularly revealed by investment in human capital, which in the national accounts is not included as saving or investment at all. For instance, the ratio of total R and D expenditures to GDP, which reached a peak in the mid-1960s, has not been surpassed since then; the ratio of civilian R and D to GDP reached a plateau in the early 1980s.[32]. Since the mid-1960s both Germany and Japan have shown a steadily rising share of the ratio of total R and D to GDP that surpassed similar statistics in the United States by the late 1980s. If only civilian R and D is considered, then R and D expenditures as a percent of GDP are roughly one-half those of Japan, Germany, and Sweden, a possible explanation of the dramatic decline of the U.S. trade balance in high technology goods during the 1980s.

Another indicator of the spirit of capitalism is innovation and invention, but these are difficult to measure. Nevertheless, the available scraps of evidence point toward a pessimistic conclusion and some clues are provided by statistics on patents. The patents granted to domestic individuals and groups per million adults between twenty and sixty-five has declined from 462 in 1951–55 (or 656 in 1966–70) to 337 in 1986–90.[33] In recent years such patents have begun to increase, although it is not clear whether this represent a temporary or permanent change. Of course, many serious problems arise in interpreting patent statistics as a measure of inventive activity and, moreover, these

32. Department of Commerce, Bureau of the Census (annual-b, 1993).The data on Japan, Germany, and Sweden come from U.S. National Science Board (1991), p. 4. According to the U.S. National Science Board (biennial-1989), Table 7.14, the trade surplus of high-technology goods (measured in current prices) disappeared by the end of the 1980s; in constant prices [(ibid., 1991), Table 6.8], the balanced halved over the decade but still remained positive.

33. The patent data (as well as the copyright data discussed later) come from U.S. Department of Commerce, Bureau of the Census (1975 and annual-b, various years). The population data come from U.S. Council of Economic Advisors (annual, 1993). These results for patents granted cannot be traced to any change in the ratio of patent applications to patents granted, which is quite irregular but was roughly the same in the two periods considered. Two useful studies exploring the difficulties in interpreting patent statistics are Griliches (1990) and Comanor and Scherer (1969).

include changing criteria by which patents are granted and a decline in the propensity to patent inventions of a given quality. Nevertheless, the 27 percent decline in patents granted per adult from the early 1950s (or the 49 percent decline from the late 1960s) is so marked that it raises the possibility about an important change in the spirit of capitalism in the United States.[34]

This decline in the relative volume of R and D is reinforced by events in the sphere of finance. As noted in Chapter 5, corporate debt soared in the 1980s for a variety of reasons. This type of financial restructuring has the disadvantage of raising interest costs and creates incentives for management to reduce relative expenditures on investment, including R and D, where the time horizon is long. Empirical evidence is available to suggest that this is what happened.[35]

Other indicators of the enervation of the capitalist spirit focus directly on the activities of the firm. The average index of net business formations was only 29 percent higher in the 1980s than in the 1950s, even though the average GDP in the latter decade was 146 percent higher.[36] Indeed, net business formations was roughly the same in the 1970s and 1980s and showed no sign of rising from this plateau in the early 1990s. Although incorporations had increased faster than the GDP, so had business failures. If the spirit of capitalism can be measured by successful business formations, then such information does not bode well for the future. Furthermore, as discussed in Chapter 6, the linkage between executive compensation in these firms and firm profits is becoming weaker. A key aspect of capitalism, namely economic reward for successful economic performance, is being undermined. This is also disturbing. Although the values of managers in the United States are highly individualistic (evidence is presented in Appendix Note 10.1), this does not mean that capitalism is alive and well, since such attitudes can lead to the seeking of rents, not profits, so that the economy is no better off.

34. Although it is argued that the decline in patents granted to individuals reflects the well-known substitution of organized research by enterprises and laboratories replacing the solitary inventer. individuals may be losing their zeal for such a challenge. That is, the person who used to be a solitary inventor is no longer puttering in his cold garage on a new project, but is sitting with a beer in one hand in his warm living room in front of the TV watching a football game.

      Another possibility is that many of the recent innovations, for instance, those arising from various types of continuous improvement drives by enterprises are simply not being patented.

      It is also noteworthy that the number of copyrights granted per million adults rose 66 percent between 1951–5 and 1986–90. One interpretation (among many) of this steady increase suggests that considerable creative energy has been diverted from technological activities such as inventing, to the arts.

35. The evidence on these matters is presented by Hall (1990); other studies are summarized by Hall (1991).

36. This discussion is based on data from U.S. Department of Commerce, Bureau of the Census (Annual-b, various editions) and (1975), Series V21 and V22.

It is sometimes argued that the spirit of capitalism ebbs because its vigor cannot withstand the relentless expansion of governmental regulation. The data presented in Chapter 9 suggest that the relative degree of regulation – at least as measured by the direct costs to the government of carrying out such activities – began to decline slightly in the late 1970s. Little credible evidence is at hand that the United States has begun to approach the point of declining entrepreneurial vigor arising from this quarter, despite the self-serving complaints of many business people.

In sum, the spirit of capitalism is a cultural aspect crucial for the functioning of the U.S. economic system, not to mention the path of evolution it will take in the future. Most indicators of its enervation are quite imperfect and, moreover, ambiguous. Several particular indicators – the saving rate, R and D expenditures, new patents, net business formation, and linkage of excutive compensation and performance – suggest that an enervation may be taking place. The case, however, is not strong. Various indicators of the work ethic are even more ambiguous. Although the decline in the quality of primary and secondary education and the amount of schoolwork carried out certainly point to a decline, attempts to measure such a decline among actual members of the work force have not been successful. I believe that this cultural change represented by an enervation of the capitalist spirit will have an impact on the future of capitalism in the United States, but the empirical evidence that is presented above is not sufficiently strong to rest much of my argument upon it. As a result, I will focus most of the following discussion on the other three indicators – increased structural complexity, increased world economic integration, and decreased social cohesiveness.

Other important forces of systemic change

Others have advanced still different candidates for the crucial underlying forces of systemic change and it is worthwhile to glance briefly at them.

Many have pointed to problems of the physical environment. If economic difficulties will occur because raw materials and energy become more scarce and expensive (an assumption that can be challenged), this may have an adverse influence on the distribution of income and a corresponding impact on patterns of consumption.[37] The planet may also suffer from a crisis of over-population and increasing inequality between rich and poor nations. Similarly, problems arising from global warming may lead to more governmental regulation but, as indicated in Chapter 9, alternate methods of handling such problems are available to the government, short of a massive expansion of the public sector. Although these and other forces will undoubtedly change the economy and

37. The environmental catastrophe that so may are predicting appears overdrawn. Some brief comments on this matter are presented in Appendix Note 10.4.

key economic variables, it is difficult to see how these changes would affect economic institutions and the U.S. economic system, the focus of this study.

Changes in technology may influence the economic system and a prime candidate is computerization and the growth of information technology. Again, this will have an important impact on the economy but, as indicated in Chapter 6, its direct impact on economic institutions per se is ambiguous. For instance, ever decreasing information costs can lead either to greater decentralization or greater centralization, depending on how the technology is used; the outcome is not incised in stone in advance.

Scenarios of alternate capitalisms

The mass media in the United States did a disservice to the public in its paeans of praise for the "triumph of capitalism" following the collapse of communism in Eastern Europe, because it diverted attention from more serious issues: What kind of capitalism will, or should, we have?

One scenario of the future of the U.S. economic system is simply more of the same, a possibility discussed earlier in the chapter. In this section I sketch four more scenarios. The first is a general exhaustion of the system, a possibility that deserves serious consideration. The other three are labeled: an American-style finance capitalism, an atomic capitalism, and a remodeled capitalism, that is, a capitalism operating with different values and procedures. I do not bother to sketch a social-democratic welfare state or a laissez-faire system, both of which seem unlikely. Nor do I discuss other improbable developments such as a technoutopia, a single-world economy guided by a centralized world federation of nations, or a theocratic economy–polity.

A general exhaustion

An exhaustion of capitalism does not necessarily mean the evaporation of private property, or the disappearance of buying and selling of goods on some type of market for private profit; these have existed for millennia and undoubtedly will persist for millennia in the future. Instead, the exhaustion of capitalism as an economic system means the decline in its capacity for change, an existential collapse as it were. As Robert Heilbroner argues:[38] "If capitalism is anything, it is a social order in constant change – and beyond that, change that seems to have a direction, an underlying principle of motion, a logic."

As noted above, the United States manifested a greater deceleration of growth of GDP per economically active than any other highly industrialized nation between 1950 and 1990.[39] The collapse of U.S. capitalism could come

38. Heilbroner (1993), p. 41.
39. The data underlying this claim are presented in Pryor (1994b).

about simply as a continuation of current trends in labor productivity, reinforced by further decline in saving and investment, especially if investment risks rise as a result of declining social cohesiveness. The decline also might be fueled by a possible decline in the willingness of the population to work hard or to allow those who do to enjoy the fruits of their labor. As noted previously, however, this change in the work ethic is problematic.

After such a collapse, the United States would simply become a mediocre economic entity with few ideas, a stifling economic climate, little change, and fewer hopes. A rough parallel is provided by Argentina which, up to World War I, was generally considered as the richest and fastest growing Latin American economy and a potential world economic power. As a result of a combination of external economic shocks and inappropriate economic policies, the economy did not follow the expected trajectory thereafter and Argentina became known for its economic problems, rather than its successes.

Increasing structural complexity would no longer be such a problem if such exhaustion occurred because economic growth, a major cause of the increase in complexity, would be very slow. In this case, the major source of rising structural complexity would come through increasing economic internationalization, at least if the nation chose to participate in the world economic integration.

This exhaustion could be accelerated by further loss of social cohesiveness, with implications for both our private and business lives. Fewer people would want to leave their homes, preferring to spend their time surfing on the 500 channels available to them; and social interactions would become more limited. In the economic realm, property would become less easy to protect, a result of rising crime and a weakening of the effectiveness of government to enforce business contracts. The economic stagnation, combined with the ever increasing inequalities of income and wealth, could lead to a new type of class struggle – between those with and without human capital. The former could sustain a high living standard, the latter would suffer from unemployment, poor health, poverty, and anger. Governmental action to rectify the situation would also be limited, in major part because of the lack of social cohesiveness would create a policy gridlock to resolve the problem. Whatever the exact cause of collapse is economic, social or cultural, once a nation is started along this road, an easy turnabout is difficult to envision.[40]

40. One "traditional solution" to overcome such exhaustion and to reignite the engines of economic is, of course, an authoritarian government that would create a force-fed capitalism. In nations such as Singapore, such a solution has produced spectacular results. But this "solution" presupposes a relatively simple or small economy, with a supply of docile and trained workers. The increasing structural complexity in the United States, combined with the apparent decline of the work ethic, would make a successful outcome of such authoritarianism in the United States a highly questionable method of resuscitating the moribund economic system. And the increasingly deep world economic integration will also remove from consideration usage of certain governmental policy tools to carry out such direct management of the economy.

*Scenarios of change in the organization and
control of production*

Major changes in the organization and control of production are, I believe, the most far-reaching systemic changes that could occur in the coming decades. Three scenarios have some probability of occurring: finance capitalism, atomic capitalism, and remodeled capitalism. They are sketched in the following discussion and analyzed at considerable length in Appendix Note 10.3.

Finance capitalism: "Third-party capitalism" provides a label for several different types of capitalism in which institutions, rather than individual owners of the means of production, exercise major decision-making powers in the crucial productive institutions. Finance capitalism represents the most likely form that such a third-party capitalism could take.

The motive force of finance capitalism are two types of increasing structural complexity, namely the increasing aging of the population and the increasing separation of control and ultimate ownership occurring when financial intermediaries, especially pension funds, take over the oversight and control of the large corporations. The increasing share of stock ownership by financial intermediaries is documented in Chapter 6; finance capitalism implies that the passive holding of such stock is transformed into actual control, a step that would require a number of changes in laws and government regulations now restricting such activities.

Finance capitalism is consistent with trends toward internationalization, a breakdown in social cohesiveness, and an enervation of the capitalist spirit. Financial intermediaries can easily operate in a world market and, indeed, an increase in their power over the operation of enterprises represents a type of convergence of the organization of industry in the United States with that in some continental European nations and Japan. Under certain circumstances finance-capitalism can accelerate the decline in social cohesiveness, by creating a type of dual economy, with two groups of firms. One group is well financed and capital intensive, with a well-trained and well-paid work force. The other group has little contact with these large financial intermediaries and lacks the resources to invest in the latest technologies, so that their productivity and, of course, their wages are much lower than in the first group. The only way of social and economic mobility is through the bureaucracy of enterprises in the first group. Thus it is bureaucratic imperatives, rather than the dynamism of small-scale capitalism, that drives the system. Such an economy adapts to the enervation of the capitalist spirit by bureaucratizing the innovative function. With the exception that ownership remains private, such a world has considerable similarity to the future described by Joseph Schumpeter.

Atomic capitalism: This is the label for an economy where production is carried out in relatively small enterprises and where one type of structural complexity, namely the separation of ownership and control, is reversed. It represents almost the antithesis of finance capitalism.

The motive force of atomic capitalism are developments described in Chapter 6. They include the decline in aggregate concentration and the average sizes of productive enterprises in recent decades; the intention of managers (revealed by the survey data) to simplify procedures and processes, to decentralize, and to focus more attention to their core businesses; and the evidence that investment in information processing leads to smaller enterprises because their transaction costs in monitoring subcontractors and suppliers are lowered.

It might be questioned whether such a systemic change is consistent with increasing internationalization of economic activity. Experience from other nations such as Germany and Taiwan, where small firms in certain sectors have been able to compete internationally, suggests that under certain institutional arrangements, atomic capitalism is viable in an increasingly interdependent world. Because atomic capitalism is more dependent upon contracts with subcontractors, rather than inhouse production, the decline of social cohesiveness would have to be reversed, at least to the extent that contract enforcement would be strengthened and risks arising from crime would be held steady or reduced. Moreover, for atomic capitalism to function effectively, the spirit of capitalism would need to be strength ened so that there is a large core of individuals that are willing to take up the risks of such production directly, or to participate in such an enterprise in the form of *employee stock ownership plans* (ESOPs).

Remodeled capitalism: This is the label for an economic system that has adapted to the increasing structural complexity. It reflects an enhanced valuation of human capital through a greater use of skills and a greater education of the labor force. Among other things, production would increasingly shift toward those sectors in which the United States has a comparative advantage (Chapter 8).

Remodeled capitalism certainly is consistent with an increasing internationalization and, indeed, would lead to a shift in production toward that type of production requiring high inputs of skills in which the nation has a comparative advantage (Chapter 8). It would require a reversal of the decline in social cohesiveness of the nation, and a reintegration of the currently disadvantaged groups into the economic process. In the private sector work would have to be restructured along many dimensions that would include: reward for achievement through closer ties of remuneration to total results, power sharing, and job enrichment. In the public sector more funds would have to be allocated toward providing the necessary education and social capital. Moreover, to anticipate the changes in the economy requiring effective intervention, the government would have to function with a more unified long-term vision of the future impact of its current policies. Finally, such an economic system might require a certain changes in values, particularly among managers, away from the extreme individualism of current American managers (Appendix Note 10.1) and toward a managerial style that is more inclined toward decentralization and reliance on the knowledge and skills of others.

The motive force toward a remodeled capitalism is not material, but psychological – a greater realization of the citizenry about the current trajectory of institutions in both the public and private sectors. Unfortunately, I find few indications that the requisite national dialogue about the economic system is taking place. Although this book, as well as many others that are oriented more toward policy analysis of the system, represent attempts to frame some of these issues, the election of public officials and decisions about institutional policy, both in the public and private sectors, appear to be made predominantly on the basis of considerations other than these long-term factors. Of particular importance, the decrease in social cohesiveness and the enervation in the capitalist spirit have yet to be addressed in a serious and comprehensive fashion by the public at large.

A brief summary

After casting doubt on the notion that the economic system is functioning so poorly that its performance alone would force a change in the system, I define four major forces that I believe to influence the evolution of the economic system: increasing structural complexity, increasing world economic integration, decreasing social cohesiveness, and an enervation of the capitalist spirit. The middle two forces are reflected in important ways in structural complexity, even though they also represent independent forces as well. Taking these into account, I describe two extremes – no change from present trends and a general exhaustion of the system, the latter being merely an accelerated version of the former. I also briefly examine three other scenarios that lie in between – an American-style finance capital, an atomic capitalism, and a remodeled capitalism with different values and procedures in both the public and private sectors . For each I indicate briefly how they reinforce or act against the four major forces of change.

I do not believe any of the three scenarios lying between the extremes will come about in a pure form. Nor do they exhaust the various possibilities of the changes that U.S. capitalism might take. Nevertheless, since these three scenarios are, in many respects, not mutually exclusive, I also believe that some elements in one system might be combined with other elements of another system to yield a hybrid that would have sufficient integrity to be stable. The exact composition of the mix that would characterize this future economic system would depend on a mix of economic, political, social, and cultural considerations that defy prediction.

In this context it is also worth noting that the four major forces previously outlined are also operating with varying degrees of strength in other industrialized nations as well. These nations are at quite different starting points: on the one hand, most do not feature the extreme inequalities nor have they reached the loss of social cohesiveness found in the United States. On the other hand, the capitalist ethos may be weaker in some of those nations than in the United States. Despite the convergence of economic institutions encouraged by deep world economic integration, it seems highly unlikely that the capitalist systems of various nations will converge. Many critical economic institutions and many procedures and policies followed in these institutions are shaped by special national characteristics and preferences.

Epilogue

This book, as a whole, has focused on changes in structural complexity and these five scenarios represent different manifestations of such changes. The no-change scenario indicates a continuation of current trends of structural complexity. The exhaustion of capitalism scenario exemplifies a deceleration of the growth of structural complexity because the economy is stagnating. The scenario of finance capitalism depicts the acceleration of the separation of ownership from effective control, a particular type of structural complexity. The scenario of atomic capitalism represents a decrease in structural complexity in the sense of a compression of the size distribution of enterprises, and an increase in such complexity in the sense of a more dense network of communications between an expanded universe of firms. Finally, the remodeled capitalism represents an increase in the share of the labor force engaged in the generation, collection, and analysis of information.

Previous chapters examine the meaning and impact of structural complexity on particular parts of the economy from the end of World War II to the present. Structural complexity proves to have a variety of manifestations and these, in turn, have quite different impacts on the behavior of the economy. Although in many cases structural complexity is increasing, in some cases that I discuss, it is not. In some cases the impact of structural complexity represents a serious policy problem, for instance, the secular increase in unemployment; in other cases the impact of rising complexity is less serious than feared, for instance, on the volatility of financial variables.

In this book I have marched the reader through many different parts of the economy. Although I have tried to show how the structural complexity of the economy is changing and how these changes effect the operation of the economy, this exercise has a still more important purpose. As noted in the first chapter, structural complexity is a perspective, not a theory. The concept leads us, however, to ask questions about the evolution of the institutions of the economic system more systematically, and also to ask a variety of new questions about institutional changes. It provides a framework in which old theories can be reinterpreted and new theories can be constructed. It forces us to collect new types of information about the economy that allow us to investigate more systematically the long-run changes in our economic institutions. And finally, it helps us to understand more clearly many disparate phenomena in different sectors of the economy and to perceive the relationships between them, where no links were seen before. The discussion in this study have focused on only a small number of the many questions that can be investigated using the concept of structural complexity.

As structural complexity of the economy increases, so do our lives. Use of the concept of structural complexity to understand this changing world allows us to function with greater insight and effectiveness. It may not reduce the increasing difficulties of our daily existence, but at least we will have a greater understanding of what is happening.

Appendix notes

Notes to Chapter 1

Note 1.1: The meaning of complexity

Complexity is a term with several related meanings. This note explores three major sets of definitions so that perspective can be gained on the approach followed in this book.

Structural complexity concerns properties of a system at one point in time; *dynamic or behavioral complexity* refers to the behavior of a system over time generated by the rules of the system; and *subjective complexity* focuses either on the way in which the system is perceived by others or to properties of the system that arise not from any particular rules but from the purposes and goals of individuals in the system. Unfortunately, this terminology is not standardized. For instance, paralleling my distinction between "structural" and "behavior" complexity, Alexei N. Severtsov distinguishes between "morphological" and "biological" complexity (Urbanek, 1988). McShea (1991) calls "structural complexity" what I call "behavioral complexity." If I understand him correctly, Çambel, (1993) calls "static complexity" what I designate "subjective complexity."

Dynamic complexity focuses particularly on the self-organizing behavior of systems. For instance, biologists have investigated how birds flock together again after they fly around obstacles and chemists have investigated how systems behave when they are far from equilibrium (Nicolis and Prigogine, 1989). In both cases the self-organization is generated by the nonlinear equations describing the system. Along the same lines economists have examined sunspot equilibria, speculative bubbles on the stock market, unemployment as a hysteresis phenomenon, and more general path-dependent historical processes such as the adoption of particular standards or technologies (e.g., Anderson, Arrow, and Pines, 1988; Barnett, Geweke, and Shell, 1989; David, 1985). This type of complexity is the focus of some fascinating research carried out under the aegis or under the influence of the Santa Fe Institute. This type of complexity is not, however, the focus of this study.

Subjective complexity can refer to how complicated the phenomenon under investigation is considered by the person under investigation. In the case of a policy decision, this may refer to the amount of information required to make the decision, or the number of alternatives considered, or the trade-offs between particular outcomes. In the case of tax legislation this may refer to the provisions of the law, the computational requirements to comply, or the amount of time to complete a tax form. In the social sciences psychologists investigate the related concept of cognitive complexity, which some such as Streufert and Swezey (1986) define in terms of multidimensional information processing in problem solving. In machines or consumer durables, subjective complexity refers to the ease of operating the object (a useful study is by Sedgwick, 1993). Such a definition is independent of the structural meaning of complexity since we can have complications and problems with relatively simple structures. This study does not deal directly with complexity in this sense, except in so far as structural complexity leads to complications.

These various approaches toward complexity are related, not just with regard to the information approach that is common to them. For instance, Kauffman (1993) and others describe some interesting links between structural and dynamic complexity in analyzing the development of morphological forms. In economics it would certainly be useful to study the relation between the structural complexity of markets and the types of price behavior over time that they generate.

In specific disciplines ranging from mathematics, biology, and engineering to sociology and theology, other definitions of complexity exist as well. In some cases, for instance algorithmic complexity or complexity as measured by fractal dimensions, the meanings of complexity are quite precise. In other cases, especially in the social sciences, the meanings of the concept are more ambiguous. In some cases scholars have explored complexity from a very broad perspective, for instance, the behavior of nonlinear dynamic systems, or the application of "hierarchy theory." In other cases the focus of study is much narrower. Since "complexity" is becoming a buzz-word in academic discourse, I try to be very explicit in the first chapter about how I use the concept.

Note 1.2: Use of the Theil statistic

I use the Theil statistic (Theil, 1967) throughout this study to explore changes in structural complexity. Employed in the physical sciences as a measure of entropy, it is sometimes used in the social sciences as a measure of the potential information of the data about a system. This is based on the notion that the information conveyed by any piece of data is, on the average, inversely proportional to the probability that the particular value of the data would occur. For example, where the population is evenly divided between several religions, we gain more information from learning a person's religion where there are ten religions than where there are two. In the former case, the probability of a person having a given religion is 10 percent; in the latter case, 50 percent. Moreover, we gain more information from the data about a person's religion in a country with ten religions if the population is evenly divided among them, than in a situation where 99 percent of the population professes a particular religion.

Theil (1967) has popularized the following formula to measure the expected informational content in economic situations:
where H = expected information context; ln is the natural logarithm, and p = probability of the event i (the sum of the probabilities = 1).

$$H = \Sigma \, p_i \ln \left(\frac{1}{p_i} \right),$$

To show how to use the formula in the examples about religion, we first determine the share of each religion in the total; these represent the probabilities of a given person professing any particular religion. If the population in a nation is 180 and there is but one religion, $H = 0$ [using the convention that log $(1/0) = 0$]. This occurs because the probability of everyone having that single religion is 100 percent and the log of this probability is zero. In other words, the information content of learning anyone's religion is nil since the population is religiously homogeneous. If each of the 180 people has a different religion, $H = 5.193$; in this case 1/180 is the probability of any person having a given religion and the summation in the formula above occurs over all religions. This value of H represents complete religious heterogeneity and is the highest H that can be achieved. If the population is split evenly among ten religions, $H = 2.303$; and if half of the population has one religion and the remaining half is split evenly among nine other religions, then $H = 1.732$. If the population is larger than 180, the measure of extreme heterogeneity increases because the number of possible religions increases.

We can calculate a Theil statistic for any distribution, for instance age, per capita incomes, number of employees in different size firms, or people professing a given religion. But we must be careful in interpreting the results in terms of structural complexity because the meaning of H for the analysis depends upon the type of distribution.

Differently stated, heterogeneity and inequality are not the same, although both represent aspects of structural complexity. Suppose, for instance, we are dealing with a problem where the

Table A.1. *Examples of Theil averages*

Labor force Establishment	Country A	Country B	Country C	Country D
1	200	100	100	1
2	200	150	100	1
3	200	200	100	1
4	200	250	100	1
5	200	300	600	996
Total workers (N)	1000	1000	1000	1000
Arithmetic average	200	200	200	200
Theil statistic of shares (H)	1.61	1.54	1.23	.032
Theil average: antilogarithm (ln N – H)	200	213	293	969

focus is on the shares per se such as the share of the population having a given religion or age. Then the greatest homogeneity occurs when the population is all in one category (where $H = 0$), while the greatest heterogeneity occurs when the population is evenly split among the N categories (where $H = \ln N$; the proof is given in Theil, 1967, p. 25). If, on the other hand, we are dealing with a distribution where the focus is on *per capita* values, the highest Theil coefficient refers to complete equality, while the lowest Theil coefficient refers to complete inequality.

A "Theil average" is simply the antilogarithm of $(\ln N - H)$, where $\ln N$ is the natural logarithm of the number of individuals in the distribution. The properties of such an average can be seen by several numerical examples presented in Table A.1.

For calculating statistics characterizing the size distribution of employment of firms in four countries, the formula can be easily applied. The Theil statistics (H) are presented on the penultimate line of the table. Because attention is on the average employment size, rather than shares, interpretation of the H is similar to that of per capita income. That is, distributions with relatively equal employment sizes have larger H coefficients than distributions featuring an unequal distribution with one large firm and several very small firms.

For all countries the arithmetic size average enterprise is 200, but this does not tell us very much since the distributions are clearly different. For the Theil average, the probability that a worker is in a particular establishment is merely the ratio of the workers in that unit to the total number of workers. A larger Theil average indicates that the size distribution of firm size is more unequal and that the economy is dominated by one very large firm.

Notes to Chapter 2

Note 2.1: Educational and religious heterogeneity

Readily available statistics allow measurement of the heterogeneity of formal educational credentials. These are presented in Table A.2. The major problem with these data, namely that they do not measure actual skills and knowledge, is discussed in Chapter 2.

For the measurement of religious heterogeneity, the basic data on membership in different church denomina tions come primarily from various issues of: National Council of the Churches of Christ in the U.S.A., *Yearbook of American and Canadian Churches*. Although this is the most complete census of its kind, the data do not seem of high quality and several problems arise in their use.

Table A.2. *Trends in education of the population 25 and over*

Year	1950	1960	1970	1980	1990
No education	2.6%	2.3%	1.6%	1.0%	0.7%
1–4 years	8.5%	6.1%	3.9%	2.6%	1.7%
5–8 years	37.2%	31.4%	22.9%	14.6%	8.3%
9–12 years	38.7%	43.8%	50.5%	49.9%	49.8%
13–15 years	7.3%	8.8%	10.6%	15.7%	18.5%
16 years and over	6.2%	7.7%	10.7%	16.3%	21.1%
Median (education years)	9.3	10.6	12.1	12.5	12.7
Absolute Theil	2.03	2.00	1.91	1.81	1.74
Relative Theil	92.6%	91.2%	87.0%	82.3%	79.5%

Notes: A larger Theil statistic reflects greater heterogeneity. The data come from U.S. Department of Commerce, *Bureau of the Census* (1964, Table 76; 1973/4, Table 75; and 1984, Table 262); and Kominski and Adams (1992, Table 1). For calculating the Theil coefficients, data are disaggregated into nine categories.

(a) Often membership data could not be obtained exactly for the year in the table; in such cases I took the closest year. In cases where data were available only in different decades, I made logarithmic interpolations.

(b) Although the sample includes a total of 389 religious denominations and other bodies and the data source is the largest census of its kind, Islam – with a membership of six million adherents in the United States in 1990 (*Yearbook* 1992) – is not included. Moreover, several smaller religions that do not reveal their membership were also omitted, for instance, the Christ Scientists. In some cases the churches changed their name so that the total religious groups in this census actually number less than 389.

(c) The membership data may be inflated since members, who have left the church, may still be retained on the rolls.

The data are presented in Table A.3 and include calculation of both absolute and relative Theil statistics; the latter run from 0 (all people belong to one church) to 1.00 (the population is evenly divided among all churches). The absolute Theil coefficients show an increasing homogeneity, which reflects in large part movement toward church consolidation. The relative Theil coefficient shows no trend at all, which means that the relative dispersal of the population among the existing churches has been about the same. Similar statistics were calculated using number of clergy per church, rather than church membership; the same trends were obtained.

Note 2.2: Further details on wage and salary inequalities

Table A.4 presents several sets of data showing the inequality of various types of wage and salary income over time. To explain these changes, three approaches are found in the economic literature and I briefly discuss each.

Between-group and within-group differences: Overall income inequality can vary because the inequality within particular groups (intragroup) changes; because the average wages between particular groups (intergroup) changes; and because the share of the population in the different groups (for instance, high- and low-wage groups) changes. These factors can interact. For instance, a change in the share of families in low- and high-income groups can, at the same time, cause changes in the average income of the two groups, as well as changes in the degree of income

Table A.3. *Religious heterogeneity in the United States*

	Inclusive membership (1000s)	Number of religious denominations	Theil statistic Absolute	Relative
1950	94,361	254	2.99	0.54
1960	124,662	260	3.04	0.55
1970	132,015	221	2.87	0.53
1980	140,850	190	2.89	0.55
1990	149,503	175	2.67	0.52

Notes: A larger Theil statistic reflects greater heterogeneity. The sources are discussed in the text of Appendix Note 2.1.

inequality within and between the two groups. For analytical convenience, however, it is often enough to focus on the impact of within-group differences from those of between-group differences. To see how such data can be interpreted in the light of overall trends in inequality, several examples are useful to consider:

A simple case is the analysis of wages classified by gender of recipient. It is well-known that the ratio of wages of men and women declined over the period at the same time that the number of women in the labor force rose from 33 percent in 1958 to 45 percent in 1988 (U.S. Council of Economic Advisors, annual, 1993). Unambiguously, changes in between-group wage differences by gender led to a decrease of the overall inequality of wages and salaries over the entire period.

Another aspect of the problem is illustrated by the impact of between-group differences of wages classed by race of recipient. The ratio of wages of blacks to whites remained roughly constant in the 1950s, rose in the 1960s and 1970s and remained roughly constant in the 1980s. But because blacks are such a small percentage of the population, the overall impact of these between-group changes and overall wage inequalities was very small.

Analysis of earnings differences between groups classed by educational status provides another clue into the changing wage inequalities, since the earnings ratios of individuals with higher levels of education to those with lower levels fell in the 1970s but rose in the 1980s (Katz and Murphy, 1992). At the same time the share of the labor force with higher education rose. For most years, except the early 1970s, the overall impact of between-group differences by education combined by shifts between groups was to increase overall inequalities (Grubb and Wilson, 1992). The extreme case is poorly educated males, who have suffered not just a decline in relative wages, but an absolute decline as well.

Turning now to aggregate trends in wage inequality, between-group differences, no matter how measured, do not seem to have played a major role. Taking the between-group differences by three major demographic variables – age, gender, and education – together, Grubb and Wilson (1992) find that their impact on change in overall inequalities was small over the twenty-one-year period. This is because the share of overall inequality explained by the group differences declined from about 47 percent to 39 percent between 1967 and 1988. The growing labor earnings inequality explained by years of education and, to a lesser extent, experience was offset by the effects of changes in the gender composition of the labor force. They also examine the between-group differences by major labor market factors such as industry structure (11 classes), occupational structure (9 classes), and work status (5 classes: full-year, some-overtime; full-year; full-year, part-time; part-year, full-year; part-year, part-time). For these variables they also find the impact on changes in the overall inequality was relatively small. The share of inequality explained by these factors declined from about 56 percent to 52 percent. It is noteworthy that work status explains by far the largest share of inequality of any single variable, a result found by others as well (for instance, Sattinger, 1985). I argue in Chapter 3 that this work status variable is related to the skills and education of the individual. It is interesting that the variable reflecting the share of the labor force in different industrial sectors, which received so much hysterical attention during the "deindustrialization debate" turned out to have a relatively minor impact on changes in income inequalities.

In the 1980s rising within-group wage differences appeared to play some role in explaining changes in income inequality than did between-group differences. Grubb and Wilson, who have the finest division of demographic groups of any study currently available, show that such within-in-group differences accounted for about 30 percent of all differences in 1970, a percentage slowly rising to 32 percent by 1988. Other studies, discussed by Levy and Murnane (1992), show a considerably larger contribution of within-group variation to the increasing wage inequality.

Supply and demand factors: The supply and demand approach for different types of labor is a second way in which problems of changing wage inequalities can be approached.

Supply induced changes in wage differentials arise from changes in the relative size of particular demographic groups. The more a specific demographic group in the labor force increases in comparison to other groups, the more the wages of this group fall in comparison to other groups, other things being equal. This is particularly noticeable with regard to income differentials due to education. This differential began significantly to increase only in the 1980s. During the post World War II era up to the 1980s, the percentage of the young labor force with university degrees was steadily rising. Since these newly educated workers were replacing an older generation with much less education, the share of college educated workers rose significantly. After 1970, however, the share of those graduating from universities increased much less quickly and, moreover, they were replacing a working cohort with more education. As a result, the share of the entire work force with university degrees increased much more slowly and, because the demand for such workers continued to rise, the ratio of their salaries to those with just a high school education rose. Levy and Murnane (1992) present quantitative evidence showing that the spurt in years of education of the labor force in the 1970s (Table A.2) led to a decline in the education differential; and the relative decline in the increase of years of education in the 1980s led to the reverse phenomenon (Burtless, 1990). Such evidence is reinforced by work by Bishop (1992), who takes into account on the supply side not only years of education, but also the quality of the education as well.

The degree of importance placed on supply-side factors in various empirical investigations varies considerably. Grubb and Wilson (1992) find that other supply factors played a considerably important role; Katz and Murphy (1992), who have a less detailed breakdown of demographic groups, but a more systematic analysis of supply factors, find that labor supply considerations were particularly important in the 1970s, but not in the 1980s where the educational differential played a particularly important role. Studies by Bound and Johnson (1991) and Levy and Murnane (1992) supply supporting evidence to the Katz and Murphy result. Because an increasing share of legal immigrants have a low level of education, Borjas, Freeman, and Katz (1992) argue that immigration had a significant effect on wages of low-skilled workers in the 1980s. This is exacerbated by illegal immigrants who have a lower average level of education than legal immigrants.

Demand-induced changes in wage differentials arise from changes in the demand for particular types of labor. Such changes in labor demand may be indirect and arise from a changing demand for the products of particular domestic industries, either because of changes in income, tastes, or a substitution of foreign and domestically produced goods. Or such demand changes for labor may occur directly because of a biased type of technological change where relatively more of a particular type of labor is required than another. In these two cases the relative wages of those groups expanding the fastest also rise the fastest.

Regarding the shift in product demand, a number of researchers present empirical evidence of the importance of foreign trade, particularly since wages at the low end of the scale in the late 1970s and early 1980s began to fall in absolute terms as the ratio of foreign trade to total produc-

Table A.4. Trends in wages and salaries inequalities

	Grubb-Wilson estimates: Theil statistics					Karoly estimates			Henle estimates	
	Total nation	Within-group contribution	Between-group contribution (%)	All men	All women	Theil: total nation	Gini: total nation	Logarithm variance: total nation	Men Gini	Women Gini
1958									.327	.389
1959									.324	.385
1960									.337	.384
1961									.343	.399
1962									.336	.393
1963									.336	.396
1964									.336	.391
1965									.334	n.a.
1966									.342	.396
1967	.337			.248	.342	.339	.441	1.605	.335	.392
1968	.336			.248	.355	.339	.442	1.624	.337	.395
1969	.352			.258	.348	.356	.453	1.761	.344	.390
1970	.358	.104	.254 (70.9)	.286	.367	.361	.456	1.801	.350	.402
1971	.358	.101	.256 (71.5)	.272	.356	.360	.456	1.753	.357	.400
1972	.363	.109	.254 (70.0)	.277	.356	.365	.459	1.751	.365	.403
1973	.363	.104	.259 (71.3)	.271	.355	.366	.461	1.746	.360	.404
1974	.359	.106	.253 (70.5)	.275	.345	.361	.459	1.718	.361	n.a.
1975	.353	.100	.258 (72.1)	.278	.341	.353	.455	1.684	.367	.400
1976	.360	.102	.258 (71.7)	.280	.345	.353	.456	1.687	.371	.401
1977	.360	.103	.257 (71.4)	.282	.336	.353	.456	1.684	.374	.394

1978	.356	.103	.253	(71.1)	.276	.333	.347	.453	1.638
1979	.351	.106	.245	(69.8)	.275	.330	.339	.448	1.664
1980	.347	.103	.244	(70.3)	.276	.326	.366	.446	1.642
1981	.360	.108	.253	(70.3)	.298	.324	.350	.453	1.675
1982	.372	.113	.258	(69.4)	.317	.337	.358	.458	1.744
1983	.369	.113	.256	(69.4)	.317	.340	.355	.457	1.770
1984	.378	.115	.263	(69.6)	.325	.344	.362	.460	1.765
1985	.375	.117	.258	(68.8)	.323	.344	.359	.459	1.706
1986	.378	.120	.258	(68.2)	.326	.350	.359	.459	1.721
1987	.372	.118	.254	(68.3)	.325	.344	.359	.459	
1988	.367	.116	.251	(68.4)	.319	.344			

Notes: All estimates are annual wages and salaries of workers 16 years and over who have positive wage and salary incomes. The sources are Grubb-Wilson (1992), Henle (1972) and Karoly (1988), cited by Levy and Murnane (1992). An increasing Theil statistic indicates increasing inequality.

tion rose (see Chapter 8). At first glance it appears that such trade increased competitive pressures, particularly upon industries relying primarily on unskilled labor. According to this argument, the United States is losing its comparative advantages in these areas because the productivity differentials do not offset the low wages in these industries in foreign countries.

As I show empirically in Chapter 8 (Table 8.5), one important premise of the argument appears correct: the United States is losing its competitiveness in those industries featuring a high ratio of unskilled to total labor. Some empirical studies, for instance, Murphy and Welch (1991), examine the problem from a different perspective to show directly that wages of those unskilled workers facing foreign competition have declined vis-à-vis average wages. But a number of other empirical studies provide evidence that trade flows explain only a relatively small percentage of the changes in wage structure. For instance, Lawrence and Slaughter (1993) argue that if foreign competition is the major cause, then relative import prices of products with a high unskilled-labor intensity should have fallen, but they did not. Although this is an interesting finding, it does not answer the empirical results that those industries with a high unskilled-labor component are also those whose final sales in the United States feature an increasingly higher percentage of imports.

Another key demand factor is technological change biased against unskilled labor, a factor that I believe plays the most important role in the changing wage inequalities. Some investigators such as Bound and Johnson (1992) or Katz and Murphy (1992) provide evidence that the technological change occurring in industry has particularly favored those with a higher degree of formal education. This was particularly so in the 1980s when the U.S. manufacturing sector began a concerted effort to meet the new competitive challenges. Some industries with a high degree of unskilled labor flourished, but they also revealed a shift in the composition of their labor force toward more skilled workers. The wide-scale introduction of computers into white and blue collar work increased the demand for an educated labor force that could adapt to the new methods. Indeed, Krueger (1991) shows workers using computers on their job earn roughly 10 to 15 percent more than others, other things held constant, and that these workers are more likely to be more educated and earning more than the average. Similarly Grogger and Eide (1993) present evidence showing that the demand for particular types of educated labor, not just educated labor in general, is also important in understanding changes in relative wages. Shifts in college trained young workers toward majors in college yielding higher paying jobs have been an important response.

The argument about technological change can also be used to explain the widening of within-group wage and salary differentials. As I point out in the discussion about Table 2.3 in the text, the share of the labor force that has mastery of basic skills does not appear to have greatly changed. If this is so, then the shift in demand toward skilled and adaptable workers has widened the wage gap among workers with a particular level of formal education because it has increased the demand for that share of this demographic group with an actual mastery of basic intellectual skills. Other reasons have also been offered for explaining the widening of within-group differentials, but they do not seem very convincing to me.

The unmeasured skill differences that might underlie the increasing within-group wage differences can also refer to other intellectual factors not tied to mastery of basic skills. These would include such skills such as the ability to communicate effectively with other people (discussed in a quantitative fashion in Chapter 3, or the ability to take initiative in the work process; or adherence to particular work norms such as close attention to quality or the ability to work at high intensity without monitoring, which is in part a cultural difference. Some detailed evidence provided by Borjas (1992) also suggests that work attitudes provided by ethnicity are an important factor explaining wages so that increasing wage dispersion might be tied to increasing ethnic heterogeneity. Such a result also suggests we must be careful in dealing with cultural heterogeneity since it has important qualitative dimensions not reflected in a simple quantitative measure.

Even increasing heterogeneity of the family structure can play a role: for instance, Blackburn (1990) presents evidence that intragroup variation in earned income is higher for unmarried than married men and that the growth of unmarried men in the labor force explains 15 percent of the widening intragroup earnings among men from the late 1960s to the mid 1980s. Unfortunately, such evidence tying ethnic and family heterogeneity to increasing intragroup income inequality is fragmentary and much more research is required before the link is established with any certainty. Most of the explanations of the within-group wage differentials are cross-section studies that have focused on such factors as industry-specific differentials, plant-specific differentials, or unmeasured person-specific differentials in IQ (these studies are summarized by Levy and Murnane, 1992). None of these studies, however, explain why such differentials have been increasing.

Institutional changes: Some economists contend that changes in the wage setting institutions have also influenced the increasing wage inequality. For instance, Richard Freeman (1993) argues that labor unions have been an important cause of narrowing of wage differentials between similar jobs. Thus the decline in the importance of unionism, which I discuss in Chapter 4, has released an important constraint on wage equalization so that there are fewer jobs with high pay that can be filled by unskilled workers.

Although union activity has undoubtedly influenced wage differentials in some industries, the role of unions was sufficiently small by 1980 that this could hardly have served as a major influence for the economy as a whole. The evidence for other variants of the hypothesis linking wage-setting institutions to income differentials is also mixed (Levy and Murnane, 1992). Although some also have pointed toward the falling real value of the minimum wage as a source of increased inequality, empirical study of the problem by Blackburn, Bloom, and Freeman (1990) suggests that this has not been an important factor explaining the increasing inequality of earnings.

Another possible institutional explanation focuses on increased bu. `aucratization. Corporate and governmental organizations generally feature a relatively stable pyramidal hierarchy and relative stable income differentials from level to level. As the organization grows, the levels of bureaucracy increase so that the income differences between the top and the middle incomes increase. I present data in Chapter 5 that cast doubt on the common notion that administrative hierarchies are flattening. In the same chapter I also show that although top salaries as a multiple of average wages do not seem to be increasing over the long run, this ratio has increased considerably since 1970. It is not known, however, how much the increase in top salaries has pulled up salaries at lower levels of the administrative hierarchy so the overall impact on wage and salary differentials is clouded.

Other explanations: It is also useful to note several explanations found in the literature that do not explain changes in the inequality of labor incomes:

- Age distribution: Although median income is correlated with age, shifts in the age distribution provide very little explanation for the increase in inequality (Asher and DeFina, 1984). For wages alone, I present evidence below that the age distribution played a quite secondary role.
- Skill mismatches: As I argue in Chapter 3, the skill level of the occupational structure is increasing and, moreover, in so far as many jobs require several different but highly specific skills, it becomes increasingly difficult for employers to fill such positions without increasing wages. Although the existence of such skill mismatches has been argued with considerable vigor (Johnston and Packer, 1987), little systematic evidence has yet been brought forward that such mismatches greatly change to the wage structure (Levy and Murnane, 1992).
- Macroeconomic factors: These trends cannot be explained by such macroeconomic variables such as the rate of growth of labor productivity or per capita income or the rate of unemployment or inflation (Cutler and Katz, 1991; Ruggles and Stone, 1992; Blank and Card, 1993).

Table A.5. *Relative importance of direct and indirect consumption of raw materials and agricultural goods*

Unit	Average household income before taxes ($)	Average household consumption ($)	Metals minerals	Nonmetallic minerals	Coal	Petroleum natural gas	Agricultural products	Total
			Percentage of money income before taxes (%)					
All households	23,464	21,975	.1	.2	.8	6.3	6.4	13.8
Lowest 20%, by income	3,169	10,894	.4	.7	3.4	26.1	25.9	56.4
Second 20%, by income	10,250	14,337	.2	.3	1.3	10.6	11.3	23.7
Third 20%, by income	18,340	19,469	.1	.2	.9	7.6	7.9	16.8
Fourth 20%, by income	29,008	26,138	.1	.2	.7	5.9	6.2	13.1
Highest 20%, by income	56,426	41,825	.1	.1	.5	4.3	4.5	9.5

Notes: Sources and methods are described in the text of the appendix.

Note 2.3: The raw material content of consumption at different income levels

Consumption includes not only direct purchases of the raw material, but the raw material embodied in all items purchased by the consumer (direct and indirect consumption). Estimates can be made using an input-output table and information on family budgets (see Table A.5).

I calculated my estimates in three steps. First, I took 1984 household budget data from the U.S. Department of Labor (1989a) and arranged them according to the categories of the 1982 input-output table (from *Survey of Current Business,* 71, No. 7, July 1991, pp. 30–72). Second, I multiplied the expenditures by the coefficients of the inverse matrix, commodity by commodity to derive the first approximation of the direct and indirect usage. Third, I compared the derived amounts for the average household to the results from a similar exercise using the vector of total consumption; this led to a series of small additional adjustments to the BLS data to achieve consistency of the aggregates from the two sources.

Unfortunately, the budget surveys of the Bureau of Labor Statistics raise several technical issues: First, total expenditures do not equal total income plus changes in net worth. This occurs not only because of an under-reporting of income, but also because business losses are not fully reflected in the change in net worth. It is, however, likely that the income rankings of the consumers would be roughly the same if income were fully reported. Thus the directions of the trends of direct and indirect raw material consumption are the same, even if the exact percentages are not. Second, the purchase of consumer durables such as automobiles are counted in the year of purchase, even though the individuals (especially those in lower income groups) bought the durable on an installment plan. A more correct procedure would focus on the actual annual usage of the durable, rather than its initial purchase. As a result, the total expenditures are inflated, an effect important in the lower quintiles of the income distribution. I would like to thank Mr. John Rogers of the Bureau of Labor Statistics for a useful discussion with me of these problems.

Note 2.4: A simulation model of population and economic growth

The model is written on the spreadsheet EXCEL. Using a 386 personal computer of average speed, each simulation for sixty years can be made in less than a second if data for decades, rather than single years, are used. The advantage of a simulation model over a standard type of demographic–economic analytic model is that it allows the analyst to take more complicated types of interrelations into account.

The model has four modules: population, labor force, macroeconomic variables, and microeconomic variables. The coefficients of the model are similar to some basic parameters of the U.S. economy, but can be changed for simulation purposes. The baseline assumptions are usually the values of the key variables in 1990.

Population module: The population projections for different age groups are based of assumptions about age-specific mortality rates, age-specific birth rates, and age-specific immigration rates. For each decade, each age cohort is multiplied by the ten-year survival rate (the share of people in that cohort who live to the end of the decade) and then moved to the next age group. The model calculates the number of births from the number of women in each age group (the total population in that age group divided by two, since roughly half are women) times the age specific birth rate. Survival rates and age specific birth rates are projected for the next decade by means of particular assumptions that can be changed.

The calibration of the model for the U.S. economy uses readily available data. The 1990 population and survival rates were calibrated from data presented in Spencer (1989). I used later estimates of immigration, but assumed the same age distribution as the Census Bureau's 1989 estimates. The age-specific birth rates of women for 1988 are taken from U.S. Bureau of the Census (annual-b, 1990); they were adjusted so that the number of births is equal to the number of babies born in 1990.

Labor module: The labor force projections are based on assumptions about labor force participation rates at different age groups and the "effectiveness" of the labor force. The "effective labor force" is the labor force at different age groups multiplied by adjustment factors so that each age group is allowed to have a different productivity, depending on its education and age-cohort characteristics. These adjustment factors take two factors into account:

(a) **Education:** The impact of increased education on production is modeled simply by multiplying the age-specific productivity by a factor reflecting the changing stock of education of that age group. In the early 1990s the median years of education in the different age cohorts of the working population (excluding those under 25) were roughly the same, according to data from the report of the Bureau of Labor Statistics cited in Chapter 2; so I have not attempted any more complex modeling. Changing the assumption about the stock of education by, let us say, 4 percent means that education acts to increase the productivity of an average worker 4 percent more than the baseline case in the next decade. Underlying this kind of approach is a human capital theory that more education allows a worker to be more productive. For simplicity, the model assumes that education, either in school or on the job, increases the same amount for various age groups. A more complicated model would allow the effects of education of one particular cohort to follow that cohort as it ages.

(b) **Age-based productivity:** This is based on the vague notion that in comparison with workers in their middle years, the young work less effectively because of higher absenteeism, more job switching, lower socialization into the labor force, and so forth, while the old work less effectively because of less strength and physical facilities. The ratios in the table are completely arbitrary and can be easily changed in the labor force module. A more complex modeling would allow "cohort effects" to occur. For instance, if a group from 15 to 25 has high unemployment in several years, it might work less effectively in the next decade.

The participation ratios were calibrated from data in U.S. Department of Labor, Bureau of Labor Statistics (1988). I adjusted these labor force data to include the armed forces.

Macroeconomic module: The macroeconomic module is for a closed economy and shows the relation between technology, the capital stock, investment, and production. It has a very simple structure that allows various assumptions to be made concerning the rate of technical change, the capital stock depreciation rate, the share of property income (the capital coefficient), the share of government investment in the gross domestic product (GDP), and the share of business and foreign investment in total property income.

Gross domestic product (GDP) is a function of the level of technology (Z), the stock of K, and the effective labor force (L). It is calculated from a production function, which I assume to be: $GDP = a(1+Z)^t K^b L^{1-b}$, where a is a constant selected so that GDP roughly equals the U.S. value in 1990, t is time (where 1990 = 0), Z is the rate of technical change, and b is the "capital coefficient." The level of technology is reflected in $(1+Z)^t$. The remaining part of the production function features constant returns to scale. With some elementary calculus it can be easily shown than the capital coefficient b is also the share of total income accounted for by property income. The model allows this capital coefficient to be changed over time.

The capital stock (K) is the fixed net reproducible wealth excluding consumer durables and consists of equipment and structures. It increases as investment is pumped into the system; and it decreases because of depreciation. In 1990 gross private investment as a share of K amounted to 7.0 percent. If we assume that government investment (roads, dams, buildings, etc.) was another 1.1 percentage points, total investment amounted to about 8.1 percent of total (net) K. In the same year, the depreciation rate was 5.4 percent, so that the net growth of the capital stock was 2.7 percent. This, I should point out, was also the average rate at which K increased between 1985 and 1990.

The macroeconomic module requires a simplifying assumption, namely that the increase in the capital stock over the decade is equal to the rate at the beginning of the decade. This is not quite correct, but a more exact solution would require much more computing capacity and would slow the model to a crawl. This approximation, however, does not greatly distort reality.

Individual savings are an integral part of the micromodel and are modeled carefully (see below). I assume that all individual savings are invested, although much of this investment is actually carried out by the business sector. The remaining savings and investments are modeled more crudely. More specifically, I have made government investment a simple share of GDP that can be increased or decreased by assumption; in 1990 it was about 2.3 percent of GDP. I made business and foreign investment a simple share of total property income, a ratio that can also be changed by assumption. The ratio was calibrated for 1990 by subtracting from total 1990 investment the investment of the government and the investment financed by individuals from their savings, a method that allows consistency with the actual 1990 aggregates. Since the share of property income can also be varied, business and foreign investment can be changed in two different ways: a change in the base and a change in the ratio to that base.

The coefficients and data in this module were calibrated from readily available information and provided few problems. The capital stock data come from the U.S. Department of Commerce, Bureau of the Census (annual-b, 1990) and were projected from 1988 to 1990, taking into account increases in prices as well as the volume of total capital. The GDP and depreciation data come from the U.S. Council of Economic Advisors (annual, 1991).

The microeconomic module: The microeconomic module focuses exclusively on individual savings and income. The income model is very simple and assumes that the per capita income of a person in a given ten-year age cohort increases at the same rate as total per capita income.

The savings function raises some problems. The model calculates savings from average savings rates for each age cohort that, in turn, are based on the average savings rates of people in that cohort in 1990. This "empirical savings function" approach is rather different from other studies that employ either life-cycle or other theoretical models to predict the savings ratio or that try to determine savings as the difference between income and imputed "needs" (Cutler, et al., 1990).

Although my average savings rates in the initial year are calculated from actual data, the coefficients can be changed over time by assumption. The total individual savings generated by these functions are combined with the savings of the government and the business/foreign sector (see above) to generate total gross investment.

Problems arise in calculating the actual savings rates in 1990 of different age cohorts because various U.S. governmental sources give quite different estimates for personal savings. My calculations are based on adjustment of data by age group in 1987 presented in U.S. Department of Labor, Bureau of Labor Statistics (1989a). The Bureau of Labor Statistics estimates the net change of consumer wealth as the net change in assets minus net change in liabilities, but for purposes of the model, it is necessary to remove consumer durables (e.g., household furnishing and equipment) from these estimates.

These BLS data raise some additional problems because the savings data of household are presented by age of household head and my estimates of average saving by age group required several simplifying assumptions: Husbands and wives (henceforth householders, although only one may be present in the family unit) are of the same age. Furthermore, except for the exogenous investment by the government and business sectors, all income, wealth, and savings belong exclusively to, and arise from, the activities of the householders. Since I do not have government, busi-

Table A.6. *Some simulation results of the population and economic growth model*

	Average annual growth rates of per capita GDP (%)			
Change in assumption	1990–2000	2000–2010	2010–2030	2030–2050
Base-line results	1.50	1.44	1.22	1.29
Age-specific mortality rates fall 10% a decade	1.50	1.37	1.08	1.06
Age-specific birth rates fall 10% a decade	1.53	1.55	1.38	1.39
Age-specific immigration rates rise 10% a decade	1.50	1.44	1.22	1.30
Years of education per person in 15–25 cohort rises 5%a decade (in a cumulative fashion)	1.56	1.58	1.52	1.73
Technological change rises to 11% a decade	1.59	1.55	1.34	1.41
Technological change rises to 15% a decade	1.95	1.99	1.81	1.90
Savings rate increases 10% a decade	1.57	1.56	1.36	1.44

ness, or foreign sectors, I adjust incomes so that aggregate household income is equal to GDP, and from these income data I calculate the average propensity to save. Because the rates are quite jagged and may incorporate some sampling error, I "smooth" the series by increasing the saving rate for the 45- to 75-year brackets, but in a manner to keep total saving the same. Finally, I adjust these 1987 data to 1990 by multiplying them by a coefficient representing the change in individual saving estimated by the Federal Reserve Bank (reported by U.S., Council of Economic Advisors, annual, 1990, p. 319) between these two years.

To determine if the results from these savings rates made any sense, I also tested two "theoretical" savings functions, namely one based on Keynesian ideas, the other on the life cycle hypothesis. Since all three simulations gave quite similar results, I have reported only the results using the "actual" savings function discussed above.

As noted above, the sum of individual, governmental, and business/foreign investment as well as the depreciation rate determine the growth of the capital stock. With this information plus data on the effective labor supply and technology, a GDP is calculated. This, in turn, allows calculation of the GDP per effective worker, which is then used with the average income in the previous period to calculate the average incomes in each age group during this period. A slight problem arises because the model does not separate labor and property income for the individual income classes and, at this point, a slight adjustment is made. This income data multiplied by the selected average propensities to save determine total individual saving, and the calculations for the next decade begin.

Last words on the model: Clearly the model of the economy is oversimplified. But it allows us to gauge the orders of magnitudes of certain changes in the key economic variables. More realistic projections would require much more equations that would model the government, business, and foreign sectors more explicitly. Nevertheless, this simple model allows the interaction of many variables to be examined in a systematic manner.

A few simulation results: The basic statistic reported below is annual growth of GDP per capita; and for the sake of comparison it is worth noting that in the 1960s, 1970s, and 1980s these statistics were respectively 2.17 percent, 2.66 percent, and 2.12 percent (derived from a regression analysis and standard NIPA data). In the same years the decade averages of the growth of total factor productivity were respectively 12.5 percent, 2.1 percent, and 9.0 percent.

The baseline projection makes the following assumptions: No change in mortality, no change in birth rate, no change in the annual immigration, no change in the level of education, and a decade growth of total factor productivity of 10 percent (0.96 percent annually). The impacts of changes in assumptions are detailed in Table A.6.

Note 2.5: Statistical notes for Chapter 2

Table 2.1: Data on racial composition come from U.S. Department of Commerce, Bureau of the Census (1953), Table 38; Spencer (1989); and Day (1993). Data on the foreign born come from U.S. Department of Commerce, Bureau of the Census (Annual-b, 92, Table 45). Projections are based on the Day (1993) population estimates (middle series), the middle assumption for net immigration, namely 880,000 a year, and the assumption that 15 percent of the foreign born die each decade.

Table 2.2: The data for Part A come from Saluter (1989). In Part B the divorce rate data come from Norton and Miller (1992); the data on illegitimate births, from U.S. Department of Commerce, Bureau of the Census (Annual-b, 1993, Table 98; 1992, Table 89; and 1975, p. 52). The data on families with two parents present from U.S. Department of Commerce, Bureau of the Census (1964), Tables 80 and 90; and Norton and Miller (1992).

Table 2.3: The data for Part B come from National Center for Education Statistics (1993); the data in Part A come from unpublished data supplied by the Educational Testing Service. Average years of schooling come from Kominski and Adams (1992), p. 7. Data in Part C come from Mullis (1991) and unpublished information supplied by Educational Testing Service.

Table 2.4: The data come from U.S. Department of Commerce, Bureau of the Census (1953, Table 94; 1964, Table 155; 1973, Table 50; 1983, Table 41), Spencer (1989, p. 43) and Day (1993).

Table 2.5: For the estimates from estate tax returns, the data sets are: Lampman (1962), pp. 24, 202 (basic variant) extended through 1956 and Smith (1984), p. 422; the latter data are from 1958 through 1976. Both define wealth in a conventional sense. Wolff–Marley (1989), pp. 782–3 define net worth in two ways: the "narrow" sense (their W1) is the cash surrender value of total assets less liabilities; the "wide" definition (their W4) includes the expected present value of social security benefits plus private pensions. Both sets of data refer to all individuals in the population. The Wolff estimates using the household survey data come from Wolff (1994). Other estimates are made by Kennickell–Woodburn (1992) and Wolff–Marley (1989).

Diagram 2.1: Data on the ratio of family income of the top quintile to the bottom quintile come from Hanson (1990), p. 16. The other two series come from U.S. Department of Commerce, Bureau of the Census (1992), Table B-7; (1993), Tables B-3 and B-7; and (1977), Table 13.

Table A.7. *Characteristics of all U.S. jobs*

	1950	1960	1970	1980	1990	Male/female gap over time
Data skills	4.18	4.28	4.47	4.68	4.96	Gap closing (women higher)
Skills with things	4.05	3.92	3.84	3.71	3.50	Gap small, no trend (women higher)
General educational development	4.78	4.90	5.08	5.26	5.49	Difference closed
Specific vocational preparation	4.91	4.91	5.03	5.20	5.39	Gap closing (men higher)
Strength required	3.94	3.58	3.26	3.11	2.98	Gap closing (men higher)
Physical demands	5.16	4.83	4.54	4.33	4.15	Gap closing (men higher)
Adverse environmental conditions	1.30	1.09	0.92	0.84	0.81	Gap constant and large (men higher)
Total physical demands	2.77	2.35	1.98	1.86	1.78	Gap constant
Undesirable working conditions	.32	.30	.26	.23	.25	Gap increasing (men higher)

Notes: Estimating procedures are described in the text; the scales have been transformed to range from 0 (low) to 10 (high). The particular occupational characteristics are discussed briefly in the text and more thoroughly in various articles in Miller et al. (1980). The data skills variable ranges from comparing and copying to coordinating and synthesizing. The skill with things ranges from handling and feeding to precision working and setting up. The specific vocational preparation variable ranges from short demonstrations to over ten years. The strength variable ranges from "sedentary" to very heavy work. The physical demands variable is a composite variable taking into account stooping, kneeling, crouching, handling, and so forth. The adverse environmental conditions entry is a similar composite variable. The total physical demands and the undesirable working conditions variables are composite variables resulting from a factor analysis and are highly correlated to some variables above them in the list.

Notes to Chapter 3

Note 3.1: Determination of the skill level of the occupational structure

The skill ratings of specific occupations come from Roos and Treiman (1980), who based their calculations on weighted averages of the occupations in the U.S. Department of Labor's publication *Dictionary of Occupational Titles* (DOT). Some problems in using their data arise because their estimates are matched to the 1970 census (which include 1960 occupational data as well). In other censuses, the occupations are classified somewhat differently, especially for the census in 1980 and 1990.

Consequently, I employed a four-step procedure in making my estimates. First, for each occupation in the other census years that were not listed in the Roos and Treiman calculations, I used weighted averages of analogous occupations. Second, for each of the three census years, I calculated average ratings for both years listed (e.g., 1980 and 1970). Third, I compared the ratings for the same years but from different censuses and made appropriate adjustments of the aggregate results to obtain a consistent series. As it turned out, these adjustments were relatively minor. Finally, I transformed each set of ratings into a scale ranging from 0 to 10.

For Tables 3.1 and 3.2 in the text and Table A.7 in this note, the data on occupations come from U.S. Department of Commerce, Bureau of the Census (1964), Table 201; (1973/4), Table 221; (1984), Table 276; and (1992a). Some adjustments were made to increase comparability; particular difficulties arose for 1970 in the 1970 census, since a sizable share of the labor force was not distributed among the individual occupations in the major occupational categories. In such cases, I have adjusted each occupation within the group by the same percentage.

Note 3.2: Calculations of wage rigidity

Table A.8 reports regression results calculated by following the method of Robert J. Gordon (1983), equation 1. Similar results with regard to wage rigidity were obtained by using his equation 5 instead. I have used all of his variables excepting the crude materials variable, for which I used a different and, I believe, more suitable series.

Most of the data come from various editions of U.S. Council of Economic Advisors (annual). For estimating the potential GDP to calculate the GDP gap, I employed the following procedure. From data on the actual GDP per population between 20 and 65, I calculated exponential curves from a given peak (that is, highest GDP/population) to all other peaks within a twelve-year period. Then I selected the highest interpolated exponential curve for any given peak to calculate the potential GDP for the intermediate points. For 1990 and beyond, I extrapolated the curve connecting the 1989 peak with a previous peak. For the period 1950 to 1955 the calculation of potential GDP was sensitive to the assumptions made about handling 1945, which was the previous peak. I have reduced the GDP in 1945 to reflect both the higher labor participation rate and the longer hours worked during World War II than in the 1950 to 1955 period.

For the statement in Chapter 5 that business cycles have not changed in severity since the mid-1950s, I simply regressed the logarithm of the ratio of actual GDP to potential GDP for the period. The following results were obtained for the period from 1950 through 1991:

$$\ln(\text{GDP gap}) = .621 - .000299 \text{ Year}, \ R^2 = .0175$$
$$\phantom{\ln(\text{GDP gap}) = }(0.089) \quad (0.843) \qquad \qquad (T \text{ statistics are presented in parentheses})$$

Since the results are sensitive to the manner in which the high GDPs per adult during World War II are adjusted when calculating the potential GDPs for the 1945–55 period, it is also worthwhile to calculate the results from 1955 through 1991:

$$\ln(\text{GDP gap}) = -.0302 + .0000305 \text{ Year}, \ R^2 = .00002$$
$$\phantom{\ln(\text{GDP gap}) = }(0.040) \quad (0.079) \qquad \qquad (T \text{ statistics are presented in parentheses})$$

Neither calculation shows any significant change in the ratio of potential to actual GDP.

Table A.8. *Wage rigidity regressions, 1950–1991*

Dependent variables Independent variables	Logarithm of changes in nominal wages			Logarithm of changes in real wages		
Constant	+.0386* (3.86)	.00317 (0.838)	+.444* (5.45)	+.0804* (4.45)	-.00177 (0.321)	+.0768* (4.75)
$\log(w_{t-1}/w_{t-2})$ Lagged change in wages.	+.385* (3.45)	+.553* (4.70)	+.389* (3.50)	+.0895 (.544)	+.643* (4.41)	+.0843 (0.52)
$\log(p_{t-1}/p_{t-2})$ Lagged change in prices.	+.718* (6.23)	+.580* (4.60)	+.684* (6.32)	+.155 (1.64)	+.215 (1.79)	+.175* (2.09)
$\log(Y^a/Y^p)$ Ratio of actual to potential GDP.	-.0986 (0.45)	-.511* (2.39)	+.0884* (1.97)	+.202 (0.75)	-.349 (1.12)	+.0772 (1.66)
$\log(Y^a_t/Y^p_t) - \log(Y^a_{t-1}/Y^p_{t-1})$ Change in ratio of actual to potential GDP	+.125* (2.88)	+.135* (2.67)	+.135* (3.21)	+.0769 (1.41)	+.112 (1.61)	.0704 (1.35)
Korean War year Dummy variable.	-.139 (1.80)	-.0188* (2.12)	-.0149 (1.95)	-.00623 (.87)	-.00157 (0.17)	-.00572 (0.81)
Nixon price/wage control year Dummy variable	+.0188* (2.11)	+.136 (1.33)	+.0164 (1.94)	+.0384* (3.57)	+.0260 (1.95)	+.0400* (3.98)
$\log(r_{t-1}/r_{t-2})$ (Lagged change in raw material prices)	-.0460* (2.05)	-.0585* (2.27)	-.0360 (1.87)	-.0785* (2.68)	-.120* (3.38)	-.0849* (3.34)
Year* $\log(Y^a_t/Y^p_t)$ Artificial variable for testing changes in wage rigidity	+.00276 (0.87)	+.00933* (3.15)	—	-.00185 (0.47)	+.00587 (1.27)	—

Year	$-.000489^*$	—	$-.000560^*$	$-.00106^*$	—	$-.00101^*$
	(3.56)		(5.05)	(4.69)		(5.00)
Adjusted coefficient determination	.9036	.8695	.9042	.7780	.7078	.8256
Durban–Watson statistic	1.96	1.97	1.87	1.76	1.93	1.75

Where:

w = average nonagricultural gross hourly earnings in private sector

p = GDP deflator

Y^a = actual real GDP (nominal wage divided by implicit consumption price deflator in GDP)

Y^p = full employment GDP

r = producer prices for crude materials for further processing

Korean War dummy variable = $-.5$ in 1950; $-.5$ in 1951; and 1 in 1952

Nixon price/wage control dummy variable = .5 in 1972; .5 in 1973; $-.3$ in 1974; and $-.7$ in 1975

Year = Actual year $-$ 1900

T statistics are placed under the calculated coefficients; statistically significant coefficients (.05 level) are marked with an asterisk. Only natural logarithms are used.

Note 3.3: Other statistical notes for Chapter 3

Table 3.3: The main source of unemployment data is U.S. Council of Economic Advisors (annual). Data for the total armed forces (not just resident armed forces) come from Department of Labor (annual-b, 1982) and U.S. Department of Commerce, Bureau of the Census (annual-b, 1992). The two series are not quite the same and the data in the 1980s were adjusted to achieve comparability with the earlier data. Data on discouraged workers (those who claimed that they wanted work but didn't look, either because of job market conditions or because, for personal reasons, they didn't think they would be hired), as well as data on persons on part-time work for economic reasons come from various issues of U.S. Department of Labor (annual-a, annual-b, 1982).

Table 3.4: Raw data on literacy come from National Center for Educational Statistics (1993), Tables 2-2A to 2-2C.

Table 3.5: Turbulence: Data on employment by U.S. states (Alaska and Hawaii are omitted) come from U.S. Department of Labor, Bureau of Labor Statistics (1974, 1985, 1989b, 1992). Some small adjustments to achieve comparability had to be made for the District of Columbia, Maryland, Michigan, Virginia, and Wisconsin. Data on full-time equivalent employees for various industries come from Department of Commerce, Bureau of Economic Analysis (1986 and 1992/3), supplemented by Department of Commerce, Bureau of Economic Analysis (monthly), (Vol. 72, No. 1; January 1992). Data on employment by occupations come from U.S. Department of Labor, Bureau of Labor Statistics (1974, 1982, 1988), supplemented by Department of Labor (annual-a), various years. For the highly detailed occupational calculations, data are drawn from the same sources as Table 2.2. The turbulence statistic for 1950–60 is .134; for 1960–70, .153; for 1970–80, .121. The number of occupational categories is an average for the three census volumes. The jump in turbulence in 1960–70 may be a statistical artifact that arises from the adjustment for comparability discussed in the note for Table 2.2.

Incentives: Data on unemployment insurance payments come from U.S. Council of Economic Advisors (annual), 1993; and U.S. Department of Commerce, Bureau of the Census (annual-b and 1975). Data on average number of weeks of unemployment of those exhausting unemployment benefits come from U.S. Department of Labor, Employment and Training Administration (1983) and yearly supplements. Minimum wage data come from U.S. Department of Commerce (annual-b, various years); the data are weighted by month if the minimum wage changed during the year. The average weekly and hourly compensation and wages/salaries are derived from data on total compensation and wages/salaries for all domestic industries, divided by data on equivalent full-time employment (divided by 52) and total number of hours worked. The basic data come from U.S. Department of Commerce, Bureau of Economic Analysis (1986 and 1992/3), supplemented by U.S. Department of Commerce, Bureau of Economic Analysis (monthly, Vol. 72, No. 1, January 1992).

Job vacancy data: The Conference Board publishes the help-wanted index. A corrected version from 1951 to the present was supplied by Kenneth Goldstein on March 2, 1993 and I would like to express my gratitude to him. For the corrections to this index to take into account changes in the occupational composition of employment, changes in employers' advertising practices, and declines in newspaper competition I draw data from Abraham (1987) for the years 1960 through 1985. For the five-year period from 1950 through 1954 I assumed these corrections would amount to 3.8 percent; for 1955 through 1959, 4.8 percent; and 1985 through 1990, 3.8 percent.

Notes to Chapter 4

Note 4.1: Statistical notes for Chapter 4

Table 4.1: Although I made certain small changes, the classification of industries and occupations generally follows that of Wolff and Baumol (1989). The major trends are also the same.

For the individual industries, the data for 1950 and 1960 include all members in the labor force who are fourteen or over; the data for 1970 and 1980 include all members in the labor force who are sixteen and over. The impact of this definitional change is minuscule. For occupations, which are much more sensitive indicators of the movement into services, I have used the concept of experienced labor force. This excludes the unemployed who have not previously worked or who were formerly in the army. These estimates involved using data for two decades that are presented according to the same definitions in each census, and then using the percentage differences between the data for the same year from two different censuses to make adjustments to the aggregates to make them consistent. In several cases I made some additional adjustments, but in no case did such adjustments significantly change the results.

The major data sources are: U.S. Department of Commerce, Bureau of the Census (1964, Tables 201, 211; 1984, Tables 276, 285; 1992-a). I have used other censuses, however, and unpublished materials from the 1990 census on the distribution of employment by industry supplied by the U.S. Bureau of the Census. The data for both the civilian labor force and the armed services come from the same sources. The number of homemakers is specified in the 1950 census; thereafter, I had to rely on the annual data presented in various issues of *Employment and Earnings.*

For the classification of occupations and industries, I use the categories and the definitions of Wolff and Baumol (1989). For given years their results and mine differ slightly for several reasons. We use somewhat different concepts of the labor force. They were apparently working at a less detailed level of aggregation. And they handled the adjustments of the data from various years to the 1970 census definitions slightly differently. My time series is also longer than theirs, but the trends are the same for both sets of calculations.

Table 4.2: The Pencavel and Hartsog estimates are presented in Pencavel and Hartsog (1984). However, I drop their estimate for 1975–79 because it is so different from the other estimates as to appear unreasonable, both to them and to me. The wage differential estimates attempt to hold the industry constant.

Data on union membership. The basic data on members of union come from the *Current Population Survey* and are reported by Chang and Sorrentino (1991) for the 1970s and 1980s. In the 1950s and 1960s the Bureau of Labor Statistics (1980) estimated labor union membership from data supplied by the unions. I have assumed that the overstatement of membership based on the latter data was a constant percentage of a more accurate measuring of union membership obtained from the former source. Certain other small adjustments were made to obtain greater comparability over time.

Data on union wage differentials. The Pencavel-Hartsog estimates (1984) follow the method pioneered by H. Gregg Lewis, but with the regressions recalculated in a modified fashion. Johnson (1984) employs another and more crude usage of the Lewis technique for the same period. The most satisfactory methodology uses cross-section evidence from the Current Population Survey and holds a series of variables constant that also influence wage differentials; unfortunately comparable data exist only for a limited number of years: for instance, a study by Ashenfelter (1978) covers 1967 through 1975; and a study by Blanchflower and Freeman (1992) covers only the 1985–7 period. These two studies show a lower differential than those reported in Table 2.4; they also suggest a rise in the differential between 1967 and 1985, although the comparability of the two studies is not clear.

My own method employs data from the Bureau of Labor Statistics (1989a) and subsequent bulletins reporting the employment cost indices for December of 1975 to the present. From the indices of changes in wage costs in both union and nonunion enterprises and data on the absolute level of wages for a single year, I calculated the ratios.

Notes to Chapter 5

Note 5.1: Changes in the ownership of wealth

This Appendix Note documents the trends in the ownership of wealth briefly summarized in Chapter 5. The discussion serves as a bridge between the analysis of the distribution of wealth in Chapter 2 and the government policies generating wealth discussed in Chapter 9.

Changes in ownership by major groups: Conclusions about trends in the ownership of wealth depend upon the exact definition of wealth employed in the analysis. I use several different definitions to illustrate different types of trends.

Over the post World War II period the composition of tangible wealth (reproducible assets and land) has not significantly changed. From 1950 through 1990, residential structures and consumer durables constituted about 40 percent; nonresidential buildings and equipment plus inventories, about 38 percent; and land, about 22 percent (calculations made from data from Board of Governors of the Federal Reserve, 1991). Thus, ownership shares are not complicated by shifts in the composition of the types of major assets.

Table A.9 shows that individuals and corporations hold about one half of fixed reproducible assets (tangible assets excluding land and inventories) in the United States and that this share has not greatly changed over the postwar period. The share held by nonprofit institutions has increased considerably, but is still quite small. The nation is far from the third-sector nirvana painted in such glowing terms by many futurists, many of whom rely on grants from the third-sector to fund their work. Although this trend will probably continue, the share of assets controlled by nonprofit institutions will remain small for the foreseeable future.

The share of fixed reproducible assets held by the government has declined steadily over time. The decline during the 1980s when political conservatives occupied the U.S. presidency during most of the time was less, rather than greater, than in the 1970s. "Creeping socialism," at least defined in terms of ownership, was a myth the moment that this slogan entered political discourse. Furthermore, the privatization of governmental assets that has received attention will not make a significant dent in the share of assets held by the government because the volume of such asset sales is so small in comparison to the total. This theme receives much more extensive discussion in Chapter 9.

More important changes reflect the growing internationalization of production and wealth. Although both the relative importance of U.S. assets held by foreigners and foreign assets held by U.S. residents increased, the former rose much faster than the latter. The increase in foreign ownership of U.S. domestic wealth was particularly rapid during the 1980s, when it more than doubled. Its future trend depends in good measure on whether the United States can bring the deficit in its current accounts of the balance of payments under control.

Turning to total financial assets, the major change is a fall in the share of assets held by households and a rise in the share held by private financial institutions. This is one facet of the rise in the financial intermediation ratio discussed below. Internationalization has also proceeded apace. The share of financial assets held by foreign residents has risen over the period. Although the relative level is still small, the 1980s witnessed a significant increase; moreover, for certain types of financial wealth the share held by foreigners is significant. For instance, in 1990 foreigners held 14.5 percent of the $3.211 trillion debt of the federal government. The ratio of foreign financial assets owned by U.S. residents to total financial assets did not, however, essentially change over the period.

The relative importance of tangible and intangible wealth: Tangible capital in the form of plant, equipment, inventories, and land is but one form of wealth. As I discuss, intangible wealth in the

Table A.9. *The pattern of ownership (%)*

	1950	1960	1970	1980	1990
Part A: Total fixed reproducible assets in the U.S.					
Share of assets directly held by:					
Persons, sole proprietorship, partnerships	51.0	49.7	47.5	49.4	51.0
Nonprofit organizations	2.3	2.5	3.1	3.0	3.4
Corporate and other private organizations	22.4	23.9	24.9	26.8	27.0
Government	24.3	23.9	24.4	20.8	18.6
Part B: Domestic wealth					
Ratios to domestic wealth of:					
U.S. assets owned by foreign residents	1.5	1.8	2.3	3.7	8.0
Foreign assets owned by U.S. residents	3.3	3.9	4.6	6.2	5.8
Part C: Total private financial assets in the U.S.					
Share of assets directly held by:					
Households	63.2	62.6	58.7	55.7	51.1
Farm businesses	.7	.4	.3	.2	.2
Nonfarm, noncorporate businesses	1.8	1.3	.8	1.3	1.5
Nonfinancial corporations	8.9	8.3	8.7	8.6	7.6
Private financial institutions	25.4	27.4	31.5	34.3	39.6

Notes:
- *Part A:* Total reproducible fixed assets includes plant and equipment, residential housing, and consumer durables; it excludes land and financial assets. I use the current-cost, net stock concept. The data come from U.S. Department of Commerce, Bureau of Economic Analysis (1993), Table A13 and *Survey of Current Business* 73, No. 8 (September 1993). For 1990 some small estimates had to be made.
- *Part B:* Domestic wealth includes total reproducible assets (structures, equipment, inventories, and consumer durables) and land. I use again the current-cost, net stock concept. The data come from the Board of Governors of the Federal Reserve System (1993), Tables B11 and B109.
- *Part C:* The data come from Board of Governors of the Federal Reserve System (1991).

form of human capital (particularly investment in education) and pension rights, (particularly claims on the social security system) are considerably greater in value. In four decades following World War II, such intangible wealth increased more rapidly than tangible wealth although this trend may be leveling off.

It is unfortunate that many forms of intangible wealth cannot be measured. In an elegant discussion of the role of government, Charles A. Reich (1964) outlines a variety of mechanisms by which the government creates such intangible wealth. These run the spectrum from claims on welfare payments to the distribution of income-creating franchises, such as TV channels, to the creation of other privileges such as special tariffs. But some forms of intangible wealth, particularly the creation of human capital, have received the greatest attention by economists and the quantitative materials about such matters are plentiful. Net household claims on the social security system include claims based on contributions up to now plus the discounted value of future claims minus future payments into the system.

The most startling conclusion yielded by studies of intangible wealth is that such wealth is by far the most important component of personal wealth. For instance, Edward N. Wolff (1987b) calculates that in 1969, human capital accounted for roughly 70 percent of the total stock of household wealth in the United States. In addition, net claims on social security accounted for about 15 percent, and finally tangible wealth accounted for the remaining 15 percent. The exact shares of these three types of wealth differ, however, depending on assumptions about such matters as the discount rate, the growth of income, and the growth of social security payout rates. I must add that net claims on social security, as a share of total household wealth, rose steadily from the late 1930s to the late 1970s. Since then the evidence is less clear cut, but certain data suggest that this share leveled off in the 1980s (Wolff, 1989).

Jorgenson and Fraumeni (1989) look at another part of the intangible wealth puzzle and focus on human versus nonhuman wealth. The former consists primarily of human capital and the latter consists of tangible wealth plus net claims on the rest of the world and on the government (excluding social security). According to their calculations, human wealth fluctuated between 92 and 94 percent of total wealth in the period between 1949 and 1984.

Although the Wolff and Jorgenson–Fraumeni estimates differ about relative magnitudes and include somewhat different items of wealth, the major point should be clear: the ordinary concept of wealth that focuses exclusively on tangible capital captures only a small fraction of our total wealth.

Will the relative importance of human capital increase in the future? At first sight it seems obvious that human capital will increase faster, since the average level of education is increasing *pari passu* with the level of technology. But, as discussed in Chapter 2, the quality of this human capital may be decreasing. Moreover, as noted in Chapter 4, the technological complementarities between physical and human capital are not at all clear. With such theoretical uncertainties, it seems more sensible to turn to the data.

Regarding relative rates of change of human and physical capital, unfortunately the various sources give different results. As noted, Wolff finds the volume of intangible wealth increasing faster than tangible wealth. Jorgenson–Fraumeni (1989) present data in constant prices showing a slightly faster growth of physical than human capital. Three earlier estimates (summarized by Williamson and Lindert, 1980, p. 70) show human capital increasing faster than physical capital. These various growth rates are influenced not only by the definition of wealth employed, but also by whether current or constant price series are used.

The impact of the social insurance system on total household wealth needs several words of explanation. For the moment, let us assume a situation in which the social insurance system is completely financed by a pay-as-you-go tax system on the working population and where the social insurance tax rate remains fixed. The annual share of such taxes for social insurance increase at a rate determined by the rates of growth of the labor force and of productivity, and the same is true of the capitalized value used to measure social insurance wealth as well. If the ratio of physical capital to output remains constant (in actuality, it has slightly decreased over the last 35 years), the ratio of social insurance wealth to nonhuman wealth remains constant as well. This means that a change in the ratio of nonhuman to human wealth can occur for three reasons: (a) the social insurance system increases in scope of coverage or payout, for instance, with an increase in health-care coverage; (b) the ratio of physical capital to output falls; (c) or the ratio of human capital to physical capital rises. Currently, factors (b) and (c) seem to be working in opposite directions; so the key factor is the change in the social insurance system. If some form of governmentally sponsored universal health-care coverage eventually emerges and if it is totally self-supporting, the net wealth effect should be minimal, even though for some income classes, a significant increase or decrease might occur. As a result, it does not seem likely that the net increase in wealth deriving from social insurance claims will increase as fast in the future as in the past.

Given these conflicting considerations, only a few relatively weak conclusions are possible. The importance of the government in the creation of the overwhelming bulk of total wealth will undoubtedly continue. Nevertheless, the relative importance of such governmentally created human capital vis-à-vis physical capital depends on extensions of the scope of the social insurance system or of educational expenditures, the two most important components of such governmentally created human capital. In the near future, this does not seem highly likely and, as a result, a marked change in the relative importance of human and physical capital appears unlikely as well.

Note 5.2: Detailed results of the volatility tests

Table A.10A. Changes in volatility over time: Monetary and financial indicators

	Frequency, number of series	Significance tests (%)																
		1960–9 to 1950–9			1974–8 to 1960–9			1983–90 to 1974–8			1974–8 to 1950–9			1983–90 to 1950–9			1983–90 to 1960–6		
		+	0	–	+	0	–	+	0	–	+	0	–	+	0	–	+	0	–
Stocks and bond yields	M 17*	12	12	75	53	35	12	35	29	35	25	19	56	50	12	38	76	6	18
Bonds: 3 years and over	M 8	0	12	88	25	62	12	75	25	0	0	25	75	62	25	12	100	0	0
Bills, commercial paper, prime rate, federal funds rate, discount rate	M 6*	0	0	100	50	33	17	0	0	100	20	20	60	0	0	100	33	17	50
Stock indexes	M 3	67	33	0	100	0	0	0	67	33	100	0	0	100	0	0	100	0	0
Money and credit	M 7*	20	0	80	57	14	29	43	29	29	20	20	60	20	20	60	57	14	29
Money	M 5*	33	0	67	40	40	20	40	20	40	33	0	67	33	0	67	40	20	40
Credit	M 2	0	0	100	100	0	0	50	50	0	0	50	50	0	50	50	100	0	0
Exchange rate index	M 1	0	0	100	100	0	0	100	0	0	100	0	0	100	0	0	100	0	0
Exchange rates	M 10	20	60	20	100	0	0	70	10	20	90	10	0	90	10	0	100	0	0

Notes: M = monthly; * means that some series aren't complete for the entire period. The sources and other comments are presented in the Statistical Notes.
The bond yields include: Aaa corporate bonds, Aa corporate bonds, A corporate bonds, Baa corporate bonds, Aaa state/local bonds, Baa state/local bonds,
long-term government bonds, five-year government bonds, three-year government bonds, one-year T bills, six-month commercial paper, the discount rate,
the prime rate, the effective rate on federal funds.
The stock indices include: Standard & Poor's 500, Dow Jones industrial average, NYSE common stock price index.
The money series include: M1, M2, M3, liquidity, monetary base.
The credit series include: commercial and industrial loans outstanding, consumer installment credit.
The exchange rate series include: Belgium, Canada, France, Germany, Italy, Japan, Netherlands, Sweden, Switzerland, United Kingdom. The Federal
Reserve Bank index, which started in 1967, was extended back to the late 1940s using the same weights.
The + column indicates the percentage of cases in which the volatility was significantly greater in the later period than in the earlier; the – column indicates
the percentage of cases in which the volatility was significantly smaller in the later period than in the earlier; and the 0 column indicates where no significant trend could be found.

Table A.10B. *Changes in volatility over time: Production, price, and labor indicators*

	Frequency, number of series	Significance tests																	
		1960–9 to 1950–9			1974–8 to 1960–9			1983–90 to 1974–8			1974–8 to 1950–9			1983–90 to 1950–9			1983–90 to 1960–9		
		+	0	–	+	0	–	+	0	–	+	0	–	+	0	–	+	0	–
GDP, current, NSA	Q 1	0	0	100	0	100	0	0	0	100	0	0	100	0	0	100	0	0	100
Major components	Q 5	20	20	60	20	0	80	0	40	60	0	40	60	0	0	100	0	0	100
GDP, constant, NSA	Q 1	0	100	0	0	0	100	0	0	100	0	0	100	0	0	100	0	0	100
Major components	Q 5	0	40	60	0	60	40	0	40	60	0	20	80	0	0	100	0	0	100
Major physical production series	M 4	25	25	50	75	25	0	50	25	25	50	25	25	50	25	25	75	0	25
National inc. (current)	Q 1	0	0	100	100	0	0	0	0	100	0	100	0	0	0	100	0	100	0
Nat. inc. components	Q 2	0	0	100	50	50	0	0	50	50	0	50	50	0	0	100	50	0	50
Major price indices	M 3	0	0	100	100	0	0	0	0	100	33	33	33	0	33	67	100	0	0
GDP deflator, NSA	Q 1	0	0	100	0	0	100	0	0	100	0	0	100	0	0	100	0	0	100
Employment, unemploy.	M 3	0	0	100	0	100	0	0	0	100	0	0	100	0	0	100	0	0	100
Mnf. hours, hourly wage	M 2	50	50	0	50	50	0	0	0	100	50	50	0	0	0	100	0	0	100
Help wanted ad index	M 1	0	0	100	100	0	0	0	100	0	0	0	100	0	0	100	100	0	0

Notes: M = monthly; Q = quarterly; NSA = not seasonally adjusted. The quarterly data for the last period are 1983–9. The sources and other comments are presented in the Statistical Notes.

The GDP components include: consumption, investment, government expenditures, exports, and imports.

The major physical production series include: industrial production, housing starts, production of electrical power, new plant and equipment

The national income components include: compensation of employees, corporate profits after tax.

The major price deflators include: consumer price index, producer price index, index of sensitive material prices.

The GDP deflator is estimated on a nonseasonal adjusted basis.

The employment and unemployment series include: nonagricultural employees, total civilian unemployed, unemployment rate.

The + column indicates the percentage of cases in which the volatility was significantly greater in the later period than in the earlier; the – column indicates the percentage of cases in which the volatility was significantly smaller in the later period than in the earlier; and the 0 column indicates where no significant trend could be found.

Note 5.3: Statistical notes for Chapter 5

Table 5.1: For the business failure series, the data for 1984 and later years are not completely comparable with the data before that date. For the series on delinquent mortgages published by the Mortgage Bankers of America, both delinquent and foreclosed mortgages refer to mortgages of 1 to 4 units; the delinquent mortgages refer to mortgages more than 30 days delinquent. The series are drawn from a somewhat different universe than the SAIF, which is more complete but does not extend as far back.

To estimate total short-term liabilities of nonfarm, noncommercial businesses, I include both noncorporate and corporate businesses. For the former I take the sum of all trade debt plus one half of all bank and other loans that were not for mortgages. For the latter I take the sum of trade payables plus trade debt plus commercial paper outstanding plus all acceptance liabilities to banks plus one half of bank loans (nonmortgage), of loans from abroad, and of nonbank financial loans.

Savings and loan data extend only through 1989; these data also do not include assets of banks with negative net worth but not yet declared bankrupt.

Financial interrelations and financial intermediation ratios. The underlying data come from Board of Governors of the Federal Reserve System (1991).

Financial ratios for households and for nonfinancial, nonfarm corporate businesses. The financial data come from Board of Governors of the Federal Reserve System (1991); the national account data come from U.S. Department of Commerce (1992/3), supplemented by NIPA data (especially Tables 1.14 and 8.17) from computer disks supplied by the Bureau of Economic Analysis, U.S. Department of Commerce.

Financial ratios of FDIC members. The underlying data come from FDIC (1993).

Table 5.2: Number of financial crises. Wolfson (1986, 1990); the individual crises are listed in footnote 14 in the text.

Business failure data. Dun & Bradstreet (1993).

Deposits of failed commercial banks. FDIC (annual; and 1993). The estimate for the denominator comes from data from Board of Governors of the Federal Reserve (1993).

Assets of all commercial banks. Board of Governors of the Federal Reserve System (1976) and Board of Governors (monthly, various issues).

Gross loan write-offs and total loans and leases of FDIC members. Federal Deposit Insurance Corporation (1993). The trends of net write-offs show an even faster rise since the ratio of net to gross write-off rose over the 40-year period.

Savings and loan bank bankruptcies. The data series from 1950 through 1979 were supplied by Martin Wolfson, to whom I am grateful. The 1980 through 1989 data come from unpublished series supplied by the Office of Thrift Supervision.

MBA delinquency and foreclosure data. Mortgage Bankers Association, letter. In early years this represented a complete sample; in later years, the sample was restricted. The number of foreclosures and delinquencies is somewhat different from the SAIF data.

SAIF delinquency and foreclosure data. From U.S. Office of Thrift Supervision (1989) and earlier versions of the same publication published by the Federal Home Loan Bank (FHLB). Before 1989 the Savings Association Insurance Fund (SAIF) was called the Federal and Savings Loan Insurance Corporation (FSLIC). For the number of delinquent and foreclosed mortgages, these data are broader than the MBA data and also somewhat different; the trends, however, are the same for both series.

AOUSC personal bankruptcy data. Administrative Office of the United States Courts supplied me with data on the number of business and nonbusiness bankruptcies. I would like to thank Susan Tuck for her assistance. The data on the population age 20 and over come from U.S. Council of Economic Advisors (1993).

Table 5.3: I have drawn monthly series from a variety of sources including: Board of Governors of the Federal Reserve System (1976; annual; monthly) and computer diskettes of various series purchased the Federal reserve; the U.S. Department of Commerce, Bureau of Economic Analysis (1992/3), computer diskettes of the NIPA, and computer diskettes of a variety of series appearing in *Survey of Current Business*; other publications of the U.S. government; and the Citibank mini-database; and Conference Board data on help wanted advertisements.

Official estimates are available for both seasonally adjusted and nonseasonally adjusted current price national account data. For constant price series, only seasonally adjusted estimates are available. I estimated constant price nonseasonally adjusted series by applying the seasonal adjustment series from the current price data. As it turned out, both the seasonally adjusted and the nonseasonal adjusted series for both current and constant price series yielded the same trends in volatility.

Some series we investigated did not extend back to 1948. If the series started in the early part of the period under examination, I calculated the average for the period using the available data; if the series started in the toward the end of the period under examination, no average was calculated.

Notes to Chapter 6

Note 6.1: Financial fragility in the nonfinancial corporate sector

Following the approach outlined in Chapter 5, financial fragility in the nonfinancial corporate sector is manifested by a faster growth of debt than physical assets. One consequence is a rising share of the total cashflow accounted for by gross interest payments. This means that any downturn in economic activity raises the specter both of an inability to service this debt (insolvency) and bankruptcy (a negative net worth). For instance, using the financial data from a sample of firms, Bernanke, Campbell, and Whited (1990) simulate the same kind of recession that occurred in 1973–4 for the financial structure in 1988. They show that in the second year of such a hypothetical event, 25 percent of the firms would become insolvent and 10 percent would become illiquid.

Some aggregate indicators of financial fragility are shown in the top part of Table A.11. The problem of financial fragility does not lie with changes in total *property income*: Although the ratio of property income to net worth has declined, so did the corporate tax rate so that the ratio of after-tax property income to either net worth or total assets did not significantly change. (Significance is determined by fitting an exponential curve to the annual data and determining whether the calculated trend coefficient is significantly different from zero at the .95 level of confidence.) But the ratio of posttax *profits* to both net worth and total assets did decline significantly, reflecting the fact that net interest payments increased as a share of total property income. Thus, the sector had a smaller profit share to reinvest.

Although it is possible that the nonfinancial corporate sector could obtain sufficient investment funds from internal sources by lowering the dividend payout rate, a strategy used from the 1950s

Table A.11. *Profit and financial indicators of the nonfinancial, corporate sector (%)*

Current prices, Average annual percentages	1951–5	1956–60	1961–5	1966–70	1971–5	1976–80	1981–5	1986–90
Fragility indicators								
Ratio of gross interest to cash flow	10.6	13.9	17.7	26.7	35.5	34.4	57.5	64.7
Ratio of total liabilities to domestic factor payments	92.9	100.6	104.1	107.5	110.0	96.0	103.3	124.6
Ratios of property income to assets.								
Pretax property income (profits + net interest) to net worth	12.5	10.4	12.5	12.9	10.0	8.7	7.9	9.7
Posttax property income (profits + net interest) to net worth	5.9	5.5	7.7	8.2	6.3	5.5	5.9	7.1
Posttax property income (profits + net interest) to total assets	3.8	3.6	4.8	4.8	3.8	3.6	3.9	4.1
Posttax profits to net worth	5.4	4.9	6.6	6.4	4.0	3.5	3.3	4.0
Posttax profits to total assets	3.5	3.2	4.1	3.8	2.4	2.3	2.2	2.3
Ratios of property income to domestic factor payments (DFP)								
Pretax property income (profits + net interest) to DFP	22.1	20.0	21.6	20.2	17.0	16.7	15.9	16.4
Posttax property income (profits + net interest) to DFP	10.4	10.6	13.3	12.7	10.7	10.5	11.9	12.1
Pretax profits to DFP	21.3	18.7	19.8	17.5	13.1	12.9	10.6	11.1
Posttax profits to DFP	9.5	9.4	11.5	10.0	6.8	6.7	6.6	6.7
Dividend behavior								
Ratio of retained earnings to posttax profits (excluding price adjustment	58.1	54.0	54.5	51.6	60.1	66.4	36.4	22.8
Ratio of retained earnings to posttax profits (including price adjustment)	69.1	59.7	49.3	49.3	87.9	108.9	42.0	20.9

Notes: All profit calculations, unless noted, include inventory and fixed capital price adjustments so that any monetary profits arising from differences in book and market value are excluded. Domestic factor payments are expenditures for wages plus profits plus interest payments.
Profit data come from Tables 1.16 and 8.17 of the national accounts, Department of Commerce (1992), supplemented by later data from *Survey of Current Business*, October 1991. The asset data, annually valued at current prices, come from Board of Governors of the Federal Reserve (1991). The asset data exclude corporate farms, but the slight upward bias to the ratios of profit rates to assets should be minuscule.

through the 1970s, the opposite occurred during the 1980s. This appears an important source of the problem. The same trends are apparent when profits are more strictly defined with price adjustments included. This means that in the 1980s, the nonfinancial corporate sector became more dependent upon outside sources of finance. This, I should add, contributed to the overall decline in savings in the economy discussed in greater detail in the last chapter of the book.

The increasing financial fragility of the nonfinancial, corporate sector, as measured by the ratio of gross interest payments to cashflow, can have two major causes: increasing interest rates or a rising ratio of liabilities to income. The latter phenomenon can, in turn, be traced to such factors as a higher dividend payout rate or lower profits, both of which require more external financing of investment.

A simple simulation model allows an understanding about the relevant magnitudes of the various causal factors. I started with data on liabilities, net profits, dividends and retained earnings, cashflow, gross interest, and capital consumption. The ratios of gross interest payments to liabilities and of posttax to pretax profits are used for determining actual interest rate and profit tax series. In the discussion below, these are called "actual" data. These various actual series are used in calculating the "constructed" series, which designate what would happen if certain key variables of the economy were changed.

For year t, constructed gross interest payments are determined as the actual interest rate times the constructed liabilities in year t. Constructed pretax profits are calculated as actual pretax profits in year t plus the difference between actual and constructed gross interest payments in year t. Posttax profits in year t are pretax profits in the same year, multiplied by the actual tax rate. Constructed retained earnings are simply posttax profits multiplied by the assumed fixed retained earnings ratio. Constructed liabilities in year t are equal to constructed liabilities in year $t-1$ plus the change in actual liabilities in years t and $t-1$ plus the difference in actual and constructed retained earnings in year $t-1$. Strictly speaking, this should be the difference in actual and constructed retained earnings in year t. But such a slight deviation was necessary to make the model recursive so that simultaneous equations would not need to be solved for each year's solution.

If, for instance, the ratio of retained earnings to profits (excluding the price adjustments) remained at the 1951–5 level, the results with respect to fragility would not have been much different. If, on the other hand, the profit retention rate had been held at a constant 75.7 percent for the entire period, by 1985–90 the ratio of liabilities to domestic income would have been the same as in the 1951–5 period. However, the ratio of gross interest payments to cashflow would have been 40.0 percent in the latter period, which would have reflected the increase in the interest rate. Thus, both rising interest rates and the fall in the profit retention rate in the 1980s played important roles in increasing the financial fragility of the nonfinancial, corporate sector.

The simultaneous increased dividends and increased borrowing of the 1980s has several explanations. Of course, some enterprises may not have had profitable opportunities in which to invest their cashflow and, as a result, paid higher dividends. But the Bernanke, Campbell, and Whited (1990) study, which looks at individual firms, reports that the macroeconomic trends are reflected in the balance sheets of the particular enterprises as well.

Clearly the increasing reliance on credit was a matter of deliberate choice between risk and return by corporate decision makers. Contrary to myth, the level of corporate taxes appeared to play no contributory role since tax liabilities as a share of gross profits significantly declined, albeit at a very slow pace. It should be added that the data presented in Chapter 5 in Table 5.2 show that the risk-return choices made during the 1980s were accompanied by increased bankruptcy and other types of financial distress. Of course, the unmeasured costs of these events were borne not only by the sector itself, but by those workers who became unemployed as a result. In other words, there was a negative externality resulting from this decision by corporate leaders on other parts of the economy.

Whatever the costs to society, underlying the risk-return decisions by enterprise decision makers were certain incentives that appear closely tied to the system of corporate taxation that encouraged such behavior. It does not seem beyond imagination for the government to arrange tax and other incentives to the nonfinancial corporate sector that would encourage a higher ratio of retained earnings and a lower degree of financial fragility. Of course, lower interest rates that could arise from more responsible fiscal policies could also play an important role.

Note 6.2: *The structure of production units*

This Appendix Note deals first with indicators reflecting the structure of productive units in the manufacturing sector. Then the analysis turns to the calculation of Theil statistic for almost the entire economy to determine whether structural complexity of the size distributions of establishments and enterprises has changed.

Establishments: On the establishment level in the manufacturing sector in the period from 1958 through 1987, specialization and concentration on the main line of production have increased. The percentage of production accounted for by the principal products has increased; the share of production accounted for by establishments outside the four-digit industry has decreased; and vertical integration appears to have decreased slightly as well. Technological economies of scale appear the major driving force in this reduction in intraestablishment complexity.

These generalizations are based on data from U.S. Bureau of the Census, Department of Commerce (1961, 1991a). The starting point is a classification of all production establishments by the U.S. Bureau of Census according to the shipments of their major product.

The *specialization ratio* is defined as shipments of primary products to total products of each industry; and these are weighted by the value added in each industry to obtain an aggregate ratio. Between 1958 and 1987, this ratio rose from 89.56 to 91.69 percent, which indicates that manufacturing establishments are very slowly becoming more specialized. The *coverage ratio* is defined as the ratio of products of a given four-digit industry shipped by establishments in this industrial classification to the total shipments of this product by all establishments. These are also weighted by the value added in each industry to obtain an aggregate ratio. Between 1958 and 1987, this ratio rose from 87.51 to 91.96 percent. In neither case do the results seem significantly influenced by the composition of production, at least on a two-digit level.

Enterprises: The data on productive establishments are much less complete than for establishments and, as a result, our conclusions are more uncertain.

The vertical integration of production probably remained relatively constant in the period following World War II. The horizontal integration of production appears to have increased up to the middle or late 1970s and then decreased thereafter.

The generalization about vertical integration is based on the ratio of sales to value added which, as Scherer and Ross (1990 pp. 94 ff) have argued at some length, is an imperfect indicator of vertical integration. Laffer (1969) presents data for this indicator showing that from 1948 through 1965, it remained roughly the same for production as a whole, holding the composition of production constant. Although Laffer (1969) was able to use data on corporate sales and GDP from various sectors to calculate vertical integration from 1929 through 1965 for the economy as a whole, I could not find data series for later years that are comparable. Data on payrolls and sales are available, however, for the years 1972 through 1987 (U.S. Bureau of the Census, 1991b, Table 12) for selected sectors (mining, construction, manufacturing, wholesale and retail sales, and selected services). Using data on total compensation and corporate profits from Tables 6.2B–6.2C and 6.16B–6.16C of the national accounts (U.S. Department of Commerce, Bureau of Economic Analysis, 1992/3, Table 1.18), a rough approximation to the value-added by two digit industries can be estimated. ratios of these pseudo value-added statistics to payrolls were applied to the payroll data in the enterprise statistics to estimate the value added in the various two-digit industries. These results were then used in the calculation of the sales/value-added ratios.

For the period 1972 through 1987 these sales/value-added ratios fell from 4.72 to 4.48. If, however, the composition of production is kept constant and the aggregate ratios are recalculated, they rise from 4.72 to 4.74. In other words, the degree of vertical integration did not essentially change. For the manufacturing sector, Laffer shows a slight increase in vertical integration for 1948 through 1965. My results for the manufacturing sector show that the sales/vale-added ratio rose from 3.33 to 3.45 from 1972 to 1987. If the composition of production is kept constant, the ratios rose from 3.33 to 3.54, that is, the degree of vertical integration fell.

The disaggregated data on sales and value added for more than 400 four-digit industries can also be used to examine changes in vertical integration. From 1958 to 1987 the ratio of sales to value added fell from 2.26 to 2.12, which indicates an increase in vertical integration. If, however, the structure of production at a two-digit level is held at the 1958 proportions, the ratio falls from 2.26 to 2.18, which is much less impressive.

The generalization about the horizontal integration of production is based on two quite different data sets. For the early part of the period: the average number of lines of business for the top 200 manufacturing enterprises (ranked by sales) rose from 4.76 in 1950 to 10.89 in 1975 (Ravenscraft and Scherer, 1987, p. 30). Economies of scope and the business necessity of entering new markets when existing product lines reach maturity are the major driving forces for this increase in intraenterprise complexity. Nevertheless, Lichtenberg (1990) presents evidence that such diversification probably peaked in the early 1970s and that since then, the degree of enterprise diversification has significantly decreased. A considerable fraction of this change came through divestitures of units previously acquired in mergers.

Size distribution of productive units: On a descriptive level the problem of structural complexity of the size distribution of enterprises or establishments for the entire economy can be handled straightforwardly. Although the size distribution of enterprises (or firms) and establishments (or plants) producing goods and services can be measured by sales, assets, and other financial measures, I use a labor force measurement that is not influenced by the price level. Given the overwhelming number of very small enterprises and establishments, it is also useful to follow standard procedures and calculate the various statistics for units that have twenty or more employees. Table A.12 presents data on the share of workers in different size units for a thirty-year period. Several unexpected conclusions can be drawn from these data:

- *Average size:* Although the average size of enterprises and establishments increased from the early part of the century up to the 1960s in some sectors such as manufacturing (Pryor, 1973b, Chaps. 5 and 6), these average sizes, measured in terms both of simple arithmetic averages and weighted averages based on the Theil statistic, began to decline in the 1980s. These changes are especially apparent when examining the enterprises and establishments that have twenty or more employees. One factor underlying this change has been the decline in the share of the labor force working in manufacturing where the sizes of production units are larger than in most other sectors. But other causal factors are also at work that are difficult to isolate.
- *Structural complexity:* Calculations of the Theil statistics show that the complexity of the productive system measured either from data on enterprises or establishments is trending slowly and irregularly upward. This has occurred primarily because the number of units is increasing. The percentage of employment in the various size categories is erratic with no discernible trends.

Another measure of complexity, following the approach of Simon (1969), focuses on the vertical interactions of the system and the degree to which hierarchical levels of decision making are increasing, as manifested by the relative spread of multiplant firms. Although the universes covered by the measures for enterprises and establishments in Table A.12 are slightly different, a rough measure of the extent of multiplant enterprises would be the ratio of the average size enter-

Table A.12: *Percentage of the labor force in different size units of productions*

Employee size category	Enterprises				Establishments			
	1958	1967	1977	1987	1958	1967	1977	1987
Distribution of labor force in different size units (%)								
Less than 20 employees	23.3	21.7	19.8	20.8	28.7	25.1	27.1	27.0
20–99 employees	18.0	19.2	17.9	19.1	23.9	24.3	27.4	29.5
100–499 employees	13.9	13.2	12.3	14.2	22.3	23.0	23.0	24.1
500–999 employees	4.9	4.2	4.3	4.7	8.9	9.7	7.9	6.9
1,000 and over employees	—	—	—	—	16.3	17.8	14.5	12.5
1,000–4,999 employees	11.3	9.7	10.1	10.0	n.a.	n.a.	n.a.	n.a.
5,000–9,999 employees	5.8	5.3	5.0	4.9	n.a.	n.a.	n.a.	n.a.
10,000 and over employees	23.0	27.6	30.6	26.3	n.a.	n.a.	n.a.	n.a.
Employee size: arithmetic average:								
All units	17	18	21	21	12	15	15	14
All units with more than								
19 employees	139	141	148	137	99	100	91	83
Employee size: Theil average:								
All units	366	458	584	453	86	103	84	74
All units with more than								
19 employees	1281	1529	1782	1380	255	268	216	183
Theil statistic of complexity of employment size structure:								
All units	11.3	11.4	11.3	11.8	13.1	13.1	13.6	14.0
All units with more than								
19 employees	9.8	10.0	9.9	10.5	11.7	11.9	12.3	12.7

Notes: The Theil averages are based on the same approach as the Theil statistic and are described in Appendix Note 1.2. An increasing Theil statistic represents an increase in structural complexity. Both Theil statistics are calculated with more detailed size distribution data than presented in the table. For enterprises, there are nine size classes of units with twenty or more workers; for establishments, six size classes. The enterprise data exclude farms, the government sector, and selected branches of transportation, communications, and services. Since the data for the four years are slightly different in the industries omitted, the data are not completely comparable. These non-comparabilities should, however, make very little difference. Since the raw data for 1958 and 1967 exclude construction as well, I have subtracted the construction sector from the data in 1977 and 1987; this adjustment for comparability also makes little difference to the final results. I have also eliminated all firms with no paid employees.

The establishment data exclude farms, the government sector, the self-employed, and several branches of transportation.

The enterprise data come from Department of Commerce, Bureau of the Census (1963b, 1972, 1981, 1991b). The establishment data come from Department of Commerce, Bureau of the Census (annual-a, various issues). The data for 1958 are for the first quarter of 1959 since data were not published for 1958. For this year I also made estimates for employment in each employment size class by assuming that they were the same as the average size establishment in 1964, adjusting so that the total employment in 1959 was the same as reported.

Table A.13. *Share of business receipts of enterprises with different forms of ownership (%)*

	1947	1960	1970	1980	1988
Corporations	71.8	79.8	85.4	89.9	89.6
Partnerships	11.7	6.9	4.6	4.2	4.2
Nonfarm proprietorships	16.5	13.4	10.0	6.0	6.1

Note: For 1947 and 1960 a rough adjustment is made to exclude farm receipts from nonfarm proprietorships to achieve comparability; errors introduced in this estimation should be very small. The data come from U.S. Department of Commerce, Bureau of the Census (1975), Volume 2, p. 911; and U.S. Department of Commerce, Bureau of the Census (annual-b, 1992), p. 519.

prise to average size establishment. Such a calculation has the most meaning when arithmetic average sizes are used. Such an exercise shows an increase in structural complexity over the entire period, although it should be added that the rate of increase tapered off between 1977 and 1987.

Trends in the form of enterprise ownership. Changes in the form of enterprise ownership follow well-known paths and require little discussion. The data in Table A.13 show that corporations accounted for an increasing share of business receipts up to 1980; thereafter the trend begins to level off. At the same time, the share of business receipts of partnerships and proprietorships both fell until 1980. Although the relative importance of corporations may increase slightly, I see no strong forces in the next several decades that would greatly change the situation existing at the end of the 1980s.

Note 6.3: Trends in executive compensation

The trends in executive compensation discussed in the text are based on data presented in Table A.14.

The Lewellen (1968, pp. 137, 147; and 1975) data cover the 50 largest industrial corporations (in terms of sales) in the Fortune 500. The pretax estimates of nonsalary elements are the amounts of salary and bonus that would yield the equivalent posttax return. Thus in 1960 when the marginal tax rate was particularly high, the difference between pretax and posttax incomes was, according to this method of estimation, very great. Lewellen also valued stock options according to the income actually realized, taking the actual prices of stocks in subsequent years.

The *Forbes* estimates are made from compensation data from the annual survey in *Forbes* plus additional data on the 50 largest industrial corporations from the annual survey in *Fortune*. The *Forbes* survey values stock options in terms of the realized values. Thus, options not yet cashed in by CEOs, when they have retired, are not included, which means that the value of these options is considerably understated.

The Hay data come from Hay Management Consultants (annual: 1991, 1981). In 1980, their sample is drawn from firms with sales over $4 billion; in 1990, over $5 billion. The value of various types of benefits is drawn from a larger sample that suggests that benefits and perquisites were 34.3 percent of base salary (excluding bonuses). Since it is possible that these other types of compensation have been a more important part of compensation for CEOs of the largest companies, these data understate the actual amount. I doubt, however, that the differences are great. They value the stock options according to a rough estimation method that takes into account estimates of the future price of the stock and the discount rate. This method results in higher values of stock

Table A.14. *CEO remuneration and compensation in large industrial corporations*

	1940	1950	1960	1970	1980	1990
Bases of comparison: Average compensation for all workers in the economy, current $ (ACAWE):						
Average pretax compensation	1,376	3,198	5,247	8,689	18,814	31,294
Average posttax compensation	1,335	2,916	4,622	7,549	16,542	26,407
Salary and bonus of top CEOs as a multiple (divided by) ACAWE:						
Lewellen estimates: pretax average	95.5	45.6	33.8	32.4	n.a.	n.a.
Lewellen estimates: posttax average	57.3	27.4	17.4	20.0	n.a.	n.a.
Forbes estimates: pretax, average	n.a.	n.a.	n.a.	26.0	36.4	46.2
Forbes estimates: pretax, median	n.a.	n.a.	n.a.	26.2	36.1	44.2
Hay Group: pretax, average	n.a.	n.a.	n.a.	n.a.	n.a.	41.7
Hay Group: pretax, median	n.a.	n.a.	n.a.	n.a.	33.6	39.1
Top CEO pension payments, other benefits, and deferred compensation as multiple of ACAWE:						
Lewellen estimates: pretax average	51.1	57.6	103.0	n.a.	n.a.	n.a.
Lewellen estimates: posttax average	19.1	13.9	10.9	9.8	n.a.	n.a.
Hay Group: pretax, average (rough est.)	n.a.	n.a.	n.a.	n.a.	n.a.	8.4
Top CEO value of stock options as multiple of ACAWE:						
Lewellen estimates: pretax average	0.0	3.5	187.4	n.a.	n.a.	n.a.
Lewellen estimates: posttax average	0.0	0.8	19.7	3.6	n.a.	n.a.
Hay Group: pretax, average	n.a.	n.a.	n.a.	n.a.	n.a.	77.9
Hay Group: pretax, median	n.a.	n.a.	n.a.	n.a.	n.a.	31.3
Total top CEO compensation as multiple of ACAWE:						
Lewellen estimates: pretax average	146.6	106.7	324.3	n.a.	n.a.	n.a.
Lewellen estimates: posttax average	76.5	42.4	48.5	33.6	n.a.	n.a.
Forbes estimates: pretax, average	n.a.	n.a.	n.a.	30.0	58.2	85.1
Forbes estimates: pretax, median	n.a.	n.a.	n.a.	28.8	46.3	68.6
Estimate A (see text): pretax average	146.6	106.7	324.3	n.a.	n.a.	135.3
Estimate B (see text): posttax average	76.5	42.4	48.5	33.6	n.a.	112.9

Notes: The estimates of average pretax compensation of full-time employees come from the official national account and product data, Tables 6.2 B and 6.5 A (Department of Commerce, Bureau of Economic Analysis, 1992/3). The average tax rate is estimated from data from Table 2.1 of the national accounts as the ratio of personal tax and nontax payments to total personal income. The *Forbes* data come from: Volumes 107, No. 10; Volume 127, No. 12; and Volume 147, No. 11.

options than the *Forbes* method, because some account is taken of nonrealized increases in the value of these options. I would like to thank Robert C. Ochsner for these data although neither he nor the Hay Group is responsible for the ways in which I have made use of their raw data.

The salary and bonus data from the various sources appears roughly comparable. Such data suggest that relative CEO salary levels were roughly the same in 1990 as in 1950. The mean and median salary plus bonus payments are not greatly different.

For pension payments, benefits, and deferred compensation, the decline in the marginal tax rates during the Reagan era would close the gap between pretax and posttax compensation according to the method used by Lewellen. Assuming that such benefits avoid all taxes, the Hay Group estimate of pretax payments would be roughly 11.2 times the average pretax compensation if we use the Lewellen method of valuation. This is the "Lewellen equivalent."

Stock options raise the greatest comparability problems. Moreover, the differences between the median and average are also greatest because of the wide range in stock options received by the CEOs in the sample.

Although it is not possible to make estimates for 1990 that correspond with those of Lewellen for earlier years, we can make some rough calculations to determine relative orders of magnitudes. For the pretax average, it is useful to start with the *Forbes* estimate of salary and basic bonus, since it is more consistent to the Lewellen data than that of the Hay group. To this is added the Lewellen equivalent for the Hay estimates of pension payments, other benefits, and deferred compensation (see above) that are normally not taxed. And finally, the Hay estimate of the pretax value of stock options, which in 1990 were taxed at the same rate as regular income, are added. This is Estimate A presented in Table A.14.

Deriving a rough estimate of the posttax total compensation requires some additional assumptions. Let us assume that the CEO paid an average tax of 30 percent on wages, salaries, and stock options and no tax on the other benefits. From this we can derive Estimate B in the table. It is on the bases of Estimates A and B that I make the statement in Chapter 6 that relative executive compensation on a pretax basis has not greatly changed since 1940, but that it has probably risen in posttax terms.

Note 6.4: More data from the company survey

See Tables A.15, A.16, and A.17 on pages 310–316.

Note 6.5: Statistical Notes for Chapter 6

Table 6.1: The data for the first four lines in Table 1 come from U.S. Department of Commerce, Bureau of the Census (1986a). For the bottom three lines in the same table, the data on employment in the world's largest enterprises come from *Fortune,* Vols. 60, No. 1 (July 1959); 60, No. 2 (August 1959); 70, No. 1 (July 1964); 70, No. 2 (August 1964); 87, No. 5 (March 1973); 88, No. 3 (September 1973); 107, No. 9 (May 2, 1983); and 108, No. 4 (August 22, 1983). From the lists of the largest corporations in and outside the United States, I tried to eliminate those companies in both lists owned by a parent company in the other list. Although it was also my intention to consolidate companies in Japan that were members of the same *keiretsu* (industrial group), this proved impossible, so that aggregate concentration may be somewhat understated. On the other hand, to the extent that employment in any joint venture between the various top one hundred corporations is counted by both partners, the degree of aggregate concentration may be understated. For the twenty-two industrial nations, I also eliminated those enterprises in the top 100 based in the developing nations.

The denominator of the aggregate concentration ratio for the United States was drawn from U.S. Department of Commerce, Bureau of Economic Analysis (1986, pp. 272–3). For the broader samples, the denominator represents the economically active in mining and manufacturing in the world capitalist system, that is, all countries except the thirty-three Marxist regimes identified by Pryor (1992b). For the twenty-two industrial nations, I used the economically active in mining and manufacturing of the important industrial nations in the OECD.

The data on economically active for a number of years for 101 nations came from International Labour Office (1990, Table 2A; and 1991, Table 2) and Taiwan (1984). The economically active in 1958, 1963, 1972, and 1982 were estimated by standard interpolation and extrapolation techniques. The countries for which data on economically active were not available represented about 10 percent of the total population; all were low-income nations. The economically active in manufacturing and mining in these nations were estimated on a continent by continent basis, assuming that their ratio of economically active in these two industries to total population was the same as the low-income nations on the same continent for which data were available. The population data came from United Nations (1979, 1988).

Table 6.2: Part A: The data come from the Board of Governors of the Federal Reserve, Flow of Funds Accounts, Z1 release, Table L.215; diskettes, October 29, 1993. The totals may not add because of rounding.

Part B: the data come from Larner (1970), Table 2.

Notes to Chapter 7

Note 7.1: The data set of domestic prices

It is difficult to obtain comparable retail price data of particular goods and services in different cities. The Bureau of Labor Statistics (BLS), which collects price information for calculation of the Consumer Price Index, uses a probability sample. Among other things, this means that not exactly the same goods and services are included for any two cities or at any two periods of time. Thus, these data cannot be employed in their raw form but must be transformed in some appropriate way.

The exact statistical methods employed in these estimates are discussed in detail in Pryor (1995). It is useful, however, to consider at this point what biases my statistical methods might impart to the results. Since the data used in this study are average prices of aggregates, each composed of relatively substitutable products, such data should obviously reduce the spatial variation at one point in time. Barring some extreme cases that do not seem to occur, it is difficult to see any major impact such aggregation should have on the *trend* of the spatial variation. More intractable is the problem arising from the weighting of the aggregates. The average prices for each aggregate are calculated for a one-year period in the late 1980s according to the Consumer Price Index weights in use at that time. These were extrapolated backwards in time with the use of time series of the aggregates, which were periodically reweighted.

It is impossible to determine the bias imparted by this procedure. In an attempt to take such matters into account, I calculated the trends not just from 1950 through 1992, but also for a shorter time period where the bias imparted by the reweighting is not so strong. This did not change the overall results. Further, the results do not appear influenced by changes in the measurement of goods and services included. Except rental equivalents of owner-occupied housing, the BLS has not made major changes. Moreover, any such changes would occur in all cities where the data were collected and should have less impact on the CV than in the price increases per se.

The detailed results of the calculations are shown in Table A.18, page 317.

Note 7.2: Further data on concentration ratios

See Table A.19 on page 318.

Note 7.3: Further comments on price volatility

This Note has three parts. The first discusses some commonly advanced reasons why price volatility of basic commodities should be decreasing. The second looks at more exotic reasons invoked to explain changes in volatility. The final section outlines the theoretical argument by Dornbusch (1985) linking raw material volatility to the volatility of internationally traded commodities. I also present the detailed data on exchange rate, price, and production volatility.

Note 6.4: More data from the company survey

Table A.15. *Mastering structural complexity by more resources to information processing*

	Total	Mining	Construction	Manufacturing		Transportation commerce, public utilities	Trade			Finance, insurance, real estate	Services
				Nondurables	Durables		Wholesale	Retail			
Number of firms in sample	206	2	7	48	64	16	12	13	30	14

Average scores:

1A: How the ratio of expenditures for data processing to sales changed in the last decade? Scale: decreased = −1; same = 0; increased = +1.

	Total	Mining	Construction	Nondurables	Durables	Transportation	Wholesale	Retail	Finance estate	Services
	+.44	+1.00	.00	+.44	+.27	+.88	+.50	+.46	+.62	+.36

1B: How will this ratio change in the next decade? Same scale as above.

	+.18	+.50	−.57	+.25	+.19	+.19	+.08	+.38	+.34	−.21

2A: How has the status of information officers in the company changed? Same scale as above

	+.46	+.50	+.57	+.53	+.16	+.40	+.50	+.77	+.72	+.64

2B: How will this ratio change in the next decade? Same scale as above.

	+.29	.00	.00	+.26	+.27	+.13	+.50	+.54	+.28	+.43

3A: How has the budget of the controller's office changed as a percent of sales? Same scale as above.

	−.28	.00	+.29	−.23	−.39	−.50	−.08	−.23	−.10	−.57

3B: How will this ratio change in the next decade? Same scale as above.

	−.45	−.50	−.14	−.53	−.46	−.56	−.42	−.31	−.23	−.71

4A: How have expenditures for legal matters changed as a percent of sales? Same scale as above.

	+.77	+1.00	+.43	+.75	+.81	+.81	+.67	+.62	+.77	+.93

4B: How will this ratio change in the next decade? Same scale as above.

	+.41	+1.00	+.14	+.39	+.49	+.38	+.33	+.46	+.30	+.50

Average scores:

	Total firms	Enterprise size: Number of workers and employees			
		500–999	1,000–4,999	5,000–9,999	10,000 and over
Number of firms in sample	206	76	85	20	25
1A: How the ratio of expenditures for data processing to sales changed in the last decade? Scale: decreased = −1; same = 0; increased = +1.	+.44	+.41	+.39	+.55	+.60
1B: How will this ratio change in the next decade? Same scale as above.	+.18	+.16	+.12	+.35	+.32
2A: How has the status of information officers in the company changed? Same scale as above.	+.46	+.28	+.56	+.45	+.64
2B: How will this ratio change in the next decade? Same scale as above.	+.29	+.28	+.27	+.20	+.44
3A: How has the budget of the controller's office changed as a percent of sales? Same scale as above.	−.28	−.26	−.26	−.15	−.48
3B: How will this ratio change in the next decade? Same scale as above.	−.45	−.49	−.37	−.40	−.60
4A: How have expenditures for legal matters changed as a percent of sales? Same scale as above.	+.77	+.82	+.74	+.65	+.80
4B: How will this ratio change in the next decade? Same scale as above.	+.41	+.51	+.38	.00	+.56

Table A.16. *Reducing structural complexity by decentralization*

	Total	Mining	Construction	Manufacturing		Transportation, commerce, public utilities	Trade		Finance, insurance, real estate	Services
				Nondurables	Durables		Wholesale	Rerail		
Number of firms in sample	206	2	7	48	64	16	12	13	30	14

Average scores:

5A: Has responsibility for operations in the past decade been decentralized by creating more profit centers in the past decade?
Scale: fewer centers = −1; same = 0; more centers = +1.

	Total	Mining	Construction	Nondurables	Durables	Transp.	Wholesale	Rerail	Finance	Services
	+.50	+1.00	+.14	+.37	+.55	+.33	+.50	+.38	+.69	+.71

5B: How will this change in the next decade? Same scale as above.

	+.18	+.50	−.14	+.24	+.14	+.06	+.25	+.38	+.27	.00

6A: Has responsibility for operations been decentralized by grouping operating divisions and creating overall group leaders in the past decade?
Scale: fewer groupings = −1; same = 0; more groupings = +1.

	+.41	+1.00	+.57	+.42	+.40	+.19	+.58	+.38	+.25	+.69

6B: How will this change in the next decade? Same scale as above.

	+.22	+1.00	+.14	+.16	+.17	−.13	+.25	+.31	+.41	+.46

7A: Has the relation between compensations for workers and employees in different operations and the results of their work been changed in the past decade?
Scale: less closely tied = −1; same = 0; more closely tied = +1.

	+.61	+.50	+.83	+.57	+.53	+.38	+.67	+.77	+.72	+.85

7B: How will this change in the next decade? Same scale as above.

	+.61	+1.00	+.17	+.53	+.56	+.75	+.50	+.77	+.69	+.77

8A: Have relations in the past decade between suppliers changed in the last decade so that there are more competitive relations with more supplies or closer relations with fewer suppliers.
Scale: more competitive with more = −1; same = 0; closer relations with fewer suppliers = +1.

	+.46	−.50	+.29	+.46	+.67	+.31	+.58	+.25	+.38	+.15

8B: How will this change in the next decade? Same scale as above.

+.26 +1.00 +.43 +.21 +.39 +.50 +.58 -.17 +.04 -.14

9A: How has vertical integration changed in the past decade?
Scale: decreased = 1; same = 0; increased = +1.

+.07 -1.00 -.14 -.02 +.25 +.07 +.45 -.08 -.04 -.17

9B: How will this change in the next decade? Same scale as above.

+.05 -1.00 -.14 -.02 +.26 -.07 +.18 -.17 +.12 -.42

Average scores:

| | Enterprise size: Number of workers and employees | | | | |
	Total firms	500–999	1,000–4,999	5,000–9,999	10,000 and over
Number of firms in sample	206	76	85	20	25

5A: Has responsibility for operations in the past decade been decentralized by creating more profit centers in the past decade?
Scale: fewer centers = -1; same = 0; more centers = +1.

| | +.50 | +.47 | +.49 | +.47 | +.64 |

5B: How will this change in the next decade? Same scale as above.

| | +.18 | +.23 | +.21 | +.11 | .00 |

6A: Has responsibility for operations been decentralized by grouping operating divisions and creating overall group leaders in the past decade?
Scale: fewer groupings = -1; same = 0; more groupings = +1.

| | +.41 | +.42 | +.43 | +.24 | +.40 |

6B: How will this change in the next decade? Same scales as above.

| | +.22 | +.23 | +.18 | +.33 | +.20 |

7A: Has the relation between compensations for workers and employees in different operations and the results of their work been changed in the past decade?
Scale: less closely tied = -1; same = 0; more closely tied = +1.

| | +.61 | +.49 | +.66 | +.75 | +.67 |

Table A.16. (cont.)

Average scores:

	Total firms	Enterprise size: Number of workers and employees			
		500–999	1,000–4,999	5,000–9,999	10,000 and over
Number of firms in sample	206	76	85	20	25

7B: How will this change in the next decade? Same scale as above.

	+.61	+.60	+.59	+.70	+.60

8A: Have relations in the past decade between suppliers changed in the last decade so that there are more competitive relations with more supplies or closer relations with fewer suppliers.
Scale: more competitive with more = –1; same = 0; closer relations with fewer suppliers = +1.

	+.46	+.39	+.46	+.75	+.46

8B: How will this change in the next decade? Same scale as above.

	+.26	+.17	+.23	+.40	+.50

9A: How has vertical integration changed in the past decade?
Scale: decreased = 1; same = 0; increased = +1.

	+.07	+.11	–.03	+.30	+.09

9B: How will this change in the next decade? Same scale as above.

	+.05	.00	+.05	+.45	–.13

Table A.17. *Evading structural complexity by simplification*

	Total	Mining	Construction	Manufacturing		Transportation, commerce, public utilities	Trade		Finance, insurance, real estate	Services
				Nondurables	Durables		Wholesale	Retail		
Number of firms in sample	206	2	7	48	64	16	12	13	30	14

Average scores:

10A: How has *attention in operations* to the core businesses or closely related businesses changed in the past decade?
Scale: less focus on core business = −1; same = 0; more attention to core business = +1.

	Total	Mining	Construction	Nondurables	Durables	Transportation	Wholesale	Retail	Finance	Services
10A	+.60	+1.00	+.14	+.48	+.63	+.50	+.67	+.64	+.76	+.77

10B: How will this change in the next decade? Same scale as above.

	Total	Mining	Construction	Nondurables	Durables	Transportation	Wholesale	Retail	Finance	Services
10B	+.46	+1.00	+.43	+.38	+.45	+.44	+.58	+.64	+.28	+.85

11A: How has *product standardization* proceeded in the past decade?
Scale: less standardization = −1; same = 0; more standardization = +1.

	Total	Mining	Construction	Nondurables	Durables	Transportation	Wholesale	Retail	Finance	Services
11A	+.48	.00	+.14	+.42	+.47	+.36	+.42	+.92	+.50	+.77

11B: How will this change in the next decade? Same scale as above.

	Total	Mining	Construction	Nondurables	Durables	Transportation	Wholesale	Retail	Finance	Services
11B	+.43	+1.00	+.14	+.28	+.44	+.64	+.58	+.67	+.40	+.54

12A: How has *process standardization* proceeded in the past decade? Same scale as above.

	Total	Mining	Construction	Nondurables	Durables	Transportation	Wholesale	Retail	Finance	Services
12A	+.66	+1.00	+.14	+.55	+.76	+.57	+.75	+.92	+.54	+.85

12B: How will this change in the next decade? Same scale as above.

	Total	Mining	Construction	Nondurables	Durables	Transportation	Wholesale	Retail	Finance	Services
12B	+.65	+1.00	+.29	+.57	+.79	+.50	+.75	+.83	+.55	+.62

13A: How as *standardization of procedures* proceeded in the past decade? Same scale as above.

	Total	Mining	Construction	Nondurables	Durables	Transportation	Wholesale	Retail	Finance	Services
13A	+.58	+1.00	+.71	+.45	+.63	+.50	+.58	+.92	+.43	+.69

13B: How will this change in the next decade? Same scale as above.

	Total	Mining	Construction	Nondurables	Durables	Transportation	Wholesale	Retail	Finance	Services
13B	+.54	.00	+.57	+.50	+.51	+.46	+.92	+.85	+.41	+.62

14A: How has the *process-of-change* proceeded in the past decade?
Scale: more large changes = −1; same = 0; more incremental changes = +1.

	Total	Mining	Construction	Nondurables	Durables	Transportation	Wholesale	Retail	Finance	Services
14A	−.08	−1.00	+.29	−.21	−.08	+.20	−.33	+.23	−.12	−.09

14B: How will the process-of-change proceed in the next decade? Same scale as above.

	Total	Mining	Construction	Nondurables	Durables	Transportation	Wholesale	Retail	Finance	Services
14B	+.54	+1.00	+.71	+.64	+.43	+.43	+.42	+.92	+.41	+.73

Table A.1. (cont.)

	Average scores:				
		Enterprise size: Number of workers and employees			
	Total firms	500–999	1,000–4,999	5,000–9,999	10,000 and over
Number of firms in sample	206	76	85	20	25
10A: How has attention in operations to the core businesses or closely related businesses changed in the past decade? Scale: less focus on core business = −1; same = 0; more attention to core business = +1.	+.60	+.53	+.59	+.63	+.80
10B: How will this change in the next decade? Same scale as above.	+.46	+.46	+.42	+.55	+.48
11A: How has product standardization proceeded in the past decade? Scale: less standardization = −1; same = 0; more standardization = +1.	+.48	+.40	+.54	+.58	+.44
11B: How will this change in the next decade? Same scale as above.	+.43	+.53	+.46	+.25	+.21
12A: How has process standardization proceeded in the past decade? Same scale as above.	+.66	+.58	+.67	+.74	+.80
12B: How will this change in the next decade? Same scale as above.	+.65	+.67	+.64	+.55	+.75
13A: How as standardization of procedures proceeded in the past decade? Same scale as above.	+.58	+.51	+.60	+.63	+.68
13B: How will this change in the next decade? Same scale as above.	+.54	+.61	+.46	+.50	+.63
14A: How has the process-of-change proceeded in the past decade? Scale: more large changes = −1; same = 0; more incremental changes = +1.	−.08	−.07	−.06	−.56	+.24
14B: How will the process-of-change proceed in the next decade? Same scale as above.	+.54	+.58	+.61	+.47	+.27

Table A.18. *Measurements of retail price behavior: Percentages*

Good or service	First year of series	Average annual price changes		Five city statistics								
				Average coefficient of variation		Average annual change of CV		Random walk process		"Corrected" average" annual change of CV		True test"
		First year to 1993	1976–93	First year to 1993	1976–93	First year to 1993	1976–93	First year to 1993	1976–93	First year to 1993	1976–93	
Alcoholic beverages	1976	—	4.82	—	7.91	—	+.51	—	Yes	—	None	No
Cereal and bakery products	1950	4.60	5.47	5.33	5.89	+1.49	+2.96	Yes	?	None	+3.80	Yes
Dairy products	1950	3.54	3.93	4.49	5.13	+.97	-3.81	?	No	None	-3.12	No
Fruits and vegetables	1950	4.63	6.22	8.78	7.38	-1.50	+0.95	?	?	None	None	Yes
Meat, poultry, fish, eggs	1976	—	3.81	—	3.74	—	-3.98	—	?	—	None	Yes
Canned and prepared foods, baby foods, snacks, and other foods	1976	—	5.18	—	4.75	—	None	—	?	—	None	Yes
Men and boys clothing	1950	2.55	2.96	11.05	12.20	+.92	-.54	?	?	+.30	None	Yes
Women and girls clothing	1950	2.02	2.29	17.00	15.10	-.75	-1.74	?	No	None	None	Yes
Footwear	1950	3.38	3.46	16.25	12.83	-1.50	-2.26	?	Yes	None	None	Yes
Motor fuels	1978	—	4.52	—	7.51	—	+.76	—	?	—	None	No
Private transportation	1950	3.89	5.26	6.30	4.65	-2.30	-7.55	Yes	?	None	-5.27	No
Piped natural gas and electricity	1950	4.27	6.08	22.38	18.13	-1.32	+.44	?	No	None	None	No
House furnishings & operations	1976	—	3.53	—	10.33	—	+2.55	—	?	—	+2.25	Yes
Housing rents	1957	3.84	5.53	12.40	15.40	+2.18	+3.82	?	?	+2.83	None	No
Shelter (rents & rental equivalent)	1953	4.94	6.75	27.37	28.62	None	None	?	?	None	None	No
Entertainment (e.g., books, movies) and so forth)	1976	—	4.94	—	12.25	—	+1.22	—	?	—	+1.81	No
Medical services	1967	8.26	8.56	10.85	10.71	None	+2.14	?	?	None	+1.25	No

Notes: Data sources are discussed in the text. The CV is the unweighted standard deviation. Gasoline is one part of the private transportation series; housing rents is one part of the shelter series. The meaning of "true test" is discussed in the text.
The presence of a random-walk process is determined with the use of the Dickey-Fuller test on a synthetic regression. This calculation, and the "corrected" trend calculation are described in the text.

Table A.19. *Weighted concentration ratios, 1958 and 1982, two-digit basis*

	Domestic concentration ratios				Trade adjusted concentration ratios			
SIC	DP-CR4 1958	DP-CR4 1982	DP-CR8 1958	DP-CR8 1982	TA-CR4 1958	TA-CR4 1982	TA-CR8 1958	TA-CR8 1982
Manufacturing sector	36.2	35.8	48.2	47.6	35.7	32.6	47.4	43.5
20 Food and kindred products	32.1	38.3	46.2	51.3	31.1	36.8	44.8	49.3
21 Tobacco products	78.2	88.1	97.4	98.2	78.2	87.2	97.4	97.1
22 Textile mill products	29.2	35.3	41.7	49.7	27.8	32.5	39.7	45.8
23 Apparel and related products	14.8	22.5	22.3	31.1	14.6	19.1	22.0	26.3
24 Lumber and wood products	12.5	19.5	19.5	27.6	12.0	18.2	18.8	25.8
25 Furniture and fixtures	17.1	21.4	25.2	30.1	17.1	20.2	25.1	28.6
26 Paper and allied products	31.4	31.1	46.0	46.4	29.8	29.6	43.6	43.9
27 Printing and publishing	18.1	19.6	25.7	28.1	18.0	19.4	25.6	27.9
28 Chemicals and allied products	37.6	34.1	51.9	48.5	37.1	32.7	51.2	46.5
29 Petroleum and coal products	30.3	28.5	52.1	47.5	29.0	26.5	49.8	44.2
30 Rubber and miscellaneous plastics	21.7	20.0	28.0	27.7	21.9	17.7	28.3	24.5
31 Leather and leather products	22.7	28.2	32.5	40.6	17.5	16.0	25.1	23.2
32 Stone, clay, and glass products	36.9	36.9	47.3	49.7	36.1	34.4	46.2	46.3
33 Primary metal industries	44.3	37.4	57.9	53.0	42.5	32.1	55.8	45.5
34 Fabricated metal products	31.4	24.3	40.3	32.8	31.3	23.3	40.1	31.5
35 Machinery (except electrical)	36.1	32.1	48.3	42.7	35.6	29.3	47.6	39.0
36 Electrical equipment and supplies	41.6	38.9	53.5	51.7	41.4	34.4	53.3	45.6
37 Transportation equipment	65.7	64.0	78.7	75.7	65.9	55.5	79.1	66.2
38 Instruments and related products	41.0	44.8	52.6	55.4	40.0	39.9	51.4	49.4
39 Miscellaneous manufactures	23.0	27.9	33.2	38.8	20.7	22.2	29.9	30.7

Notes: DP-CR = domestic concentration ratios; TA-CR = trade-adjusted concentration ratios; the numerals 4 and 8 stand for the number of firms in the calculation. The concentration ratios are for product classes. The 1982 SIC classification is for 1982, and 1982 value-added weights are used to calculate the averages. The data sources are described in Pryor (1994a).

Possible causal influences: Economists have advanced several common reasons for expecting a decline in volatility of internationally traded basic commodities.

- **Market size:** It is commonly believed that as the market size of any particular good or service increases, both prices and total quantities of production should become more stable. This is because random shocks are an important cause of short-term fluctuations of both the supply curve (for instance, a harvest failure or the flooding of a mine or a strike) and the demand curve (for instances, short-term changes in tastes or income). With an expansion of the market size, these individual shocks become less important since they are diffused over a broader market area. Furthermore, in a larger area they may be offset by shocks in the opposite direction in other parts of the market. This proposition about market size can also be examined from the opposite perspective. Simulation models show quite readily that certain types of trade barriers narrowing markets (such as quotas or the European Community's variable levy on agricultural goods) increase price fluctuations in the rest of the world (Pryor, 1981).

- **Development of forward markets:** The development of forward markets in the post World War II era should also lead to a decrease in price and production volatility. This is because such forward markets allow the risk to be shifted from producers to professional risk takers so that, under normal conditions, they allow stabilizing speculation to take place (Sarris, 1984).
- **Macroeconomic volatility:** In as far as macroeconomic volatility is decreasing, microeconomic volatility should be decreasing as well. The calculations in Appendix Note 5.2, Table A.10B, document the decline in quarterly volatility of most macroeconomic variables in the United States. This suggests that shocks to individual markets caused by changes in aggregate demand should be decreasing.

Other causal influences: Economists have advanced a series of more exotic influences on the volatility of basic material prices and quantities that deserve brief mention. In some cases it is unclear in which direction these factors influence the volatility. These factors include:

- **Production lags:** This argument focuses on the period of production and the lags between the decision to start production and the sale of the good. The greater the lag, the greater is the possibility that differences will arise between the projected and the actual market price, and that the amount produced will overshoot or undershoot the quantity of production appropriate to the current market price. Such a mismatch between current price and supply causes price and quantity fluctuations. These are analyzed as part of the standard economic theory about "cobwebs," so named because of the appearance of the supply and demand diagram used to illustrate the analysis.

  The relevance of this argument is open to questions for many types of production. Certainly it does not have a great deal of force in many types of basic material production, which are conditioned on seasonal or similar considerations. Moreover, the higher the ratio of capital to labor in the production process, the more costly are short-run changes in production since hiring more workers may bring only a small increment of production with the existing machinery when production is close to full capacity. As a result, short-term volatility of production is dampened. Furthermore, greater mechanization often shortens, rather than increases, production lags. From this approach it is quite unclear how production and price volatility will change over time.
- **Expectations:** Many production decisions are made on the basis of prices expected in the future. The greater the variation of these expectations, the greater will be the variations in production, holding other things constant such as the cost of moving from one production level to another. To the extent that these expectations are made on the basis of past prices, then the volatility of production depends on the degree to which belief is placed in the information content of these past prices. Thus in a situation where past prices have fluctuated, future production will fluctuate more if producers believe such price information is meaningful. In as far as the improvement of information gathering occurring with the fall of information costs is believed by producers to give higher quality information, then production may fluctuate more than before on the basis of the same price changes. If fluctuating exchange rates have less information content than before (so that producers give less weight to them in their formation of price expectations), then production fluctuations may decline for exchange rate fluctuations of a given magnitude. Although other variations on this theme can be mentioned, this approach does not seem promising to tell us how price and quantity volatility has changed.
- **Market structure:** It is often argued that prices are most volatile under perfect competition and that, as the structure of industry becomes more oligopolistic, prices become more "administered" and stable, remaining on a rough plateau for long peri-

ods and then taking discrete jumps to another plateau. This theory, which has been associated with the name of Gardiner C. Means to explain industrial prices, has been challenged both theoretically (Carlton, 1989) and empirically (Stigler and Kindahl, 1970). Carlton (1986) has reanalyzed the Stigler–Kindahl data and obtained more nuanced results.

For the commodities in my sample, the evidence of increasing cartellization over the long run is thin. Of course, cartels have appeared in the short run for a number of commodities, but few maintain their effectiveness over the long-term. I should add that the evidence of increasing competitiveness is also thin. When examining the raw price data for the 1950s and 1960s, one does find a constant nominal price lasting for many years for certain commodities such as phosphate rock, a pattern not found for the 1970s and 1980s.

Changes in competitiveness undoubtedly influenced the degree of volatility of some commodities. Nevertheless, this factor could not have had a significant influence on the entire index.

- **External shocks:** The change in price volatility could be caused by increased shocks to the system that do not influence production. Although basic commodity prices are sensitive to business-cycle conditions and to other exogenous shocks, world business cycles do not seem to have become more pronounced. It might be argued that other shocks to the system, induced by governmental policy, weather, or political events, may have increased over time and, as a result, may have induced greater volatility to the economy as a whole and to prices in particular, this also does not seem likely. More specifically, the data in Table 7.5 showing volatility of the real U.S. GDP as well as the combined GDP of 31 nations in the world show no significant trend over time. Although this might explain why production volatility of the commodities did not increase, this explanation must be ruled out to explain the volatility of commodity prices.
- **Trade barriers:** The change in price volatility might have been caused by some change in trade barriers. Although certain trade barriers in the international market have increased, a market narrowing process that increases world price volatility, has occurred more often in the trade of agricultural goods, rather than the other types of basic commodities shown in the tables. Further, the role of international futures or forward markets appears to have increased, not decreased, so that this could not have caused the increase in price volatility. Moreover, such arguments explain nothing about the relative stability of production volatility.
- **Other factors:** A variety of other factors such as a change in the degree of speculation can be mentioned, but I could find no evidence to suggest that they might have played an important role. The price volatility might have also arisen from some interaction with trends in the real prices of commodities. However, a regression with these variables shows little relation between the trend of real prices of particular commodities and their volatility. Almost 70 percent of the series had a downward trend in deflated prices and there was some tendency, albeit not statistically significant, for price volatility to be greater when the trend of relative prices was declining. But no matter how skillfully the variables are transformed and dummy variables introduced into the regressions to explain price volatility, no more than about one-sixth of the variance could ever be explained. This explanation, of course, says nothing about production volatility.

Volatility of exchange rates and prices of internationally traded commodities: Rudiger Dornbusch (1985) has carefully specified the relation between volatility of exchange rates and the prices of internationally traded goods. His argument assumes a three-country world with a commodity exporter (country EX), a commodity importer (country IM), and the United States, which can either export or import commodities and in whose currency all basic commodity prices are denominated. He outlines three situations:

(a) If the dollar appreciates and the other two currencies remain in fixed proportion, the dollar price of the commodity will fall. This is because the initial rise in dollar prices occurring with the appreciation will result in country IM reducing its imports and substituting a domestic commodity for the higher dollar priced import. If the United States is an exporter of the commodity, country IM will also increase its imports from country EX and reduce them from the United States. Although these increased exports may raise the marginal costs of production in country EX, it is unlikely that the rise in marginal costs will be greater than the amount of the appreciation, so that the dollar price will remain higher (even while the price in currency EX is also higher). If the United States is an importer, it will increase its imports from country EX, since the commodity is relatively cheaper, while reducing its own production. Again, it is unlikely that the increase in marginal costs of country EX will offset the impact of the appreciation. From a similar argument it can be shown that a depreciation of the dollar, with the currency rates of the other two countries remaining the same, will result in a fall in the dollar price of the commodity. If the appreciation in the U.S. currency is caused by a rise in the interest rate, or another element increasing the cost of raw material production, then the appreciation of the currency is associated with a change of basic commodity prices through the supply side as well (Schwartz, 1986).

(b) If the currency of country EX appreciates vis-à-vis the dollar and the currency of country IM, the dollar price of the commodity will rise. If the U.S. is an importer, country IM will be paying a higher dollar price to country EX and, while the United States will be importing less from EX and producing more, its marginal (dollar) costs of production will rise. If the United States is an exporter, country IM will import less from country EX and more from the United States. Although the shift in the demand curve for country EX's exports will shift so that the effects of the appreciation are partially offset, the marginal (dollar) costs of production in the United States will rise so that the overall dollar price remains higher. From a similar argument it can be shown that a depreciation of the currency of country EX will result in a fall in the dollar price.

(c) If the currency of country IM appreciates vis-à-vis the dollar and the currency of country EX, the dollar price of the commodity will rise. This is because it will appear to consumers in country IM that the supply curve has shifted downward and they will import more, thus raising the marginal costs (measured in dollars) of country EX and the United States as well if it is an exporter. If the United States is an importer the dollar price will still rise, caused by the increase of demand by country IM of the commodity exports from country EX.

Detailed results of the calculations

Table A.20 presents the results of the exchange rate. In this, as in the following tables, I measure volatility without making any strong assumptions about long-run price changes by measuring volatility against a moving average exchange rate over several years. More specifically, I first calculate five-year moving averages of the exchange rate (in the other tables, averages of price or quantity of each good in question); then I compute the average of the squared percentage variations of the actual exchange rate from this "standard" exchange rate for a set of five-year periods; and finally I take a square root so that the results represent a statistic similar to a coefficient of

Table A.20. *Annual volatility of dollar exchange rates*

	Average percentage deviations from a 5-year moving average (%)					
	1950–69 Nominal E.R.	1970–9 Nominal E.R.	1980–9 Nominal E.R.	1950–69 Real E.R.	1970–9 Real E.R.	1980–9 Real E.R.
Canada	2.0	2.2	2.5	2.7	3.0	3.1
Mexico	4.5	8.3	29.7	4.8	6.5	15.7
Japan	2.9	7.0	8.2	1.5	7.2	8.9
Australia	1.5	5.0	6.0	2.4	6.1	6.5
Belgium	1.2	5.0	10.4	1.3	5.1	10.5
France	3.2	6.1	9.9	3.0	6.0	9.8
Germany	1.4	5.1	9.9	2.1	5.4	10.8
Italy	1.1	6.1	9.6	1.4	4.7	9.6
Netherlands	3.1	4.9	10.1	1.7	5.0	10.2
United Kingdom	3.6	5.9	7.4	4.6	5.0	8.6
Saudi Arabia	2.9	2.7	0.7	n.a.	15.1	8.0
Hong Kong	1.7	2.4	3.8	2.0	3.5	4.9
South Korea	19.8	5.7	4.4	17.3	5.2	3.8
Taiwan	7.4	1.2	3.7	8.6	6.0	12.8
India	4.9	2.4	3.7	4.4	5.3	4.2
USA (weighted)	.7	2.2	18.3	2.7	2.1	6.6
USA (weighted excluding Mexico)	.6	2.2	4.1	2.9	2.1	4.6

Notes: The exchange rate data come from various issues of International Monetary Fund (annual) and from the CD-ROM of the basic IFS data; the GDP deflators came from World Bank (irregular, various issues); OECD (irregular, various editions); and, for particular nations, from national sources.

variation. For "real" exchange rate changes, I deflate by an index of the ratios of the GDP deflators for the country under examination and the United States. This measurement of volatility, it should be noted, is somewhat different from that employed in Table 5.4 but it is, I believe, more suited for current price data.

The statistic of volatility is analogous to a coefficient of variation and is calculated in the manner described in the text. For the real exchange rates, the nominal exchange rates were deflated by an index representing the ratio of the GDP deflators of the United States and the country involved. For the United States, the indices of exchange rates for each country (with 1970 = 1.000) were weighted by the average share of U.S. exports and imports with those countries and the weights were changed to correspond with the opening year of each decade. Because few countries published data for the earliest and latest years, the averages are calculated from 1951 through 1988, rather than 1950 through 1989. Because Mexico has a relatively high weight and manifests extremely high currency fluctuations, the index is calculated both with and without that nation.

In Table A.21 I present the results of the calculations of volatility of prices of internationally traded basic materials.

Finally, in Table A.22 I give the results of the calculations of the volatility of production of internationally traded basic materials.

Table A.21. *Annual price volatility of basic commodities*

	Number of products	Average percentage deviation of prices from a 5-year moving average (%)							
		1950–4	1955–9	1960–4	1965–9	1970–4	1975–9	1980–4	1985–9
Current prices									
Crops	14	8.3	6.2	12.1	9.6	25.1	14.6	17.7	15.7
Animal products	5	15.3	12.2	11.3	13.8	25.0	20.4	9.2	14.9
Tree and forest products	14	16.7	10.3	6.2	9.7	17.6	16.4	14.8	14.2
Raw materials	12	7.7	7.8	4.4	5.5	16.0	12.4	11.2	13.0
Fuels	3	2.7	3.1	1.0	2.5	13.7	11.1	8.9	11.9
Fishery products	7	13.5	9.0	8.5	8.3	15.4	13.2	11.2	9.8
All basic commodities	55	9.8	7.5	7.0	7.9	19.3	14.4	13.1	13.9
All basic commodities except fishery products	48	9.7	7.4	7.0	7.8	19.4	14.5	13.2	14.0
Deflated prices									
Crops	14	8.2	6.2	12.2	9.7	25.0	14.2	17.6	15.4
Animal products	5	14.7	12.4	11.2	13.9	24.6	21.4	10.0	15.3
Tree and forest products	14	16.5	10.3	6.3	9.6	17.2	16.6	15.0	14.1
Raw materials	12	7.3	7.7	4.4	5.3	15.6	11.9	11.3	13.2
Fuels	3	2.8	2.8	1.1	2.0	12.3	9.6	8.3	11.6
Fishery products	7	12.4	9.0	8.4	8.1	15.9	13.7	10.9	9.9
All basic commodities	55	9.6	7.4	7.1	7.7	18.8	14.1	13.1	13.8
All basic commodities except fishery products	48	9.5	7.4	7.0	7.7	18.9	14.1	13.2	13.9

Notes: For each year the prices are annual averages. The constant prices are current prices deflated by GDP deflator.
The price data come from International Monetary Fund (annual, various issues); from the CD-ROM of the basic IFS data; and from U.S. Department of Commerce, Bureau of the Census (annual-b, various years); the value weights come from United Nations (1978), supplemented for several crops by data from Food and Agricultural Organization (annual-a, 1977) and, for fishery products, from rough estimates made on the basis of data contained in Food and Agricultural Organization (annual-b, 1978), Volumes 44 and 45.

Table A.22. *Annual production volatility of basic commodities and of several aggregate series*

	Number of products	Average percentage deviation of prices from a 5-year moving average (%)							
		1950-4	1955-9	1960-4	1965-9	1970-4	1975-9	1980-4	1985-9
Crops	13	n.a.	n.a.	3.9	3.5	3.7	4.0	5.6	4.7
Animal products	5	n.a.	n.a.	1.4	1.5	2.0	1.5	1.0	.6
Tree and forest products	14	n.a.	n.a.	3.8	3.1	4.5	4.7	3.9	8.2
Raw materials	11	n.a.	n.a.	3.3	2.6	2.4	3.2	2.9	4.5
Fuels	3	5.0	2.6	1.5	1.9	1.4	1.8	2.1	1.7
All commodities	46	n.a.	n.a.	3.6	3.0	2.6	3.2	3.3	3.7
U.S. GDP volume	—	2.1	1.4	.8	1.0	1.9	1.9	1.8	.8
Combined GDP volume, 31 nations	—	.9	1.1	1.2	.8	1.2	1.1	1.2	.6

Notes: The statistics of production volatility are calculated in the same manner as in Table A.21 and A.22. The various series are also weighted by the same weights.

For the agricultural commodities, the basic data come from FAO Agrostat computer disks. For 1958 through 1961 these series were supplemented by data drawn from FAO (annual-a) and FAO (annual-c). The raw material and fuel data come primarily from various issues of United Nations (annual-b), supplemented for fuels by United Nations (1976). In most cases the series had to be spliced together to achieve consistency.

For the U.S. GDP the data come from U.S. Council of Economic Advisors (annual, 1992) and U.S. Department of Commerce, Bureau of Economic Analysis (annual, 1986), Table 1.6. The 31 nations include fifteen OECD nations plus Brazil, China, India, Indonesia, and Mexico; their combined GDP is calculated by summing the individual GDPs calculated in international dollars (chain index). The basic data come from a disk obtained from the NBER and prepared by Robert Summers and Alan Heston (1991). The GDP data were supplemented for 1988–91 by data from IMF (monthly, October 1992) and, for 1948–50, from a CD-ROM version of the same data.

Notes to Chapter 8

Note 8.1: Internationalization of the U.S. economy

Internationalization is a broad concept covering such phenomena as openness, market integration, and interdependence. The latter concept, in turn, focuses on structural interdependence, mutual dependence or vulnerability, correlation of economic shocks, and policy interdependence. These various concepts have exact yet different meanings and a given set of economic events may have implications for several of them. Thus, according to one definition, such events may indicate internationalization has increased; while, according to another definition, internationalization has decreased.

The purpose of this exercise is to supplement the qualitative discussions in Chapters 8 and 10 by examining briefly some evidence of trends in the internationalization of the United States. In the following discussion I generally follow the explication of concepts provided by Cooper (1985).

Openness: This phenomenon is usually approached in terms of the relative importance of exports or imports in the economy as a whole. An extensive discussion of this problem occurs in the first section of Chapter 8. But the concept can also refer to immigration and emigration (the former receives attention in Chapter 2) and the flow of capital (which receives brief attention in Chapter 5).

Market integration: As discussed in Chapter 7, market integration is usually discussed in terms of the law-of-one-price, either in its static or dynamic sense. This type of discussion, however, takes different paths, depending on the phenomena under examination. It is useful to discuss separately the markets for goods, labor, and financial.

- **Markets for goods:** As discussed in Chapter 7, although it is commonly assumed that the law-of-one-price holds for homogeneous raw materials on an international level, evidence has been offered that this is not necessarily the case, even after lags and other difficulties have been taken into account. For heterogeneous goods, the phenomenon of pricing-to-the-market acts contrary to the law-of-one-price. For instance, Krugman (1989) shows that when exchange rate changes occur, the domestic prices do not change in the same degree as the exchange rate. Furthermore, these heterogeneous goods constitute a much higher share of foreign trade than a century ago, when a large part of foreign trade consisted of raw materials or simple, standardized goods. In this special sense, the integration of world markets has diminished.
- **Markets for labor:** Clearly the law-of-one-price does not hold in its static sense and, indeed, wage differentials among nations are powerful stimuli for immigration. In a dynamic sense, wages in industrial nations have converged since World War II. As Ehrenberg (1994) emphasizes, nations have also cooperated for many years in developing common labor-market standards. Although the process was initially encouraged by the International Labour Office, in recent years much of this standardization has occurred in interregional organizations and free trade associations. Moreover, among industrialized nations, considerable institutional convergence has also occurred. Although the standardization of labor norms and institutional convergence have proceeded most rapidly in the European Community, such free trade areas as NAFTA contain provisions for a certain narrowing of the gap in labor-market norms and procedures.
- **Markets for money and other assets:** Determining whether the law-of-one-price holds for financial markets raises some difficult conceptual issues. According to a relatively standard argument [see, for instance, Herring and Litan (1995), who also summarize some of the empirical evidence], the lowest level of internationalization occurs

when interest rates for loans in a given currency such as dollars are the same in two countries. A somewhat more advanced level of internationalization occurs when interest rates in domestic currencies are similar after taking into account the forward premium of one country's currency in terms of the other. A still higher level of internationalization is achieved when equality of real interest rates occurs. The available evidence suggests that, according to these criteria, a global money market appears to be slowly emerging.

The analysis is, however, complicated by a number of difficulties. One problem is the degree to which the process of market integration is hindered by capital controls or is influenced by different taxes (see, for instance, Eichengreen, 1990). Another problem concerns problems of whether ownership risks in one country parallel those of another (discussed in several papers in Stansell, 1993). And still another difficulty arises in the impact of different and often conflicting national monetary and fiscal policies that influence these financial markets. These and other problems make empirical analysis challenging.

Although analysis of the market of assets is usually carried out in terms of asset price convergence, the topic can also be approached by examining asset ownership. In this sense, internationalization increases as a larger share of the capital of a nation is held by foreign owners and, in turn, foreign assets constitute a larger share of domestic portfolios. Complete integration of asset markets occurs when investors are completely indifferent as to the nation in which their investments are located. Among other things, this implies that the share of a portfolio in securities of an investor's own country is inversely related to the size of the country in which the investor lives.

A very slow trend in this direction is occurring. Golub (1990) shows that the average share of foreign assets to total domestic assets held (both equities and bonds) slowly rose in most of the 12 nations under investigation between the 1970s and the first half of the 1980s. Some data for the United States on the foreign asset ownership and ownership by foreigners of American assets are presented in Table 5.1.

Interdependence: Interdependence refers to the influence on the margin that one economy has on another. Cooper (1985) discusses four types of phenomena that reflect such interdependence in different ways.

- **Structural interdependence:** This refers to the impact that one economy has on another through trade and is sometimes designated as "sensitivity interdependence." An important aspect of such structural interdependence is reflected in the price and income elasticities of exports and imports, which appear to have increased in the United States in the post–World War II period. Some evidence on this matter is presented in Table A.23.

  The estimates for the income elasticities of the U.S. demand for imports and the foreign demand for U.S. exports are relatively unsophisticated. They suggest that the income elasticities of both imports and exports (the latter are calculated with regard to the combined GDP of the United State's largest trade partners) have become greater than unity and that these elasticities have increased over time.

  The price elasticities, derived in a more sophisticated manner, show that for imports, the price elasticity has generally increased. For exports, the pattern is irregular and several explanations might be offered. For instance, since multinational firms account for most U.S. exports, the problem may lie in the different trade-offs between changing exports from U.S. plants or changing production of foreign plants that they have made when the U.S. dollar has changed over the years.

- **Mutual dependence or vulnerability:** This concept refers to a situation in which a country is vulnerable to the economic actions of another. It focuses, for instance, on

Table A.23. *Selected elasticities of U.S. exports and imports*

	1948	1960	1970	1980	1987
Income elasticities:					
U.S. import demand	.908	.957	.997	1.037	1.065
Demand for U.S. exports	1.09	1.17	1.23	1.29	1.35
Price elasticities:					
U.S. import demand	−.183	−.404	−.593	−.803	−.842
U.S. export supply	2.203	2.392	1.853	.859	1.418

Notes: The price elasticity calculations come from Kohli (1990) and are "own-price elasticities." For determining the income elasticity of demand for U.S. imports and exports for the period from 1950 through 1990, the formulae are (with standard errors in parentheses):

$$Im = -2.66 + 0.214\ ImPr_{t-1} + .716\ Y_{t-1} - .00725\ t*ImPr_{t-1} + .00401\ t*Y_{t-1}$$
$$(1.45)\quad(.499)\qquad(.230)\qquad(.00695)\qquad\qquad(.00069)$$
$$Ex = 5.27 - 10.93\ WY_{t-1} + .00618\ t*WY_{t-1}$$
$$(.017)\quad(4.08)\qquad(.00207)$$

Im = logarithm imports at constant prices
Ex = logarithm export at constant prices
$ImPr$ = logarithm of index of import prices relative to GDP prices
Y = logarithm GDP at constant prices
WY = logarithm of trade weighted GDPs of fifteen largest U.S. trade partners
t = year

For the import equation, the calculated price elasticities are quite similar to those of Kohli for the early years, but rise at a slower rate. For exports a difficult problem arose concerning the proper prices to use. In the regression above I have used only world GDP; measures of the real exchange rate or of a modified real exchange rate in which the U.S. export price index, rather than GDP index, is used to calculate the real exchange rate yielded about the same income elasticities; except for the latter price variable, the estimated price elasticities made little sense.

The data on U.S. imports, exports, and GDP come from U.S. Council of Economic Advisors (annual 1990, 1991) and from U.S. Department of Commerce, Bureau of the Census (1970, 1979, 1985). Other U.S. data come from U.S. Department of Commerce, Bureau of Economic Analysis (1986). The fifteen nations used to construct the exchange rate and world GDP indices are Australia, Belgium, Canada, France, West Germany, Hong Kong, South Korea, India, Italy, Japan, Mexico, Netherlands, Saudi Arabia, Taiwan, and the United Kingdom. These indices were reweighted every ten years to take into accounts shifts in trade. The national account data come from OECD (irregular, 1970, 1992) and, for the non-OECD nations, from various World Bank, United Nations, and, when necessary, national sources. The exchange rate data come from International Monetary Fund (monthly).

how costly it would be for a country to do without the transactions with another, even after a period of adjustment. It is multidimensional and, moreover, is difficult to measure without examining highly detailed microdata. Determination of raw materials vulnerability is, nevertheless, somewhat easier since it allows a rough picture to be gained without making such detailed estimations. Some relevant data and discussion on this matter can be found in the discussion on openness in Chapter 8.

Table A.24. *Correlation of fluctuations from growth trends of the United States with other G-7 nations (coefficients of determination)*

	Canada	France	Germany	Italy	Japan	U.K.	Total G-7 excluding U.S.
1950–1969	.5640	.3284	.1689	.2617	.5051	.3776	.4473
1970–1989	.3329	.3399	.3967	.2647	.3251	.6936	.6204

Notes: For the 40 year series for the each country, as well as for the entire G-7 bloc excluding the United States, I first determined the long-term trend of the GDP by calculating a regression of the following form: $\log Y_t = a + b\,T + cT^2$. Then I regressed the ratio of the regression residuals as a percentage of forecasted GDP of each country with that of the United States.

The data came from OECD (1970, 1991), supplemented for several early years for Italy and Japan by other sources. The weights for the overall index are the dollar value of the GDP for 1970, as found in the computer disks accompanying Summers and Heston (1988).

- **Parallel shocks:** According to this definition, interdependence increases according to the degree to which economies are subject to the same shocks, whether these shocks occur exogenously or are transmitted from one country to another. Within the United States, for instance, it has been found that the single most important variable explaining the level of aggregative economic activity in individual states is the level for the nation as a whole. This meaning of interdependency implies that the business cycles of particular nations are increasingly correlated with those of other nations.

One way of measuring this phenomenon is to determine whether the fluctuations around the trend growth in various nations are correlated, an exercise carried out in Table A.24. For simplicity I have chosen the G-7 nations as the basis of comparison because they represent America's largest trade partners. In comparing these correlations for the twenty years between 1950 and 1970 with the twenty years between 1970 and 1990, two conclusions can be quickly drawn. Between individual countries and the United States, no conclusions can be drawn: for two nations (Germany and the United Kingdom), such similarity in the pattern of economic fluctuations increased; for two other nations (France and Italy), no great change occurred; and for two nations (Canada and Japan) the similarity of business cycle patterns decreased. For the G-7 nations as a whole, however, the patterns of fluctuations became considerably more similar and, in this sense, interdependence increased.

Policy interdependence: Two distinct notions of interdependence are involved here. The concept can imply that there is similarity in the objectives of policy, that is, that one country becomes increasingly concerned about country B attaining some policy target. A dramatic case occurs in a mutual defense alliance, where the security of all nations depends on each fulfilling certain tasks. In the sphere of economics, adverse economic events in one country can have a strongly negative impact on economic events in another nation so that one nation has an important interest in the success of the other. The concept of policy interdependence can also imply that the nations actually coordinate particular economic policies. For instance, the G-7 nations have tried to coordinate exchange and monetary policy; and the major thrust of the Economic Community is to coordinate a much broader spectrum of economic policies as well.

It is difficult to quantify this type of integration. Most importantly, most of the evidence is of a qualitative nature that involves the creation and functioning of economic institutions and policy making. The most relevant evidence includes the actions of various international or intranational organizations such as the GATT, the IMF, the European Union, or specialized agencies such as

Table A.25. *Direction of U.S. merchandise trade (%)*

	1929	1939	1950	1960	1970	1980	1988
Exports:							
All industrial nations	73.9	68.0	58.7	65.1	70.0	61.0	65.0
Canada	18.4	15.4	19.8	18.5	21.0	16.0	21.6
Japan	5.0	7.3	4.1	7.0	10.8	9.4	11.8
Other	50.4	45.3	34.8	39.6	38.2	35.6	31.6
Developing countries	26.1	32.0	41.3	34.9	30.0	39.0	35.0
Mexico	2.6	2.6	5.1	4.0	3.9	6.9	6.4
Other NICs	2.5	3.1	5.0	4.1	6.1	8.6	11.7
Other	21.0	26.3	31.2	26.7	20.0	23.5	16.9
Note: Canada and Mexico	21.0	18.0	25.0	22.6	25.0	22.9	28.1
Imports:							
All industrial nations	53.0	50.6	44.5	59.3	73.8	51.8	63.4
Canada	11.4	14.7	22.1	19.8	27.8	16.9	18.3
Japan	9.8	6.9	2.1	7.8	14.7	12.5	20.4
Other	31.8	29.0	20.3	31.6	31.3	22.3	24.7
Developing countries	47.0	49.4	55.5	40.7	26.2	48.2	36.6
Mexico	2.7	2.4	3.6	3.0	3.1	5.1	5.3
Other NICs	5.0	4.8	8.2	5.0	6.5	8.7	16.4
Other	39.3	42.2	43.8	32.7	16.6	34.4	14.9
Note: Canada and Mexico	14.1	17.1	25.7	22.8	30.8	22.1	23.6

Notes: Industrial countries include all nations in Europe plus Australia, Canada, Japan, New Zealand, and South Africa. The NICs (newly industrialized countries) include Brazil, Hong Kong, Korea (South), Mexico, Singapore, and Hong Kong.
The data come from U.S. Department of Commerce, Bureau of the Census (1975) plus various issues of U.S. Department of Commerce, Bureau of the Census (annual-b).

WHO, FAO, the Bank for International Settlements, or the International Organization for Standardization. But also of great importance are the more informal arrangements such as the G-7 meetings or the various bilateral or multilateral meetings called for special purposes. For analyzing changes in internationalization, it is important to focus on what these various bodies and meetings actually accomplish, in contrast to public declarations of intention.

The attempts to coordinate policy appear to be increasing, although the success of such endeavors can be disputed. This topic has received wide discussion in the economic literature. In recent years it has been the focus of the analysis of "shallow" versus "deep" integration, where the former refers to arrangements focusing primarily on trade and finance, while the latter refers to much closer coordination of policy, regulations, and institutions.

Note 8.2: The direction of trade

The direction of trade can also influence the complexity of domestic production. If U.S. exports turn more toward the developing nations, then it seems likely that the nation would be exporting less technologically complex goods than if the direction of trade turned more toward Europe. Changes in the direction of U.S. trade thus deserve a quick glance and the relevant data are presented in Table A.25.

Several aspects of data deserve mention. The bulk of U.S. trade has always been carried out with industrial nations and, although these shares have jumped around considerably from decade to decade, the relative importance of the industrial nations is slowly rising for imports and is roughly constant for exports. Moreover, within the developing nations, the share of U.S. trade with the NICs (newly industrialized countries) has grown very fast, while U.S. trade with other developing nations has fallen, particularly for imports. Trade with Canada and Mexico, the immediate neighbors of the United States, has remained at roughly 25 percent of both imports and exports since the 1950s; no historical increase in across-border trade seems to underlie the drive for a three-nation free-trade area.

Note 8.3: Additional data on job characteristics and trade

Table A.26. *Job characteristics of manufacturing production and trade*

	Total production	Exports	Imports	Total production	Exports	Imports
	1958: 1958 labor force weights			1982: 1982 labor force weights		
Data skills	3.69	4.07	3.33	3.97	4.51	3.82
General educational development	4.35	4.59	4.10	4.41	4.69	4.21
Specific vocational preparation	4.58	4.87	4.32	4.70	5.01	4.50
Skills with things	4.38	4.74	4.22	4.49	4.79	4.70
Strength required	3.61	3.56	3.75	3.40	3.24	3.26
Physical demands	4.84	4.95	4.91	4.73	4.72	4.71
Adverse environmental conditions	1.20	1.20	1.31	1.17	1.10	1.15
Total physical demands	1.88	1.87	2.03	1.77	1.69	1.68
Undesirable working conditions	.36	.32	.42	.35	.28	.32

Notes: Estimating procedures are described in the text; the scales have been transformed to range from 0 (low) to 10 (high). The particular occupational characteristics are discussed briefly in the text and more thoroughly in various articles in Miller et al. (1980). The data skills variable ranges from comparing and copying to coordinating and synthesizing. The specific vocational preparation variable ranges from short demonstration to over ten years. The skill with things ranges from handling and feeding to precision working and setting up. The strength variable ranges from "sedentary" to very heavy work. The physical demands variable is a composite variable taking into account stooping, kneeling, crouching, handling, and so forth. The adverse environmental conditions is a similar composite variable. The total physical demands and the undesirable working conditions variables are both composite variables resulting from a factor analysis and are highly correlated to some of the variables above them in the list. To achieve greater comparability, the 1982 estimates are calculated on the basis on the bases of the 1958 industrial classification.

Table A.27. *Disaggregated change in job characteristics of manufacturing production and trade*

Part A: Absolute levels

Data set W	Total production	Exports	Imports	Data set X	Total production	Exports	Imports
	1958: 1958 labor force weights				1982: 1982 labor force weights		
Substantive skills	3.35	3.60	3.10		3.48	3.82	3.31
General educational development	4.35	4.59	4.10		4.41	4.69	4.21
Interaction skills	1.44	1.43	1.35		1.50	1.64	1.50
Motor skills	5.38	5.55	5.29		5.34	5.40	5.38

Data set Y				Data set Z			
	1958: 1982 labor force weights				1982: 1958 labor force weights		
Substantive skills	3.45	3.74	3.25		3.40	3.74	3.21
General educational development	4.44	4.70	4.24		4.31	4.62	4.10
Interaction skills	1.46	1.46	1.32		1.55	1.60	1.52
Motor skills	5.42	5.59	5.44		5.30	5.40	5.21

Part B: Percentage changes representing shifts in production methods reflected by changes in occupational mix

	Data set Y/Data set W			Data set X/Data set Z		
Substantive skills	+3.0%	+3.9%	+4.8%	+2.4%	+2.1%	+3.1%
General educational development	+2.1	+2.4	+3.4	+2.3	+1.5	+2.7
Interaction skills	+1.4	+2.1	−2.2	−3.2	+2.5	−1.3
Motor skills	+0.7	+0.7	+2.8	+0.8	0.0	+3.3

Part C: Percentage changes representing shifts in industrial (or trade) mix

	Data set Z/Data set W			Data set X/Data set Y		
Substantive skills	+1.5%	+3.9%	+3.5%	+0.9%	+2.1%	+1.8%
General educational development	−0.9	+0.7	0.0	−0.7	−0.2	−0.7
Interaction skills	+7.6	+11.9	+12.6	+2.7	+12.3	+13.6
Motor skills	−1.5	−2.7	−1.5	−1.5	−3.4	−1.1

Part D: Percentage changes representing shifts in both industrial and occupational methods

	Data set X/Data set W		
Substantive skills	+3.9%	+6.1	+6.8
General educational development	+1.4	+2.2	+2.7
Interaction skills	+4.2	+14.7	+11.1
Motor skills	−0.7	−2.7	+1.7

Notes: The scales have been transformed to range from 0 (low) to 10 (high). The various occupational skills are discussed in the text. To achieve greater comparability, the 1982 estimates are calculated on the bases of the 1958 industrial classification.

Note 8.4: Additional data on competitiveness

Table A.28. *Changes in competitiveness of selected U.S. manufacturing industries, 1958–82 (%)*

SIC number	Industry	Net exports as a percent of production			Average annual growth of:	
					Production	Total factor production
Greatest increases in net exports		1958	1982	Change		
3721	Aircraft	8.1	59.5	51.4	1.7	1.2
2611	Pulp mills	−27.9	−3.1	24.9	3.2	1.0
3643	Current carrying wiring devices	5.1	29.5	24.4	1.3	−1.2
3829	Miscellaneous measuring and controlling devices	20.2	43.7	23.6	n.a.	n.a.
3728	Aircraft and space vehicle equipment	5.0	26.5	21.5	.6	.1
2411	Logging camp products	−1.9	18.8	20.7	4.0	2.3
3511	Turbines and turbine generator sets	7.0	27.5	20.5	.5	−.7
3825	Instruments to measure electricity	4.8	23.2	18.4	4.6	−.2
3573	Electronic computing equipment	4.9	17.3	12.4	20.5	12.9
3533	Oil field machinery	36.2	48.3	12.2	6.0	.2
Greatest decreases in net exports						
3574	Calculating and accounting machines	2.9	−88.4	−91.3	n.a.	n.a.
3651	Radio and TV receiving set	3.4	−82.9	−86.3	7.0	5.9
3171	Women's handbags and purses	−2.1	−76.8	−74.8	1.5	2.7
3873	Watches, clocks, and watch cases	−14.8	−74.2	−59.4	2.3	4.3
3552	Textile machinery	15.6	−35.5	−51.0	−.5	1.8
3144	Women's footwear except athletic	−.9	−46.1	−45.1	−1.1	1.2
3161	Luggage	−4.3	−47.0	−42.7	2.1	2.0
3021	Rubber and plastic footwear	−5.5	−47.3	−41.8	7	1.6
3811	Engineering and scientific instruments	3.7	−30.5	−34.2	1.6	1.1
2271	Woven carpets and rugs	−.7	−32.8	−32.2	−4.8	2.4

Note: n.a. = not available.

Ratios of net exports (exports minus imports, so that a negative number indicates net imports) to production were calculated for 431 four-digit industries; the industries were then arranged according to the changes in these ratios. For the table, only those industries with 15,000 or more workers in either 1958 or 1982 were selected. The trade data were supplied from Laurence Katz from the NBER sample described by Abowd (1991); the production data are unofficial calculations of the U.S. Department of Labor, Bureau of Labor Statistics; the total factor productivity data were calculated from weighted averages of labor supply and capital stock in each industry; the capital stock data were supplied by the U.S. Department of Commerce, Office of Business Economics. More details of the data are provided in Appendix A.5.

Table A.29. *Important industries with the greatest prediction errors for changes in competitiveness*

SIC number	Industry	Change in net exports (%)		Prediction errors (%)	Average annual growth of:	
		Actual	Predicted		Production	Total factor productivity
Greatest negative prediction errors (most overoptimistic estimates of changes in competitiveness)						
3651	Radio and TV receiving sets	−86.3	−9.9	−76.4	7.0	5.9
3574	Calculating and accounting machines	−91.3	−29.1	−62.2	n.a.	n.a.
3171	Women's handbags and purses	−74.8	−17.3	−57.5	1.5	2.7
3873	Watches, clocks and watch cases	−59.4	−5.0	−54.4	2.3	4.3
3552	Textile machinery	−51.0	−6.7	−44.4	−.5	1.8
3811	Engineering and scientific instruments	−34.2	−.8	−33.4	1.6	1.1
3161	Luggage	−42.8	−15.8	−26.9	2.1	2.0
3144	Women's footwear except athletic	−45.1	−19.6	−25.6	−1.1	1.2
3281	Cut stone and stone products	−27.7	−4.3	−23.4	−.3	2.4
3795	Tank and tank components	−25.2	−2.6	−22.6	6.2	2.1
Greatest positive prediction errors (most overpessimistic estimates of changes in competitiveness)						
3721	Civilian aircraft	51.4	.1	51.3	1.7	1.2
2611	Pulp mill products	24.9	−1.1	26.0	3.2	1.0
3643	Current carrying wiring devices	24.4	−.1	24.5	1.3	−1.2
2252	Miscellaneous hosiery	.0	−22.4	22.4	n.a.	n.a.
2834	Pharmaceutical preparations	−1.2	−22.0	20.7	5.7	2.3
3728	Aircraft parts and auxiliary equipment	21.5	1.4	20.1	.6	.1
3825	Instruments to measure electricity	18.4	−1.6	20.0	4.6	−.2
2411	Logging camps products	20.7	2.5	18.2	4.0	2.3
3524	Lawn and garden equipment	10.3	−5.7	16.0	n.a.	n.a.
2341	Women's and children's underwear	−3.0	−17.9	14.8	2.0	1.9

Note: n.a. = not available.
The regression residuals (the difference between predicted and actual values) are calculated from Formula 1 in Table 8.4. Two criteria are used for including the industry in the table. First, the industries must have had 15,000 or more workers in either 1958 or 1982. Second, the regression residual in Formula 2 in Table 8.4 must be equal or greater than the predicted value, at least when the relevant data are available.

Note 8.5: Statistical notes for Chapter 8

Table 8.1: First half of table: Data from U.S. Department of Commerce (1986); *Survey of Current Business* Volumes 70, 71, and 74, July 1990, November 1991, and June 1994; and U.S. Council of Economic Advisors (annual, 1990, 1991).

Second half of table: Columns 1 and 2, my calculations from U.S. Department of Commerce, Bureau of the Census (1970) and from N.B.E.R. data (Abowd, 1991). Column 3, International Monetary Fund (annual), various issues; data for 1930s for 1938 and from IMF, December 1952. Columns 4, 5, and 6, U.S. Department of Commerce, Bureau of the Census (1975), p. 888 and U.S. Department of Commerce, Bureau of the Census (annual-b, 1991), p. 814.

Table 8.2: The underlying statistical materials come from U.S. Department of Commerce, Bureau of the Census (1970, 1979, 1985, 1994). Other data come from U.S. Department of Commerce, Bureau of Economic Analysis/Office of Business Economics (1954, 1986) and Survey of Current Business, 73 , No. 11 (November 1993).

Tables 8.3, 8.4, and A.28: The basic source of the data on exports, imports, and production in current prices according to the four-digit SIC classification is the National Bureau of Economic Analysis Immigration, Trade, and Labor Markets Data Files. This is described by John M. Abowd (1991) and I would like to thank Professor Lawrence F. Katz for giving me a copy. The sample was reduced by removing a number of industries where the industrial classification had changed so greatly that I had doubts about the comparability of the data or which were so heterogeneous that I believed the net export ratios made little sense. I also eliminated those industries in which the absolute value of either the net export ratios or the change in net exports were greater than unity; this was because these extreme values tended to dominate the regressions.

The data on production in constant prices, as well as labor hours, come from data disks supplied by the U.S. Department of Labor, Bureau of Labor Statistics. These data have not received the final imprimatur of the BLS and must be considered unofficial.

The data on gross capital stock come from data disks supplied by the U.S. Department of Commerce, Bureau of Economic Analysis.

The data on employment in various industries by level of skills come from U.S. Department of Labor, Bureau of Labor Statistics (1969 and 1981). They are for 1960 and 1978 and are presented in these publications primarily on a three-digit basis.

The total factor productivity indices were calculated by weighing indices of the growth of the gross capital stock and the growth of employment hours. The weights were determined by the relative share of labor and property income, which raised some problems since the relevant data on the shares of labor income and "other value added" from the various *Censuses of Manufactures* (U.S. Department of Commerce, Census Bureau, 1961, 1966) are different from those in the calculations of the national accounts (U.S. Department of Commerce, Bureau of Economic Analysis, 1985). The latter are given on a two-digit basis and I have adjusted the Census Bureau weights on a four-digit basis so that on a two-digit basis they add up to the BEA weights.

Ratios of R and D expenditures to sales for 1976 come from the U.S. Federal Trade Commission (1982); unfortunately, these are on a three-digit basis. More detailed ratios of R and D expenditures are calculated from the detailed 1972 input/output tables (U.S. Department of Commerce, Bureau of Economic Analysis, 1979).

Table A.30. *Distribution of federal governmental transfers*

Income class (total money income including transfers and realized capital gains)	1990: Average annual transfers/household ($)				1990 tax expenditures per household
	Social Security	Military civilian pensions	Other	Total transfers	
$10,000 and under	1,741	46	2,493	4,280	Not
$10,001–$20,000	2,751	191	2,007	4,949	known
$20,001–$30,000	2,551	375	1,658	4,583	
$30,001–$40,000	2,262	535	1,522	4,318	
$40,001–$50,000	1,787	651	1,238	3,676	
$50,001–$75,000	1,649	734	1,164	3,548	
$75,001–$100,000	1,637	1,128	1,224	3,968	
Over $100,000	1,845	1,142	1,277	4,263	
All income groups	2,147	430	1,736	4,312	$2,956

Notes: Tax expenditures are revenue losses attributable to provision in the federal tax laws that allow a special exclusion, exemption, or deduction from gross income or that provide a special credit, a preferential rate of tax, or a deferral of tax liability. They are generally higher for individuals with higher incomes.

The transfer estimates come from information privately supplied by the Congressional Budget Office. Income categories are defined in terms of "complete incomes." The income units are defined more broadly than by the Census Bureau (the Census would count three unrelated individuals living together as a household; CBO would count as three families) so that the numbers of families, especially at the low income levels, are greater than households reported by the U.S. Department of Commerce, Bureau of the Census (1991c). The tax expenditure data come from U.S. Department of Commerce, Bureau of the Census (annual-1993, p. 334), supplemented by my own estimates. For comparability with the transfer data, the average is calculated using the CBO definition of household; if the Census definition is used, the average tax expenditure per household is $3,248.

Notes to Chapter 9

Note 9.1: Particular economic features of the federal governmental sector

This research note deals with two issues: the distribution of transfers to families at different income levels and the impact of governmental regulatory expenditures on the economy.

Transfer by income level: Federal transfers by level of income can be quickly treated. Table A.30 presents data on the transfers of the federal government, divided into income group of the recipients. The meaning of these data is discussed in Chapter 9.

Costs of governmental regulations: I present data on the direct costs to the government's regulating the economy in Table 9.3. These do not, however, reflect the costs imposed on the private sector, which require the calculation of four different kinds of costs:

- **Direct compliance costs:** These include the capital expenditures for equipment required by the regulations and the current costs of operating such equipment. These costs are experienced not just by business but by consumers (for instance, catalytic converters for cars, which involve not just an initial purchase but higher gas consumption) and by government itself.
- **Process costs:** These include the paperwork burden associated with compliance and are experienced primarily by business and lower level governmental agencies. Many analysts combine these with compliance costs. Some data on such costs are available from survey results. For instance, the Office of Management and Budget estimates that about five billion hours were needed to comply with government paperwork requirements in 1988, of which more than four billion related to tax compliance (Hopkins, 1992, p. 15). If the opportunity cost of this labor is $25 an hour, this amounts to 2.6 percent of the GDP. Other analysts such as Litan and Nordhaus (1981, p. 20) argue that filling out an "income tax form is a regulatory burden in the same sense as spending time waiting for red lights to change" and exclude it from their estimates. The Litan/Nordhaus and the Hopkins estimates are the costs of regulation and are roughly comparable, once this tax compliance item is taken into account.
- **Indirect of hidden costs:** These include the reduction of production efficiency (for instance, the lower agricultural production because certain pesticides are banned); the costs of plant closings due to an inability to meet pollution standards; the costs of construction and other delays; the costs of lower economic growth because of lower investment and other responses; the costs of research and development costs for meeting regulatory standards; welfare losses to the consumer due to the higher costs of products or the inability to obtain products; and various nonmarket costs (for instance, volunteer labor for recycling). These hidden costs are particularly difficult to estimate and results vary. For instance, Denison (1985, p. 112) estimated that from 1973 to 1982, various regulations regulating pollution and worker safety and health reduced the average annual growth rate of the entire economy by .12 percentage points. Jorgenson and Wilcoxen (1990) estimated the same datum for pollution regulation alone as .19 percentage points for the 1973–85 period. And Gray (1987) estimated the cost of the Environmental Protection Agency (EPA) and the Office of Safety and Health Administration (OSHA) regulations on the growth between 1958 and 1978 of the manufacturing sector alone as .44 percentage points annually.

  If Gray's estimate held for the production of all goods and if such production were the only sector adversely influenced by regulations of OSHA and EPA, the annual growth rate of the GDP would be .17 percentage points lower. If the nongoods producing sector were influenced half as much as those sectors producing goods, the growth rate of the GDP would be .30 percentage points lower.
- **Transfer costs:** These arise when the higher costs to one population group are offset by lower costs to another group. Tariffs, for instance, raise costs to consumers, but domestic producers benefit by receiving a higher price for their goods. Most consumer safety regulations raise the cost to the consumer but, at the same time, give the consumer a higher quality product so that the consumer expenditures are transferred to the producer. Or a worker who now works in a safer environment but receives the same wage has, in effect, experienced a real wage increase. Although transfers should not be included in the cost calculations, it is often difficult to exclude them, especially in a partial-equilibrium type of analysis.

The cost estimates shown Table A.31 are very rough and, moreover, they vary considerably. Although they appear to decline between 1977 and 1988, this may be an artifact of the method of estimation since part of the estimates were based on multiples of direct costs of government regulatory activities that declined during the period.

Table A.31. *Very rough estimates of costs of federal regulation to the private sector*

			As percent of GDP
1976	Weidenbaum (1978, p. 16)	Compliance and process costs	3.7
1977	Litan and Nordhaus (1981, p.23)	Compliance and some process costs	1.8 to 4.8
1977	Hopkins (1992, p. 2)	Compliance and process costs	4.1
		Transfer costs	4.8
1988	Hahn and Hird (1991, p. 250, 56)	Compliance and process costs	1.7 to 2.3
		Transfer costs	3.5 to 4.3
1988	Hopkins (1992, p. 2)	Compliance and process costs	3.3
		Transfer costs	2.3

Notes: These data represent very rough estimates and are indicative only of gross orders of magnitude. Hopkins' data are taken from a graph and may be slightly inaccurate. His data are also presented in 1988 dollars and therefore had to be reflated with a GDP deflator. He includes paperwork costs for taxes as part of a government regulation cost, but these are excluded in the above table.

Note 9.2: Simulation model of the federal governmental sector

The simulation model is basically a set of accounting identities. It assumes smooth exponential growth of the GDP, constant ratios of the change in expenditures (or taxes) to the GDP, and a tax-GDP interaction variable reflecting a slowdown in economic growth that might occur if the tax/GDP ratio rises because of the disincentive effects. It also assumes a constant real interest rate and a monetary interest rate equal to the real interest rate plus the rate of price increase, and constant parameters.

Of course, one key behavioral variable is the percentage change in governmental expenditures as GDP increases. This reflects the changes both in the present structure of entitlement (expenditures made automatically if the recipient meets certain eligibility rules) and changes in discretionary expenditures. Similarly, the tax variable reflects the impact of both the present tax structure and future changes in this structure.

Most of the simulation runs assume that the rate of taxation does not influence economic growth. In the last set of simulations, this assumption is changed and a tax-GDP interaction variable is introduced that lowers economic growth as the ratio of tax revenues to GDP rises. More specifically, the formula employed is:

$$r_t^{GDP} = r^{base} \left[1 + Z \left(\frac{Rev_{1990}}{GDP_{1990}} - \frac{Rev_t}{G} \right) \right] + r^{PRICE}$$

where r^{GDP}_t is the rate of growth of nominal GDP; r^{base} is the "underlying real growth rate" before interaction with the rate of taxation; Rev/GDP is the ratio of tax revenues to GDP; r^{PRICE} is the rate of growth of the GDP deflator; and Z is the tax-GDP interaction variable. If the tax/GDP is .01 above the 1990 base and if the tax-GDP interaction variable is 20, this means that the real growth rate is 80 percent of what it would have been if the tax/GDP ratio had remained the same as in 1990.

Although we cannot easily predict the changes in the key variables of the model, we can investigate the quantitative impacts of a range of possible changes and the results of such an accounting exercise are presented in Table A.32. The model is calibrated using 1990 as the base point. It

Table A.32. *Simulation of interest payments and debt of federal government*

Variable that is changed (%)		Ratio of gross interest/public expenditures (%)	Ratio of gross interest/GDP (current $) (%)	Ratio of debt to GDP (current $) (%)	Ratio of expenditures to GDP (current $) (%)	Ratio of revenues to GDP (current $) ($)	Ratio of 2010 to 1990 GDP Current $	Constant $
1990	—	19.6	4.5	59.8	23.0	18.8	—	—

Base Simulation: Growth of real GDP, 2.0%; price growth, 3.5%; income elasticities of expenditure and revenue, 1.0; real interest rate, 4.0%; no interaction of taxation and GDP

Variable that is changed (%)		Ratio of gross interest/public expenditures (%)	Ratio of gross interest/GDP (current $) (%)	Ratio of debt to GDP (current $) (%)	Ratio of expenditures to GDP (current $) (%)	Ratio of revenues to GDP (current $) ($)	Ratio of 2010 to 1990 GDP Current $	Constant $
2010	—	23.2	5.3	71.0	23.0	18.8	2.92	1.49
Set of variants: Real GDP growth								
2010	1.0	26.0	6.0	79.8	23.0	18.8	2.41	1.22
2010	2.0	23.2	5.3	71.0	23.0	18.8	2.92	1.49
2010	3.0	20.7	4.8	63.6	23.0	18.8	3.52	1.81
Set of variants: Price growth								
2010	2.0	22.1	5.1	84.8	23.0	18.8	2.19	1.49
2010	3.5	23.2	5.3	71.0	23.0	18.8	2.92	1.49
2010	5.0	23.6	5.4	60.2	23.0	18.8	3.87	1.49
2010	6.5	23.6	5.4	51.7	23.0	18.8	5.11	1.49
Set of variants: Income elasticities of expenditures								
2010	0.90	20.1	4.2	55.4	20.7	18.8	2.92	1.49
2010	1.00	23.2	5.3	71.0	23.0	18.8	2.92	1.49
2010	1.10	25.8	6.6	87.7	25.5	18.8	2.92	1.49
2010	1.20	28.0	7.9	105.6	28.3	18.8	2.92	1.49
Set of variants: Income elasticities of revenues								
2010	0.90	27.3	6.3	83.7	23.0	16.9	2.92	1.49
2010	1.00	23.2	5.3	71.0	23.0	18.8	2.92	1.49
2010	1.10	18.7	4.3	57.4	23.0	20.8	2.92	1.49
2010	1.20	14.0	3.2	42.8	23.0	23.1	2.92	1.49

Set of variants: Both income elasticities of expenditures and revenues

2010	0.90	24.7	5.1	68.2	20.7	16.9	2.92	1.49
2010	1.00	22.2	5.3	63.6	23.0	18.8	2.92	1.49
2010	1.10	21.8	5.6	74.1	25.5	20.8	2.92	1.49
2010	1.20	20.5	5.8	77.4	28.3	23.3	2.92	1.49

Set of variants: Real interest rate

2010	3.0	20.1	4.6	71.0	23.0	18.8	2.92	1.49
2010	4.0	23.2	5.3	71.0	23.0	18.8	2.92	1.49
2010	5.0	26.2	6.0	71.0	23.0	18.8	2.92	1.49

Set of variants: Tax-GDP interaction variable (both expenditure and revenue elasticities = 1.1)

2010	0	21.8	5.6	74.1	25.5	20.8	2.92	1.49
2010	20	23.0	5.8	77.8	25.4	20.7	2.72	1.38
2010	40	24.2	6.1	81.3	25.2	20.6	2.55	1.29
2010	80	26.5	6.6	88.0	24.9	20.4	2.29	1.15

Note: These calculations are strictly an accounting exercise and all behavior is reflected in the assumptions that are varied. The "tax-GDP interaction variable" is defined in the text. The income or revenue elasticities are the percentage change in governmental expenditures or revenues occurring with a 1 percent increase in GDP. They results are calibrated with 1990 data from U.S. Department of Commerce, Bureau of the Census (annual-b, 1993, p. 328). From 1970 to 1990, constant GDP rose about 2.7 percent annually; and the GDP deflator, about 6.2 percent annually (ibid., p. 442). In the same time period the revenue and expenditure elasticities were, respectively, .987 and 1.098.

should be noted that the interest expenditures in the simulation results in Table A.32 are gross expenditures for 1990 and thus the 1990 figure differs from the interest payments presented in Table 9.2 in three ways: it covers only the Federal government, it is only for 1990, rather than the five-year period, and it is gross (and thus excludes interest payments to the social security system and other governmental agencies).

The results show that the faster the growth of real GDP, the lower is the interest burden both in terms of the GDP and also of total budgetary expenditures. The faster the growth of prices, the higher the interest burden (because of higher interest rates). This is partially offset by a falling ratio of debt to GDP.

The income elasticities of expenditures and revenue operate as one would expect. For instance, one set of elasticities that would balance the budget by 2010 are .9 for expenditures and 1.1 for tax revenues.

Any increase in the ratio of taxes to GDP has a cost since, as previously argued, higher levels of taxes may increase work disincentives and other distortions. It is, therefore, useful to consider what happens when the level of taxes to the GDP feeds back upon the GDP growth rate. In the last set of simulations I assume that both government expenditures and taxes increase 1.1 percent for every 1 percent increase in GDP. Tax-interaction variables of 10, 20, and 40 mean that for every 1 percent increase in the ratio of taxes to GDP, the annual real GDP growth rises respectively only 90 percent, 80 percent, and 60 percent as fast as it normally would (the "normal" real growth in this simulation is assumed to be 2 percent; the price increase of 3.5 percent is not affected). As the last column shows, real growth over the 20-year period is reduced from 49 percent to respectively 38 percent, 29 percent, and 15 percent.

It is impossible to predict accurately the political forces that will lead to a particular set of income elasticities of expenditures and taxes. My own belief is that the extension of the governmental health program, if it occurs, will lead to an income elasticity of demand of about 1.1 percent and it seems politically unlikely that the income elasticity of tax revenues will be much greater than this. (By way of contrast, the U.S. Office of Management and the Budget [1993, pp. 39, 40, 44] foresees the income elasticity of expenditures to be .67 percent between 1992 and 1998; and for taxes, 1.14 percent). If a feedback between the level of taxes and GDP growth occurs and if my tax predictions are correct, the simulation results show we have one more reason to expect a declining growth rate.

Note 9.3: Statistical notes for Chapter 9

Table 9.1: Public expenditure and labor force data come from Department of Commerce, Bureau of Economic Analysis (1982/3), supplemented by various issues of *Survey of Current Business*. Capital stock data are

Table 9.2: The data come from the U.S. Department of Commerce, Bureau of Economic Analysis, computer diskettes, June 1993, for the National Income and Product Accounts. The data are drawn specifically from Tables 3.16 and 3.17 and represent a considerable reorganization of the data. Veterans expenditures, for instance, are allocated to education, health, and general welfare. Data from these NIPA tables are not available before 1952.

Table 9.3: The data are drawn from the worksheets of Winston and Crandall (1994) and were updated for 1989 and 1990 with the aid of U.S. Office of the Budget (annual).

Table 9.4: Administration costs come from DuBoff (1993); text pages explaining law from U.S. Congress, Joint Committee on Taxation (1976, 1987); other data come from Krueger and Duncan (1993).

Notes to Chapter 10

Note 10.1: Values held by managers

To isolate different values and attitudes of managerial cultures in various countries, the Center for International Business Studies (Amstelveen, Netherlands) administered a questionnaire to 15,000 middle-upper managers who were participating in its program and who came from 15 nations. The Center posed these managers a series of administrative dilemmas and some results are presented in Table A.33. Significant differences occur between nations, and the strong individualism in many responses of the U.S. managers should be readily apparent.

Note 10.2: U.S. macroeconomic performance

Changes in the three traditional success criteria – economic growth, inflation, and unemployment – are presented in Part A of Table A.34 (pages 344–345) from 1950 through 1990. The GDP growth rates in the 1980s were below the 40-year average and the results suggest a deceleration in GDP growth. The inflation rate, as represented by the price index for the GDP, shows an irregular rise and then fall in the late 1980s. The civilian unemployment rates show a slowly rising trend, and the more thorough statistical analysis in Chapter 3 confirms these visual impressions.

The decline in growth has been attributed to many factors, of which the decline in savings and investment has received widespread attention. As a share of GDP, investment has fallen slightly (Part B, Table A.34); it is noteworthy that in constant prices this decline is not evident because the prices of investment goods have risen less rapidly than the GDP deflator. The decline in savings has been much greater, especially by individuals and the government, but such a fall in domestic saving has been partially offset by the rise in foreign saving placed in the United States. Let me add that the declining growth rate of production and the rising unemployment are not, as some such as Heilbroner (1993) have recently argued, due to secular stagnation, that is, the long-run failure to maintain aggregate demand. Rather, as I argue in Chapter 3, the secular rising rate of unemployment is due to an increasing lack of appropriate skills, which is a supply side phenomenon.

A critical important factor underlying the decelerating growth of GDP has been the deceleration in productivity, which can only in part be traced to the decline in investment. In comparison to 28 other industrial nations from 1950 through 1988, the United States experienced the most rapid deceleration of growth of labor productivity (Pryor, 1994). It is, therefore, worthwhile to attempt to disentangle some of the issues here by examining labor productivity growth in various sectors. I carry out this task by estimating quadratic trend equations of GDP per worker and extrapolating.

The results of this exercise, presented in Table A.35 (page 346), show a dramatic decline in labor productivity. Even though I do not believe that actual labor productivity growth will be negative in the decades of the 1990s and 2000s, such a mechanical exercise shows dramatically the deceleration of growth in all sectors except wholesale trade. The situation is worst in the services and, given the large relative size of the service sector (in 1990, GDP originating in services amounted to 54 percent of the total), it is clear that the services are driving the results of the calculation for the entire GDP.

But there is less in these results than meets the eye. Some growth deceleration occurring in the 1950 through 1990 period occurred because of a shift toward the services, a phenomenon that should taper off as the entry of women into the labor force tapers off, as I argue in Chapter 4. If no shift to the service sector had occurred, the growth rate of overall productivity would have been .18 percent higher per year. (This was estimated by weighing the sectoral productivity growth rates by the GDP originating in each sector in 1950.) Moreover, the estimate of a quadratic trend may not fully take into account events in the latter part of the period where productivity began to increase, particularly in the production of goods and trade. If a cubic trend calculation, rather than

Table A.33. *Value positions of managers of various nations*

1. Which position or value is more fundamental in the following alternatives? (a) A company is a system designed to perform functions and tasks in an efficient way; people are hired to fulfill these functions – and are paid for the tasks they perform. (b) A company is a group of people working together. The people have social relations with other people and with the organization. The functioning is dependent on these relations.

Tasks and function	U.S.	Sweden	U.K.	Germany	France	Japan	Social relations
	74%	56%	55%	41%	35%	29%	

2. Which position or value is more fundamental in the following alternatives? (a) The only real goal of a company is making profit. (b) A company, besides making profits, has a goal of attaining the well-being of various stakeholders, such as employees, customers, etc.

Profits only	U.S.	U.K.	Sweden	Germany	France	Japan	All stakeholders
	40%	33%	27%	24%	16%	8%	

3. Which of the two following considerations are more important to you in hiring a new employee to work in your department? (a) The new employee must have the skills, the knowledge, and a record of success in a previous job. (b) The new employee must fit into the group or team in which he/she is to work.

Individual capacity	U.S.	Germany	U.K.	France	Sweden	Japan	Fitting into team
	92%	87%	71%	57%	53%	49%	

4. Does job skill or power legitimize the boss?

Job skills	Germany	U.S.	France	Sweden	U.K.	Japan	Power
	80%	78%	75%	70%	64%	27%	

5. An employee has worked fifteen years for the company and has performed his job in a satisfactory way. For various reasons, last year the results of his work dropped to an unsatisfactory level. There are no reasons to believe the situation will improve. Which is more appropriate to view the situation? (a) Job performance should remain the criterion for dismissal, regardless of the age or the person and his previous record. (b) Because he has worked fifteen years in a satisfactory manner, the company has a responsibility for the person and should take his whole record into account.

Failed objective tive standards	U.S.	U.K.	Japan	Germany	France		Company responsibility
	77%	42%	34%	31%	26%		

6. (a) Individuals can work on their own. In this case people are pretty well their own bosses and decide things personally as they get along in the business. Such people look out for themselves and do not expect others to look out for them. (b) Another way is to work in a group in which all work together. Everyone has something to say in the decisions that are made and everyone can count on each other.

Their own boss	U.S.	Sweden	Japan	U.K.	France	Germany	In a group
	42%	41%	40%	23%	12%	12%	

7. (a) The work of a department can best be done if the individual members and the company agree on objectives, and it is then left to the individual to decide how to attain these goals. (b) The work can best be done if the manager sets the objectives and also directs the members of the department in completing the various tasks that need to be done.

Freedom within agreed objectives	France	Japan	Germany	U.S.	U.K.	Sweden	Manager sets goals and means
	88%	76%	73%	70%	67%	57%	

Source: Hampden-Turner and Trompenaars (1993). "Germany" refers to the former West Germany.

a quadratic trend calculation, is made, the annual productivity increase in the 1990s is much slower than in the 1950 to 1990 period, but it begins to recover in the first decade of the 2000s.

Moreover, the recent stagnation of labor productivity in the services, which underlies the extrapolated decline of productivity in coming decades, does not accord with our observations from life. As I emphasize in the text, the measurement of productivity changes in the services is highly problematic and, as a result, it is quite possible that the strange results of the statistical exercise in Table A.35 are being driven in part by measurement errors.

But in several parts of this study, I suggest for different reasons that economic growth might slow for factors having nothing to do with measurement error. Indeed, these factors may play the most causal role in the deceleration of the growth of labor productivity.

As noted in the text, it seems premature to say that the government knows how to deal with inflation. But barring any major supply shocks such as the oil shocks in 1970 and 1980, the necessity of controlling inflation also does not appear to be the key to predicting systemic change.

Finally, cyclical activity causing wild swings in unemployment also does not appear to be sufficiently serious to serve as an impetus for systemic change. Current discussion in the economic profession has moved far from the Marxian prediction of an ever increasing severity of the business cycle. In a series of essays, Christina Romer has presented some compelling evidence to support the notion that the severity of the business cycles, especially as measured in terms of total deviation from long-term trends, has not greatly changed in the last century. Most economists (for instance, Diebold and Rudebusch, 1992) argue that business cycles have become less severe as we have learned to tame them with fiscal and monetary policy. My own evidence on business cycles (Appendix Note 4.1) suggests that in terms of deviation from the trend, their severity has not significantly changed since the mid 1950s. This means that unemployment has not yet been influenced by the rising level of financial distress – as manifested by business failures, bank failures, personal bankruptcies, delinquent mortgages, and so forth (Chapter 5).

Note 10.3: Additional remarks on alternate scenarios for capitalism

This note expands the discussion of three scenarios for the development of U.S. capitalism that are tersely mentioned in the text: finance-capitalism, atomic-capitalism, and remodeled-capitalism. Finance-capitalism is but one of several different types of third-party capitalism, and several of these other types are briefly discussed as well.

Third-party capitalism: "Third-party capitalism" provides a label for several different types of capitalism in which institutions, rather than individual owners of the means of production, exercise major decision-making powers in the crucial productive institutions. It represents an acceleration of a particular type of structural complexity associated with an increasing separating of control and ultimate ownership and a rising importance of financial to tangible "real" assets. Several different types of third-party capitalism can be envisioned.

Finance-capitalism, American style. The most likely third-party capitalism is what can be called "finance-capitalism, American style," an economic system dominated by financial intermediaries. As argued in Chapter 6, this is a manifestation of increased structural complexity in the financial field. Finance-capitalism is consistent with the increasing world economic integration and, indeed, represents a type of convergence of American economic institutions with some nations of continental Europe and Japan. It is also consistent with a decline in social cohesiveness. In so far as finance-capitalism capital would encourage entrepreneurship by providing ready finance, it would address some aspects of the enervation of the spirit of capitalism.

As shown in Table A.36 (page 347) and discussed in greater detail in Chapter 5, financial intermediaries (pension funds, insurance companies, mutual funds, bank holding companies, and

Table A.34. Some indicators of U.S. economic performance

	1951–5	1956–60	1961–5	1966–70	1971–5	1976–80	1981–5	1986–90	1951–90
Part A: Traditional indicators, annual average percentages									
GDP growth	4.5	2.2	4.6	3.1	2.3	3.2	2.5	2.7	3.1
GDP deflator growth	2.5	2.6	1.8	4.3	7.0	7.8	5.6	3.7	4.4
Civilian unemployment	3.8	5.2	5.5	3.9	6.1	6.8	8.3	5.9	5.7
Part B: Investment, saving, and depreciation as a percent of GDP (NIPA accounts)									
Gross domestic investment	23.4	22.0	21.4	21.5	20.3	21.3	20.7	19.4	21.3
of which private	16.1	15.6	15.6	15.9	16.4	18.1	17.4	16.0	16.4
of which government	7.3	6.4	5.8	5.6	3.9	3.2	3.3	3.5	4.9
Gross saving	23.4	22.0	21.4	21.5	20.3	21.3	20.7	19.4	21.3
Personal saving	4.6	4.8	4.6	5.1	6.0	5.0	5.6	3.3	4.9
Business saving	11.3	12.0	12.3	11.6	11.9	13.3	13.5	12.8	12.3
Government saving	6.9	6.2	5.7	5.1	2.7	2.5	.4	1.1	3.8
Saving from (+), to (−) abroad	.0	−.5	−.9	−.4	−.4	.0	1.2	2.5	0.2
Statistical discrepancy	.6	−.5	−.2	.0	.2	.5	.0	−.2	.1
Depreciation	17.5	16.8	14.8	14.6	14.4	15.3	15.5	14.9	15.5
Part C: Personal saving as a percent of personal disposable income									
NIPA Accounts:									
Voluntary saving	6.7	6.7	6.6	7.3	8.4	7.1	7.7	4.6	6.9
Involuntary saving (social insurance and private pension plans)	3.0	2.7	2.7	3.1	2.8	2.5	0.4	−0.8	2.0
Total saving excluding durables	9.7	9.5	9.3	10.4	11.2	9.6	8.1	3.7	8.9
Net purchase of consumer durables	4.0	2.3	1.9	4.4	4.5	5.3	2.9	3.3	3.6
Total saving including durables	13.7	11.8	11.2	14.8	15.7	14.8	11.0	7.1	12.5

Flow of funds:

Voluntary saving, pension saving, life insurance saving	13.9	11.5	12.1	13.8	13.8	12.9	12.3	11.7	12.8
Vary and involuntary social insurance savings	16.1	13.4	14.1	16.1	15.6	14.2	13.1	13.2	14.5

Notes: In contrast to the standard national income product and income accounts (NIPA), I have added government investment (and the saving corresponding to this investment) into the estimates in the appropriate places. Depreciation includes not only depreciation from private capital but depreciation and disposal from the government capital account at current cost valuation. The personal saving percentage in Part B and Part C of the table differ because the denominators are, respectively, the GDP and personal disposable income. The various totals may not add because of rounding.

The data from the NIPA come from Department of Commerce, Bureau of Economic Analysis (1992/93) and Survey of Current Business 73, No. 112 (November 1993); the NIPA investment data come from Department of Commerce, Bureau of Economic Analysis (1993) plus my own estimate for 1990. Consumer durable data come from the same source, Table A.18, with my own estimate for 1990.

Involuntary savings includes both personal and employee contributions to social insurance (NIPA: 2.1 and 6.10) minus payouts from the OASDI and the government employees retirement benefits (NIPA: 6.11C) plus employer payments to pension and profit sharing systems and group life insurance minus benefits paid by pension and profit sharing and group life insurance (NIPA: 6.11C). This provides only a very crude measure of involuntary savings from private pension plans; it also does not apparently include private individual life insurance plans.

The flow of funds, Set 1, are calculated by the Federal Reserve Bank and come from Council of Economic Advisors (annual-1994, p. 303). Personal saving in insurance and pension funds is defined in terms of reserves of all types. Saving through nonrealized capital gains are included. Involuntary savings consists only of employer and employee contributions to the social insurance fund minus outpayments of the social insurance fund and the government employee pension fund (NIPA: Table 6.10 and 6.11).

Table A.35. *Labor productivity trends in the United States (%)*

	Extrapolations using a quadratic trend		
	1950–90	1990–2000	2000–10
Gross domestic product	+1.2%	–.3%	–.9%
Production of goods	+1.6	+.6	+.2
Agriculture, fishing, forestry	+1.4	+.6	+.3
Mining	+1.0	–4.1	–6.1
Construction	–.5	–2.2	–2.9
Manufacturing	+2.3	+1.8	+1.5
Production of goods/services	+1.6	+.6	+.2
Transportation, communication, public utilities	+2.9	+.7	–.2
Wholesale trade	+2.7	+3.0	+3.1
Retail trade	+.5	–.1	–.4
Production of services	+.6	–.7	–1.3
Finance, insurance, real estate	+.8	–1.4	–2.3
Personal and other services	+.3	–1.5	–2.2
Government	+.2	–.0	–.1

Notes: For the various sectors these represent gross product originating per full-time equivalent worker. They are derived from data for the 1950–90 period using the following regressions: $X_t = a_0 + a_1 T + a_2 T^2$, where the X is the particular variable under examination, T is the year, and the lower case letters are the calculated coefficients. The basic data come from tables in Chapter 6 of the national income and product accounts. For the gross product originating, the underlying data for 1977–90 come from the recent calculations (*Survey of Current Business* 73, No. 5, May 1993). For 1950–77 the basic data come from older estimates for earlier years that were calculated using a different methodology; these come from U.S. Department of Commerce, Bureau of Economic Analysis (1986).

The division into industries is somewhat different from that used in the calculations in Chapter 3.

other types of trusts) are holding an increasing share of financial assets, particularly corporate stocks. Focusing just on the traded corporate equities held by these intermediaries, in the mid 1990s this share is roughly 50 percent (Blair, 1994). According to data presented by Brancato (1989, p. 40), institutional investors held over 40 percent of the stock in 41 out of the top 50 firms. Furthermore, these institutional investors are highly concentrated. For instance, out of the 1,000 largest public and private pension funds, the top 25 control 37 percent of the assets. This reflects a type of separation of ultimate ownership from control, either direct or indirect, over productive assets.

As elaborated in Chapter 6, in the period from 1950 to 1990, governmental regulations and tax laws aimed at the different types of financial intermediaries limited the share of stock that these intermediaries could hold in any one enterprise and discouraged their participation in management of the affairs of the corporation. Moreover, until recently, individual financial intermediaries could not easily coordinate the exercise of their voting rights of their ownership shares to influence the corporate boards of directors without having to mount a full-scale proxy fight, which could be quite costly. Despite their potential power, most of these financial intermediaries had to be content being passive investors.

Table A.36. *Measures of the importance of financial intermediaries and ESOPs (%)*

	1951–5	1956–60	1961–5	1966–70	1971–5	1976–80	1981–5	1986–90
Financial intermediaries								
Ratio of total financial assets of financial corporations to total financial assets	26.0	26.7	28.8	30.4	33.7	34.9	36.2	39.3
Employee stock ownership plans (ESOPs)								
Employees covered by ESOPs to total employees outside of agriculture and government	n.a.	n.a.	n.a.	n.a.	n.a.	3.4	7.4	10.8

Notes: Financial asset data comes from Table 5.2 (financial intermediation ratio). The ESOP data come from U.S. Department of Commerce, Bureau of the Census (annual-b, 1992, p. 543) and a letter from the National Center for Employee Ownership. These data differ from a shorter series from the U.S. General Accounting Office (1986-b, p. 5) data, which are 5.0 percent (1976–80) and 8.4 percent (1981–5). The data on employees come from U.S. Council of Economic Advisors (annual, 1993, pp. 394–5).

This situation had some adverse consequences. Of greatest importance, many institutional investors had no permanent stake in the companies whose equities they held. Rather, these investors were judged by the return they could obtain and, if a stock was not doing well, they would sell it. Empirical evidence on this matter is, however, difficult to interpret because of the differences between long-term rhetoric of the institutional managers and the short-term actions, particularly regarding the way by which fund managers are evaluated. An interesting study of this problem is by O'Barr, Conley, and Brancato (1992), Chapter 7, who also have a discussion on the way in which financial intermediaries participate in corporate governance (Chapter 8). In many cases this, in turn, encouraged a short-term mentality by the executives of the productive enterprises so that their stock price would not be depressed and bought up by corporate raiders. Symptoms of this short-term perspective included high dividend payouts, scrimping on R and D expenditures, and reducing employee training expenses.

This strategy of stock turnover has not been available to some very large financial intermediaries such as pension funds that hold significant blocks of stock in many companies, for instance, the California Public Employees Retirement System (CalPERS). These intermediaries have been locked in and could not sell their large blocks of shares of poorly performing companies without greatly depressing market values and experiencing capital losses.

An interesting development toward American-style finance-capitalism occurred in 1990 when CalPERS started to target the 24 worst performing companies in its portfolio to influence their management. This step had some success not just in ousting poor managers but also in improving CalPERS portfolio performance (Minow, 1994). In the middle 1990s, however, the management of CalPERS appears to have lost some zest for such activities. A more important further step was a change in the regulations of the Securities and Exchange Commission in October 1992 to allow large shareholders to take collective actions against corporations without having to mount a full-scale proxy battle. This technical change has important consequences since it allows groups of pension funds to cooperate for enhancing their influence of their ownership stakes.

In the early 1990s stockholder activism, led primarily by financial intermediaries, resulted in the ousting of chief executives at IBM, Westinghouse, American Express, Kodak, General Motors, and other corporations, and this appears a harbinger of what might come. "Relationship investing" by investment banks became an important battle cry because it represents more involvement than a short-term "white-knight" fund. Their purchase of large blocs of stock, accompanied either by membership in the board of directors or greater informal long-term influence, was another aspect of the same trend. Some novel proposals were floated. For instance, Robert Monks has proposed the creation of the American equivalent of the Supervisory Boards in Germany, a council outside the Board of Directors where holders of very large blocks of stock are allowed privileged access to corporate information to improve the quality of their influence on the firm.

The development of American-style finance-capitalism is constrained in two major ways. In the mid 1990s most types of financial intermediaries are still actively discouraged by various laws and governmental regulations from playing an active role in the affairs of the companies in which they hold ownership stakes. Any easing of legal constraints would have to occur across the board for all financial intermediaries because of shifts of funds from one type of financial intermediary to other. For instance, there has been a slow shift in the pension world from defined-benefit plans, which saddle the enterprise with high liabilities in the future, to defined-contribution plans, in which the enterprise contributes to pension funds vested in each recipient – for instance, a 401(K) plan – and the individual, in turn, can place these funds in financial intermediaries such as mutual funds that operate under different regulatory regimes than the pension plans.

Moreover, the legal measures to encourage such "relationship investing" by large institutions would have to take into account that most institutional investors have few incentives to engage in this activity – the costs are high and the expertise must be developed (Blair, 1994). One study, for instance, showed that only one-fifth of the proxy fights over corporate governance in the 1990 proxy season were made by institutional investors (Gordon and Pound, 1993). This reticence reflects some of the difficulties of "relationship investing," even though recent evidence that in some types of industries large stockholding can serve as effective monitors of managerial behavior (Zeckhauser and Pound, 1990).

American-style finance-capitalism would differ from the varieties of this system that are found in Germany (discussed by such early twentieth-century Marxists as Rudolf Hilferding) or in Japan. Most importantly, it would not be centered on a single bank. Moreover, without the creation of special mechanisms, the financial intermediaries might not receive the constant stream of inside information that German and Japanese banks often receive (although the value of this information can be disputed). As a result, the representatives of the financial intermediaries would be much less informed and able to focus only on the extreme cases. American-style finance-capitalism would also not feature the interlocking directorships occurring in Japan that arise from significant ownership stakes of one corporation in another. Indeed, exponents of relationship investing have decried multiple directorships by one person since it enhances the power of management by diluting the attention any single director can focus on any one given firm. It would also not feature the significant participation in the monitoring of management by enterprise workers occurring in Germany.

Although designed for another purpose, American-style finance-capitalism would act with arguable success to combat the enervation of the capitalist spirit along a particular dimension by improving management to increase its accountability to the major shareholders. This trend would also be congruent with the internationalization of financial markets.

Such a change in the economic system does not address the information problems arising from increased structural complexity and, in addition, it might exacerbate the decline in social cohesiveness. More specifically, because the attention and expertise of large financial intermediaries are finite, they might not effectively serve as venture capitalists and, indeed, their participation might be limited to a certain set of privileged enterprises. For these enterprises, close ties with the financial intermediaries through relationship investing would not only allow some useful oversight but would also encourage and facilitate the flow of capital to them. Some smaller enterprises might be able to flourish without capital injections by such financial intermediaries, however, if they could tap specialized venture capital funds. Nevertheless, the danger would exist that such a development might strengthen already existing forces encouraging the creation of a dual economy within the productive sector: One set would be well-financed, economically progressive firms, which could afford the research and development to keep them on the technological frontier and that could maintain and further train a skilled and motivated work force. Another set would be poorly-financed, economically stagnant firms, which would find it difficult to break out of their low-level equilibrium and which would have less capable workers receiving little additional training because of lack of enterprise funds for this purpose.

I should add that some parts of the stagnant sector would not be without wealth since this sector would also include the apparently expanding underground or shadow economy that can be financed through crime. The size of the underground economy appears to be large, but its size is open to considerable dispute: for the 1980s various estimates (reported by Schoepfle et al., 1992) ranged from 2 percent to 40 percent of the GDP, with the range between 5 and 15 percent of the GDP finding the most acceptance. Carson (1984) presents various estimates for the period from 1974–81 ranging from 5 to 33 percent of the GDP. A majority of the estimates also seem to fall within the 5 to 15 percent range, exemplified by Greenfield's (1993) recent estimate of roughly 6 or 7 percent of the GDP. Although commonly believed that the underground economy has been expanding in relative importance, the evidence is controversial, for instance, the estimates provided by O'Neill (1983).

Nevertheless, it seems likely that American-style finance-capitalism might exacerbate the tendency toward a dual economy and greater economic inequality; and it would only partially address the challenges of the cultural forces previously discussed.

Corporatism. Corporatism is another type of third-party capitalism. It designates an economic system where representatives of management, government, and usually labor set certain policies for the various individual industries as a whole; individual shareholders thus exercise only very partial powers of control. I present a much more extended discussion of corporatism in Pryor (1988).

Corporatism must be fostered by the state since the policies made by the corporate bodies violate current U.S. anti-trust laws in many nations since they cover wages, prices, investments, product standards, and possibly market shares. As shown in the experience in West Europe, such corporatism can be institutionalized in different ways and, it should be added, corporatism has several definitions as well.

The introduction of any kind of corporatism in the United States does not appear likely for three reasons: First, holding other factors constant, corporatistic economies perform no better along several criteria than more traditional capitalist economies. Second, those economies featuring a high degree of corporatism have been small open economies with ethnically homogeneous populations, conditions that certainly do not describe the United States. Finally, such tripartite institutions are not necessarily stable. Often the various industrial agreements could not be maintained so that the institutions themselves eventually collapsed.

A dominant nonprofit sector. Still another type of third-party capitalism would feature a dominant nonprofit sector; their equity shares are literally owned by no one. Nonprofit enterprises, seen as the middle way between the extremes of capitalist and socialist firms, have some vocal advocates who claim that this is a way to overcome some of the disadvantages of individual share ownership. Two types of nonprofit institutions should be distinguished: 501-c3 and 501-c4 organizations (the designations refer to their tax code number), which include religious, charitable, and social welfare organizations; and other nonprofits that include labor, business, agricultural organizations, social and recreational clubs, mutual retirement and insurance funds (many of which are now going public), war veterans' organization, and so forth. According to the data I present elsewhere (Pryor, 1994c), both types are growing at roughly the same rate, but the former (called hereafter the "independent sector") account for roughly 10 times the income originating (value added) as the latter.

The data on the nonprofit sector reveal a paradoxical picture. Contributions to charities, measured as a share of national income, show no trend between the late 1950s and the late 1980s. On the other hand, GDP originating from the nonprofit sector as a share of the GDP or the income originating as a percent of national income (as well as the share of total fixed reproducible assets shown in Table 5.1) show a remarkable increase. What has happened is that the independent sector was increasingly financed both by payment for services (tuition paid to nonprofit schools or direct reimbursement for expenses paid to nonprofit hospitals) and by various levels of government. The latter have used the nonprofits as agents for their own purposes, so that we are witnessing the growth of "nonprofits for hire" (Smith and Lipsky, 1993), a phenomenon occurring in many other countries as well.

The nonprofit organizations are most active in health, education, and welfare. For instance, in 1992, 80 percent of the depreciable assets of nonprofits were held by hospitals, schools, universities, and churches (unpublished data from Department of Commerce, Bureau of Economic Analysis). The nonprofits have grown rapidly, primarily because the sectors in which they are found have grown rapidly. This can be seen from GDP originating from nonprofit organizations (NIPA Table 1.7) as a share of GDP originating from private health, education, and social organizations (NIPA Table 6.2). This ratio was roughly constant from 1951–5 to 1986–90. So a relative increase in the share of such services does not account for the growth of the nonprofits. Contrary to popular belief, the special tax status of the nonprofits does not appear to have played a significant role in this growth.

In any case, it seems highly unlikely that this type of third-party capitalism will significantly influence the operation of the economic system in the coming decades.

Atomic-capitalism. "Atomic-capitalism" is a label for an economy where production is carried out in relatively small enterprises. It represents a parallel to forces in financial markets where financial assets are stripped into their components, each of which is separately sold. It signifies a reversal of a trend of the last two centuries toward giant enterprises and a replacement of enterprise hierarchies with market transactions. In one sense this represents a decrease in structural complexity since the size distribution of enterprises becomes compressed. In another sense, however, it represents an increase in structural complexity since information flows, which previously had been confined within a single firm, are replaced by a more dense network of communication within the expanded universe of enterprises.

Several harbingers of such a development might be noted. The first is found in Tables 6.2 and A.12 showing some decreases in aggregate concentration and the average sizes of productive enterprises and establishments in the last few decades. This is supported by the survey evidence in Chapter 6 suggesting that enterprise managers plan to meet the challenges raised by ever-increasing structural complexity of the environment by simplifying procedures and processes, decentralizing, and focusing more attention to their core businesses. An obvious step is to subcontract many functions previously carried out within the firm itself. At present, for instance, many firms subcontract functions such as payroll management to outside contractors who are more familiar with the most advanced computer programs and techniques to accomplish the task, thereby allowing the firm managers to focus more on the business at hand. Some empirical evidence suggests that heavy investment in information processing encourages such a tendency (Brynjolfsson et al.,1993). Finally, various attempts by the federal government to apply different policies to different size firms (for instance, exempting small companies from particular worker-benefit requirements) encourage the unbundling of firms into smaller units.

These processes can, however, be carried much further as they have in certain areas such as certain parts of Italy and France, but not in others such as Japan (Piore and Sabel, 1984, and Lorenz, 1988). Indeed, the core firm could subcontract out research and development, design, sales, and manufacturing work to peripheral supplier firms specializing in a single technology. Moreover, the core firm need not have ownership in the peripheral firms; if it did not, it would have more freedom of action. Activities of the different firms could be coordinated by close electronic linkages to create what one software visionary, Jim Manzi (1994), calls "electronic keiretsu." These links enable the cooperating companies to pool information, skills, and technology, a sort of economic salvation by group-ware. These processes, however, demand more than electronic communication; they require trust as well, if not in society as a whole, then at least between the contractors.

The massive subcontracting envisioned, combined with a considerable decentralization, imply a mutation from a multidivisional firm to a holding company; and the replacement of a vertical hierarchy with a type of more loosely structured "network organization." It is based on the assumption that the latest information technologies have resulted in three very important shifts in relative costs and benefits: First, the costs saved by having a specialist produce a particular good or saving outweigh the costs of subcontracting (the transaction costs of negotiating and enforcing the contract). Second, the falling costs of information more than offset the rising transaction costs arising from the monitoring of quality of the good or service that reflects the increased technological complexity of the goods and services sold. Finally, the savings in administrative costs outweigh the benefits of cross-fertilization between divisions, especially regarding a core technology.

Some of these smaller enterprises might be owned by the managers and created through some type of leveraged buyout. According to the standard argument, by uniting ownership with experienced managerial abilities, this development provides the incentives for a reinvigoration of capitalism. As noted in a brief review of the evidence in Chapter 6, it is not clear that these firms perform better than other firms.

The subcontracting firms might be owned wholly or in part by the core firm, with the rest of the equity dispersed. In the first case the central firm serves as a holding company; in the second case, it retains much more freedom of action. This could lead, however, to a type of dual economy that is found to a certain extent in Japan, where the contracting firms are fiercely competing against each other and facing market risks much greater than the core firms. That is, normal market risks would be shifted from the core firm to the smaller firms on the periphery by several mechanisms. Technological shifts could quickly wipe out the comparative advantage of the peripheral firm as the core firm negotiates a new contract with another firm. Moreover, during business downturns, the core firm could employ some of its redundant workers to fulfill the tasks of the peripheral firms, thereby placing the burden of layoffs entirely on the smaller firms. By such an action the core firms, of course, can offer much more employment security than the satellite firms and thereby take advantage of the additional human capital that the workers would be willing to invest in themselves.

The wages of workers in these supplying firms would undoubtedly be lower than in the core firm (to a certain extent this has also happened in the United States). This is because they would be in more direct competition with foreign firms, rather than being sheltered under the umbrella of the domestic multidivisional firm, as the wage contour approach of Dunlop (1957) toward the labor market would suggest. Labor unions would be further weakened. Such a trend might also be quite congruent with world economic integration since it would accelerate the impulse to contract abroad for certain functions to be fulfilled by relatively low paid workers, rather than within the firm itself.

Some of these subcontracting enterprises, especially those where the primary assets are the knowledge and skills of the employees, might also be owned either directly by the employees or set up as producer cooperatives. A variety of anecdotes can be found in the daily press about the growing economic strength of traditional producer cooperatives, or employee-owned enterprises. Although time-series data on cooperatives of various types are scarce, one series – the ratio of current income of (traditional) cooperatives to the total current income of nonfarm proprietors – shows clearly that the relative importance of cooperatives is minuscule and has no apparent upward trend (this comes from the national income and product accounts, Table 8.20). Some, such as Jon Elster and Karl Ove Moene (1989), argue that producer cooperatives have not flourished in the United States because of the hostile legal environment, as well as the adverse self-selection occurring when such cooperatives are formed. Although they believe that under the proper circumstances, these factors could be overcome, the changes in the legal and economic environment to allow this do not appear on the horizon.

A more likely form would be an employee-owned enterprise, where participants would own shares that could, in some instances, be distributed as part of their salaries. This could take the form of employee stock ownership plans (ESOPs), which, according to various empirical tests by Patrick M. Rooney (1992c), place a firm somewhere in the middle of the continuum between a true worker cooperative and a standard profit maximizing firm. Although employee stock purchase plans existed for many years, ESOPs in their current form are creatures of a 1974 law. This provides ESOP firms with some favorable tax advantages to both employers and employees, and in recent years tax motives were crucial in the formation of more than three quarters of these plans (U.S. General Accounting Office, 1986a).

As the data in Table 10.1 show, the share of workers covered by such plans has skyrocketed. In terms of ownership of total outstanding stock, these ESOPs owned roughly 1 to 2 percent (an estimate based on calculations for 1983 by Blasi, 1990). In the late 1980s among the Fortune top 100 industrial firms, one third had such plans, with the percentage of employee ownership ranging from 4.0 percent (Quaker Oats) to 32.6 percent (McDonald Douglas). More data for the Fortune 500 are presented by Blasi and Kruse (1990, p. 14 ff). I should note, however, that aggregate measurements of ESOPS do not include profit-sharing plans, many of which are actually profit-sharing trusts (Blasi, 1990). In the early 1980s the latter plans actually hold more stock than the ESOPs. In the same year other defined contribution plans such as savings plans and 401(K) plans also held roughly the same amount of stock as the ESOPs.

Depending on the manner in which Employee Stock Ownership Trusts (which hold the stock of the ESOP) are structured and the laws of the state of incorporation, the individual workers may not be able to exercise the voting rights of these shares. Analysis of the impact of these plans is further complicated because ESOP firms are much more likely to have other forms of decision-making participation as well. A final complication arises from the mixed motives for setting up ESOPs. Many start-up technology companies have used this form as a work incentive to their employees. Other ESOPs have been formed to save a failing firm – workers give wage concessions in return for stock; and still others are formed by the managers to strengthen their control over the corporation at the expense of outside stockholders (Monks and Minow, 1991).

Although the research problem on relative performance can be stated easily, statistical nightmares abound. The available data are poor and analytic problems arise because firm performance may be influenced by those factors that led to the adoption of an ESOP – self-selection bias. In a survey of the literature Conte and Svejnar (1990) show that the evidence is contradictory and ambiguous. Research on the topic continues and, for instance, Rooney (1992a, 1992b) finds that employee ownership is positively associated with the level of productivity, especially when combined with various types of arrangements for worker participation in decision making. This effect, however, appears to fade over time. He also finds that firms with both ESOPs and worker participation arrangements have better safety records than profit maximizing firms. If enterprises with ESOPs perform better, then the use of such plans may increase; given their relatively small share of stock ownership, however, it will take many decades for them to become an important institution in the economy. As a result of these complications, the question of whether ESOP firms perform better than conventionally owned firms is a matter of considerable debate.

Atomic-capitalism represents a response to the growing structural complexity by placing more allocation burdens on the market. Whether it is consistent with increasing internationalization of economic activity, where a certain size is required to function effectively on world markets, is open to question. Nevertheless, in countries such as Germany and Taiwan, these small firms have been able to compete internationally in certain sectors. More specifically, world integration may place limits on the degree to which atomic-capitalism can proceed. In the case of producer cooperatives or ESOPs, such a development might strengthen certain types of social cohesiveness in particular groups. The development of many larger number of satellite enterprises around a central enterprise might, however, strengthen the tendencies toward a dual economy and exacerbate income inequalities, thereby reducing social cohesiveness for the nation as a whole. Finally, such a trend might, under certain circumstances lead to an invigora tion of the spirit of capitalism by tying worker incomes more closely to the results of the firm.

Remodeled-capitalism: The remodeled-capitalism that I discuss represents an acceleration in structural complexity as represented by an enhanced valuation of human capital through a greater use of skills and education of the labor force. Further, a much greater share of the labor force would be engaged in the generation, collection, and analysis of information.

This requires a shift in our focus. In contrast to abstract economic theories of capitalism, which recognize no national differences in the manner in which capitalism is practiced, in actuality capitalism functions quite differently in various industrialized nations and features quite different values and managerial practices. Various commentators have held up the "Japanese model" or the "Rhine model" as worthy of emulation in the United States, which, according to Michel Albert (1993), suffers from an "obsession with individual achievement and short-term profit [that] has led it to the brink of collapse." An even more blunt assessment comes from Cenozoic Matsushita, head of Japan's largest electronics group (cited by McRae, 1994, p. 75):

> We are going to win and the industrial West is going to lose; there is nothing much you can do about it because the reasons for your failure are within yourselves. With bosses doing the thinking, while the workers wield the screwdrivers, you are convinced deep down that this is the right way to run a business. For you, the essence of management is getting ideas out of the heads of bosses into the hands of labor ... For us,

the core of management is [the] art of mobilizing and putting together the intellectual resources of all employees in the service of the firm. Because we have measured better than you the scope of the new technological and economic challenges, we know that the intelligence of a handful of technocrats, however brilliant and smart they may be, is no longer enough for a real chance of success.

The fact that in the early 1990s the Japanese economy was not performing particularly well does not mean that they are poorly positioned in the long-run.

To what extent can the United States, where values are different, adopt successful foreign models of management? This raises questions both about values and practices.

It is first necessary to isolate exactly what values we are talking about and to what extent such values are unique to this or that nation. One attempt is by Charles Hampden-Turner and Alfons Trompenaars, who posed various business problems to managers of different nations and asked them to select appropriate solutions or policies. Some of their results, presented in Appendix Note 10.1 for those who are interested, confirm the commonly stated observations that on almost all dimensions, U.S. managers hold more individualistic values than those of other nations.

The advocates of remodeled-capitalism argue that a move away from traditional methods of U.S. management becomes increasingly necessary in an environment that is growing more structurally complex. For instance, in the supervision of labor, the monitoring of work of employees is increasingly costly, especially where there is a growing need to draw upon an ever greater variety of high-level skills and knowledge of different people. This systemic change in the nature of U.S. capitalism is thus required to meet the special challenges of increasing structural complexity.

Determining whether this diagnosis is correct requires comparative study of those nations manifesting these values (Germany or Japan) with those that do not. Assuming, however, that this analysis is correct, such a change in values and managerial methods has implications for both the private and the public sector that deserve brief mention.

Private sector. For the private sector the requisite changes in managerial values and methods include closer ties of remuneration to total results, greater employee involvement and power sharing, and job enrichment. According to some businesspeople, much of the corporate downsizing that occurred in the late 1980s and early 1990s was accompanied by these changes in managerial practices for those employees who remained.

- **Closer ties of remuneration to total results:** This does not refer to traditional piece-work remuneration system, but instead includes such measures as profit sharing plans, gainsharing (group bonuses based on cost reductions or productivity improvements), stock option plans, and the like. Some data are available, such as, Kruse (1993), Cable and Wilson (1988), and Weitzman and Kruse (1990). According to Kruse (p. 9), the share of workers covered by profit sharing plans is increasing. Although most studies show that profit sharing is associated with greater productivity and/or employment stability, there are some severe statistical problems that limit these results. Kruse's own work, which employs panel study data of 500 publicly listed firms and takes into account a number of different productivity enhancing measures, shows that profit sharing probably increases productivity to a degree that is "neither so small as to be negligible, nor so large as to be implausible." The stabilizing effect on employment of such measures is even more uncertain. Such careful econometric work for other types of remuneration systems is not available.
- **Employee involvement and power sharing:** These types of measures include kaisens and quality circles, suggestion systems, surveys of employee attitudes, information sharing (of firm results, business plans, and performance of competitors), worker committees to resolve particular production problems, worker councils, codetermination, or participation on company management boards. The advocates of this view range

from the industrial democracy advocates on the left to the Roman Catholic church on the right and the benefits are alleged to range from a more stable work force to higher productivity. David I. Levine and Laura Tyson (1990) survey the vast literature on the impact of such measures and find that most studies usually show a positive, but usually small, effect on productivity. More recent studies reveal mixed results and depend upon the method of analysis: For instance, in his regression analysis of "objective" performance variables, Douglas L. Kruse (1992) generally finds positive effects as well, but the derived coefficients seldom achieve statistical significance. By way of contrast, in a study of managerial evaluations of such programs, Edward E. Lawler and his colleagues (1992) find that such measures definitely have positive results.

- **Job enrichment:** These include such measures as autonomous work teams, measures to increase group cohesiveness and solidarity (for instance, relatively narrow wage differentials), guarantees of worker rights, and continual job training programs. Long-term employment security might be included in this category as well. The impacts of such measures have not been as closely studied as those in the other two categories.

   Although many of these measures might benefit both labor and management by raising productivity, many factors other than inertia have prevented their wholesale adoption. Levine and Tyson (1990), for instance, point out several cases in which such measures are advantageous only if most other firms have also introduced them. For instance, unless all firms adopt such policies, one firm narrowing its wage differentials may find its most productive workers leaving while it is flooded with less-productive job applicants. Moreover, as Albert (1993, p. 12) and others have pointed out, many of these measures are predicated on a stable labor force and a degree of social cohesiveness that may not exist

Public sector. In remodeled-capitalism the public sector has two important roles in facilitating this shift in procedures and management techniques in the private sector.

- **Providing the necessary social capital:** Various types of programs can be envisioned to provide the necessary social capital and to upgrade continuously the skills of the labor force. In this regard, the faults of the American education system are widely known. For instance, Dertouzos et al, (1989) present a trenchant argument for the particular need of improving the job training system and this applies both to the workers currently employed and to those unable to find employment (Chapter 3). Although many enterprises have their own training and, indeed, elementary education programs, such private measures are insufficient. Moreover, employers face one critical disincentive for mounting such programs, namely the risk that the worker trained at their cost may then accept work at a high wage from other employers who do not need to bear such costs.

   A variety of solutions have been proposed in the field of formal education, for instance, a longer school year in elementary and secondary schools, closer contact of schools with firms so that training may be directed toward needed skills, apprenticeship programs, and the like. Another example of improving human capital comes from the area of health care: low cost vaccinations for children from families with incomes below a certain limit are available, but the government must develop more effective methods to encourage mothers to take advantage of the programs.

   If, as I have argued, the society is becoming ever less cohesive, then special steps must be taken to include those in the bottom social strata in the creation of such necessary social capital, for otherwise such programs reinforce the trend toward a dual economy. Part of the implementation problem also arises from social complementarities to participation in such programs: if sufficient housing, food, and care are not available for many children, they will be incapable of taking advantage of such programs. Part of the implementation problem arises from cultural complementarities to the programs: if a sixteen-year-old girl wants to bears a child out of wedlock to have someone to love and if a sixteen-year-old boy sees much higher gains in dealing drugs, they will have no interest in such educational programs to increase their human capital.

- **Long-term vision:** Although political leaders are supposed to provide a long-term vision to justify their various proposed policies, the federal government has devoted relatively few resources to long-term planning. Moreover, although some long-term planning is carried out, these efforts are usually devoted to particular problems and few of the plans are coordinated. For instance, the Social Security Administration works on projections for many decades in the future, the Department of Transportation has considered many future aspects of the American transportation system, the Department of Education has a plan for the year 2000, the Department of Energy has proposed a long-range national energy strategy, the National Critical Materials Council has worried about the long-run scarcity of minerals, or the Department of Defense Advance Research Project Agency has considered certain problems of long-run technological development. As a result, it is difficult to prioritize the various possible government initiatives proposed. I strongly suspect, for instance, that such an ordering of programs for the future would probably show that long-term educational programs to create human capital and social projects to ameliorate the conditions fostering the declining social cohesiveness would have a much larger payoff than projects more focused on the creation of physical capital. The major point is that most governmental actions are taken to meet short-term problems and that the framework in which these decisions are taken does not encourage long-term thinking.

A caveat. These shifts in the values, managerial practices, and public policies underlying a remodeled-capitalism represent attempts to adapt to the increasing structural complexity of the economy. The decentralization and the retraining to utilize more effectively the capabilities and knowledge of those lower in the organizational hierarchy represent an attempt to adapt to the explosion of knowledge accompanying such increasing complexity. Remodeled-capitalism is aimed at increasing competitiveness in international trade. If both private and public parts of the remodeling are carried out, it acts to combat the decreasing social cohesiveness; if only the private part is carried out, then it strengthens the trend toward a dual economy and greater income inequalities. The impact on the spirit of capitalism is more uncertain; such a change really does not address the cultural issues.

Unfortunately, I see no strong forces bringing about such a remodeled-capitalism in the United States, particularly in the public sector. Indeed, some such as power-sharing in production are predicated on a degree of social cohesiveness that may not exist; similarly, as I point out for programs to increase social capital, both social and cultural complementarities may render the programs ineffective. Moreover, the political constituency for the changes in the public sector that I have sketched is small, and the short-term profit implications of the changes in the private sector may not be sufficient to induce many enterprises to introduce such changes, so that only part of the productive system is remodeled. In sum, a remodeled-capitalism is easier to prescribe than to implement. It may be a desirable change to the economic system, but it is unclear whether it is probable. A nation can face a challenge to its economic existence, and yet fail to rise to the occasion and meet it.

Note 10.4: Environmental catastrophes and the economic system

The argument about the increasing scarcity of raw materials and energy is based on a simple idea: We live in a finite world and, as we extract raw materials for direct usage or production of energy, they are becoming increasingly scarce and costly. Although an increasing scarcity should be reflected in rising market prices, this does not occur. For raw materials sold on international markets, the real prices (prices adjusted by the GDP deflator) have either been stable or declining in the 1950–90 period for most products (Chapter 8). A glance at producer price indexes by stage of processing (Department of Commerce, Bureau of the Census, annual-b, 1992, p. 489) reveals a slower growth in prices of crude materials and crude foodstuffs than other categories of goods between 1950 and 1992.

Three explanations have been offered for this failure of the relative prices of raw materials, energy, and foodstuffs to rise. Some have claimed that the market prices do not accurately reflect such scarcities – that the market is shortsighted and that the businesspeople who make their living buying and selling commodities are not as smart as the academics who are armed with the "real truth," namely economic theory. Others argue that the 40-year time period that I am using is too short, and that we must look at much longer series. But a more likely explanation is that production technologies have managed to offset the costs arising from less fertile soil, poorer quality ores, or deeper pools of oil and gas. As long as production technologies increase at this rate, there is no problem. What happens if the swift pace of technological change falters?

Although it is possible that important resource constraints and rising relative raw material and energy products may be an important feature of twenty-first-century capitalism, it is also possible that this will not be the case. Although we know that an increase in relative raw material prices will undoubtedly hurt low-income groups much more than high-income groups (Appendix Note 2.3), it is unclear whether this pressure for increased inequality will actually occur. We can only consider different scenarios in which such an event does and does not occur.

With regard to global warming, changes of climate, even more difficulties arise. According to standard physics, an increase in carbon dioxide in the atmosphere will lead, other things being equal, to an increase in temperature. This occurs because this gas absorbs more infrared radiation so that a balance between the earth's energy absorption and radiation comes back into balance only at a higher temperature. But in climatology as in economics, other things do not remain equal and a considerable gap exists between predictions of global warming and actual facts about the climate (Balling, 1992).

If global warming occurs, the economic effects are far from certain – some areas and industries will be hurt, others will be helped. Internationally, the same problem occurs. For instance, if global warming leads to a rise in the sea level, the breadbasket of Bangladesh in the delta of the Ganges would be inundated and the emigration pressure from that nation to richer countries would be multiplied.

The degree to which structural strains introduced either by a rise in raw material prices or global warming can be handled by the market mechanism, rather than more direct governmental action, is also unclear. Blanket generalizations are meaningless, for the answer depends not only on the specific problem at hand, but also on the political, social, and cultural conditions at the time the decision must be taken. Again, we have only the option of considering different scenarios.

Bibliography

Aaron, Henry J., Thomas E. Mann, and Timothy Taylor, editors. 1994. *Values and Public Policy.* Washington, D.C.: Brookings.

Abowd, John M. 1991. "The NBER Immigration, Trade and Labor Market Data Files," in Abowd and Freeman, 1991: pp. 407–23.

Abowd, John M. and Richard B. Freeman, editors. 1991 *Immigration, Trade, and the Labor Market.* Chicago: University of Chicago Press for N.B.E.R.

Abraham, Katharine G. 1987. "Help-Wanted Advertising, Job Vacancies, and Unemployment," *Brookings Papers on Economic Activity,* No. 1: pp. 207–47.

———. 1990. "Restructuring the Employee Relationship: The Growth of Market-Mediated Arrangements," in Abraham and McKersie (1990): pp. 85–120.

———. 1991. "Mismatch and Labour Mobility: Some Final Remarks," in Padoa-Schioppa (1991): pp. 453–80.

Abraham, Katherine G. and Robert B. McKersie, editors. 1990. *New Developments in the Labor Market.* Cambridge, Mass.: MIT Press.

Abraham, Katherine G. and Susan S. Housman. 1993. "Does Employment Protection Inhibit Labor Market Flexibility? Lessons from Germany, France, and Belgium," National Bureau of Economic Research, working paper No. 4390. Cambridge, Mass.

Akerlof, George A. and Brian G.M. Main. 1980. "Employment Spells and Unemployment Experience," *American Economic Review 70,* No. 5 (December): pp. 855–93.

Albert, Michel. 1993. *Capitalism vs. Capitalism: How America's Obsession with Individual Achievement and Short-Term Profit has Let it to the Bring of Collapse.* New York: Four Wall Eight Windows.

Allen, Steven G. 1991. "Changes in the Cyclical Sensitivity of Wages in the United States, 1891–1987," National Bureau of Economic Research, working paper No. 3854. Cambridge, Mass.

Altonji, Joseph and David Card. 1989. "The Effects of Immigration on the Labor Market of Natives," National Bureau of Economic Research, working paper No. 3123, Cambridge, Mass.

Andersen, Esben Sloth. 1994. *Evolutionary Economics.* London: Pinter Publishers.

Anderson, Philip W., Kenneth J. Arrow, and David Pines, editors. *The Economy as an Evolving Complex System.* Santa Fe Institute Studies in the Sciences of Complexity, Volume 5. Redwood City, Calif.: Addison-Wesley, 1988.

Arthur, W. Brian. 1990. "Positive Feedbacks in the Economy," *Scientific American 265,* No. 2 (February): pp. 92–9.

———. 1993. "Why Do Things Become More Complex," *Scientific American 268,* No. 5 (May): p. 144.

———. 1994. *Increasing Returns and Path Dependence in the Economy.* Ann Arbor: University of Michigan Press.

Ashenfelter, Orley. 1978. "Union Relative Wage Effects: New Evidence and a Survey of their Implications for Wage Inflation," in Richard Stone and William Peterson, editors. *Econometric Contributions to Public Policy.* New York: St. Martin's Press: pp. 31–61.

Ashenfelter, Orley and Richard Layard, editors. 1986. *Handbook of Labor Economics.* Amsterdam: North Holland Press.

Asher, Martin A. and Robert H. DeFina. Forthcoming 1994. "Age Adjusted Income Inequality Trends."

Atkinson, A. B., J. Gomulka, and J. Mickelwright. 1984. "Unemployment Benefits, Duration and Incentives in Britain: How Robust is the Evidence," *Journal of Public Economics 23,* No. 1–2 (February): pp. 3–26.

Attali, Jacques. 1991. *Millennium: Winners and Losers in the Coming World Order.* New York: Random House.

Audretsch, David B. and Hideki Yamawaki. 1988. "R & D Rivalry, Industrial Policy, and U.S.–Japanese Trade," *Review of Economics and Statistics 70,* No. 3 (August): pp. 438–47.

Auerbach, Paul R. and John J. Siegfried. 1974. "Executive Compensation and Corporation Control," *Nebraska Journal of Economic and Business 13,* No. 3 (Summer): pp. 3–16.

Avery, Robert B., Gregory E. Elliehausen, and Arthur B. Kennickell. 1988. "Measuring Wealth with Survey Data: An Estimate of the 1983 Survey of Consumer Finances," *Review of Income and Wealth 34,* No. 4 (December): pp. 339–69.

Bacon, Jeremy 1990. *Membership and Organization of Corporate Boards,* Research Report 940. New York: Conference Board.

Bacon, Jeremy and James K. Brown. 1975. *Corporate Directorship Practices: Role, Selection and Legal Status of the Board.* New York: Conference Board.

Badaracco, Joseph L. 1988. "Changing Forms of the Corporation," in Meyer and Gustafson (1988): pp. 67–91.

Beason, Richard and David Weinstein. 1993. "Growth, Economies of Scale, and Targeting in Japan," Harvard Institute of Economic Research Discussion Paper 1644. Cambridge, Mass.: processed.

Baily, Martin Neil and Robert J. Gordon. 1988. "The Productivity Slowdown, Measurement Issues, and the Explosion of Computer Power," *Brookings Papers on Economic Activity,* No. 2: pp. 347–433.

Bakrone-Adesi, Giovanni and Bernand Yeung. 1990. "Price Flexibility and Output Variability: The Case for Flexible Exchange Rates," *Journal of International Money and Finance 9,* No. 3 (September): pp. 276 –99.

Balling, Robert C. Jr. 1992. *The Heated Debate: Greenhouse Predictions vs Climate Reality.* San Francisco: Pacific Institute for Public Policy.

Banerjee, Abhijet V. and Michael Spagat. 1991. "Production Paralysis and the Complexity Problem: Why do Centrally Planned Economies become Prematurely Gray," *Journal of Comparative Economics 15,* No. 4 (December): pp. 646–60.

Bennett, William J. 1993. *The Index of Leading Cultural Indicators 1,* (March). Washington, D.C.: Empower America, The Heritage Foundation, and the Free Congress Foundation.

Barnett, William A., John Geweke, and Karl Shell, editors. 1989. *Economic Complexity: Chaos, Sunspots, Bubbles, and Non-Linearities.* New York: Cambridge University Press.

Barro, Robert J. and Jong-Wha Lee. "Losers and Winners in Economic Growth," National Bureau of Economic Research, working paper No. 4341. Cambridge, Mass.

Barth, James R., R. Dan Brumbaugh, Jr., and Robert E. Litan. 1992. *The Future of American Banking.* Armonk, New York: M.E. Sharpe.

Bartlett, Robin L., James H. Grant and Timothy I. Miller. 1992. "The Earnings of Top Executives," *Quarterly Review of Economics and Finance 32,* No. 1 (Spring): pp. 38–49.

Baumol, William J. 1967. *Business Behavior, Value, and Growth,* revised edition. New York: Macmillan.

Baumol, William J., Sue Ann Batey Blackman, and Edward N. Wolff. 1989. *Productivity and American Leadership: The Long View.* Cambridge, Mass.: MIT Press.

Beach, Charles M. and S.F. Kaliski. 1987. "The Distribution of Unemployment Spells: Canada, 1978–82," *Industrial and Labor Relations Review 40*, No. 2 (January): pp. 254–67.

Beason, Richard and David E. Weinstein. 1993. "Growth, Economies of Scale, and Targeting in Japan (1955–1990)." Harvard Institute of Economic Research, Discussion Paper 1644.

Becketti, Sean and Gordon H. Sellon, Jr. 1990. "Has Financial Market Volatility Increased?" in Davis (1990): pp. 3–19.

Bell, Daniel. 1973. *The Coming of Post-Industrial Society: A Venture in Social Forecasting*. New York: Basic Books.

———. 1976. *The Cultural Contradictions of Capitalism*. New York: Basic Books.

Belman, Dale. 1992. "Unions, the Quality of Labor Relations, and Firm Performance," in Mishel and Voos (1992): pp. 41–108.

Benabau, Roland. 1993. "Workings of a City: Location, Education, and Production," *Quarterly Journal of Economics 108*, No. 3 (August): pp. 519–52.

Bell, Linda and Richard Freeman. 1994. "Why Do Americans and Germans Work Different Hours?" National Bureau of Economic Research, working paper No. 4808. Cambridge, Mass.

Bennett, James T. 1991. "Private Sector Unions: The Myth of Decline," *Journal of Labor Research 11*, (Winter): pp. 307–22.

Bennett, William J. 1993. *The Index of Leading Cultural Indicators*. Washington, D.C.: Heritage Foundation.

Benston, George J. 1985. "The Self-Serving Management Hypothesis," *Journal of Accounting and Economics 7*, Nos. 1–3 (April): pp. 67–84.

Berke, Richard L. 1994. "Fears of Crime Rival Concern over Economy," *New York Times*, January 23: p. 1.

Berle, Adolf A. and Gardiner C. Means. 1933. *The Modern Corporation and Private Property*. New York: Macmillan.

Bernanke, Ben S. and John Y. Campbell. 1988. "Is There a Corporate Debt Crisis," *Brookings Papers on Economic Activity*, No. 1 (Spring): pp. 83–125.

Bernanke, Ben S., John Y. Campbell, and Toni M. Whited. 1990. "U.S. Corporate Leverage: Developments in 1987 and 1988," *Brookings Papers on Economic Activity*, No. 1 (Spring): pp. 255–87.

Berndt, Ernst R. and Laurits R. Christensen. 1974. "Testing for the Existence of a Consistent Aggregate Index of Labor Inputs," *American Economic Review 64*, No. 2 (June): pp. 391–404.

Berndt, Ernst R., Catherine J. Morrison, and Larry S. Rosenblum. 1992. "High-Tech Capital Formation and Labor Composition in U.S. Manufacturing Industries: An Exploratory Analysis," National Bureau of Economic Research, working paper No. 4010. Cambridge, Mass.

Betts, Julian R. 1993. "Does School Quality Matter? Evidence from the National Longitudinal Survey of Youth," La Jolla, Calif.: University of California at San Diego, processed.

Bezeau, Lawrence M. 1979. "Complexity as a Characteristic of Policies in Albert Breton's Economic Theory of Representative Government," Public Choice 34, No. 3–4: pp. 493–8.

Bishop, John H. 1989. "Is the Test Score Decline Responsible for the Productivity Growth Decline," *American Economic Review 79*, No. 1 (March): pp. 178–98.

———. 1990. "The Worsening Shortage of College Graduate Workers," working papers 90–15, Center for Advanced Human Resource Studies, School of Industrial and Labor Relations, Cornell University (Ithaca: processed).

———. 1992. "Achievement,Test Scores, and Relative Wages," in Kosters (1992): pp. 146–85.

———. 1993a. "Improving Job Matches in U.S. Labor Markets," *Brookings Papers on Economic Behavior: Microeconomics*, No. 1: pp. 335–90.

———. 1993b. "Overeducation," working paper 93–06, Center for Advanced Human Resource Studies, School of Industrial and Labor Relations, Cornell University (Ithaca: processed); to appear in *International Encyclopedia of Education*, 2nd edition.

Blackburn, McKinley L. 1990. "What Can Explain the Increase in Earnings Inequality Among Males?" *Industrial Relations 29,* No. 3 (Fall): pp. 441–56.

Blackburn, McKinley L., David E. Bloom, and Richard Freeman. 1990. "The Declining Economic Position of Less Skilled American Men," in Burtless (1990): pp. 31–67.

Blair, Margaret M., editor. 1993a. *The Deal Decade: What Takeovers and Leveraged Buyouts Mean for Corporate Governance.* Washington, D.C.: Brookings Institution.

Blair, Margaret M. 1993b. "Financial Restructuring and the Debate about Corporate Governance," in Blair (1993a): pp. 1–17.

———. 1994. *Ownership and Control: What's at Stake in the Corporate Governance Debates.* Washington, D.C.: Brookings Institution.

Blair, Margaret M. and Girish Uppal. 1993. *The Deal Decade Handbook.* Washington, D.C.: Brookings Institution.

Blanchard, Olivier Jean and Lawrence H. Summers. 1988. "Hysteresis and the European Unemployment Problem," in Cross (1988): pp. 306–64.

Blanchflower, David G. and Richard B. Freeman. 1992. "Unionism in the United States and other Advanced O.E.C.D. Countries," *Industrial Relations 31,* No. 1 (Winter): pp. 56–80.

Blank, Rebecca M. 1990. "Are Part-Time Jobs Bad Jobs?" in Burtless (1990): pp. 123–55.

Blank, Rebecca H. and David Card. 1993. "Poverty, Income Distribution and Growth: Are They Still Connected," *Brookings Papers on Economic Activity,* No. 2: pp. 285-341.

Blankenhorn, David. 1995. *Fatherless America.* New York: Basic Books.

Blasi, Joseph Raphael. 1988. *Employee Ownership: Revolution or Ripoff.* Cambridge, Mass.: Ballinger Publisher.

———. 1990. "Comment," in Blinder, editor. (1990): pp. 172–81.

Blasi, Joseph Raphael and Douglas L. Kruse. 1990. *The New Owners.* New York: Harper Collins.

Blinder, Alan S. 1988. "Life Cycle Savings vs. Intergenerational Transfers: Comments," in Kessler and Masson (1988): pp. 68–76.

Blinder, Alan S., editor. 1990. *Paying for Productivity: A Look at the Evidence.* Washington, DC: Brookings Institution.

Bliss, Chester I., Karl W. Deutsch, and Alexander Eckstein. 1962. "Population, Sovereignty, and the Share of Foreign Trade," *Economic Development and Cultural Change 10,* (July): pp. 353–66.

Block, Fred. 1990a. *Postindustrial Possibilities: A Critique of Economic Discourse.* Berkeley: University of California Press.

———. 1990b. "Bad Data Drive Out Good: The Decline of Personal Savings Reexamined," *Journal of Post Keynesian Economics 13,* No. 1: pp. 3–20.

Bloom, David and Richard Freeman. 1991. "The Fall in Private Pension Coverage in the United States," NBER Working Paper No. 3973.

Board of Governors of the Federal Reserve System. Monthly. *Federal Reserve Bulletin.* Washington, D.C.

———. 1976. *Banking and Monetary Statistics, 1941–1970.* Washington, D.C.

———. 1991. *Balance Sheets for the U.S. Economy, 1945–90.* Washington, D.C.

———. 1993. *Balance Sheets for the U.S. Economy, 1945–92.* Washington, D.C.

Bok, Derek. 1993. *The Cost of Talent: How Executives and Professionals Are Paid and How it Affects America.* New York: Free Press.

Bonner, John Tyler. 1988. *The Evolution of Complexity.* Princeton: Princeton University Press, 1988.

Borcherding, T.E. 1985. "The Causes of Government Expenditure Growth: A Survey of the U.S. Evidence," *Journal of Public Economics 28,* No. 3 (December): pp. 359–82.

Borjas, George J. 1992. "Ethnic Capital and Intergenerational Mobility," *Quarterly Journal of Economics 207,* No. 1, pp. 123–51.

————. 1994. "The Economics of Immigration," *Journal of Economic Literature 32*, No. 4 (December): pp. 1667–1718.

Borjas, George J., Richard B. Freeman, and Lawrence F. Katz. 1992. "On the Labor Market Effects of Immigration and Trade," in George J. Borjas and Richard B. Freeman, editors. *Immigration and the Work Force.* Chicago: University of Chicago Press: pp. 213–44.

Bosch, Gerhard, *et al.* 1993. *Times are Changing: Working Time in 14 Industrialised Countries.* Geneva: International Institute for Labour Studies.

Bosworth, Barry, Gary Burtless, John Sabelhaus. 1991. "The Decline of Savings: Evidence from Household Surveys," *Brookings Papers on Economic Activity,* No. 1: pp. 183–257.

Bothwell, James L. 1980. "Profitability, Risk, and the Separation of Ownership from Control," *Journal of Industrial Economics 28*, No. 3 (March): pp. 303–11.

Boudreaux, Kenneth J. 1973. "'Managerialism' and Risk Return Performance," *Southern Economic Journal 39*, No. 3 (January): pp. 366–73.

Bound, John and George Johnson. 1991. "Wages in the United States during the 1980s and Beyond," in Kosters (1991): pp. 77–103.

————. 1992. "Changes in the Structure of Wages in the 1980's: An Evaluation of Alternative Explanations," *American Economic Review 82*, No. 3 (June): pp. 371–92.

Bowers, Norman. 1980. "Probing the Issue of Unemployment Duration," *Monthly Labor Review 103*, No. 7 (July): pp. 23–32.

Boyajian, George and Tim Lutz. 1992. "Evolution of Biological Complexity and its Relation to Taxonomic Longevity in the Ammonoidea," *Geology 20*, No. 11 (November): pp. 983–6.

Brancato, Carolyn Kay. 1989. *Leveraged Buyouts and the Pot of Gold: 1989 Update,* Report for the Subcommittee on Oversight and Invesigations of the Committee on Energy and Commerce, U.S. House of Representatives. Washington, D.C.: G.P.O.

Braudel, Fernand. 1982. *The Perspective of the World,* Volume 3, *Civilization and Capitalism: 15th–18th Century.* New York: Harper and Row.

Brill, Edward A. and Daniel R. Halem. 1994. "Foreign, U.S. Labor Laws Could Clash," *National Law Journal,* Monday, February 28, p. S.20.

Brown, Charles, James Hamilton, and James Medoff. 1990. *Employers Large and Small.* Cambridge, Mass.: Harvard University Press.

Brunello, Giorgio. 1991. "Mismatch in Japan," in Padoa-Schioppa (1991): pp. 140–82.

Bryant, Ralph C. and others. 1989. "Domestic and Cross-Border Consequences of U.S. Macroeconomic Policies," in Ralph C. Bryant, *et al.,* editors. *Macroeconomic Policies in an Interdependent World.* Washington, DC: Brookings.

————. Forthcoming. "Coordination of National Macroeconomic Policies in an Integrated World Economy," a monograph in the Brookings Project on Integrating the World Economy, edited by Henry Aaron, *et al.* Washington, D.C.

Brynjolfsson, Erik. 1993. "The Productivity Paradox of Information Technology." *Communications of the ACM (Association for Computing Machinery) 36*, No. 12 (December): pp. 67–77.

Brynjolfsson, Erik, Thomas W. Malone, Vijay Gurbaxani, and Ajit Kambil. 1993a. "Does Information Technology Lead to Smaller Firms?" MIT, Sloan School Working Paper 3142, Cambridge, Mass.

Brynjolfsson, Erik and Lorin Hitt. 1993b. "New Evidence on the Returns to Information Systems," MIT, Sloan School Working Paper 3571, Cambridge, Mass.

Bui, Nhuong and John Pippenger. 1990. "Commodity Prices, Exchange Rates and Their Relative Volatility," *Journal of International Money and Finance 9*, No. 1 (March): pp. 3–21.

Burch, Philip H., Jr. 1972. *The Managerial Revolution Reassessed: Family Control in America's Large Corporations.* Lexington, Mass: Lexington Books.

Burley, Peter and John Forster, editors. 1994. *Economics and Thermodynamics.* Boston: Kluwer Academic, 1994.

Burtless, Gary. 1990. "Earnings Inequality over the Business an Demographic Cycle," in Burtless, editor. (1990): pp. 77–122.

Burtless, Gary, editor. 1990. *A Future of Lousy Jobs: The Changing Structure of U.S. Wages.* Washington, D.C.: Brookings.

Cable, John and Nicholas Wilson. 1988. "Profit-Sharing and Productivity: An International Comparison," *Warwick Economic Research Papers,* No. 301. Warwick, England: processed.

Cage, Mary Crystal. 1994. "Beyond the B.A.," *The Chronicle of Higher Education.* January 26: pp. A29–A31.

Calder, Kent E. 1993. *Strategic Capitalism: Private Business and Public Purpose in Japanese Industrial Finance.* Princeton: Princeton University Press, 1993.

Çambel, A. B. 1993. *Applied Chaos Theory: A Paradigm for Complexity.* Boston: Academic Press.

Card, David. 1989. "The Impact of the Mariel Boatlift on the Miami Labor Market," National Bureau of Economic Research, working paper No. 3069. Cambridge, Mass.

Card, David and Allan B. Krueger. 1992a. "Does School Quality Matter? Returns to Education and the Characteristics of Public Schools in the United States," *Journal of Political Economy 100,* No. 1 (February): pp. 1–40.

———. 1992b."Quality and Black-White Relative Earnings: A Direct Assessment," *Quarterly Journal of Economics 107,* No. 1 (February): pp. 151–200.

Carlton, Dennis W. 1986. "The Rigidity of Prices," National Bureau of Economic Research, working paper No. 1813. Cambridge, Mass.

———. 1989. "The Theory and Facts of How Markets Clear: Is Industrial Organization Valuable for Understanding Macroeconomics," in Richard Schmalensee and Robert Willig, editors. *Handbook of Industrial Organization,* Volume 1. New York: Elsevier: pp. 910–46.

Carnevale, Anthony Patrick. 1991. *America and the New Economy.* San Francisco: Jossey Bass Publishers.

Carson, Carol S. 1984. "The Underground Economy: An Introduction," *Survey of Current Business 64,* Number 5 (May): pp. 21–38.

Caskey, John P. and Steven M. Fazzari. 1992. "Debt, Price Flexibility and Aggregate Stability," *Revue d'economie politique 102,* Number 4 (July): pp. 519–43.

Caves, Richard E. 1988. "Trade Exposure and Changing Structures of U.S. Manufacturing Industries," in Michael A. Spence and Heather A. Hazard, editors. *International Competitiveness.* Cambridge Mass.: Harper and Row, Ballinger.

Caves, Richard E. and Michael Porter. 1976. "Barriers to Exit," in Robert T. Masson and P. David Qualls, *Essays on Industrial Organization in Honor of Joe S. Bain* (Cambridge: Ballinger, 1976): pp. 39–69].

Cetron, Marvin and Owen Davies. 1989. *American Renaissance: Our Life at the Turn of the 21st Century.* New York: St. Martin's Press.

Chaison, Gary N. and Dileep G. Dhavale. 1990. "A Note on the Severity of the Decline in Union Organizing Activity," *Industrial and Labor Relations Review 43,* No. 4 (April): pp. 366–73.

Chang, Clara and Constance Sorrentino. 1991. "Union Membership in 12 Countries," *Monthly Labor Review 114,* No. 12 (December): pp. 46–53.

Charreaux, Gérard. 1991. "Structure de propriété, relations d'agence et performance financière," *Revue économique 42,* No. 3 (May): pp. 521–52.

Chavez, Linda. 1992. "Commentary," in Chiswick (1992): pp. 297–9.

Chiswick, Barry R. 1986. "Is the New Immigration Less Skilled than the Old," *Journal of Labor Economics 4,* No. 2: pp. 168–92.

Chiswick, Barry R. and Paul W. Miller. 1992. "Language in the Immigrant Labor Market," in Chiswick (1992): pp. 229–97.

Chiswick, Barry R., editor. 1992. *Immigration, Language, and Ethnicity: Canada and the United States.* Washington, D.C.: American Enterprise Institute.

Clark, Kim B. and Lawrence H. Summers. 1979. "Labor Market Dynamics and Unemployment: A Reconsideration," *Brookings Papers on Economic Activity*, No. 1: pp. 13–72.

Clark, Rebecca L. and Jeffrey S. Passell. 1993. "Studies are Deceptive," *New York Times*, (September 3): p. 23.

Cohen, Stephen S. and John Zysman. 1987. *Manufacturing Matters: The Myth of the Post Industrial Economy*. New York: Basic Books.

Collins, Norman R. and Lee E. Preston. 1961. "The Size Structure of the Largest Industrial Firms, 1909–1958," *American Economic Review 51*, No. 5 (December): pp. 986–1011.

Coleman, James et al. 1966. *Equality of Educational Opportunity*. Washington, D.C.: GPO.

Comanor, William S. and F.M. Scherer. 1969. "Patent Statistics as a Measure of Technical Change," *Journal of Political Economy 77*, No. 3 (May): pp. 392–9.

Conte, Michael A. and Jan Svejnar, 1990. "The Performance Effects of Employee Ownership Plans," in Blinder, editor. (1990): pp. 143–72.

Cooper, Richard N. 1968. *The Economics of Interdependence: Economic Policy in the Atlantic Community*. New York: McGraw Hill, 1968.

———. 1985. "Economic Interdependence and Coordination of Economic Policies," in Ronald W. Jones and Peter B. Kenen, editors. *Handbook of International Economics*, Vol. 2. Amsterdam: North Holland Publishing Company, pp. 1195–1234.

Corrigan, E. Gerald. 1991. "The Risks of Financial Crises," in Feldstein (1991): pp. 44–53.

Corson, Walter and Jean Grossman. 1986. *An Evaluation of the Federal Supplemental Compensation Program*, U.S. Department of Labor, Employment and Training Administration, Unemployment Insurance Service Occasional Paper 86–3. Washington, D.C.

Cosh, A.D. and A. Hughes. 1987. "The Anatomy of Corporate Control: Directors, Stockholders, and Managerial Remuneration in Giant U.S. and U.K. Corporations," *Cambridge Journal of Economic 11*, No. 4 (December 1987): pp. 285–315.

Cotta, Alain. 1991. *Le capitalisme dans tous ses états*. Paris: Fayard.

Crockett, Jean. 1991. "Savings in the Twenty-First Century, " unpublished paper.

Cross, Rod, editor. 1987. *Unemployment, Hysteresis and the Natural Rate Hypothesis*. New York: Blackwell.

Crystal, Graef S. 1991. *In Search of Excess: The Overcompensation of American Executives*. New York: Norton.

Cutler, David M. and Lawrence F. Katz. 1991. "Macroeconomic Performance and the Disadvantaged," *Brookings Papers on Economic Activity*, No. 2: pp. 1–75.

——. 1992. "Rising Inequality? Changes in the Distribution of Income and Consumption in the 1980s," National Bureau of Economic Research, working paper No. 3964. Cambridge, Mass.

Cutler, David M. and Louise M. Sheiner. 1993. "Policy Options for Long-Term Care," National Bureau of Economic Research, working paper No. 4302. Cambridge, Mass.

Cutler, David M., Douglas W. Elmendorf, and Richard J. Zeckhauser. 1993. "Demographic Characteristics and the Public Bundle, " National Bureau of Economic Research, working paper No. 4283. Cambridge, Mass.

Cutler, David M., et al. 1990. "An Aging Society: Opportunity or Challenge?" *Brookings Papers on Economic Activity*, No. 1: pp. 1–73.

Daly, Bonita A. and Thomas C. Omer. 1990. "A Comment on 'A Behavioral Study of the Meaning and Influence of Tax Complexity," *Journal of Accounting Research 28*, No. 1 (Spring): pp. 193–7.

Danziger, Sheldon and Peter Gottschalk, editors. 1993. *Uneven Tides: Rising Inequality in America*. New York: Russell Sage Foundation.

David, Paul. 1985. "Clio and the Economics of QWERTY," *American Economic Review 75*, No. 2 (May): pp. 332–7.

———. 1990. "The Dynamo and the Computer: An Historical Perspective on the Modern Productivity Puzzle," *American Economic Review 80*, No. 2 (May 1990): pp. 355–61.

Davis, Mary. 1993. "The Gautreaux Assisted Housing Program," in G. Thomas Kingsley and Margery Austin Turner, *Housing Markets and Residential Mobility*. Washington, D.C.: Urgan Institute Press: pp. 243–55.

Davis, Steven J. and John Haltiwanger. 1992. "Gross Job Creation, Gross Job Destruction, and Employment Reallocation," *Quarterly Journal of Economics 103*, No. 3 (August)" pp. 819–63.

Davis, Lance E. 1986. "Comment on Wallis and North," in Engerman and Gallman (1986): pp. 149–59.

Davis, Thomas E., editor. 1990. *Financial Market Volatility and the Economy*. Kansas City: Kansas City Federal Reserve Bank.

Day, Jennifer Cheeseman. 1993. *Population Projections of the United States, by Age, Sex, Race, and Hispanic Origin: 1992 to 2050*. Bureau of the Census, Current Population Reports, P25–1092. Washington, D.C.: GPO.

Deckop, John R. 1988. "Determinants of Chief Executive Officer Compensation," *Industrial and Labor Relations Review 41*, No. 2 (January): 215–27.

De Long, J. Bradford and Lawrence H. Summers. 1986. "The Changing Cyclical Variability of Economic Activity in the United States," in Gordon (1986): pp. 679–719.

Demsetz, Harold. 1983. "The Structure of Ownership and the Theory of the Firm," *Journal of Law and Economics 26*, No. 2 (June): pp. 375–90.

Demsetz, Harold and Kenneth Lehn. 1985. "The Structure of Corporate Ownership: Causes and Consequences," *Journal of Political Economy 93*, No. 6 (November/December): pp. 1155–77.

Denison, Edward F. 1979. Acounting for Slower Economic Growth. Washington, D.C.: Brookings Institution.

——— 1985. *Trends in American Economic Growth, 1929–1982*. Washington, D.C.: Brookings Institution.

Dertouzos, Michael L., et al. 1989. *Made in America: Regaining the Productive Edge*. Cambridge, Mass.: MIT Press.

Dickens, Rodney. 1987. "Variability in Some Major UK Asset Markets since the Mid-1960s: An Application of the ARCH Model," in Charles Goodhart, David Currie, and David T. Llewellyn, editors. *The Operation and Regulation of Financial Markets*. Dobbs Ferry, New York: Sheridan House: pp. 231–70.

Diebold, Francis X. and Glenn A. Rudebusch. 1992. "Have Postwar Economic Fluctuations been Stabilized?" *American Economic Review 82*, No. 4 (September): pp. 993–1006.

Disraeli, Benjamin. 1845 (1981). *Sybil; or the Two Nations*. New York: Oxford University Press.

Dornbusch, Rudiger. 1985. "Policy and Performance Links between LDC Debtors and Industrial Nations," *Brookings Papers on Economic Activity*, No. 2 (Fall): pp. 303–68.

Dosi, Giovanni, Keith Pavitt, and Luc Soete. 1990. *The Economics of Technical Change and International Trade*. New York: New York University Press.

Douglas, Evan J. and Rexford E. Santerre. 1990. "Incentive Contracts and Stockholder Monitoring: Substitute Sources of Executive Compliance," *Quarterly Review of Economics and Business 30*, No. 2 (Summer 1990): pp. 24–31.

Drucker, Peter F. 1993. *Post-Capitalist Society*. New York: HarperCollins.

DuBoff, Richard B. 1993. "The Growth of Federal Regulation: A Brief Economic History," Preliminary draft.

Dun and Bradstreet Corporation. 1993 *Business Failure Record*. New York.

Dunlop, John T. 1957. "The Task of Contemporary Wage Theory," in John T. Dunlop, ed., *The Theory of Wage Determination* (London: Macmillan): pp. 3–27.

Dye, Thomas R. 1983. "Who Owns America: Strategic Ownership Positions in Industrial Corporations," *Social Science Quarterly 64*, No. 4 (December): pp. 865–71.

Dyl, Edward A. 1988. "Corporate Control and Managerial Compensation: Evidence of the Agency Problem," *Managerial and Decision Economics 9*, No. 1 (March 1988): pp. 21–5.

Easterlin, Richard A. and Eileen M. Crimmins. 1991. "Private Materialism, Personal Self-Fulfillment, Family Life, and Public Interest," *Public Opinion Quarterly 55,* No. 4 (Winter): pp. 499–539.

Edwards, Richard. 1993. *Rights at Work: Employment Relations in the Post-Union Era.* Washington, D.C.: Brookings Institution.

Ehrenberg, Ronald. 1994. *Labor Markets and Interating National Economies.* Washington, D.C.: Brookings.

Ehrlich, Isaac. 1973. "Participation in Illegitimate Activities: A Theoretical and Empirical Investigation," *Journal of Political Economy 81,* No. 3 (May/June): pp. 521–66.

Eichengreen, Barry. 1990. "One Money for Europe? Lessons from the U.S. Currency Union," *Economic Policy: A Forum for Europe 10,* April: pp. 118–173.

Eisner, Robert. 1989. *The Total Incomes System of Accounts.* Chicago: University of Chicago Press.

Elliott, J.W. 1972. "Control, Size, Growth, and Financial Performance of the Firm," *Journal of Financial and Quantitative Analysis 7,* No. 1: pp. 1309–20.

Elster, Jon and Karl Ove Moene. 1989. "Introduction," in Elster and Moene, editors. *Alternatives to Capitalism.* New York: Cambridge U. Press: pp. 1–35.

Engel, Charles. 1992. "Real Exchange Rates and Relative Prices: An Empirical Investigation," National Bureau of Economic Research, working paper No. 4231. Cambridge, Mass.

Engerman, Stanley L. and Robert E. Gallman, editors. 1986. *Long-Term Factors in American Economic Growth.* Chicago: University of Chicago Press.

Esping-Andersen, Gøsta. 1990. *The Three Worlds of Welfare Capitalism.* Princeton: Princeton University Press.

Farber, Henry S. 1986. "The Analysis of Union Behavior," in Ashenfelter and Layard, Volume II (1986): pp. 1039–91.

Farber, Henry S. and Alan B. Krueger. 1992. "Union Membership in the United States: The Decline Continues," *Working Paper 306,* Industrial Relations Section, Princeton University.

Farley, Reynolds. "Residential Segregation of Social and Economic Groups Among Blacks, 1970–1980," in Jencks and Peterson (1991): pp. 274–99.

Federal Deposit Insurance Corporation (FDIC). Annual. *Annual Report.* Washington, D.C.

———. 1993. *Historical Statistics on Banking: 1934–91.* Washington, D.C.: FDIC.

Federal Home Loan Bank (FHLB). Irregular. *Savings and Home Financing Source Book.* Washington, D.C.

Federal Reserve Bank of Kansas City, editor. 1988. *Financial Market Volatility.* Kansas City.

Feenstra, Robert C., editor. 1988. *Empirical Methods for International Trade.* Cambridge, Mass.: MIT Press.

Feldstein, Martin, editor. 1991. *The Risk of Economic Crisis.* Chicago: University of Chicago Press, 1991.

Feldstein, Martin and James M. Poterba. 1984. "Unemployment Insurance and Reservation Wages," *Journal of Public Economics 23,* No. 1–2 (February): pp. 141–67.

Finnerty, Joseph E., Myung-Gun Choo, and Sidney F. Sufrin. 1979. "Business Control, Ownership and Performance," *Rivista Internazionale di Scienze Economiche e Commerciali 26,* No. 6 (June): pp. 573–86.

Folger, Robert and Janet Belew. 1985. "Nonreactive Measurement: A Focus for Research on Absenteeism and Occupational Stress," in L. L. Cummins and Barry M. Straw, editors. *Research in Organizational Behavior,* Vol. 7. Greenwich, Connecticut: JAI Press: pp. 129-70.

Food and Agricultural Organization. Annual-a. *Trade Yearbook.* Rome.

———. Annual-b. *Yearbook of Fishery Statistics,* Rome.

———. Annual-c. *Yearbook of Forest Product Statistics.* Rome.

Freeman, Richard B.. 1992. "Is Declining Unionization of the U.S. Good, Bad, or Irrelevant," in Mishel and Voos (1992): pp. 143–72.

———. 1993. "How Much as De-Unionization Contributed to the Rise in Male Earnings Inequality," in Danziger and Gottschalk (1993): pp. 133–65.

Freeman, Richard B. and James L. Medoff 1984. *What Do Unions Do?* New York: Basic Books.

Freeman, Richard B. and Marcus E. Rebick. 1989. "Crumbling Pillar? Declining Union Density in Japan," *Journal of the Japanese and International Economics 3*, No. 3 (December): pp. 578–605.

Frenkel, Jacob A. and Michael Mussa. 1980. "The Efficiency of Foreign Exchange Markets and Measures of Turbulence," *American Economic Review 70*, No. 2 (May 1980): pp. 374–81.

Friedman, Benjamin. 1991. "The Risks of Financial Crisis," in Feldstein (1991): pp. 19–43.

Froot, Kenneth A. and Paul Klemperer. 1988. "Exchange Rate Pass-Through When Market Share Matters," National Bureau of Economic Research, working paper No. 2542. Cambridge, Mass.

Fuller, Wayne A. 1976. *Introduction to Statistical Time Series.* New York: Wiley.

Galor, Oded. 1993. "Income Distribution and Macroeconomics," *Review of Economic Studies 60*, No. 1 (January): pp. 35–52.

Gambetta, Diego, editor. 1988. *Trust: Making and Breaking Cooperative Relations.* New York: Basil Blackwell.

Galbraith, John Kenneth. 1967. *The New Industrial State.* Boston: Houghton Mifflin.

Garfinkel, Irwin and Sara S. McLanahan. 1986. *Single Mothers and Their Children.* Washington, D.C: Urban Institute.

Garner, Alan C. 1990a. "Does Interest Rate Volatility Affect Money Demand?" in Davis, editor (1990): pp. 99–115.

———. 1990b. "Has the Stock Market Crash Reduced Consumer Spending?" in David, editor (1990): pp. 69–85.

Gell-Mann, Murray. 1994. *The Quark and the Jaguar: Adventures in the Simple and the Complex.* New York: W. H. Freeman.

Georgescu-Roegen, Nicholas. 1971. *The Entropy Law and the Economic Process.* Cambridge, Mass.: Harvard University Press.

Gergen, Kenneth J. 1992. *The Saturated Self: Dilemmas of Identify in Contemporary Life.* New York: Basic Books.

Giarini, Orio. 1985. "The Consequences of Complexity in Economics: Vulnerability, Risk, and Rigidity Factors in Supply," in United Nations University (1985): pp. 133–45.

Globerman, Steven and James W. Dean. 1990. "Recent Trends in Intra-Industry Trade and Their Implications for Future Trade Liberalization," *Weltwirtschaftliches Archiv 126*, No. 1: pp. 25–49.

Goldfield, Michael. 1987. *The Decline of Organized Labor in the United States.* Chicago: University of Chicago Press.

Goldin, Claudia. 1993. "The Political Economy of Immigration Restriction in the United States," National Bureau of Economic Research, working paper No. 4345. Cambridge, Mass.

Goldin, Claudia and Robert A. Margo. 1992. "The Great Compression: The Wage Structure in the United States at Mid-Century," *Quarterly Journal of Economics 107*, No. 1 (February): pp. 1–35.

Goldsmith, Raymond. 1985. *Comparative National Balance Sheets: A Study of Twenty Countries, 1688–1978.* Chicago: University of Chicago Press.

Goldstein, Morris, *et al.* 1993. *International Capital Markets, Part I: Exchange Rate Management and Capital Flows.* Washington, D.C.: International Monetary Fund.

Goldstein, Morris and Michael Mussa. 1993. "The Integration of World Capital Markets," Paper delivered at Federal Reserve Bank of Kansas City conference, *Changing Capital Markets.* Jackson Hole, Wyoming: processed.

Golub, Steven S. 1990. "International Capital Mobility: Net Versus Gross Stocks and Flows," *Journal of International Money and Finance 9*, No. 4 (December): pp. 424–39.

Goodhart, Charles A. E. 1988. "The International Transmission of Asset Price Volatility," in Federal Reserve Bank of Kansas City (1988): pp. 79–121.

Gordon, Lilli A. and John Pound. 1993. "Information, Ownership Structure, and Shareholding Voting: Evidence from Shareholder-Sponsored Corporate Governance Proposals," *Journal of Finance 48,* No. 2 (June): pp. 697–719.

Gordon, Robert A. 1945. *Business Leadership in the Large Corporation.* Berkeley: University of California Press.

Gordon, Robert J. 1983. "A Century of Evidence on Wage and Price Stickiness in the United States, the United Kingdom, and Japan," in James Tobin, editor. *Macroeconomics, Prices, and Quantities.* Washington, D.C.: Brookings, 1983: pp. 85–133.

————, editor. 1986. *The American Business Cycle Changes.* Chicago: University of Chicago Press.

Gould, Steven Jay. 1981. *The Mismeasurement of Man.* New York: W.W. Norton.

Gramlich, Edward M., Richard Kasten, and Frank Sammartino. 1993. "Growing Inequality in the 1980s: The Role of Federal Taxes and Cash Transfers," in Danziger and Gottschalk (1993): pp. 225–51.

Gray, Wayne B.. 1987. "The Cost of Regulation: OSHA, EPA and the Productivity Slowdown), *American Economic Review 77,* No. 5 (December): pp. 998–1006.

Greenfield, Harry I. 1993. *Indivisible, Outlawed, and Untaxed: America's Underground Economy.* Westport, Connecticut: Praeger.

Greenwood, Daphne T. 1987. "Age. Income, and Household Size: Their Relation to Wealth Distribution in the United States," in Wolff (1987a): pp. 121–40.

Griliches, Zvi. 1990. "Patent Statistics as Economic Indicators: A Survey," *Journal of Economic Literature 27,* No. 4 (December): pp. 1161–1707.

Griliches, Zvi, editor. 1992. *Output Measurement in the Service Sectors.* Chicago: University of Chicago Press.

Grogger, Jeff. 1993. "Does School Quality Explain the Recent Black/White Trend." Santa Barbara, Calif.: University of California at Santa Barbara, processed.

Grogger, Jeff and Eric Eide. 1993. "Changes in College Skills and the Rise in the College Wage Premium," Santa Barbara, University of California at Santa Barbara, processed.

Grubb, W. Norton and Robert H. Wilson. 1989. "Sources of Increasing Inequality in Wages and Salaries, 1960–80," *Monthly Labor Review 112,* No. 4 (April): pp. 3–13.

——. 1992. "Trends in Wage and Salary Inequality, 1967–88," *Monthly Labor Review 115,* No. 6 (June): pp. 40–8.

Grubel, Herbert G. and Michael A. Walker, editors. 1978. *Unemployment Insurance: Global Evidence of its Effects on Unemployment.* Vancouver: Fraser Institute.

Habib, Jack. 1985. "The Economy and the Aged," in Robert H. Binstock and Ethel Shanas, editors. *Handbook of Aging and the Social Sciences.* New York: Van Nostrand Reinhold: pp. 479–503.

Hacker, Andrew. 1992. *Two Nations: Black and White, Separate, Hostile, Unequal.* New York: Charles Scribner's Sons.

Hahn, Robert W. and John A. Hird. 1991. "The Costs and Benefits of Regulation: Review and Synthesis," *Yale Journal on Regulation 8,* No. 1 (Winter): pp. 233–79.

Hahn F.H. and Robert M. Solow. 1986. "Is Wage Flexibility a Good Thing," in Wilfred Beckerman, editor. *Wage Rigidity and Unemployment.* Baltimore: Johns Hopkins University Press: pp. 1–21.

Hall, Bronwyn H. 1990. "The Impact of Corporate Restructuring on Industrial Research and Development," *Brookings Papers on Economic Activity: Microeconomics.* (Washington, D.C.: 1990).

————. 1991. "Corporate Restructuring and Investment Horizons," National Bureau of Economic Research, working paper No. 3794. Cambridge, Mass.

Hammermesh, David S. 1982. "The Interaction between Research and Policy: The Case of Unemployment Insurance," *American Economic Review 72*, No. 3 (May: Papers and Proceedings): pp. 237–41.

Hampden-Turner, Charles and Alfons Trompenaars. 1993. *The Seven Cultures of Capitalism*. New York: Currency-Doubleday.

Hanushek, Eric A. 1986. "The Economics of Schooling: Production and Efficiency in Public Schools," *Journal of Economic Literature 24*, (September): pp. 1131–77.

Hanson, Mary F. 1990. *Trends in Income, by Selected Characteristics: 1947 to 1988*, U.S. Department of Commerce, Bureau of the Census, Current Population Reports P60–167. Washington, D.C.: GPO.

Harrison, Roderick and Claudette E. Bennett. 1995. "Racism and Ethnic Diversity," in Reynolds Farley, editor. 1995. *State of the Union: America in the 1990's*. Vol. 2. New York: Russell Sage Foundation, pp. 141–211.

Hay Management Consultants. Annual. *Executive Compensation Report*. Philadelphia.

Hayghe, Howard V. 1991. "Volunteer in the U.S.: Who Donates the Time," *Monthly Labor Review 114*, No. 2 (February): pp. 17–24.

Hedges, Janice Neipert. 1973. "Absence from Work – A Look at Some National Data," *Monthly Labor Review 96*, No. 2 (July 1973): pp. 24–30.

——. 1975. "Unscheduled Absences from Work – An Update," *Monthly Labor Review 98*, No. 8 (August): pp. 33–42.

——. 1977. "Absence from Work – Measuring the Hours Lost," *Monthly Labor Review 100*, No. 10 (October 1977): pp. 16–23.

Heilbroner, Robert. 1993. *21st Century Capitalism*. New York: W. W. Norton.

Henle, Peter. 1972. "Exploring the Distribution of Earned Income," *Monthly Labor Review 95*, Number 12 (December): pp. 16–27.

Herman, Edward S. 1981. *Corporate Control, Corporate Power*. New York: Cambridge University Press.

Herring, Richard J. and Robert E. Litan. 1995. *Financial Regulation in a Global Economy*. Washington, D.C.: Brookings Institution.

Herrnstein, Richard J. and Charles Murray. 1994. *The Bell Curve: Intelligence and Class Structure in American Life*. New York: Free Press.

Hibbs, Douglas A., Jr. 1987. *The Political Economy of Industrial Democracies*. Cambridge, Mass.: Harvard University Press.

Hickok, Susan. 1990. "Factors Behind the Shifting Composition of U.S. Manufactured Goods Grade," Federal Reserve Bank of New York, Research Paper 9036. New York.

Hodgkinson, Virginia, et al. c. 1992. *Nonprofit Almanac, 1992–1993*. San Francisco: Jossey-Bass Publishers.

Holderness, Clifford G. and Dennis P. Sheehan. 1988. "The Role of Majority Stockholders in Publicly Held Corporations," *Journal of Financial Economics 20*, (January): pp. 317–46.

Holl, Peter. 1975. "Effect of Control Type on the Performance of the Firms in the U.K.," *Journal of Industrial Economics 23*, No. 4 (June 1975): pp. 257–71.

Holzer, Harry J. 1986. "Black Youth Nonemployment: Duration and Job Search," in Richard J. Freeman, Richard J. and Harry J. Holzer, editors. *The Black Youth Employment Crisis*. Chicago: University of Chicago Press, (1986): 23–75.

——. 1990. "Job Vacancy Rates in the Firm: An Empirical Analysis," National Bureau of Economic Research, working paper No. 3524. Cambridge, Mass.

Hopkins, Thomas D. 1992. "The Costs of Federal Regulation," National Chamber Foundation, Washington, D.C.

Horowitz, M. and I. Herrnstadt. 1966. "Change in Skill Requirements of Occupations in Selected Industries," in National Commission on Technology, *Technology and the American Economy*, Appendix Volume 2, *Changes in Skill Requirements of Occupations in Selected Industries*. Washington, D.C.: GPO.

Houthakker, H. S. and Stephen Magee. 1969. "Income and Price Elasticities in World Trade," *Review of Economics and Statistics 51*, No. 2 (May): pp. 111–26.

Howe, Neil and Phillip Longman. 1992. "The Next New Deal," *Atlantic Monthly 290*, No. 4 (April): pp. 88–99.

Howell, David R. 1994. "The Skills Myth," *The American Prospect 18*, (Summer): pp. 81–90.

Howell, David R. and Edward N. Wolff. 1991. "Trends in the Growth and Distribution of Skills in the U.S. Workplace, 1960–85," *Industrial and Labor Relations Review 44*, No. 3 (April): pp. 486–502.

Howell, David R. and Edward N. Wolff. 1993. "Changes in the Information-Intensity of the U.S. Workplace Since 1950: Has Information Technology Made a Difference?" working paper RR # 93–08, C.V. Starr Center for Applied Economics, New York University. New York, New York.

Hubbard, R. Glenn, editor.1990. *Asymmetric Information, Corporate Finance, and Investment*. Chicago: University of Chicago Press.

———. 1991. *Financial Markets and Financial Crisis*. Chicago: University of Chicago Press.

Huddle, Donald L. 1993. "A Growing Burden," *New York Times*. (September 3): p. 23.

Hughes, Jonathan R.T. 1991. *The Governmental Habit Redux*. Princeton: Princeton University Press.

International Labour Office. Annual. *Yearbook of Labour Statistics*. Geneva.

——. 1990. *Yearbook of Labour Statistics: Retrospective Edition, 1945–1989*. Geneva.

International Monetary Fund. Annual. *International Financial Statistics Yearbook*. Washington, D.C.

Jacoby, Sanford M. and Anil Verma. 1992. "Enterprise Unions in the United States," *Industrial Relations 31*, No. 1 (1992): pp. 137–59.

Jargowsky, Paul A. and Mary Jo Bane. 1991. "Ghetto Poverty in the United States, 1970–1980," in Jencks and Peterson (1991): pp. 235–73.

Jencks, Christopher. 1991. "Is the American Underclass Growing?" in Jencks and Peterson (1991): pp. 28–103.

Jencks, Christopher and Paul E. Peterson, editors. 1991. *The Urban Underclass*. Washington, D.C.: Brookings Institution.

Jensen, Michael C. 1994. "A Revolution Only Markets Could Love," *Wall Street Journal*, January 3.

Jensen, Michael C. and Kevin J. Murphy. 1990. "Performance Pay and Top-Management Incentives," *Journal of Political Economy 98*, No. 2 (April): pp. 225–65.

Johnson, George E. 1984. "Changes Over Time in the Union-Nonunion Wage Differential in the United States," in Jean-Jacques Rosa, editor, *The Economics of Trade Unions: New Directions*. Boston: Kluwer-Nijhoff Publishing.

Johnson, George E. and Richard Layard. 1986. "The Natural Rate of Unemployment : Explanation and Policy," in Ashenfelter and Layard (1986), Volume 2: pp. 921–99.

Johnston, William B. and Arnold E. Packer. 1987. *Workforce 2000*. Washington, D.C.: Hudson Institute.

Jones, J.C.H., L. Laudadio, and M. Percy. 1973. "Market Structure and Profitability in Canadian Manufacturing Industry: Some Cross Section Results," *Canadian Journal of Economics 6*, No. 3: pp. 356–68.

Jorgenson, Dale W. and Barbara M. Fraumeni. 1989. "The Accumulation of Human and Nonhuman Capital, 1948–1984," in Lipsey and Tice (1989): pp. 227–87.

Jorgenson, Dale W. and Peter J. Wilcoxen. 1990.. "Environmental Regulation and U.S. Economic Growth," *RAND Journal of Economics 21*, No. 2 (Summer): pp. 314–40.

Judis, John B. 1994. "Can Labor Come Back," *The New Republic.* (May 23): pp. 25–32.

Juhn, Chinhui, Keven M. Murphy and Robert H. Topel. 1991. "Why Has the Natural Rate of Unemployment Increased Over Time?" *Brookings Papers on Economic Activity*, No. 2: pp. 75–142.

Kalt, Joseph P. 1988. "The Impact of Domestic Environmental Regulatory Policy on U.S. International Competitiveness," in Spence and Hazard (1988): pp. 221–62.

Kamin, Jacob Y. and Joshua Ronen. 1978. "The Effects of Corporate Control on Apparent Profit Performance," *Southern Economic Journal 45*, No. 1 (July): pp. 181–91.

Kammerchen, David R. 1968. "Ownership and Control and Profit Rates," *American Economic Review 58*, No. 3 (June): pp. 432–48.

Kania, John J. and John R. McKean. 1976. "Control and the Contemporary Corporation: A General Behavioral Analysis," *Kyklos 29*, No. 2: pp. 272–92.

Karoly, Lynn A. 1988. *A Study of the Distribution of Individual Earnings in the United States from 1967 to 1986*, Ph. D. Dissertation, Yale University, cited by Levy and Murnane (1992).

Karoly, Lynn A. Forthcoming. "Trends in Income Inequality: The Impact of, and Implications for, Tax Policy," in Joel B. Slemrod, editor. *Tax Progressivity.* New York: Cambridge University Press.

Karoly, Lynn A. and Gary Burtless. 1994. "The Effects of Rising Earnings Inequality on the Distribution of U.S. Income," Paper presented at the RAND/NICHD conference, "Reshaping the Family: Social and Economic Changes and Public Policy," January 20–1.

Katz, Lawrence F. and Bruce D. Meyer. 1990. "The Impact of the Potential Duration of Unemployment Benefits on the Duration of Unemployment," *Journal of Public Economics 41*, No. 1 (February): pp. 45–72.

Katz, Lawrence and Kevin M. Murphy. 1992. "Wages, 1963–1987: Supply and Demand Factors," *Quarterly Journal of Economics 107*, No. 1 (February): pp. 35–79.

Kauffman, Stuart A. 1993. *The Origins of Order: Self-Organization and Selection in Evolution.* New York: Oxford University Press.

Kaufman, Bruce E. 1982. "The Determinants of Strikes in the United States, 1900–1977," *Industrial and Labor Relations Review 35*, No. 4 (July): pp. 473–90.

Kaus, Mickey. 1992. *The End of Inequality.* New York: Basic Books.

Kearns, Robert L. 1992. *Zaibatsu America: How Japanese Firms are Colonizing Vital U.S. Industries.* New York: Free Press.

Kennedy, James. 1993. "An Analysis of Revisions to the Industrial Production Index," *Applied Economics 25*, No. 2 (February): pp. 213–19.

Kennedy, Paul M. 1993. *Preparing for the Twenty First Century.* New York: Random House.

Kennickell, Arthur B. and R. Louise Woodburn. "Estimation of Household Net Worth Using Model-Based and Design-Based Weights: Evidence from the 1989 Survey of Consumer Finances," Board of Governors of the Federal Reserve Bank, distributed paper, April 1992.

Kessides, Ioannis N. 1990. "Market Concentration, Contestibility and Sunk Costs," *Review of Economics and Statistics 72*, No. 4 (November): pp. 614–22.

Kessler, Denis and André Masson. 1988. *Modelling the Accumulation and Distribution of Wealth.* Oxford: Clarenden Press.

Kessler, Denis and Edward N. Wolff. 1991. "A Comparative Analysis of Household Wealth Patterns in France and the United States," *Review of Income and Wealth 37*, No. 3 (September): pp. 249–66.

Kindleberger, Charles P. 1989. *Economic Laws and Economic History.* New York: Cambridge University Press.

Kirby, Michael J.L. 1985. "Complexity, Democracy, and Governance," in United Nations University (1985): pp. 329–37.

Kirsch, Irwin S. and Ann Jungeblut. 1985. *Literacy: Profiles of America's Young Adults.* Princeton, N.J.: Educational Testing Service.

Klein, Bruce W. 1986. "Missed Work and Lost Hours, May 1985," *Monthly Labor Review 109,* No. 11 (November): pp. 26–30.

Knacks, Stephen. 1990. "Why We Don't Vote – Or Say Thank You," *Wall Street Journal,* December 31.

Kohli, Ulrich. 1990. "Price and Quantity Elasticities in U.S. Foreign Trade," *Economic Letters 33,* No. 3 (July): pp. 277–81.

Kokoski, Mary F. 1991. "New Research on Interarea Consumer Price Differences," *Monthly Labor Review 114,* No. 7 (July): pp. 31–4.

Kokoski, Mary, Patrick Cardiff, and Brent Moulton. 1992. "Interarea Price Indices for Consumer Goods and Services: An Hedonic Approach Using CPI Data," unpublished, Department of Labor, Bureau of Labor Statistics.

Kominski, Robert and Andrea Adams. 1992. "Educational Attainment in the United States," U. S. Census Bureau, *Current Population Report, Series P-20,* No. 462. Washington, D.C.: GPO.

Konstant, Raymond A. and Irvin F. O. Wingeard. 1968. "Analysis and Use of Job Vacancy Statistics, Part II," *Monthly Labor Review 91,* No. 9 (September): pp. 18–21.

Kosters, Marvin H., editor. 1991. *Workers and Their Wages.* Washington, D.C. : American Enterprise Institute.

Kostiuk, Peter F. 1990. "Firm Size and Executive Compensation," *Journal of Human Resources 25,* No. 1 (Winter): pp. 90–105.

Kotlikoff, Laurence and Lawrence H. Summers. 1988. "The Contribution of Intergenerational Transfers to Total Wealth: A Reply," in Kessler and Masson (1988): pp. 53–67.

Kotz, David M. 1978. *Bank Control of Large Corporations in the United States.* Berkeley: University of California Press, 1978.

Kristol, Irving. 1978. *Two Cheers for Capitalism.* New York: Basic Books.

———. 1992. "The Cultural Revolution and the Capitalist Future," *The American Enterprise 3,* No. 2 (March): pp. 44–51.

Kristov, Lorenzo, Peter Lindert, and Robert McClelland. 1992. "Pressure Groups and Redistribution," *Journal of Public Economics 48,* No. 2 (July): pp. 135–65.

Krueger, Alan. 1991. "How Computers have Changed the Wage Structure: Evidence from Microdata, 1984–89," National Bureau of Economic Research, working papers No. 3858. Cambridge, Mass.

Krueger, Anne O. and Roderick Duncan. 1993. "The Political Economy of Controls: Complexity," National Bureau of Economic Research, working papers No. 4351. Cambridge, Mass.

Krugman, Paul. 1989. *Exchange-Rate Instability.* Cambridge, Mass.: MIT Press.

———. 1990. *The Age of Diminished Expectations.* Cambridge, Mass.: MIT Press.

Kruse, Douglas L. 1993. *Profit Sharing: Does It Make a Difference?* Kalamazoo, Michigan: Upjohn Institute for Employment Research.

Kuznets, Simon. 1959. *Six Lectures on Economic Growth.* Glencoe, Illinois: Free Press.

Laband, David N. and John P. Sophocleus. 1992. "An Estimate of Resource Expenditures on transfer Activity in the United States," *Quarterly Journal of Economics 107,* No. 3 (Autumn): pp. 950–83.

Laffer, Arthur. 1969. "Vertical Integration by Corporations, 1929–1965, " *Review of Economics and Statistics 51,* Number 1 (February): pp. 91–3.

Lamet, Joachim, Josef Richter, Werner Teufelsbauer. 1972. "Patterns of Industrial Structure of Economic Development," *European Economic Review 3,* No. 1: pp. 47–63.

Lampman, Robert J. 1962. *The Share of Top Wealth-Holders in National Wealth, 1922–56.* Princeton: Princeton University Press.

Larkey, Patrick D., Chandler Stolp, and Mark Winer. 1984. "Why Does Government Grow?" in Trudi C. Miller, editor. *Public Sector Performance: A Conceptual Turning Point.* Baltimore: Johns Hopkins: pp. 65–101.

Larner, Robert J. 1970. *Management Control and the Large Corporation.* Cambridge, Mass.: Dunellen.

Lasch, Christopher. 1995. *The Revolt of the Elites and the Betrayal of Democracy.* New York: W. W. Norton.

Lawler, Edward E., III et al. 1992. *Employee Involvement and Total Quality Management.* San Francisco: Jossey-Bass.

Lawrence, Robert Z. and Matthew J. Slaughter. 1993. "Trade and US Wages: Great Sucking Sound or Small Hiccup," *Brookings Papers on Economic Activity, Microeconomics,* No. 2: pp. 161–227.

Lawriwsky, Michael. 1984. *Corporate Structure and Performance.* London: Croom Helm.

Lazonick, William. 1988. "Financial Commitment and Economic Performance: Ownership and Control in the American Industrial Corporation," *Business and Economic History 17,* 2nd Series (Williamsburg, Virginia): pp. 115–28.

Leach, Dennis. 1987. "Ownership Concentration and Control in Large U.S. Corporations in the 1930s," *Journal of Industrial Economics 35,* No. 3 (March): pp. 333–42.

Leach, Dennis and John Leahy. 1991. "Ownership Structure, Control Type Classification, and the Performance of Large British Companies," *Economic Journal 101,* No. 409 (November): pp. 1418–37.

Leamer, Edward E. 1984. *Sources of International Comparative Advantage: Theory and Evidence.* Cambridge, Mass.: MIT Press.

———. 1992. "Testing Trade Theory," National Bureau of Economic Research, working papers No. 3957. Cambridge, Mass.

Leonard, Jonathan S. 1992. "Unions and Employment Growth," *Industrial Relations 31,* No. 1 (Winter): pp. 80–95.

Levin, Sharon G. and Stanford L. Levin. 1982. "Ownership and Control of Large Industrial Firms: Some New Evidence," *Review of Business and Economic Research 18,* No. 1 (Fall): pp. 37–49.

Levine, David I.. and Laura D'Andrea Tyson. 1990. "Participation, Productivity, and the Firm's Environment," ia Blinder (1990): 183–244.

Leigh, J. Paul 1983. "Sex Differences in Absenteeism," *Industrial Relations 22,* No. 3 (Fall 1983): pp. 349–61.

Levy, Frank and Richard J. Murnane. 1992. "U.S. Earnings Levels and Earnings Inequality: A Review of Recent Trends and Proposed Explanations," *Journal of Economic Literature 30,* No. 3 (September): pp. 1333–81.

Lewellen, Wilbur G. 1968. *Executive Compensation in the Large Industrial Corporation.* New York: Columbia University Press for National Bureau of Economic Research.

———. 1971. *The Ownership Income of Management.* New York: Columbia University Press for National Bureau of Economic Research.

———. 1975. "Recent Evidence in Senior Executive Pay," *National Tax Journal 28,* No. 2 (June): pp. 159–73.

Lewellen, Wilbur G. and Blaine Huntsman. 1970. "Managerial Pay and Corporate Performance," *American Economic Review 60,* No. 3 (June): pp. 710–20.

Lewin, Roger. 1992. *Complexity: Life at the Edge of Chaos.* New York: Macmillan.

Lichtenberg, Frank R. 1990. "Industrial De-Diversification and its Consequences for Productivity," National Bureau of Economic Research, working paper No. 3231. Cambridge, Mass.

———. 1992. *Corporate Takeovers and Productivity.* Cambridge, Mass.: MIT Press.

———, 1993. "The Output Contribution of Computer Equipment and Personnel: A Firm-Level Analysis," National Bureau of Economic Research, working paper No. 4540. Cambridge, Mass.

Lilien, David M. 1982. "Sectoral Shifts and Cyclical Unemployment," *Journal of Political Economy 70,* No. 4 (August): pp. 777–93.

Lincoln, James R. 1989. "Productivity, Motivation, and Work Attitudes in the United States and Japan," *Advances in the Study of Entrepreneurship, Innovation, and Economic Growth 3:* pp. 119–55.

Lindbeck, Assar. 1987. "The Advanced Welfare State," Seminar Paper 395, Institute for International Studies. Stockholm: processed.

———. 1993. "Overshooting, Reform, and Retreat of the Welfare State," Seminar Paper 552, Institute for International Economic Studies. Stockholm: processed.

Linder, Staffan Burenstam. 1978. *The Harried Leisure Class.* New York: Columbia University Press.

Lindert, Peter H. Forthcoming 1993. "The Rise of Social Spending, 1880–1930," *Explorations in Economic History.*

Lipsey, Robert E. and Helen Stone Tice, editor. 1989. *The Measurement of Saving, Investment, and Wealth,* National Bureau of Economic Research, Vol. 52, Studies in Income and Wealth. Chicago: University of Chicago Press.

Litan, Robert E. and William D. Nordhaus. 1981. *Reforming Federal Regulation.* New Haven: Yale University Press.

Litan, Richard J., et al., editors. 1988. *American Living Standards: Threats and Challenges.* Washington, D.C.: Brookings Institution.

Löfgren, Karl-Gustav and Lars Engström. 1989. "The Duration of Unemployment: Theory and Empirical Evidence," in Bertil Holmlund, Karl-Gustav Löfgren, and Lars Engström, *Trade Unions, Employment, and Unemployment Duration.* Oxford: Clarendon Press: pp. 133–221.

Long, William F. and David J. Ravenscraft. 1993. "Decade of Debt: Lessons from LBOs in the 1980s," in Blair (1993a): pp. 205–38.

Lorenz, Edward H. 1988. "Neither Friends nor Strangers: Informal Networks of Subcontracting in French Industry," in Gambetta (1988): pp. 194–211.

Lybeck, J.A. and M. Henrekson, editors. 1988. *Explaining the Growth of Government.* New York: Elsevier Science Publishing Company.

McDonald, Charles. 1992. "U.S. Union Membership in Future Decades: A Trade Unionist's Perspective," *Industrial Relations 31,* No. 1 (Winter 1992): pp. 13–31.

McEachern, William A. 1975. *Managerial Control and Performance.* Lexington, Mass.: D.C. Heath.

———. 1976. "Corporate Control and Risk," *Economic Inquiry 14,* No. 2 (June): pp. 270–9.

McKenzie, Richard B. 1990. "The Retreat of the Elderly Welfare State," Publication 102 of Center for the Study of American Business.

McKenzie, Richard B. and Christina Klein. 1992. "The 1980s: A Decade of Debt?" Policy Study Number 114, Center for the Study of American Business, Washington University, St. Louis.

McKinnon, Ronald I. 1990. "Interest Rate Volatility and Exchange Risk: New Rules for a Common Monetary Standard," *Contemporary Policy Issues 8,* No. 2 (April): pp. 1–18.

McKinsey Global Institute. 1993. *Manufacturing Productivity.* Washington, D.C.: McKinsey and Company.

McLanahan, Sara. 1989. "The Two Faces of Divorce: Women's and Children's Interests," Discussion Paper 903–89, Institute of Research on Poverty, Madison, Wisconsin.

———. 1994. "The Consequences of Single Motherhood," *The National Interest 18,* (Summer): pp. 48–58.

McLanahan, Sara and Larry Bumpers. 1986. "Intergenerational Consequences of Family Disruption," Discussion Paper 806–86, Institute of Research on Poverty, Madison, Wisconsin.

McRae, Hamish. 1994. *The World in 2020.* New York: Harper

McShea, Daniel W. 1991. "Complexity and Evolution: What Everybody Knows," *Biology and Philosophy 6:* pp. 303–24.

Machlup, Fritz. 1962. *The Production and Distribution of Knowledge in the United States.* Princeton: Princeton University Press.

Maddison, Angus. 1987. "Growth and Slowdown in Advanced Capitalist Nations," *Journal of Economic Literature 25,* No. 2 (June): pp. 649–98.

Magnet, Myron. 1993. *The Dream and the Nightmare: The Sixties Legacy to the Underclass.* New York: William Morrow.

Main, B.G.M. 1991. "Top Executive Pay and Performance," *Managerial and Decision Economics 12,* No. 3 (June): pp. 217–31.

Malabre, Alfred L. and Lindley H. Clark, Jr. 1992. "Productivity Statistics for the Service Sector May Understate Gains," *Wall Street Journal,* (August 12): p. A1.

Mandel, Michael J. and Christopher Farrell. 1992. "The Immigrants: How They're Helping to Revitalize the U.S. Economy," *Business Week,* (July 13): pp. 114–22.

Mankiw, N. Gregory, David L. Runkle, and Matthew R. Shapiro. 1984. "Are Preliminary Announcements of the Money Stock Rational Forecasts?" *Journal of Monetary Economics 14,* No. 1 (July): pp. 15–27.

Mankiw, N. Gregory and M. Shapiro. 1986. "News or Noise: An Analysis of GNP Revisions," *Survey of Current Business 66,* No. 3 (May): pp. 20–5.

Manthy, Robert S. 1978.. *Natural Resource Commodities – A Century of Statistics.* Baltimore: Johns Hopkins University Press for Resources for the Future.

Manzi, Jim. 1994. "Computer Keiretsu: Japanese Idea, U.S. Style," *New York Times,* (February 6): p. F-14.

Marcotte, Dave E. 1994. "The Declining Stability of Employment in the U.S.: 1976–1988," lecture presented at Brookings Institution, Washington, D.C. April.

Marris, Robin. 1964. *The Economic Theory of Managerial Capitalism.* New York: Free Press.

Maskus, Keith E. 1990. "Exchange Rate Risk and U.S. Trade: A Sectoral Analysis," in Davis, editor (1990): pp. 86–99.

Massey, Douglas S. and Eggers, Mitchell L. 1990. "The Ecology of Inequality: Minorities and the Concentration of Poverty, 1970–1980," *American Journal of Sociology 95,* No. 5 (March): pp. 1153–88.

Massey, Douglas S. and Nancy A. Denton. 1993. *American Apartheid: Segregation and the Making of the Underclass.* Cambridge, Mass.: Harvard University Press.

Masson, Robert Tempest. 1971. "Executive Motivation, Earnings, and Consequent Equity Performance," *Journal of Political Economy 79,* No. 6 (December): pp. 1278–93.

Marston, Richard C., 1990. "Price Behavior in Japanese and U.S. Manufacturing," National Bureau of Economic Research, working paper No. 3364. Cambridge, Mass.

Mayer, Susan E. 1991. "How Much Does a High School's Racial and Socioeconomic Mix Affect Graduation and Teenage Fertility Rates," in Jencks (1991): pp. 321–41.

Meissenheimer, Joseph L. 1990. "Employee Absences in 1989: A New Look at Data from the CPS," *Monthly Labor Review 113,* No. 8 (August 1990): pp. 28–33.

Meeks, Geoffrey and Geoffrey Whittington. 1975. "Growth and Profitability," *Journal of Industrial Economics 24,* No. 3 (September): pp. 1–14.

de Melo, Jaime and Shujiro Urata. 1986. "The Influence of Increased Foreign Competition on Industrial Concentration and Profitability," *International Journal of Industrial Organization 4,* No. 3: pp. 287–304.

Meyer, John R. and James M. Gustafson, editors. 1988. *The U.S. Business Corporation: An Institution in Transition.* Cambridge, Mass.: Ballinger.

Michael, Donald N. 1968. "On Coping with Complexity: Planning and Politics," *Daedalus,* No. 4 (Fall): pp. 1179–93.

Miller, Ann R., Donald J. Treiman, Pamela S. Cain, and Patricia A. Roos, editors. 1980. *Work, Jobs and Occupations: A Critical Review of the Dictionary of Occupational Titles.* Washington, D.C. : National Academy Press.

Miller, Ronald E. and Peter D. Blair, 1985. *Input-Output Analysis: Foundations and Extensions.* Englewood Cliffs, New Jersey: Prentice-Hall.

Milliron, Valerie C. 1985. "A Behavioral Study of the Meaning and Influence of Tax Complexity," *Journal of Accounting Research 23*, No. 2 (Autumn): pp. 794–816.

Minow, Nell. 1994. "Do Your Duty, Retirement Managers," *New York Times*, (January 30): p. F-11.

Minsky, Hyman P. 1982. *Can "It" Happen Again? Essays on Instability and Finance.* Armonk, New York: M. E. Sharpe.

Mishel, Lawrence and Jared Bernstein. 1993. *The State of Working America: 1992–93.* Washington, D.C.: Economic Policy Institute.

Mishel, Lawrence and Ruy A. Teixeira. 1991. "The Myth of the Coming Labor Shortage," *The American Prospect*, No. 4 (Fall): pp. 98–103.

Modigliani, Franco. 1988. "Measuring the Contribution of Intergenerational Transfers to Total Wealth: Conceptual Issues and Empirical Evidence," in Kessler and Masson (1988): pp. 21–53.

Monks, Robert A.G. and Nell Minow. 1991. *Power and Accountability.* New York: Harper Brothers.

Monson, R. Joseph, John S. Chiu and David E. Cooley. 1968. "The Effect of Separation of Ownership and Control on the Performance of the Large Firm," *Quarterly Journal of Economics 83*, No. 3 (August): pp. 435–51.

Moore, William J. and Robert J. Newman. 1988. "A Cross-Section Analysis of the Postwar Decline in American Trade Union Membership," *Journal of Labor Research 9*, No. 2 (Spring 1988): pp. 111–25.

Moore, William J., Robert J. Newman and Loren C. Scott. 1989. "Welfare Expenditures and the Decline of Unions," *Review of Economics and Statistics 71*, No. 3 (August): pp. 538–42.

Morck, Randall, Andrei Shleifer, and Robert W. Vishny. 1985. "Management Ownership and Corporate Performance," National Bureau of Economic Research, working paper No. 2055. Cambridge, Mass.

Morrall, John F. 1992. "Control of Regulation: A Washington Perspective," in Thomas D. Hopkins, editor. *Regulatory Policy in Canada and the United States.* Rochester, New York: Rochester Institute of Technology, processed.

Morrison, Catherine J. and Ernst R. Berndt. 1991. "Assessing the Productivity of Information Technology Equipment in U.S. Manufacturing Industries," National Bureau of Economic Research, working paper No. 3582. Cambridge, Mass.

Mueller, Dennis C., editor. 1983. *The Political Economy of Growth.* New Haven: Yale University Press.

Mueller, Dennis C. 1986. *Profits in the Long Run.* New York: Cambridge University Press.

———. 1989. "The Size of Government," in Dennis C. Mueller, *Public Choice II.* Cambridge: Cambridge University Press.

Mueller, Dennis C. and Peter Murrell. 1986. "Interest Groups and the Size of Government." *Public Choice 48*, No. 2: pp. 125–45.

Mueller, Willard F. and Larry G. Hamm. 1974. "Trends in Industrial Market Concentration, 1947 to 1970," *Review of Economics and Statistics 56*, No. 4 (November 1974): pp. 511–20.

Mulgan, G. J. 1991. *Communication and Control: Networks and the New Economics of Communications.* New York: Guilford Press.

Muller, Edward N. 1988. "Democracy, Economic Development, and Income Inequality," *American Sociological Review 53*, No. 1 (February): pp. 50–69.

Mullis, Ina V.S. et al. 1991. *Trends in Academic Progress,* National Center for Educational Statistics. Washington, D.C.: U.S. Department of Education.

Murnane, Richard J. 1988. "Education and the Productivity of the Work Force: Looking Ahead," in Litan (1988): pp. 215–45.

Murphy, Kevin M. and Finis Welch. 1991. "The Role of International Trade in Wage Differentials," in Kosters (1991): pp. 39–69.

Murrell, Peter. 1983. "The Comparative Structure of the Growth of the West German and British Manufacturing Industries," in Mueller (1983): pp. 109–32.

———. 1982. "Comparative Growth and Comparative Advantage: Tests of the Effects of Interest Group Behavior on Foreign Trade Patterns," *Public Choice* 38, Number 1: pp. 35–53.

Naples, Michele Irene. 1982. *The Structure of Industrial Relations, Labor Militance and the Rate of Growth of Productivity: The Case of United States Mining and Manufacturing, 1953–1977.* Unpublished Ph.D. dissertation, University of Mass.

Nasar, Sylvia. 1992. "More College Graduates Taking Low-Wage Jobs," *New York Times.* (August 7, 1992): p. D-5.

National Center for Education Statistics. 1993. *Adult Literacy in America.* Washington D.C.: GPO.

National Center for Employee Ownership, Inc. Bimonthly. *Employee Ownership Report.* Oakland, Calif.

National Council of the Churches of Christ in the U.S.A. . Annual. *Yearbook of American and Canadian Churches.* Nashville: Abingdon Press.

Nelson, Michael A. 1990. "Decentralization of the Subnational Public Sector: An Empirical Analysis of the Determinants of Local Government Structure in Metropolitan Finance," *Southern Economic Journal 57,* No. 2 (October): pp. 443–57.

Nelson, Richard. 1995. "Recent Economic Theorizing About Evolutionary Change," *Journal of Economic Literature* 33, No. 1 (March): pp. 48–91.

Nelson, Richard R. and Sidney G. Winter. 1982. *An Evolutionary Theory of Economic Change.* Cambridge, Mass.: Belknap Press.

Neumark, David and William Wascher 1991. "Can We Improve Upon Preliminary Estimates of Payroll Employment Growth?" *Journal of Business Economics and Statistics 9,* No. 2 (April): pp. 197–205.

Neun, Stephen P. and Rexford E. Santerre. 1986. "Dominant Stockholder and Profitability," *Managerial and Decision Economics 7,* No. 3 (September): pp. 207–10.

Neumann, George R. and Ellen R. Rissman. 1984. "Where Have All the Union Members Gone?" *Journal of Labor Economics 2,* No. 2 (April): pp. 175–92.

Newhouse, Joseph P. 1992. "Medical Care Costs: How Much Welfare Loss," *Journal of Economic Perspectives 6,* No. 3 (Summer): pp. 3–21.

Nicolis, Grégoire and Ilya Prigogine. 1989. New York: W. H. Freeman and Company.

Nicolson, Walter. 1981. "A Statistical Model of Exhaustion of Unemployment Benefits," *Journal of Human Resources 16,* No. 1 (Winter): pp. 129–41.

Nietzsche, Friedrich. 1901 (1986). *The Will to Power,* edited by Walter Kaufmann. New York: Vintage Books.

Niskanen, William. 1975, "Bureaucrats and Politicians," *Journal of Law and Economics 28,* No. 3 (December) pp. 617–44.

Nitecki, Matthew H., editor. 1988. *Evolutionary Progress.* Chicago: University of Chicago.

Norton, Arthur and Louisa F. Miller. 1992. *Marriage, Divorce and Remarriage in the 1990's,* Bureau of the Census, Current Population Reports P23–180. Washington, D.C.: GPO.

O'Barr, William M., John M. Conley, and Carolyn Kay Brancato. 1992. *Fortune and Folly: The Wealth and Power of Institutional Investing.* Homewood, Illinois: Irwin.

Oliner, Stephen and Daniel Sichel. 1994. "Computers and Productivity Revisited: How Large is the Puzzle," unpublished working paper.

Olson, Mancur. 1982. *The Rise and Decline of Nations: Economic Growth, Stagflation and Social Rigidities.* New Haven: Yale University Press.

O'Neill, Molly. 1993. "Drop the Mop. Bless the Mess: The Decline of Housekeeping," *New York Times,* (April 11): p. 1.

O'Neill, David M. 1983. "Growth of the Underground Economy, 1950–81: Some Evidence from the Current Population Survey," Joint Economic Committee, U.S. Congress, *Study*. Washington, D.C.: GPO, December.

Orfield, Gary. *The Growth of Segregation in American Schools: Changing Patterns of Separation and Poverty Since 1968*. Washington, DC: National School Boards Association.

Organization for Economic Cooperation and Development (OECD). Irregular. *National Account Statistics*. Paris.

———. 1970. *National Accounts of the OECD Countries, 1950–1968*. Paris.

———. 1991. *National Accounts, Main Aggregates*, Vol. 1, *1960–89*. Paris.

———. 1992c: *Employment Outlook*, (July). Paris.

———. 1992a. *National Accounts, Detailed Tables*, Vol. 2, *1978–1990*. Paris.

———. 1992b. *Technology and the Economy*. Paris.

Owen, John D. 1988. "Work Time Reduction in U.S. and Western Europe," *Monthly Labor Review 111*, No. 12 (December): pp. 41–5.

Padoa-Schioppa, Fiorella, editor. 1991. *Mismatch and Labour Mobility*. New York: Cambridge University Press.

Pagden, Anthony. 1988. "The Destruction of Trust and its Economic Consequences in the Case of Eighteenth-century Naples," in Gambetta (1988): pp. 127–42.

Paldam, Martin and Peder J. Pedersen. 1984 "The Large Pattern of Industrial Conflict: A Comparative Study of 18 Nations,1919–79." *International Journal of Social Economics 11*, No. 5: pp. 3–28.

Palmer, John P. 1973a. "The Profit-Performance Effects of the Separation of Ownership from Control in Large U.S. Industrial Corporations," *Bell Journal of Economics 4*, No. 1 (Spring): pp. 293–303.

———. 1973b. "The Profit-Variability Effect of the Managerial Enterprise," *Western Economic Journal 11*, No. 2 (June 1973): pp. 228–31.

———. 1975. "A Further Analysis of Profit Variability and Managerialism," *Economic Inquiry 13*, No. 1 (March): pp. 124–7.

Pappas, Gregory, Susan Queen, Wilbur Hadden, and Gail Fisher. 1993. "The Increasing Disparity in Mortality between Socioeconomic Groups in the United States, 1960 and 1986," *The New England Journal of Medicine 329*, No. 2 (July 8): pp. 103–9.

Parker, Jeffrey. 1992. "Structural Unemployment in the United States: The Effects of Interindustry and Interregional Dispersion," *Economic Inquiry 30*, No. 1 (January): pp. 101–16.

Pedersen, Lawrence and William K. Taub. 1976. "Ownership and Control in Large Corporations Revisited," *Antitrust Bulletin 21*, No. 1 (Spring): pp. 53–66.

Peltzman, Sam. 1980. "The Growth of Government," *Journal of Law and Economics 23*, No. 2 (October): pp. 209–28.

———. 1989. "The Economic Theory of Regulation after a Decade of Deregulation," *Brookings Papers on Economic Activity: Microeconomics*. Washington, D.C.: pp. 1–42.

———. 1992. "Voters as Fiscal Conservatives," *Quarterly Journal of Economics 107*, No. 2 (May 1992): pp. 327–61.

Pencavel, John H. 1970. *An Analysis of the Quit Rate in American Manufacturing Industry*. Princeton, New Jersey: Industrial Relations Section, Department of Economics.

Pencavel, John and Catherine E. Hartsog. 1984. "A Reconsideration of the Effects of Unionism on Relative Wages and Employment in the United States, 1920–1980," *Journal of Labor Economics 2*, No. 2 (April): pp. 193–233.

Penner, Rudolph G. 1986. "Prepared Statement," in U.S. Congress, Joint Economic Committee, Subcommittee on Economic Resources, Competitiveness and Security Economics. *Demographic Changes in the United States: The Economic and Social Consequences into the 21st Century*. Washington, D.C.: GPO.

Peters, Edgar E. 1991. *Chaos and Order in the Capital Markets: A New View of Cycles, Prices, and Market Volatility*. New York: Wiley.

Peterson, Paul E. 1991. "The Urban Underclass and the Poverty Paradox," in Jencks and Peterson (1991): pp. 3–28.

Piel, Gerald. 1992. *Only One World: Our Own to Make and to Keep*. New York: W.H. Freeman.

Pierce, James L. 1991. *The Future of Banking*. New York: 20th Century Fund.

Piore, Michael J. and Charles F. Sabel. 1984. *The Second Industrial Divide: Possibilities for Prosperity*. New York: Basic Books.

Pollin, Robert. 1990. *Deeper in Debt: The Changing Financial Conditions of U.S. Households*. Washington, D.C.: Economic Policy Institute.

Porat, Marc Uri. 1977. *The Information Economy: Definition and Measurement*. U.S. Department of Commerce, OT Special Publication 77–12 (1), Washington, D.C.: GPO.

Pratt, John W., David A. Wise, and Richard Zeckhauser. 1979. "Price Differences in Almost Competitve Markets," *Quarterly Journal of Economics 93*, No. 2 (May): pp. 189–211.

Primont, Diane F. and Mary F. Kokoski. 1991. "Differences in Food Prices Across U.S. Cities: Evidence from CPI Data, " U.S. Department of Labor, Bureau of Labor Statistics, BLS working paper, No. 209.

Pryor, Frederic L. 1968. *Public Expenditures in Communist and Capitalist Nations*. London: Allen and Unwin; and Homewood, Illinois: Irwin.

———. 1973a. "The Impact of Social and Economic Institutions on the Size Distribution of Income and Wealth: A Simulation Study," *American Economic Review, 62*, No. 1 (March): pp. 339–50.

———. 1973b. *Property and Industrial Organization in Communist and Capitalist Nations*. Bloomington, Indiana: University of Indiana Press.

———. 1977. "Some Costs and Benefits of Markets: An Empirical Study," *Quarterly Journal of Economic 91*, No. 1 (February 1977): pp. 81–102.

———. 1981. "Static and Dynamic Effects of Different Types of Trade Barriers: A Synthesis Using a General Equilibrium Model," *Eastern Economic Journal, 7*, No. 2 (April): pp. 59–74.

———. 1983a. "Some Economics of Sloth," *The Social Science Review 5*, No. 1 (Fall): pp. 82–102.

———. 1983b. "A Quasi-Test of Mancur Olson's Hypothesis," in Dennis Mueller, editor. (1983): pp. 90–105.

———. 1984a. "Incentives in Manufacturing: The Carrot and the Stick," *Monthly Labor Review 107*, No. 7 (July): pp. 40–3.

———. 1984b. "Rent Seeking and the Growth and Fluctuation of Nations: Empirical Tests of Some Recent Hypotheses," in David Collander, editor. *Neoclassical Political Economy*. Cambridge, Mass.: Ballinger: pp. 155–77.

———. 1987. "Testing Olson: Some Statistical Problems," *Public Choice 52*: pp. 223–6.

———. 1988. "Corporatism as an Economic System," *Journal of Comparative Economics 12*, No. 3 (September}: pp. 317–44.

———. 1990. *The Political Economy of Poverty, Equity, and Growth: Malawi and Madagascar*. New York: Oxford University Press for the World Bank.

———. 1992a. "A Puzzle about Intra-Industry Trade: A Comment," *Weltwirtschaftliches Archiv 128*, No. 4: pp. 742–6.

———. 1992b. *The Red and the Green: The Rise and Fall of Collectivized Agriculture in Marxist Regimes*. Princeton: Princeton University Press.

———. 1993. "The Roman Catholic Church and the Economic System: A Review Essay," *Journal of Comparative Economics, 17*, No. 1 (March 1993), pp. 129–51.

———. 1994a. "The Evolution of Competition in the United States," *The Review of Industrial Organization, 25*, No. 2: pp. 121–33.

————. 1994b. "Growth Deceleration and Transaction Costs: A Note," *Journal of Economic Behavior and Organization. 25*, No. 3: pp. 121–33.

————. 1994c. "Reflections and the Non-Profit Sector," *Comparative Economic Studies 36*, No. 1 (Spring): pp. 69– 81.

————. 1995. "Behavior of Retail Prices: A Note on Market Integration in the U.S.," *Eastern Economic Journal*, No. 1 (Winter), pp. 83–97.

Pryor, Frederic L. and Elliott Sulcove. 1995. "A Note on Volatility," *Journal of Post-Keynesian Economics 17*, No. 4 (summer): pp. 525–44.

Quinn, Robert P., Graham L. Staines, and Margaret R. McCullough. 1974. *Job Satisfaction: Is There a Trend*, U.S. Department of Labor, Manpower Administration, *Manpower Research Monograph 30*. Washington, D.C.: GPO.

Radice, H.K. 1971. "Control Type, Profitability and Growth in Large Firms," *Economic Journal 81*, No. 323 (September): pp. 547–63.

Ravenscraft, David J. and F. M. Scherer. 1987. *Mergers, Sell-Offs, and Economic Efficiency.* Washington, D.C.: Brookings.

Ravitch, Diane. 1993. "When School Comes to You," *Economist 328*, (September 11): pp. 43–9.

Reich, Charles A. 1964. "The New Property," *Yale Law Journal 73*, (April): pp. 733–87.

Reich, Robert. 1991. "Up the Workers," *The New Republic*, (May 13): pp. 21–5.

————. 1993. "Companies are Cutting their Hearts Out," *New York Times Magazine*, (December 19): pp. 54–5.

Reinemer, Vic. 1979. "Stalking the Invisible Investor," *Journal of Economic Issues 13*, No. 2 (June): pp. 391–405.

Ricketts, Erol and Ronald Mincy. 1990. "Growth of the Underclass, 1970–80," *Journal of Human Resources 25*, No. 1 (Winter): pp. 37–44.

Rochell, Carlton C.. 1987. *Dreams Betrayed: Working in the Technological Age.* Lexington, Mass.: Lexington Books.

Roe, Mark J. 1990. "Political and Legal Restraints on Ownership and Control of Public Companies," *Journal of Financial Economics 27*, No. 1 (September): pp. 7–41.

————. 1993. "Takeover Politics," in Blair (1993a): pp. 321–53.

Romer, Christina D. 1992. "Remeasuring Business Cycles," National Bureau of Economic Research, working paper No. 4150. Cambridge, Mass.

Rooney, Patrick Michael. 1992a. "Employee Ownership and Worker Participation: Effects on Firm-Level Productivity in the United States," Indianapolis: Indiana University — Purdue University *IUPUI Working Paper*, No. 92: p. 1.

————. 1992b. "Employee Ownership and Worker Participation: Effects on Health and Safety," *Economic Letters 39*, No. 3 (July): pp. 323–8.

————. 1992c. "ESOPS, Producer Co-ops, and Traditional Firms: Are They Different?" *Journal of Economic Issues 26*, no. 2 (June): pp. 593–603.

Roos, Patricia A. and Donald J. Treiman. 1980. "DOT Scales for the 1970 Census Classification," in Miller *et al.* (1980): pp. 336–89.

Rose, Andrew. 1991. "Why has Trade Grown Faster than Income," *Canadian Journal of Economics 24*, No. 2 (May 1991): pp. 417–27.

Rose, Stephen J. 1993. "Declining Family Incomes in the 1980s: New Evidence from Longitudinal Data," unpublished paper.

Ross, Arthur M. 1958. "Do We Have a New Industrial Feudalism?" *American Economic Review 48*, No. 5 (December): pp. 903–20.

Ruggles, Patricia and Charles F. Stone. 1992. "Income Distribution over the Business Cycles: The 1980s were Different," *Journal of Policy Analysis and Management 11*, No. 4: pp. 715–22.

Rutledge, Carl L. and Mary L. Leonard. 1992. "Pollution Abatement and Control Expenditures, 1972–90," *Survey of Current Business 72*, No. 6 (June): pp. 25–41.

Ryscavage, Paul and Peter Henle. 1989. "Earnings Inequality Accelerates in the 1980's," *Monthly Labor Review 113*, No. 12 (December): pp. 3–15.

Sachs, Jeffrey D. and Howard J. Shatz. 1994. "Trade and Jobs in U.S. Manufacturing," *Brookings Papers on Economic Activity*, No. 1: pp. 1–85.

Saluter, Arlene F. 1989. *Changes in American Family Life*, Bureau of the Census, Current Population Reports P23– 163. Washington, D.C.: GPO.

Sanford, Charles E., Jr.1994. "Financial Markets in 2020," *Economic Review of the Federal Reserve Bank of Kansas City 79*, No. 1 (First quarter):19–29.

Santerre, Rexford E. and Stephen P. Neun. 1986. "Stock Dispersion and Executive Compensation," *Review of Economics and Statistics 68*, No. 4 (November): pp. 685–87.

———. 1989. "Managerial Control and Executive Compensation in the 1930s: A Reexamination," *Quarterly Journal of Business and Economics 28*, No. 4 (Autumn): pp. 100–9.

Sarris, Alexander. 1984. "Speculative Storage, Futures Markets, and the Stability of Commodity Prices," *Economic Enquiry 22*, No. 1 (January): pp. 80–108.

Sattinger, Michael. 1985. *Unemployment, Choice, and Inequality*. New York: Springer-Verlag.

Sawhill, Isabel V. and Mark Condon. 1992. "Is U.S. Income Inequality Really Growing," *Policy Bites* (Urban Institute) 13. June.

Scherer, F.M. 1976. "Industrial Structure, Scale Economies, and Worker Alienation," in Robert T. Masson and P. David Qualls, editors. *Essays on Industrial Organization in Honor of Joe S. Bain*. Cambridge, Mass.: Ballinger Publishing Company.

———. 1988. "Corporate Ownership and Control," in Meyer and Gustafson (1988): pp. 43–67.

———. 1992. *International High-Technology Competition*. Cambridge, Mass.: Harvard University Press.

Scherer, F.M. and David Ross. 1990. *Industrial Market Structure and Economic Performance*, Third edition. Boston: Houghton Mifflin.

Schmandt, Henry J. and G. Ross Stephens. 1960. "Measuring Municipal Output," *National Tax Journal 13*, No. 4 (December): pp. 369–75.

Schoepfle, Gregory K., et al. 1992. "The Underground Economy in the United States," United States Department of Labor, *Occasional Papers on the Informal Economy*, No. 2 (September). Washington, DC: Processed.

Schor, Juliet B. 1991. *The Overworked American*. New York: Basic Books.

Schor, Juliet B. and Samuel Bowles. 1987. "Employment Rents and the Incidence of Strikes,"a *Review of Economics and Statistics 69*, No. 4 (November): pp. 584–92.

Schumpeter, Joseph A. 1942. *Capitalism, Socialism, and Democracy*. New York: Harper and Brothers.

Schwartz, Nancy E. 1986, "The Consequences of a Floating Exchange Rate for the U.S. Wheat Market," *American Journal of Agricultural Economics 68*, No. 2 (May): pp. 428–33.

Scott, John. 1986. *Capitalist Property and Financial Power*. New York: New York University Press.

Sedgwick, John. 1993. "The Complexity Problem," *Atlantic Monthly*, (March): pp. 96–104.

Shapiro, Harvey. 1961. "Measuring Local Government Output: A Comment," *National Tax Journal 14*, No. 4 (December): pp. 394–7.

Sharpe, Rochelle. 1993. "In Latest Recession Only Blacks Suffered Net Employment Loss," *Wall Street Journal*, (September 14): pp. A1, A12–3.

Shiller, Robert J. 1992. "Volatility," in Peter Newman, *et al.*, editors, *The New Palgrave Dictionary of Money and Finance*.New York: Stockten Press, Volume 3: pp. 762–5.

Shleifer, Andrei and Robert W. Vishny. 1988. "Value Maximization and the Acquisition Process,": *Journal of Economic Perspectives 2*, No. 1 (Winter): pp. 7–20.

Simon, Herbert A. 1969. "The Architecture of Complexity," in *The Sciences of the Artificial*. Cambridge, Mass.: MIT Press: pp. 84–118.

————. 1977. *Models of Discovery and Other Topics in the Methods of Science*. Boston: Reidel.

Slemrod, Joel. 1992. "Taxation and Inequality: A Time-Exposure Perspective," National Bureau of Economic Research, working paper No. 3999. Cambridge, Mass.

Smith, James D., editor. 1980. *Modeling the Distribution and Intergenerational Transmission of Wealth*. Chicago: University of Chicago Press.

————. 1984. "Trends in the Concentration of Personal Wealth in the United States, 1958 to 1976," *The Review of Income and Wealth, 30*, No. 4 (December 1984): pp. 419–29.

Smith, John Maynard. 1988. "Evolutionary Progress and Levels of Selection," in Nitecki (1988): pp. 219–30.

Smith, Steven R. and Michael Lipsky. 1993. *Nonprofits for Hire*. Cambridge, Mass.: Harvard University Press.

Solon, Gary. 1985. "Work Incentive Effects of Taxing Unemployment Benefits," *Econometrica 53*, No. 2 (March): pp. 295–305.

————. 1992. "Intergenerational Income Mobility in the United States," *American Economic Review 82*, No. 3 (June): pp. 393–498.

Sorensen, Robert. 1974, "The Separation of Ownership and Control and Firm Performance: An Empirical Analysis," *Southern Economic Journal 41*, Number 1 (July): pp. 145–8.

Spencer, Gregory. 1989. *Projections of the Population of the United States, by Age, Sex, and Race: 1988 to 2080*. Bureau of the Census, Current Population Reports P25–1018. Washington, D.C.: GPO.

Spence, A. Michael and Heather A. Hazard, editors. 1988. *International Competitiveness*. Cambridge, Mass.: Harper and Row.

Spenner, Kenneth I. 1983. "Deciphering Prometheus: Temporal Change in Work Content," *American Sociological Review 48*, (December): pp. 824–37.

Stano, Myron. 1975. "Executive Ownership Interests and Corporate Behavior," *Southern Economic Journal 42*, No. 2 (October 1975): pp. 272–8.

Stansell, Stanely R., editor. 1993. *International Financial Market Integration*. Oxford, England: Blackwell Publishers.

Stigler, George J. and Claire Friedland. 1983. "The Literature of Economics: The Case of Berle and Means," *Journal of Law and Economics 26*, No. 2 (June): pp. 237–69.

Stigler, George J. and James K. Kindahl. 1970. *The Behavior of Industrial Prices*. New York: Columbia University Press for National Bureau of Economic Research.

Stodder, James. 1995. "The Evolution of Complexity in Primitive Economies," *Journal of Comparative Economics 19* (February): pp. 1–32; and (April): pp. 190–211.

Stone, Charles F. and Larry Radbill. 1993a. "Longitudinal Evidence on Earnings: Some Preliminary Findings from the PSID," Paper presented at the annual meetings of the Eastern Economic Association, March 21.

————. 1993b. "Trends in Family Income and its Distribution: New Evidence on Mobility and Inequality," September: processed.

Stout, Hilary. 1989. "Shaky Numbers: U.S. Statistics Mills Grind Out more Data That Are Then Revised," *Wall Street Journal 114*, No. 43 (Aug 31, 1989), pp. 1–2.

Streufert, Siegfried and Robert W. Swezey. 1986. *Complexity, Managers, and Organizations*. San Diego: Academic Press, 1986.

Summers, Larry H. 1991. "Macroeconomic Consequences of Financial Crises," in Feldstein (1991): pp. 135–57.

Summers, Robert and Alan Heston. 1988. "A New Set of International Comparisons of Real Product and Price Level Estimates for 130 Countries, 1950–1985," *Review of Income and Wealth 34*, No. 1 (March): pp. 1–25.

————. 1991. "The Penn World Table (Mark 5): An Expanded Set of International Comparisons, 1950–1988," *Quarterly Journal of Economics, 106*, No. 2 (May): pp. 327–68.

Sutton, John. 1991. *Sunk Costs and Market Structure*. Cambridge, Mass.: MIT Press.

Sveikauskas, Leo. 1983. "Science and Technology in United States Foreign Trade," *Economic Journal 93*, No. 3 (September): pp. 542–54.

Sweden, Statens offentliga utredningar, Finansdepartementet. 1968. *Industrins struktur och konkurrensförhållanden.* Stockholm: 1968.

Taiwan, Directorate General of Budget, Accounting and Statistics, 1984. *Statistical Yearbook of the Republic of China 1984.* Taipai.

Taylor, Daniel. 1979. "Absent Workers and Lost Work Hours, May 1978," *Monthly Labor Review 102*, No. 8 (August 1979): pp. 49–55.

Theil, Henri. 1967. *Economics and Information Theory.* Chicago: Rand McNally.

Tilly, Chris. 1991. "Reasons for Continuing Growth of Part-Time Employment," *Monthly Labor Review 114*, No. 3 (March): pp. 10–18.

Tinbergen. Jan. 1975. *Income Distribution: Analysis and Policies.* Amsterdam: North-Holland Publishing Co.

Toffler, Alvin. 1981. *The Third Wave.* New York: Bantam Books.

——. 1990. *Powershift: Knowledge, Wealth, and Violence at the Edge of the 21st Century.* New York: Bantam Books.

Troy, Leo. 1990. "Is the U.S. Unique in the Decline of Private Sector Unionism?" *Journal of Labor Research 11*, No. 2 (Spring): pp. 111–43.

Turner, John A and Daniel J. Beller, editors. 1992. *Trends in Pensions 1992.* Washington, D.C.: GPO.

United Nations. Annual-a. *Yearbook of Industrial Statistics* (formerly called *The Growth of World Industry*). New York.

——. Annual-b. *Yearbook of International Trade Statistics.* New York.

——. 1976. *World Energy Supplies, 1950–1974,* Statistical Papers, Series J., No. 19. New York.

——. 1979. *Demographic Yearbook: Historical Supplement.* New York.

——. 1988. *Demographic Yearbook 1986.* New York.

——. 1992. *National Account Statistics: Main Aggregates and Detailed Tables.* New York.

United Nations University. 1985. *The Science and Praxis of Complexity.* Tokyo: United Nations University Press.

U.S. Congress, Joint Committee on Taxation. 1976. *General Explanation of the Tax Reform Act of 1976.* Washington, D.C.:GPO.

——. 1987. *General Explanation of the Tax Reform Act of 1986.* Washington, D.C.: GPO.

——. 1993. *Estimates of Federal Tax Expenditures for Fiscal Years 1993–1998.* Washington, D.C.: GPO.

U.S. Council of Economic Advisors. Annual. *Economic Report of the President.* Washington, D.C.: GPO.

U.S. Department of Commerce, Bureau of the Census. Annual-a. *County Business Patterns.* Washington, D.C.: GPO.

——. Annual-b. *Statistical Abstract of the United States.* Washington, D.C.: GPO.

——. Monthly. *Survey of Current Business.* Washington, D.C: GPO.

——. 1953. *Census of Population: 1950,* Vol. II, *Characteristics of the Population, Part 1, United States Summary.* Washington, D.C.: GPO.

——. 1961. *1958 Census of Manufactures,* Vol. 1, *Summary Statistics.* Washington, D.C.: GPO.

——. 1963a. *Census of Population: 1960,* Vol. I, *Characteristics of the Population, Part 51, Wisconsin.* Washington, D.C.: GPO.

——. 1963b. *1958 Enterprise Statistics.* Washington, D.C.: GPO.

——. 1964. *Census of Population: 1960,* Vol. I, *Characteristics of the Population, Part 1, United States Summary.* Washington, D.C.: GPO.

——. 1966. *1963 Census of Manufactures,* Vol. 1, *Summary and Subject Statistics.* Washington, D.C.: GPO.

384   **Economic evolution and structure**

———. 1970. *U.S. Exports and Imports Classified by OBE End-Use Commodity Categories, 1923–1968.* Washington, D.C.: GPO.

———. 1972. *1967 Enterprise Statistics.* Washington, D.C.: GPO.

———, 1973/74. *1970 Census of Population,* Vol. I, *Characteristics of the Population,* Part 1, *United States Summary.* Washington, D.C.: GPO.

———. 1975. *Historical Statistics of the United States.* Washington, D.C: GPO.

———. 1976. *1972 Census of Manufactures.* Washington, D.C.

———. 1977. *Money Income in 1975 of Families and Persons in the United States,* Current Population Reports P6–105. Washington, D.C. GPO.

———. 1979. *U.S. Commodity Exports and Imports as Related to Output, 1972 and 1971.* Washington, D.C.

———. 1981. *1977 Enterprise Statistics.* Washington, D.C.: GPO.

———. 1983. *1980 Census of Population,* Vol. I, *Characteristics of the Population,* Part 1, *United States Summary.* Washington, D.C.: GPO.

———. 1984. *1980 Census of the Population,* Vol. 1, Chapter D, *Detailed Characteristics of the Population,* Part 1, U.S. Summary. Washington, D.C.: GPO.

———. 1985. *U.S. Commodity Exports and Imports as Related to Output, 1982 and 1981.* Washington, D.C.

———. 1986a. *1982 Census of Manufactures,* Subject Series, *Concentration Ratios in Manufacturing.* Washington, D.C.: GPO.

———. 1986b. *1982 Census of Manufacturers,* Subject Series, *General Summary.* Washington, D.C.: GPO.

———. 1991a. *1987 Census of Manufacturers,* Subject Series, *General Summary.* Washington, D.C.: GPO.

———. 1991b. *1987 Enterprise Statistics.* Washington, D.C.: GPO.

———. 1991c. *Money Income of Households, Families, and Persons in the United States: 1990,* Current Population Report, P60–174. Washington, D.C.: GPO.

———. 1992a. *1990 Census of Population,* Supplementary Reports, *Detailed Occupation and Other Characteristics from the EEO File for the United States.* Washington, D.C.: GPO.

———. 1992b. *Money Income of Households, Families, and Persons in the United States: 1991,* Current Population Report, P60–180. Washington, D.C.: GPO.

———. 1993. *Money Income of Households, Families, and Persons in the United States: 1991,* Current Population Report, P60–184. Washington, D.C.: GPO.

———. 1994. *U.S. Commodity Exports and Imports as Related to Output, 1991 and 1990.* Washington, D.C.

U.S. Department of Commerce, Bureau of Economic Analysis/Office of Business Economics. Monthly. *Survey of Current Business.* Washington, D.C.

———. 1954. *National Income, 1954 Edition.* Washington, D.C.: G.O.O.

———. 1965. "Transactions Table of the 1958 Input-Output Study and Revised Direct and Total Requirements Data," *Survey of Current Business 45,* No. 9 (September): pp. 33–50.

———. 1979. *The Detailed Input-Output Structure of the U.S. Economy: 1972.* Washington, D.C.: GPO.

———. 1985. *Foreign Direct Investment in the United States: Revised 1982 Estimates.* Washington, D.C.

———. 1986. *The National Income and Product Accounts of the United States, 1929–82.* Washington, D.C.: GPO.

———. 1987. *Fixed Reproducible Tangible Wealth in the United States, 1925–85.* Washington, D.C.: GPO.

———. 1992/3. *National Income and Product Accounts of the United States,* Vols. 1 and 2. Washington, D.C.: GPO.

————. 1993. *Fixed Reproducible Tangible Wealth in the United States, 1925–89*. Washington, D.C. GPO.

U.S. Department of Education. 1993a. *Adult Literacy in America: A First Look at the Results of the National Adult Literacy Survey*. Washington, D.C.: GPO.

————. 1993b. *Reading Report Card on Schools*. Washington, D.C.: GPO.

U.S. Department of Labor. Annual-a. *Employment and Earnings*. Washington, D.C.: GPO.

————. Annual-b. *Employment and Training Report of the President*. Washington, D.C.: GPO.

————. 1977. *Dictionary of Occupational Titles*. Washington, D.C.: GPO.

————. 1989. *Consumer Expenditure Survey, 1984–1986*, Bulletin 2333. Washington, D.C.: GPO.

U.S. Department of Labor, Bureau of Labor Statistics. 1965, "Interindustry Employment Requirements," *Monthly Labor Review 88*, No. 7 (July): pp. 841–51.

————. 1969. *Tomorrow's Manpower Needs*, Vol. 4, *The National Industry-Occupational Matrix and Other Manpower Data*, Bulletin No. 1606.

————. 1974. *Handbook of Labor Statistics*, BLS Bulletin 1825. Washington, D.C.

————. 1980. *Handbook of Labor Statistics*, BLS Bulletin 1979. Washington, D.C.

————. 1981. *The National Industry-Occupation Employment Matrix, 1970, 1978, and Projected 1990*. Vol. 1, Bulletin 2086.

————. 1982. *BLS Labor Force Statistics Derived from the Current Population Survey: A Databook*, Vol. 1. BLS Bulletin 2096. Washington, D.C.

————. 1983. *Handbook of Labor Statistics*, BLS Bulletin 2175. Washington, D.C.

————. 1985. *Handbook of Labor Statistics*, BLS Bulletin 2217. Washington, D.C.

————. 1988. *Labor Force Statistics Derived from the Current Population Series, 1948 to 1987*, BLS Bulletin 2307. Washington, D.C.: GPO.

————. 1989a. *Consumer Expenditure Survey, 1984–1986*, Bulletin 2333. Washington, D.C.: GPO.

————. 1989b. *Employment Cost Indexes and Levels, 1975–89*. BLS Bulletin 2339. Washington, D.C.

————. 1989c. *Handbook of Labor Statistics*, BLS Bulletin 2340. Washington, D.C.

————. 1992. *Employment, Hours, and Earnings, States and Earnings*. BLS Bulletin 2411. Washington, D.C.

U.S. Department of Labor, Employment and Training Administration. 1978. *The Public Employment Service and Help Wanted Ads*, R&D Monograph 59. Washington, D.C.: G.P.P.

————. 1983. *Unemployment Insurance Financial Data*, ET Handbook 394. Washington, D.C.

U.S. Federal Trade Commission, Bureau of Economics, 1982. *Statistical Report, Annual Line of Business Report, 1976*. Washington, D.C.

U.S. General Accounting Office. 1986a. *Employee Stock Ownership Plans: Benefits and Costs of ESOP Tax Incentives for Broadening Stock Ownership*. Washington, DC: processed.

————. 1986b. *Employee Stock Ownership Plans: Interim Report on a Survey and Related Employment Trends*. Washington, DC: processed.

————. 1987. *Employee Stock Ownership Plans: Little Evidence of Effects on Corporate Performance*. Washington, D.C.

U.S. Office of Management and the Budget. Annual. *Budget of the United States Government*. Washington, D.C.: GPO.

————. 1993. *Mid-Session Review of the 1994 Budget*. Washington, D.C.: GPO.

U.S. Office of Thrift Supervision. 1989 and irregular. *Savings and Home Financing Source Book*. Washington, D.C.

U.S. National Science Board. Biennial. *Science and Engineering Indicators, 1991*. Washington, D.C.: GPO.

Urbanek, Adam. 1988. "Morpho-Physiological Progress," in Nitecki (1988): pp. 195–216

Veum, Jonathan R. 1992, "Accounting for Income Mobility Changes in the United States," *Social Science Quarterly 73*, No. 4 (December): pp. 773–85.

Voge, Jean. 1983. "The Political Economics of Complexity: From the Information Economy to the 'Complexity' Economy," *Information Economics and Policy 1*, No. 1: pp. 97–114.

Volcker, Paul A. 1991. "Financial Crises and the Macroeconomy," in Feldstein (1991): pp. 174–9.

Waldo, Daniel R., Sally T. Sonnefeld, David R. McKusick, and Ross H. Arnett, III. 1989. "Health Expenditures by Age Group, 1977 and 1987," *Health Care Financing Review 10*, No. 4 (Spring): pp. 111–20.

Wallerstein, Judith S. and Sandra Blakeslee. 1989. *Second Chance: Men, Women, and Children a Decade After Divorce.* New York: Ticknor and Fields.

Wallis, John Joseph and Douglass C. North. 1986. "Measuring the Transaction Sector in the American Economy, 1870–1970," in Engerman and Gallman (1986): pp. 95–148.

Warsh, David. 1984. *The Idea of Economic Complexity.* New York: Viking Press.

Warner, Andrew M. 1992. "Does World Investment Demand Determine U.S. Exports," International Finance Discussion Papers No. 423, Board of Governors of the Federal Reserve Bank. Washington, D.C.

Warren, Melinda. 1994. "Reforming the Federal Regulatory Process: Rhetoric or Reality?" " Occasional Paper 138, Center for the Study of American Business, Washington University. St. Louis.

Warren, Melinda and James Lis. 1992. "Regulatory Standstill: Analysis of the 1993 Federal Budget," Occasional Paper 105, Center for the Study of American Business, Washington University. St. Louis.

Warshawsky, Mark J. 1991. "Is there a Corporate Debt Crisis? Another Look," in Hubbard (1991): pp. 207–30.

Wattenberg, Ben. 1987. *The Birth Dearth.* New York: Pharos Books.

———. 1991. *The First Universal Nation: Leading Indicators and Ideas about the Surge of America in the 1990s.* New York: Free Press.

Weede, Erich. 1987. "A Note on Pryor's Criticism of Olson's Rise and Decline of Nations," *Public Choice 52.* pp. 215–22.

———. 1990. "Redistribution and Income Inequality in Industrial Democracies," *Research in Social Movements, Conflict and Change 12.* Greenwich, Connecticut: JAI Press: pp. 301–26.

Weidenbaum Murray. 1978. *The Cost of Federal Government Regulation of Business.* Joint Economic Committee, Congress of the United States. Washington, D.C.: GPO.

———. 1979. *The Future of Business Regulation: Private Action and Public Demand.* New York: American Management Assoociation.

Weiss, Leonard W. 1983. "The Extent and Effects of Aggregate Concentration," *Journal of Law and Economics 26*, No. 2 (June): pp. 429–57.

Weisskopf, Thomas E., Samuel Bowles, and David M. Gordon. 1983. "Hearts and Minds: A Social Model of U.S. Productivity Growth," *Brookings Papers on Economic Activity,* No. 2: pp. 381–442.

Weitzman, Martin L. and Douglas L. Kruse. 1990. "Profit Sharing and Productivity," in Blinder, editor. (1990): pp. 95–141.

White, Michael J. 1987. *American Households and Residential Differentiation.* New York: Russell Sage.

Whitehead, Barbara DeFoe. 1993. "Dan Quayle Was Right," *The Atlantic Monthly,* (April): pp. 47–84.

Williams, George C. 1966. *Adaption and Natural Selection: A Critique of Some Current Evolutionary Thought.* Princeton: Princeton University Press.

Williamson, Jeffrey G. and Peter H. Lindert. 1980. *American Inequality: A Macroeconomic History.* New York: Academic Press.

————. 1980. "Long-Term Trends in American Wealth Inequality," in Smith (1980): pp. 9–93.

Williamson, Oliver E. 1963. "Managerial Discretion and Business Behavior," *American Economic Review 53,* No. 5 (December 1963): pp. 1032–58.

Wilson, Jack W., Richard E. Sylla, Charles P. Jones. 1990. "Financial Market Panics and Volatility in the Long Run, 1830–1930," in Eugene N. White, editor. *Crashes and Panics: The Lessons from History.* Homewood, Illinois: Dow Jones-Irwin: pp. 85–1988.

Wilson, James Q. 1994. "Culture, Incentives, and the Underclass," in Aaron, *et al.* (1994): pp. 54–87.

Winston, Clifford. 1993. "Economic Deregulation: Days of Reckoning for Microeconomists," *Journal of Economic Literature 23,* No. 3 (September): pp. 1263–89.

Winston, Clifford and Robert W. Crandall. 1994. "Explaining Regulatory Policy," *Brookings Papers on Economic Activity,* forthcoming.

Wolff, Edward N., editor. 1987a. *International Comparisons of the Distribution of Household Wealth.* Oxford: Clarenden Press.

————. 1987b. "The Effects of Pensions and Social Security on the Distribution of Wealth in the U.S.," in Wolff (1987a): pp. 208–47.

————. 1989. "Trends in Aggregate Household Wealth in the U.S., 1900–83," *Review of Income and Wealth 35,* No. 1 (March): pp. 1–31.

————. 1994. "Trends in Household Wealth in the United States, 1962–1983 and 1983–1989," Working Paper 94–03, C. V. Starr Center for Applied Economics, New York University.

Wolff, Edward N. and William J. Baumol. 1989. "Sources of Postwar Growth of Information Activity in the United States," in Lars Osberg, Edward N. Wolff, and William J. Baumol, editors. *The Information Economy: Implications of Unbalanced Growth.* Ottawa: Institute for Research on Public Policy.

Wolff, Edward N. and Marcia Marley. 1989. "Long-Term Trends in U.S. Wealth Inequality: Methodological Issues and Results," in Lipsey and Tice (1989): pp. 765–844.

Wolfson, Martin E. 1986. *Financial Crises: Understanding the Postwar U.S. Experience.* Armonk, NY: M.E. Sharpe.

———— 1990. "The Causes of Financial Instability," *Journal of Post Keynesian Economics 12,* No. 3 (Spring): pp. 333–55.

Woolhandler, Steffie, David U. Himmelstein, and James P. Lewontin. 1993. "Administrative Costs in U.S. Hospitals," *New England Journal of Medicine 329,* No. 6 (August 5): pp. 400–4.

World Bank. Irregular. *World Tables.* Washington, D.C.

Wright, Neil R. 1978. "Product Differentiation, Concentration, and Changes in Concentration," *Review of Economics and Statistics 60,* No. 4 (November 1978): pp. 628–31.

Wuthnow, Robert. 1994. *God and Mammon in America.* New York: The Free Press.

Yan, Chiou-Shuang and Edward Ames. 1965. "Economic Interactions," *Review of Economic Studies 32,* No. 4 (October): pp. 299–310.

Yankelovitch, Daniel. 1994. "How Changes in the Economy are Reshaping American Values," in Henry J. Aaron, *et al.* (1994): pp. 16–54.

Yellen, Janet L. "Comment and Discussion," *Brookings Papers on Economic Activity,* No. 2: pp. 127–33.

Young, Allan H. 1987. "Evaluation of GNP Estimates," *Survey of Current Business 67,* No. 8 (August): pp. 18–42.

Zeckhauser, Richard J. and John Pound. 1990. "Are Large Shareholders Effective Monitors?" in Hubbard (1990): pp. 149–80.

Zimmerman, David J. 1992. "Regression toward Mediocrity in Economic Stature," *American Economic Review 82,* No. 3 (June): pp. 409–29.

Zuboff, Shoshana. 1988. *In the Age of the Smart Machine: The Future of Work and Power.* New York: Basic Books.

Index